HUMANISTIC LETTERS

HUMANISTIC LETTERS

The Irving Babbitt–Paul Elmer More Correspondence

Edited by Eric Adler

UNIVERSITY OF MISSOURI PRESS
COLUMBIA

Copyright © 2023 by
The Curators of the University of Missouri
University of Missouri Press, Columbia, Missouri 65211
Printed and bound in the United States of America
All rights reserved. First printing, 2023.

Library of Congress Cataloging-in-Publication Data

Names: Babbitt, Irving, 1865-1933 author. | More, Paul Elmer, 1864-1937
   author. | Adler, Eric, 1973- editor.
Title: Humanistic letters : the Irving Babbitt-Paul Elmer More
   correspondence / edited by Eric Adler.
Description: Columbia : University of Missouri Press, 2023. | Includes
   bibliographical references and index.
Identifiers: LCCN 2023017162 (print) | LCCN 2023017163 (ebook) | ISBN
   9780826222909 (cloth) | ISBN 9780826274915 (ebook)
Subjects: LCSH: Education, Humanistic. | Babbitt, Irving,
   1865-1933--Correspondence. | More, Paul Elmer,
   1864-1937--Correspondence.
Classification: LCC LC1011 .B185 2023 (print) | LCC LC1011 (ebook) | DDC
   370.11/2--dc23/eng/20230620
LC record available at https://lccn.loc.gov/2023017162
LC ebook record available at https://lccn.loc.gov/2023017163

♾™ This paper meets the requirements of the
American National Standard for Permanence of Paper
for Printed Library Materials, Z39.48, 1984.

Typeface: Minion Pro

For Julian

Contents

Acknowledgments		ix
INTRODUCTION		3
CHRONOLOGY		59
CHAPTER 1	1895–1898	87
CHAPTER 2	1899–1907	111
CHAPTER 3	1908–1911	141
CHAPTER 4	1912–1914	177
CHAPTER 5	1915–1916	221
CHAPTER 6	1917–1918	255
CHAPTER 7	1919–1921	283
CHAPTER 8	1922–1925	311
CHAPTER 9	1926–1929	345
CHAPTER 10	1930–1934	375
APPENDIX A		405
APPENDIX B		411
APPENDIX C		415
Biographical Register		417
Bibliography		445
Index		469

Acknowledgments

NUMEROUS PEOPLE HELPED make the publication of this book possible. Claes Ryn deserves special mention, as a constant source of knowledge, guidance, and encouragement. He agreed that a volume devoted to the Babbitt–More correspondence would be welcome and thus provided me with access to the Irving Babbitt Papers (IBP) at the Harvard University Archives (HUG 1185; courtesy of the Harvard University Archives). Claes allowed me to reprint in the Introduction of this book small portions of an article that will appear in the journal he co-edits: "On the Politics of the New Humanism," *Humanitas* (forthcoming). He also lent me Folke Leander's insightful unpublished manuscript on the philosophy of Paul Elmer More. Without Claes's indefatigable counsel and support, this book would not exist.

The staff of the Harvard University Archives has been exceedingly helpful. It digitized the typescript of the correspondence for me, along with many original letters from Babbitt and handwritten copies of More's originals. The staff also diligently answered all my queries about the correspondence and the IBP in general.

Charles Doran and AnnaLee Pauls from the Princeton University Library Special Collections also aided the project. Charles facilitated the staff's digitizing of More's original letters from the Paul Elmer More Papers (PEMP) at Princeton and provided information for me about publication through the literary rights of Arthur Hazard Dakin Jr. Since Dakin passed away in 2001 and had no heirs, Paul Fine (the grandson of Paul Elmer More) kindly provided his approval to publish materials in the PEMP. Margo Lalich (Paul More's great-granddaughter) deserves thanks for sending me a More family tree.

Various people aided the project at different stages. Among them I would like to mention Teresa Bejan and Jessica Hooten Wilson (who gave me ideas for finding a publisher for the correspondence), and Thomas R. Nevin (who offered information about the IBP, Babbitt's family, and kindred topics).

The anonymous readers for the University of Missouri Press (one of whom subsequently outed himself as Michael Federici) provided very useful feedback, which improved the manuscript and saved me from various blunders. The staff of the University of Missouri Press (especially David Rosenbaum, Mary S. Conley, Deanna Davis, and Drew Griffith) has been exceedingly helpful throughout the publication process. I am particularly thankful to David for his support for this project from the start. Susan Curtis deserves kudos for her fantastic job of copyediting. Nate Mills should be thanked for creating a wonderful index for the book.

This book would never have seen the light of day without the constant encouragement and good cheer of my family: Amy Adler, Joel Adler, Julian Calvert Adler, Nancy Adler, Lili Katz-Jones, Calvert Jones, Julian Jones, and Patricia Wallace.

My son Julian is an endless source of joy. It is a pleasure to dedicate this book to him.

HUMANISTIC LETTERS

INTRODUCTION

"THE DIVERSITY OF created beings is very great, and one is hardly likely to do justice to all: but these seem to me the two *wisest* men that I have known."[1] Thus did the poet and critic T. S. Eliot sum up his impressions of Irving Babbitt (1865–1933) and Paul Elmer More (1864–1937), the two leading figures of the so-called New Humanism,[2] an informal school of literary and social criticism that thrived during the late nineteenth and early twentieth centuries.

At different times in Eliot's life, these two men played a prominent role in his intellectual, moral, and aesthetic development. Babbitt, a professor of French and comparative literature at Harvard University and the author of numerous books and essays, had cast his spell during Eliot's senior year in college,[3] when Eliot, enrolled in Babbitt's course ostensibly devoted to French literary criticism, marveled at the deep learning and torrential energy Babbitt displayed in his classroom. Although he would later express some reservations about Babbitt's approach to Humanism, Eliot testified that Babbitt had shaped his thought and taste in essential ways. "Yet to have been once a pupil of Babbitt's," Eliot wrote in a tribute to his former teacher, "was to remain always in that position, and to be grateful always for (in my case) a very much qualified approval."[4]

If anything, Paul Elmer More had an even greater impact on Eliot.[5] More, like Eliot a native of St. Louis,[6] enjoyed a distinguished career as a literary

---

1. Eliot 1937b: 374 (emphasis in the original).
2. In the Chronology, Introduction, notes, and Biographical Register of this book, the capitalization of *Humanism* and *Humanist* will refer to the New Humanism and New Humanist, whereas the lowercase terms will describe *humanism* and *humanist* generically.
3. See Eliot 2015: 810.
4. Eliot in Manchester and Shepard 1941: 103. On Eliot's criticisms of the New Humanism, see, e.g., Birzer 2015: 233-35.
5. On Eliot's friendship with More, see, e.g., Wilson 1948: 4-5; Dakin 1960: 267; Hanford 1961: 166; Duggan 1966: 123; Tanner 1971, esp. 212 and 1987: 12. For discussions of More's influence on Eliot, see, e.g., Tanner 1971, 1987: 237, and 1998: 189-90.
6. Although More was Eliot's elder, they moved in similar circles in St. Louis. More, in fact, had taught Eliot's older brother ancient Greek at the Smith Academy, a role he would have played for Eliot too, if More had not left the Academy for graduate studies at Harvard.

critic, editor, and academic. Twice a serious candidate for the Nobel Prize in Literature,[7] More was a prolific and wide-ranging author with a lyrical prose style that earned praise even from his detractors. Although throughout much of his life he took his philosophical cues from his good friend Babbitt, by the early 1920s More had partly retreated from the New Humanism, embracing a Platonic Christianity at odds with Babbitt's ecumenical approach to revealed religion. Eliot, like More a Christian convert of Anglican leanings, considered *The Greek Tradition*, More's multi-volume contribution to Christian apologetics, a masterwork that profoundly affected his religious convictions.[8] Many examples of Eliot's literary criticism—most famously, perhaps, his celebrated essay "Tradition and the Individual Talent"—betray the influence of Babbitt and More.[9]

Eliot was far from alone in demonstrating the impact of the New Humanism on his work. As a Harvard faculty member, Babbitt had the opportunity to shape some of the best minds of the early twentieth century. His former pupils included the esteemed critics Walter Lippmann, Van Wyck Brooks, Harry Levin, Norman Foerster, Austin Warren, and Stuart P. Sherman, the noted Vergilian scholar Brooks Otis, and the future Harvard president Nathan Pusey. Even those who proved more critical of the New Humanism—including Lippmann and Brooks—appreciated Babbitt's probing intellect and pedagogical gifts.[10] Through his writings, moreover, Babbitt had sway over non-Harvardians; important thinkers whose writings reveal the influence of the New Humanism include the philosopher Benedetto Croce, the intellectual historian Arthur O. Lovejoy, the classical scholar Werner Jaeger, and the historian Jacques Barzun.

For a brief time in the late 1920s and early 1930s, moreover, the New Humanism attracted considerable attention in American—and even European—culture. When Norman Foerster's edited collection *Humanism and America*, a New Humanist manifesto of sorts, complete with contributions from Babbitt and More, appeared in print in early 1930, the book helped spark a debate that dominated American intellectual circles for the better part of a year. The Humanists received such widespread interest, in

---

7. In 1930 and 1932. See, e.g., Collins 1930b: 70; Dakin 1960: v; Duggan 1966: 9; Hoeveler 1977: 12; Tanner 1987: 1-2 and 1998: 186.

8. Eliot 1937a and 1937b: 373.

9. See, e.g., Nevin 1984: 31; Tanner 1971 and 1998: 189-90.

10. See, e.g., Brooks 1954: 118, 121-22. For estimations of Babbitt as a teacher, see the contributions to Manchester and Shepard 1941.

fact, that on May 9, 1930, Babbitt debated the critics Carl Van Doren and Henry Seidel Canby in front of a packed audience at Carnegie Hall in New York City.¹¹ Magazines and newspapers devoted much energy to attacking and defending the movement.¹²

Even Babbitt's and More's prominent detractors testified to their intellectual stature. The novelist Sinclair Lewis, who had beaten out More for the Nobel Prize in Literature in 1930, disparaged the New Humanism in his victory speech.¹³ There were even earlier hints of his dislike for Babbitt and More. Lewis likely thumbed his nose at their movement by naming his novels *Babbitt* (1922), about an uninspired middle-class businessman, and *Elmer Gantry* (1927), about a hypocritical minister, after the New Humanism's two leading lights.¹⁴ Lewis was far from alone in his disapproval; indeed, in an essay from 1928 called "The Demon of the Absolute," More, looking back on his writing career with his tongue only partly in cheek, lamented, "I was at once the least read and most hated author in existence."¹⁵

Yet even stalwart critics appeared impressed with Babbitt's and More's output. The famed libertarian journalist H. L. Mencken, a veteran of various intellectual scrapes with the Humanists,¹⁶ christened More "perhaps the nearest approach to a genuine scholar that we have in America, God save us all!"¹⁷ In a 1930 letter to the poet John Peale Bishop, furthermore, the noted literary critic Edmund Wilson, though far from a fan of the New Humanism,¹⁸ explained, "the doctrine of Babbitt and More (they are quite impressive in some ways when you come to read them) looms as the only systematic attempt in sight to deal with large political, social, moral, and aesthetic questions, in relation to each other, in a monumental and logical

---

11. For an analysis of this debate dedicated to criticizing the New Humanism, see Colum 1930.
12. See, e.g., Jones 1928; anon. 1930; Canby 1930; Rand 1932; Maynard 1935.
13. Hindus 1994: 39.
14. See Dakin 1960: 295; Dunham 1966: 159.
15. More 1928a: 3. Dakin (1960: 208) quotes from a December 29, 1922, letter to his friend Prosser Hall Frye, in which More wrote, "I have gained the rather sad preeminence of being at once the least read and worst hated author in the country." On Frye, see his entry in the Biographical Register.
16. See, e.g., Mencken 1920: 18-25 and 1922: 176-79; Sherman 1923: 1-12; Babbitt 1924: 274, 1940: 218-19, and 1968: 201-34; More 1928a: 76; Shafer 1935c: 114-19. Cf. Jones 1928; Hanford 1961: 168; Spiller 1963: 1148, 1152-53. On Mencken, see his entry in the Biographical Register.
17. Mencken 1922: 178.
18. See Wilson 1930.

way."[19] Although their influence has ebbed and flowed in the decades following their deaths, Babbitt and More still deserve consideration as among the most important literary and social critics in American history.

The New Humanism, moreover, should not be merely the object of historical curiosity. On the contrary, the movement Babbitt and More spearheaded has much to teach us today. This conclusion seems especially salient in our anti-humanistic age. A major thrust of the New Humanism was its critique of the sidelining of the classical and modern humanities in our higher education—a move that Babbitt, More, and their followers deemed disastrous for human happiness and the continuation of civilization. As American institutions of higher learning grow ever more utilitarian and vocational in their emphases, the New Humanism's trenchant critique of our nation's professionalized universities remains highly valuable for intellectuals worried about the fate of our nation and its culture.

This introduction aims to provide readers with the essential biographical and intellectual background necessary to appreciate and contextualize the Babbitt–More correspondence. The Babbitt–More correspondence, which extends from the early days of the authors' academic careers in the 1890s all the way to Babbitt's death in 1933, offers an intimate portrait of the New Humanist movement that readers cannot glean elsewhere. Previously locked away in university archives,[20] the letters between Babbitt and More clarify the (occasionally clashing) perspectives of two intellectual giants, as they attempted to foster a major critical and cultural movement. The correspondence offers readers a window into Babbitt's and More's intellectual and critical aims that is not available from their published work alone. Indeed, one cannot understand the goals and development of the New Humanism without reading this correspondence.

Especially since much that has been written about Babbitt and More remains unreliable—influenced by the polemical criticisms the two men weathered in the controversies their work helped inaugurate—it seems essential to discuss Babbitt's and More's ideas with care. Though of necessity brief, the introduction will also point to fuller analyses of the New Humanism that provide dependable estimations of the movement. By its end we shall see that Babbitt's and More's writings, though hardly immune to criticism, deserve a wide readership.

---

19. Wilson 1977: 193 (the letter is dated January 15, 1930).
20. On the location of the original letters in this correspondence, see below.

On the "Warring Buddha of Harvard"

Although some of his critics would presume that he was born with a proverbial silver spoon in his mouth, Irving Babbitt in important respects did not lead a privileged early life.[21] Born on August 2, 1865, in Dayton, Ohio, Babbitt was the fourth of five children of Edwin Dwight Babbitt (1828–1905) and Augusta (Darling) Babbitt (1836–1876). Irving's father Edwin, although calling himself a doctor, was actually something of a spiritual guru of decidedly crankish proclivities.[22] Throughout his career Edwin inaugurated various educational ventures of dubious quality; at one point, for example, he served as the dean of a Los Angeles institution called the College of Fine Forces. Edwin maintained his faith in pseudo-science of all sorts, billing himself as a "magnetist," a "psycho-physician," and a "chromo-therapist," who vouched for the purported health benefits of colored lights. Despite penning numerous self-help books, Edwin was unable to parlay his enthusiasms into a stable career and thus proved a poor provider for his family.

Thanks to his father's precarious undertakings, Irving moved around quite a bit as a youngster, with stops in New York City and East Orange, New Jersey.[23] When Irving's mother passed away soon after his eleventh birthday in 1876, Irving's grandparents took him and his siblings in to live with them on their farm in Madisonville, Ohio.[24] By 1881 Edwin had remarried and thus Irving and his younger sister Katharine moved to his new home in Cincinnati.[25] All the while Irving Babbitt attended public schools. In 1884 he graduated second in his class from Cincinnati's Woodward High School.[26]

Since his family did not possess the requisite funds to allow him to attend his dream school of Harvard, Babbitt spent a post-graduate year in high

---

21. Unfortunately, Babbitt, unlike More, has not been the subject of a full-length biography. In fact, published information about Babbitt's life relies heavily on a brief biographical portrait his wife, Dora Babbitt, composed after her husband's death (see D. Babbitt in Manchester and Shepard 1941: ix-xiii), occasionally supplemented by details found in Dakin's (1960) biography of More. Since Dora Babbitt's narrative often lacks firm dates, we are less informed about aspects of Babbitt's life than we would like. For other biographical analyses of Babbitt, see, e.g., Barney 1974: 29-58, 238-39; Hoeveler 1977: 5-10; Nevin 1984: 5-7, 12-23; Slayton 1986; Brennan and Yarbrough 1987: 1-27, 58-78; Ryn 1991: xii-xix, 1995b: xv-xix, and 1997: 10-12; Panichas 1999: 194-206; Adler 2020: 166-70.

22. On Edwin Babbitt, see, e.g., Levin 1966: 331-32; Barney 1974: 29-30; Brennan and Yarbrough 1987: 3, 6-10; Hindus 1994: 18; Ryn 1995b: xv and 1997: 10.

23. D. Babbitt in Manchester and Shepard 1941: ix.

24. D. Babbitt in Manchester and Shepard 1941: ix.

25. D. Babbitt in Manchester and Shepard 1941: x.

26. Giese in Manchester and Shepard 1941: 20 n. 1.

school, where he studied civil engineering and chemistry.[27] Finally Babbitt's uncles—one of whom had hired Babbitt the previous summer as a helper on his ranch in Wyoming[28]—loaned him the money, and thus Babbitt began his college career at Harvard in the fall of 1885.[29] By this time the elective system, one of the signature reforms of Harvard president Charles W. Eliot (1834-1926), was in effect. This approach to the curriculum, which would earn Babbitt's lifelong criticism,[30] afforded undergraduate students maximum choice in regard to coursework. Babbitt, who soon discovered that he was overprepared for Harvard,[31] chose classes mostly in the ancient and modern languages.[32] He graduated magna cum laude with honors in classics in 1889.[33]

Although one can find examples of his father's influence on Babbitt's views,[34] it was at Harvard that Babbitt revolted from the pseudo-spiritual hokum prized by Edwin and pioneered many of the ideas ultimately associated with the New Humanism. Unfortunately, Babbitt found few valuable intellectual and moral models amongst the Harvard faculty. As he bemoaned in some of his writings, the teaching of ancient and modern literature at Harvard was dominated by a cabal Babbitt labeled the Philological Syndicate.[35] Enraptured with the supposedly scientific approach to literature pioneered in the German research universities, many language professors at Harvard prized the minute philological analysis of literary texts. Babbitt, who found this perspective dry and trifling, aimed to avoid the Philological Syndicate's pedantry as much as possible.[36] He took it as a badge of honor that at one time during his undergraduate career he possessed the record for the most skipped classes at Harvard.[37] When he deigned to attend, moreover, Babbitt could prove a pest in the classroom for members of the Philological

---

27. D. Babbitt in Manchester and Shepard 1941: xi.
28. D. Babbitt in Manchester and Shepard 1941: x.
29. D. Babbitt in Manchester and Shepard 1941: xi.
30. Babbitt's criticisms of curricular free election are legion. See especially Babbitt 1940: 198-224, 1986, and 1991: 66 n. 1.
31. D. Babbitt in Manchester and Shepard 1941: xi.
32. For a full listing of Babbitt's undergraduate coursework, see Barney 1974: 238.
33. D. Babbitt in Manchester and Shepard 1941: xi; Levin 1966: 333; Ryn 1991: xiii.
34. Warren (1956: 145), for example, maintained that Babbitt's partial respect for Emerson stemmed from his father. Brennan and Yarbrough (1987: 10) also note that Edwin admired Buddha; his son Irving would maintain a strong attachment to Buddhism.
35. See, e.g., Babbitt 1986: 141, 148. Cf. Giese in Manchester and Shepard 1941: 1. Chief among the Syndicate at Harvard was George Lyman Kittredge, from whom Babbitt earned the uncharacteristically low grade of a C- in his "English 2" course during his senior year (see Barney 1974: 238). Levin (1991: 28) mentions Kittredge as the key figure in the Syndicate. On Kittredge, see his entry in the Biographical Register.
36. Giese in Manchester and Shepard 1941: 15.
37. Giese in Manchester and Shepard 1941: 15.

Syndicate, whom he would pepper with queries undermining their scholarly narrowness.[38]

Babbitt's attitude toward scientific philology—so characteristic of his fierce opposition to the zeitgeist of his age—undeniably affected his academic career. Immediately upon graduating from Harvard, Babbitt, who had to pay back his family for the loans he received, took a job teaching introductory ancient Greek and Latin at the College of Montana in Deer Lodge, a modest institution in a tiny mill town.[39] Although he disliked the daily gerund-grinding the position entailed, Babbitt remained a faculty member there for two years, until he had saved up enough money for graduate studies. He first spent a year at the Sorbonne, where he studied Sanskrit, Pali, and Indian philosophy with Sylvain Lévi.[40] In 1892 Babbitt began work on similar topics at Harvard. There he met Paul Elmer More as the only other student in the advanced class in Oriental studies taught by Professor Charles R. Lanman.[41] Babbitt and More became best friends and Babbitt, with some intellectual assistance from More, it appears, slowly converted More to his philosophy of life. It was in graduate school at Harvard, moreover, that Babbitt enrolled in a class on Dante with Charles Eliot Norton, a polymath professor of art history whose moralistic approach to literature and the arts provided a welcome respite from the Philological Syndicate. Although their rationales for humanistic study differed in essential ways,[42] throughout his life Babbitt considered Norton a crucial mentor.[43]

Having received his A.M. in 1893,[44] Babbitt decided against earning a Ph.D., since he disdained the narrow and technical approach to literature it fostered. He thus left Harvard for a job as a sabbatical replacement at Williams College, where he served as an instructor of French, Spanish, and

---

38. Giese in Manchester and Shepard 1941: 1. Hence Giese noted Babbitt's undergraduate nickname among the classroom backbenchers: "Assistant Professor Babbitt."
39. D. Babbitt in Manchester and Shepard 1941: xi-xii; Douglas in Manchester and Shepard 1941: 26; Hoeveler 1977: 8; Slayton 1986: 229; Brennan and Yarbrough 1987: 15-16.
40. D. Babbitt in Manchester and Shepard 1941: xii; Lévi in Manchester and Shepard 1941, esp. 34; Slayton 1986: 229. On Lévi, see his entry in the Biographical Register.
41. D. Babbitt in Manchester and Shepard 1941: xii; Dakin 1960: 48-49; Brennan and Yarbrough 1987: 18; Ryn 1991: xiv. For a full listing of Babbitt's graduate coursework at Harvard, see Barney 1974: 239. On Lanman, see his entry in the Biographical Register.
42. On Norton's rationale for the modern humanities on the basis of what would be called "Western civilization," see Turner 1999: 384-88; Adler 2020: 79-81. On Babbitt's universalistic rationale for the humanities, see below. On Norton, see his entry in the Biographical Register.
43. For discussions of Norton's influence on Babbitt, see, e.g., Giese in Manchester and Shepard 1941: 14-15; Barney 1974: 39; Nevin 1984: 17-18; Brennan and Yarbrough 1987: 19-20; Turner 1999: 345. See also More 1967c: 97-113.
44. Slayton 1986: 230; Ryn 1991: xiv and 1995b: xvi. *Contra* Withun 2017: 26 (who claims that Babbitt earned a Ph.D.).

Italian.⁴⁵ Although he only remained at Williams for one academic year, there Babbitt made an important contact: Frank Jewett Mather Jr. (1868–1953), then a faculty member in Williams' English department.⁴⁶ Mather, whose career would extend to numerous years in journalism and a faculty position in art history at Princeton University, was another convert to the New Humanism and a lifelong friend of both Babbitt and More—a core part of the movement's inner circle.

In 1894 Babbitt became a member of the Harvard faculty. Although he longed to teach ancient Greek and Latin, the classics department had no openings, and it is likely that its professors, recalling Babbitt as an obstreperous undergraduate, would have disapproved of him joining their ranks.⁴⁷ But the firing of a teacher in the French department for plagiarism compelled its chairman, Ferdinand Bôcher, to hunt for a last-minute replacement, and thus Babbitt was hired as an instructor in French and, eventually, comparative literature.⁴⁸ It was an appointment the department would soon regret: Bôcher and his fellow senior faculty members of the Romance languages esteemed scientific philology and thus found Babbitt's perspective on scholarship irksome.

Babbitt's outsized opinions and combative character did not endear him to many of his colleagues. In part as a result of his verbal bellicosity, G. R. Elliott, another convert to the New Humanism, dubbed Babbitt the "Warring Buddha of Harvard."⁴⁹ William F. Giese, a friend and follower from Babbitt's undergraduate days, reported that Babbitt, when still a lowly instructor at Harvard, once informed his chairman that French was "only a cheap and nasty substitute for Latin."⁵⁰ Routinely ignored by his colleagues in both the Romance languages and the classics, Babbitt was almost let go at various times from Harvard. But he managed to remain a faculty member there for the rest of his life. In comparison with his friend More, in fact, Babbitt would experience a sedentary existence. Married in the summer of 1900 to Dora (Drew) Babbitt, a former pupil of his at Radcliffe College,⁵¹ Babbitt

---

45. D. Babbitt in Manchester and Shepard 1941: xii; Slayton 1986: 230. See also Mather in Manchester and Shepard 1941: 42.

46. Mather in Manchester and Shepard 1941: 42; More in Manchester and Shepard 1941: 336; Dakin 1960: 81-82. On Mather, see his entry in the Biographical Register.

47. See Hoeveler 1977: 9. Cf. Panichas 1999: 198.

48. Mercier 1928: 49; D. Babbitt in Manchester and Shepard 1941: xii; Hough 1952: 135; Slayton 1986: 230; Brennan and Yarbrough 1987: 20; Ryn 1995b: xvi-xvii; Panichas 1999: 198.

49. Elliott 1938: 56. On Elliott, see his entry in the Biographical Register.

50. Giese in Manchester and Shepard 1941: 4.

51. The marriage ceremony occurred in London on June 12 of that year. See D. Babbitt in Manchester and Shepard 1941: xii; Nevin 1984: 13; Slayton 1986: 231; Ryn 1991: xv and 1995b: xviii; Panichas 1999: 199. On Dora Babbitt, see her entry in the Biographical Register.

for decades rented a home at 6 Kirkland Road near the Harvard campus.[52] With the exception of numerous summers spent in New Hampshire, some trips to Europe, and stints as a visiting faculty member and guest lecturer in France and the United States, there Babbitt would stay. In 1902 Babbitt earned the title of assistant professor.[53] Thanks, it seems, to an offer of employment from the University of Illinois, in 1912 Babbitt was promoted to a full professorship.[54]

Despite his unfashionable views on the academy, Babbitt became one of Harvard's most prominent scholars and teachers. He was a lecturer of boundless enthusiasm and a seemingly inexhaustible array of learned quotations, and all his courses, in opposition to the dominant academic trends, connected literary study to the crucial art of living well. As *Irving Babbitt: Man and Teacher* (1941), a valuable collection of reflections on his life,[55] attests, Babbitt earned a devoted following and by the end of his career Harvard students flocked to his classes. Although a late bloomer on the scholarly front (his first monograph did not appear in print until he was forty-two years old), Babbitt published books and articles of wide significance, which helped attract many readers to the New Humanism. For such influential scholarship Babbitt received many accolades. He was invited to deliver prestigious lectures at institutions such as Yale,[56] Stanford,[57] and Brown;[58] he won election to the French Institute in 1926[59] and the Academy of Arts and Letters in 1930.[60] Unfortunately, Babbitt did not live a very long life. He passed away aged sixty-seven in his home in Cambridge on July 15, 1933, having suffered for at least a year from ulcerative colitis.[61] As but one mark of his impact, in 1960 the Harvard president Nathan Pusey, one of Babbitt's former pupils, inaugurated the Irving Babbitt Professorship of Comparative Literature.

---

52. Slayton 1986: 231; Ryn 1991: xv.
53. D. Babbitt in Manchester and Shepard 1941: xii; Hough 1952: 135; Nevin 1984: 13; Brennan and Yarbrough 1987: 22; Ryn 1991: xiv-xv.
54. D. Babbitt in Manchester and Shepard 1941: xii; Dakin 1960: 113; Levin 1966: 321-22. See also Nevin (1984: 23-24), who discusses the contact in 1911 between Evarts Greene (1870-1947), a dean at Illinois, and Babbitt regarding potential employment there.
55. Manchester and Shepard 1941.
56. See Slayton 1986: 233; Panichas 1999: 202.
57. See Slayton 1986: 233.
58. See Slayton 1986: 234.
59. D. Babbitt in Manchester and Shepard 1941: xii; Brennan and Yarbrough 1987: 72-73.
60. D. Babbitt in Manchester and Shepard 1941: xii-xiii; Dakin 1960: 295; Slayton 1986: 234; Ryn 1991: xviii.
61. D. Babbitt in Manchester and Shepard 1941: xiii; Hough 1952: 136; Slayton 1986: 235; Ryn 1991: xvii and 1995b: xix.

Historical and "Psychological" Humanism

Babbitt's books all differ in their emphases. Thus, for example, *Literature and the American College* (1908) criticizes the anti-humanistic drift of higher education in the US; *The New Laokoon* (1910) presents a morally informed theory of aesthetics; *Rousseau and Romanticism* (1919) provides a forceful attack on sentimental naturalism; and *Democracy and Leadership* (1924) defends its author's anti-imperialist and anti-statist political commitments. But even casual readers of Babbitt's books will recognize that they interlock in essential ways. Indeed, all Babbitt's writings, regardless of their ostensible focus, argue in favor of his philosophy of life, which he would label humanism but would more commonly be branded the New Humanism.[62]

As its name intimates, the New Humanism bears a strong relationship with the historical humanist movement, especially in its classical and Renaissance manifestations. Thus, in his first monograph Babbitt expatiated on the meanings of the Latin words *humanitas* and *humanus* as part of his attempt to unearth the foundations of historical humanism.[63] Like the ancient and Renaissance humanists before him, Babbitt placed great emphasis on curricular matters, since he recognized that at its root humanism is a pedagogical tradition first articulated in the works of Cicero and reconceptualized and revivified in Renaissance Italy.[64]

But Babbitt was not concerned merely with unearthing humanistic history. Rather, he also used his description of the historical humanist movement as a launching point for his personal vision of the Good Life. For this reason, Babbitt could speak of humanism both as a historical and, as he termed it, a "psychological" phenomenon.[65] Although versed in humanist history, Babbitt aimed to reimagine the movement, allowing it to incapsulate what he took to be the essence of humanist wisdom. To this end, he could label as "humanists" many figures not strictly associated with the historical humanistic tradition. Babbitt, for example, deemed Socrates the West's inaugural humanist[66] and considered Aristotle its quintessential exemplar,[67] though of course Socrates and Aristotle, like the ancient Greeks more generally, would not have used such a Latin term to designate their philosophies.

Moreover, Babbitt spied essential elements of humanist wisdom in non-Western traditions. A thinker with strong syncretistic impulses, in his

---

62. Brennan and Yarbrough (1987: 19) note that Babbitt disliked the adjective "New" attached to his Humanism. Cf. Kimball 1995: 175.
63. Babbitt 1986: 73-77.
64. Histories of the humanities are legion. See, e.g., Proctor 1998 and Adler 2020: 33-87.
65. Babbitt 1930: 30.
66. Babbitt 1986: 124.
67. E.g., Babbitt 1991: 86.

writings he deemed Buddha a deeply important humanist thinker and tied Confucius to the movement as well. In a striking example of intellectual ecumenism for the early twentieth century, for example, Babbitt maintained in an article from 1921, "The Western traditions have been partly religious, partly humanistic. The names that sum up these two aspects of tradition most completely are those of Aristotle and Christ, corresponding in a general way to those of Confucius and Buddha in the Far East."[68] As far as Babbitt was concerned, humanist wisdom concerned far more than its historical foundation in Roman antiquity would suggest.

Babbitt's idiosyncratic perspective on the nature of humanism earned numerous critics. To some, Babbitt had appropriated a pleasant-sounding term for his own purposes and ran roughshod over the history of humanism.[69] Such criticisms have validity: Babbitt's creative refashioning of the movement entailed some conclusions seemingly at odds with humanist history. Chief among them was Babbitt's largely (but not entirely) critical perspective on Renaissance humanism, which he perceived as unduly centrifugal in its tenor.[70] How could a philosophy called the New Humanism, Babbitt's detractors wondered, disparage such a key humanist figure as Petrarch?[71]

But these critics often failed to recognize the value of Babbitt's thorough reconceptualization. His approach entailed a more detailed and specific analysis of humanist goals and values than his predecessors in Roman antiquity or the Italian Renaissance had mustered. Moreover, Babbitt's greatly broadened Humanism allowed the movement to speak more meaningfully to the vicissitudes of the present. Indeed, as we have already hinted, Babbitt vouched for an expanded and updated humanist canon, which would prove more capable of meeting the intellectual and moral needs of his day.

Humanism vs. Naturalism

How did he do this? A major part of Babbitt's refashioning surrounded the philosophical dualism he recognized in much classical, Buddhist, Hindu, and Christian thought. All true humanists, he maintained, have at least implicitly comprehended that human life is dual: human beings possess both impulsive desires (what the French philosopher Henri Bergson called the *élan vital* and Babbitt equated with the lower will) and the ability to restrain or affirm these desires (what Babbitt deemed the *frein vital*, inner check, or higher

---

68. Babbitt 1921: 86.
69. E.g., Cowley 1930: 64-65; Hazlitt 1930: 96; Wilson 1930: 47-48.
70. For some examples of Babbitt's criticisms of Renaissance humanism, see Babbitt 1910a: 88, 1912e: 222; 1986: 76-79. On this topic, see Mercier 1928: 51; McMahon 1931: 17.
71. See, e.g., Babbitt 1986: 91, 138, 164. Cf. Babbitt 1986: 187-88.

will).[72] Although critics often presumed that Babbitt's arguments on this score implied a strictly negative vision of morality,[73] his position (admittedly not advanced with exceptional clarity) was distinctly different. Elaborating on his views in *Rousseau and Romanticism*, for example, Babbitt maintained:

> Like all the great Greeks Aristotle recognizes that man is the creature of two laws: he has an ordinary or natural self of impulse and desire and a human self that is known practically as a power of control over impulse and desire. If man is to become human he must not let impulse and desire run wild, but must oppose to everything excessive in his ordinary self, whether in thought or deed or emotion, the law of measure. This insistence on restraint and proportion is rightly taken to be the essence not merely of the Greek spirit but of the classical spirit in general.[74]

By associating the inner check—a term Emerson had discovered when reading an essay on Hindu philosophy[75]—with Aristotle's law of measure, Babbitt underscored *both* its affirming and its restraining capacities.[76] Hence the philosopher Folke Leander, one of the most perceptive interpreters of the New Humanism, explained Babbitt's and More's vision of the inner check thus: "The moral sense begins its work as an inner check but proceeds by means of deliberation to acceptance of some course of action as good. The course of action which is approved participates in the good; the initial check ('Is this good?') which sets us deliberating, is an intuition of the ethical ultimate, the One, the good or whatever we prefer to call it."[77]

With a nod to Diderot, Babbitt called the struggle between human beings' impulsive desires and their inner check "the civil war in the cave."[78] Individuals, he stressed, must learn to nourish their beneficent impulses and restrain those that are destructive to productive and respectful life. For this reason Babbitt (like the historical humanists before him) placed cardinal

---

72. On Babbitt's and More's vision of the inner check, see above all Leander 1974: esp. 3-4, 6-7, 20; Ryn 1977: esp. 254, 1991: xxxiii-xxxvi, and 1997: esp. 30-32, 150. Cf. Mercier 1948: 20.

73. E.g., Cowley 1930: 67-68; Hazlitt 1930: 95; Mumford 1930: 345-46, 348, and 351; Tate 1930: 141; Wilson 1930: 46; Dewey 1984: 264.

74. Babbitt 1991: 16.

75. Babbitt 1940: 151 (who notes that Emerson originally spied this term in a piece by Colebrook on the Vedanta); Levin 1966: 337.

76. Cf. Mather 1930a: 159; Leander 1970: 13-17, 52, 77-100, 147, 163; Ryn 1977: 254, 1991: xxvi, 1995b: xxxiii, and 1997: 31-32; Jamieson 1986: 158.

77. Leander 1974: 4.

78. E.g., Babbitt 1940: 155, 157, 228 and 1991: 150, 204.

importance on a particular conception of education: a proper approach to pedagogy, he argued, centered on the study of literary and artistic masterpieces from the past.[79] Such works, which provide the most profound visions of the Good, the True, and the Beautiful, thought Babbitt, could spur on the young to cultivate their inner check, thus enabling them to live more ethically sound and happier lives.

Babbitt spied twin threats to this inner-focused Humanist wisdom, both of which he identified with so-called humanitarianism. He labeled one "scientific naturalism" and considered Francis Bacon its progenitor;[80] he called the other "sentimental naturalism" and deemed Jean-Jacques Rousseau, the most influential philosopher associated with the romantic movement, its most powerful advocate.[81] Babbitt keenly recognized that both these brands of naturalism possess certain common principles, which allowed them to prove mutually reinforcing. They both earned the moniker "naturalist" insofar as they denied the inner dualism Babbitt considered key to Humanism in favor of a monistic interpretation of human life.

Sentimental naturalists such as Rousseau contended that human beings were intrinsically good, and that society and its institutions had corrupted them.[82] Thus Rousseau and his fellow romantics preached the cultivation of one's innate impulses. They eschewed the civil war in the cave in favor of an outer militancy: the true fight, they posited, was between human beings and society.[83] Babbitt recognized that this Rousseauistic perspective has the benefit of appealing to human vanity, since it inevitably blames external forces for all the world's evils and thereby exonerates individuals for their malefactions. But he considered it misguided. Rousseau believed that human beings, if they stayed true to their impulsive selves, would naturally cultivate a brotherhood of man.[84] This conclusion, thought Babbitt, was a cardinal example of Rousseau's idyllic imagination.[85] He and his fellow romantics failed to recognize the baleful elements of human nature—that human beings possess base inclinations just as much as beneficent ones. In reality, Rousseau's sentimentalized brotherhood, however plaintively vouched for, would prove

---

79. For some examples of Babbitt expressing a preference for certain literary works in the college curriculum, see Babbitt 1986: 75, 122, 164. Cf. Connely in Manchester and Shepard 1941: 185.
80. See, e.g., Babbitt 1986: 89-101.
81. See, e.g., Babbitt 1940: 225-47, 1986: esp. 88-108, and 1991.
82. See, e.g., Babbitt 1940: 227 and 1991: 153, 256.
83. See, e.g., Babbitt 1940: 228.
84. For Babbitt's criticisms of Rousseau on this score, see, e.g., Babbitt 1986: 104.
85. See, e.g., Babbitt 1940: 232.

no match for people's selfish will to power.[86] Without regard for personal improvement through the cultivation of one's inner check, thought Babbitt, supposed humanitarianism based on Rousseauistic wishful thinking would court violence, chaos, and misery.[87]

Unfortunately, Babbitt contended, another sort of naturalism, which antedated the romantic movement, reinforces the pseudo-humanitarianism he associated with Rousseauism. According to Babbitt, scientific naturalists such as Bacon deny human dualism in part by eschewing the goal of character development in favor of gaining power over the natural world. They aim not to learn from the masterworks of the past about the best ways to live, preferring instead, as Babbitt expressed it, "the glorification of man's increasing control over the forces of nature under the name of progress."[88] Like the Rousseauists, the Baconians denied the true dualism in favor of a struggle between humankind and the world. By gaining dominion strictly over things, Babbitt feared, the scientific naturalist of necessity lost control over himself. Although Babbitt saw great value in scientific discoveries,[89] he warned that the complete displacement of humanism with sentimental and scientific naturalism was a recipe for disaster. Such naturalists, with their implicit denial of the inner check, have cooperated in undermining humanist wisdom. As he stressed in *Rousseau and Romanticism*, "The man who does not rein in his will to power and is at the same time very active according to the natural law is in a fair way to become an efficient megalomaniac."[90]

A Problem of Pedagogy

It was therefore disastrous, thought Babbitt, that American higher education in his day actively undermined humanism in favor of sentimental and scientific naturalism. In various books and articles Babbitt excoriated the drastic changes that had taken place in US colleges since the dawn of the American university movement in the second half of the nineteenth century. Although by no means a curricular reactionary,[91] Babbitt recognized that the new professionalized universities by design sideline the humanities. "Our

---

86. Babbitt was critical of Nietzsche's championing of a "will to power"; see, e.g., Babbitt 1924: 259. For More's more detailed criticism of Nietzsche from a New Humanist perspective, see More 1967a: 147-90. On the origins of this essay/pamphlet, see below, chapter 4.

87. On this topic, see, e.g., Mercier 1928: 64-65, which discusses Babbitt's link between rampant naturalism and the outbreak of World War I.

88. Babbitt 1940: 229.

89. See, e.g., Babbitt 1910a: 210-11, 1912e: 452, 1924: 258, 1930: 32, 1986: 105, and 1991: 368. On this topic, see also Mather 1930a: 156; Jewett 2012: 199.

90. Babbitt 1991: 366.

91. See, e.g., Babbitt 1986: 109-10, 115-16, 119-23, 127, 184.

reformers said with truth that the old college curriculum needed broadening," he wrote. "What they have actually done is not to broaden this curriculum, but to change its essence."[92] For all their faults, Babbitt maintained, the classical colleges of early America at least provided a curriculum of substance that compelled students to experience humanist masterworks. The architects of the American universities, by contrast, hoped to minimize the influence of the classical humanities and theology on education, aiming to center higher learning on the scientific method.[93] Charles W. Eliot, the longstanding president of Harvard and Babbitt's pedagogical bête noir,[94] for example, helped popularize a fully elective curriculum for undergraduates at his institution that he likened to social Darwinism. "In education, as elsewhere," Eliot opined in an essay on liberal education originally published in 1884, "it is the fittest that survives."[95]

By eliminating curricular prescription in favor of election, Eliot demonstrated his Rousseauistic and Baconian bona fides. According to Eliot's scheme, Babbitt noted in *Literature and the American College*, "There is no general norm, no law for man, as the humanist believed, with reference to which the individual should select [courses]; he should make his selection entirely with reference to his own temperament and its (supposedly) unique requirements. The wisdom of all the ages is to be naught as compared with the inclination of a sophomore."[96] Indeed, Eliot openly disparaged the inner-focused humanism Babbitt prized. As part of his ninetieth birthday celebration at Harvard, Eliot repeated to students the advice of the minister Edward Everett Hale: "Look forward and not backward—Look out and not in."[97] To Eliot, a scientific naturalist par excellence, education's goals were service and power;[98] to the humanist, by contrast, they were wisdom and character.[99]

Though it was no easy task, Babbitt considered it essential to revivify the humanities, to enable them to provide a genuinely humanist contrast to the naturalism dominant in American education and American life.

---

92. Babbitt 1940: 63-64.
93. On this topic, see, e.g., Jewett 2012; Adler 2020: esp. 50-87.
94. For Babbitt's criticisms of Eliot, see, e.g., Babbitt 1924: 301-2, 1940: 198-224, 1968: 227-28, and 1986: 95-99, 122, 204. On these criticisms, see, e.g., Veysey 1965: 248; Hawkins 1972: 298; Hoeveler 1977: 9, 112; Smilie 2010: 135-69. In an April 1, 1906, letter to More found in chapter 2 of this book, Babbitt noted that he sees his book *Literature and the American College* in part an attack on Eliot's views.
95. Eliot 1898: 120.
96. Babbitt 1986: 96.
97. Quoted in James 1930 2: 309.
98. See, e.g., Eliot 1899: 441, 1923: 36, 39, and 1926: 168, 171. Cf. Boyd 1934: 33, who accurately portrays Eliot as a Baconian.
99. E.g., Babbitt 1924: 303.

But he found that few of his colleagues had the stomach for such combat. Unfortunately, Babbitt lamented, many humanities professors in his day had themselves eschewed humanism in favor of minute, professionalized research Babbitt linked to scientific naturalism. They did not aim to contemplate the wisdom found in masterworks of the past in an attempt to discover an appropriate philosophy of life. On the contrary, representatives of the Philological Syndicate confined themselves to linguistic trifling that helped serve the scientific naturalist's cult of progress.[100] "With the invasion of this hard literalness," Babbitt fretted, "the humanities themselves have ceased to be humane."[101] In such circumstances, he maintained that a humanist revival was required to ensure individual and civilizational flourishing. He warned that "Man is in danger of being deprived of every last scrap and vestige of his humanity by this working together of romanticism and science."[102]

The New Humanism's Radical Omni-Culturalism

Babbitt naturally deemed the disappearance of genuine humanism from American higher education a catastrophe. Without a humanist counterweight to the regnant naturalism, he thought, human beings would continue to usher in conflict and misery. And Babbitt recognized that wistful laments about the bygone days of higher learning would not provide much help. Solutions to contemporary educational problems could not be rooted in the past. Far from the pedagogical reactionary of popular imagination,[103] Babbitt thus became a humanist trailblazer of sorts, who argued in favor of a radical expansion of the humanist canon.

Babbitt's thoroughgoing enlargement of the humanistic tradition centered on an issue he called the Platonic problem of the One and the Many. In *Literature and the American College*, Babbitt noted the crucial importance of this concept for the continuation of civilization: "To harmonize the One and the Many," he wrote, "this indeed is a difficult adjustment, perhaps the most difficult of all, and so important, withal, that nations have perished from their failure to achieve it."[104] Even the ancient Greeks, in many respects Babbitt's model of a salubrious ancient humanism, served as a warning in this regard. "The critical moment of Greek life was, like the present," he contended in his second monograph, "a period of naturalistic eman-

---

100. See, e.g., Babbitt 1986: 135. Cf. Babbitt 1940: 191.
101. Babbitt 1986: 84.
102. Babbitt 1991: 262.
103. E.g., Canby 1930: 1122; Harris 1970: 52; Butts 1971: 347, 398; Brennan and Yarbrough 1987: 108; Smilie 2016: 113-14.
104. Babbitt 1986: 84.

cipation, when the multitude was content to live without standards, and the few were groping for inner standards to take the place of the outer standards they had lost. The Greek problems were like our own problems of unrestraint; for what we see on every hand in our modern society, when we get beneath its veneer of scientific progress, is barbaric violation of the law of measure."[105]

In his early dialogues Plato defined the One and the Many as a metaphysical problem. For example, he wondered what is the one thing common to all, say, just actions that makes them just. Babbitt, although indebted to Plato's analysis on this score, transferred the problem of the One and the Many to the human soul. He equated a human being's impulsive desires (that is, the lower will) with the Many and linked the inner check (that is, the higher will) with the One.[106] To Babbitt, one's quotidian impulses serve to distance people from one another, whereas the inner check (which Babbitt linked to Buddhism, Hinduism, and the Christian spirit of grace) speaks to what is common among human beings. Sentimental and scientific naturalism, when unrestrained by a spirit of dualistic Humanism, prove pernicious because they reinforce a metaphysics of the Many, without the crucial counterbalancing of a metaphysics of the One. Literary works may be deemed masterpieces, Babbitt thought, if they possess a transcendent quality that blends the One and the Many, which allows them to offer readers a sense of what human life is like in toto. As Babbitt put it in a review from 1918, "the creator of the first class gets his general truth without any sacrifice of his peculiar and personal note; he is at once unique and universal."[107] By reveling in individualistic impulsiveness, Babbitt suggested, romantic literature ignored a more profound investigation of the human condition, which underscores both the differences and similarities between people.

Hence Babbitt hunted for examples from various cultures of similar approaches to the challenges of life. For instance, he noted that "the experience of the Far East completes and confirms in a most interesting way that of the Occident. We can scarcely afford to neglect it if we hope to work out a truly ecumenical wisdom to oppose the sinister one-sidedness of our current naturalism."[108] According to Babbitt, Eastern sages such as Confucius

---

105. Babbitt 1910a: 251. Although enraptured by aspects of Greece (especially Athens) in the classical period, Babbitt also noted many perceived weaknesses of ancient Greek culture. See, e.g., Babbitt 1910a: 250-52 and 1912e: x.

106. See, e.g., Babbitt 1910a: 216, 245, 1912c: 453-454, 1930: 32, 1940: 220, and 1986: 84-86, 163. On Babbitt's understanding of the One and the Many, see, e.g., Mercier 1928: 52 and 1936: 70; McMahon 1931: 64, 80; Hoeveler 1977: 36-38; Ryn 1977: 252-53 and 1997: 29-30.

107. Babbitt 1918: 139.

108. Babbitt 1991: lxxix.

and Buddha supply lessons about the cardinal necessity of an inner check that parallel the insights discoverable in Aristotle's *Nicomachean Ethics* and Christian theology.[109] This crucial correspondence among seminal thinkers from disparate cultures suggested to Babbitt that he had hit upon a key aspect of the wisdom of the ages.

As some astute scholars have noted, Babbitt's Humanism was in essential respects rooted in Eastern philosophy. Louis J. A. Mercier, one of Babbitt's colleagues at Harvard and a fellow Humanist, remarked, for example, that "Babbitt was not a humanist in the purely classical tradition. He thoroughly understood classical humanism from the start, but it early seemed to him that it did not take all the facts of human nature into consideration."[110] Critical of what he perceived to be the overly intellectualized approach to existence he witnessed in the Greek tradition, Babbitt highlighted the crucial role of the will and the imagination in human flourishing. These were features of what he took to be ancient Eastern humanism.[111] Whereas Socrates and Cicero had demonstrated excessive optimism about the power of reason to shape human life, Buddhism—especially in its earlier Lesser Vehicle formulation—supplied for Babbitt a more realistic impression of congenital human weaknesses and stressed the larger role of character.

Although in his writings he underscored the virtues of classical and Far Eastern thought, Babbitt at least implicitly argued in favor of a radical omniculturalism that saw value in the examination of *all* human civilizations for traces of humanistic wisdom. Given the cardinal importance of the problem of the One and the Many to his thought, Babbitt naturally stressed that there is such a thing as a common humanity. Every human tradition, he argued, by virtue of being human, has contributed to the wisdom of the ages, a nucleus of universal human experience that could help us fight against pure naturalism and determine salubrious standards for living well.

Babbitt's approach to Humanism was thus notably cosmopolitan (especially for its time). This cosmopolitanism would prove attractive to Paul Elmer More, Babbitt's long-standing best friend and a critic similarly drawn to the study of Eastern civilizations.

---

109. For examples of Babbitt's penchant to include the Far East in his expansive vision of humanism, see Babbitt 1921, 1924: 34, 163, 1930: 27-28, 30-31, 37, 40-41, 1968: xvi, 54, 235-61, 1940: 141-69, 190, 202-5, 1986: 83, 206, and 1991: lxxviii-lxxix, 148, 150, 343.
110. Mercier 1948: 14. On Mercier, see his entry in the Biographical Register.
111. On the relationship between the will, the intellect, and the imagination in Babbitt's philosophy, see above all Ryn 1997. Cf. Ryn 1991: xxvi-xxvii.

On the "Hermit of Princeton"

Paul Elmer More's early life bears some striking resemblances to that of his best friend Irving Babbitt.[112] More, like Babbitt a product of the American Midwest, was born on December 12, 1864, in St. Louis, Missouri.[113] Chiefly of English stock, he was the seventh of eight children of Enoch Anson More (1821–1899) and Katharine Hay (Elmer) More (1825–1914). Paul More's family saw its fair share of financial hardships. His father, who had fought on the Union side in the Civil War, was an intermittently successful businessman.[114] At one time after his marriage, he had built up a profitable career as a bookseller in Dayton, Ohio.[115] But Enoch abandoned this trade in a family move to St. Louis, to follow a minister with considerable influence over the Mores.[116] His further business ventures—including wholesale grocery and hardware—experienced various ups and downs. Without an inheritance from his wife's father in 1883, in fact, Enoch More's family may have collapsed altogether.[117]

In this same year Paul More graduated from Central High School in St. Louis, a public institution, and began attending nearby Washington University,[118] from which he would graduate with a B.A. in 1887.[119] By this time More, a bookish undergraduate whose intellectual pursuits included writing poetry and essays for the school newspaper,[120] had caused considerable anxiety in his family by announcing his break from Christianity.[121] More's parents were strict Calvinists and in an autobiographical reflection

---

112. As noted above, we have much fuller biographical information about More than about Babbitt. The chief reason for this is Dakin's (1960) exhaustive biography of More. To this biography can be added other reflections on More as a person: e.g., Clemens 1939; L. T. More 1940 and 1942; Oates 1946; Shafer 1948; Wilson 1948: 3-14; Dunham 1966. More 1936c also provides some autobiographical reflections, though he found the genre "distasteful" (1).

113. Shafer 1935c: 59; Mather 1938: 368: Hough 1952: 172; Davies 1958: 25; Dakin 1960: 4; Hanford 1961: 163.

114. Shafer 1935c: 61; Dakin 1960: 4.

115. Shafer 1935c: 61; Dakin 1960: 4.

116. Shafer 1935c: 61 (who suggests that the move occurred "about 1860"); Dakin 1960: 4 (who says it took place in 1859).

117. Dakin 1960: 13.

118. Dakin 1960: 13.

119. Shafer 1935c: 64; Mather 1938: 368; Oates 1946: 303; Dakin 1960: 20.

120. See, e.g., Shafer 1948; Dakin 1950: 89 and 1960: 18-19.

121. Dakin 1960: 18-19. It is uncertain precisely when this occurred, but Dakin suggests that in December of 1886 More appears to have published an anonymous article in the Washington University student publication *Student Life* in which he talks about his religious break and consequent crisis of faith. According to More's younger brother (L. T. More 1942: 52), More broke from Calvinism around age thirteen. According to Duggan (1966: 21), this break occurred when More was in his late teens or early twenties. For More's disavowal of Christianity, see also More 1909a: 65-66.

written towards the end of his life, More reported that a sermon he experienced one Sunday devoted to universal human depravity helped crystalize his growing doubts about the Christian faith. "With something like a paroxysm of certainty," he wrote, "with bitter actual tears of regret, I cast off...the faith that had nurtured the better part of my childhood and youth."[122]

Upon his graduation from college, More became a teacher of Latin and other subjects at the Smith Academy in St. Louis, a job he would hold through 1892,[123] save for one year traveling in Europe.[124] But he found teaching a trying profession. A reserved man whom G. R. Elliott later dubbed the "Hermit of Princeton,"[125] More proved less adept in the classroom than the gregarious and opinionated Babbitt.[126] Thus More yearned to move on from the Smith Academy. In 1890 he had published his first book, *Helena and Occasional Poems*, which helped affirm his aspirations as a creative writer. Two years later More earned an M.A. from his alma mater for a thesis written in Latin.[127] In May of that same year he informed Professor Lanman that he aimed to study Sanskrit, Pali, ancient Greek, and Latin at Harvard, hoping to earn a Ph.D.[128] He would matriculate there in the fall and befriend Babbitt as Lanman's graduate student of ancient Indian literature and philosophy.[129]

More's introverted nature was not the only trait that distinguished him from his new friend Babbitt. Early on in his college career, Babbitt began cobbling together the intellectual structure for the New Humanism, a philosophy to which he would be devoted for the remainder of his life. Indeed, as More would suggest in a post-mortem tribute to his friend, "The astonishing fact, as I look back over the years, is that he [Babbitt] seems to have sprung up, like Minerva, fully grown and fully armed. No doubt he made vast additions to his knowledge and acquired by practice a deadly dexterity in wielding it, but there is something almost inhuman in the immobility of his central ideas."[130]

---

122. More 1936c: 24.
123. Shafer 1935c: 64; Hough 1952: 173; Dakin 1960: 21.
124. This travel occurred in 1888 and 1889; see Dakin 1960: 22-34.
125. Elliott 1938: 56.
126. As More himself noted. See More 1894: 3 (through a fictionalized but autobiographical character) and 1915b: 651. On More as a teacher, see also Shafer 1935c: 80-81; Oates 1946: 314-15; Davies 1958: 29, 52-53; Dakin 1960: 21, 53-54, 213, 296.
127. Shafer 1935c: 64; Mather 1938: 368; Oates 1946: 303; Hough 1952: 173; Davies 1958: 28.
128. Dakin 1960: 41. Dakin specifies that More wrote the letter on May 24.
129. Dakin 1960: 48-49.
130. More in Manchester and Shepard 1941: 325. Cf. Mather in Manchester and Shepard 1941: 43-44; Dakin 1960: 323; Hoeveler 1977: 9; Panichas 1999: 40; Smilie 2010: 26.

By contrast, More, although often pigeonholed as a follower of Babbitt, was something of an intellectual seeker, constantly revising his outlook on life. After his break with Calvinism, More launched into successive phases of romanticism, rationalism, classicism, Platonism,[131] and ultimately, as we shall discuss, an idiosyncratic brand of Platonic Christianity.[132] When he met Babbitt at Harvard, More was enchanted by a mystical Vedantic Hinduism, which he conceived of as an improvement on his boyhood Calvinism.[133] Although never strictly speaking a Hindu,[134] More clearly found in what he called the "forest philosophy"[135] an attractive spiritual alternative to Christianity.

But this does not imply that More's intellectual and religious journey was without its constants. Indeed, in countless heated conversations with Babbitt at Harvard, More managed to shed much of his erstwhile romanticism and convert to many of the ideas central to the New Humanism.[136] Relatedly, around this time More had an epiphany of sorts when reading Ferdinand C. Baur's *Das Manichäische Religionssytem* (1831),[137] a book that jumpstarted his lifelong commitment to philosophical dualism.[138] Through this book More grew enchanted with dualistic perspectives on human existence, which would prove key to the New Humanism and serve as an organizing thread throughout More's intellectual and spiritual perambulations.[139] In the whole of his writing career, one can find key staples of Babbitt's thought—for

---

131. More did, however, demonstrate an attachment to Plato throughout much of his writing career. For an example of More's early interest in Plato, see, e.g., More 1894: 6-7. Cf. More 1909a: 321-55. On More's Platonism, see, e.g., Davies 1958: 98-99; Duggan 1966: 27-31.

132. For useful discussions of the successive intellectual/spiritual phases of More's life, see, More 1936c; Davies 1958: esp. 35.

133. More 1936c: 26-27; Duggan 1966: 24-27.

134. See Shafer 1935c: 93; Tanner 1987: 30. Cf. Leander 1938: 440.

135. See More 1909a: 1-42.

136. More in Manchester and Shepard 1941: 324-25.

137. Baur 1973.

138. Late in life More claimed (see Dakin 1960: 314) to have happened upon this book in 1891, before he attended Harvard. Cf. Shafer 1935c: 67; Davies 1958: 45; Tanner 1987: 29. But Dakin (1960: 44 n. 23) supplies evidence to suggest that More read Baur's book slightly later, only after he came to Cambridge. See also Warren 1969: 1099.

139. On the crucial importance of dualism to More's thought, see, e.g., More 1894: 138, 1899a: 13-15, 1909a: 18, 41, 69, 119, 146-47, 172, 177, 221, 243-44, 266-67, 321-23, 1910a: 86, 1915a: 214-15, 1917b: 79-117, 1921: esp. vi-vii, 53, 199-200, 1924: esp. 2, 5, 207-9, 1928a: x, 1936c: 17-18, 1936d: 163, 1937b, 1967a: xiii, 247-302, 1967c: 89-90. For scholarly recognition of the importance of dualism for More, see, e.g., Shafer 1935c: 155; Mather 1938: 370; Harding 1954: 36; Dakin 1960: 323; Otis 1965: 58; Duggan 1966: 28-29, 45-49; Warren 1969: 1099; Leander 1974: esp. 3-4; Hoeveler 1977: 13; Kuntz 1980; Tanner 1987: *passim* but esp. 3, 5, 10-11, 13, 27-36, 63, and 100; Lambert 1999: 49.

example, the inner check[140] and the One and the Many[141]—also appearing in More's books and essays.

For all the differences in his personality and intellectual journey, however, More did see eye to eye with Babbitt in regard to the Philological Syndicate and the unbecoming narrowness of American graduate study. Although in April of 1893 he delivered a conference presentation that led to a published scholarly article on Hinduism and Manichaeism,[142] More ultimately decided against writing a dissertation, venturing out on the academic job market without a Ph.D. in hand. After serving for a year as Lanman's assistant in Indo-Iranian languages,[143] More landed a position in 1895 as an instructor of Sanskrit and classical literature at Bryn Mawr College.[144] By this time, More had again demonstrated his literary ambitions: in 1894 he published *The Great Refusal, Being Letters of a Dreamer in Gotham*, an epistolary novel that provided a fictionalized take on one of his own failed love affairs.

More found teaching at Bryn Mawr no more rewarding than he had earlier at the Smith Academy. He thus resigned from the position in 1897, when M. Carey Thomas, Bryn Mawr's president, refused his demand for higher pay and less work.[145] This departure led More to embark on one of the most storied episodes in the history of the New Humanism. At the conclusion of the 1896-97 academic year, More, now in his early thirties and unclear about his vocational path, rented a small cabin in an isolated spot on the Philbrook farm in remote Shelburne, New Hampshire, where he would retreat from civilization to read, write, and determine his next steps.[146] By that time engaged to Henrietta ("Nettie" or "Net") Beck (1867-1928), a childhood friend from St. Louis, More lacked the requisite funds for marriage and was in

---

140. E.g., More 1915a: 115, 1917b: 146, 196, 1967a: 247-48, 250-511, 277. According to Wilson (1948: 9), More said that he had used the term "inner check" before Babbitt did. Given its origins in the Vedanta, this seems likely to be true. On More's use of this term, see, e.g., Shafer 1935c: 167; Leander 1937a: 126, 1938: 446 and 1974; More in Manchester and Shepard 1941: 335-36; Oates 1946: 313; Tanner 1987: 37-38.

141. E.g., More 1908d: 56, 1909a: 322, 332, 352-53, 1910a: 210, 268-69, 1917b: 214, 1936d: 17-18. On More's views on the One and the Many, see Davies 1958: 101-3.

142. More 1896. Although published in 1896, More delivered the original paper at a scholarly conference in April of 1893.

143. Shafer 1935c: 70; Mather 1938: 368; Dakin 1960: 51; Hanford 1961: 163; Aaron 1963: 1; Duggan 1966: 15.

144. Shafer 1935c: 79; Mather 1938: 368; Hough 1952: 175; Davies 1958: 29; Dakin 1960: 51.

145. Dakin 1960: 55-56. Cf. Davies 1958: 29.

146. Shafer 1935c: 84, 86; Mather 1938: 368; Hough 1952: 175; Davies 1958: 29; Dakin 1960: 55-56. For More's brief discussions of his retreat to Shelburne, see, e.g., More 1904: 1-21 and 1908d: 43. See also L. T. More 1940, a retrospective account of More's younger brother, who spent time with him at the cabin. Davies (1958: 53-55) suggests that More's failure to win the hand of Sadie Brank, another love interest, also encouraged his departure for Shelburne.

much need of direction.[147] He ultimately stayed in the cabin in Shelburne for two years and three months,[148] by which time he had determined to embark on a career as a critic. In 1898 More began contributing literary criticism to the *Atlantic Monthly* and the *New World*.[149] His book-length translation of Sanskrit poetry, *A Century of Indian Epigrams*,[150] which appeared in the same year, both reinforced his interest in Hindu dualism and turned out to be his final major poetic effort. Although he would co-author another epistolary novel with Corra Mae Harris (1869–1935) in 1904,[151] More had cast aside a career as a creative writer.

Now certain of his calling in life but unsure how to make ends meet, in the autumn of 1899 More departed Shelburne for Harvard, where he would aid Lanman with a translation project.[152] Desperate for additional funds, he also began work on a brief biography of Benjamin Franklin, the chief advantage of which was the $350 advance he received for the project.[153] On June 12, 1900—the exact same day that Babbitt married—More and Henrietta were wed.[154] The couple moved to East Orange, New Jersey, where More hoped to pick up more freelance writing jobs but soon discovered that he required a steadier paycheck.

More was thus fortunate to receive an offer in early 1901 to join the staff of the *Independent*, a prominent liberal periodical based in New York City.[155] Although chiefly serving as its literary editor, More also began contributing numerous pieces to the publication. During his career in journalism, in fact, More demonstrated his almost preternatural productivity as an essayist and reviewer. Despite his full-time job and the demands of his family, he

---

147. On the specifics of this engagement, which occurred in the fall of 1895, see Dakin 1960: 52. On Henrietta Beck More, see her entry in the Biographical Register.
148. Shafer 1935c: 87. He had a few visitors at the cabin, including Babbitt and his younger brother Louis T. More. See Louis T. More 1940. On Louis More, see his entry in the Biographical Register.
149. E.g., More 1898a and b. Cf. Dakin 1950: 90.
150. More 1899a. Babbitt 1899 is a review of this book.
151. More and Harris 1904. The book was published in April of that year (see Dakin 1950: 96). For more on Harris and her views, see below.
152. Shafer 1935c: 101-2; More 1936c: 33 and in Manchester and Shepard 1941: 329; Brown 1939: 476; Mather 1938: 369; Davies 1958: 29.
153. Shafer 1935c: 102; Dakin 1950: 92 and 1960: 74 n. 3 (which specifies that the biography was published ca. October of 1900).
154. Dakin 1960: 78.
155. Dakin (1960: 87) informs us that More was offered the job by January 30, 1901, and began his position on April 1. See also Shafer 1935c: 102; Mather 1938: 369; Oates 1946: 306; Hough 1952: 175; Hanford 1961: 163. Cf. Davies 1958: 30, who may be confused about the start date.

managed to contribute hundreds of pieces on a wide variety of subjects.[156] More decided to reprint some of the more substantial of these writings in his *Shelburne Essays*, of which there were eleven volumes, published between 1904 and 1921.[157] These books, which highlight their author's limpid prose, capacious learning, and forceful literary judgments, helped cement More as arguably the greatest voice in American literary criticism in the early twentieth century.

By the time the first volume of the *Shelburne Essays* had seen the light of day, More had departed from the *Independent*'s staff to start work as the literary editor of the New York *Evening Post*.[158] In addition to his editorial work, More continued his prodigious output as a writer; much of his writing at this time appeared in both the *Evening Post* and the *Nation*, two titles that were then under the same ownership and shared much published material in common.[159] More wrote so much, in fact, that he seems to have spent little time with his family, even though Henrietta had given birth to a daughter, May Darrah More, in February of 1902.[160] On July 1, 1906, a few days after Alice, the Mores' second daughter, was born,[161] More added even more to his plate: he became the literary editor of the *Nation*, while retaining his position at the *Evening Post*.[162] This move must have entailed an increase in More's prestige, since the *Nation*, a periodical founded in the aftermath of the Civil War, was among the most storied political magazines in the US.

May of 1909 marked another key turning point in More's career. On the sixth of that month, Hammond Lamont, the editor-in-chief of the *Nation*, passed away after a botched operation; less than a week later More was appointed as his successor.[163] This was a position of great stature, and through

156. See Dakin 1950, which provides a fuller bibliography than does Young 1941. Neither is complete, however, since More wrote many unsigned pieces and even as thorough a researcher as Dakin was not able to track them all down.

157. For information on the publication dates of these volumes, see the Chronology.

158. This switch in jobs occurred in 1903. See Shafer 1935c: 109; Mather 1938: 369; Oates 1946: 306; Hough 1952: 175; Dakin 1960: 94.

159. See Shafer 1935c: 109; Duggan 1966: 15.

160. Dakin 1960: 93, who specifies the date as February 24. On Mary Darrah More, see her entry in the Biographical Register.

161. Alice was born on June 28, 1906; see Dakin 1960: 99, who notes that after the birth Henrietta's "health was permanently undermined." On Henrietta More's health problems, see below. On Alice More, her daughter, see her entry in the Biographical Register.

162. Dakin 1960: 98; Hanford 1961: 163.

163. Dakin (1960: 109) specifies that Lamont died on May 6 and that More was officially appointed his replacement on the 11th (109 n. 2). He further notes (108) that on April 21, More had written a letter to his brother Louis, suggesting that Lamont may leave the magazine's staff to take a faculty position at Williams College; he hoped that, if this happened, someone other

herculean efforts More managed to turn the magazine into the most respected cultural review in the US. Now a major voice in American letters, More continued contributing essays and reviews and delivered various lectures across the country.

However appealing the esteem that he accrued as a result of his lofty position at the *Nation*, More found the constant drudgery associated with the position tiresome. He had shown himself an able editor, but More much preferred to advance his own writing career. In addition, More's acrimonious relationship with Oswald Garrison Villard, the owner of the New York Evening Post Company and the publisher of the *Nation*, caused increasing strains. By this time Villard had drifted to the political Left and occasionally complained about pieces appearing in the *Nation* that matched More's Tory predilections. More found Villard's meddling in editorial affairs irksome.[164]

An unexpected loss allowed More to escape from the ball-and-chain of his editorial duties. In early 1911 Mary D. Richardson, Henrietta More's aunt and the widow of a successful businessman, died.[165] Henrietta had for years taken care of her paralytic aunt, who left her with a surprisingly large inheritance.[166] Thus, as her husband's position at the *Nation* grew less rewarding, Henrietta, who feared the job's impact on More's health, possessed the requisite funds to enable him to leave. More resigned his position at some point in the summer of 1913,[167] though he would remain the editor-in-chief through the middle of March, 1914,[168] thereafter to stay on nominally as the *Nation*'s "advisory editor."[169] To soothe her husband's ego, Henrietta agreed that he would cover his own personal expenses through freelance writing and lecturing.[170] She purchased a family home on Nassau Street in nearby Princeton, New Jersey, a town that allowed the Mores to escape the hustle and bustle of New York City and keep close with Frank Jewett Mather, More's and Babbitt's dear friend, who now served as a faculty member in Princeton's art history department.

---

than More would be made the editor-in-chief. On Hammond Lamont, see his entry in the Biographical Register.

164. Dakin 1960: 145-46. See also Wilson 1948: 9.
165. Anon. 1911; Dakin 1960: 113-14. The death was announced on January 3.
166. Dakin 1960: 113-14.
167. Dakin (1960: 144) specifies that on August 17, 1913, More wrote to his older sister Alice, informing her that he had resigned from the *Nation* and aimed to stay on only as long as it took to reorganize the office.
168. As of March 15, 1914, More's position as editor ended (Dakin 1960: 144-46). On his departure, see also Shafer 1935c: 109, 206; Mather 1938: 370; Oates 1946: 306; Dakin 1950: 7; Hough 1952: 175-76; Duggan 1966: 89; Warren 1969: 1107; Hanford 1961: 163.
169. Dakin (1950: 7) notes that More was the *Nation*'s advisory editor from 1914 to 1917.
170. Dakin 1960: 145.

More's newfound freedom afforded him the opportunity to work on a different sort of intellectual project.[171] Although he continued to produce essays and reviews for the popular press, the number of these pieces notably declined as More turned to a book project that would ultimately span numerous volumes. More had grown deeply attached to Platonic philosophy, especially in what he took to be its dualistic foundation. In late 1917 the Princeton University Press published his book *Platonism*, which had first seen life as a series of lectures delivered at the university.[172] When he started work on the book More continued to keep Christianity at arm's length,[173] but this soon changed.[174] *Platonism* became the introductory volume of a five-part series More called *The Greek Tradition*. In these books More would contend that Christianity, especially in the orthodox expression of it codified by the councils of Nicaea and Chalcedon, amounted to the proper culmination of Platonic dualism. As More announced in *The Religion of Plato*, the second installment of *The Greek Tradition*:

> My belief then is that Greek literature, philosophic and religious, pagan and Christian, from Plato to St. Chrysostom and beyond to that of the Council of Chalcedon in 451 A.D., is essentially a unit and follows at the centre a straight line. This body of thought I call the Greek Tradition, since the main force in preserving it intact while assimilating large accretions of foreign matter was the extraordinary genius of the Greek speech. The initial impulse to the movement was given by a peculiar form of dualism developed by Plato from the teaching of his master Socrates.[175]

Throughout the remainder of his life More's work would focus chiefly on philosophy and theology. More, again a Christian believer, drew closer to

---

171. After his retirement from the *Nation*, More served in an unofficial and, ultimately, official capacity as an editor for Henry Holt's *Unpopular Review*, which changed its name to *Unpartizan Review* soon before Holt ended its print run in 1921. See, e.g., Sherman and More 1929: 52; Dakin 1960: 151. See also Shafer 1935c: 206. On Henry Holt, see his entry in the Biographical Register.

172. See More 1917b: i. Dakin (1950: 170) notes that More delivered these lectures in October and November of 1917 and that the book was published in December of the same year. See also Shafer 1935c: 206-7; Mather 1938: 370; Dakin 1960: 170; Oates 1946: 307.

173. For examples of More's earlier criticisms of Christianity, see, e.g., More 1909a: 44, 121, 246, 326. Cf. More 1909a: 243.

174. On the hints from the Babbitt–More correspondence about the timing of this change, see below. According to Mather (1938: 371), More's wife likely influenced More's later turn towards Christianity.

175. More 1921: vi.

a heterodox Anglicanism. As we shall see, this change, accompanied as it was with criticisms of other approaches to faith, caused consternation for Babbitt, whose Humanism had always been decidedly ecumenical in spirit.

A few years after the Mores had arrived in Princeton, the university decided to take advantage of the proximity of such an esteemed intellectual, courting him to join the philosophy faculty as a part-time lecturer by the spring of 1918.[176] He would teach undergraduate and graduate classes at Princeton one semester of the academic year, first in philosophy and eventually in the classics department, [177] until his retirement in 1933.[178] The teaching provided More some intellectual stimulation and a paycheck, without proving so onerous as to keep him from his writing. This task possibly took on added social benefits as of 1928, since in January of this year Henrietta, whose health had declined after the birth of their daughters, passed away.[179]

In addition to *The Greek Tradition*, More's later output included three volumes of *New Shelburne Essays*, one of which, *On Being Human* (1936), offers an essay on his relationship with Babbitt[180] and some uncharacteristic forays into contemporary literary criticism. In a piece originally appearing in a French journal, for example, More excoriated many then-famous authors, memorably likening John Dos Passos's *Manhattan Transfer* (1925) to "an explosion in a cesspool."[181] His interests remained chiefly theological, however. As his final intellectual task, completed only a few days prior to his death from cancer on March 9, 1937,[182] More revised *Pages from an Oxford Diary* (1937), a memoir of sorts about his stay in England written more than a decade earlier, which describes his conversion to Christianity.[183]

---

176. The imprecise accounts of More's lectureship at Princeton render it difficult to determine when he began teaching there. See, e.g., Mather 1938: 370; Dakin 1960: 177-78, 182-83, 211; Hoeveler 1977: 11; Ryn 1995b: xxii. In a letter to Babbitt from July 26, 1918, More appears to suggest that he was teaching at Princeton in the spring 1918 semester. See chapter 6. This is likely the first semester in which he offered a class there.

177. Dakin (1960: 236) notes that More agreed to switch from the philosophy to the classics department at Princeton on January 28, 1926. Although he esteemed his colleagues in philosophy, More thought that his lack of technical training in the discipline made classics a more reasonable home for him.

178. Dakin (1960: 321) notes that April 13, 1933, marked More's retirement from Princeton.

179. Dakin (1960: 254) notes her death on the 20th of the month. The funeral was held three days later at the Mores' home at 245 Nassau Street in Princeton.

180. More 1936d: 25-42.

181. More 1936d: 63.

182. Mather 1938: 372; Dakin 1960: 386; Hanford 1961: 164. On More's battle with prostate cancer, see Mather 1938: 372; Oates 1946: 316; Dakin 1960: 372, 375, 382.

183. On the discovery of this manuscript shortly before More's death and his decision to edit it for publication, see Mather 1938: 372; Davies 1958: 63; Dakin 1960: 386.

A Plutarchan Literary Critic

As we have already discussed, in large measure due to Babbitt's influence, More's writings, especially prior to their author's return to Christianity, demonstrate many overlapping themes with Babbitt's—to such a degree, in fact, that we can safely conclude that for decades Babbitt and More were the leaders of the self-same philosophical and cultural movement. The *Shelburne Essays*, arguably More's chief claim to fame, typically render a verdict on their literary subjects on the basis of authors' confirmation or rejection of Humanist principles. Writers who affirm a dualistic conception of human existence receive More's plaudits, whereas monistic writers often earn condemnation, at least on this score. One might conclude that this tendency undercuts the value of the judgments found in the *Shelburne Essays* and helps demonstrate that More—despite the awe-inspiring range of his criticism—tended to view literature in unbecomingly narrow and moralistic terms.

Such an assessment does not hold up to scrutiny, however. To be sure, in places one can find More's criticism a tad predictable, especially when many examples of it are read in quick succession. Since he tended to weigh the ultimate success or failure of individual writers in large measure through the lens of ethical dualism, at times one can guess what More's reaction will be to a given author before one commences reading an essay. But this feature of More's criticism pales in comparison with his writings' many laudable traits. Furthermore, the intellectual context of late-nineteenth and early-twentieth-century America helps explain More's insistence on the moral qualities of literature. The wild popularity of romanticism and naturalism helped cement an art-for-art's-sake aesthetic as the age's dominant literary and critical force. More and Babbitt thus underscored the moral nature of creative writing not because they perceived that this was its lone value, but rather because they recognized the lowly place then accorded to it.

It must also be noted that More did not simply praise or condemn authors on the grounds of their philosophies of life alone. More aesthetically inclined than Babbitt, he was capable of detecting the strengths of well-wrought literary works, even when he disagreed with what he took to be their animating spirit. Thus, for example, though he found fault with Wordsworth's untrammeled romanticism, More recognized his creative gifts. About Wordsworth's oeuvre overall, he maintained, "It is perfectly true that we may read through pages of weary metaphysics and self-maunderings of tortured prose, and then suddenly come upon a passage whose inevitable beauty flashes upon the soul like a burning search-light."[184] More also correctly classed Walt Whitman among "the great and not the minor poets,"[185] despite noting similar romantic tendencies in his writings.[186] Though appalled by Kipling's apologetics for imperialism, furthermore, he was capable of detecting his charms. "When to Kipling's instinctive utterance of the popular needs are added his wit and dramatic power, his skill in telling a story, his mastery of the clinging epithet, his pulsating language and sturdy rhythms," More wrote in an essay comparing Kipling and Edward FitzGerald, "it is easy to understand his immense vogue."[187] More even praised lesser writers such as the socialist political scientist and philosopher G. Lowes Dickinson, whom he deemed a talented stylist, regardless of the differences in their ideological perspectives. "His language is shot through with imagination, above its utilitarian values," More ventured.[188]

Most crucially, More's focus on literary criticism as criticism of life allows his writings to sparkle with an immediacy and excitement atypical of such essays. More's work, in addition to serving as a cultural Baedeker on its own, demonstrates the vital importance of literature for living well. Like the New Humanism more generally, More's essays demonstrate that literature matters in the most urgent and profound respects. This quality helps grant More's criticism an enthusiasm that is catching—even among those who disagree with his broader judgements. In addition, More's almost preternatural frame of reference—his capacious learning in the annals of literary history from antiquity to the present—ensures that he could trace the history of ideas in literature in profound ways and provide critical assessments based on a learnedness rare even among professional critics. To a greater degree than Babbitt, moreover, More in the *Shelburne Essays* attempted to provide rounded estimates of writers,[189] remarking on their strengths even when he found their approach to life unpalatable.

In a few of his missives to Babbitt, More noted his affection for the ancient Greek biographer and moral philosopher Plutarch. At the conclusion of a letter from July 15, 1919, for instance, More suggested to Babbitt that Plutarch is "a kindred spirit."[190] This remark provides a useful window into

---

184. More 1910a: 44. For his full estimation, see 27-48.
185. More 1906: 200.
186. More 1906: 180-211.
187. More 1905b: 112.
188. More 1910a: 182. For his full judgment of Dickinson, see 170-94.
189. Babbitt occasionally suggested that this was not his aim; see, e.g., Babbitt 1986: 69-70.
190. See below, chapter 7.

More's critical mission. Like the great Platonist from Chaeronea, More aimed in his literary criticism to determine the essence of an individual. Hence More's deep interest in the biographies of authors whose writings he analyzed: he hoped to discover whether the philosophies of existence detectable in their works allowed them to live sound and rewarding lives. As readers of the *Shelburne Essays* will note, this tendency made writers' letters especially attractive to him; his critical reviews abound in discussions of authors' correspondence. Although More's biographical proclivities would become passé with the vogue for the New Criticism soon after his death, they help enliven his critical essays, which otherwise contain few genuflections to popular taste and often assume a grounding in literary and philosophical history that must have been rare among readers of his (or any) day.

In part due to the undeniable strengths of the *Shelburne Essays*, some have concluded that More was a more penetrating and successful literary critic than was Babbitt.[191] One can certainly understand such a view, but it misinterprets Babbitt's purpose. As others have noted,[192] Babbitt was not so much a literary critic as a cosmopolitan philosopher of literature. He intended to provide for others the intellectual means through which they could properly approach creative writing. Thus, much of his work focused less on individual novelists and poets and more on figures, such as Rousseau, who granted critics the principles by which they could view art and literature overall. Although More offered his insights into major literary critics such as Sainte-Beuve and Matthew Arnold,[193] throughout much of his career he was far closer to what one may term a "working critic," and therefore he expended much greater effort sizing up the merits and demerits of individual creative authors. For this reason, perhaps, scholars of literature have often preferred to focus on More's work, whereas philosophers, political theorists, and intellectual historians have typically demonstrated greater interest in Babbitt's.

We must also not overlook aspects of Babbitt's published oeuvre that appear more successful than More's. Babbitt was surely the more insightful political theorist. *Democracy and Leadership* (1924), the book that provides Babbitt's fullest expression of his Burkean approach to politics, remains a classic of American conservative thought.[194] Although marred by Babbitt's typically meandering prose style, the monograph displays the strengths of its author's

---

191. E.g., Otis 1965: 58.
192. E.g., Spiller 1963: 1148; Levin 1966: 346. Cf. Maynard 1935: 586; Mercier in Manchester and Shepard 1941: 204.
193. See, e.g., More 1905b: 54-81 (on Saint-Beuve) and 1910a: 213-44.
194. For helpful analysis of Babbitt's views on the relationship between democracy and imperialism, see Smith 2019.

systematic application of Humanist principles to political life. In it, Babbitt powerfully appeals to a Washingtonian vision of American republicanism, which views constitutional checks and balances as a governmental corollary to a person's *frein vital*. He frets about the rise of a Jeffersonian—ultimately Rousseauistic—approach to governance, which lauds the fleeting whims of the populace. Though clearly animated by the advent of World War I,[195] *Democracy and Leadership* continues to resonate with later generations of political thinkers.[196]

By comparison, *Aristocracy and Justice* (1915), More's only book-length discussion of politics, although not without its merits, seems much less successful.[197] In these essays More dilated on the problem of cultivating what he termed a "natural aristocracy"—that is to say, an aristocracy of intelligence and character, rather than of birth or wealth—in a democratic society such as the United States, which lacks the aristocratic trappings of Europe.[198] Although hardly the anti-democratic screed of his detractors' imaginations,[199] the book provides a few stark and polemical judgments on which More's critics pounced. "To the civilized man," More intoned in the volume, "*the rights of property are more important than the right to life.*"[200] Critics fumed at this callous overstatement, often without placing it in the proper context of More's argument. In a misleading denunciation, for example, Van Wyck Brooks maintained that More "has not been able to feel human values finely because to have done so would have been to upset his whole faith in a society based not upon the creative but upon the acquisitive instincts of men, a society ruled over by the 'natural aristocracy.'"[201] In reality, More expressed acute criticisms of plutocrats—men who, in his judgment, lacked any vital principle of restraint—and the sort of society that would champion them as moral exemplars.[202] But such uncharacteristically bellicose language on his part provided fodder for his critics.

---

195. As Smith (2019: 103) perceptively notes.

196. E.g., Ryn 1978; Smith 2019; Garrison and Holston 2020.

197. Notably, Mather (1938: 370) and Warren (1969: 1106), two men highly sympathetic to the New Humanism, considered it one of his least successful volumes.

198. See More 1915a: esp. 3-38. More's decision to compose the political essays included in this book seems related to the fomenting of World War I.

199. See, e.g., Kazin 1982: 297, who portrayed More as an opponent of democracy.

200. More 1915a: 136 (emphasis in the original).

201. Brooks 1918: 72-73. See also 84. For another example of critics homing in on More's polemical praise of private property, see, e.g., Kazin 1982: 299. Cf. Davies (1958: 17), who similarly discusses More's "extreme economic conservatism."

202. E.g., More 1901, 1902, 1915a: 21, 30, 60, and 1936d: 142. Cf. More 1910a: 254-56 (a critique of laissez-faire economics) and 1915a: 141, 169, 172, 228 (which supplies criticisms of free-market economics). See also Duggan 1966: 86.

More's political writings, furthermore, are less prone than Babbitt's to steer clear of the nitty-gritty policy issues of their day. Accordingly, More's essays on political topics possess less lasting value and occasionally showcase views that have not aged well, to say the least. Although both Babbitt and More, for example, appear to have opposed women's suffrage[203] and were hardly feminists, only More included criticisms in his writing of feminism and "the peculiar characteristics and limitations of the female sex"[204] that seem risible today.[205]

Babbitt also mustered more compelling and systematic criticisms of American higher education than did More. This is an important conclusion since the New Humanism's critique of the university movement in the US remains arguably its signal accomplishment. In *Literature and the American College* and other writings focused on the shortcomings of the professionalized, pseudo-humanitarian academy in America, Babbitt unearthed the unsound philosophical moorings that he blamed for warping higher learning. Even many readers critical of the New Humanism saw value in Babbitt's powerful analyses of what ailed colleges and universities in his day.[206] Given the directions in which American higher education has moved in the decades following Babbitt's death, moreover, the criticisms he articulated continue to resonate. Indeed, Babbitt provided a radical critique of the professionalized university that remains highly valuable for those concerned about our ongoing crisis for the humanities.[207]

More too spilled much ink on educational matters, and he, like Babbitt, often stressed the philosophical premises surrounding the demotion of the classical humanities.[208] The study of ancient Greek literary masterpieces, he

203. On Babbitt's opposition, see Nevin 1984: 119. On More's opposition, see Dakin 1960: 126. Cf. More 1967a: 237-38.

204. More 1915a: 143.

205. For other examples of More's anti-feminism, see More 1915a: 143, 241-42. For examples of his sexism, see, e.g., More 1905b: 126-27, 133-34, 1908d: 75, 1910a: 120, 1967a: 129, 1967b: 74, and 1967c: 280. Despite More's sexism, though, he was capable of articulating pro-women attitudes: e.g., More 1903b: 338-39, 1904: 200, 1908d: 224-25, 239. Babbitt also demonstrated sexist attitudes in his writing: e.g., Babbitt 1986: 125, 134-35, 139. Cf. Giese in Manchester and Shepard 1941: 18-19; Maag in Manchester and Shepard 1941: 80; Nevin 1984: 28-29; Brennan and Yarbrough 1987: 2; Graff 1987: 107.

206. E.g., Canby 1930: 1122; Colum 1930: 1064; Winters 1930: 329; Maynard 1935: 578. See also Eliot 1964: 434 n. 2; Hovey 1986; Hindus 1994: 45. In this context, it is interesting to note that no contribution to Grattan 1930a, a book dedicated to criticizing the New Humanism, focused its attack on Babbitt's critique of American higher education.

207. On this topic, see, e.g., Hovey 1986; Adler 2020.

208. See, e.g., More 1905b: 197, 1910a: 256-57, 1915a: 60, 63-64, 84, 88-94, 1916a: 695, 1967a: 236, and 1972: 263, 265-66; More in Dakin 1950: 42. Cf. More 1903c, 1915a: 36 and 1972: 256-61.

maintained, possessed unrivaled importance for the nation's young because these works' instinctive humanism fights against the dominant naturalism of the age. "If Greek affords no discipline corrective of the influence of science and different from that of the languages in which modern tendencies are expressed," he argued, "the study of it is merely an enormous waste of time."[209]

But More often genuflected to the shopworn, skills-based defenses of the classical humanities that had served as the bread and butter of the much-maligned Philological Syndicate. As part of his defense of the classics, More contended that ancient Greek and Latin have value because they "act as a tonic exercise to the brain."[210] Such arguments had been a disaster for educational traditionalists in the late nineteenth century,[211] and More, unlike Babbitt, continued to rely on this losing position well into the early decades of the twentieth.

Platonized Christianity and the Fate of the New Humanism

By focusing too much on the disparate nature of Babbitt's and More's accomplishments, one can overlook their power in tandem. Indeed, Babbitt, the penetrating philosopher of literature, and More, the elegant and sensitive literary critic, masterfully complemented one another's intellectual gifts. It is no wonder, then, that Babbitt grew distraught over More's partial departure from the New Humanism in favor of Platonic Anglicanism. To make matters worse for Babbitt, More's review in the pages of the *Bookman* of *Humanism and America*, the collective manifesto that received so much attention in the American press in 1930, reiterated some of the reservations Babbitt's socially conservative critics had expressed about the movement.[212] Like other Christian detractors of the New Humanism, More now relayed doubts about Babbitt's latitudinarianism.[213] Humanism, he stressed, cannot flourish without a theistic undergirding. "Why should I propose to myself a line of life which requires a constant exercise of choice and restraint, in

---

209. More 1910a: 257.
210. More 1915a: 48. For similar skills-based defenses of the classical languages, see, e.g., More 1903a: 512, 1915a: 46-49, and 1972: 262. Cf. More 1916a: 695.
211. On the congenital downsides of such arguments, see, e.g., Proctor 1998: 99-103, 106, 110, 112; Adler 2020: 70-71, 84-85.
212. More 1930b. Mercier (in Manchester and Shepard 1941: 195-96), Babbitt's colleague at Harvard, reports that Babbitt was bothered by this review.
213. For similar critiques of Humanism's ecumenism, see, e.g., Chesterton 1929; Tate 1930; Maynard 1935: 588; Eliot 1964: 419-38. Cf. Grattan 1930b: 22; Rascoe 1930: 119.

themselves painful to the natural man, unless something of value is to be attained thereby?"[214]

In an attempt to satisfy potential followers of both religious and secular inclinations, Babbitt provided many responses to this question. "The two most notable manifestations of the humanistic spirit that the world has seen, that in ancient Greece and that in Confucian China," he asserted, "did not have the support of Christianity or any other form of revealed religion."[215] Despite such appeals, however, More's criticisms—especially insofar as they provided fodder for conservative Christians skeptical about Humanism— exposed the divisions among the Humanists on religious matters. Whereas Louis J. A. Mercier energetically maintained the correspondence between Humanism and Catholicism,[216] for instance, Frank Jewett Mather[217] and Norman Foerster[218] hinted that the New Humanism was incompatible with revealed religion. Although unlikely to have been the main reason for the retreat of the New Humanism from the vanguard of American intellectual life, the movement's incapacity to provide a united front on such a crucial issue could not have helped win converts.

The Babbitt–More correspondence hints at Babbitt's unease with More's partial withdrawal from the movement.[219] According to More, the two friends remained closer intellectually than Babbitt presumed. In a July 4, 1922, letter to the literary critic Percy H. Houston, for example, More maintained that "Our difference—his and mine—is rather, I think, a matter of emphasis than of fundamental disagreement."[220] Moreover, More's later focus on Christian apologetics should not obscure the fact that the two leading lights of the New Humanism never saw eye-to-eye on various matters. Prior to his conversion

214. More 1936d: 17-18.
215. Babbitt 1930: 37. For useful analyses of Babbitt's approach to religion, see, e.g., Leander 1937a: 147-61; Warren 1956: 157-59; Ryn 1995b: xii, xxx-xxxii; Panichas 1999: 83-106; Holston 2020.
216. Mercier 1936: esp. 178-87.
217. Mather 1930b: 747. In an April 1, 1930, letter to Robert Shafer, More referred to Mather as an "outspoken" agnostic (for the text of the letter, see Dakin 1960: 283).
218. Noted by Mercier (1936: 172). But cf. Foerster 1929, which broadcasts its author's skeptical attitude toward religion yet maintains that Humanism can be compatible with it.
219. Many discussions of their break underscore Babbitt's sense of unease. On this break see, e.g., Elliott 1937c and 1938: 103-15; Eliot 1937b: 374; Mercier in Manchester and Shepard 1941: 195-96; Otis in Manchester and Shepard 1941: 309; Rice in Manchester and Shepard 1941: 250, 260-61; Warren in Manchester and Shepard 1941: 214; Mercier 1948: 24-28; Dakin 1960: 221-22, 241-42, 255-57; Hanford 1961: 165; Duggan 1966: 141-42; Warren 1969: 1099; Kazin 1982: 295; Brennan and Yarbrough 1987: 73-74; Tanner 1987: 38-39. More himself discussed the break; see More in Manchester and Shepard 1941: 328-31.
220. Quoted in Dakin 1960: 222.

to Christianity, More favored a mystical, Vedantic Hinduism and esteemed Plato as the greatest Greek philosopher. Babbitt, by contrast, hewed closest to a Hinayana Buddhism stripped of all mythological baggage and considered Aristotle his chief Western intellectual model.[221] Babbitt's discussion of More's essay called "The Forest Philosophy of India" in the correspondence[222] hints at early differences in their approaches and suggests that their disagreements were from the start highly religious in character.[223] Although undeniably More's turn away from literary criticism towards theology widened their intellectual and spiritual distance, the two men betrayed disparate visions from the start.

The Polemical War over the New Humanism

Such a recognition was easily lost in the bellicose arguments over the New Humanism that took center stage in the late 1920s and early 1930s. After Babbitt and More for decades lamented the minimal impact of their movement on American culture, suddenly in these years umpteen learned journals and newspapers featured articles adjudicating the battle over the New Humanism.[224] Unfortunately, the polemical nature of these arguments ensured that Babbitt's and More's views seldom received the careful analysis they deserve. On the contrary: the culture warriors who weighed in on the New Humanism typically provided critiques filled with misconceptions and distortions.

Many critics mischaracterized Babbitt and More as strictly backward-looking figures. "Humanistic values are derived from past formulations," groused C. Hartley Grattan, a dogged opponent of the New Humanism, "particularly from formulations arrived at in a primitive society where the authors could not conceivably imagine many of the most vital and complex problems of modern living."[225] In reality, Babbitt had stressed the

---

221. From early on, moreover, More offered criticisms of Aristotle. See, e.g., More 1905a: 188, 1921: 313-14, and 1924: 136-39. Cf. More 1923: 204-5, 1924: 136, 1928a: ix-x, xii, and 1937b: 72. Leander (1970: 125-26, 142-43) provides a useful discussion of the differing attitudes to religion, mysticism, and happiness Babbitt and More harbored from their earliest days together in graduate school. Despite his conversion to many of Babbitt's ideas, Leander stresses, More "retained his theosophic, Vedantist bias" (126).

222. See Babbitt's July 3, 1907, letter to More in chapter 2.

223. Interestingly, prior to his turn to Christianity, More perceived many similarities between it and Buddhism. See, e.g., More 1904: 239, 242-43. Cf. More 1909a: 150-51.

224. For pieces addressing the controversy over the New Humanism, see, e.g., anon. 1930; Canby 1930; Colum 1930; the contributions to Grattan 1930a; Rand 1932; Maynard 1935. For a lament from More about the New Humanism's obscurity, see More 1928a: 73-76.

225. Grattan 1930b: 28.

crucial importance of the individual's creative refashioning of tradition for the needs of the present. "The task of assimilating what is best in the past and the present, and adapting it to one's own use and the use of others," Babbitt wrote, "so far from lacking in originality, calls for something akin to creation."[226] He had, moreover, underscored the value of the natural and social sciences as part of his (confusingly termed) attempt to "become a complete positivist."[227] Even so, detractors pilloried the New Humanism as a reactionary approach to life ill-equipped to deal with the contemporary world.[228]

Some naysayers misunderstood Babbitt's and More's conception of the inner check, incorrectly concluding that it suggested a strictly passive approach to morality. The philosopher John Dewey, whose progressive vision of education earned much criticism from the Humanists,[229] for example, deemed Babbitt's and More's philosophy a "doctrine of restraint and negation" alone.[230] On this score, the Southern Agrarian poet and critic Allen Tate agreed; according to the New Humanism, he opined, "The good man is he who 'refrains from doing' what the 'lower nature dictates,' and he need do nothing positive."[231] Careful readers of Babbitt's and More's writings would have spied the affirmative qualities of the inner check, but the raucous debates over the New Humanism ran roughshod over such subtleties.

Unfortunately, the pugnacious rows Babbitt and More helped inspire towards the end of their lives have also affected the character of many later estimations of their movement. Thus, some more recent writers have committed similar errors in their discussions of the New Humanism. According to the literary critic R. P. Blackmur, for example, Babbitt "was a praiser of gone times because he had none of his own."[232] The educational historian Laurence Vesey, misunderstanding Aristotle's conception of leisure, concluded that Babbitt deemed laziness a key feature of a proper approach to liberal culture.[233] Catherine Oglesby, seemingly uninformed about major

---

226. Babbitt 1986: 125. Cf. Babbitt 1940: 44-45.
227. Babbitt 1991: lxxi. On Babbitt's confusing embrace of the term "positivism" to describe his outlook, see, e.g., Ryn 1991: xxix-xxx, 1995a, and 1997: 91.
228. E.g., Jones 1928: 158; Canby 1930: 1122; Blackmur 1955: 147; Butts 1971: 398.
229. See, e.g., Babbitt 1924: 312-13, 1940: 211-12, and 1991: 388; Mather 1930a: 156-57; More 1936d: 117-43.
230. Dewey 1984: 264.
231. Tate 1930: 141. For congruent opinions, see Wilson 1930: 46; Maynard 1935: 579.
232. Blackmur 1955: 147.
233. Veysey 1965: 188.

aspects of More's thought, portrayed him as a hyper-rational stoic.[234] In an almost hysterical denunciation of the New Humanism, the literary scholar William V. Spanos managed to misinterpret numerous ideas foundational to the movement: "this inhumane and alienating will to power," he announced, "this impulse to discipline beginnings from the end, is enacted, however unevenly, at every site on the continuum of being, whatever the particular site Babbitt chooses to focus, by his utterly exemplary, exhausted, insistently graceless, tendentious, and judgmental discourse."[235] It is hard to know where to begin correcting such misimpressions, which treat Babbitt—who, like More, was heavily critical of Nietzsche—as a proponent of the will to power.[236]

Shortcomings, Intellectual and Tactical

The unreliable character of many criticisms should not lead us to conclude that Babbitt's and More's writings possess no downsides. Sometimes, in fact, the spirited critiques of the New Humanism—even when overblown—possessed at least kernels of truth. For example, polemical detractors have dismissed More as a Puritan.[237] To some degree, this assessment relates to More's estimation of the American revivalist preacher Jonathan Edwards. He deemed Edwards "the greatest theologian and philosopher yet produced in this country."[238] But More also clarified that he found Edwards' fire-and-brimstone theology repulsive.[239] Occasionally critics failed to note More's reservations about Edwards, instead portraying More as a knuckle-dragging Calvinist. Even so, it seems clear that in some respects More's reactions to literature could be squeamish.[240] When analyzing the plot of Proust's *À la recherché du temps perdu* (1913-27), for example, More referred to "a passionate display of anomalous love (I prefer this less repulsive phrase for homosexuality) intensified by sadism."[241] Though he recognized

---

234. Oglesby 2008: 51-70, esp. 51, 54-55, 60. More was critical of what he took to be overly rationalistic understandings of human existence (see, e.g., More 1924: 5) and despised Stoicism as fatalistic monism (see., e.g., More 1921: vi-vii and 1923: 65-93).

235. Spanos 1985: 43-44.

236. On Babbitt's and More's anti-Nietzscheanism, see above.

237. E.g., Mencken 1922: 176; Hough 1924: 1408; Maynard 1935: 588. On such charges see, e.g., Brown 1939: 478, 488; Warren 1969: 1105; Lambert 1999: 50; Domitrovic 2003: 345.

238. More 1967c: 53. See also More 1900: 2, 111 and 1967c: 35-65.

239. As Kuntz (1980: 390) correctly notes. Cf. More 1967b: 28 and 1967c: 7, 25. See also Tanner 1987: 73, 179.

240. For a similar estimation, see Duggan 1966: 56-58. Cf. Leander 1938: esp. 453; Aaron 1963: 5-6.

241. More 1936d: 44-45.

that Joyce's *Ulysses* (1922) was far from pornographic, moreover, More expressed disdain for its occasional lapses into obscenity.[242] He even deemed Mark Twain's *The Adventures of Tom Sawyer* (1876) a pernicious model for young readers.[243]

We may safely chalk up such judgments to More's personal background and the era in which he grew up. It is unfair to pronounce upon More's critical achievements and failures without rooting them in their historical and intellectual context. But, more significantly, More in places proved an unreliable assessor of contemporary literature. He was too quick to dismiss the moral qualities in Dostoyevsky's work,[244] for example, and could not recognize how Joyce's later stream-of-consciousness style could promote reflections on the ethical life of which More may have approved.[245] As Francis Duggan notes, More seemed either so impatient "with the formal experimentation of certain modern writers" or revolted by "their frank protestations of sordidness, crime, and sensuality"[246] that he too categorically dismissed many authors now heralded in the modernist canon.

Even when he displayed his squeamishness, More possessed an elegant prose style, which helped him earn many plaudits. The same cannot be said for Babbitt. To be sure, Babbitt was a master of the punchy phrase and the sententious quip. Hence of the two men he is consistently the more humorous and quotable author. But Babbitt's writings seem undercut by serious problems of arrangement. This is a topic about which More himself contributed a valuable assessment:

> A rhetorician would say that he [Babbitt] did not know how to manage his paragraphs. Instead of finishing one link of his argument and proceeding to the next one and so on from premise to conclusion, he is somewhat inclined to crowd his whole thesis, at least implicitly, into each single paragraph, so that the book, despite the inexhaustible variety of his illustrations, gives the impression of endless repetition. That

---

242. More 1936d: 298-300.
243. More 1915b: 651. It is important to recognize, however, that More could also provide anti-prudish estimations of writers: e.g., More 1905b: 207-8, 1906: 148, and 1967b: 286-87. Cf. More 1928a: 103.
244. See, e.g., More 1967b: 298-300. Cf. More's heavy criticism of G. B. Shaw at 303.
245. See More 1928a: 39-40 and 1936d: 69-96, esp. 69-70, where More partly recognizes Joyce's strengths as a moralist. On More's changing attitude toward Joyce, see also Wilson 1948: 10. For examples of More's heavy criticisms for then-contemporary authors, see, e.g., More 1920b and 1928a: 53-76.
246. Duggan 1966: 131.

is undoubtedly a fault of construction, and has stood in the way of his full recognition as a thinker.[247]

Babbitt also occasionally failed to define his terms precisely—a regrettable lapse for a writer whose invocation of idiosyncratically understood concepts such as the "inner check," "the higher will," and "a complete positivist" could cause confusion among readers.[248] Many of Babbitt's friends and admirers noted that he was a more powerful speaker than writer,[249] and undeniably his faults in the latter category helped feed misimpressions about his ideas.

Although More's prose did not suffer from similar demerits, he too could relay the principles of the New Humanism in a confusing manner. His essay "Definitions of Dualism," from the eighth installment of the *Shelburne Essays*,[250] provides a perfect case in point. The Babbitt–More correspondence demonstrates that both men took pains to ensure that this piece—which arguably amounts to the most detailed encapsulation of his critical philosophy that More ever mustered—contains as reliable a window into the New Humanism as possible. Unfortunately, though, More chose to explain this philosophy through ninety separate maxims, rather than one logically connected essay. Indeed, the structure of "Definitions of Dualism" has caused considerable troubles for interpreters—even sympathetic interpreters—who aim to make sense of More's Platonic dualism.[251]

Other downsides associated with the New Humanism likely stem from matters of emphasis. Babbitt and More proved so distraught about the rampant downgrading of free will and the individual's moral responsibility in contemporary society that they gave short shrift to the economic and social forces that provide parameters for human beings' daily lives. Perhaps relatedly, both Babbitt and More presented a one-sided impression of the romantic movement, which failed to take full account of its disparate—and

---

247. More in Manchester and Shepard 1941: 326.
248. As Hazlitt (1930: 91-92) and Nevin (1984: 40) reasonably note.
249. Elliott 1938: 56, 88; Elliott in Manchester and Shepard 1941: 326; Nevin 1984: 25, 29. Cf. Dakin 1960: 105 n. 60; Hindus 1994: 39.
250. More 1967a: 247-302.
251. See, e.g., Duggan 1966: 35-36; Leander 1970; Kuntz 1980. Cf. Leander 1937a and 1974. On More's choice for the structure of "Definitions of Dualism," Leander (1970: 4) writes: "We all live in a haze; a central area is illuminated by the light of clear thought but all around it is darkness. It was a strong feeling of this aspect of our human predicament that caused More to write a series of definitions instead of attempting a fully systematic presentation." Leander's manuscript chiefly aims to provide a full accounting for More's pre-Christian philosophy, since More never did so.

even countervailing—tendencies.²⁵² Ever since Arthur Lovejoy memorably deemed Babbitt a romantic in his anti-romanticism,²⁵³ it became common for critics of the New Humanism to note the tension between its full-throated attack on romanticism and its heralding of the Golden Mean.²⁵⁴ This point was arguably more clever than significant. Still, Babbitt and More seem not to have recognized that they too were partly products of the romantic movement. In their theories of knowledge, for example, the leaders of the New Humanism betray the influence of romanticism.²⁵⁵

Fascism, Monarchism, and ... the New Humanism?

Although critics have occasionally focused on these and kindred shortcomings, far more attention in the battle over the New Humanism stressed the movement's political bona fides. Many attempts to discredit Babbitt and More lapsed into exercises of guilt by association. The two men's occasional carelessness in cultivating intellectual allies appears to have encouraged this approach among anti-Humanist culture warriors.²⁵⁶

The vast majority of these critiques surrounded a man by the name of Seward Collins (1899–1952).²⁵⁷ Collins, a wealthy socialite, journalist, and editor, had drifted erratically in his political commitments, from progressivism, Southern Agrarianism, the New Humanism, and Distributism, to a flirtation with a self-styled American Fascism. In the early 1920s when still affiliated with the political Left, Collins had denigrated More's work in his column for the *Brooklyn Daily Eagle*. About *The Greek Tradition*, a few volumes of which were already in print, for example, Collins declared, "It is pathetic at the moments it is not disgusting."²⁵⁸ He was then a member of the progressive journalistic smart set in New York City, on good terms with, for example, his old college chum Edmund Wilson (who had procured for

---

252. On this score, see, e.g., Hoeveler 1977: 43-44, 54; Ryn 1995b: xliv and 1997: 45-46, 52.
253. Lovejoy 1920: 302.
254. E.g., Wilson 1930: 47; Dewey 1984: 265.
255. On this topic, see the insightful analyses of Ryn 1991: xxi, 1995b: xliv, and 1997: 45-46, 52. Ryn focuses on Babbitt, but his criticisms relate to More's views as well.
256. As Rice (in Manchester and Shepard 1941: 256) notes.
257. On Collins, see above all Stone 1960; Tucker 2006. See also Hoeveler 1977: 24. For examples of discrediting the New Humanism by reference to Collins see Brody 1930; Frohock 1940: 329; Kazin 1982: 293. For more on Collins, see his entry in the Biographical Register and below.
258. Collins 1922b. See also Collins 1922a. On More's reaction to such criticism from Collins, see Dakin 1960: 217.

Collins a position at *Vanity Fair*)²⁵⁹ and Dorothy Parker (whom he almost wed).²⁶⁰

By 1929, however, Collins had shifted to the Right, for a spell embracing the New Humanism with enthusiasm.²⁶¹ In fact, around this time Collins had transformed the *Bookman*, the journal he owned and edited,²⁶² into a veritable monthly organ of the movement, routinely featuring articles and reviews from its exponents and excoriating its detractors with gusto.²⁶³ As the Babbitt–More correspondence attests²⁶⁴ and Collins himself lamented,²⁶⁵ the two leaders of the New Humanism appeared skeptical of him. Even so, perhaps pleased to have a regular outlet in which to publish, they and some of their followers continued to pen pieces for the *Bookman*.

As of 1933, Collins, by now enthralled with Distributism and so-called Fascism, shut down the *Bookman* and launched the *American Review* in its stead.²⁶⁶ A more deliberately political enterprise, Collins deemed the *Review* a "Right-Wing miscellany"²⁶⁷ that would feature contributions from Distributists, Southern Agrarians, neo-scholastics, and New Humanists, among others.²⁶⁸ Its pages included some disturbing views and rhetoric, not least from Collins himself, who had by then drifted away from the New Humanism towards some brand of monarchism.²⁶⁹ About Hitler's rise in Germany, for example, Collins wrote in the May 1933 issue, "One would gather from the fantastic lack of proportion of our press—not to say its gull-

---

259. Tucker 2006: 57.
260. Tucker 2006: 70-71. Tucker also notes (83-85) that Collins earned kudos on the Left for his support for Sacco and Vanzetti in 1927 and 1928.
261. See Tucker 2006: 91-92.
262. Collins purchased the *Bookman* in July of 1927 (anon. 1928; Stone 1960: 4; cf. Tucker 2006: 82-83). When its editor, Burton Rascoe, resigned on April 13, 1928 (Tucker 2006: 86), Collins took over his position.
263. For examples of his defenses of the New Humanism, see Collins 1930a and b. On this topic, see Brennan and Yarbrough 1987: 72.
264. See More's November 18, 1932, letter to Babbitt below, chapter 10. Hoeveler (1977: 24 n. 35) notes More's skepticism of Collins. Tucker (2006: esp. 109) informs us that Collins was an unreliable editor. On this topic, see below.
265. As noted by Tucker 2006: 94.
266. The first issue of the *American Review* appeared in April of 1933.
267. Collins 1934: 118.
268. On the groups Collins hoped to feature in the magazine, see Collins 1933a.
269. Tucker (2006) tries to diminish the horrors of Collins's views. To be sure, Collins appears not to have supported "Fascism" in the strict Italian sense. Nor were flirtations with Fascism on the part of American intellectuals in the 1920s and 1930s unique to him. But Tucker seems engaged in a kind of special pleading. Tucker's views on the New Humanism are also unreliable.

ibility and sensationalism—that the most important aspect of the German revolution was the hardships suffered by Jews under the new régime. Even if the absurd atrocity stories were all true, the fact would be almost negligible beside an event that shouts aloud in spite of the journalistic silence: the victory of Hitler signifies the end of the Communist threat, *forever*."[270] Other contributors to the *American Review* ventured similarly troubling perspectives. The Southern Agrarian historian Frank L. Owsley, for example, broadcast his anti-Black racism in a discussion of the infamous Scottsboro trial.[271] R. L. Burgess took to the *Review*'s pages to wax historical on the supposed superiority of American Protestants to Catholics and Jews.[272] Protestants such as himself, Burgess counseled, should admit that "there is a rough truth to the essentials of the [Ku Klux] Klan position" on racial matters.[273]

Babbitt was gravely ill by the time Collins abandoned the *Bookman* for the *American Review*. Although Collins published Babbitt's essay "Buddha and the Occident" in two installments in its pages after the author's death,[274] Babbitt never actively contributed to the magazine. Moreover, the New Humanist pieces in the *American Review*, confined to literary criticism, educational animadversions, and reflections on Babbitt and More, appear entirely unobjectionable.[275] But it remains a black mark on the movement that so many figures associated with it—including More himself—continued to write for Collins's periodical after he and some of its contributors trumpeted their unsavory opinions.[276]

---

270. Collins 1933b: 247-48 (emphasis in the original). For other problematic views articulated by Collins, see, e.g., Collins 1933b: 253 (praise for Mussolini), 256 (Nazism has much to teach us).

271. Owsley 1933.

272. Burgess 1934.

273. Burgess 1934: 450. Tellingly, perhaps, when Collins published his own (1934: 123) and R. A. McGowan's (1934) rebuttal to this article, both Collins and McGowan defended Catholics and not Jews from Burgess's attack.

274. Babbitt 1936a and b.

275. Contributions by the Humanists to the *American Review* include Elliott 1933a and b, 1936a and b, and 1937a, b, and c; Foerster 1933 and 1937b; More 1933, 1935a and b, 1936c; Giese 1935; Shafer 1935a, b, and d; Warren 1936a and b and 1937; Leander 1937b and c. More, Mercier, Warren, and other Humanists also wrote book reviews for the magazine. Tucker (2006: 127) reasonably concludes that the *American Review* featured a jumble of opinions, many of them contradicting one another. Collins himself (1934: 126-27) noted that Babbitt would have disagreed with much appearing in the *Review*'s pages. Numerous major writers contributed to the publication, including Hilaire Belloc, Cleanth Brooks, G. K. Chesterton, Ananda K. Coomaraswamy, Christopher Dawson, T. S. Eliot, Randall Jarrell, Wyndham Lewis, John Crowe Ransom, Allen Tate, Mark Van Doren, Robert Penn Warren, and Yvor Winters. So, the Humanists were far from alone in making the mistake of aiding Collins.

276. Although Hoffman Nickerson wrote for the *Review* (see, e.g., Nickerson 1933) and also contributed to *Irving Babbitt: Man and Teacher* (see Manchester and Shepard 1941: 91-94),

The choice of many Humanists to stick with the *American Review* became an obvious tactical blunder. In February 1936, the journalist Grace Lumpkin published an interview she conducted with Collins in the pro-Communist journal *Fight*. Collins, who was tricked into believing that Lumpkin was a political ally, expressed all sorts of offensive and foolish beliefs. "Yes, I am a fascist," he told Lumpkin. "I admire Hitler and Mussolini very much."[277] Asked about the Nazis' maltreatment of the Jews, Collins opined, "It is not persecution. The Jews make trouble. It is necessary to segregate them."[278] As Michael Jay Tucker, Collins's biographer, notes, the resulting article, called "I Want a King," made Collins "look like a raging idiot, opposed to everything modern, up to and including indoor plumbing."[279] Lumpkin's piece, soon picked up by the New York press, contributed to the Southern Agrarian defection from the *American Review*.[280] Collins' periodical, now starved of contributors, ceased publication in 1937. Despite the controversy, some Humanists continued to publish in the *American Review* until its demise.[281]

We have no reason to suspect that More agreed with Collins's extremist views. He, like Babbitt, had criticized anti-Semitism in his published work and praised Emile Zola—an author he otherwise disliked—for his courageous stand in the Dreyfus affair.[282] Among the Humanist circle were at least a couple of men of Jewish descent;[283] by contrast, the *American Review*

Tucker (2006: 104) stresses that he was a protégé of Hilaire Belloc, not a Humanist. Cf. Collins 1934: 121-22.

277. Lumpkin 1936: 3.
278. Lumpkin 1936: 14.
279. Tucker 2006: 155.
280. Stone (1960: 16-18) portrays the Southern Agrarian break from Collins as ideological in character. According to Tucker (2006: 155-57), however, the Agrarians were mainly fed up with Collins's editorial deficiencies. He notes (109-10) that Collins was a disorganized editor who may have suffered from clinical depression.
281. More's final piece for the magazine appeared in the November 1936 issue (see More 1936c). Especially given Collins's erratic approach to editing, it is conceivable that More wrote the piece prior to Lumpkin's publication of her interview with Collins. By this time, moreover, More was already suffering from the prostate cancer that would lead to his death.
282. More 1903d: 562. For Babbitt's support of Dreyfus, see Babbitt 1912e: 315. For other hints of More's support for Jews, see, e.g., More 1915a: 151-89 (esteem for Disraeli) and 1924: 28 (a sympathetic take on Jewish ethnic exclusivity in antiquity); Dakin 1960: 10, 167-69. Tucker (2006: 145-46, 193) suggests that Collins's anti-Semitism stemmed from his embrace of Hilaire Belloc, a Distributist who expressed anti-Jewish attitudes.
283. E.g., Bernard Bandler II and Harry Levin. On Bandler, see his entry in the Biographical Register. Levin was perhaps not strictly speaking a Humanist, but he did admire Babbitt and served as the inaugural Irving Babbitt Professor of Comparative Literature at Harvard. For Levin's largely sympathetic assessments of Babbitt, see Levin 1940 and 1966: 321-47.

included no Jewish contributors.[284] Babbitt and More had also expressed their preference for democratic republicanism over monarchy.[285] Although a critic of a political culture that embraces the instantaneous whims of the populace, Babbitt in *Democracy and Leadership* argued in favor of constitutional checks and balances. For his part, More spilled much ink articulating his desire for a kind of "natural aristocracy" that could help guide American democracy on a more salubrious path. "The cure of democracy is not *more* democracy, but *better* democracy," he wrote.[286] Babbitt and More, moreover, with their hostility to nationalism, imperialism, and warmongering, were deeply hostile to Fascism.[287]

But the New Humanists' cavorting with Collins allowed critics of Babbitt and More to paint them as political extremists. Even before the birth of the *American Review*, naysayers denigrated the New Humanism by linking it to Collins. In a letter to the editor appearing in the *New Republic*, for example, a man named Alter Brody wrote that, "Stripped, with Mr. Collins' aid, of its philosophic verbiage, the New Humanism emerges as the intellectual program of the Boston Chapter of the Daughters of the American Revolution, differing from the Ku Klux Klan by being more exclusive."[288] Similarly, in the Marxist journal *New Masses*, V. F. Calverton concluded that, "In the final analysis...the new humanists are the intellectual fascists of the present (and the forthcoming) generation."[289] Such charges were off-base and unfair, but they helped minimize Babbitt's and More's intellectual and cultural influence.

---

284. Stone 1960: 11. Dorothy Parker, once Collins's love interest, was half-Jewish, and Collins almost married her. But their romantic relationship occurred prior to Collins's fascination with the anti-Semitic Belloc.

285. According to Stone (1960: 9), moreover, Collins "did not seriously believe monarchy could be fashioned from the democratic party system."

286. E.g., More 1915a: 29 (emphasis in the original). For other examples of More's views on democracy, see, e.g., More 1908d: 26, 28-29, 1909a: 271-72, 1910a: 179, 1915a: 3-38, 1917b: 67, 1936d: 154, 1967a: 282-83, and 1967c: 105-7.

287. On Babbitt's disdain for Fascism, see Chalmers 1941: 390; Hoeveler 1977: 181. For an example of More's anti-militarism, see, e.g., More 1915g. For Babbitt's anti-nationalism, see, e.g., Babbitt 1940: 192-93 and 1986: 170-72. Babbitt included a sentence in *Democracy and Leadership* (Babbitt 1924: 312) that has not aged well: "Circumstances may arise when we may esteem ourselves fortunate if we get the American equivalent of a Mussolini; he may be needed to save us from the American equivalent of a Lenin." It should be noted that this book was published in 1924, well before all the horrors of Fascism had manifested themselves to Americans. Furthermore, the sentiment Babbitt offered does not imply support for Mussolini. Cf. Goldman in Manchester and Shepard 1941: 235, who notes that when they met in 1923 Babbitt was hostile to European right-wing authoritarian movements.

288. Brody 1930.

289. Calverton 1930: 10. Yunck (1963) demonstrates that Collins's enthusiasm for a harsh review of Ernest Hemingway's *A Farewell to Arms* that appeared in the *Bookman*—though

Babbitt was an especially undeserving target of these criticisms. After all, his insistence on an essential unity to human knowledge—a cardinal feature of his emphasis on the problem of the One and the Many—is but one example of his deliberate opposition to the race-thinking so prevalent in the late nineteenth and early twentieth centuries. Indeed, Babbitt's critique of scientific naturalism included the Baconians' embrace of eugenics and kindred expressions of racism. "It gives a man a fine expansive feeling to think that he is endowed with certain virtues simply because he has taken the trouble to be born a Celt or a Teuton or an Anglo-Saxon," he wrote.[290] Among Babbitt's enthusiastic students at Harvard were large numbers of Asians, who flocked to his classes due to his penchant for blending Eastern and Western wisdom.[291] Babbitt was also the chief intellectual influence on the Black anthropologist Allison Davis (1902–1983) during his graduate school days at Harvard[292] and an inspiration to the Jewish literary critic Harry Levin (1912–1994), in 1960 named the first occupant of the Irving Babbitt Professorship of Comparative Literature at Harvard.[293]

One finds hints that More, although by no means a bigot in the Collins mold, was less committed than was Babbitt to the New Humanism's brand of intellectual and spiritual ecumenism.[294] Corra Mae Harris, More's co-author of the epistolary novel *The Jessica Letters*, for example, had commenced her writing career with a letter to the editor of the *Independent* from 1899, in which she took exception to the paper's editorializing against lynching, declaring that the "negro is a brute product" and "the mongrel of civiliza-

---

not written by a Humanist—compelled Hemingway to write scornfully about the New Humanism.

290. Babbitt 1912e: 31. For other criticisms of racism, eugenics, and race-thinking, see, e.g., Babbitt 1912e: 161, 1924: 210, 1968: 235-37. For occasional lapses into race-thinking, see, e.g., Babbitt 1924: 209-10 (a passage that appears to grant partial credence to the idea of inferior ethnic groups, a sentiment that clashes with the universalist message in his work), 1940: 1-20 (stereotypes about the Spanish), 21-47 (stereotypes about the English), and 1986: 110 (about Anglo-Saxons' supposed lack of ideas). See also Brennan and Yarbrough 1987: 126, 128.

291. See, e.g., Mercier 1928: vi; Aldridge 1993: esp. 332.

292. Varel 2018: 32.

293. It should be noted that in his letter to More of March 5, 1896, Babbitt expresses some casual anti-Semitism when discussing a rival job candidate—in a short passage Dora excised from the typescript of the correspondence (but which has been restored in this edited collection). Here Babbitt in private correspondence seems not to have lived up to the spirit of ecumenism he elsewhere championed in his writings.

294. There are important signs of cosmopolitanism in More's writings, however, which nod to the greatness of non-Western civilizations. See, e.g., More 1899a: 18, 1905a: esp. 48, 1905b: 265, 1909a: 1-42, 1917b: 14-15, and 1924: 108-11.

tion."²⁹⁵ More, who did not take up a staff position at the *Independent* until two years after the printing of this missive, never published anything that suggests sympathy with Harris's perspective on the matter. In fact, he barely discussed race relations in his voluminous writings²⁹⁶ and in his correspondence with Harris he did not address the issue.²⁹⁷ But More does appear to have been more attached to his ethnic heritage than was Babbitt. A devoted Anglophile, he altered his essays to reflect British spelling when they appeared in book form.²⁹⁸ By the end of his career, in opposition to Babbitt's religious syncretism, More was dilating on the superiority of his brand of Christianity to all other faiths.²⁹⁹ It seems likely that part of Anglicanism's appeal to him, moreover, was its Englishness.

In a letter to Babbitt from December 21, 1915, More criticized Albert Foucher for suggesting that Hindu and Chinese subjects should be added to the college curriculum.³⁰⁰ Such additions were integral to Babbitt's radically expanded humanist canon.³⁰¹ One also notes More's greater regard for race-thinking in some of his writings.³⁰² In sum, on the topic of race More was a more conventional exponent of his time than was Babbitt. After all, the mania for Darwinism in the late nineteenth century encouraged among American intellectuals all sorts of objectionable pseudoscientific estimations of ethnic groups. But perhaps we ought to hold More to a higher standard than his contemporaries, given his paramount interest in the proper moral parameters for living.

In some instances, criticisms of Babbitt's and More's political views appear to have stemmed from their tactical blunders. As we have already discussed, the two men were famous—in some circles infamous—for their hostility to what they called *humanitarianism*. It may have helped Babbitt's and More's cause if they had directed their antipathy toward *pseudo-humanitarianism*,

---

295. Harris 1899: 1354. On Harris and her complicated legacy, see, e.g., Badura 2000; Oglesby 2008.

296. For a rare example of such a discussion, see More 1905b: 32-33, which demonstrates his support for abolitionism.

297. See Oglesby 2008: 62. Although Oglesby provides a misleading and unflinchingly negative portrait of More and his influence on Harris (51-70), she does not blame him for her racism.

298. On this topic, see Duggan 1966: 88.

299. See, e.g., More 1924: 292 and 1937b: 145; More and Cross 1935: xx. See also More's letter to Babbitt from March 26, 1923, which includes criticisms of non-Christians More suggests that Babbitt will dislike.

300. See below, chapter 5.

301. See, for example, Babbitt's support for "a broadened and enriched classical tradition" in his letter to More from May 17, 1908.

302. E.g., More 1904: 87, 1905a: 106-8, 117, 165, 197, 1905b: 93, 223, 1921: viii. See also Ryn 1997: 48, who suggests that More disliked Italians.

rather than humanitarianism per se. Their use of the label *humanitarian* encouraged careless observers to conclude that they were haughty aristocratic types who lacked feeling for the less fortunate. Nothing could be further from the truth.[303] In fact, the New Humanists proved as critical of Nietzschean anti-altruism as they were of Rousseau's chimerical brotherhood of man. Both Babbitt and More scoffed at plutocrats in whose acquisitiveness they spied a stunning lack of the Humanist virtue of self-restraint.[304] They worried that much supposedly humanitarian rhetoric about the poor actually served to excuse people from the more onerous and selfless work of aiding those in need. All that pseudo-humanitarianism of the Rousseauistic type necessitated, they feared, was the complacent self-advertising of concern for the downtrodden—stripped of any concomitant requirement to make the personal sacrifices requisite to help others.[305]

The Legacy of Babbitt, More, and the New Humanism

Even before the deaths of Babbitt and More the New Humanism retreated from the forefront of American culture. The Great Depression rendered Babbitt's and More's anti-statist politics unpopular. Additionally, the second generation of Humanists lacked the intellectual firepower of the movement's progenitors. Babbitt's former student Stuart P. Sherman was a facile writer and capable critic, yet he both withdrew from Humanism in favor of a more robust commitment to populism and pre-deceased Babbitt and More. T. S. Eliot obviously became the most famous writer connected to the movement, but, as we have seen, his devout Anglicanism compelled him to articulate reservations about Babbitt's ideas.[306] Robert Shafer was an energetic exponent of Humanism, but his rambling book-length analysis of More's work demonstrates that he had little to add to the movement besides tenacity.[307] Of such second-generation Humanists, Norman Foerster, another of Babbitt's former undergraduates, was arguably the most prolific and successful. Yet Foerster's contributions to Humanist educational theory, while highly read-

---

303. Cf. Babbitt 1986: 105, 113, 127, 209 and 1991: 368; More 1915a: 209-10 and More in Dakin 1950: 42, which vouch for the benefits of genuine humanitarianism.

304. For Babbitt's criticisms of wealthy business leaders see, e.g., Babbitt 1940: 214-15 and 1986: 92, 107. Cf. Babbitt 1910a: 233 and 1940: 214; Kirk 1960: 479-80. For More's criticisms of plutocrats, see above.

305. For hints that More considered supposed humanitarians to be pseudo-humanitarians, see, e.g., More 1967a: 184-86 and 1967b: 63-64. He actually esteemed genuine humanitarianism: see, e.g., More 1915a: 209-10. On More's view of humanitarianism, see the helpful insights of Tanner 1987: 57-63, 220.

306. See, e.g., Eliot 1964: 419-38 and above. For Babbitt's criticisms of Eliot's position, see, e.g., Babbitt 1928, 1930: 37, 49, and 1940: 204.

307. Shafer 1935c. On Shafer, see his entry in the Biographical Register.

able and updated to fit the pedagogical and curricular context of the decades following Babbitt's death, do not advance much beyond Babbitt's original ideas.[308] In part for these reasons, the New Humanism, which had failed to spark a movement among creative writers and artists animated by its principles, ceased to remain a major force in American culture.

But this retreat does not imply that Babbitt and More have faded into obscurity. During their lifetimes, More appears to have been the better known of the two. He had contributed far more frequently to the popular press and thereby reached a wider circle of readers. For good reason, then, he—and not Babbitt—was a serious candidate for the Nobel Prize in Literature. Yet their fortunes shifted after their deaths. Although More was fortunate to receive much fuller biographical treatment at the hands of his friend Arthur Dakin Jr.,[309] he has been the subject of fewer posthumous analyses. Some of these analyses are very perceptive: Folke Leander, Francis Duggan, and Stephen Tanner have contributed especially helpful scholarship on More's voluminous output.[310] Overall, though, interest in More—once among the most famous literary critics in America—has faded.

To some degree, comparative disinterest in More is a matter of timing. He did not live long enough to witness the birth of the so-called New Criticism, which would render his biographically focused and moralistic criticism old-fashioned by comparison. Indeed, even before More's death academic literary criticism in the US had moved in directions antithetical to his work. This fact may make More's criticism even more valuable as a counterpoise to the intellectual zeitgeist, but it has also contributed to More's comparative obscurity.

In his later years, as we have noted, More was also a well-known Christian apologist. Russell Kirk, the prominent American conservative deeply influenced by the New Humanism,[311] considered him especially successful in this regard; similarly, T. S. Eliot deemed *The Greek Tradition* More's finest work.[312] Yet it is easy to recognize why these volumes remain little read today. *The Greek Tradition*, although containing many striking and original insights, requires of its readers such a strong philosophical background that

---

308. See, e.g., Foerster 1937a, 1946, and 1969.
309. Dakin 1960. See also Dakin 1950, which includes a helpful listing of many of More's writings.
310. See, e.g., Leander 1937a and 1974; Duggan 1966; Tanner 1987.
311. On Babbitt's influence on Kirk, see Birzer 2015: 30-38, 239-40; on More's influence on Kirk, see Birzer 2015: 38-42.
312. See, e.g., Eliot 1937a and b: 373; Warren 1969: 1110. Cf. Duggan 1966: 108-15, 143.

it was unlikely to attract much interest. These volumes, with their penchant for turning Plato into a New Humanist *avant la lettre*,[313] also failed to win much favor among professional philosophers.[314] In comparison with a lucid example of apologetics such as C. S. Lewis's *Mere Christianity* (1952), *The Greek Tradition* seems almost impenetrable.[315] More's own approach to religion, moreover, was highly idiosyncratic. For this reason, it appears, More decided against a deathbed communion.[316] And undoubtedly his religious idiosyncrasies rendered his work less appealing to fellow Christians.[317]

Although scholarly interest in Babbitt has ebbed and flowed in the decades after his passing, his work has garnered greater intellectual attention than has his best friend's. Political philosophers appear especially intrigued by Babbitt's oeuvre. A fair amount of this interest stems from Claes G. Ryn, for decades Babbitt's most penetrating and reliable interpreter.[318] Ryn's former students have contributed numerous books and essays that touch on Babbitt's work. Most recently, for example, William S. Smith has composed the first book-length study of Babbitt's views on foreign relations[319] and Justin Garrison and Ryan Holston edited a volume showcasing the value of Babbitt's and Ryn's approach to politics.[320] In the realms of literary criticism and education, moreover, one can spy continued fascination with Babbitt.[321] Indeed, it seems reasonable to suggest that we are witnessing the start of a Babbittian renaissance.

One hopes that this holds true for both Babbitt and More. Their writings, after all, although not without their blemishes, possess great value. This conclusion appears especially clear in the context of the contemporary professionalized university, which fosters a narrow and trifling approach to literary scholarship that rightly earned the New Humanists' scorn. As our culture grows steadily anti-humanistic and increasingly utilitarian (for reasons Babbitt and More articulated), their writings can supply a tonic reaction to

---

313. On this topic, see, e.g., Dakin 1960: 237.
314. For reviews of volumes in More's *The Greek Tradition* series, see, e.g., Bury 1918; Shorey 1918; Moore 1919; Bush 1922; Otis 1965: 59: Lambert 1999: 53. On such criticisms, see Dakin 1960: 236-39.
315. As the Babbitt–More correspondence hints, More was friendly with Lewis and influenced him. See, e.g., Dakin 1960: 358-60; Lambert 1999: 53; Birzer 2015: 38.
316. See Dakin 1960: 384.
317. As Lambert (1999: 53) notes.
318. Ryn, in turn, was a student of Folke Leander, a scholar who contributed valuable assessments of the New Humanism.
319. Smith 2019.
320. Garrison and Holston 2020.
321. See, e.g., Panichas 1999; Adler 2020.

the status quo. Babbitt and More demonstrated that literary and artistic masterworks are essential to the Good Life, and this lesson appears more urgent today than ever.

The Babbitt–More Correspondence

The extant original letters Babbitt and More wrote to one another can be found in two places: those composed by Babbitt are housed among the Irving Babbitt Papers (IBP) at the Harvard University Archives (HUA); those written by More are located among the Paul Elmer More Papers in the Princeton University Library's special collections. In addition, the IBP include a typescript of the extant letters, produced by Dora Babbitt, Irving Babbitt's widow.[322] Dora also made handwritten copies of More's letters prior to producing the typescript, many of which are included in the IBP at Harvard. Dora's typescript served as the basis for the edited version of the correspondence found in this book, although recourse to the original letters (and Dora's handwritten copies) has also been made when necessary. The typescript does not always record precisely what appears in the original letters, often, it seems, from a desire to excise material that seems too personal, inconsequential, or potentially offensive.[323] Attempts have been made to include these excised bits, but Babbitt's and More's penmanship did not always allow for such inclusions. As is typical of a correspondence that lasted decades, Babbitt and More were not always consistent in their use of underlining, spelling, and punctuation. This volume attempts to reproduce the original letters, at the expense of orthographical consistency. Very occasionally, punctuation has been added to individual letters in brackets, when this additional punctuation will help readers get a sense of

---

322. Dakin (1960: 368) reproduces part of a March 31, 1935, letter from More to Dora Babbitt, arguing against Dora's idea of publishing her husband's letters. A September 4, 1985, letter from George F. Howe, Irving Babbitt's son-in-law, to the Princeton University Library found in the Paul Elmer More Papers at Princeton, specifies that Dora attempted to get the correspondence published but was unable to do so. The HUA discussion of the IBP notes that Dora inspected and labeled many of the materials in the collection, prior to its move to the HUA (see the "Custodial History" of the IBP at https://hollisarchives.lib.harvard.edu/repositories/4/resources/4108). Thomas Nevin, the author of a fine book on Irving Babbitt (Nevin 1984), informed me that Harry Levin, the first Irving Babbitt Professor of Comparative Literature at Harvard, previously attempted to publish the correspondence with Harvard University Press. When Harvard declined, he abandoned the project. Harvard's rejection of the project is unfortunate, given how crucial the Babbitt–More correspondence is to a proper appreciation of the New Humanist movement.

323. The offense that appears to have concerned her surrounds the occasional criticisms of people who were (or who Dora may have thought were) still alive.

Babbitt's or More's meaning. Words Babbitt or More underlined in their handwritten letters have been converted to italics. The typescript contains a comparatively small number of footnotes that supply needed context. Readers will note that in this book these have been greatly supplemented with additional—and more extensive—notes.

As will become clear to readers of this correspondence, numerous letters between Babbitt and More have gone missing. The collected correspondence commences with letters from Babbitt without any responses from More for a few years. One will also note that the collection becomes fuller as time progresses, with noticeable gaps in 1921 and, unfortunately, 1930, the year of the New Humanism's greatest renown. Dora's typescript contains two items in an appendix, both of which have been retained in this book: an undated letter from More to Babbitt; and detailed notes from Babbitt's response to More's essay "Definitions in Dualism."

In this book there have been a few additions to and one subtraction from the typescript of the correspondence. A letter from More to Babbitt from May 27, 1908, was filed in Box 1 of the IBP at the HUA in the folder "Family Correspondence, 1865, 1884–1937." Accordingly, Dora did not include it in her typescript of the Babbitt–More correspondence. Readers will find this (important) letter restored to the correspondence in this book. For reasons that are not fully clear, Dora added to the typescript a December 30, 1918, missive from Babbitt to More's younger brother Louis Trenchard More. This letter has been moved from the chronological Babbitt–More correspondence proper to the appendix (see Appendix C). Dora also appended to her typescript some letters from Paul More to her, the first of which comes from 1908, when Irving Babbitt was out of the country, and a number beginning in early 1933, when he was gravely ill. Although Irving Babbitt was not their intended recipient, these letters have been retained in the correspondence, since they speak to important matters, not least of which is More's impressions of Babbitt directly after he passed away. The Paul Elmer More Papers include two additional letters to Dora—from March 10, 1934, and January 24, 1936—which Dora chose not to include in the typescript of the correspondence. Since the former letter includes More's memories of Babbitt, it has been included in this book; the latter missive deals chiefly with the stalled efforts of Babbitt's pupils to compose an edited collection of reminiscences about Babbitt, and has thus been excluded.

Readers of this correspondence will find a treasure trove of information that illuminates much about Babbitt, More, and the New Humanism, in addition to American culture, academia, journalism, literary criticism, religion, and social life in the late nineteenth and early twentieth centuries. Such readers can obviously discover this material on their own. But it seems prudent to present a few remarks about the correspondence's insights into the New Humanist movement.

Although More elsewhere criticized Babbitt's casual attitude towards letter-writing,[324] one will note that the two men remained in sufficiently close contact to aid one another in the development of their respective writings. They served as careful and faithful editors of one another's work for decades, and it remains striking how frank they could be in their assessments. Though they often couched their criticisms in the context of general approval, Babbitt and More could prove insightful, penetrating, and even withering critics. More, for example, candidly assessed the perceived demerits of Babbitt's writing style in numerous letters to his friend.[325] For his part, Babbitt took the liberty of informing More when he believed More's interpretation of Buddhism was misguided.[326]

It is also useful to note those writings that drew Babbitt's and More's particular attention and those writings they either chose not to discuss or passed over quickly. With the notable exception of More's translation of *A Century of Indian Epigrams*, Babbitt scarcely touched on More's creative work. Although he provided a couple of quick jokes at the expense of More's *The Great Refusal*, for example, he displays no real interest in the novel. In the extant letters, moreover, nowhere did Babbitt mention *The Jessica Letters*. In all, one senses that both Babbitt and More considered More's poetry and fiction undeserving of much attention. Babbitt's comparative concern for More's *Indian Epigrams* likely relates both to their greater quality and, most importantly, the philosophical and religious themes found therein. Of More's criticism, Babbitt demonstrates special interest in "Definitions of Dualism." Since this was arguably More's fullest contribution to an explication of the philosophy surrounding the New Humanism, Babbitt's concern is unsurprising.

Readers of the letters will also recognize Babbitt's and More's cardinal focus on intellectual matters. Although they occasionally swapped gossip and discussed their families, the correspondence has an overwhelmingly cerebral cast—more than one might have expected, given their close friendship. Babbitt, in fact, appears throughout the letters particularly intent on the

---

324. See Dakin 1960: 368.
325. Cf. Babbitt's November 21, 1917, letter to More, in which he justifies this style as necessary to keep his job at Harvard.
326. See Babbitt's letter of August 6, 1931, to More and More's response from August 12, 1931.

creation of a literary and social movement. His regard for tactical matters is especially marked. Babbitt repeatedly urged More, for example, to consider issues of presentation in his books: he worried that the haphazard arrangement and genre-crossing found in most installments of the *Shelburne Essays* would ensure that they received less attention than they deserve. This issue weighed on More too; when he moved to a new publisher for the *Shelburne Essays*, he contemplated pioneering definite themes and subtitles, to garner more interest in the individual volumes.[327] Overall, however, More comes across as less anxious about the pragmatic matters associated with his writings. He even joked in one letter about his laissez-faire policy in courting reviews.[328]

From the start, in fact, More appears to have been less comfortable as part of any "movement." Though he did not shun fame, when he became prominent in American intellectual circles More appears rather blasé about having obtained a measure of it.[329] Babbitt too comes across as uninterested in personal prominence. But he thought the ideas encapsulated in the New Humanism were central to warding off the dangers that rampant naturalism had courted. Thus, Babbitt showed far greater interest in presenting Humanism in a manner maximally attractive to readers. For example, he fretted about being pigeonholed as a Tory or a reactionary, since these designations could alienate some prospective followers.[330] More, on the other hand, happily embraced the label of a reactionary—provided it was rightly understood.[331] Babbitt saw the New Humanism as "an international movement" and pined for positive reactions in the press to help advance its cause.[332] More seems almost aloof about such issues—willing to consider them, but overwhelmingly because he aimed to please his friend.

This difference in outlook may help qualify the portrait of More as a Humanist apostate. Given his nonchalance about his membership in any sort of literary or social movement, we should not be shocked to discover More's reluctance to contribute to Foerster's collective Humanist manifesto.[333] To be

---

327. See More's August 18, 1912, letter to Babbitt.
328. See More's May 3, 1913, letter to Babbitt.
329. Cf. More's May 23, 1906, letter to his older sister Alice (quoted in Dakin 1960: 98-99), in which More asserts that he was desperate for fame since his youth but, now that he has some, it means nothing to him.
330. See Babbitt's February 13, 1916, letter to More. For Babbitt's criticisms of reactionary politics, see, e.g., Babbitt 1910a: xiii, 1912e: 315, 381, and 1940: 90.
331. See More's March 6, 1916, letter to Babbitt. Cf. More 1910a: 267-68; Shafer 1935c: 170.
332. See Babbitt's September 4, 1919, letter to More.
333. See especially More's March 29, 1929, letter to Babbitt. Note also More's January 17, 1920, letter, in which he expresses his interest in withdrawing from the fight over Humanism.

sure, by that time More had to some extent moved away from Humanism toward his own Platonized semi-Anglicanism. But he seems always to have been skittish about playing a part in an organized movement—whereas Babbitt aimed first and foremost to create one. Even towards the very end of his life, when already hobbled by the illness that would eventually kill him, Babbitt worried that More's turn to Christian theology would muddy the movement's message.[334] Babbitt remained to the end concerned about the group's self-presentation and urged More not to overemphasize the differences in their views.

The correspondence also offers clues about the nature of Babbitt's and More's intellectual break. This break (which, it should be stressed, was only partial) appears to have been longer in the making than most estimations of the New Humanism suggest. As early as 1912, Babbitt remarked on More's preference for Plato and contrasted it with his own attachment to Aristotle.[335] Although scholars typically note that More's turn back to Christianity occurred between the publication of his books *Platonism* (1917) and *The Religion of Plato* (1921),[336] in a letter from early 1915 Babbitt recognized that More, though typically supporting conclusions compatible with his own, was "inclined to put greater stress on the religious side of the problem."[337] Perhaps More's decision to quote some Greek from John Chrysostom in a letter to Babbitt from December 9, 1917, provides the first explicit signal of More's move towards Christian themes and topics in his work, which would occupy much of his attention throughout his later career.

It is possible that as he began focusing on Christian apologetics More grew reluctant to receive Babbitt's criticisms of his writings. He offered to Babbitt, for example, the opportunity to read *The Religion of Plato* only in proofs, suggesting that there was insufficient time for him to examine the original manuscript.[338] And he did not send the manuscript of *Hellenistic Philosophies* to Babbitt, despite Babbitt's eagerness to comment on it.[339] When More had Babbitt examine *The Christ of the New Testament* (1924), moreover, he urged a quick turn-around time and informed him that the

---

334. See Babbitt's April 17, 1932, letter to More.
335. See Babbitt's December 5, 1912, letter to More. Cf. More's January 6, 1915, letter, in which he playfully labels Babbitt "a stark anti-Platonist." See also Babbitt's February 12, 1915, letter, in which he criticizes More's Platonism.
336. E.g., Shafer 1935c: 254-55; Mather 1938: 370; Davies 1958: 35. Cf. Duggan 1966: 141-42.
337. See Babbitt's February 12, 1915, letter to More.
338. See More's June 23, 1921, letter to Babbitt.
339. See More's January 2, 1923, and February 9, 1923, letters to Babbitt.

manuscript would not please him in important respects.[340] Although they continued to edit one another's drafts throughout their lives, More appears to have made attempts to minimize the possibility of obtaining Babbitt's full feedback, perhaps due to a desire to avoid an open disagreement with his dear, yet combative, friend.[341]

Readers interested in Babbitt's and More's partial intellectual parting may deem May 14, 1924, an especially noteworthy date. Babbitt's letter from this day, an exhaustive criticism of More's *Hellenistic Philosophies*, then already in print, lays bare Babbitt's critique of More's views on Aristotle and expresses disquiet over More's "changes" to his "base line." More's defense of his position and continued attack on Aristotle in his letter of May 24, 1924, only further cemented their differences. By June 9, 1924, More informed his friend Maurice Baum that Babbitt perceived an intellectual chasm between them.[342]

These differences, it should be underscored, were chiefly religious in character. On the political front, Babbitt and More remained largely sympatico. In fact, it seems noteworthy that in their letters Babbitt and More seldom expressed serious reservations about Frank Jewett Mather—arguably the third leg of the New Humanist tripod—despite the fact that Mather had written about his "extreme" leftism in the pages of the *New Republic*.[343] Although much has been made of the supposedly rigid views of Babbitt in connection with the "defections" of Stuart Sherman and T. S. Eliot, when it came to the leftist Mather, Babbitt continued to support his work. This fact suggests something unacknowledged about the New Humanism: it was not as narrowly political as some have presumed, a movement to be identified strictly with More's shrill embrace of private property or Babbitt's disparagement of Wilsonian idealism. Mather had been one of Babbitt's initial converts to Humanism and remained close to More and Babbitt throughout his life. And in their extant correspondence the leaders of the New Humanism ventured few criticisms of Mather's notably disparate approach to politics because they considered him a Humanist regardless. The same may be said in regard to some second-generation Humanists, such as Gorham Munson and Odell

---

340. See More's December 6, 1923, letter to Babbitt.
341. Leander (1970: 139) provides a variant rationale for Babbitt's comparative silence on More's Christian apologetics: "In view of the fact that Babbitt's comments on *The Greek Tradition* were reduced to a few slight hints, it is hard to escape the impression that he had become painfully aware of More's emotional reactions."
342. See Dakin 1960: 222.
343. In Mather 1930a: 156, the author referred to himself as "a Humanist of the extreme left."

Shephard, who identified to varying degrees with the political and economic Left.[344]

Recognition of this fact may help spread Babbitt's and More's influence. Although, as we have already mentioned, a wide variety of twentieth- and twenty-first-century thinkers betray such influence, surely traditionalist conservatives have embraced Babbitt's and More's work most enthusiastically. Both men have been labeled (with varying degrees of accuracy) conservatives and traditionalists. But, as their biographies, correspondence, and published writings attest, they were highly idiosyncratic traditionalists. Babbitt felt so repulsed by the arid literary instruction on offer during his undergraduate days at Harvard that he seldom troubled himself to attend class. More ultimately embraced such a heterodox case for a kind of Platonic Anglicanism that it is difficult for all but technically trained philosophers to make an accurate estimation of his religious views. Especially since their powerful criticisms of modern society remain all the more accurate and worthwhile today, it seems high time for a broader array of scholars and intellectuals to turn back to the New Humanism.

---

344. On this topic, see the entries for Munson and Shepard in the Biographical Register.

CHRONOLOGY

1864
Dec. 12   Paul Elmer More is born in St. Louis, Missouri, the seventh of eight children of Enoch Anson More (1821–1899) and Katharine Hay (Elmer) More (1825–1914).

1865
Aug. 2   Irving Babbitt is born in Dayton, Ohio, the fourth of five children of Edwin Dwight Babbitt (1828–1905) and Augusta (Darling) Babbitt (1836–1876).

1870
April 9   Paul More's younger brother Louis Trenchard More (1870–1944) is born.

1876
Aug. 7   Irving Babbitt's mother Augusta Babbitt passes away a few days after Irving's eleventh birthday. Soon thereafter, Augusta's parents have Irving, his older brother Tom, and his younger sister Katharine, live with them in Madisonville, Ohio, close to Cincinnati.

1881   Edwin Babbitt, Irving's father, remarries and settles in Cincinnati, Ohio. Irving and his younger sister Katharine move in with him and attend Woodward High School, a public school.

As readers of this chronology will note, for some entries we have exact or approximate dates within a given calendar year. For others, such dates are unknown. Events that can only be identified by their calendar year have been added to the chronology without an italicized note (e.g., *Dec. 12*) next to them. They have often been placed in the sequence of a given year when they were most likely to have occurred. Since Paul Elmer More was the subject of a lengthy biography (Dakin 1960) and Irving Babbitt thus far has not received such biographical treatment, readers will recognize that the chronological entries for More are fuller and often more exact than those for Babbitt.

1883

March 11 — Lucius Quintus Cincinnatus Elmer (1793–1883), Paul More's maternal grandfather, passes away and leaves a legacy to More's mother, through which the More family avoids starvation and Paul has the opportunity to attend Washington University in St. Louis.

June 15 — Paul More graduates from Central High School, a public school in St. Louis.

Fall — Paul More begins attending the College of Liberal Arts of Washington University.

1884

Spring — Irving Babbitt graduates second in his class of ca. 50 from Woodward High School.

Summer — Irving Babbitt joins his older brother Tom to work on his uncle Albert Babbitt's Bar-Circle Ranch in Cheyenne, Wyoming.

Fall — Having graduated from high school, Irving Babbitt, lacking sufficient funds to attend Harvard University, returns to Woodward High School for the academic year 1884–85, where he studies chemistry and civil engineering.

1885

Fall — Irving Babbitt enters Harvard as a freshman.

1886

Spring — Irving Babbitt meets his lifelong friend, the future academic William F. Giese.

Dec. — Paul More likely publishes an anonymous article in the Washington University student publication *Student Life*, which discusses his anguished break from Calvinism.

1887

June 9 — Paul More receives his B.A. from Washington University, *cum laude*. Upon graduation, he becomes a Latin teacher at Smith Academy in St. Louis, a job he would hold until 1892, save one year spent in Europe (see below).

July — Irving Babbitt arrives in Europe with his Harvard classmate, the fellow Woodward High graduate Alfred Potts

	Butterworth. The two would travel there for the 1887–88 academic year.
1888	Paul More, on leave from his job at the Smith Academy, begins his travels in Europe, where he will stay into 1889. During this time, he proposes marriage to Mary Gates Cone, who refuses.
1889	
Spring	Irving Babbitt graduates *magna cum laude* with honors in classics from Harvard University.
Fall	Needing to pay back a loan for his Harvard tuition to his uncles, Irving Babbitt begins to teach Latin and Greek at the College of Montana in Deer Lodge, where he serves as a faculty member for two years (the academic years 1889 to 1891).
1890	
Spring	Through a pupil at the Smith Academy, Paul More meets Sarah Warfield Brank, the love of his life and the disguised subject of More's epistolary novel *The Great Refusal* (1894). Paul More publishes his first book, *Helena and Occasional Poems*.
1891	Irving Babbitt begins to study Sanskrit, Pali, and Indian philosophy at the École des Hautes Études in Paris under Sylvain Lévi.
	Around this time, Paul More reads Ferdinand Baur's book *Das Manichäisches Religionssystem* (1831), which encourages More's lifelong interest in philosophical dualism.[1]
1892	
May 24	Paul More informs Professor Charles R. Lanman of Harvard University that he aims to study Sanskrit, Greek, and Latin in the following year at Harvard, hoping ultimately to earn a Ph.D.
	Paul More receives his M.A. from Washington University for a thesis written in Latin.

---

1. It is not certain that this took place in 1891. See the Introduction.

Fall	Irving Babbitt and Paul More begin their graduate studies at Harvard and meet one another as the only two students in Professor Lanman's advanced class in Oriental studies.

1893

April	Paul More delivers an address that leads to his first scholarly article, "The Influences of Hindu Thought on Manichaeism." It would appear in the *Proceedings of the American Oriental Society* in 1896.
June	Irving Babbitt and Paul More both earn an A.M. from the Harvard Graduate School. More continues as a student there, also serving as an assistant in Sanskrit during the 1894–95 academic year.
Aug. 19	Paul More informs Professor Lanman that he no longer wants to earn a Ph.D., preferring to occupy his time with general reading.
Fall	Irving Babbitt starts his appointment for the 1893–94 academic year as an instructor in Romance languages at Williams College. He teaches French, Spanish, Italian, and a course on Dante. At Williams Babbitt meets Frank Jewett Mather Jr., a faculty member in English.

1894

May	Charles W. Eliot, the President of Harvard University, dismisses a French professor for plagiarism, creating a position in the department that would be filled by Irving Babbitt.
Fall	Irving Babbitt joins the Harvard faculty as an instructor of French, a rank he would hold until his promotion to assistant professor in 1902. Paul More publishes *The Great Refusal, Being Letters of a Dreamer in Gotham*.[2]

1894–95	Paul More serves as an assistant to Professor Lanman in Indo-Iranian languages, teaching Sanskrit for three hours per week, a position he holds through the 1894–95 academic year.

---

2. Dakin (1950: 183) lists a February 23, 1895, piece as the earliest review of the book. This suggests that *The Great Refusal* was published late in 1894.

1895

Spring — Martha Carey Thomas, the President of Bryn Mawr College, offers a faculty job in Sanskrit and classical literature to Paul More, which he quickly accepts.

Summer — Irving Babbitt spends the summer with Frank Jewett Mather Jr. in Florence.

Sept. 1 — Paul More begins teaching Sanskrit, Latin, and Greek at Bryn Mawr, a post he would hold through the conclusion of the 1897 academic year.

Fall — Paul More successfully proposes marriage to his childhood friend Henrietta Beck. They are both too poor to wed, so they remain apart while engaged.

Babbitt delivers a lecture at the University of Wisconsin called "The Rational Study of the Classics." It foreshadows what would become the New Humanism.

1896

Early — Irving Babbitt begins teaching at Radcliffe College to supplement his income.

Irving Babbitt starts to inquire through Paul More about vacancies in the classics department at Bryn Mawr; he asks his college friend William Giese, a professor of French and Spanish, about possible vacancies at the University of Wisconsin.

Summer — Irving Babbitt visits France and buys ca. three hundred books to help him prepare for advanced French courses he will begin to teach. He returns to Cambridge ca. September 2.

Summer — Paul More visits Professor Ephraim Emerton of Harvard and his family at their cottage in Shelburne, New Hampshire.

1897

March — Irving Babbitt publishes his first article, "The Rational Study of the Classics," in the *Atlantic Monthly*.

Paul More resigns from Bryn Mawr College when President Thomas will not acquiesce to More's demand for higher pay and less work.

Summer — Paul More begins renting out a little red cottage on the Philbrook farm in Shelburne, New Hampshire.

	He will ultimately remain there for two years and three months.
1898	Paul More begins contributing literary criticism to the *Atlantic Monthly* and *New World*. Irving Babbitt's edition of H. Taine's *Introduction à l'histoire de la littérature anglaise* is published.
Feb.–July?	Paul More leaves the cottage in Shelburne for some months at home in St. Louis, where he takes care of his father. On his way back to Shelburne, he visits Irving Babbitt in Cambridge.
Sept.	Paul More publishes *A Century of Indian Epigrams, Chiefly from the Sanskrit of Bhartrihari*.
Dec.	Paul More publishes *The Judgment of Socrates*, his translation of Plato's *Apology*, the *Crito*, and a portion of the *Phaedo*, with an introductory essay by More.
1899	
Jan. 28	Enoch Anson More, Paul More's father, passes away. Paul More visits Irving Babbitt in Cambridge after attending the funeral in St. Louis.
Ca. May	Paul More publishes his translation of Aeschylus's *Prometheus Bound*, with notes and an introduction.
Summer	Louis More, More's mother, Prosser Hall Frye, and Irving Babbitt all visit Paul More in Shelburne, New Hampshire.
Oct. 1	Paul More aims to accept Professor Lanman's offer to work at Harvard on a translation of the Sanskrit text the *Pancatantra*, since he cannot find any other academic employment.
Fall	Paul More leaves his remote cottage in Shelburne, New Hampshire, returning to Harvard to work for Professor Lanman.
Winter	Paul More begins work on a biography of Benjamin Franklin.
1900	
June 12	Irving Babbitt marries twenty-three-year-old Dora May Drew (1877–1944), his former Radcliffe student, in London.
June 12	Paul More marries Henrietta Beck. The couple moves to East Orange, New Jersey, where More begins work as an indigent freelance critic.

	Irving Babbitt rents a three-story house at 6 Kirkland Road, Cambridge, which will be his family's home for the remainder of his life.
	Louis T. More, Paul More's brother, becomes a professor of physics at the University of Cincinnati, a position he will hold until his retirement in 1940.
Ca. Oct.	Paul More's brief biography of Benjamin Franklin is published.

1901

April 1	Paul More joins the staff of the *Independent*, a liberal periodical based in New York City, chiefly as its literary editor.
Mid-April	Irving and Dora Babbitt visit Paul and Henrietta More for a week in East Orange, New Jersey.
June	The *Atlantic Monthly* publishes More's essay "A Hermit's Notes on Thoreau," the first piece ultimately to appear in More's voluminous *Shelburne Essays*.
Oct. 2	Irving and Dora Babbitt's daughter Esther Babbitt (1901–1984) is born.

1902

	Irving Babbitt's edition of Renan's *Souvenirs d'Enfance et de Jeunesse* is published.
Feb. 24	Paul and Henrietta More's daughter, Mary Darrah More (1902–1975), is born; it is a difficult birth for Henrietta.
	Irving Babbitt is promoted to assistant professor at Harvard.
Sept.	Paul More takes a furlough from his job at the *Independent* for two weeks to care for Henrietta, who is still suffering from the difficult birth of their daughter.
Early Dec.?	Paul and Henrietta More spend a week on vacation in Cambridge, Massachusetts, as guests of the Babbitts.

1903

June 2?	Paul More's mother and invalid sister Alice (1849–1930) move out of the More house in East Orange, New Jersey, to a place in Bridgeton, New Jersey.
June 12	Irving and Dora Babbitt's son Edward Sturges Babbitt (1903–1997) is born.

Oct. 23 or 24	Rollo Ogden, the editor of the New York *Evening Post*, offers Paul More a job as the *Post*'s literary editor, which More accepts.
By Dec. 1	Paul More leaves the staff of the *Independent* to start as the literary editor of the New York *Evening Post*. Much of More's writings for the *Post* also appears in the *Nation*, which was then under the same ownership.

1904

April	Paul More and Corra May Harris anonymously publish their co-written epistolary novel *The Jessica Letters*.
Summer	Paul and Henrietta More, along with some family, spend time with the Babbitts on vacation at Biddeford Pool, Maine.
Ca. mid-Sept.	The first series of Paul More's *Shelburne Essays* is published.

1905

	Irving Babbitt's edition of Voltaire's *Zadig and Other Stories* is published.
May	The second series of Paul More's *Shelburne Essays* is published.
Late spring/ early summer	More's edition of *The Complete Poetical Works of Lord Byron* is published.
June 28	Edwin Dwight Babbitt, Irving Babbitt's father, passes away.
Sept.	The third series of Paul More's *Shelburne Essays* is published.

1906

First half	Henrietta More, in poor health, spends much time in bed, scarcely able to walk around the house.
Early Apr.	Henrietta More has an appendectomy.
June 28	Paul and Henrietta More have a daughter, Alice More (1906–1971). The birth permanently undermines Henrietta's health.
July 1	Paul More becomes the literary editor of the *Nation*, while retaining his position as the literary editor at the New York *Evening Post*.
Summer	Paul More's mother and sister Alice move from Bridgeport, New Jersey, back to St. Louis.
Dec.	Irving Babbitt visits Paul More in New Jersey for a couple of days.
Dec.	The fourth series of More's *Shelburne Essays* is published.

1907
Feb. 27   Paul More speaks to the Wednesday Club in St. Louis on "The Centenary of Longfellow."
                    Irving Babbitt is granted his first sabbatical (for the 1907–08 academic year) to finish his first book.

1908
Feb. 6   Paul More signs a lease for an apartment at 260 West 99th Street in New York City, so Henrietta can help take care of her sickly aunt, Mary D. Richardson.
Feb. 10   Paul More is elected to the National Institute of Arts and Letters.
Ca. March 31   Paul More and his family move into their new apartment in New York City.
April   The fifth series of Paul More's *Shelburne Essays* is published.
May 1   Paul More delivers a lecture to the English Club at Bryn Mawr College on "Sir Thomas Browne."
By May 18   Irving Babbitt's first book, *Literature and the American College*, is published.
August   Irving Babbitt visits Paul More at his summer place in Essex, New York, where Babbitt upbraids More about Plato.
By Sept.   Paul More refuses election to the American Academy of Arts and Letters.
Oct. 7   Walter Lippmann, an undergraduate in one of Irving Babbitt's courses at Harvard, writes a letter of complaint to Babbitt for linking socialism to Rousseauism in a class lecture.
Dec. 31   Irving Babbitt informs Paul More that he prefers A. Lawrence Lowell for the presidency of Harvard.

1909   Irving Babbitt's classes at Harvard become more popular with students than they had been in the past. T. S. Eliot, a senior at Harvard, enrolls in one of Babbitt's courses.
Jan. 6–19   Paul More delivers the Nathaniel Ropes Lectures at the University of Cincinnati.
Jan. 12   Paul More delivers the lecture "Tennyson" at Denison University.
Late Feb./early March   The sixth series of Paul More's *Shelburne Essays*, called *Studies of Religious Dualism*, is published.

May 6	Hammond Lamont, editor-in-chief of the *Nation*, passes away.
May 11	Paul More is appointed the editor-in-chief of the *Nation*. He resigns as the literary editor of the New York *Evening Post*.

1910

Early Feb.	Paul More delivers a speech on "Criticism" at the Women's Club of St. Louis.
Feb. 12	Paul More delivers his speech "Criticism" at the (Yale) University Club in New Haven, Connecticut.
March 17–20	Paul More visits Irving Babbitt in Cambridge and agrees to proofread the manuscript of Babbitt's second book, *The New Laokoon*.
May 3	Paul More delivers his speech on "Criticism" at Columbia University.
Summer	Irving Babbitt and Frank Jewett Mather Jr. visit Paul More for some time while he vacations in Essex, New York.
Ca. Nov. 12	The seventh series of Paul More's *Shelburne Essays* is published.
	Irving Babbitt publishes his second book, *The New Laokoon*.
	Irving Babbitt's edition of Racine's *Phèdre* is published.

1911

Jan. 3	Mary D. Richardson, the aunt of Henrietta More, passes away, leaving Henrietta an unexpectedly large inheritance. When they return from the funeral, the Mores move into Richardson's old house at 780 West End Avenue in New York City.
Feb. 24	Evarts Greene, the Dean of the College of Arts and Literature at the University of Illinois, writes a letter to Irving Babbitt, informing him of the lay of the land at Illinois, where Babbitt is interested in a faculty position.
March 13	A. Lawrence Lowell, the President of Harvard, writes a letter to Irving Babbitt, informing him that the Harvard Corporation believes it unwise to promote Babbitt to a full professorship.
March 16–23	Paul More delivers five lectures on romanticism at the University of Wisconsin.

March 20	A. Lawrence Lowell writes a letter to Irving Babbitt's colleague Charles Hall Grandgent, the Chairman of the Committee on Studies in the Humanities at Harvard, explaining the decision not to promote Babbitt to a full professorship.
March 24–25	Paul More speaks in Milwaukee, Wisconsin, on Cardinal Newman and Walter Pater.
March 27–31	Paul More repeats the five lectures he had given at Wisconsin at the University of Illinois.
Sept. 9	Paul More and his family move to a house at 159 West 92nd Street in New York City.
	Stuart P. Sherman, Irving Babbitt's former student, helps obtain for Babbitt an offer of employment at the University of Illinois.

1912

Feb.	Irving Babbitt, having received an offer of a faculty position from the University of Illinois, is promoted to a full professorship of French literature at Harvard.
	Paul More's book *Nietzsche* is published.
April 18	Paul More delivers a lecture called "Philosophy Is a Science of Life" at Lehigh University.
May 25	Paul More, without his family, boards a ship to set sail for England, where he intends to stay for ca. eight to ten weeks.
July 29	Paul More arrives back in Essex, New York, after his trip to England. He then returns home to New York City.
	Irving Babbitt's third book, *The Masters of Modern French Criticism*, is published.

1913

Feb. 17–21	Paul More delivers a series of lectures at the University of Kansas.
March	The eighth series of Paul More's *Shelburne Essays*, called *The Drift of Romanticism*, is published.
April 4	Paul More lectures at the University of Michigan on "The Paradox of Oxford."
Later in April	Paul More spends two days in Cambridge, MA, visiting with the Babbitts.
June 12	Washington University grants Paul More an honorary degree of Doctor of Laws.

Aug. 17	Paul More informs his sister Alice More that he has resigned from the *Nation* and will stay on as its editor only as long as it takes to reorganize the office for his successor.

1914

Jan. 11	In a letter to Paul More, Irving Babbitt details his efforts to get More a position in the classics department at Harvard.
Jan. 23	Oswald Garrison Villard, the President of the New York *Evening Post* Company, informs Paul More that he will remain the editor of the *Nation* until March 15, 1914.
March 15	Paul More officially leaves the editorship of the *Nation*, becoming an advisory editor instead (a position he will hold from 1914 to 1917), and moves with his family to a home at 245 Nassau Street in Princeton, New Jersey.
March 20	Paul More attends an advisory committee meeting for the Harvard Graduate School. He stays in Cambridge with the Babbitts.
April 10	Paul More is by his mother's side when she passes away of pneumonia in Bridgetown, New Jersey.
April 13	Paul More brings his mother to St. Louis for her burial there.
Dec.	Paul More is elected to the Nassau Club in Princeton, New Jersey.

1915

March 17	Paul More delivers a lecture to the Nassau Club of Princeton, in which he argues for the classics and philosophy as the core of education.
March 22	Paul More delivers an address at a Princeton University Phi Beta Kappa dinner in which he defends private property as essential to the stability and progress of society.
April 18	Paul More delivers an address to celebrate the opening of the library Mary D. Richardson (his aunt-in-law) bequeathed to the St. Louis Art Museum.
June 7	Paul More delivers a lecture on Benjamin Disraeli for the Phi Beta Kappa chapter of Indiana University.
Oct.	The ninth series of *Shelburne Essays*, called *Aristocracy and Justice*, is published.
Nov. 18	Paul More is elected to the American Academy of Arts and Letters.

1916

Jan.	Irving Babbitt spends the month in Princeton, New Jersey, at the close of his "semi-sabbatical," working on his book *Rousseau and Romanticism*.
Feb.	Paul More reads the lecture "The Spirit and Poetry of Early New England" at the Present Day Club of Princeton, New Jersey.
March 29–April 12	Paul More delivers the Percy Turnbull Memorial Lectures at the Johns Hopkins University.
May 15	Paul More debates Willard Huntington Wright on "Nietzsche and Progress" at the Get-Together Club in Hartford, Connecticut.
July	Paul More accompanies his sister Alice to the Maine General Hospital in Portland, where she receives an exploratory operation.
Mid-Sept.	Paul More visits Irving Babbitt at Squam Lake, New Hampshire.
By the end of Oct.	Alice More, Paul's sister, moves into her new apartment in Princeton, New Jersey, at 293 Nassau Street.

1917

Feb. 22	Paul More delivers an address to the University Club in New York City.
March 23	Paul More delivers a lecture called "The Spirit and Poetry of Early New England" at Trinity College (now Duke University) in Durham, North Carolina.
April 19	Paul More attends the semicentennial dinner for the *Nation* at the Biltmore in New York City.
April 26	Paul More delivers his William Vaughn Moody Lecture, called "Standards of Taste," at the University of Chicago.
June	Paul More receives honorary Doctor of Letters degrees from Columbia University and Dartmouth College.
Oct.–Nov.	Paul More delivers the Louis Clark Vanuxem Lectures at Princeton University, based on the material for his forthcoming book *Platonism* (1917).
Dec.	Paul More's book *Platonism* is published.

Dec. 31	Paul More reprises his lecture "Standards of Taste" at the Middlesex Women's Club in Lowell, Massachusetts. During the trip More visits with the Babbitts.

1918

Jan. 30	Irving Babbitt lectures at Princeton University and visits with the Mores on his trip.
Feb. 13	Paul and Henrietta More attend the funeral of Henrietta's mother in St. Louis. Henrietta returns to Princeton ailing from kidney problems.
Mid-Sept.	Paul More entertains Irving Babbitt at his summer abode in Essex, New York.
Fall	Paul More begins his formal appointment as a lecturer in Greek philosophy in Princeton University's philosophy department. During this semester More offers a course on "Platonism and Christian Theology."

1919

March 21	Paul More offers an opening address on humanism at the Latin Conference of Mount Holyoke, Smith, Vassar, and Wellesley colleges.
April 25	Paul More delivers a lecture on the importance of Latin and ancient Greek at Vassar College.
May 24	Irving Babbitt publishes his fourth book, *Rousseau and Romanticism*.
June 3	Paul More offers an address on humanism at the Allegheny College chapter of Phi Beta Kappa.
June 16	Paul More receives an honorary Doctor of Letters from Princeton University.
Ca. June 24	Irving Babbitt lectures at Indiana University.
Summer	Irving Babbitt begins work on the book that will ultimately be called *Democracy and Leadership*.
Nov.	The tenth series of Paul More's *Shelburne Essays*, called *With the Wits*, is published.

1920

Jan.	Irving Babbitt delivers a lecture to graduate students at Harvard called "The Discipline of Ideas in Literature."
Jan. 17	Irving Babbitt is elected to the National Institute of Arts and Letters.

March	Irving Babbitt is the Larwill lecturer at Kenyon College in Gambier, Ohio.
March 13	Paul More reads the lecture, "Samuel Butler of Erewhon," at the Century Association in New York.
August	Paul More visits the Babbitts at their summer cottage in Chesham, New Hampshire.
Dec. 7	Paul More presents the Annie Talbot Cole Lecture at Bowdoin College on "The Spirit and Poetry of Early New England."
	Paul More begins to edit the book section of Henry Holt's *Unpartizan Review*, a job he will continue through 1921, when Holt ceases publication of the magazine.

1921

March 9–10	Robert Frost spends the night at Paul More's house, after Frost gives a reading and delivers a talk to the Freneau Club at Princeton University.
March	The eleventh and final series of Paul More's *Shelburne Essays* is published.
April 18	Paul More offers a lecture on "Scholarship" to the Phi Beta Kappa chapter at Cincinnati.
Oct.	Paul More publishes *The Religion of Plato*, the first volume of *The Greek Tradition*.
Oct.	Irving Babbitt is the Harvard lecturer at Yale University, a position he will hold through February of 1922.
Early Nov.	Paul More speaks at Lake Forest College in Illinois on "Religion and Social Discontent."

1922

Jan.	Chinese intellectuals influenced by Irving Babbitt found a monthly journal in China called the *Critical Review*.
Early Jan.	Paul More travels to Cambridge to attend a Visiting Committee of the Harvard Graduate School. In a letter of January 14, 1922, to his sister Alice, More describes Babbitt as old and weary.
Feb. 22	Paul More lectures on "English and Englistic" at a gathering of the American Academy of Arts and Letters, held at the University Club in New York City.
March 9–11	Paul More speaks to Princeton undergraduates about religion and Christianity.
April	Irving Babbitt is the West lecturer at Stanford University.

Oct.	Paul More delivers a lecture at Wells College in Aurora, New York, where he is the guest of Professor Robert Shafer, whom More meets for the first time.
Dec. 29	In a letter to his friend Prosser Hall Frye, Paul More claims that he is "at once the least read and the worst hated author in the country."

1923

March–May	Irving Babbitt is the James Hazen Hyde Lecturer and exchange professor at the Sorbonne.
Late May?	At some point after his Sorbonne lectures are completed, Irving Babbitt briefly visits with his former student T. S. Eliot.
June?	Paul More attends the graduation of his daughter Darrah from Vassar College and then delivers the commencement address at Oberlin College on "The Demon of the Absolute."
Nov. 14	In a letter to his brother Louis, Paul More explains that Henrietta has malignant breast cancer and will have an operation to remove it.
Dec.	Paul More's *Hellenistic Philosophies*, the second volume of *The Greek Tradition*, is published.

1924

Feb. 11	Paul More speaks on "The Demon of the Absolute" at the Twentieth Century Club in Pittsburgh.
Feb.	Henrietta More suffers from tonsillitis, grippe, and laryngitis.
April 24	Stuart P. Sherman leaves his position on the faculty at the University of Illinois for a job as the literary editor of the New York *Herald Tribune*.
May 14	Irving Babbitt writes a lengthy letter to Paul More, suggesting a possibly irreversible intellectual break between them.
May 14?	Irving Babbitt's fifth book, *Democracy and Leadership*, is published.
May	Paul More's *The Christ of the New Testament*, the third volume of *The Greek Tradition*, is published.
Spring	Paul More seeks the signatures of Brander Matthews and Stuart Sherman, in hopes of getting Irving Babbitt elected to the American Academy of Arts and Letters.
June 9	Paul More writes a letter to Maurice Baum, informing him that Irving Babbitt believes that there has been an

	intellectual break between Babbitt and More, based on Babbitt's Aristotelianism and More's Platonism.
July 4	Paul More writes to Percy H. Houston, describing his intellectual disagreements with Irving Babbitt and informing Houston that Babbitt had recently spent time in Princeton, talking while More listened.
July 12	Paul More, on leave from Princeton, and his family sail from New York City for England. He will visit England, Italy, and Greece, returning in the summer of 1925.
Sept. 2	Stuart P. Sherman arrives in New York City, where he begins preparations for the literary review of the New York *Herald Tribune*.

1925

Ca. first six weeks	Paul More, staying at the Isis Hotel in Oxford, begins writing the notes that would ultimately be published posthumously as *Pages from an Oxford Diary*.
Spring	Paul More and his family continue their extended trip to Europe with time in Italy and Greece.
May 12	Irving Babbitt delivers a lecture, "The Primitivism of Wordsworth," at Bowdoin College.
May 13	Irving Babbitt takes part in a "Round Table Conference" at Bowdoin College.
June 17	Irving Babbitt delivers the commencement address at the College of Wooster, called "The Role of the Critic in American Life."
July 24–27	Paul More rooms at Balliol College, Oxford, to attend a joint session of the Aristotelian Society and the Mind Association.
Aug. 3	Paul More and his family leave Southampton on board a ship headed to the United States.
Nov. 14	Irving Babbitt's sister, Katharine Babbitt, is hit by a car when crossing a highway in Farmington, Connecticut.
Nov. 17	Irving Babbitt's sister, Katharine Babbitt (1871–1925), passes away in a hospital in Hartford, Connecticut.

1926

Jan. 28	Paul More accepts the offer of Professor Edward Capps to teach two courses per year in Princeton's classics department,

	starting the next academic year, and thus officially transfers from philosophy to the classics at Princeton.
Spring term	Paul More replaces Professor Charles Burton Gulick for a semester in Harvard's classics department. He lectures on Plato and Greek philosophy and teaches an ancient Greek course at Radcliffe. While in Cambridge, More meets regularly with Irving Babbitt.
May 3	Paul More addresses the Harvard Philosophical Club on "The Demon of the Absolute."
Ca. June	Paul More speaks on the distinctions between humanism and humanitarianism to the Harvard Classical Club.
July 6	Paul More writes to Percy H. Houston, informing him that Irving Babbitt is the only professor at Harvard who "had a true message for the hungry student."
July 23	Paul More writes to Irving Babbitt about his work on a second edition of *Platonism*, admitting that the book does not fit with some aspects of later volumes in *The Greek Tradition*.
Aug. 21	Stuart P. Sherman dies in a drowning accident.
Sept.?	Paul More visits the Babbitts at their vacation place in Dublin, New Hampshire.
Sept. 13–17	Paul More attends the Sixth International Congress of Philosophy in Cambridge.
Oct. 8	Paul More writes to Robert Shafer, informing him that he has reluctantly accepted the *Revue de Paris*'s suggestion that he write an article on contemporary American literature.
Oct. 13	Irving Babbitt delivers the lecture "Humanist and Specialist" to celebrate the dedication of the Marston Hall of Languages at Brown University in Providence, Rhode Island.
	Irving Babbitt is elected to the French Institute.
	The second edition of Paul More's *Platonism* is published, which is now listed as a "Complementary Volume" in *The Greek Tradition* series.
1927	
Jan.	Paul More reads his article "The Modern Current in American Literature" at both the Present Day Club and the Nassau Club of Princeton, New Jersey.
Jan. 18	Paul More sends off his piece on contemporary American literature to the *Revue de Paris*, translated into French by Professor Louis Cons of Princeton University.

May 18	Paul More informs his brother Louis that Henrietta is in bad condition and some pain.
June 25	Henrietta More purchases the lot in Princeton, New Jersey, at 59 Battle Road.
July	Seward Collins purchases the *Bookman* from George H. Doran and begins to serve as the publication's publisher.
Sept. 1	Paul and Henrietta More's daughter Darrah marries Harry Boehme Fine at St. John's Episcopal Church in Essex, New York.
Sept.	Paul More's *Christ the Word*, the fourth volume of *The Greek Tradition*, is published.
Oct. 12	Paul More writes to Irving Babbitt with his critique of Babbitt's recently composed essay "Buddha and the Occident."
Dec. 17	Paul and Henrietta More's daughter Alice marries Edmund Gilbert Dymond.
	Norman Foerster commences work on his edited collection, *Humanism and America*.

1928

Jan. 14	Henrietta More suffers an attack of nephritis with dilation to the heart.
Jan. 20	Henrietta More passes away.
Jan. 23	Paul More holds Henrietta More's funeral at their home at 245 Nassau Street, Princeton.
Feb.	Irving Babbitt attacks H. L. Mencken in an essay called "The Critic and American Life," which is published in the *Forum*.
Feb. 12	Paul More reports in a letter to William Peterfield Trent that his daughter Darrah and her husband have come to live with him until he can find a smaller house.
March 24	Paul More informs Prosser Hall Frye that his sister Alice, now old and quite deaf, has left Bridgetown to come live with him at his house in Princeton.
April	Upon the resignation of Burton Rascoe, Seward Collins becomes the editor of the *Bookman*.
June 24	Paul More writes a letter to Robert Shafer, agreeing with him that only the younger Humanists should contribute to Foerster's collection *Humanism and America*.
July 17	Paul More writes to Robert Shafer about the latter's plans to write a study of More.

	Irving Babbitt takes a pleasure trip to Italy, Greece, France, and England.
July 28	Paul More and Stanley Went (a former employee at the *Nation*) set sail from New York City to England.
Aug. 6	Paul More and Stanley Went arrive in Liverpool.
Aug. 8	Paul More arrives at his daughter Alice's house in Cambridge, England. At some point soon after, More meets up with the Babbitts at nearby Ely.
Sept.	Paul More's first volume of *New Shelburne Essays*, called *The Demon of the Absolute*, is published.
Sept. 9	Paul More and his daughter Alice arrive back at Cambridge, England, having taken a road trip around the country together.
Late Sept.	Paul More meets T. S. Eliot for the first time.
Oct. 8– end of Oct.	Paul More stays at the Isis Hotel in Oxford, England.
Nov. 30	Paul More, still in England, informs his sister Alice that "I shall certainly see T. S. Eliot with whom I have contracted rather an intimate acquaintance."
Dec. 14?	Paul More begins the trip back from England to the United States.

1929

Jan. 24	Paul More writes to Robert Shafer, informing him that Norman Foerster tasked Babbitt, Mather, and More with contributing to *Humanism and America*, despite More's disinclination to do so. More feels that he has little choice but to accept the invitation.
Feb. 10	Paul More's daughter Darrah gives birth to a daughter, Mary Darragh Fine.
March 28	In a letter to G. R. Elliott, Paul More notes that he and Elliott both recognize that humanism without religion is futile.
March 29	Paul More explains in a letter to Irving Babbitt that he agreed to contribute to Foerster's collection *Humanism and America* with great reluctance.
April 17	Paul More delivers an address at Amherst College on "Humanism and Religion." He meets with Dora Babbitt at Amherst.
May 19	In a letter to Irving Babbitt, Paul More again suggests that he does not want to contribute to Foerster's *Humanism and America*.

June 10	Paul More tells Archibald Allan Bowman in a letter that he took up Princeton President John Grier Hibben's and trustee Melanchthon W. Jacobus's suggestion that he teach a course on the origins of Christianity at Princeton.
July 5	In a letter to Norman Foerster, Paul More says that he does not want to contribute to *Humanism and America*.
July 7	Paul More informs Prosser Hall Frye in a letter that he has sold his house on Nassau Street and that workmen are putting up a new one on his plot on Battle Road.
Summer	Rumors swirl that Paul More will win the Nobel Prize in Literature.
Summer	T. S. Eliot reports to Paul More that he cannot find a publisher for *Pages from an Oxford Diary*, which More wanted published anonymously and had entrusted to Eliot the winter before.
Sept. 7	Paul More writes to Seward Collins about Allen Tate's essay critical of the New Humanism, informing Collins that he agrees with Tate in principle that humanism cannot succeed without religion.
	Paul More recycles sections of his essay "The Demon of the Absolute," retitles them "The Humility of Common Sense," and sends them to Norman Foerster as his contribution to *Humanism and America*.
Nov.?	Irving Babbitt sees More at Princeton after delivering a lecture in Atlantic City.
Ca. Nov. 22	Paul More and his sister Alice move to the new house at 59 Battle Road, Princeton.

1930

Jan.?	Paul More travels to Berkeley, California, where he will teach two courses at the University: an undergraduate course on Plato and a graduate seminar on Aristotle.
Jan. 24	Paul More writes from Berkeley to his sister Alice, informing her that the hubbub about the New Humanism has made him rather famous there.
Feb. 10	The Division of Modern Language at Harvard votes down Irving Babbitt's proposal to establish an A.M. degree with honors.
Late Feb.	Norman Foerster's edited collection *Humanism and America* is published.
	Controversy rages over the New Humanism.

March	The *Bookman* carries Paul More's review of Foerster's collection *Humanism and America*, called "A Revival of Humanism."
Early March?	Irving Babbitt is the Clyde Fitch Lecturer at Amherst College, where he offers an address called "Humanism and Education."
March 7	Paul More reads a revised version of his review of *Humanism and America* to an audience at Berkeley.
March 29	In a letter to his sister Alice, Paul More reports that he is famous there.
April 26	With the spring term concluded, Paul More leaves Berkeley for a trip to San Francisco.
April 29	Paul More delivers a lecture in Los Angeles, California.
April 30	The publisher of C. Hartley Grattan's edited collection, *A Critique of Humanism*, sends Irving Babbitt a galley copy of the book, in advance of Babbitt's Carnegie Hall debate over the New Humanism.
Early May	Paul More leaves California and visits with his brother Louis in Cincinnati for a few days, ultimately heading home to Princeton.
May 9	Irving Babbitt debates Carl Van Doren and Henry Seidel Canby at Carnegie Hall in New York City.
May 26	C. Hartley Grattan's edited collection, *A Critique of Humanism*, is published.
	Irving Babbitt's former pupil Norman Foerster becomes the director of the School of Letters at the University of Iowa, where he attempts to put some of Babbitt's curricular ideas into effect.
Sept.	Paul More's sister Alice, now aged 81, collapses and is on bedrest.
Oct. 5	Alice More, Paul's older sister, passes away.
Nov.?	Irving Babbitt is elected to the American Academy of Arts and Letters.
Dec. 12	Sinclair Lewis receives the Nobel Prize in Literature and in his acceptance speech he criticizes the New Humanism as a "doctrine of death."

1931

Winter	Irving Babbitt delivers the Alexander Lectures at the University of Toronto.

April 4	Paul More, along with his brother Louis, sets sail for Britain, aiming to see a new grandchild, born to his daughter Alice.
April?	Paul More's daughters Alice and Darrah both have sons.
Ca. May 20	T. S. Eliot attempts to set up a meeting for Paul More with an English publisher for the book that would ultimately be called *Anglicanism*.
July 18	Paul More departs England for the United States, reading the proofs of *The Catholic Faith*.
Aug.?	Paul More attempts to get Mary, his cook for twenty-five years, into a sanitarium, because she had been stricken with tuberculosis.
Oct. 22	Paul More writes a letter to Robert Shafer describing his "noetic life," for Shafer's intended volume on More.
Nov.	Paul More, with Babbitt's help, becomes a member of the American Academy of Arts and Sciences.
Nov.	Paul More's *The Catholic Faith*, the final volume of *The Greek Tradition*, is published.
Nov.	Paul More attends the funeral of Louis T. More's wife in Cincinnati.

1932

Jan.	Irving Babbitt publishes his sixth book, *On Being Creative and Other Essays*.
Jan.	Irving Babbitt's health begins to decline.
Jan.	Paul More delivers a lecture on Proust to the philosophical club at Princeton, which ultimately would lead to an article in the April 1933 issue of the *American Review*.
April 17	In a letter to Paul More, Irving Babbitt explains that he will address the controversy surrounding the New Humanism and religion in an appendix to his planned book, *Humanism and Education*.
May 1–2	Irving Babbitt delivers the commencement address at Drew Seminary in New Jersey. After the address, Babbitt visits with Paul More. More reports to his brother Louis that Babbitt looks old "and has a disfiguring eruption on his cheek." During the visit, More tactfully criticizes *On Being Creative and Other Essays*.
June	Irving Babbitt receives an honorary Doctorate of Humane Letters from Bowdoin College.

June	Paul More works on his Lowell Lectures, which will ultimately spawn his book *The Sceptical Approach to Religion*.
July	Illness begins to affect Irving Babbitt, who suffers from a persistent fever.
Fall semester	Paul More offers his last course at Princeton, a graduate class on Aristotle.
Mid-Oct.	Paul More presents an early version of one of his Lowell Lectures, "Rationalism and Faith," at a conference of Episcopal clergy at Mahopac, New York.
Nov.	T. S. Eliot, on a nine-month stay at Harvard, visits with Irving Babbitt twice, before Babbitt's illness renders further contact impossible.
Nov. 10	Irving Babbitt delivers his final public lecture to the American Academy of Arts and Letters, "Style in a Democracy."
Nov. 15	Paul More writes a letter to Robert Shafer, underscoring that Irving Babbitt came up with the first impetus for the New Humanism, though More was chiefly responsible for the conception of a philosophical dualism. He adds that Babbitt is not well.

1933

Start of year	Rumors again swirl that More will win the Nobel Prize in Literature.
March	Seward Collins publishes the final issue of the *Bookman*.
March	Paul More lectures at a preparatory school in New Lebanon, New York.
March	Paul More lectures on "A Sceptical Approach to Religion" at Williams College.
March 23	Paul More introduces T. S. Eliot to an audience at Princeton. Eliot delivers a talk on Biblical influences on English literature, and More entertains Eliot and some others at his house at 59 Battle Road.
April	Irving Babbitt, weakened by illness, stops lecturing to his students at Harvard.
April	Seward Collins's *American Review* launches as the successor to the *Bookman*. The first issue features an essay by Paul More on Proust.

April 7	Paul More begins his voyage from New York City to England, where he will work on gathering material for his co-edited volume on Anglicanism.
April 13	Paul More officially retires from teaching at Princeton University.
May 11	In a letter to Christian Gauss, Paul More reports that he enjoys the company of C. S. Lewis.
May 14	Paul More writes to Irving Babbitt about Seward Collins's new *American Review*, informing him that he likes the publication, though he has qualms about Distributism.
May 26	Paul More writes to his brother Louis, explaining that Irving Babbitt's daughter Esther told Robert Shafer that Babbitt is bedridden with round-the-clock nursing care.
July 10	Paul More writes to Babbitt, hoping his health improves and telling him that he should finish his current project on humanism and education.
July 15	Irving Babbitt passes away in his home in Cambridge, having completed all his work for the spring term at Harvard.
July 17	Paul More informs Dora Babbitt in a letter that he did not consider his move to Christianity a break from Irving Babbitt.
July 24–26	Paul More entertains T. S. Eliot at the Isis Hotel in Oxford, England.
Aug. 4	Paul More makes his way from Liverpool to Montreal, to head back to the United States.
Aug. 12	Paul More arrives in Essex, New York.
Sept. 16	Paul More writes a letter to Prosser Hall Frye, criticizing Robert Shafer's book on More, because it focuses too much on Shafer and too little on More.
Fall	Oxford University Press publishes Louis J. A. Mercier's *The Challenge of Humanism*.

1934

Feb.	Paul More delivers his Lowell Lectures each Monday and Wednesday of the month at the Lowell Institute in Boston to a small audience. These lectures would ultimately be published as *The Sceptical Approach to Religion*.
April	Paul More repeats his Lowell Lectures in Cincinnati, where they are more successful.

May 23	Paul More delivers a commencement address called "Church and Politics" at the General Theological Seminary in New York.
Early July	Paul More heads to his vacation place at Essex, New York, aiming to read the proofs for *The Sceptical Approach to Religion*.
Sept.	Paul More leaves Essex for Princeton, feeling tired and unwell.
Oct.	Paul More's second volume of *New Shelburne Essays*, called *The Sceptical Approach to Religion*, is published.
Winter	Still tired and unwell, Paul More helps Samuel Pendleton Cowardin Jr. with their textbook, *The Study of English Literature*.

1935

Early	Paul More contemplates writing an essay on James Joyce for Seward Collins's *American Review*, despite Collins's unpredictable behavior towards More.
Feb. 21	Paul More signs what turns out to be his final will.
April	Doctors give Paul More a clean bill of health, failing to find symptoms of any malignant growth in his body.
May	Paul More's edited collection with Frank Leslie Cross, *Anglicanism*, is published.
May 17	Paul More is operated on at Presbyterian Hospital in New York for carcinoma of the prostate, despite being told that he only has a fibroid tumor. The operation prolongs More's life but leaves him physically disabled.
Early June	Although barely surviving the operation, Paul More begins to recover. His daughters care for him at his home on Battle Road in Princeton.
Sept.	Paul More, having returned from his vacation spot in Essex, New York, receives various guests, because he has become too weak to leave his home.

1936

Feb.	The Communist journal *Fight* publishes Grace Lumpkin's deceitfully procured interview from the previous month with Seward Collins, in which Collins praises Hitler and suggests that Jews deserve the treatment the Nazis are giving them. Various Southern Agrarian contributors to the *American*

	Review, already irate with Collins due to his editorial incompetence, begin denouncing him and his journal.
End of March	Paul More recognizes that he is dying of a malignant cancer, but he refuses to ask his doctor about it.
Spring	A split over the *American Review* intensifies, led by the Southern Agrarian Herbert Agar, who detests Seward Collins's self-styled American Fascism.
April	Paul More's essay on John Bailey appears in the *American Review*.
May	Paul More's essay "How to Read *Lycidas*" is published in the *American Review*.
May	Paul More's textbook with Samuel Pendelton Cowardin Jr., *The Study of English Literature*, is published.
Sept.	The third volume of More's *New Shelburne Essays*, called *On Being Human*, is published. It is More's final collection of literary essays.
Sept.?	Paul More dictates his autobiographical "Marginalia" to his daughter Darrah, which he does not complete. A first installment alone is published, in the November, 1936, issue of the *American Review*.
Thanksgiving	Paul More is so emaciated that a nurse must help More's daughter Darrah take care of him.
	Irving Babbitt's translation of the *Dhammapada* is published posthumously.

1937

Early Feb.	Bishop Matthews from the Episcopal Church asks Paul More if he would like to be confirmed. More says that he will think it over and ultimately decides against it.
Early Feb.	Paul More's daughter Darrah discovers the manuscript of *Pages from an Oxford Diary*; Whitney J. Oates convinces More to publish it.
Feb. 5	The *Princeton Alumni Weekly* publishes T. S. Eliot's article "Paul Elmer More," which More's daughter Darrah reads to him, to More's delight.
Feb. 23	Paul More finishes revising *Pages from an Oxford Diary* on his death bed.
March 9	Paul More passes away at ca. 9:00 AM.
March 11	Paul More is buried.
By Sept.	Paul More's *Pages from an Oxford Diary* is published posthumously.

CHAPTER ONE
1895–1898

Harvard University
Cambridge
December 23, 1895

My dear More,

Do you still hold to your purpose of going to St. Louis during the Christmas recess?[1] If you have made any change in your plans and are likely to be in New York, I should of course be extremely sorry not to know of the fact. With your Hindoo respect for a vow, you would not[,] I fancy, write first even though you were going to pass the holidays within hailing distance of me. Some odd bits of information about you and your work have come to my ears this autumn, the report that you were teaching a class of forty girls in Homer (through Sawyer) none of them good-looking (Lanman)[2]—*ce qui n'est pas drôle*. You should, however, according to Mather,[3] find a compensation in the sentimental interest they must take in you. They will, he says, ascribe to you all the adventures of the hero of the "Great Refusal"—except dying on Staten Island.[4]

I have of course missed you very much this year—so far as I have had time to miss any one. My work has been a wretched grind. I have nearly three hundred men under my instruction without counting a hors-d'oeuvre like my class at Radcliffe. I cannot endure this kind of thing much longer. I might

---

1. On September 1, 1895, More began his job as an Associate in Sanskrit and Classical Literature at Bryn Mawr College, a position he would hold until his resignation in 1897. See Dakin 1960: 51. Since More was a native of St. Louis, Babbitt here asks More if he aims to go home for the winter break.
2. Babbitt suggests that he heard this detail about More's teaching at Bryn Mawr from Charles R. Lanman, who previously taught both Babbitt and More during their graduate studies at Harvard. On Lanman, see his entry in the Bibliographical Register.
3. Frank Jewett Mather Jr., Babbitt's friend and fellow Humanist since their days as faculty members at Williams College, who subsequently became close to More as well. On Mather, see his entry in the Biographical Register.
4. In late 1894 More had published the epistolary novel *The Great Refusal, Being Letters of a Dreamer in Gotham*, which was secretly based on More's own relationship with Sarah Warfield Brank (see Dakin 1950: 90 and 1960: 37, 50-51).

be willing to sacrifice myself for Greek but I am not going to turn myself into a teaching automaton in order that Harvard sophomores may read French novels of the decadence in the original.

I have of course had no time to do anything with Pâli or other outside work. I have read in connection with one of my French courses six volumes of Taine's "Origines." Taine has the dry and mechanical intellectual habit of a 14th century schoolman: there is as Amiel[5] says somewhere, something in his style that suggests the grinding of pulleys and the click of machinery—something that takes hold of the throat like the gases from a chemical laboratory: and yet his book by its massiveness and logical consistency ends by imposing respect if not admiration. Some shortcomings may be overlooked in a writer, who, like Taine, possesses real virility of thought and expression, at a time when literature seems to have fallen almost entirely under the influence of women.

What progress are you making with the Bhartrihari?[6] I feel a great interest in your Sanskrit translations: some of the work of this kind in the "Great Refusal" is altogether admirable, and I hope you will continue until you have the material to form a volume.

I ordered your La Fontaine[7] and Ronsard[8] last autumn immediately after your speaking to me about the matter. I received recently a note from Flammarion[9] saying that there was still some formality for me to comply with in order to open up an account with them—all this in spite of the special arrangement I made with them when in Paris. I have written a rather tart rejoinder, and do not know what the outcome of the affair will be, but in any case will see that your order reaches you in the next few weeks.

I have let two or three days slip by before finishing this letter and I presume you have already left Bryn Mawr.[10] The letter will follow you, however, and the very fact of my having written it ought, with your knowledge of my habits, to indicate how deeply desirous I am of hearing from you. Turner[11]

---

5. The Swiss philosopher, critic, and poet Henri-Frédéric Amiel (1821–1881).

6. More would publish his book of translations called *A Century of Indian Epigrams: Chiefly from the Sanskrit of Bhartrihari* in 1898. The introduction to the book takes the form of a letter to Babbitt (see More 1899a: 1-19).

7. The French poet and fabulist Jean de La Fontaine (1621–1695).

8. The French poet Pierre de Ronsard (1524–1585).

9. Flammarion, a publishing company founded in 1876 by Ernest Flammarion, is headquartered in Paris.

10. For the winter recess, Babbitt means.

11. There appears only to have been only one Harvard faculty member with the last name Turner at this time: the engineer Daniel Lawrence Turner (1869–1942), who had served as an

sends his regards and other members of Table 16, if they knew I were writing, would doubtless do the same.

Very sincerely yours,
Irving Babbitt.

Harvard University
Cambridge
March 5, 1896

My dear More,

The receipt of your letter was one of the very few real pleasures I have had during these recent times. During the mid-year period and for some time afterwards I lived in a nightmare of examination books, and I have not even yet entirely shaken off the numbness of mind that comes from the prolonged application of it to an entirely distasteful task. I somewhat relieved my feelings by giving about fifty "Ds" and "Es" to men who took my Fr. 1B in the hope that it would be a "snap." One of these victims told me pathetically that "there was not any chance of a man's finding a 'snap' at Harvard now unless he fell into it by accident." I answered that only full professors could afford to give "snaps" at Harvard and that it wasn't always safe even for them.

Let me thank you heartily for the kind way in which you have thought of me in connection with the possible vacancy at Bryn Mawr. Curiously enough, almost the very day of the receipt of your letter, there reached me a letter from Giese containing similar inquiries in regard to a vacancy in U. of Wisconsin.[12] I enclose G's letter the blotted appearance of which you will excuse. I read it while walking along the street in a snowstorm. I can't say how I should regard an offer from Wisconsin or from Bryn Mawr before having a talk with President Eliot.[13] I am intending to see him sometime during the next few days and after my conversation with him hope to arrive

---

instructor in surveying and railroad engineering since 1893. Turner's tenure as an instructor at Harvard overlapped with More's time as a graduate student there, so the two could have known one another.

12. Babbitt, who as this and the previous letter intimate, was irritated by his lowly rank, pay, and teaching assignments at Harvard, had inquired about other academic positions. William F. Giese was an undergraduate classmate of Babbitt and a professor of French and Spanish at the University of Wisconsin. On Giese, see his entry in the Biographical Register. On Babbitt's hunt for a new position, see Nevin 1984: 12.

13. Charles W. Eliot, a chemist who served as the president of Harvard from 1869 until 1909, was Babbitt's pedagogical bête noir. On Eliot, see his entry in the Biographical Register.

at a clearer notion of my present situation. I am heartily sick of the work I am doing now and do not care to go on unless I see something very definitively ahead of me.[14]

Even though I were not to accept an outside offer, it might be extremely useful for me to get one for the way in which I might use it to strengthen my position at Harvard: so that I think it might be well for you to suggest my name to Miss Thomas[15] should there be a vacancy at Bryn Mawr in classics. In the meanwhile I should like to get fuller information about the place—hours and kind of work, probable salary and chances of promotion.

I should be more reconciled to my position at Harvard if I were permitted to give some advanced work. I hoped to be able to do so next year, but the present outlook is not encouraging. I had wanted to give a half-course, primarily for graduates, with some such title say as "Literary Schools in France during the XIXth Cent., with special reference to the origins of the Romantic Movement." The more important of the lectures, especially those relating to the influence of Rousseau and Chateaubriand[,] I intended to write down and by a careful revision of them later hoped to get the material for a small volume. I shall lose nothing, however, by holding back my ideas on this subject, such as they are, until they are thoroughly mellowed by reflection or to use the expression of Joubert,[16] sufficiently "passées par l'âme." A friend like yourself, who knows how ready I am to deliver myself of crude and rash generalizations in conversation, will possibly be somewhat surprised at this commendable slowness on my part to put my theories in print and may regard as indolence what is really caution. I am not, however, so subject to violent *partis-pris* as would appear from my talk. A certain cold judicial habit of mind is I fancy much more essential in me than my vehemence of expression which comes in part from humorous exaggeration and partly from a mere impatience of the blood joined to my natural combative instincts in the face of contradiction.

I received a second letter from Giese a few days ago which, however, does not add much to the information contained in the first. The man who takes the position in Latin could hope for the full professorship and the head of

---

14. Since his hiring in 1894, Babbitt remained an instructor in Harvard's French department, a position he would hold until his promotion to assistant professor in 1902.

15. Martha Carey Thomas (1857–1935), a linguist and the second president of Bryn Mawr College (pr. 1894–1922), had hired More as an Associate in Sanskrit and Classical Literature for a two-year term in 1895. When Thomas refused More's appeal for increased pay and a decreased workload in 1897, More resigned. See Dakin 1960: 51-56, 103.

16. The French essayist and critic Joseph Joubert (1754–1824).

the department at the end of a year with a salary of $2500: he might also substitute for one of his Latin courses a course in Greek. It appears that they are coquetting with a certain Gudemann [sic] of Philadelphia.[17] Mather[,] who knows him[,] tells me that he amply satisfies the expectations ruined by his name, being a runty little German Jew and pedant of the worst type. Mather added with a tinge of melancholy (he has been refused promotion at Williams) that in a few years no one who is seamly [sic?] and not a Jew would have any chance of getting on in university work in this country.

Would you, by the way, care for the Wisconsin position yourself? If, as is rumored among certain people here in Cambridge, you are engaged to be married you may be thinking about salaries.[18] If you decide to enter the lists, I should of course retire immediately and work for you with a will. This rumor of your engagement, by the way, merits an official confirmation or denial. So many members past and present of Table 16 have succumbed of late that I feel no one is safe. Turner is said to have been very successful in his matrimonial venture, but I confess to my shame that I have not as yet found time to call on the young *ménage*.

I am counting on seeing you here during the April recess. It will be a great disappointment for me if you do not come and I need scarcely add for many other friends whom you have in Cambridge. Your plans for next summer would be of great interest to me if you have made any as yet and care to state them. My present intention is to remain in this country though friends who think they know my habits tell me that about May 1st I am going to be looking up the steamer sailings for Europe.

The two epigrams were much appreciated. I prefer on the whole, the one translated from the Sanskrit. A small volume composed of work as good as that or of the quality of some of the epigrams you have inserted in the "Great Refusal" would, in my opinion, be a real contribution to literature. The plan

---

17. Babbitt must here refer to the Jewish-American classical philologist Alfred Gudeman (1862–1942), who from 1893 to 1901 taught at the University of Pennsylvania. After earning a doctorate at the University of Berlin, Gudeman, despite his scholarly productivity, had no luck finding lasting employment in American academia, undoubtedly thanks to anti-Semitism. He thus returned to Germany, where he ultimately was killed in the Holocaust. On Gudeman, see Hurley 1990. The position at the University of Wisconsin was accepted by Moses Slaughter (see Babbitt's September 2, 1896, letter below).

18. More had successfully proposed to Henrietta ("Nettie" or "Net") Beck, a childhood friend from St. Louis, in 1896 (see Dakin 1960: 52; the Chronology; and Henrietta Beck More in the Biographical Register). But, due to More's poverty, the two would not get married until June 12, 1900 (see Shafer 1935c: 102; Mather 1938: 369; Hough 1952: 175; Dakin 1960: 78; Duggan 1966: 15).

of study you have marked out for yourself seems to me worthy of all praise. You will not I am sure, allow an undue devotion to scholarship to impair your capacity for original work.

***19

I hope you will let me hear from you as soon as you can, telling me what you think about the Wisconsin vacancy and informing me of any new development at Bryn Mawr: a possible opening there in Greek might be of extreme interest to me.

Very sincerely yours,
Irving Babbitt.

Harvard University
Cambridge
June 2, 1896
(finished June 10)

My dear More,

I trust that none of your family or friends have suffered through the St. Louis cyclone;[20] the actual loss of life seems, so far as I can judge from the papers, to have been confined to the lower classes. I have not, however, had the patience to wade through all the hysterical superlatives and lurid rhetoric of the press accounts and hope you will write a line to reassure me.

I certainly owe you a very humble apology for my delay in answering your extremely interesting letter of last April, containing as it did the announcement of your engagement. As to this last event, I am going to refrain from comment except to express my satisfaction that your choice has fallen on a Western rather than on an Eastern girl. These New England women are entirely too thin-blooded to suit my taste. Your Cambridge friends were variously affected by the report of your engagement—Few[21] sends his congratulations, Marks[22] his commiserations, etc.

---

19. It is unknown what is missing from Babbitt's letter here, since the original of the second half of this missive appears to have been lost.

20. On May 27, 1896, a tornado caused major damage to downtown St. Louis, Missouri, and other nearby areas. It killed ca. 255 people.

21. William Preston Few (1867–1940) received his Ph.D. in English philology from Harvard in 1896. Since he had earned his A.M. at Harvard in 1893, Few overlapped with More as a graduate student there. Few would later serve as the president of Duke University.

22. Lionel Simeon Marks (1871–1955) was a British engineer on the faculty of Harvard since 1894.

One reason for my delay in writing, as you may no doubt have surmised, has been the lack of leisure resulting from my efforts to get my lecture for Madison into shape.[23] This proved to be more of a task than I had anticipated—it takes a surprising amount of manuscript to fill an hour. When the time came to start for Wisconsin I had about half finished and the rest of the address was composed on the North Shore Limited en route for Chicago. I had to copy it in a frightful hurry on a train going fifty miles an hour from Chicago to Madison and the result was that when I came to deliver it I had the greatest difficulty in reading in places my own manuscript. I was not in the slightest degree nervous but as the result of my stumbling undoubtedly gave the impression of being so. The hall was execrable, a great barnlike place with a hundred and fifty or two hundred people scattered around in the back of it.

It was unfortunate that my lecture was spoiled by the ineffective delivery as in itself it seemed to me fairly satisfactory; it at least represented fairly both in form and substance what I am capable of doing. I may revise it and try to get it published as a magazine article and in that case I should like you to look over it and give me the benefit of your criticism.

I made use, by the way, of your translation of the Sanskrit epigram on the philologians, giving you of course due credit for it.[24]

My present feeling is that the chances are decidedly against my getting an offer from Wisconsin. Even if I did get it, I think it is extremely doubtful whether I should accept it. President Adams[25] sounded me as to whether I would take the position and I answered as I was in duty bound to do, that this was somewhat problematic.

I could not of course put forward your candidacy in a formal way while remaining in the field myself, but I spoke of you in general terms to the President and hope to have a chance to present your name before any final decision is reached. I am now expecting word of some kind from Madison daily and as soon as it comes, will lose no time in informing you.

My situation at Harvard will be slightly improved the coming year. I am entirely relieved of French A. The advanced half course of which I spoke to you in my last letter was barred out of Harvard by the philological

---

23. In 1895 Babbitt delivered a lecture at the University of Wisconsin called "The Rational Study of the Classics." Babbitt turned this lecture into an article of the same title, which appeared in the *Atlantic Monthly* in March 1897. See Babbitt 1897b. This, in turn, became one chapter of Babbitt's first book, *Literature and the American College* (1908). On the article, see, e.g., Foerster 1930: vii.

24. See Babbitt 1897b: 360.

25. Charles Kendall Adams (1835–1902) was a historian who served as the president of the University of Wisconsin from 1892 until 1901.

syndicate but I have succeeded in getting two advanced half courses—one on the origins of Romanticism and one on literary criticism in France during the XIXth cent. accepted at Radcliffe. If these courses succeed there I should get at least one of them accepted at Harvard the following year.[26]

I have been kept from finishing this letter for a number of days by the duties of my final examinations and in the meanwhile I have received your letter as well as the one enclosed from Giese. It is a great disappointment to me not to be able to see you here in Cambridge sometime this month. My plans for the summer are quite unsettled. I may be abroad during July and the early part of August but should in any case be able to see you at Biddeford Pool[27] or Cambridge toward the end of August or in September.

It would appear from Giese's letter that we are both barred out from the position at Madison. I am somewhat consoled when I think of all the anxious deliberation I have been spared by not getting the offer. I am still going to make some efforts in your behalf though I must say that the outlook is not promising.

I shall be forced to work on the average about twelve hours a day this summer in order to get my Radcliffe courses into shape, but promise if you write me to answer with reasonable promptness.

Sincerely in haste,
Irving Babbitt.

---

65 Hammond Street
Cambridge
2 September 1896

My dear More,

I am just back from Paris where I have been spending the last two months. I had intended to remain about a week or two longer and visit Sylvain Lévi[28] in Switzerland but was unable to secure accommodations on any steamer

---

26. This appears to be the end of the original portion of the letter, composed on June 2. Babbitt wrote the remainder on June 10.

27. More spent parts of his summer at Biddeford Pool in Maine as early as 1893. See Dakin 1960: 45.

28. Babbitt studied Pali and Sanskrit with Lévi as a graduate student in 1891–92 at the Sorbonne. On Lévi, see his entry in the Biographical Register.

sailing after Aug. 22nd. My stay in Paris was marked by no special incident. I explored most of the second hand book shops in the Latin Quarter under the guidance of Giese, attended in a rather languid and perfunctory way some of the lectures given under the auspices of the *Alliance Française* and did a certain amount of reading in preparation for my Radcliffe courses. I bought altogether about three hundred books, most of them intended to serve as a special apparatus for next year's work.

I believe I mailed you Giese's postal card, telling of the nomination of a certain Slaughter of Iowa[29] to the Wisconsin professorship. I had just finished when I received word from Giese, a letter in your behalf to President Adams. I regret now that I did not sacrifice myself resolutely several weeks earlier and devote my entire attention to backing you, but Giese seems to feel quite certain that the result would not have been changed.

I write this note mainly to find out whether you are now at Biddeford Pool in accordance with your plan as expressed in your last letter to me, and if so, to make arrangements to visit you there.[30] I have so much work to do in preparation for the college opening that my stay will have to be very brief but I look forward with great anticipation to the pleasure of seeing you again nevertheless.

Let me have a line from you assuring me that you are at the Pool and giving me any information you may deem useful, as to the ways and means of getting there, etc. If I do not hear from you within the next three of four days I am going to write to your address in Saint-Louis. I have promised by the way to see Lanman if I go to Maine. Would it not be possible for us to visit him and the Sheldons[31] together?

Sincerely in haste,
Irving Babbitt.

---

29. Moses S. Slaughter (1860–1923), who earned a Ph.D. from the Johns Hopkins University in 1891, had taught in Iowa prior to becoming a professor of Latin at the University of Wisconsin in 1896.

30. Dakin (1960: 51) notes that More visited the Harvard history professor Ephraim Emerton (1851–1935) and his family at their cottage in Shelburne, New Hampshire, in the summers of 1895 and 1896. These visits presumably gave More the idea of renting a small cabin on the Philbrook farm in Shelburne from 1897 to 1899. More had taken a graduate course with Emerton, whom he subsequently befriended. See Dakin 1960: 47, 51, 65.

31. Edward Stevens Sheldon (1851–1925) was a professor of Romance languages at Harvard from 1894 until he retired in 1921. Dakin (1960: 47) tells us that More studied with Sheldon as a graduate student at Harvard.

65 Hammond Street
Harvard University
Cambridge
16 October, 1896

My dear More,

 I trust you will pardon my delay in answering your very welcome letter of recent date. The beginning of the college year here at Harvard is, as you know, a trying season. – Geneviève is pronounced without nazalization [sic] and with suppression of course of the medial mute *e* – *Gen'viève*.

 No class at Radcliffe, only two applicants, one short of the necessary number. In this case it is not a miss but the lack of a miss which is as good as a mile. It doesn't look as though I succeeded in making much of an impression last year on the Radcliffe community. I can bear up with heroic equanimity under its disfavor but am less easily reconciled to the financial loss involved which is serious.

 I have been asked to do some advanced work at Harvard—one lecture a week on French literary criticism to a single graduate student—but am not sure as yet whether I shall accept.

 I agree with the scientific men in regarding Dick Norton's utterances on art and science—so far as I can judge of them from what you tell me—as crude and sophomoric.[32] He should begin by an hour of preliminary definition as to just what he means by art and what by science to make the establishing of a mechanical opposition between the two justifiable. Some grievous charges may be brought against contemporary science, but such as it is, it sometimes seems to me more deserving of respect than contemporary art and literature. Purely voluptuary art—art designed to produce aesthetic titillations merely—such art, for instance, as inspires most of the pictures in a Paris Salon, may become a veritable malady and it has already passed into that stage in some of the European countries. *Quot artes, tot concupiscentiae.*[33] Science at least helps to preserve the human personality from being dissolved in pure sensation. Art only fulfils a high function when it is used to throw a

---

 32. Richard Norton (1872–1918) was a Harvard-trained archaeologist who in April 1895 became a professor at Bryn Mawr (Turner 1999: 366) and was thus More's colleague. He was the son of the polymath Harvard professor Charles Eliot Norton, with whom Babbitt studied as a graduate student. On Charles Eliot Norton, see his entry in the Biographical Register.

 33. Here Babbitt is providing a humorous nod to the Roman playwright Terence's famous line *quot homines tot sententiae* ("There are as many opinions as there are people"). Babbitt's version means "There are as many arts as there are sensual desires."

veil of divine illusion over some essential truth. As Joubert says: "L'illusion et la sagesse réunies sont le charme de la vie et de l'art." Sainte-Beuve[34] is right in lamenting the failure of art and literature toward the beginning of this century to enter heartily into the deeper thought and aspirations of the new age and try to interpret them; the reaction of Chateaubriand and of the Romantic writers and artists toward the middle ages was altogether futile. By a divorce of faculties of the mind that should coöperate, science tends more and more to arid analysis and dry intellectualism while art runs the risk of degenerating into mere dilettanteism and virtuosity. The whole subject is discussed in an interesting way in Guyau's *Problèmes de l'esthétique contemporaine*,[35] a book, by the way, which I think would interest you. Scherer's[36] article on the elder Ampère is an interesting study of a man in whom the scientific and imaginative habits of mind were blended.

I shall be deeply interested in what you write on the subject of melancholy among the Greeks.[37] You may give me some very useful hints for my course on Romanticism—in case it is ever given. I have found very suggestive remarks on the subject in various passages of Sainte-Beuve and am prepared to send you a list of references in case you think it would prove useful.

I have ordered books sent directly from Paris to Bryn Mawr, but there may be some delay on account of binding. I hope you will find time to write me occasionally. It looks this year as though you were to be busier than I am.

Sincerely,
Irving Babbitt.

---

65 Hammond Street
Cambridge
15 February, 1897

My dear More,

Your recent letter and the manuscript which followed it both called for my immediate acknowledgement; my failure to make this acknowledgement is

---

34. The French literary critic Charles Augustin Sainte-Beuve (1804–1896).
35. The French philosopher Jean-Marie Guyau (1854–1888) published this book in 1884.
36. The German historian of literature Wilhelm Scherer (1841–1886).
37. It is possible that Babbitt here refers to More 1898a, although this piece does not focus particularly on melancholy. Babbitt would later title one of the chapters of *Rousseau and Romanticism* "Romantic Melancholy" (1991: 306-52) and in it he would highlight the ancient Greek conception of melancholy.

due in the present case not so much to my natural dilatoriness as to the very peculiar pressure under which I have been for a number of days back. I had in the first place, my batch of mid-year examination books, the correction of which could not be postponed. I have besides had other occupations and anxieties the nature of which I may explain to you when we next meet. It will be some time yet before I can hope to have any real leisure and you will, I hope, pardon me if even now after all my delay, I only have time to send you a hasty line.

Your dedication[38] to me came as a most pleasant surprise. I have appreciated it deeply both for the honor I feel it to be in itself and for other reasons you will readily understand. I should be only too proud to have my name connected in any way with work of such undoubted excellence as much of that in your collection of epigrams seems to me to be. As to the practical question whether it would be best to run your dedicatory letter and your introduction together as you have done, I hesitate about giving an opinion. I should certainly suggest some changes. The whole question seems to me an extremely delicate one and, being interested as I am, I do not feel altogether qualified to decide it. I should like, if you do not object, to submit in confidence your dedicatory letter to Norton[39] and get the benefit of his wide experience in matters of this kind. If he should advise keeping the dedication but separately, I should be inclined to submit to his judgment, and if, again, he advised the entire suppression of the dedication, I should, though with extreme reluctance, feel disposed to acquiesce. The great advantage of the letter in its present form is that it affords you a means of escaping from academic stiffness in your discussion of Bhartrihari and then besides there are a couple of extremely happy quotations which it would be a pity to lose.

I have read and re-read your epigrams during the past few days and examined most of them line by line and word by word. It has been a pleasure rather than a task for me to do so. A number of the more recent epigrams, or at least of those I had not as yet seen seem to me thoroughly good and indicate that you are gaining an ever greater mastery of your form. There are, however, some epigrams which I should advise you to reject altogether or to rewrite, and others which seem to me susceptible of improvement in single lines. I am going to use my pencil freely as you suggest. You seem to me already to have in sight the material of a little volume which is likely to add to your reputation both as a scholar and a writer. If you feel that your position at Bryn Mawr needs strengthening, it would of course be well to publish as

---

38. Of More's *A Century of Indian Epigrams*; see More 1899a: 1-19.
39. Charles Eliot Norton, a Harvard professor and a key mentor to both Babbitt and More.

soon as possible. Would it not, however, be a good idea to take your time with your book, and in the meanwhile to publish some of the best of your verse in one of the magazines? I think it very likely that if you sent fifteen or twenty of the best of the epigrams with a prefatory note, to Scudder,[40] he would be able to make use of them for the *Atlantic*; or you might write a regular article mingling prose and verse, under the title "Quatrains from Bhartrihari" or something of the sort. There is just a chance of my seeing Scudder inside the next two or three weeks. Would you like me to bring up this project in a discreet way in course of conversation with him and get his opinion of its feasibility? You may have noticed from the advertising pages of the Feb. *Atlantic* that my article on the classics is booked for the March number.[41] I had also hoped to get ready an article on Brunetière[42] apropos of his visit to this country but I despair of finding time to write it in my disjointed existence here at Harvard—the "multitude of little things and their relentless feud"[43] in the midst of which I pass my life.

If there is no hitch in seeing Norton, I hope to return you your MS. with another letter toward the end of this week. My delay seems on the face of it unpardonable but I think you would pardon it if you knew all the circumstances. Excuse the desperate haste in which I have had to write this evening, and believe me,

Heartily yours,
Irving Babbitt.

---

65 Hammond Street
Cambridge
23 March, '97

My dear More,

I must find time for a hasty line in answer to your letter received this morning. I wish to thank you very much for the efforts you have been making in my behalf at Bryn Mawr. I really do not know what attitude I should take toward an offer from Miss Thomas[44] if it came to me before the middle of April; after that date, for reasons I have not time to detail here, I shall be

---

40. Horace Scudder (1838–1902) was then the editor of the *Atlantic Monthly*.
41. See Babbitt 1897b.
42. See Babbitt 1897a, an article on Brunetière that appeared in the June issue of the *Atlantic*.
43. Babbitt here quotes from one of More's translated epigrams; see More 1899a: 114.
44. Martha Carey Thomas, the president of Bryn Mawr College. On Thomas, see Babbitt's letter of March 5, 1896, above.

in a position to speak more definitively. I am working with might and main at present on an article on Brunetière which I should like to finish and send off by April 10th in time for insertion in the May *Atlantic*.[45] I fear that if I had to consider the Bryn Mawr matter between now and then it would interfere with the completion of my article. If you could hit upon some perfectly discreet way of obtaining a stay of proceedings until the last half of April I should be much obliged to you. I may by the way send you some sheets of my Brunetière article for criticism and in that case should have to ask you to return them in a day or two after receipt.

I am very much interested in the progress of your volume of epigrams. I only hope you will have an *accès de verve* such as you lyrical people are subject to, and do a dozen or fifteen more epigrams as good as the best of your present collection or else so revise a number of those you have already done as to bring them up to the standard of your best work.

Excuse haste.

Sincerely your friend,
Irving Babbitt.

---

65 Hammond Street
Cambridge
6 May, 1897

My dear More,

Many thanks for your observations on my mss. I found many of them useful though I was too hurried in finishing my article to make all the changes you suggested. I finally got my paper off to Scudder at the fifty-ninth minute of the eleventh hour; he at once returned it to me with a very kind letter saying that he had not anticipated so long a paper (about 8000 words in its complete form) and that he could not possibly find room for it in the June *Atlantic*, the only number in which he cared to print an article on Brunetière. He would, he added, be very glad to publish a paper of 5000 words and asked me, accordingly, whether I could not cut my mss. down to that length, reserving myself the privilege of publishing rejected portions in an article by itself.[46] He gave me a little over a day in which to do this abridging, and get mss. back to *Atlantic*. You can imagine that this task of mutilating my own work was not precisely an agreeable one, but I accomplished it, nevertheless,

---

45. Babbitt 1897a, which appeared in the June number.
46. Babbitt later significantly reworked this article to serve as a chapter of his book *The Masters of Modern French Criticism*. See Babbitt 1912e: 298-337.

and the result will appear in the June *Atlantic*. My article has suffered seriously both in form and substance by the excisions, but whether it has been completely ruined others can judge better than myself.

The *Atlantic* has written me, by the way, soliciting contributions for its "Men and Letters" department. I may send a short article, unsigned of course, for this department, on your Indian Epigrams in case you get them published.[47]

The news of your resignation from Bryn Mawr came as a great surprise not only to me but to all your friends here in Cambridge.[48] Lanman thinks you have been very imprudent. A mere disagreement about salary seems on the face of it a rather insufficient motive for taking so serious a step. Still I have such confidence in your good sense that I am going to await further details before commenting on your action either one way or the other. I have heard by the way a number of times from independent sources that you are succeeding as a teacher at Bryn Mawr.[49]

I very much envy your year of prospective solitude.[50] *Reste à voir* whether you actually carry your little scheme out. If I am thwarted here at Harvard much longer by such men as Sumichrast,[51] I am likely to retire in disgust, too, and go out and cultivate some abandoned farm.

I have consulted with Lanman about material likely to be useful in your lecture. The reference for the monk who cried *aho nikhans* is Jātaka 10; the preceding Jātaka (9) about the king who had only 84,000 thousand years to live might also furnish an amusing illustration. See also for good anecdote trans. of Dhammapada, pp. 38–39, note. For different sects see references in Fausböll's introduction to translation of Sutta-Nipāta,[52] -- also first two Suttas of Dīyha-Nikāya and possibly in the commentary to them published also in the Pāli Text Soc. It might be well to look through Spence Hardy's

---

47. See Babbitt 1899, an anonymous review of More's epigrams that also appeared posthumously in Babbitt 1940: 141-49.

48. On More's resignation from Bryn Mawr in 1897, see Dakin 1960: 55-56.

49. Dakin (1960: 53-54) reports that More, lacking Babbitt's energy and self-confidence, was somewhat underwhelming in the classroom at Bryn Mawr.

50. Upon his departure from Bryn Mawr in the summer of 1897, More would famously spend two years and three months in comparative solitude in a little red cabin on the Philbrook farm in Shelburne, New Hampshire.

51. Frederick Cesar de Sumichrast was a fellow member of the French department at Harvard and a detractor of Babbitt. On Sumichrast, see his entry in the Biographical Register.

52. Viggo Fausböll (1821-1908) was a Danish Pali scholar and professor who translated the *Dhammapada* (1855) and the *Sutta-Nipata* (1885).

"Eastern Monachism"[53] and you might also glean something to your purpose occasionally from Warren's book.[54]

I am delighted at the prospect of seeing you here in June and hope you will decide for a two weeks rather than a one week stay. I am going to be very much rushed for two or three weeks but after that hope to be comparatively free.

Very sincerely,
Irving Babbitt.

My sister[55] is with me at present and desires to be remembered to you.

---

65 Hammond Street
Cambridge
16 November, 1897

My dear More,

My delay in writing has been due to the preparation of my lecture which came last Friday. I did not begin seriously the composition of it until the Sunday before and so was very much rushed at the last moment. My date was about the worst that could possibly have been chosen; rain, eve of Yale Game, free Glee Club concert, meetings of Grad. Club, Harvard Union, etc. and so I had a small audience. I intend of course to use my material for an article in the *Atlantic*. I have not decided, however, whether to publish at once or to wait until I have finished two companion articles—"Poe and the French Decadents" and "Journal of the Goncourts." I wish you to look my paper over and give me the benefit of your criticism before I send it to Page.[56]

I am heartily glad that Houghton Mifflin have accepted your "Epigrams." I have never had any special fault to find with the present title but of course it will do no hurt to try and find a better one. I should for some reasons

---

53. R. Spence Hardy (1803–1868) was a scholar of Buddhism. His book *Eastern Monachism* was published in 1860.
54. Babbitt presumably refers to the work of Henry Clarke Warren (1854–1899), a scholar of Pali and Sanskrit.
55. Katharine Babbitt, with whom Babbitt was very close. On Katharine, see her entry in the Biographical Register.
56. Walter Hines Page (1855–1918), then the editor of the *Atlantic Monthly*.

have preferred to see the book published next spring rather than next fall;[57] I think I could have my review ready for insertion, say in the May *Atlantic*.[58] Lanman might advertise your book in connection with his Baltimore lectures and besides these lectures might call the attention of the public to the subject of Sanskrit poetry in a way that would help the sale of your book. I leave the decision on the whole matter in your hands and in those of H. M.[59] I shall be interested to learn H. M.'s estimate of the cost of publication and shall of course put this amount at your disposition whenever you need it. I should advise you in the meanwhile to rewrite or find substitutes for some few of the epigrams—a half dozen perhaps—which are not equal in execution to the others and to do everything in your power to free your little book from every blemish.

I have had a great deal of pleasure in reading over your essay on Delphi in its completed form.[60] It seems to me a thoroughly good piece of work, though I have some criticisms of details. There is not as much ease of style at the beginning of the essay as later on, and the reader at times is perhaps conscious of an undue compression. There is a sort of *cui bono* atmosphere which hangs over the last few pages of your article. The reader is carried on in a fine forward sweep of large and sound generalization but is left at the very end with the melancholy feeling that after all the human spirit may be fatally condemned to be blighted by some unfriendly excess and indeed become the victim of its own virtues. But possibly this is the impression you wished to give. – There are in addition to this general criticism some few queries as to details of expression which I will make later.

I should not on the whole advise the article for the *Atlantic*. It think it extremely important that you keep on good terms with the *Atlantic* and with this end in view not risk any experiments. It will be entirely in its place in the *New World*, and I do not doubt will very greatly increase your chances of getting a good position in the classics. It seems extremely desirable to me that you state either in a note or in some other form that the article is

---

57. Houghton Mifflin eventually published the book in September of 1898 (Dakin 1950: 90 and 1960: 68).

58. Babbitt's anonymous review appeared in the October 1899 issue of the *Atlantic*. See Babbitt 1899.

59. Houghton Mifflin.

60. "Two Famous Maxims of Greece," which originally appeared in the March 1898 issue of the *New World* (More 1898a) and later under the title "Delphi and Greek Literature" in the second series of More's *Shelburne Essays*. See More 1905b: 188-218.

an introductory chapter to a book you are preparing on Greek Ethics. Seen from this point of view, it will impress the reader as a much stronger piece of work than if taken as a detached fragment.

The letter from White[61] is extremely gratifying. M. H. Morgan,[62] by the way, approached me lately and threw out a hint that if I cared to give up modern languages I might get a position in the classics here. He gave me a warm invitation to come around and call on him. I am going to make use of this opening to talk to him of you and your work, and thus strengthen if possible, the impression he has received through White.

Do you find all the material you need in the Gaston Paris I sent you? I can supplement it if you so desire by the medieval part of the encyclopaedic history of Fr. Lit. now being published under the direction of Petit de Juleville. Marcou[63] has my copy but if you think it will prove useful you must let me know and I will get it back from him. I also have text of Chrétien de Troyes' *Yvain*, etc. Do you know enough old French for it to be of service to you? I will rummage over my books now that I have more leisure and may find something else to your purpose.

What time in the winter do you expect to be in Cambridge? Let me have a line telling me your decision as to date of publication of Epigrams.

Sincerely,
I. B.

P.S. Flammarion did not send books in the way I directed and so incurred an extra expense of 2 Fr. not covered by my remittance and which they wish you to pay. I will see that the matter is settled.

---

61. Presumably Babbitt here refers to John Williams White (1849–1917), a longstanding Hellenist in Harvard's classics department. See S. Douglas Olson's entry on White in the *Database of Classical Scholars*: dbcs.rutgers.edu.

62. Morris H. Morgan (1859–1910), a classical philologist who worked on both Greek and Latin, was then a member of Harvard's classics department. See William M. Calder III's entry on Morgan in the *Database of Classical Scholars*: dbcs.rutgers.edu.

63. Philippe Belknap Marcou (1855–1927), then a faculty member of Romance languages at Harvard. Brennan and Yarbrough (1987: 21) note that Marcou, one of the senior professors of French when Babbitt was hired, was a philologist who disliked Babbitt's views on the humanities. Marcou's graduate training at the University of Berlin and thesis there, "Der historische Infinitiv im Franzoesischen," speak to his predilection for scientific philology. On Marcou, see Rivet 1928.

65 Hammond Street
Cambridge
5 August, 1898

My dear More,

I have been over your essay on Byron carefully two or three times.[64] I have found the thought of it interesting and think that the expression of a considerable part of it is already in excellent shape. There does not seem to me however as much charm and finish of expression in the work as a whole as you have shown yourself capable of elsewhere; and this is but natural if, as you say, the essay in its present form is a mere *ébauche*.

I was already familiar with your ideas about the "intellectual" qualities of Byron and think that when you get in all your modifying clauses I am going to agree with you in the main. I am very much hampered, however, in judging your essay by the fact that I have done no critical reading in Byron or Keats or Shelley for a number of years and do not know what I should think of their relative value if I read them through carefully now. You are likely to awaken contradiction in asserting that in his "art and perception of beauty" Byron stood above the other poets of his time including of course Keats.

Your comparison of the metaphors of Shelley and Byron may seem to some disproportionate to the length of your essay. I think that nearly everything you say on this point is sound. I fear, however, that some of your distinctions may seem rather fine-drawn to the average reader; and in a subject of this kind you cannot be too careful to avoid misunderstandings. For instance, the great danger of Classical metaphors, etc. is that they tend to become too intellectual and abstract and so lose the right sensuous quality and refuse to visualize. The germ of the "printer's devil" personifications of pseudo-classicism is to be found in true classicism. Molière's figures constantly tend to become incoherent—"Le *poids* de sa grimace où *brille* l'artifice, etc."[65] Besides, only one class of "romantic" metaphors run to an excessive temerity—especially those which try to render certain shades of sensation, color and sound. Another class of images no less romantic are extraordinary for their plastic precision and firmness of contour—for instance the images

---

64. More would publish a biographical sketch of Byron in the December 1898 issue of the *Atlantic Monthly*, which would ultimately serve as the introduction to More's 1905 edition of Byron's complete poetry. See More 1898b and 1905a: xi-xxi; Dakin 1960: 63.

65. Babbitt here quotes a line from the first scene of Act 5 of Molière's play *Le Misanthrope*.

of Victor Hugo, Leconte de Lisle, Heredia, etc., only I do not look upon the images of these men as in the highest sense poetical because they have not undergone the subtle transformation which lifts them from the region of nature into the region of the human soul. All this is of course familiar to you, but I am not sure that your discussion of the question does not in one or two places leave the way open to some misapprehension.

I am not certain that your treatment of the psychological side of Byron is altogether adequate. I can only say that personally I should have given rather more space to a study of the peculiar nature of his "egotism" and "subjectivity" and also to showing in what respects he was medieval and feudal in his attitude toward life and in what respects he was a child of the modern spirit. It might also have been well to make a little clearer the significance of the irony that appears in Byron and other modern writers. Allar's[66] analysis of the different forms the *mal du siècle* assumed might be of some service to you. Still you have the right in a brief introduction to neglect certain sides of so large a subject, and you must not regard any of my remarks as more than first impressions which I might modify on further reflection.

I have got very little done during the past month and have suffered greatly from the heat, and it does not reflect credit on my intelligence that I have remained in Cambridge at all under the circumstances. I hope to get out of here early next week. I am thinking of going into some farm house near Centre Harbor, N. H. on the neck of land between Lake Winnipesaukee and Squam Lake. I may have to modify my plans however in order to accommodate a young man I have arranged to tutor during the latter part of the summer. I am going to give him about two hours a day and expect to get about $250 out of the transaction. I of course do not enjoy the prospect of this kind of summer work, but found the financial side of the proposition too tempting.

Remember me kindly to the Emertons. I am going to let you have a line as soon as I am settled for the summer.

Very sincerely yours,
Irving Babbitt.

---

66. The typewritten version of this letter informs readers that the name is a guess because the "name is illegible in the original letter."

Squam Lake, N. H.
25 August, 1898

My dear More,

I have hired a little cottage not far from the lakeshore here, and am very comfortably settled in it along with the student I am tutoring. We board at a neighboring farmhouse. There is excellent boating, fishing, bathing, and a large variety of pleasant walks. We are about a mile from the "Whittier pine" and from the house where Whittier[67] spent his summers for a great many years. Lake Winnipesaukee and other lakes are from two to four miles away.

I have been wondering whether you could not come down and visit me for a few days.[68] I should certainly run up and see you if I were not hindered by my tutoring. Could you not go over to Pinkham Notch to the railroad and then take the stage from West Ossipee to Centre Harbor where I should meet you? We can put you up in our cottage and I think you would find it extremely pleasant here. I should like to get your oral comment on the proof of my George Sand article which I enclose.[69] And then I should like to talk with you more in detail about your Byron and a number of other matters.

I am anxious to get the benefit of your suggestions on my George S. and your opinion of the emendations I am making. I of course need to get the proof back as soon as possible.

I have not accomplished much in the way of work up here. I have just finished reading Fielding's Tom Jones and have enjoyed it hugely in spite of the 18th cent. coarseness and the 18th cent. sentimentality—the transports, gushing tears and all that sort of thing.

I am intending to return to Cambridge about the middle of September— possibly a little later. I am going to have all the bother of furnishing my new rooms. My P.O. address here is Centre Harbor, N. H.

Very sincerely yours,
Irving Babbitt.

---

67. John Greenleaf Whittier (1807–1892), the American poet and abolitionist.
68. More was then still in his small cabin in Shelburne, NH, in the northernmost part of the state.
69. See Babbitt 1898, from the October 1898 number of the *Atlantic*, which later appeared under a different title in Babbitt 1940: 121-49.

Squam Lake, N. H.
17 September, 1898

My dear More,

Many thanks for the careful way in which you went over my George Sand; I found many of your suggestions excellent and have adopted most of them. The trouble I have had getting rid of the crudities of expression in this article will teach me to avoid in future *dictating* my work at the eleventh hour. Page[70] seems to have a glut of "correspondence" at present and I do not know when he intends to publish the G. S. I looked in the Sep. *Atlantic* by the way, for your English paper: I found an article by a nihilist, one by an anarchist and one by Copeland,[71] but nothing of yours.

I have found it curiously hard to make up my mind about the sonnet you sent me. It is not nearly so easy for some reason or other, to judge objectively a friend's verse as it is his prose. I have always told you that in your love-poems you tend to become a little what the French call *alambique*. This present poem has less of this quality than other work you have done but is possibly not without traces of it. I like some of the lines in the earlier part very much, but am just a trifle in doubt about the ending. The unwonted metrical form coming in conjunction with the rare rhyme word "pleasaunce" and with the overflow "thy presence—I go—" seem to me to destroy in some measure that easy swing and cumulative effect that should mark the close of a sonnet. Besides, the phrase "sweeter than sound of waters" smacks to me vaguely of Shelley. The phrase "leafy bowers" at the beginning also seems to me to be written from the memory rather than the imagination. Judging the work, then, by a severe standard, I should say that it had great excellencies of detail but as a whole, it does not deserve to rank with many of the epigrams which are so good as to leave no room whatsoever to doubt. My advice is that you send it to Page but in such a way as to make it easy for him to return it if it does not exactly hit his fancy.

I have received a copy of the epigrams and am very much pleased with the way H. M.[72] have done their part in the work. I am impressed in looking over the little book not only with the merit of separate epigrams but with the happy arrangement and the careful composition of the whole. I really envy

---

70. Walter Hines Page, the editor of the *Atlantic*.

71. Charles Townsend Copeland (1860–1952), the poet, professor, and writer. For the piece in question, see Copeland 1898.

72. Houghton Mifflin, the publisher of More's *A Century of Indian Epigrams*. See More 1899a.

you for having got something done which seems to me to contain so much of the right kind of originality. I am sure that the epigrams will gain you reputation in the long run, and I hope that they may obtain some recognition immediately. But as to this latter point it is not safe to feel any certainty. You must remember how much the spirit of your little book runs counter to the optimistic and humanitarian temper of the present age. But you may find an audience of dissenters.

I wish I could report more progress on my review. I hope, however, to have it done in time for the December *Atlantic* and I am not sure that this is not plenty soon enough.[73] The conditions of my life here are singularly unfavorable for doing anything of this kind. I spend the mornings walking, the afternoons rowing and swimming, and the evenings tutoring. I like the neighborhood so well that I may return another year. The water to my thinking is a luxury not to be dispensed with—not to speak of its scenic advantages.

I left your Greek paper with Toy.[74] If he has not written you about it, I will call and see him immediately on my return to Cambridge. He spoke to me of sending it to the French review.

Let me know as soon as possible how much the balance of the loan will be and I will remit at once. I intend to return to Cambridge next Monday so that my P.O. address will be as usual.

Sincerely,
Irving Babbitt.

---

73. Babbitt's review of More's *A Century of Indian Epigrams* did not in fact appear until the October 1899 issue of the *Atlantic*. See Babbitt 1899.
74. Presumably Babbitt means Crawford Howell Toy (1836–1919), a professor of Hebrew and Oriental languages at Harvard.

CHAPTER TWO

1899–1907

Shelburne, N. H.
26 April 1899

My dear Babbitt,

    I am in debt to you for two letters, and such indebtedness is so rare and so pleasant on the whole that I find it hard to cancel. I came to Shelburne instead of going to New York or Cambridge for several reasons, the chief being, if truth must be told, the rapidly emptying state of my purse. I received an account of the sales of The Epigrams in February. Something above three hundred copies had been sold up to that date—not a tremendous number you will admit. I fear too the demand for the book has ceased as no new edition has been called for. The money for the first sales I was constrained to embezzle for personal expenses. I have at last fully made up my mind that it will be better for me to get back to teaching again and do what writing I may in my leisure hours.[1] Starving grows a monotonous occupation after a while, and in fact they do say men have died of it. I have written to Lanman asking him to set me rolling once more and have received from him rather an encouraging letter. I judge from what he says he is endeavoring among other things to get me an appointment at Harvard next year. I doubt his success in that very much, and indeed I hope he will fail there and succeed elsewhere.[2]

    My Prometheus is in the press and will be out very soon.[3] I am now wrestling with a translation of the Oedipus. Plato I found hard, Prometheus harder, and this Oedipus I begin to fear is beyond my powers—in fact I begin to doubt whether it is within the limits of possibility to make a really readable version of any Greek tragedy without taking liberties that no one

---

    1. More would eventually leave Shelburne for Cambridge, MA, in autumn of this year. There he would work as an assistant to Professor Lanman. See Shafer 1935c: 10; Brown 1939: 476. Cf. Mather 1938: 369; Hough 1952: 175.
    2. Dakin (1960: 73) quotes a letter More wrote to his mother on October 1, 1899, in which he discusses Lanman's offer to More to work as a translator of a Sanskrit text for Lanman at Harvard. See Dakin 1960: 73-74.
    3. Indeed, Dakin (1950: 91 and 1960: 64-65) tells us that Houghton Mifflin published More's translation of Aeschylus' *Prometheus Bound* ca. May of 1899. See More 1899c.

would excuse. In a few days I shall send you the first two hundred lines of my translation; and as you have time won't you go over it pretty carefully and tell me what you think of it so far. I have decided not to attempt to retain the antistrophic form of the choral odes, for the effort would only hamper me without serving any real purpose in the English. I confess frankly my version so far does not read to me like poetry.[4] – I hardly think I shall be in Cambridge this spring. Shelburne will be my home through most or all of the summer. I am delighted to hear you mean to stay home and work, and I hope you have some plan in mind that will give you plenty of room and free swing. I should like to have the pleasant task of reviewing a book of yours. – I have written to Scudder[5] asking him whether he cares to publish a volume of essays on Greek literature to include The Two Famous Maxims,[6] Nemesis,[7] and several others of this sort. If I could find a publisher for such a book I would have the pleasure of sitting down to a task into which I could put my whole heart—which is more than I can say of this translation business. Scudder has not replied yet, and the probabilities no doubt are against me. – My reading lately has been largely in Spanish which interests but does not satisfy—except Don Quixote which I am going through now and which leaves nothing to desire. Even La Vida es Sueño[8] was lacking in some last touch of self[-]restraint or conscious thought which went far to lessen its peculiar charm. It seemed as if Calderon had never sounded the depth of his own intuition. Quevedo's Sueños[9] are immensely clever but the Spanish is too hard to make them agreeable reading for me as yet. While in Saint Louis I went through a lot of novels chiefly by Galdos [sic].[10] They are powerful but not agreeable. Perhaps the brutality of Spanish provincial life is the cause of this. "Gloria" is certainly one of the greatest tragedies I ever read in prose—a much greater book I think than Doña Perfecta which is about the most revolting of all I have read of his. But I won't weary you with a lecture on Spanish Literature, but save my accumulated wisdom until we meet. I hope very much I may see something of you somewhere or other during the

---

4. More never published a translation of Sophocles' *Oedipus Tyrannus*.
5. On Horace Scudder, then the editor of the *Atlantic Monthly*, see above.
6. More had published "Two Famous Maxims of Greece" in the March 1898 issue of the *New World*. See Moore 1898. This later appeared under the title "Delphi and Greek Literature" as a chapter of More's second edition of *Shelburne Essays*. See More 1905b: 188-218.
7. More had published "Nemesis, or the Divine Envy" in the December 1899 issue of the *New World*. See More 1899b. It later appeared in the second edition of the *Shelburne Essays*. See More 1905b: 219-53.
8. A play written by Pedro Calderón de la Barca (1600-1681).
9. Francisco de Quevedo (1580-1645) wrote the satirical prose work *Los Sueños*.
10. The Spanish novelist Benito Pérez Galdós (1843-1920).

summer. Jeune hermite, vieux diable—is good. I hope I began my hermit life too late to come under either category.

Sincerely your friend
Paul E. More

P.S. I find on my desk a letter I wrote you some time since but did not send off. No doubt the present letter is a repetition of the old, but I send them both. It will completely cancel my debt in correspondence you see. – Can anything be done now to get my nephew L. Elmer More,[11] into Memorial[12] next year. He expects to enter as a freshman. If it is permitted, will you put his name down on the waiting list?

---

6 Kirkland Road
Cambridge
March 3, 1902[13]

My dear More,

I had already partly finished a letter to you when your letter came; and now I feel that I must make a fresh start and begin with the proper congratulations. You must feel greatly relieved at your wife's having come through safely.[14] Let us hear from you soon again confirming your first good news in regard to her condition and that of the child.

You will probably be bored by the card of introduction I enclose for M. Mabilleau[15]—but then you are under no obligation to use it. He will be in New York until about March 10th. He is a scientific humanitarian or

---

11. On Lucius Elmer More (1880–1961), the son of Paul Elmer More's sister Mary Caroline More (1856–1948), see Dakin 1960: 76. Lucius attended Harvard as an undergraduate.

12. A footnote in the typescript of this letter notes that "Memorial Hall was then the students' dining-hall" (at Harvard).

13. Much time has passed since the previous letter in the collection and this one, and much of significance had happened to Babbitt and More. Both men were now married to their respective wives, having wed on the same day (June 12, 1900). Babbitt had moved with his wife into a three-story house on Kirkland Road, which he would rent for the remainder of his life. After working for Charles Lanman from 1899 to 1900, More moved with his wife to East Orange, New Jersey, and worked as a free-lance critic, until he joined the staff of the *Independent* in New York City as the publication's literary editor.

14. More's wife Henrietta (Beck) More gave birth to a daughter, Mary Darrah More, on February 24, 1902. See Dakin 1960: 93. On Henrietta More and Mary Darrah More, see their entries in the Biographical Register.

15. Leopold Mabilleau (1853–1941), the Director of the Musée Social of Paris, who in 1902 was lecturing at various educational institutions in the US, including Harvard in February of this year. See anon. 1902.

sociologist, that is to say, a man without imagination, just as the sentimental humanitarian is usually a man of perverted imagination. But, aside from this fact, he is one of the most interesting Frenchmen I have met lately—a large, genial man of the world who has had an unusually broad training. He has written a number of interesting books—on Victor Hugo (Hachette's *Grand Écrivains Français* series) on the atomistic philosophy, etc. He can talk English but would probably be more interesting if you allowed him to hold up his end of the conversation in French. You may want to get an article out of him for the Independent.[16] I am also sending a card to Mather and suggested to him that you and he might like to go up to the Reform Club together some afternoon.

I fear that you thought my criticism of your article somewhat Philistinish in tone but I am anxious to see you get a fuller recognition from the public, and in my opinion this article would be a stumbling block even to the average intelligent reader—to the reader I mean who might appreciate the rest of the volume. I am anxious to see the new essays you mention.

I have actually got to work upon my educational article but am making rather slow progress. It is a discouragingly large subject to develop in a few pages of a magazine.[17] The copy of the *Souvenirs*[18] you mention must have been sent by the publishers. I have mailed another copy to Orange.[19] – My wife sends regards and will write to Mrs. More in a day or so.

Sincerely.
I. B.

---

6 Kirkland Road
Cambridge
10 April, 1902

My dear More,

I wish to consult you about a practical point and hope you will allow me to use a pencil so that I can be most expeditious. Perry[20] and I are having some

---

16. The typewritten manuscript contains the note "P. E. M. was literary editor of the *Independent*, N. Y., (1901–1903)."

17. Perhaps Babbitt refers to his article "The Humanities," which appeared in the June 1902 number of the *Atlantic*. See Babbitt 1902.

18. Babbitt's edition of Renan's *Souvenirs d'Enfance et de Jeunesse* appeared in print in 1902. See Renan 1902.

19. East Orange, New Jersey, where More and his family then lived.

20. The writer and literary critic Bliss Perry (1860–1954) was then the editor of the *Atlantic Monthly*. Later a professor at Harvard, Perry was contacted after Babbitt's death by Odell

dispute in regard to the title of my article.²¹ I have suggested three titles none of which he is willing to accept. In order of my preference they are: (1) "The College and the Humane Ideal." (2) "A Plea for Humane Scholarship." (3) "The Need of a New Humanism." Perry wants to call the paper simply "The Humane Ideal." His reason is that he has two other educational articles in the number and does not wish to give his title-page too academic an aspect. Does the title he suggests seem to you too vague and meaningless and would you advise me to take a firm stand in the matter? I am anxious to keep on good terms with Perry, but I do not wish to impair the effectiveness of my article. It is an extremely definite treatment of an extremely definite subject, and I do not see any use in disguising the fact. Does your editorial experience lead you to suppose that with Perry's title the article would have much less chance of being read and appreciated?

I was much interested in your letter that came yesterday. I agree with the details of your criticism of Dante but not with your total impression. The poetry of Dante has flashes of supernatural light and hints of things far beyond the reach of the senses such as hardly exist in other poets. Carlyle has said the right thing for once when he remarks that Dante is not world-wide but world-deep. His dominant note is intensity. He sings the triumphant grappling of the free individual will with sin and evil. This is inspiring even though the terms in which he states the problem have become obsolete.

You do not quote correctly my Renan introduction.²² I do not say that the historic sense has "become universal and descended to the lowest grades of intelligence," but that it has come to appeal to the Philistine, which is a very different thing. The Philistine is often a man of vigorous though perverted intelligence and there have been Philistines of genius (as Arnold says Luther and Cromwell were). It is true that the rank and file of English and Americans have a naïve dream of perfectibility through science or some such agency. Yet millions of copies of historical novels have been sold in England and America during the past few years and this fact also has its significance. It means that many men have come to possess, if only in rudimentary form, that imaginative sense of historical differences which was the possession of a comparative few at the beginning of the century. This sense does not, as you seem to think, result from taking the past seriously as an authority. On the

---

Shepard as a possible contributor to the edited collection *Irving Babbitt: Man and Teacher* (Manchester and Shepard 1941). In his personal copy of the book, Shepard noted Perry's negative reply to this request: "I detested the man and loathed his opinions" (189).

21. Presumably the article to which Babbitt is referring ultimately earned the title "The Humanities." See Babbitt 1902.

22. See Renan 1902: xii for the passage discussed here.

contrary—as Santayana has very neatly shown in his book[23]—the historical sense only became possible when men had ceased to take the past as an authority, when they no longer looked upon themselves and it as common partakers in an absolute ideal; when, in short, they had arrived at the degree of detachment that made it possible for them to see in the past, not a standard, but the mere *relative* product of the circumstances of time and space. The sentimental yearning of men like Chateaubriand and Walter Scott toward the past is not the essential factor, it is only a phase of that dilettantism into which the historical sense so easily degenerates. This dilettante solace is evidently what the average man seeks in the historical sense; it is a cheap way of satisfying his craving for novelty and strangeness—the masquerading instinct in short. Yet even so it has its philosophical import. It indicates that the feeling for relativity and diversity is gaining ground, and the growth of this feeling in the modern world has resulted in an immense decrease in fanaticism and to offset this gain, a great falling off in vital conviction. I sometimes wonder whether it is possible to combine the historical sense with any respect for absolute standards. Renan, for example, has a marvelous instinct for historical atmosphere, but little or no sense for the absolute human element that binds together the men of different periods. Emerson, on the other hand, sees all the personages of the past whether Plato or Confucius—in the same atmosphere or rather lack of atmosphere, and is solely interested in measuring the absolute elevation of their characters with reference to an inwardly perceived ideal. It should perhaps be our ambition to combine the gift of Renan with the gift of Emerson.

The article of Ghent[24] you refer to is a fairly accurate account of present conditions and tendencies. I was very far, however, from being impressed by it. It struck me as the nightmare of a disgruntled humanitarian who finds the public none too ready to swallow his own socialistic nostrum and so despairs of all remedy. It is filled, too, with the true Jacobin virus,—with a more or less covert attempt to stir up hatred and distrust between the different classes. I deprecate this, because so far as I have any vision of the future at all, it is one of frightful social convulsions brought about by the present materialism and childish illusions as to the real facts of human nature. Bella, horrida bella![25] Only I have a special dislike for these lurid speculations as to the future of

---

23. Cf. Santayana 1900: 170–73.

24. Babbitt here refers to "The Next Step: A Benevolent Feudalism," an article by the socialist writer W. J. Ghent (1866–1942), which had then recently appeared in the *Independent*. See Ghent 1902.

25. Babbitt quotes from Vergil's *Aeneid*, 6.86 ("Wars, horrid wars!").

society. Tu ne quaesieris, scire nefas.[26] – I hope that your own point of view will not be too much affected by the special humanitarian atmosphere of the Independent sanctum reinforced by the Carthaginian commercialism of New York. – Send me just a line on receipt of this giving your opinion about title. I am expecting proof at any moment.

Sincerely,
I. B.

---

6 Kirkland Road
Cambridge
28 September, 1905

Dear More,

I reached Boston about three yesterday and am now keeping bachelor's hall. I am already plunged into the details of another year's work. I do not much like the process of getting back into harness.

I telephoned as soon as possible over to the Massachusetts General[27] but found that Mather had gone.[28] I hope that I shall have a chance to see him later.

I was much gratified at Thayer's[29] review of your book in the Graduates' Magazine.[30] He really praises you in the right vein. I am somewhat amused at Thayer's polemical flourishes. His favorite phrase in conversation in speaking of his magazine is "explode a bomb-shell," and he has evidently intended to do this in the case of Hamilton Mabie.[31]

I hope that my occasional cavils in conversation at minor points in your essays do not disguise my own very high opinion of your critical work. The fact that it has such a small sale brings home to one in discouragingly concrete form how little audience there is for real criticism in this country.

---

26. Babbitt quotes the start of the first line of Horace's *Odes* 1.11 ("May you not seek, it is wrong to know").
27. Babbitt refers to the Massachusetts General Hospital in Boston.
28. The typescript version of this letter notes that Mather had typhoid fever. On this topic, see Morgan 1989: 109.
29. On William Roscoe Thayer, the editor of the *Harvard Graduates' Magazine* and one of More's friends, see his entry in the Biographical Register.
30. Thayer (anonymously) reviewed the first series of More's *Shelburne Essays* (More 1904) in the December 1904 issue of his magazine. See Thayer 1904.
31. Hamilton Wright Mabie (1846–1916) was an American writer and editor. In his brief review Thayer (1904: 345) praised More as a critic in part by juxtaposing him with Mabie.

All this would change fast enough if there were college teachers capable of inspiring in their students a taste for intelligent reading. To be fully appreciated many of your essays require the training that only the right kind of collegiate education can give.

Let me know when you receive that volume of Cestre's[32] and I will most likely be willing to review it. I am much interested in the subject.

With kind regards to Mrs. More.

Very sincerely yours,
Irving Babbitt.

---

6 Kirkland Road
Cambridge
6 December, 1905

Dear More,

I am afraid I shall have to beg off from writing the review that you are kind enough to offer me. The writing of the review itself would not probably take much time but I should have to devote at least one afternoon to a careful reading of the book, and I do not wish to have my attention diverted even to this extent from other tasks on which I am engaged. Everything seems to conspire here at best to give one's life a scrappy and piece-meal character and to throw obstacles in the way of sustained effort. I am making progress on my volume of educational essays[33] but not so much as I should like. I have not given much thought to the title yet. What do you think of the title I enclose—with the epigraph from Emerson?[34] It may make up for its lack of lightness by the clearness with which it indicates just what the book is about.

---

32. Babbitt refers to a book by Charles Cestre (1871–1958), a former graduate student in French at Harvard who earned his M.A. there in 1898. Babbitt ultimately reviewed this book (Cestre 1905) in an anonymous piece (previously unknown to be the work of Babbitt) in the *Nation* in 1906. See Babbitt 1906c and below. From 1918 to 1945 Cestre was a professor of American literature and civilization at the Sorbonne. On Cestre's life, see Barnes 1959. For Cestre's reminiscences about Babbitt, see Cestre in Manchester and Shepard 1941: 52-56.

33. Babbitt's first book, *Literature and the American College: Essays in Defense of the Humanities*, which would appear in print in 1908. See Babbitt 1986.

34. The book ultimately commenced with this epigraph from Emerson's "Ode Inscribed to W. H. Channing": "There are two laws discrete/ Not reconciled,—/ Law for man, and law for thing;/ The last builds town and fleet,/ But it runs wild,/ And doth the man unking" (Babbitt 1986: v).

Perry sent me back my essay on criticism with the statement that he already had an essay on the "Mission of the Literary Critic"[35] and was well loaded up with papers on related topics. He professes to want to print something by me and urges me to send him an essay on some other subject. I am beginning to look with suspicion on the whole race of review editors—as such. The profession seems about as conducive to slimy diplomacy as that of college president. My essay certainly lacks what Hazlitt would call "gusto" (a distinctly romantic quality that my work will perhaps never possess). It also lacks the smartness and journalistic over-emphasis that takes the place of true gusto in so much contemporary writing. On the other hand it contains in its highly condensed form, an amount of careful thought that neither you nor Perry perhaps has given me full credit for.

I am looking forward with much interest to that visit of yours. Mather's prolonged absence must be an extra burden for you but I hope that in spite of this you will soon be able to fix a date for your coming.[36] Your activity (of mind) during the past few months has certainly earned you a breathing spell. My first thought, by the way, on reading Mark Twain's speech on his seventieth birthday was how heartily you would echo his sentiment that "exercise is loathsome."[37]

The comparison between Harvard and Yale in the last number of the *Graduates' Magazine* has stirred up a fearful pother here.[38] Thayer has certainly succeeded in "exploding a bomb-shell" (to quote his favorite phrase); only some day he may find himself directly over one of his own bombs. He is supposed to be the author of the present article and may lose his editorship. How thin-skinned the Americans are as compared with the English in matters of this kind! If you have kept track of the matter and are of my way of thinking, I should be glad if you could get a word in Thayer's favor into the *Post*.

My wife joins me in kind regards to you and Mrs. More.

Sincerely yours,
Irving Babbitt.

---

35. See Bradford 1904.
36. In late October 1903 More left the *Independent* to accept a job as the literary editor of the New York *Evening Post* (see Dakin 1960: 94; cf. Shafer 1935c: 109; Mather 1938: 369; Hough 1952: 175; Aaron 1963: 1; Duggan 1966: 15). Mather, who from 1901 to 1906 served as an editorial writer for the *Evening Post* and an assistant editor of the *Nation*, was More's coworker. See Morgan 1989: 109. In 1905 Mather, having suffered an attack of typhoid fever, traveled with his wife to Italy, where he attempted to recover. Although Mather continued to write pieces for the *Post* and the *Nation*, his absence meant that he could not assist More with various editorial duties.
37. For the text of this speech, delivered on December 5, 1905, see Twain 1905.
38. See Thayer 1905.

6 Kirkland Road
Cambridge
17 January, 1906

Dear More,

I was genuinely disappointed at your inability to come to Cambridge last week. I had really made up my mind that you were coming and had already sent out invitations for people to meet you. I hope that the immediate cause of your inability to come—Mrs. More's indisposition[39]—is already a thing of the past. I hope that you will find it convenient to work in your trip at some other date—the sooner the better. Entirely apart from the pleasure you may get from a trip to Cambridge, I think it is good business for you to come here from time to time just as it is good business for a Cantabrigian to take an occasional run to New York. Remember that you could if you so desired spend the mornings in working in my upstairs study.

I received some time ago a letter from a Mr. Witter Bynner, speaking in behalf of Phillips, McClure & Co. and at your suggestion, and inquiring whether I am likely to do any publishing in the near future. I am obliged to you for giving me this little boost, though I do not know much about the character of this particular publishing firm. A few days later Bynner turned up in Cambridge, and called here when I was out. He told the maid that he would come again the next morning but has never reappeared. Before coming to Cambridge he must have received a letter from me in which I stated my intention of publishing a volume of educational essays. I am a bit mystified by his whole proceeding. I wonder whether after his first call on me he learned something from one of the many friends (!) I have here among the classical people and the philological moderns that chilled his enthusiasm. If you happen to have any light on the subject let me know, but do not go out of your way to get information.[40]

I have just received an elaborate volume from Cestre on *La Révolution Française et les poètes Anglais* (Hachette).[41] There are over a hundred pages

---

39. More's wife Henrietta, who had experienced difficulties when giving birth to their first child, Mary Darrah More, on February 24, 1902 (see Dakin 1960: 93), was to experience a challenging year health-wise in 1906. In early April of that year, she had an appendectomy (Dakin 1960: 99). According to Dakin (1960: 99) the birth of their second child, Alice More, on June 28, 1906, left Henrietta's health "permanently undermined." On Henrietta and Alice More, see their entries in the Biographical Register.

40. Babbitt would ultimately publish his book of educational essays, *Literature and the American College*, with the Houghton Mifflin Company in 1908.

41. See Cestre 1905. Babbitt would review this book anonymously in the *Nation*. See Babbitt 1906c and below.

on the origins of the English romantic movement which look as though they would be a corrective to the one-sided presentation of Messrs. Phelps and Beers.[42] Would you like me to review this book? I think I can find time—only you must let me know your latest date and your limit as to length. If you wish to take this book in hand yourself I shall cheerfully resign it.

Would you prefer to the quotation from Emerson on the title page of my book ("Things are in the saddle" etc.)[43] the following from Sir Joshua Reynolds: "A provision of endless apparatus, a bustle of infinite inquiry and research may be employed to evade and shuffle off real labor—the real labor of thinking."[44] This sentence seems to me to hit the bullseye pretty squarely so far as education in this country is concerned.

I should like to talk over in detail with you some of your recent writing but am too indolent to commit my views to paper. Try to set another date for your Cambridge trip and let me know as soon as you have done so. You forgot, by the way, to tell me anything about Mather. I am much interested in knowing how he is convalescing.[45] Give my kindest regards to him if he is in New York.

Sincerely yours,
Irving Babbitt.

---

6 Kirkland Road
Cambridge
1 April, 1906

Dear More,

We have had another bad scare in our family since I last wrote. Our cook was also ill with scarlet fever and succeeded in hiding her illness from us for about two weeks, the case being very light and permitting her to attend to her work as usual. Finally when she began to "peel" she was detected and

---

42. The literary historian and poet Henry Augustin Beers (1847–1926) was a professor at Yale University. William Lyon Phelps (1865–1943), a literary critic, was his colleague on the Yale faculty.

43. Unless he was misremembering, Babbitt seems originally to have selected a longer portion of Emerson's "Ode Inscribed to W. H. Channing," since the line here quoted appears in the stanza previous to the one ultimately used as the epigraph for *Literature and the American College*.

44. For the original quote from "The Twelfth Discourse" of the English painter Sir Joshua Reynolds (1723–1792) and context, see Johnson 1891: 283. Although he did not use this quotation as an epigraph, it appeared in the first chapter of *Literature and the American College*; see Babbitt 1986: 72.

45. On Mather's attack of typhoid fever, see above and the entry on Mather in the Biographical Register.

bundled off to the hospital in a jiffy. In the meanwhile both of the children[46] and the rest of us had been exposed to the limit. Curiously enough neither of the children has as yet come down. They are not out of danger as yet but should be inside the next two or three days. Mrs. Babbitt is getting along nicely but has several weeks of quarantine still ahead of her.

Mather's editorial has made some stir here.[47] It was generally assumed at first (by President Eliot as well as by others) that you wrote it, and I was glad to be able to contradict this notion, though I was of course careful not to reveal the real authorship. The editorial is a good one but I wish that I had had a chance to make some suggestions before it appeared. Its serious defect is that it does not seem (as they say of the buying or selling in the stock market) "well-informed." So far from planning to over-emphasize the mediaeval field in his new department, Schofield[48] has got together a tremendous list of comparative courses extending from pre-historic times down to the literature of last year. I heard Grandgent[49] say to Schofield: "Just like the Post. It hastens to kick before the facts are known for fear that when it knows the facts it may have nothing to kick about." The real scandal is that a man has been appointed to a full professorship of *literature* at the chief American university, who has never done anything literary and whose whole training has been philological; and not only this but he has been put at the head of a department of *literature*. And what has happened in the case of Schofield has happened in the case of at least a score of other philologists who now hold nearly all the important professorships of *literature* (ancient and modern) in the great universities of the country. The philologists would assert that no other type of man is available, but this is arguing in a vicious circle since the whole atmosphere of graduate work and the standards insisted on by these

---

46. Babbitt's daughter Esther Babbitt was born on October 2, 1901, and his son Edward Sturges Babbitt was born on June 12, 1903 (see Dora Babbitt in Manchester and Shepard 1941: xii).

47. The article (Mather 1906a), an unsigned editorial in the New York *Evening Post* (which soon after also appeared in the *Nation*), attacked Harvard's decision to appoint a medievalist (William Henry Schofield) as the chair of its comparative literature program. It denigrates much medieval literature as "barely literature at all" (257). On the cross-pollination of articles in the New York *Evening Post* and the *Nation* around this time, see the Introduction. On Schofield, see below.

48. William Henry Schofield (1870–1920) was a faculty member at Harvard who, having served since 1897 as an instructor of English, had then recently been appointed a professor and the chair of the comparative literature program. Thus Schofield, who had joined the Harvard faculty after Babbitt, earned promotion to the rank of professor prior to Babbitt. Nevin (1984: 23) notes that Babbitt's *Literature and the American College* was in part an attack on the scholarly ideals of philologists such as Schofield.

49. Charles Hall Grandgent (1862–1939) was a professor of Italian at Harvard and a devotee of German-style scientific philology.

very philologists are such as to eliminate almost automatically the opposite type of scholar. A curious fact that must also have struck you is that these philologists, almost without exception, have, according to the testimony of their admirers, a wonderful literary sense: indeed if our philological friends were taken at their own valuation of one another they would have to be set down as a lot of Sainte-Beuves. This of course comes in part from their failure to make any real distinction between historical philology (the following out of literary relationships, derivations and influences) and literature, which means, not mere dilettante appreciativeness, but the application of real standards of taste and judgment.

I believe in short that Mather's position is essentially sound but that he owes it to himself and the Post to make this position somewhat clearer; perhaps he can do this in another editorial or possibly you yourself may be willing to take a hand in the *mêlée*. The vein in my opinion is a rich one and ought to be worked further. I believe that the philological clique in spite of its apparent omnipotence is in an essentially vulnerable position because under present conditions victory belongs in the long run to those who have ideas and power of expression, and the philologues have neither. So far as their ability to reach the general public is concerned, they are an inarticulate lot.

Schofield is now posing as a much wronged individual and is receiving condolences from his friends, with a secret tickling of his vanity of course. After all Mather has not actually accused him of an intention of making his new department purely mediaeval and so owes him no apologies. If either you or Mather take up the subject again, I should advise you to eliminate, so far as possible, both Schofield and Harvard and enter into a more general discussion of the philological position.

I believe the time is ripe for an attack not only on what the philologists stand for but on what men like President Eliot stand for if anything is to remain of the American college and all that it has traditionally represented. I am making a systematic attack of this kind in the book that I am now writing and that I must have ready for the printer early next autumn.[50] I hope that I can count upon the coöperation of you and Mather in the campaign that I am planning. It will be with me a warfare of principles and I will abstain so far as possible from personalities and ill-nature. With the book of Educational Essays once out of the way, I am going to turn to the preparation of my book on French criticism and perhaps prepare the book

---

50. Babbitt refers to his first book, *Literature and the American College*, which was to appear in 1908. See Babbitt 1986.

I have promised Houghton Mifflin on English Criticism at the same time.[51] I may try to get a leave of absence for year after next (1907–08) and in case I succeed I should be able to get both books finished by the end of the leave. I also have a large amount of material for a book on Rousseau with the title *The Influence of Rousseau*, sub-title *A Study in Comparative Literature* and epigraph from Amiel: "Rousseau is an ancestor in all things."[52] It would hardly come in contact at a single point with Texte's work on Rousseau, a book by the way that is somewhat overrated.[53]

The comment that I mentioned in my last letter on your writing would deal partly with your general method and partly with details and would if put on paper require many pages. So I am going to forbear for the present in the hope that we may meet at some time in a not too distant future. This letter is already spinning out to an inordinate length—for me. My general judgment on your work is that it is excellent and that it is gradually winning you the recognition you deserve. I should suppose that this recognition must already be taking concrete form in an increased demand for your writings—at least for the Shelburne Essays.

I hope that everything is still well with Mrs. More. Give my kind regards to her, also to Mather. If there are no bad developments in the next few days, I shall soon be once more in a position to welcome either you or Mather in case you are able to take a run up to Boston.

Sincerely yours,
Irving Babbitt.

---

6 Kirkland Road
Cambridge
23 April, 1906

Dear More,

Things have been sadly upset here for the past few days because of Esther's[54] having come down with scarlet fever. All the women of the family—cook and nursemaid, my wife and sister—were either down with the disease, or

---

51. Prior to the publication of *The Masters of Modern French Criticism* (Babbitt 1912e), however, Babbitt would publish his second book, *The New Laokoon* (Babbitt 1910a). He never produced a volume devoted entirely to English criticism.

52. Babbitt's famous book on Rousseau, titled *Rousseau and Romanticism* (Babbitt 1991), would appear in 1919.

53. Joseph Texte (1865–1900) was a professor of comparative literature at the University of Lyon. The book to which Babbitt refers is Text 1899.

54. Babbitt's daughter Esther, born in 1901.

suffering from general collapse. I hurried the little boy[55] off to Boston where he spent the night in a hotel with a trained nurse, and whence he was taken to Dorchester. He has not come down as yet but it would be very strange if he escaped. Esther's case thus far has been extremely light. In fact she seems about as well as usual.

I should not care to accept any further reviewing just now. I have not finished that review of Cestre's book yet and am waiting to hear that he has got safely through with his *soutenance*. I am not familiar with the book of Paulsen's[56] you mention, unless it be an abridged translation of his history of higher education in Germany (2 vols.) which I labored through in the original German.[57] Paulsen is an able man but I find a sub-flavor of philistinism in his whole point of view.

Mather's second editorial on the philologues seems to me to come nearer the mark than his first one.[58] From your point of view and mine the way in which the editorial is made to culminate in a glorification of Bliss Perry would seem somewhat of an anti-climax.[59] Perry is an agreeable personality, a man of considerable sanity and good sense, a prime favorite with women's clubs, but from the point of view of real power not to be mentioned in the same breath with Kittredge.[60] I do not think my objection would strike the average reader, but I should say on the contrary that the editorial hits off very happily the kind of dissatisfaction now gaining ground in this country against the syndicate. It was thoroughly canvassed among the graduate students of English here at Harvard, and one of them informed me that they were inclined to look upon me as the author of it!

I hope that everything is well with Mrs. More. I am at present staying at the Harvard Union and do not expect to emerge from the present confusion even under the most favorable circumstances much before June 1st.

Sincerely yours,
Irving Babbitt.

Give my kindest regards to Mather.

---

55. Babbitt's son Edward, born in 1903.
56. Friedrich Paulsen (1846–1908), a German philosopher and educational theorist at the University of Berlin.
57. The work referred to here is likely Paulsen 1906.
58. See Mather 1906b, the *Nation*'s version of the editorial, which must have appeared earlier in the New York *Evening Post*.
59. See Mather 1906b: 297, which praises "Perry's appointment to a chair of literature at Harvard."
60. On George Lyman Kittredge, a professor of English at Harvard, a heralded Shakespeare scholar, and Babbitt's bête noir as the chief member of the "Philological Syndicate," see his entry in the Biographical Register.

6 Kirkland Road
Cambridge
5 August, 1906

Dear More,

I find it a little hard to decide off-hand about writing a paper for your educational number.[61] The offer in itself is an attractive one and I should be glad to accept it if I find that I can draw my material from the book I am preparing. I am just getting to the chapter in which I am going to take up the question of the doctor's degree and should be far enough advanced in a few days to let you have my decision—by the time, say, that you can inform me more precisely as to the amount of space you can allow for the article.[62]

I have done a good deal of scribbling this past month but can't say that I am especially pleased with the result. The weather for one thing has been abominable—a mixture of heat and humidity that has kept me from sleeping and diminished the snap that I need to recover the almost lost art of composition. I have had a good deal of trouble with the preliminary chapter of my book which is largely made up of definitions. I am sorry to have to begin with a rather arid and abstract discussion of first principles, but we are living in such an impressionist muddle nowadays that it is about the only way to avoid misunderstandings. For instance there is no use in employing such a word as humanism without first explaining what meaning one attaches to the term.

I am much interested in what you tell me about your book on India. I shall regard it as a privilege and a pleasure to look over the MS. and make any suggestions that may occur to me.

You have cut up my review rather freely but I am indifferent about changes of this kind as long as the work does not bear my signature. With the exception of the sentence on Bryan and perhaps the one immediately following it, the matter omitted seems to me strictly relevant to the subject—especially to Cestre's treatment of the subject. The list of errata you mention does not appear in my copy of the book.[63]

---

61. On July 1, 1906, More became the literary editor of the *Nation*, while retaining his position as the literary editor at the New York *Evening Post* (Dakin 1960: 98; Hanford 1961: 163).

62. In September of this year Babbitt would publish an article (Babbitt 1906b) in the *Nation* called "Literature and the Doctor's Degree," which would later serve as part of his book *Literature and the American College* (Babbitt 1986).

63. This paragraph demonstrates that Babbitt was the author of a review of Cestre 1905, which appeared in the *Nation* in September of 1906. The anonymous review (Babbitt 1906c) is not listed in the exhaustive bibliography of Babbitt's works found in Babbitt 1940: 251–59.

Schiller's review of Santayana does not seem to me to throw much new light on the subject.⁶⁴ If Santayana is a pragmatist why does Schiller need several pages in which to refute him and why does Santayana for his part look on Schiller and his whole school with something akin to detestation? Santayana lays himself open in places to the charge of being a pragmatist. I believe however that he has put himself in an untenable position in trying to establish an ideal unity of human nature without at the same time recognizing a positive principle of faith as something quite distinct from the poetic imagination. To make my meaning clear I should have to indulge in some heavy philosophizing, and I feel inclined to reserve this for cooler weather.

I wish you had told me more about Mrs. More and the new arrival in your household.⁶⁵ I hope everything is well. Give my kind regards to Mrs. More and to Mather.

Sincerely yours,
Irving Babbitt.

The Evening Post
January 18, 1907
Editorial Rooms

My Dear Babbitt:

Here is the proof of your paper which we shall probably use next week. Lamont⁶⁶ suggests that you add, if possible, a "modern instance" or two, or enlivening specifications to the first part of the paper to relieve the series of generalizations. The argument is a good one—it may work.⁶⁷ I met Todd⁶⁸ the other night, by the way, at the Century Club, but did not have many words with him. Like most of the Columbia men who have any quality at

---

64. See Schiller 1906.
65. On June 28, 1906, More's wife Henrietta gave birth to a daughter named Alice—a birth that unfortunately took a toll on Henrietta's health (see Dakin 1960: 99).
66. On Hammond Lamont, who succeeded Wendell Phillips Garrison as the editor of the *Nation* in June 1906, see his entry in the Biographical Register.
67. For the paper to which More refers (which was published as a letter to the editor in the *Nation*), see Babbitt 1907b.
68. Henry Alfred Todd (1854–1925) was a professor of romantic philology at Columbia University and in 1906 the president of the Modern Language Association (MLA), whose lecture at a meeting of the MLA Babbitt criticizes in his paper. See Babbitt 1907b.

all he is distinctly of the New York type. I also met Woodruff,[69] who has just gone to be the head of the Carnegie, and who is even more emphatically of this type. They give me a queer feeling of estrangement which it would not be easy to analyse. I presume it is at bottom a suggestion of complacent superficiality—an interest in the outer show of learning rather than the kernel. You will call it impressionism. By the way I have just been reading a book which illustrates forcibly what I have said about the present loss of the boasted historic sense. It is Bradby's "Great Days of Versailles,"[70] a thoroughly entertaining piece of work, well informed, I judge, and not ill written. All seems to be alive, the men and place, and yet withal the essential thing, what made Versailles really great, is scarcely hinted at, for the simple reason that to see this one must get out of the present and exercise the real historic sense. It suggests a good theme for an editorial. – The unexpected resuscitation of your paper in the *Graduates*' must have been annoying.[71] Thayer apparently forgot to order the thing "killed." It is a mishap which happens sooner or later to every magazine. If I forget to kill a paragraph the make-up man is sure to run it in some day when I am absent from the office. I have learnt to be careful. – I was sorry my visit to Cambridge had to be postponed, but at least I still have the pleasure of expectation. I shall be glad to read your Brunetière if you care to send it on.[72] *Putnams'* has an article prepared by H. S. Krans (a superficial youngster) on Brunetière, P. E. M., and Bernard Shaw[73]—God save the mark! 'Tis an odd juxtaposition and doesn't reflect much on the sense of the editors. – Give my kindest regards to Mrs. Babbitt and your sister, and believe me, as always,

Faithfully yours,
Paul E. More

---

69. In his letter More offers the name "Woodruff," but More here meant to refer to Robert Simpson Woodward (1849–1924), a professor of mechanics and mathematical physics at Columbia University who served as the president of the Carnegie Institute for Science from late 1904 to 1920.

70. G. F. Bradby (1863–1947) was an Oxford-trained teacher at the Rugby School. For the book in question, see Bradby 1907.

71. For the piece in question, which appeared in the December 1906 issue of Thayer's *Harvard Graduates' Magazine* and was later greatly modified before appearing as part of *Literature and the American College*, see Babbitt 1906a.

72. The April 1907 issue of the *Atlantic Monthly* would contain Babbitt's essay on Brunetière. See Babbitt 1907a.

73. See Krans 1907, which appeared in the March issue of *Putnam's Monthly*. It is partly a review of the fourth series of More's *Shelburne Essays* (More 1906).

The Evening Post
June 19, 1907
Editorial Rooms

My dear Babbitt,

I see by the Harvard Bulletin that you have been allowed a year's leave of absence, and presume from this that you have finally decided to go abroad to study and write – beatus ille qui procul collegiis![74] I really feel some jealousy of your ability to take fifteen months of self-directed work. Lou, my brother, is just ending his ferial, and reports vast pleasure and some profit.[75] And now you are going off for the same purpose. When will my turn come? Never, I fear. – I dare say you are extremely busy, but I wish you could find time to let me know definitively of your plans. They will interest me. As for me, there is no variety in view, but a plenty of business. My second essay in the series of which the last *Atlantic* paper was the first[76] is now in the hands of Prof. Geo. F. Moore[77] for the new Harvard Theological Review.[78] It is on Augustine, and quite too scholastic for the *Atlantic*. Moore said he would be glad to have the essay and would print it in the first issue of the magazine—but this was before he had read it. The *Hibbert Journal* wants me to contribute and I shall probably send the third essay—on Pascal—to them in September.[79] This, with a paper on Lady Mary Wortley promised to the *Atlantic*[80] and

---

74. More has humorously altered the first line of Horace's *Epode* 2 (*Beatus ille qui procul negotiis*, "Blessed is he who is away from work"). His new line means to say "Blessed is he who is away from colleagues," but More has used the wrong Latin word (*collegium*, "a guild, a colleagueship" vs. *collega*, "a colleague"). On Babbitt's sabbatical from Harvard in 1907, see Dora Babbitt in Manchester and Shepard 1941: xii.

75. On Louis T. More, Paul's younger brother and a physics professor sympathetic to the New Humanism, see his entry in the Biographical Register.

76. The only paper More published in the *Atlantic Monthly* in 1907 is More 1907, a piece on "The Forest Philosophy of India" that ultimately appeared in the sixth series of *Shelburne Essays* (More 1909a: 1-42).

77. George Foot Moore (1851-1931) was a Presbyterian minister and professor at the Harvard Divinity School.

78. The journal published its first issue in 1908.

79. More's essay on Augustine (More 1908a), which found a home in the *Hibbert Journal*, also appeared as a chapter in the sixth series of *Shelburne Essays* (More 1909a: 65-100). The essay on Pascal was part of the sixth series (More 1909a: 101-53) but was unpublished prior to its appearance there.

80. More 1908b, an essay that also appeared in the tenth series of *Shelburne Essays* (More 1967b: 151-85).

the insatiate hunger of the *Evening Post*, will keep me busy for some time. I am sorry I can't get your criticism of the Upanishad paper. – August my family and I spend up state at a place chosen at a venture. It is entirely in the country, where I shall see nobody—and this, unless I could see two or three chosen friends, pleases me best. Lamont is in Europe not to return until some time in July, so that I shall need a rest—or half rest. We are all well, the baby quite blooming, but still small. – With kind regards for Mrs. Babbitt,

Faithfully yours,
Paul E. More

Franconia, N. H.
3 July, 1907

Dear More,

First of all I wish to tell you how sorry I am that you were unable to make your visit to Cambridge. Of course my regret is pointed by the fact that I am going to be away next year. I know how exacting your duties at the Post are and yet suspect in your failure to come a bit of physical inertia which is in striking contrast to the activity of your mind. If I had only known that you were not going to be in Biddeford this summer,[81] I should have suggested some plan that would have brought us within hailing distance of one another and possibly together during your vacation. The cottage I have taken here belongs to Professor Beale of the Harvard Law School.[82] It is on the road between Franconia village and Bethlehem, directly opposite Mount Lafayette and looking up Franconia Notch. I am not especially attracted by the White Mountains but came here because the locality is (theoretically) immune from hay fever from which my wife suffers slightly. My own choice was for Shephard Hill, Holderness (overlooking Squam Lake) or else for Dublin. I know of desirable cottages in both places. I may feel tempted to change even yet and would like to inquire in the most tentative way whether if we went to Squam before Aug. 1st, there would be any chance of your joining us. (I do not know how binding your other contract is.) The Burr cottage that I have in mind on Shepard Hill would have lots of room for both families, also

---

81. Although More and his family occasionally spent time in the summer at Biddeford Pool, Maine (e.g., in 1905; see Dakin 1960: 93), he did not do so in 1907, preferring to go to Lakemont, New York, for a month, beginning on August 17 (Dakin 1960: 104).

82. Joseph Henry Beale (1861–1943) was a distinguished professor at Harvard Law School, from which he had graduated in 1887.

two rooms in a separate building one of which you could use as study. The cost of such an arrangement would be very moderate, certainly less, I should suppose, than that of the outing you are planning "up state."[83]

I am not planning to go abroad until I finish my book on "Literature and the American College" and arrange for its publishing. I am going to give Houghton Mifflin the first chance.[84] I have not yet decided what piece of work to take up when I have got this volume off my hands. I am hesitating between the book on French and the book on English criticism. Neilson[85] is urging me to hurry forward the latter which I have promised to do for his series and one distinct advantage will be that this book will at least be sure of a publisher. It is of course a much smaller subject but it presents itself to my mind in a scrappy way and without the coherency and symmetrical development that I find or imagine I find in the French field. If I had more time and saw more signs of eagerness on the part of Perry, there are a couple of closely related papers I should like to write on the romantic movement: one entitled *Recent books on Rousseau,* and the other *Romantic Solitude.*

I never dare to put my most serious thought into the *Atlantic* and that explains the inadequate discussion of certain topics in my paper on Brunetière that you call my attention to.[86] You evidently were not arrested by any such consideration in your article[87] in the June number and it is a concrete proof of how your reputation as an essayist is growing that you were able to impose anything so serious upon Perry at all. It is one of the most substantial pieces of philosophical writing I have seen for some time with one or two striking pieces of literary criticism thrown in. Of course my own selection from the religious philosophy of India would be somewhat different from yours—a less imaginative and poetical one you would no doubt say; and yet we are very much at one in our underlying point of view, even though it involves calling into question the fundamental postulate of European thought since Descartes. In this paper as in several others that you have published you have expressed certain ideas that I had even before I knew you so that if I ever desire to express my own views I may have to refer back to you under penalty of being thought a plagiarist. In my opinion the distortion of Greek

---

83. On More's plans to vacation in Lakemont, New York, see above.
84. Houghton Mifflin was in fact the original publisher of *Literature and the American College.*
85. William Allan Neilson (1869–1946), the future president of Smith College, then a member of Harvard's English department.
86. For the paper see Babbitt 1907a.
87. More 1907.

philosophy by Germanic intellectualism and emotionalism is of a similar nature and even more serious than the distortion of the philosophy of the Far East.

You have evidently taken up in your article and expressed with greater thoroughness and grasp on the intellectual side some of the opinions and material that you embodied some years ago in the introduction to your Indian Epigrams.[88] I should say however that your present treatment is not equal to that in natural charm of expression which artistically is one of the best things you have ever done. One has a sense of effort in places. Some of the quotations from the Upanishads are rather long and will inevitably seem uncouth to many readers, and perhaps obscure to a certain extent the structure of the article. I am trusting to memory in these comments, not having the June *Atlantic* with me, though I read the article very carefully before leaving Cambridge.

I should be interested to know what recognition if any this essay brings you. In general your very penetrating interpretation of Oriental thought does not seem to me to have attracted as yet the attention it deserves though I believe that it will be more palatable in this form than when mixed in with your general essays. I look forward with great interest to the series of chapters on religious thought of which as I understand it this paper is the first.[89] Religion at present is running more and more into an extraordinarily flimsy humanitarianism and I hope that you do not have the discouraging feeling I have in writing on topics of this kind of being without an audience. Someone has to make a beginning though it is disheartening to stand out almost alone against the main drift of one's time. One of the best signs at present is the remorseless psychological analysis that certain French writers (Lasserre,[90] etc.) are applying to the romantic movement.

I came up here about two weeks ago and thus far have finished my college work and done a large amount of general reading but no writing. I shall probably make a beginning toward the end of this week. Let me have a line about that Squam scheme though I think that there is only a slender chance at best of my being able to carry it out. Give my kind regards to Mrs. More.

Very sincerely yours,
Irving Babbitt.

---

88. See More 1899a: 1-19.

89. Babbitt here refers to More's sixth series of *Shelburne Essays*, subtitled *Studies of Religious Dualism* (More 1909a), of which the article from the *Atlantic* here discussed, "The Forest Philosophy of India," would serve as the first chapter (1-42).

90. Pierre Lasserre (1867-1930), a French writer and critic of romanticism.

P.S. Miss Maud Gorham[91] of Washington, one of my graduate students, who is writing a doctor's thesis on the 18th century novel or some such subject wishes to have access to the books of Mr. Lamont. She wishes to know whether there is any way of arranging a visit to his library while he is still abroad. I will forward to her any information you can give me on this point. I do not doubt that she will be duly grateful for any privileges granted.

The Nation 20–24 Vesey St.
New York, July 8 1907

My dear Babbitt,

I have edited a ton of bad MS., and written about twenty letters already today, so that I must now confine myself to a brief answer to your enquiries. I fear it will be impossible for us to get out of the contract at Lakemont, N. Y. August is the busy month, and our landlady has already refused other offers for our rooms. One reason, too, for our going there was the avoiding of a long journey with a young baby. But surely with the long vacation before you, you will be able to get to N. Y. for a day or two some time before you sail. I should think your next undertaking would be determined by your whereabouts. If you are in Paris you can certainly write your French book with greater ease; if in this country your English criticism. The latter is, comparatively, so slight a work that I should think you would want to get it out of the way first. – Lamont will be back early next week and I will then ask him about Miss Gorham. Neilson has already sent a similar request for some girl, I think this same Miss Gorham. Lamont's house is rented now and I don't see how I could get permission to use his books. I don't know what he does on his return. – As for the other literary matters you touch on, I wish I could make some adequate reply, but for the moment time and strength fail me—which is shabby treatment for your extraordinarily full letter. I must close with kind remembrances to Mrs. Babbitt.

Faithfully,
Paul E. More

---

91. Maud Gorham earned her A.B. (1902) and her A.M. (1906) from Radcliffe College. At the time Babbitt wrote this letter, Gorham was collecting material for a dissertation devoted to English literary criticism.

The Nation, 20–24 Vesey St.
July 10, 1907
(P.O. Box 794)

My dear Babbitt,

Your article "Literature and the Doctor's Degree"[92] was printed Sept. 20, 1906; your letter, "Value of the Doctor's Degree,"[93] January 24, 1907. – I should think a paper on recent Rousseau literature would suit Perry well, unless it is already too late. I have a long article on the subject filed from *the Revue des D. M.*[94] My paper on the Upanishad[95] attracted very little notice, so far as I know, and that little mostly from cranks. I am still fairly un-magazinable. – I wish I were out of this super heated hurly burly with you in the White Mountains, but I have three weeks more of it before any brief release. Then I shall take a box of books with me and tackle Pascal.

Faithfully,
Paul E. More.

Lakemont, N. Y.
September 8, 1907

My dear Babbitt,

Blake[96] called on me at my office and seemed a fellow pretty well able to take care of himself. I am always glad to meet any of these graduates, have a word with them, and pass them on. It is not likely, of course, that any of them can work for me immediately. – But at present I am more interested in your own work, and mighty glad to hear that your book has progressed within view of the conclusion. Essays are notoriously hard to sell, hence to publish, but I should suppose the subject of your volume, if nothing else, would carry it through with H. M. & Co.[97] Certainly I shall be glad to read

---

92. Babbitt 1906b.

93. Babbitt 1907b.

94. The *Revue des Deux Mondes*. More wrote an article on Rousseau for the *Nation* (reprinted in the New York *Evening Post*) (More 1908c), which ultimately appeared in the sixth series of *Shelburne Essays* (More 1909a: 214-41).

95. More 1907.

96. Presumably one of Babbitt's former students. Babbitt regularly recommended that his students meet More.

97. Houghton Mifflin, which was ultimately the publisher of *Literature and the American College*.

the introductory essay whenever you have it finished. I shall be here for eight or ten days more, before returning to New York. I presume from your plans that you expect to go to Paris as the MS. is handed in, and then either get ready for your volume on French criticism or perhaps actually begin the writing of it. Or will you attack Neilson's job first? Lieber Gott, how I envy your fifteen months of liberty! I do hope you will sail from New York and that you will be able to stay with us for at least a day or two. Mother and Alice will not be with us,[98] and we have always abundant spare room for guests. Schofield's announcement has just come, and I presume that the former Mrs. Cheney[99] has money. As they will be abroad this winter you may have the pleasure, and honor, of meeting them. To turn to a worthy but less fortunate subject, Mather is still in Italy and, I fear, is likely to remain there indefinitely. He reports some progress in recovery but his health is not good. Mr. Ogden, who lives in Summit and knows the family well, said to me just the other day that he had the gloomiest forebodings about Mather. There is something wrong in the family inheritance and the knowledge of this probably preys on F. J.'s mind. Meanwhile he has been sending the Nation some really admirable art letters, has sold several magazine articles, and is managing to scrape together a bare living. I do not like to think of his case, and trust yet that all will turn out well. – As for myself, I am loafing, and writing, and honestly exercising. I got away the middle of last month and joined my family here—a lovely place so far as nature is concerned, with a brave outlook over Seneca Lake, but, as I expected, serious drawbacks in the people. However, the house is almost empty now, and at the worst I could keep well to myself. My writing is the essay on Pascal which follows the St. Augustine in sequence and precedes Luther. The St. A. I sent to G. F. Moore for his new *Theological Review*,[100] but he returned it with the very just comment that *Si actum est de theologia*[101] as my thesis attempted to prove, then readers of the

---

98. More's mother, Katharine Hay (Elmer) More, and invalid sister Alice More had departed from their place in Bridgeton, New Jersey, in the summer of 1906 and were living in St. Louis at this time (Dakin 1960: 98 n. 37). Because of their respective physical conditions, they had lived with More and his wife in the past (see, e.g., Dakin 1960: 82). On both Katharine Hay More and Alice More, see their entries in the Biographical Register.

99. On September 4, 1907, William Henry Schofield, Babbitt's colleague in comparative literature at Harvard, married Mary Lyon Cheney (1868–1943), a wealthy philanthropist whose previous husband had been Charles Paine Cheney (1869–1897), a banker. On Schofield, see above, this chapter.

100. On Moore and the *Harvard Theological Review*, see above.

101. "If it was done concerning theology."

magazine would say Non licet vos esse.[102] I do not care much, as the essays really ought to be read together in a volume. The review in the *Spectator*[103] was unreservedly flattering, but my "audience" in England, as in America for that matter, is certainly few, let me hope fit. Your volume on education will probably sell more copies than all my four volumes together up to date. The first volume has just passed the thousand mark, but it is fair to add that the semi-annual sales continue undiminished. – My exercise—I see you smile— is a good walk of six or eight miles over the hills, which may not be Greek but is sufficiently agreeable. – And this ends my budget. Net[104] joins me in sending regards to Mrs. Babbitt.

Faithfully yours,
Paul E. More.

The Nation, 20–24 Vesey St.
(P.O. Box 794) New York
October 16, 1907

My dear Babbitt,

Your introductory chapter[105] is a strong piece of work and I think you need have no fear of it. It ought to make a good many ripples in the puddle. I would offer one or two suggestions. A Chapter of Definitions is something of a misnomer, as there are really very few definitions in it. Certainly I would strike out the few lines where you adopt an apologetic tone. The first paragraph does not quite please me. Can't you *begin* nearer home? At least discard that *Vides meliora*.[106] The strongest part of the essay is the use you make of Bacon and Rousseau; here, where you first introduce these names you might perhaps develop your ideas a little more freely and fully. My recollection is that the weakest link in the argument is where you pass from Renaissance humanism to the origin of modern humanitarianism. Perhaps my memory is at fault; perhaps a sentence or two here would clinch your

---

102. "It is not permitted for you to exist."
103. For the *Spectator*'s review of More's fourth series of *Shelburne Essays* (More 1906), see anon. 1907.
104. More's wife Henrietta.
105. The rough draft of the first chapter of *Literature and the American College*, which was ultimately split into the book's first three chapters. For the published version, see Babbitt 1986: 71-117. On the later division of the chapters, see below, chapter 3.
106. "You see better things." Cf. Ovid, *Metamorphoses*, 7.20-1.

ideas. I have as you see jotted down a few comments on paper and have also made a few marks in light pencil in the margin of your MS. I shall be extremely glad to see the rest of the book. How are you going to fill in the gaps before December first? I pray you be diligent. – I am back at my desk, already begrimed with the dust and sweat of journalism; my constant cry is Quo usque tandem?[107] And this Latin tag makes me think that I have been taking Terence for my morning lecture in transitu.[108] How suave and urbane and world-wise the old boy is! I read the last scenes of the Adelphi on the train this morning. How true Demea's speech is and how immoral—Re ipsa repperi facilitate nil esse homini melius neque clementia,[109] with his conclusions. Give my regards to Mrs. Babbitt. I shall hope to see you this winter.

Yours very truly,
Paul E. More.

P.S. (Oct. 21) Your note has just come. I read the MS. some days ago and wrote this letter. Then distractions came, and I neglected to wrap up the MS. As it happened it went from East Orange[110] today by express.

P. E. M.

THE NATION, 20–24 Vesey St. (P.O. Box 794)
October 31, 1907

My dear Babbitt,

I read through your MS.[111] last night and made a few marginal notes, but did not find much to criticise. The new introduction is, I think, an improvement. I did not wish you to try to conciliate those who will inevitably be offended by your position, but to get the interest and *consent* of those who are naturally your friends—two very different matters. As regards the names queried,[112] I

---

107. More here quotes the first line of Cicero's *First Catilinarian Oration*, which roughly translates as "How long, I ask you...."
108. "In passing."
109. The original typescript note reads: "*Adelphi*, Act V, Sc. 1, l. 860: 'Hard facts have taught me that a man can have no better qualities than mildness and complaisance.'"
110. In the summer of 1900 More and his new bride moved to East Orange, New Jersey (Mather 1938: 369; Hough 1952: 175; Dakin 1960: 78), which he would call home until he moved to an apartment in New York City in March of 1908 (Dakin 1960: 105). On this new apartment at 260 West 99th Street, see below, chapter 3.
111. Of *Literature and the American College*. See Babbitt 1986.
112. For chapter titles.

rather choose "What is Humanism" and "Literature and the Doctor's Degree" and "The Humanities," though here my first and third are too much alike. As regards the order, I am in doubt. "Lit. and the Dr's Degree" is the strongest of the papers after the introductory one and belongs closely with it.[113] On the other hand it might be well to insert your *Atlantic* paper[114] between them as less narrowly argumentative, and so to distribute the interest. The paper on the Dr's Degree is a strong piece of writing as it stands. One thing I note however. You here attack the historic spirit for its relativity, whereas in "The Study of the Classics" you argued for the historic method. As they stand the two papers do not seem so much to complement as to contradict each other. I think you can remedy this when you come to revise once more the earlier paper. – Liddell's equation is poem = x + HI +VF, where x = idea, HI = human interest, and VF = verse form.[115] I have given the number of the Indian Epigrams [sic] on the margin of your MS. I rather think I would omit it as offensive and not really adding to the argument. Certainly you should not bring in my name more than once, if once, in the notes.[116] We shall get the name of mutual puffing, which will aid neither of us. – Net joins me in wishing that you may come to East Orange, and if possible bring Mrs. B. We have plenty of room and should heartily enjoy a visit from you.

Very truly yours,
Paul E. More.

P.S. Your MS. goes by post today under separate cover.

THE NATION, 20–24 Vesey St. (P. O. Box 794)
November 13, 1907

My dear Babbitt,

I am sending your MS. today to your sister[117] at 15 Berkeley Street, with a few pencil annotations. I found little to criticize. This paper of course clears

---

113. It ultimately became the book's fifth chapter. See Babbitt 1986: 134-50.

114. Babbitt 1897b, which ultimately served as the book's sixth chapter. See Babbitt 1986: 151-67.

115. More discussed this equation in his review of Mark H. Liddell's book *An Introduction to the Scientific Study of English Poetry* (1902), which served as a chapter of the first series of *Shelburne Essays* (More 1904: 103-21).

116. If More is still discussing the manuscript of *Literature and the American College*, then Babbitt took his criticism, since Liddell is not mentioned in the final version of the book, and More's name appears in the preface alone (Babbitt 1986: 70).

117. Katharine Babbitt, with whom Babbitt was close. It is unclear why More sent the manuscript to her; perhaps she would produce a typescript of it.

up the historical idea. – I saw Greenslet[118] at the club last night—took dinner there with him in fact—and he seemed to think your book promised a success. He is here rooting up scandal about T. B. Aldrich, whose life he is writing[119].... We shall be delighted to share our philosophic poverty with you whenever you can visit the purlieus of Mammon.

Faithfully,
Paul E. More.

---

118. Ferris Greenslet (1875–1959), an editor at the *Atlantic Monthly* and ultimately the director of Houghton Mifflin.

119. For this biography of Thomas Bailey Aldrich (1836–1907), a longstanding editor of the *Atlantic Monthly*, see Greenslet 1908.

CHAPTER THREE
1908–1911

Old Orchard Road
Chestnut Hill, Mass.
14 January, 1908

Dear More,

    I hope that by this time the illness that you spoke of in your last letter has become an unpleasant memory. Greenslet has told me that you were looking well when he met you and so I was not prepared for any news of this kind. I was sorry to miss your opinion on the essay I sent you and yet I did not regard it as so absolutely essential in this case as in that of two other essays (the long introductory one namely and the one on the doctor's degree). Both of these latter performances struck me as being of a decidedly ticklish nature and as a matter of fact several of your suggestions have been very valuable to me. It might have been just as well to spare you the whole book except these two essays. – The book[1] has been accepted by H. M. & Co and is now being put through the press at a rather rapid rate. I hope to get all the proofs by Jan. 20. The book will probably come out in April. Perry is planning to print in April *Atlantic* the essay On Being Original[2] with a few passages omitted (ridicule of U. of Chicago, etc.) on diplomatic rather than on literary grounds. I was much pleased by the way with Mather's contribution to the Dec. *Atlantic*.[3] It shows more structural sense than I had been inclined to allow him. His underlying thesis—the need of humanizing 19th century scholarship by an application of the principle of selection—is of course in a way the underlying thesis of my book.

    The readers of H. M. & Co. were somewhat dismayed by the heavy philosophizing of my first chapter and I have finally decided to divide it into three separate chapters about uniform in length with the others. Titles to be as follows: (1) What is Humanism? (2) Two Types of Humanitarians: Bacon

---

1. Babbitt's *Literature and the American College* (Babbitt 1986).
2. This article ended up appearing in the March 1908 issue of the *Atlantic*. See Babbitt 1908.
3. See Mather 1907.

and Rousseau. (3) The College and the Democratic Spirit.[4] What do you think of this scheme?

I am not quite decided as yet on the date of my sailing for Europe. I may however take the Adriatic of White-Star Line sailing from New York to Cherbourg 29 Jan. In that case I hope to be able to visit with you at East Orange two or three days before I sail. Would it be convenient for you to put me up about that time? – I have taken a furnished house at Chestnut Hill for my family for the next four or five months. The house is spacious and if you can ever escape from your everlasting editorial routine, you will always be welcome here either before or after my departure for Europe.

I have not had time to look at the *Post* or *Nation* for months past and so do not know what you have been writing of late. I hope to catch up some day. My wife joins me in kind regards to you and Mrs. More.

Sincerely yours,
Irving Babbitt.

Old Orchard Road
Chestnut Hill, Mass.
30 January, 1908

Dear More,

I was forced at the last moment to give up my plan of sailing on the "Adriatic." The printers were slow in getting proof to me and other work piled up. I may wait now until the next eastward trip of the same steamer. This will give me an opportunity to make the preparations in this country for writing my second book. In making a start of this kind there is a distinct advantage in having access to my own books and to the Harvard stack.

You will be interested to learn that we have Mother Eddy[5] as a next-door neighbor, her bed-room commanding our place from the other side of Old Orchard Road. Her house is a somewhat gloomy pile, in appearance something intermediate between an asylum and a jail, a not inappropriate mixture if the reports of her enemies be true. About two hundred men have been busy getting the house ready for several weeks past working all night

---

4. These are in fact the titles of the book's first three chapters. See Babbitt 1986: 71-117.
5. Mary Baker Eddy (1821-1910), the founder of Christian Science. More had criticized Christian Science as "a diluted and stale product of Emersonianism" in an article included in the first series of *Shelburne Essays* (More 1904: 79; cf. 83).

as well as all day and disturbing the slumbers of the neighborhood by their hammerings. She is said to be putting $200,000 into her investment which is concrete evidence that she has made religion "hum" as they would say in Chicago.

Talking about religion, I hope that volume of essays of yours is making progress.[6] There was good stuff in your *Atlantic* paper[7] and I am looking forward with great interest to the other chapters.

I will let you know as soon as I decide on a new date for sailing. My wife joins me in regards for you and Mrs. More.

Sincerely yours,
Irving Babbitt.

East Orange
8 February, 1908

My dear Babbitt,

Printers always are slow when you wish them to be fast, and paradoxical as it may seem, fast when you wish them to be contrary. At least just now Putnams show a prodigious activity and have got ahead of my copy for the fifth volume of essays.[8] However I have but little more work to finish up that task. Meanwhile I am looking forward to your visit whenever H. M. & Co. are so good as to allow it. I was amused at your story of the Eddy household. And I too am about to move. After many delays and much doubting we have taken an apartment (tenement the wise it call [sic]) at 260 West 99th Street in the city. It is on the fourth floor of an old building without elevator, but the rooms are considerably larger than in the more modern houses within our means, and there is plenty of light. We shall move in some time toward the end of the next month.[9] Life in the suburbs has grown an intolerable burden

---

6. Babbitt means the sixth series of *Shelburne Essays: Studies of Religious Dualism* (More 1908d), which would be published in late February or early March of 1909 (Dakin 1950: 107 and 1960: 108). At the time this letter was written, More's fifth series of *Shelburne Essays* (More 1908d) was still to appear, ultimately published in April of 1908 (Dakin 1950: 104 and 1960: 106).

7. More 1907.

8. On the publication of the fifth series of *Shelburne Essays* (More 1908d), see above. As Dakin (1950: 104) specifies, G. P. Putnam's Sons was the original publisher of this volume, which was later reprinted by Houghton Mifflin.

9. For more details on this move, see above, chapter 2.

to me, and to Net also now that Mrs. Richardson[10] is an invalid in town. The children will thrive there as well as here I think, for the neighborhood is good, and the air abundant. – Let me know as far in advance as possible of your coming here so that I may avoid making any engagement for those days. – Rufus Mather[11] has returned from Italy, bringing by no means a satisfactory report of Frank; but of this we can speak when you are here. – With warmest greetings to Mrs. Babbitt.

Faithfully yours,
Paul E. More.

On Board R. M. S. "Adriatic"
Wednesday P.M.
March 4th 1908

Dear More,

We are scheduled to reach Cherbourg tomorrow at about noon after a fairly quiet trip for this time of year. I was very miserable however during the first few days because that sore throat developed into a fairly severe case of tonsilitis and kept me confined to my berth. Your remedy might have helped me if taken in time but my most serious mistake I imagine was to open the windows too wide that last night at your house and let the breeze blow in on me as I slept. – I am much pleased with this boat. She is extremely steady in a heavy sea, though having about the usual amount of jiggle and vibration, and is a model of simplicity and good taste in her furnishings. – The star passenger on this trip is J. Pierpont Morgan,[12] attended by his valet—and a private detective. It looks as if he were hurrying across to get the benefit of the cut rates—and on his own line at that. I have an opportunity to contemplate his portentous proboscis about three times a day at meals. It glows with a mellow lustre across the dining saloon. In this respect Morgan is a sort of mixture of Bardolph and Cyrano. He also has a curiously piercing eye which he occasionally fixes on me as I pass his table but he has not, I fear, awakened to the importance of getting acquainted with me. Schofield would no doubt be hobnobbing with him inside a quarter of an hour. Morgan likes to linger

---

10. Mary D. Richardson, the aunt of More's wife Henrietta, whom Dakin refers to as Mrs. Clifford Richardson throughout his biography of More (see, e.g., Dakin 1960: 411).
11. Rufus Graves Mather (1874–1952) was Frank's younger brother.
12. The American financier J. P. Morgan (1837–1913).

over his meals and so far as I can judge cleans up everything in sight. This is a habit he may have acquired in his financial deals. I fear that the "bears" may jump on the New York market now that he is away.

I have read about half a dozen books on the trip over including "Joseph Andrews."[13] There are delectable scenes but as a whole it is very inferior to "Tom Jones."[14] It occurred to me that such a scene as that between Parson Adams and Parson Trulliber would if done by Dickens have taken up from three to six times the space. Nineteenth century literature suffers from a frightful dilution.

I meant by the way to ask you for Mather's address before leaving New York. Will it be too much trouble for you to send it to my Paris address? Give my kind regards to Mrs. More. I do not envy you the job of moving those books.

Very sincerely yours,
Irving Babbitt.

The Nation 20 Vesey (P.O. Box 794)
New York May 6, 1908

My dear Mrs. Babbitt,[15]

Yes, I had a copy of the *Nation* sent to Mr. Babbitt[16] with regrets that the review[17] was not more satisfactory. I did not feel justified in reviewing the book myself, and sent it out with trepidation, fearing it might be taken the wrong way. Shorey's review is tolerable, but does not bring out the real strength of the book's argument as it should. I received a note from Goodell,[18] of Yale, the other day saying he quite agreed with the book in general—I suspect all the classical men will say this. Their "in general" means that they regard

---

13. The novel by Henry Fielding published in 1742.
14. Fielding's more famous novel of 1749.
15. This is the first letter in the correspondence addressed to Dora (Drew) Babbitt, Irving Babbitt's wife. On Dora Babbitt, see her entry in the Biographical Register.
16. A footnote in the typescript manuscript reads: "I. B. was in Europe."
17. Paul Shorey's anonymous review of *Literature and the American College* (see Shorey 1908b). The book was likely published in April of this year. On Shorey, see his entry in the Biographical Register.
18. On the Yale classical philologist Thomas Dwight Goodell (1854–1920), see Ward W. Briggs' entry in the *Database of Classical Scholars*: dbcs.rugters.edu. It should be noted that Goodell's dissertation is called "The Genitive Case in Sophokles," which is not a topic of a scholar likely to esteem Babbitt's arguments in *Literature and the American College*.

themselves naturally as an exception to the sinners. Forman,[19] one of Mr. Babbitt's old pupils, and now connected with the *North American*, is reviewing the book for that magazine;[20] I had an opportunity of bringing out one or two of the stronger points of the argument which he had overlooked. – While I am writing let me thank Miss Babbitt[21] for the two ties she sent me; I wore the brightest the other day down to Bryn Mawr where I went to lecture, and felt in consequence like a young beau—all the girls were looking at me—or it.[22] Jesting aside, the ties are handsome. – Our home address is 260 West 99th. All are well at the present moment. The baby who has been miserable (teething) for a number of weeks, has been picking up again most encouragingly. Darrah is robustious. Net and the children are to go away next month to Essex on Lake Champlain where we have taken a small cottage. I join them in August.[23]

Sincerely yours,
Paul E. More

Grand Hotel Corneille
5, Rue Corneille
Paris
17 May, 1908

Dear More,

I received your letter in acknowledgment of my book safely and should have answered it long ago. A few days ago the fifth volume of the Shelburne Essays came.[24] Most of them I had already seen but I have been going over them all again very carefully and I scarcely need add with a great deal of pleasure. I have been especially struck by the range of thought and style in this volume, the two extremes in this respect being I think, the essays on

---

19. Henry James Forman (1879–1966) was a journalist, editor, and creative writing professor who served as an associate editor of the *North American Review* from 1906 to 1910. He earned his undergraduate degree from Harvard in 1903.

20. This piece appears never to have made it to print, since the *North American Review* did not review *Literature and the American College*.

21. Katharine Babbitt, Irving's sister.

22. Dakin (1960: 106) discusses this lecture at Bryn Mawr on May 1, 1908, at which More spoke about Sir Thomas Browne.

23. On this vacation in Essex—and Babbitt's brief visit there in August—see Dakin 1960: 106-7.

24. More 1908d.

Thoreau[25] and on Donald G. Mitchell.[26] I was interested in this latter essay because it displays qualities of geniality and humor that are not usually so conspicuous in your writing. The book should establish still more securely your position in the world of letters. The world should begin to say more and more about your work what I have been saying about it for the past ten years. To convince the world nowadays it would seem to be necessary not only to have quality but to pile up a large number of volumes. You are satisfying to a surprising extent both conditions. Your chapters on religious thought[27] promise to be very important in themselves as to mark, I trust, the beginning of a happier tendency in contemporary philosophy. As much as you look down on James,[28] you and he both represent in your attitude toward what may be termed in a broad way European intellectualism, the right and the left wings of the same movement. I of course agree with all you say in the chapter on Rousseau that has just appeared.[29] How could I fail to do so, since I have been developing the same ideas in my course at Harvard for years and have indeed worked out rather fully some of the more important of them (false dualism in society, substitution of sympathy for restraint, etc.) in my book. Indeed I am so steeped in this point of view that I doubt whether I can form much notion of how this essay of yours will affect the general reader. I should say at a guess that it will prove a tough morsel for most readers, but will make a profound impression on a few.

It produced a strange impression upon me to read in the same issue of the *Nation* a review[30] of my book which did not contain the slightest hint that I had treated Rousseau's educational influence on lines similar to yours. I am naturally upset to find that my one chance of getting a serious review of my book has thus failed me. I did not wish to be puffed but I did wish to see my central point of view fairly stated and its significance in contemporary thought defined. From a purely tactical point of view, as an incident in the

25. More 1908d: 106-31.
26. More 1908d: 158-69. Donald Grant Mitchell (1822-1908), who often wrote under the penname Ik Marvel, was an American novelist and essayist.
27. Which would be collected in the then-forthcoming sixth series of *Shelburne Essays*, subtitled *Studies of Religious Dualism* (More 1909a).
28. The American pragmatist philosopher and psychologist William James (1842-1910), then an emeritus professor at Harvard. More would criticize James in an essay called "The Pragmatism of William James," which was featured in the seventh series of *Shelburne Essays* (More 1910a: 195-212).
29. The article, originally published in the April 30, 1908, issue of the *Nation*, was called "Rousseau and Education" (More 1908c); it eventually appeared as a chapter in the sixth series of *Shelburne Essays*, under the title "Rousseau" (More 1909a: 214-41).
30. Shorey 1908b.

warfare we are both carrying on against certain tendencies in contemporary life and education a review of this kind is a serious error. I view the matter not simply as a writer but as a man of action. I was I confess much startled when I learned that you had sent the book to a professor of the classics at the University of Chicago (!), and a man of German training at that.[31] The ways of the able editor, even when he happens to be my friend, have always been inscrutable to me. I should have favored somebody who was at once a man of ideas and a man of the world. Brownell[32] would have filled the bill if he could have been induced to do the job. I should judge from his essay on Lowell[33] that he has sized up very accurately the trouble with our American literary teaching. Shorey's review starts out auspiciously enough with a very fair summary of my first chapter and then suddenly ends *en queue de poisson*, in a feeble defense of the classical people that will do them no good and that leaves him no space to set forth my main argument. It is the kind of tepid stuff that will help a book on its way to oblivion. The philological syndicate is only a figment of my excited fancy, forsooth![34] One would suppose that Shorey had never heard of the combination which has boosted the author[35] of a treatise on the Spanish sibilant into the Smith professorship as the successor of James Russell Lowell (to take only one example in a hundred). It is all the kind of thing that Grandgent or Schofield might have written, except that after admitting that I had given the classical people about what they deserve, they would have tried to show that I had been unfair to the modern philologues. The review is a small thing in itself, but it comes at a very critical moment both for me personally and for the ideas I have been trying to defend for years, and so has produced in me a mood of lassitude and

---

31. Shorey, the author of the review, was a scholar of Plato and Greek philosophy who had earned a Ph.D. at Munich (see Kopff 1990: 447-48). He was to some degree critical of scientific philology and the German influence on the American academy (see Adler 2016: 63), and this is likely why More chose him as a reviewer. On Shorey, see his entry in the Biographical Register.

32. W. C. Brownell, an eminent critic sympathetic in many respects to the New Humanism. On Brownell, see his entry in the Biographical Register.

33. This essay on James Russell Lowell eventually became a chapter of Brownell's collection *American Prose Masters* (Brownell 1909: 271-335).

34. Shorey (1908b: 403) had written, "The type of pedant and Dryasdust that provokes Mr. Babbitt's satire—unread in the literature which he professes to teach, incapable of general ideas—is only too common. But the 'philological syndicate' that reserves promotion for men of this stamp is surely an exaggeration; and the young philologist who said of one of his colleagues: 'He is almost a dilettante—he reads Dante and Shakespeare'—was evidently jesting."

35. Jeremiah D. M. Ford (1873-1958), who was then the prestigious Smith Professor at Harvard, a post previously occupied by Lowell. Nevin (1984: 23) notes that Babbitt and Ford were "never on cordial terms." On Ford, see Place 1960.

discouragement that will no doubt soon wear off. I have I think at least my share of *mépris des choses fortuites*. Giese, who has just reached Paris from Italy where he has been spending the winter, tells me that he is expressing his dissatisfaction with the review in a letter to the editor of the *Nation*[36] and desires me to say to you that you can make omissions or alter his letter in any way you see fit in case it should seem suited to you for publication. Giese thinks the review will not only not help me, but will do me positive harm—it suggests that I am a clever person but rather unbalanced. Giese is planning in the near future to write a book on Victor Hugo[37] with a view to knocking out the underpinning so far as possible from his reputation. The book is likely to be amusing whatever else it may be. Giese is a wit though no one I confess would ever suspect it to look at him or to listen to his ordinary conversation.

Since my arrival in Paris I have been occupying a room *au cinquième* in this old and rather literary hotel in the heart of the Latin Quarter, the very hotel I lived in as a student at Paris the year before I met you at Harvard.[38] These upper rooms have not changed since the time the Hotel Corneille was celebrated by Balzac and Thackeray, About[39] and Du Maurier,[40] but unwonted luxuries and comforts have crept in on the lower floors. My first impression of French life on this as on previous trips was one of great suavity and finish (*la douce* France as the mediaeval epics put it). It is a curious experience to pass suddenly from a place like New York to a place like Paris with its noble and beautiful perspectives on every hand and its intense and genuine intellectual life. In all purely intellectual ways I always find this contact with Paris and with France immensely stimulating. My opportunities are unusually good because a number of the friends of my student days are now professors at the Sorbonne and the Collège de France,[41] and through them I see a great many of the so-called *intellectuels*. This whole group strikes me as extremely confident, not to say cocky at the present. The reactionary elements ever since the later stages of the Dreyfus affair[42] have been in a state of demoral-

---

36. Evidently, this letter was never published. On this topic, see below.
37. This book did not in fact appear in print until 1926. See Giese 1926.
38. In the 1891-92 academic year, Babbitt had studied Sanskrit, Pali, and Indian philosophy at the Sorbonne under Sylvain Lévi. In fall 1892, he and More began graduate study at Harvard.
39. The French novelist and journalist Edmond François Valentin About (1828–1885).
40. Presumably, Babbitt here refers to the writer and cartoonist George du Maurier (1834–1896).
41. For reminiscences of an anonymous classmate of Babbitt at the Sorbonne, see Manchester and Shepard 1941: 30-33. Lévi, Babbitt's teacher there, also contributed a short remembrance of Babbitt (Manchester and Shepard 1941: 34-35).
42. Both Babbitt (e.g., Babbitt 1912e: 300) and More (e.g., More 1903d: 562, 564) were

ization. The Revolution has passed from the acute to the chronic state and nearly everybody I meet has something of the toploftiness that one finds in people whose ideas encounter no effective opposition. Everybody is proud of *les expériences sociales* that France is making for the benefit of the world. These *expériences* so far as I can see may be reduced to one—the attempt of a great nation to dispense utterly with everything that has been traditionally recognized as religion, and to offer social sympathy as a substitute. I need scarcely add that in spite of my warm admiration for innumerable details of French life, I find that in the ultimate things of life there is a great gulf set between Frenchmen and myself—even wider than between the average American and myself. For I believe that there are still in the American consciousness some stirrings of genuine religious vitality. In France today a man is practically forced to be either a Rousseauist or a Jesuit and a refusal to accept either horn of this dilemma is taken not as a proof of superior insight but as a lack of logical thoroughness. Of course there may be other elements of French life that escape my notice and these collective judgments are always extremely risky. There are persons who see the artistic and literary problem clearly enough—the need of a reaction against the naturalistic and romantic movements and of a return to a broadened and enriched classical tradition. I heard an admirable lecture to this purport given at the Odéon by the dramatist, M. Gabriel Trarieux,[43] as an introduction to a performance of Goethe's *Iphigénie*. Lemaître's lectures on Racine—one of which I heard and found rather impressive—also tend in the same direction.[44] You will find these lectures as gathered together in book form worth reading—very much superior in any case to the Rousseau. Lemaître discovers a singular intensity of emotion under the somewhat placid surface of Racine's alexandrines and preaches a return to classic art with a sort of impressionistic trepidation. Personally I do not believe that the artistic and literary problem can be divorced from the religious problem.[45] An extreme humanitarianism is hardly compatible with humanistic standards of taste. My friend Hauvette[46] who is

---

critical of the anti-Dreyfusards.

43. The French writer, poet, and playwright Gabriel Trarieux (1870–1940).

44. Babbitt would ultimately discuss the literary critic Jules Lemaître's views on Racine at length in Babbitt 1940: 91-104, a chapter that originated as a review in the *Nation*; see Babbitt 1909a.

45. Cf. Babbitt 1924: 1: "When studied with any degree of thoroughness, the economic problem will be found to run into the political problem, the political problem in turn into the philosophical problem, and the philosophical problem itself to be almost indissolubly bound up at last with the religious problem."

46. Henri Hauvette (1865–1935).

one of the most brilliant of the younger French scholars and has been giving a course on Dante this year at the Sorbonne to an average attendance of about 300 people, admires Zola and despises Virgil!

I have been doing a great deal of dining out, theatre-going, etc. A part of my time I have been busy at the Bibliothèque Nationale and Bibliothèque Ste. Geneviève reading a vast amount of rather dismal stuff of the 16th and 17th centuries in preparation for my books on English and French criticism. I am planning to be in Paris until about July 1st and then go to England. Give my kind regards to Mrs. More.

Very sincerely yours,
Irving Babbitt.

The Nation, 20 Vesey (P. O. Box 794),
New York, May 27, 1908.[47]

My dear Babbitt,

I think you have the right to feel somewhat chagrined over the review of your book; I have myself felt so. I pitched on Shorey after considerable reflection because I know that he is himself at loggerheads with the philological syndicate. Some time ago I corresponded with him in regard to his monograph on Plato (an excellent piece of work),[48] and he then set himself apart rather bitterly from the German type of scholar. As a writer he is one of the best reviewers on our list. His review as it came to us was about double the length of what we printed. In editing Mr. L[amont] made great slices in the first part where Shorey dwelt at length and favorably on your contrast of the Rousseauists & the Baconians. I pointed out to him that this was an essential idea—but dis aliter visum.[49] The latter part of the review on the Ph[ilological] S[yndicate] he touched sparingly. I again pointed out that the review as it stood ran contrary to what the Nation has said many times editorially. He admitted this and turned the copy over to me to change this part. I edited it so as to make it far less objectionable than it was. Shorey accepted the editing without complaint. The simple fact is that L[amont], while saying nothing to me openly, is disposed to be suspicious of your

---

47. This handwritten letter was filed apart from the Babbitt-More correspondence in the Irving Babbitt Papers. It can be found in the folder marked "Family Correspondence, 1865, 1884–1937," in Box 1 of the papers.
48. Shorey 1903.
49. "It seemed otherwise to the gods."

writing. Whether this is because he thinks I may be apt [?] through friendship to grind axes or whether the English department of Harvard has inoculated him,[50] I don't know. Forman is writing a review of the book for the North American [Review], and I have tried politely as I could to direct his views; I do not know what the result will be. I have engaged TS [?] with a signed article on the book for the educational number (August 1) of the Independent.[51] It will be a matter of diplomacy to see how I can use that magazine for the good cause. Holt[52] & the rest over there you know are rank humanitarians, but Holt is pretty fair in allowing both sides of a question to be discussed when the articles are signed. I did not try the Atlantic, for I know Perry would turn down my proposal. The Atlantic, as you have no doubt learned, has been bought by Ellery Sedgwick, who after a year will edit it himself.[53] He is a small man for the place. I had hoped when I planned my Rousseau paper[54] & promised it for our educational number, that it would go in as a reinforcement of the review of your book. It is curious that L[amont] accepted with enthusiasm from me the ideas which he cut ruthlessly from the review. This was, I presume, partly because as they stood in the review they were not developed sufficiently to be quite clear & forcible, and still more because he has a constant distrust of discussing ideas of any sort in reviews. As a matter of fact I wrote on Rousseau with reluctance, but I could not escape him in any development of the idea of religious dualism. I shall when I print the book[55] next winter call attention, in a note, to your proposed work in this field. The essay has attracted considerable attention and, rather to my surprise, has been favorably received. This leads me to hope that your projected book on Rousseau, in which you will be able to treat the subject at greater length & from greater knowledge, will hit home. By the way, Spingarn[56] has just published two volumes of his English

50. Lamont had served as an instructor in Harvard's English department. On Lamont, see his entry in the Biographical Register.

51. More's nod to Babbitt's book ultimately appeared in the August 6, 1908, number of the *Independent*. See More 1908e.

52. Hamilton Holt (1872–1951), the editor and publisher of the *Independent* from 1897 to 1921, and thus More's former boss.

53. Ellery Sedgwick (1872–1960) bought the *Atlantic Monthly* in 1908 and remained its editor until 1938.

54. More 1908c.

55. More 1909a.

56. On Joel Elias Spingarn, see his entry in the Biographical Register.

Critical Essays of the 17th Century.[57] His Introduction has good material in it, and makes me feel that your treatment of English criticism may offer you a richer field that I had supposed possible. – A letter from Mather (he is now at Villa Sorgente, Capri) tells me that his health is better, but that he doubts being able to return next autumn. He praises your book as a work in the good old vein of Matthew Arnold. – Giese's letter has come and is, I am sorry to say, perfectly impossible.[58] It is practically nothing but a review of the book running counter to ours. There is nothing that can be taken out of it and printed as a Letter to the Editor. He did not send his address, and I should be obliged to you if you would inform him of the case in softened speech. – It is pleasant to hear of your good times in Paris. How I should love to be with you! But I see nothing before me but galley work at the desk and little [?] efforts to accomplish some impossible task. Fortunately, so far, my writing does not seem to have suffered, but I do not know how soon the dulling, deadening influence will make itself felt. Your good words about my fifth volume are very encouraging. – There is little else to say. In August I should join my family at Essex on Lake Champlain. I expect now to do little or no writing that month. The Plato,[59] which is to end my volume on religious dualism, is already in the stocks and will, I trust, be out of the way before then, as well as the final revision of the whole MS. I look forward to publishing in January or February.[60] – Books, books, books, they grow to be all my world. If you can venture [?] before August 1st or after September 1st, you must stop over with us for a night at least. There will be abundant room in my new tenement home (260 West 99th, fourth floor). And so, for the present, good bye.

P. E. More.

P.S. I need not add that the secrets of the office in regard to the treatment of the review be [?] for your ear alone.

P. E. M.

Grand Hotel Corneille

57. Spingarn 1908a and b.
58. On this letter, see above.
59. More 1909a: 321-55.
60. The book ultimately appeared in print in late February or early March of 1909 (Dakin 1950: 107 and 1960: 108).

5, Rue Corneille
Paris
Le 11 June, 1908

Dear More,

I was planning to keep entirely out of the controversy stirred up by Sherman's letter.[61] But Adams' communication[62] with the editorial commentary seems to me to muddle up so completely the whole question that I have been unable to refrain from perpetrating the brief letter to the editor I enclose. I assume from the Shorey incident that Lamont will have most of the deciding as to whether my letter is to be used or not.[63] Sherman wrote in a vein of romantic enthusiasm rather than of humane restraint and by his apparent suggestion that the graduate school should be used to foster original genius he has made himself vulnerable to attack. Sherman however is on a vastly higher level both in snap of expression and in grip of the ideas involved than your other correspondents.

I was very glad to get your letter of May 27th. The handling of Shorey's review by Lamont raises a doubt in my mind as to Lamont's instinct for fair play. With some account of my second chapter the review would have been tolerable, but the result of entirely cutting out this part of the review is an injustice both to Shorey and to me. Personally I do not think that Shorey was the man for the job. His paper on that great hegelizer and philologizer of Greek philosophy, Zeller,[64] makes clear that he never got beyond certain underlying assumptions of German scholarship and I doubt furthermore whether he is a man of enough intellectual power ever to break the shackles.

It is a bit of genuine good news to learn that you are planning to say something about my book in the *Independent*.[65] The only drawback is that that publication does not, I imagine, get before a very large number of the people I am trying to reach. In fact the *Nation* is about the only periodical that does, and that is why, from a purely strategical point of view, I regard the fizzle of the review there as a matter of some consequence. Still to publish

---

61. See Sherman 1908, a criticism of graduate education in America. On Stuart P. Sherman, Babbitt's former student and for a time the most promising of the younger Humanists, see his entry in the Biographical Register.

62. See Adams 1908, a riposte to Sherman 1908.

63. Evidently, Lamont chose not to publish Babbitt's letter to the editor, since it did not appear in the *Nation*.

64. Shorey 1908a.

65. See More 1908e.

an anti-humanitarian article in the *Independent* will be an inspiriting foray right into the heart of the enemy's country. – I do not by the way see any special object in referring in your forthcoming volume[66] to my intended book on Rousseau. You will however do me a great favor if you refer in a foot-note to the attack I have made on Rousseauism in the volume I have already published.[67] The reference of course should be very objective and such as it might have been if you had never known me. You speak in your article[68] of certain persons who are beginning to question the underlying postulates of Rousseauism in education. Who are these certain persons besides myself? There has been a curious absence thus far of this kind of attack in either English, German or French. A possible exception is the book of the late Thomas Davidson on Rousseau[69]: but Davidson lacked balance and his views did not gain and possibly did not deserve to gain much attention. – It looks now as though I should land directly at Boston in returning to America. If I change to New York I shall of course let you know. My kind regards to Mrs. More.

Sincerely yours,
Irving Babbitt.

---

6 Kirkland Road
Cambridge
31 December, 1908

Dear More,

Is Mather still in Sicily? I presume that neither he nor any member of his family is in the danger zone[70] but should be glad to feel sure on this point. We seem to be living in a catastrophic age and at the present rate will become hardened to great disasters. – I have of course been back in this country for several months. I spent about six weeks before the college

---

66. More 1909a.
67. More did include such a footnote to Babbitt's *Literature and the American College* in the essay on Rousseau found in the volume. See More 1909: 238 n. 1.
68. More 1908c, an earlier version of the essay in the sixth series of *Shelburne Essays* (More 1909a: 214-41).
69. Davidson 1898.
70. A footnote in the typescript of this letter reads: "Reference is to the Messina earthquake." This devastating earthquake occurred on December 28, 1908. Mather, still residing in Italy with his wife, wrote important pieces on the earthquake for the *Evening Post*. See Morgan 1989: 110.

opening with my family at Squam.⁷¹ I got away from Paris about the middle of July and spent several weeks in England mainly at Oxford and among the Lakes. I did some very strenuous tramping in the Lake country and found the whole experience distinctly worth while. My advanced courses in comparative literature are rather large this year and as usual they are keeping me extremely busy. I am trying to keep the afternoons clear for writing but it is not easy to lecture three hours in the morning and then be in good shape for independent work in the afternoon. You seem however to be able to combine a routine at least as deadening I imagine as college teaching with a high quality of writing. At the present rate you will soon have another volume of Shelburne Essays coming along. How is your book on aspects of religious thought progressing?⁷² I take a special interest in it as you know and shall be much pleased to hear that it is in the press. I hope that its structural qualities will stand out strongly and that it will not be too cluttered up with translations. That article of yours on the Teaching of the Classics⁷³ was excellent but why waste such good stuff on the *Independent*? Your allusion to my book⁷⁴ seemed to me skilful [sic] and likely to fix the reader's attention and awaken his curiosity. I wish you might work this paper up into a Shelburne Essay leaving out the allusion to the book if you think best or else relegating it to a foot-note.⁷⁵ I have been reading through Frye's⁷⁶ book⁷⁷ these last few days. In a number of the Essays he seems to be tagging on after you. The review⁷⁸ you published in the *Nation* struck me as sniffy and likely to do the book more harm than good. After all it is serious, even austere, in its intellectual quality and there is not much critical work of that kind being done in America. There are several of us who stand for somewhat similar ideas in education and literature at the present time but I fear that we are not showing much practical shrewdness in our team play.

The death of Norton⁷⁹ and the retirement of Eliot⁸⁰ would seem to mark the end of an era here at Harvard. The moment is critical and the Harvard

---

71. Squam Lake, New Hampshire, where Babbitt occasionally summered (see Dakin 1960: 162).
72. More 1909a.
73. More 1908e.
74. More 1908e: 327.
75. More chose not to do this: there is no Shelburne essay based on More 1908e.
76. On Prosser Hall Frye, a literary critic and professor at the University of Nebraska associated with the New Humanism, see his entry in the Biographical Register.
77. A footnote in the typescript of this letter informs us that Babbitt refers to Frye 1908.
78. Anon. 1908c.
79. Charles Eliot Norton, who passed away on October 21, 1908.
80. Charles W. Eliot, the longstanding president of Harvard, announced on October 26, 1908, that he would resign from the presidency, to take effect no later than May 19, 1909. See James 1930 2: 168-69.

Corporation has been and still is very much at sea. Lawrence Lowell is the best man, I should say, who has been suggested thus far but then he is over fifty![81] I wish the *Nation* might say some snappy things on this age of superstition as well as on the whole problem of the kind of man who is needed for the Harvard presidency. Unless it sees its way more clearly in some of these fundamental matters, the editorial page may lose its old reputation of ill-nature and come instead to be looked upon as insignificant. To take a small example, the editorial[82] in reply to Sherman's first letter of last May exhibited a rare degree of intellectual muddle in regard to certain crucial questions.

What chance is there of your getting up to Cambridge this winter? It would be a real piece of good news to hear that you can come. On purely practical and business grounds you should show yourself here from time to time. I had thought of running down to see you during the holidays but I have a good deal on hand and it is really your turn to visit me. I hope that you will be able to send me a line letting me know that everything is well with you and your family and also giving me the latest tidings you have of Mather. My wife joins me in New Year greetings to you and Mrs. More.

Sincerely yours,
Irving Babbitt.

The Evening Post
New York
Editorial Rooms
January 2, 1909

My dear Babbitt, – I was just about to write to you—truth!—when your letter prevented me in the old pleasant sense of that word. – Mather, and I think his family, have been at Capri since last winter, although his last letter said he was going up to Rome to look for new quarters there. He has escaped the earth quake no doubt, but otherwise the report of him is by no means good. All summer and autumn apparently he has been subject to his old headaches and sleeplessness. Since colder weather has set in, he seems to be in better condition, but one begins to fear that the family nemesis has laid hold of him never to be shaken off. I trust I am a false prophet here.

---

81. On January 13, 1909, the Harvard Corporation elected the legal scholar and political scientist A. Lawrence Lowell as Harvard's next president; he began his presidency in May of that year (Morison 1942: 439-40). Babbitt would soon sour on Lowell. On Lowell, see his entry in the Biographical Register.

82. Anon. 1908a.

No thought is more often in my mind than the waste of energy undergone from the scattering of our forces. I do believe that if you and I and Will Brown[83] and Frye and one or two more I know could get together *locally*, we might give the world a perceptible jar. But now separation and ill health and discouragement beat us down. Brown is again at Asheville recuperating—he too is I fear fallen from the ranks. What you say of Frye's book is just. The most encouraging thing about him is the astonishing growth in knowledge and ideas he has undergone in the last five or six years. I think considerable reading in Greek has anchored his mind. What you say about the review[84] of his book is unfortunately true. I seem to have exceptionally bad luck when my friends' books are reviewed. Perhaps in my anxiety to send them to the best place, I lose my head and they suffer from my confusion. – As for my own work, the volume of religious essays is all in type and will be out in three or four weeks.[85] It is pretentious, and I dread to see it go. Next week I go out to Cincinnati to deliver five lectures in their course of comparative literature just established.[86] Frye is an applicant for the chair and I hope to get in a good word for him with the president. By the way if you feel disposed to drop a line to him (not mentioning my name, of course) about Frye and his ability, judging from his book, to sit in that chair, it would no doubt help him. I know that the Columbia gang are after Dabney.[87] – I am interested to hear that you squeeze out a part of the day for your own writing. What have you on the stocks—Rousseau? – Well, here I am at the beginning of a new sheet, and my time and ideas are both at an end. – I had it firmly fixed in my mind that I should get to Cambridge this winter, but my week and a half in Cincinnati will cut me out of that, unless perhaps I may be able to get off for

---

83. A footnote in the typescript of this letter reads: "William Garrott Brown taught a few years at Harvard and was the author of *Andrew Jackson* (1900), *The Lower South in American History* (1902), *The Foe of Compromise and Other Essays* (1903), etc." Brown (1868–1913) was an essayist and historian. On his life and work, see Stephenson 1946, which notes (316) that Brown was a lecturer at Harvard in the 1901-02 academic year.

84. Anon. 1908c.

85. On the publication of More's sixth series of *Shelburne Essays* (More 1909a) in late February or early March of 1909, see Dakin 1950: 107 and 1960: 108.

86. Dakin (1960: 107) specifies that these lectures were delivered between January 6 and 19, 1909. On the lectures, see also Shafer 1935c: 206.

87. Charles William Dabney (1855–1945) served as the president of the University of Cincinnati from 1904 to 1920. More means that faculty members at Columbia University were contacting Dabney on behalf of their preferred candidate(s) for the position.

a day or two in the spring. – Meanwhile the greetings of the season to you and Mrs. Babbitt from your faithful friend

Paul E. More

The Nation
20 Vesey Street
New York, April 8, 1909

My dear Babbitt, --

    I have been hoping that I might be able to visit you this year, but the months pass and I am still bound to the "wooden prison." The fact is my trip to Cincinnati, undertaken solely for money to publish my new volume of essays, pretty well cuts me off from other travelling until summer vacation comes. We have taken the same little cottage at Essex[88] for the season. I shall send my family off some time in June, and join them for the month of July—at least such are the present plans. – Having got the last book off my hands, I feel tolerably easy; I shall scarcely try to print another until a year from this autumn, if then. Some time when you have leisure you must let me have any criticism that occurs to you in regard to this sixth volume, as I may wish to revise it for a second edition. One or two misprints I have noted, but so far none in the Greek or Latin or French. Putnams are poor printers and the whole burden of the reading falls on me. So far I have heard very little of the book, but that little has been favorable.[89] – Mather writes that his pocket has been picked for $140., making his desired trip to this country uncertain. His health too seems not so good; but on the whole I rather think he will be back in New York next winter. – Aren't you having your holidays now; and if so why can't you visit us for a few days? Nothing would give me so much pleasure, and Net would welcome you heartily. Next year, I swear by the Gods, will see me in Cambridge. Meanwhile, with kindest regards to Mrs. Babbitt, I am,

Faithfully yours,
Paul E. More

---

88. Essex, New York, a regular summering spot for More and his family.
89. On the (underwhelming) critical response to the book, see Dakin 1960: 108.

P.S. I judge from H. M. Co.'s[90] advertisements that your book has taken pretty well in the matter of sales. I know that it has deeply impressed some readers.

Cambridge
19 April, 1909

Dear More,

I wish you would give me a few days more to decide the question of reviewing Harper's book.[91] I have other work on hand during this spring recess but if I can get it out of the way, I shall be willing to undertake the job. I will in any case supply you with some notes and observations about the book that should make it easy for you to put together a review yourself. I hesitate to leave you entirely in the lurch in the matter because specialists in Sainte-Beuve are rare in America—in fact I do not happen to know of any one who has real competency. I can not promise you any very favorable review of the book. It has its strong points, but as a whole it seems to me to fall short of the mark.

I was hoping to make you a short visit in New York this spring but the present prospect is that I shall have to give up the whole scheme. I am much disappointed at your not being able to come to Cambridge. I believe that for purely worldly and practical reasons—not to put the matter on higher grounds—it would pay you to appear more frequently here. I am sorry that we cannot come together sometime in the summer. I am not quite decided where to go this coming summer. I shall probably fix upon some place in the White Mountains where my wife will escape hay fever.

One reason why I should like to see you now is that it would give me a chance to talk over with you in detail various points that have occurred to me in reading your last volume of Shelburne Essays.[92] Thank you very much for the copy you sent me which I have gone over with a good deal of care. The appearance of this volume seems to me a noteworthy event in contemporary thought but your whole point of view is so remote from the main currents of

---

90. Houghton, Mifflin and Company, the original publisher of Babbitt 1986.
91. A note in the typescript copy of the letter reads: "George McLean Harper's *Sainte-Beuve*." Babbitt ultimately would have this review (Babbitt 1909b) published in the June 24, 1909, issue of the *Nation*. For Babbitt's response to a critique of this review after its publication, see Appendix A.
92. More 1909a.

modern life that I wonder how much actual welcome the volume is likely to receive. Probably a book of one tenth its ability and at the same time more in accord with existing tendencies would be acclaimed. I shall be intensely interested to know whether you feel that you are getting a public for the kind of thinking you have put into this book and if so how large a public. I am not at all sure that you have done wisely in publishing these essays in the Shelburne series. For various reasons that I shall explain to you when we meet I should have preferred to see them come out with a separate title.

I am inclined to ask whether if only on grounds of expediency you have not in establishing your dualism insisted unduly on the sheer oppositeness of religion and ordinary life, on what you yourself call (p. 114) "the terrible cleft between the realm of nature and a power not of nature"; whether you have not made of religion something too mystically unreal, too infinitely remote from the "scene of our sorrow," something that does not come into close enough contact with the concrete and the human. Your very language seems to me in places to have fallen short of the necessary degree of vividness and perspicuity The essentially humane act after all is that of mediating between the lower and higher natures—the many and the one. To be sure you yourself have insisted on precisely this point in your essay on Plato[93] and in a way the whole book leads up to just this conclusion, but the impression that it makes as a whole is not in my opinion in entire accord with the conclusion. For example the last page of your Pascal[94] seems to me to tend too much toward entire approval. You do not insist as much as you should on a certain element of violence and excess in Pascal, of inhumanity in short. The repugnance that Pascal inspired in Goethe with his *cilice* and like austerities should not be forgotten, for most modern men are like Goethe in this respect. They are not going to be convinced so lightly that all the process of reconciliation between the flesh and the spirit that has been going on since the Renaissance has been for nothing. In other words I believe that "pure religion" is in Pascal more seriously overlaid with mediaeval theology and asceticism than you seem willing to admit.

The paper on Sir Thomas Browne[95] strikes me as unusually good—as attractive as anything in the book from a purely literary point of view. Passages of rare and unusual quality abound in all the essays, and my only query is whether you might not have won more readers if you had adopted in

93. More 1909a: 321-55.
94. More 1909a: 153.
95. More 1909a: 154-86.

places a somewhat more humane and somewhat less mystical method of presentation. There are also two or three places notably in the St. Augustine[96] which threaten to become too aridly erudite. Let me know when you come to print a second edition of either the fifth or sixth series of Shelburne Essays. There are a few misprints and other small points to which I wish to call your attention. – I have read with much interest a number of your recent papers in the *Nation* especially the one on Tennyson.[97] You have here repeated one of the main distinctions of your volume on religious dualism in a form that might I suppose bring it home to any one who has the religious sense at all. In reprinting this article I should omit the pun quoted at the beginning.[98] It does not seem to me good enough in itself to justify the intrusion in so serious a piece of work.

I wish that I might hear better reports of Mather. Send him my hearty regards if you are writing to him. My wife joins me in kind regards to you and Mrs. More.

Sincerely yours,
Irving Babbitt.

The Nation
20 Vesey Street
New York
May 7, 1909

My dear Babbitt, --

Yesterday Mr. Lamont died from the effect of a terrible operation;[99] we are all pretty well broken up over the thing both for his loss as an editor and as a man. I had come myself to grow very fond of him as I knew him better. Our staff of editorial writers on the *Evening Post* must be recruited with two or three new men immediately,[100] and I am wondering whether you can recommend any of your former or present pupils. S. P. Sherman

---

96. More 1909a: 65-100.
97. More 1909b.
98. In the later version of the piece found in the seventh series of More's *Shelburne Essays*, More did not remove the pun, but placed it later in the essay (cf. More 1909b: 82 and 1910a: 73).
99. On the death of Hammond Lamont, the editor of the *Nation*, see Dakin 1960: 109.
100. On the relationship between the *Nation* and the New York *Evening Post* at this time, see the Introduction.

we tried hard to get but could not entice him away from college, where he has just been made full professor.[101] I presume you would not yourself think of joining us—indeed I could scarcely advise you to do so, unless your way in the college world has suddenly grown very blank.[102]

--I may say, by the way, that if you care to make Harper's book the occasion for a signed essay on Ste.-B. (something not over 4500 words), I should be delighted to print it. You might in this way get into form material for your book.[103]

Yours
Paul E. More

Dublin, N. H.
27 July, 1909

Dear More,

When I wrote you last I was just on the point of leaving Cambridge for the summer. I was delayed by a job somewhat out of my usual line. My sister[104] had been translating for the National Finance Commission a volume by a French political economist on banking and I had to revise it for her with a special view to straightening out the technical terms, etc. I would not have allowed her to accept this work if I had realized how much it was going to put upon me. My college work has been very burdensome this past year and I have not made as much progress with my writing as I should have liked. Nothing has been more irksome than the reading and correcting of theses (some of them incipient doctor's theses) for my advanced students. There have been about fifty of them ranging in length from 60,000 to 4000

---

101. Although Stuart P. Sherman had previously served as a temporary member of the editorial board of the *Nation* and the *Evening Post* (Zeitlin and Woodbridge 1929: 174), when in the spring of 1909 More tried to entice Sherman to accept a permanent position on the *Post*'s staff, Sherman declined, since the University of Illinois, where Sherman was a member of the English faculty, increased his salary and made him an associate professor (Zeitlin and Woodbridge: 178-79).

102. More would be appointed Lamont's successor as editor-in-chief of the *Nation* four days after he wrote this letter to Babbitt, on May 11, 1909 (Dakin 1960: 109 n. 2).

103. Babbitt took More up on this offer, as one can see from inspecting Babbitt 1909b. That essay in turn served as the basis for a considerably augmented chapter of *The Masters of Modern French Criticism* (Babbitt 1912e: 97-188).

104. Katharine Babbitt. See her entry in the Biographical Register.

words. I am engaged at present on what is more or less a piece of hack work compared with what I should be doing. Several years ago in an incautious moment I contracted to get out an edition of Racine's *Phèdre*. I have felt that this job could not be deferred any longer and am getting it out of the way now. I hope to have the whole thing in the hands of the publishers early in August.[105] When the *Phèdre* is done I am planning to get to work on something that really interests me. I went through the field of Renaissance criticism pretty carefully in the Paris libraries last year, and the material I got then joined to the material I had already gathered, will I think furnish me out with a volume on the modern aspects of the problem that Lessing has treated in the Laokoön. I am in short going to make a contrast between the pseudo-classic and the romantic *mélange des genres*. I am not yet decided on my title. Would it be presumptuous to call my volume: *The New Laokoön*, (with sub-title) *An Essay on the Confusion of the Arts*, provided I explain in my preface that my title expresses what I think needs doing rather than what I myself would claim to have done?[106] This volume will develop the attack on the romantic and naturalistic movements I have already begun in my book on the American college and will itself need to be completed by a third volume to be entitled: *Rousseau and Romanticism*,[107] though before getting at this third volume I shall probably have to do my book on English literary criticism.

The paper you suggest on Lasserre's book would be very interesting in itself and entirely appropriate for the *Nation*. I doubt however whether it would be wise for me to be drawn aside even to this extent from my other undertakings.[108] Last winter I read before the modern language conference at Harvard a paper on "Poe and the French Decadents" which seemed to give the audience a good deal of amusement. I should be willing to turn this address into an article for the *Nation* (3500–4000 words) if I found I could do so without too much trouble. My paper ends in an attack on ultra-romanticism with mention of Lasserre and other French writers who seem to indicate the beginning of a reaction against 19th century literature. I would not need to repeat much of Page's[109] material (in his paper for the

---

105. Babbitt's edition of Racine's *Phèdre* would ultimately appear in 1910. See Babbitt 1910c.
106. This was in fact the title Babbitt chose for the book. See Babbitt 1910a.
107. Babbitt 1991.
108. But Babbitt did write a combined review of books by Lasserre and Jules Lemaître, which was published in the November 18, 1909, issue of the *Nation*. See Babbitt 1909a.
109. A footnote in the typescript of this letter identifies the person referred to here as the professor and critic Curtis Hidden Page (1870–1946), the author of Page 1909, which appeared in the January 14, 1909, issue of the *Nation*.

Nation) but simply refer back to it. Page gives some of the facts of Poe's influence in France (most of them to be found in Lanorière's[110] thesis on Poe) with a fair degree of correctness but fails almost entirely as it seems to me to interpret his facts. Let me know what you think about this Poe article as soon as convenient, remembering that I am very busy with other things and quite resigned in advance to your not wanting it.

I only wish I could see you this summer and talk over the whole situation with you. Is there any chance of your visiting us here? We have lots of room—enough for you and your whole family if necessary. I have secured for a rather nominal rental the house of the W. B. Cabots of Chestnut Hill. If you came you could have a large upstairs room for your study. I have been thinking a great deal of late of the many difficult problems that must confront you in the editing of the *Nation*—especially the chief problem of all: how is it going to be possible in this country under present conditions to run a paper with a serious intellectual purpose and at the same time make it commercially profitable. I hope you are conscious of an audience outside of the specialists, women, and dilettantes who are about the only people I can discover in this country who read anything besides the daily newspapers and cheap magazines. I have recently heard two or three dilettantes express opinions about the *Nation* that I imagine are typical. To be sure, one of them, Hancock,[111] was more or less disgruntled at something you had been writing about his book on Keats. – I should be above all gratified to learn that you had secured the right kind of lieutenant—a man who knew how to write without being a dilettante. Is Mather out of the running entirely? Have I by the way mentioned to you Van Wyck Brooks[112] as a man who may possibly be of some use to you? He has the cleverness and also something of the lack of "bottom" of men who have been under the influence of the Harvard English Department. You could get an idea of him from a book he published last year in London entitled the "Wine

---

110. The typescript of this letter in the IBP is unsure of this name's spelling; the original letter suggests that the typescript accurately reproduces the name. But I could find no work on Poe by such an author.

111. Albert Elmer Hancock (1870–1915), the literary critic, novelist, and professor of English. For his book on Keats, see Hancock 1908. A brief—and faultfinding—discussion of this book can be found in the "Notes" section of October 22, 1908, issue of the *Nation* (anon. 1908b: 386), not previously attributed to More. It is not clear from the context here, however, whether Babbitt is suggesting that More personally wrote this review or whether he attributes it to the *Nation*'s staff more generally.

112. On Brooks, one of Babbitt's former students at Harvard, see his entry in the Biographical Register.

of the Puritans"¹¹³ and also from articles of his that have appeared in the *North American Review, World's Work*, etc. He is an extremely pleasant fellow personally.¹¹⁴

Will you by the way let me have the reference for a translation of a few lines of the *Hippolytus* that you have inserted in one of your essays on Charles Lamb.¹¹⁵ Is it your own rendering? I am thinking of using it in my introduction to *Phèdre*. – My wife unites most cordially in the invitation to visit us here.

Sincerely
Irving Babbitt.

Please regard as strictly confidential what I have said in this letter about my plans for future writing.

The Nation
20 Vesey Street
New York, January 10, 1910

Dear Babbitt, – It is good to hear your prodigious activities and to know that your next book¹¹⁶ is near the birth. In what heaven of romance or criticism are you taking that *Icarusflug*? But this I shall know in good time. – I am really counting on a visit to Cambridge this year, and think March will be a good season, if it accords well with your and Mrs. Babbitt's plans and work.¹¹⁷ February will be somewhat broken up for me, as I have engaged to deliver a lecture at Yale, St. Louis,¹¹⁸ and the University of Missouri. As the same lecture serves Columbia in May¹¹⁹ I am making a fair sum of money out of it, and am preparing to deliver myself on "The Function of Criticism" in the

---

113. See Brooks 1973.
114. More did not hire Brooks as his assistant.
115. Presumably, Babbitt refers to the English translation of a passage from Euripides' *Hippolytus* found in More's essay "Charles Lamb Again" in the fourth series of *Shelburne Essays* (More 1906: 170).
116. Babbitt 1910a.
117. Dakin (1960: 111) notes that More visited the Babbitts in Cambridge from March 17–20, 1910.
118. On More's lectures on criticism at the Women's Club of St. Louis in early February and the (Yale) University Club in New Haven on February 12, 1910, see Dakin 1950: 113; 1960: 111.
119. More would deliver this address on May 3, 1910 (Dakin 1950: 113; Dakin 1960: 111).

next volume of Essays.[120] Alas, the lecture is not yet written! – I saw Schofield Saturday night at the Century Club[121] (where he appeared appropriately under the wing of Kunz, Tiffany's diamond and pearl expert) and had a talk with him on *his* department of comparative literature,[122] which he rather seems to think is revolutionizing the education of America. He spoke of the new degree to be given, L. H. D. [Doctor of Humane Letters], and of a series of volumes, the Harvard Comparative Literature, which he is to edit and finance (out of his wife's millions). He wants me to contribute a volume and offer it for the degree. I shouldn't object to doing it for prudential reasons, but do not see my way clear. Mather was also at the club with me until about 2 a.m., and appears to be holding his own in health. He is living on space rates and is entertaining a good deal in the way of reviews and editorials. He grows in some ways more genial with the years, but he is an obstinate little chap. I wish you could come to New York so we might have a foregathering. I can put you up pretty comfortably at any time. – Give the best greetings of the season to Madame, and believe me

Faithfully yours,
Paul E. More.

P.S. I presume that what Schofield said is no news to you, but he told it to me under some pretensions of confidence.

THE NATION
20 Vesey Street (P.O. Box 794)
New York, March 29, 1910.

My dear Babbitt,

I am returning the proof under another cover. The few corrections indicated were, as you understand, marked down hastily, and in some cases I might have judged differently if I had stopped longer to think. The chapter has good stuff in it. – Alice's scarlet fever shows no alarming symptoms, and Darrah has evidently escaped altogether.[123] Perhaps it would be just as

---

120. When including this essay in the seventh series of his *Shelburne Essays*, More ultimately decided to call it "Criticism." See More 1910a: 213-44; Dakin 1950: 113-14.
121. More was a member of the Century Association in New York City, which he occasionally visited. See, e.g., Dakin 1960: 107, 126, 143, 163, 188, 204.
122. On the New Humanists' animus to the work of Schofield, a scientific philologist and chair of comparative literature at Harvard, see above.
123. More is discussing the health of his daughters, Mary Darrah More and Alice More.

well if you sent the proof[124] now to the office instead of home, as I do not like to send things by post from our quarantine. – Excuse this haste.

Yours,
P.E. M.

P.S. Wm. James has an article in this week's *Nation* in which he makes an outrageous misuse of the word classic.[125] I wonder if you would care to write an editorial for me on the point. A good deal of the necessary material you can take from your book[126] with little change. Of course such an editorial would need to be couched in the most courteous, not to say deferential, language, since we have published his paper. I should have to have copy by the first delivery Monday. Drop me a line to let me know whether to expect anything.[127]

P. E. M.

Editorials run about 1000 words.

Century Club, New York
May 11, 1910

My dear Babbitt,

I am sorry you could not come down last week, as Saturday was our monthly club night and you might have met a number of the men here. However any other Saturday will do almost as well, and I still hope you will be able to leave your classes for a day or two. I went out to the Mathers' last Wednesday night and had a pleasant time with him and his wife. He has, I may have told you, accepted an offer at Princeton which will leave him a good deal of time for outside work. It looks like an ideal place, except for the smallness of the salary. He showed me his collection of Japanese swordguards, and I who generally do not care much for bric-a-brac, found them really fascinating. The instinct for beauty and fineness of craftsmanship showed by the makers and users of those bits of wrought iron is a thing

---

124. Of Babbitt 1910a. On More's agreement to proofread Babbitt's *The New Laokoön*, see Dakin 1960: 111.
125. James 1910: 313-14.
126. Babbitt 1910a.
127. The April 14, 1910, issue of the *Nation* ran an anonymous response to James' article (anon. 1910), but since it does not address James' definition of "classic," it presumably was not the work of Babbitt.

which has gone out of the world, seemingly forever. – Give my kindest regards to Mrs. Babbitt, and believe me,

Faithfully yours,
Paul E. More.

---

6 Kirkland Road
Cambridge
9 October, 1910

Dear More,

I have been looking for the galley proof of the latter part of your seventh volume[128] but it looks as though you were putting it through without the loss of time involved in sending it to Cambridge. I was of course planning to return any proof you sent me very promptly. I note with interest the concluding essay of the volume[129] in this week's *Nation*.[130] It is of course a good solid piece of philosophy that may be beyond the scope of many of your readers; but judged as a piece of philosophy it is in my opinion one of the best things you have done. It is more practically effective in its conclusion than some of your philosophical writing and may conceivably help to shake some of the more intellectual youth of the country out of their torpor.

I was laid up with a bad cold for a week after my return from Essex[131] and was then caught in the rush of the college opening. My advanced courses are very large this year—almost overwhelmingly so in fact. There are over eighty students in them at Harvard and Radcliffe (about half of this number graduates). I wonder how long Harvard will continue its present policy of giving me first rate responsibility with second rate recognition.[132]

If you fix a date in the *Nation* for the Pascal I will promise to let you have the "copy" in time. The paper is well advanced though not actually completed. I have not been able to do anything with it since the college opening. I have dawdled over this article unusually long, largely because of the

---

128. More 1910a. Dakin (1950: 122) reports that this book was published "about Nov. 12," 1910.
129. "Victorian Literature (The Philosophy of Change)" (More 1910a: 245-69).
130. More 1910b.
131. Dakin (1960: 111-12) specifies that Babbitt and Mather both visited More when he was summering in Essex, New York, during the second half of July and most of August.
132. On Babbitt's irritation with his failure to win advancement to the rank of full professor at Harvard, see the Introduction and below.

extreme difficulty of getting my ideas on this subject within the limits of a *Nation* essay. Would it be convenient for you to publish the paper early in November?[133] I presume you saw Thayer's article on my book in the last number of the Harvard Graduates' Magazine.[134] Thayer has an amusing truculence when he takes up his pen. I never realized what a fierce book I had written until I read his account of it.

I should like to know whether you get any response to that last article of yours. I hope that in proclaiming such important principles you may not turn out to be a general without any troops. That is the way I have felt about a good deal of my own writing.

Sincerely,
Irving Babbitt.

My wife joins me in kindest regards to Mrs. More.

The Nation
20 Vesey Street
New York
October 13, 1910

My dear Babbitt, –Thank you for the check and thank you also for your kind words in regard to my paper on "The Philosophy of Change."[135] As I rather feared the article, so far as any echo of it has come to me, has fallen perfectly dead. Perhaps when I reprint it in the *Evening Post* next week I may hear about it from my friends here. I have not been sending you the proof of the last part of my book because I wished to avoid every delay. My pains have proved rather useless, as the loss of a month, while part of my MS. was in the home of one of our errand boys, seems to have given the printers of Putnams an excuse for endless puttings-off. The world does not grow impatient with me. I ought to be able to use your Pascal early in November and should like to have "copy" as soon as you can get it ready. – My cold was a nasty attack of the grippe which kept me home for the best part of a week, and actually in bed for a couple of days. It left no ill effect,

---

133. This piece ultimately appeared in the November 17, 1910, issue of the *Nation*. See Babbitt 1910b.
134. Thayer 1910.
135. More 1910b.

however. I am at my desk again. The morning hour I am giving to a complete revision and rearrangement of my aphorisms.[136] I am really beginning to hope something may be made of them. Darrah and Alice caught their colds from me, but neither of them suffered much. Poor Darrah's worst affliction is from the dentist. – We are looking forward to your promised visit to New York in the Christmas holidays. My own visit to Cambridge, if made at all, must be postponed until after the first of the year. – With kind regards to Mrs. and Miss Babbitt,

Faithfully yours,
Paul E. More.

The Nation
20 Vesey Street
New York
November 12, 1910

My dear Babbitt, –

I have ordered a copy of the Seventh Series, just ready for publication, to be sent to you, and hope you will find the essays reinforced as they appear in book form.[137] I met Ferris Greenslet[138] the other night, and he told me the *New Laokoön* had received the most striking recommendation in the press, but had not sold well. Perhaps the small sale in this temporal limbo, is to be expected as much as it is to be deplored. – It is pleasant to hear that Mrs. Babbitt is so soon to visit Mrs. Richardson.[139] There is of course a hearty welcome for you at our home, if you care to come down at the same time, but I understood you were planning rather to put off your visit until the Christmas holidays. I hope you have at last thrown off your annoying cold. Nothing yet has been said to me about the situation at Columbia. From Miss Babbitt I understood there was some chance of an opening in the Un. of Illinois.[140] That place is not an intellectual paradise, but it is alive,

---

136. More here refers to his essay "Definitions of Dualism," which would make up a chapter in the eighth series of his *Shelburne Essays* (More 1967a: 247-302).
137. On the publication of More's seventh series of *Shelburne Essays* around this date, see above.
138. On Greenslet, by then the director of the Houghton Mifflin Company, see above, chapter 2.
139. On Henrietta More's aunt Mrs. Richardson, see the Introduction.
140. Babbitt, irked by his failure to win advancement at Harvard, was by this time looking around for other opportunities, either to accept one of them or to use them to help earn greater

and it might afford you an opportunity of returning to the East triumphantly. However I dare say you will hate to leave Cambridge for a mission *in partibus*. – I have been asked to give six lectures in February at the Un. of Wisconsin,[141] but it is very doubtful whether I can find time to write up so much copy. I am calculating the days. – With kind regards to the household, believe me,

Faithfully yours,
Paul E. More

P.S. I have not thanked you for the thoughtful essay on Pascal[142] which I shall probably use in the next issue.

The Nation
20 Vesey Street
New York
November 16, 1910

My dear Babbitt, – The enclosed[143] will explain itself. The point is this. I feel that it would be unwise to have your name brought up unless you are ready actually to accept a good offer—unless such an offer brought about immediate and full recognition at Harvard. I should not however tell Sherman of your decision or that I had communicated with you. This is another reason for urging haste. I must reply to him at once. My own feeling has come at last to be—I express it with great diffidence—that your future will be better served by accepting a good offer from such a place as the Un. of Ill. (unless again, of course, such an offer precipitates matters at Cambridge). I think action should be taken immediately and definitely. Please write me your decision at once, or if possible *telegraph it*. I need not say that I will write to Sherman if you decide to accept an offer, and that I will get Mather

---

standing in Cambridge. On the offer of employment to Babbitt from the University of Illinois in 1911 and its role in earning Babbitt a promotion to full professor at Harvard in 1912, see the Introduction.

141. More ultimately delivered five lectures on romanticism at the University of Wisconsin between March 16 to 23, 1911 (Dakin 1960: 114).

142. Babbitt 1910b.

143. More enclosed a recent letter to him from Stuart P. Sherman, Babbitt's former student and then a faculty member in the English department at the University of Illinois. Sherman, whom More had cultivated as a writer for the *Nation*, was instrumental in getting his university to offer Babbitt a position in 1911.

and one or two others to write. Sherman's P.S. is tempting[144] but I scarcely feel it possible to give up my place until things grow worse than they yet are. – Send me back Sherman's letter, which you will of course treat as strictly confidential.[145]

Yours,
P. E. M.

P.S. If I write, shall I lay the emphasis on English, French or Comp. Lit.?[146]

University Club
Madison, Wis.
March 16, 1911[147]

My dear Babbitt, – I have just written a long letter—rather, a second letter as the first was destroyed—to Lowell[148] and I trust I have not made matters worse by meddling.[149] I wrote pretty squarely, although I tried to be discreet. You must have been going through troubled waters, and I wish I were there to talk things over with you, and give you a chance to get rid of some bile in bad language. There must be some degenerating influence that has a hold of a man as soon as [he] is made a college president—or perhaps he is made president because he is already degenerate. – My first lecture has passed off well enough, though lecturing is certainly very distasteful to me. On Friday and Saturday of next week I lecture in Milwaukee,[150] and through the week

---

144. Sherman must have offered the possibility of a position at Illinois to More as well.

145. A footnote in the typescript version of this letter reads: "Irving Babbitt was offered a professorship at the University of Illinois, which he declined."

146. By this time Babbitt had presumably given up his former desire to become the member of a classics department. His publications and (by then) long history of teaching French and comparative literature must have made such an appointment unlikely.

147. On this date More delivered the first of five lectures at the University of Wisconsin (Dakin 1960: 114).

148. A. Lawrence Lowell, the president of Harvard.

149. Three days prior to this, on March 13, 1911, Lowell wrote to Babbitt to inform him that the members of the Harvard Corporation "were of the opinion that it would be unwise at the present time to pledge themselves to your promotion to a full professorship at the close of your present term as assistant professor. That coincides with the view that I have formed after very careful reflection" (IBP, Box 6, "Harvard Correspondence, 1886-1936").

150. Dakin (1960: 114) specifies that More would speak on Cardinal Newman and Walter Pater on March 24 and 25, 1911.

after that at Urbana.[151] – I write in haste but with a full heart. With kind regards to D.D.B.[152] I am

Faithfully yours,
Paul E. More

Dublin, N. H.
26 September, 1911

Dear More,

I wish I could talk over these aphorisms[153] with you instead of writing about them! I shall certainly be too indolent to put on paper more than a small part of the points I should bring up in conversation.[154] You seem to me to have made decided improvements in clarity and forcefulness since I looked over the first outline of the aphorisms last summer. Your thought strikes me as sound and penetrating in itself and at the same time most opportune as a protest against the present philosophical imbroglio. The form in its severe concinnity has its closest analogue, I should suppose, in certain parts of Spinoza, though I have a rather superficial knowledge of that writer.

My own views of life run so clearly parallel to yours—though refracted through a different temperament—that I am not sure my opinion is entirely trustworthy as to the effect of the aphorisms on less sympathetic readers. What is certain is that parts of them will prove hard and close reading even for those who have some philosophical training. I am still more doubtful about the effect on the ordinary reader of the *Shelburne Essays*. Work cast in this form might make a distinctly literary appeal in one of two ways: either by being extremely witty and epigrammatic or else by being lyrical and imaginative. Your gift does not seem to me to run especially to wit and epigram and though the lyric and imaginative vein that you do possess, appears strikingly in a few of the aphorisms, it does not give them their predominant tone. The great art, says Joubert, is l'art de *darder* sa pensée. I am not sure that many of your *pensées* are arresting and compelling in this purely literary sense. What I fear if you print the aphorisms in a volume of

---

151. Dakin (1960: 114) notes that More repeated the five lectures he had delivered at the University of Wisconsin at the University of Illinois from March 27 to 31, 1911.
152. Dora (Drew) Babbitt, Babbitt's wife.
153. Ultimately published as "Definitions of Dualism": More 1967a: 247-302.
154. For Babbitt's specific criticisms of More's draft of his "Definitions of Dualism," see Appendix B.

Shelburne Essays is that they will miss their true public and so pass comparatively unnoticed like the remarkable writing you put into your sixth volume. If you had put forth this sixth volume under some such title as "Studies in Religious Dualism" appending the aphorisms as the more abstract statement of the principles you illustrated concretely in the body of the book, cutting out perhaps the "Apology"[155] and rewriting parts of the "Plato"[156] and at the same time adding a few pages of general introduction to show your familiarity with the present philosophical game,—you would in my opinion have produced vastly more impression. I am not sure that I would not keep some such plan in mind as an ultimate possibility even now. The best plan for the immediate future might be to put forth the aphorisms as an independent booklet with an introduction of the kind I have mentioned and then—in addition to the ordinary critical reviews—give it a wide distribution among the philosophical reviews of the world. In lumping together such solid philosophical pabulum with what is primarily a series of literary essays do you not run some risk of confusing the *genres*? All that I have said you will of course regard as extremely tentative. I do not know what essays you are planning to include in the next *Shelburne* series and this is a drawback in arriving at an opinion.

I myself have been working this summer on the second volume of my history of French criticism which I am planning to publish before the first. The title I have taken (with your approval I believe) is "The Masters of Modern French Criticism." I have thought out the general plan of the book during the past few weeks and written the first three chapters which deal chiefly with Madame de Staël, Joubert and Chateaubriand.[157] In view of the present academic situation[158] I must get it finished in some form by next March and if possible earlier. I have been studying Bergson with some care this summer and am planning to slam him about as hard as I know how in this next volume.[159]

A professor in one of the Paris lycées has sent me a volume that he has just published on methods of teaching Fr. literature, being a sort of stenographic report of what actually takes place in his class. I may send you a note on it

---

155. More 1909a: 274-320.
156. More 1909a: 321-55.
157. See Babbitt 1912e: 1-78.
158. Babbitt here refers to his continued desire to win advancement to full professor status at Harvard and hopes that another published book will help him do so.
159. See, e.g., Babbitt 1912e: ix-x, 53-55, 252-53.

for the *Nation*, which you will publish or return to me as you see fit.[160] If you are sure on general principles that you do not want a note of this kind let me know at once.

I thought Fite's paper[161] in your last educational number was effective—much more so than that of Shorey in the previous educational number.[162] I look forward to that visit to Cambridge you speak of. It might give us an opportunity to talk over certain questions connected with the aphorisms in more detail. I leave for Cambridge tomorrow (Wednesday), the family on Friday. My wife joins me in kind regards to you and Mrs. More.

Sincerely yours,
Irving Babbitt.

---

160. This anonymous review appeared in the December 21, 1911, issue of the *Nation*. See Babbitt 1911.

161. For the paper by the American philosophy professor Warner Fite (1867–1955) to which Babbitt here refers, see Fite 1911.

162. Shorey 1911.

CHAPTER FOUR
1912–1914

6 Kirkland Road
Cambridge
25 January, 1912

Dear More,

Sidney Gunn,[1] about whom I remember speaking to you, asked me the next day for a card of introduction which I gave him. He has something [of] the air and manner of a conspirator but is in my opinion trying to do some real thinking. He has been carrying on a campaign for the good cause in "*Science*" and will probably hand you (at my request) two or three of the papers he has published there.[2] Gunn expressed to me the belief that you were exercising an important influence both by your essays and by your editing of the *Nation* on a good many young men throughout the country. I find on inquiry that the more serious graduate students here are assiduous readers of the *Nation* and approve of its present policy. I fancy the same is true of the more serious instructors. I believe you are doing more good for the general situation in your editorial capacity than you could in almost any academic position, though of course if an important offer came to you, you would be justified in not making your decision on altruistic grounds.

I am pleased that you are getting out that booklet[3] with the H. M. Co. I am planning to send you in a few days a list of foreign reviews to which copies in my opinion ought to be mailed. – I am going to give a card for you to

---

1. Sidney Allen Gunn (1876–1941), who earned an A.B. at Dalhousie University and an A.B. (1904) and A.M. (1905) at Harvard University, was a professor of English whose views aligned with the New Humanism. On Gunn's esteem for Charles Eliot Norton (one of Babbitt's mentors), see Turner 1999: 410-11.

2. E.g., Gunn 1911.

3. More 1912. The pamphlet originated as an article that first appeared in the September 21, 1911, number of the *Nation*. After reading the piece there, William Roscoe Thayer convinced More to issue it as a self-standing pamphlet and persuaded the Houghton Mifflin Company to publish it (see Dakin 1960: 119-20). The essay then appeared in the eighth series of *Shelburne Essays* (More 1967a: 147-90).

Diehl,[4] exchange professor from the Sorbonne, and have already explained to him the nature of your literary achievement. He may or may not turn up but if he does you will find that he knows enough English to piece out your knowledge of French. I hope you were not fatigued as a result of that last afternoon and evening.

Sincerely yours,
Irving Babbitt.

---

13 February, 1912

Dear More,

Dora and I have both been deeply pained to hear of the death of Mrs. Heard.[5] I hope that when the occasion presents itself you will convey our heartfelt sympathy to Mr. Heard.[6]

Accept my thanks for a copy of the "Nietzsche."[7] It strikes me as a powerful and convincing piece of writing—at least for those who can follow ideas. I am cynical enough to believe that the readers who can estimate the ideas of a book like this are none too numerous in this country. Still I think that this separate reprint is an excellent idea and that it may do a great deal to spread your reputation. – I enclose a list of foreign reviews. I may add to the list when your eighth volume appears. – I do not know anything about Royce's[8] apoplectic seizure except what I, and I presume you also have read in the papers. It is rather sinister the number of men of about his age or a few years younger who are falling by the wayside at Harvard. There was an atmosphere of strain and high pressure here during the latter part of Eliot's administration; and things have not been much improved by the advent of Lowell. Give my kind regards to Mrs. More.

Sincerely yours,
Irving Babbitt.

---

4. Charles Diehl (1859–1944), the Byzantine historian and art historian.
5. Katherine Beck Heard (1868–1912), the younger sister of More's wife Henrietta, passed away on February 9, 1912 (Dakin 1960: 138 n. 24).
6. Augustine A. Heard, Henrietta More's brother-in-law.
7. More 1912.
8. The Harvard professor of philosophy Josiah Royce (1855–1916), who suffered a stroke in 1912. On Royce, see his entry in the Biographical Register.

The Nation 20 Vesey Street
New York, February 15, 1912

My dear Babbitt, – Thank you for the list of publishers.
Here is a quotation from Nietzsche's *Ecce Homo*, of which you will highly approve: "A sedentary life, as I have already said elsewhere, is the real sin against the Holy Spirit." – You see how clearly you stand on the side of the decadents.

Yours
Paul E. More.

---

6 Kirkland Road
Cambridge
17 February, 1912

Dear More,

In addition to the "Nietzsche" I hope that you will send a copy of your sixth volume to the "Annales J. J. Rousseau." They will be sure to notice it in some way and the "Annales" reaches an influential international audience. When your eighth vol. appears I am going to advise you to send a complete set of the Shelburne Essays to the *Revue Germanique*. I shall see that Cestre who is in close touch with that publication gets a proper hint.

The signs are multiplying that the world is going to go crazy over Bergson. The last number of the *Revue des d. Mondes* proclaims[9] solemnly that he is at least as great as Kant and probably as great as Socrates. I hope that when he comes over to give his lectures at Columbia,[10] the *Nation* will take up a position on the firing line.

I should say that Nietzsche's fulmination against the sedentary life belongs to what you call (p. 19) "the inspired part of him" which is provocative; it has evidently provoked you. According to Aristotle the man who is in an extreme is wont to look on the man who is in the mean as being in the opposite extreme. Thus the man who is physically inert accuses the man who is for a normal amount of exercise of being a dromomaniac. – I see by the way that

---

9. See Le Roy 1912: 551.
10. In February of 1913, Bergson delivered lectures at Columbia, Princeton, Harvard, and the City College of New York. See McGrath 2013.

Mather has written a peace leaflet[11] and if you are in a mood for sarcasm you should find him a shining mark. I expect to see him next figuring in some peace "riot."

Sincerely yours,
Irving Babbitt.

The Nation, 20 Vesey Street
New York, February 29, 1912

My dear Babbitt, – First of all let me congratulate you on the prospect, the virtual certainty I suppose, of your advance.[12] I feel almost like quoting Scripture to your Pagan ears and saying "You have fought the god fight etc." Your title will give you a much stronger position for attack and defense. – I remember the essay[13] (returned under another cover) well enough to accept it without reading it, although it will necessitate the privilege of printing in two numbers which I have hitherto reserved as an editorial monopoly. In adapting for the *Nation* it will be well of course to lay as much emphasis as possible on the journalistic connection with [George] Saintsbury, who is after all the "official" critic of England today and who has had the honor of writing on Shakespeare and Milton in the new Cambridge History of English Literature. The last paragraph on Goethe and Saintsbury is very apt.[14] It will of course be easy, wherever you make such changes or additions for the *Nation*, to keep out the MS page as you wish it to stand in your book and reserve it for later use. Let me have copy back as soon as you can. Just now I could use it; later on I may be crowded. – I am a little in doubt about my own next volume. Most of it is ready for the press. I am now revising an introductory letter to Mather,[15] in which I take up his condemnation of my attitude towards Pater. It is an extremely difficult piece of writing, because

---

11. Mather 1912.

12. On Babbitt's advancement to the status of a full professor of French literature at Harvard, after having received an offer of employment at the University of Illinois, see, e.g., Dora Babbitt in Manchester and Shepard 1941: xii; Hough 1952: 135; Dakin 1960: 113; Levin 1966: 321-22; Nevin 1984: 24; Ryn 1991: xv and 1995b: xviii.

13. A footnote in the typescript of this letter reads: "'Are the English Critical?' *The Nation*, March 21, 28, 1912." This essay, split up into two issues of the *Nation* (Babbitt 1912a and b), posthumously appeared in the collection *Spanish Character and Other Essays* (Babbitt 1940: 21-47).

14. See Babbitt 1940: 46-47.

15. More 1967a: vii-xiv.

I am attempting at the same time to make a kind of personal *apologia* and to sum up in a formula my attitude towards romanticism. As soon as my revision is finished I am going to send it to you and to Mather and ask you to pronounce judgment. The thing ought not to be printed at all unless the tone is right. I could easily have the book ready to bring out in the autumn, but am hesitating between publication and a voyage to England with Trent.[16] Money fails for both, and I feel that for many reasons it would be good for me to take this opportunity to go abroad. On the other hand it seems to me important to get this volume off my hands. It begins to grow stale on me. Having got rid of this perillous [sic] stuff I shall probably abjure philosophy for a season and write on more purely literary and biographical topics. Houghton Mifflin will no doubt make an honest effort to launch this first volume they take up,[17] unless the "Nietzsche" should fail so signally as to damp their ardor. It would of course be a strong card for me, if you could write something. In that case, so far as benefit to me, it would be much better to print in the *Yale Review*, if Cross[18] is willing, than in the *Harvard Graduates'*.[19] – Next year when Bergson comes over I shall get some one—if you are willing; otherwise probably Fite—to expose him. Have you met Fite who is now in Cambridge? I wish you would have a talk with him and let me know how he impresses you. I have never seen him.

With kind regards to the ladies,

Sincerely,
Paul E. More.

P.S. What did you think of Fuller's review of Neilson?[20]

---

16. More set sail on May 25, 1912, for a trip of around nine weeks in England (Dakin 1960: 127; cf. More's letter to Babbitt of August 18, 1912, below). More's friend William Peterfield Trent (1862–1939) was a professor of English literature at Sewanee, the University of the South, and the founder of the *Sewanee Review*. More's *The Drift of Romanticism: Shelburne Essays, Eighth Series* (More 1967a), would be published in March of 1913 (see Dakin 1950: 143 and 1960: 139).

17. The Houghton Mifflin Company was the original publisher of More's *The Drift of Romanticism: Shelburne Essays, Eighth Series*.

18. Wilbur Lucius Cross (1862–1942), the literary critic, editor of the *Yale Review*, and future governor of Connecticut.

19. Babbitt would review More's *The Drift of Romanticism* for the *Yale Review*, in a piece (Babbitt 1913f) not listed in the extensive bibliography of Babbitt's writings affixed to *Spanish Character and Other Essays* (cf. Babbitt 1940: 254). It does appear, however, in both Young's (1941: 35) and Dakin's (1950: 188) list of reviews of More's book.

20. More here seems to mention an anonymous review (presumably written by More's friend and co-worker Harold de Wulf Fuller, then an assistant editor of the *Nation*) of William Allan Neilson's *Essentials of Poetry*, from the February 22, 1912, issue of the *Nation*. See Fuller 1912.

Cambridge, Mass.
19 March, 1912

Dear More,

The subject of my essay is not English criticism in itself but as I announce at the beginning Eng. criticism *in comparison* with that of other countries, especially France.[21] Perhaps it might be well to restate this point at the beginning of the second paper.[22] I am sorry you think that the paper as it stands over-emphasizes the French side. I am merely trying to get a background for an adequate contrast. I have indicated on a separate sheet certain passages that may go if you think necessary. I should think that the anecdotes and allusions in these passages would make the article livelier for the average reader; and there is one idea I am rather loath to sacrifice—namely that the French may lose their taste and do indeed show some signs of losing it. I have confidence in your editorial judgment and am willing to submit to it, provided I am sure you have considered the whole matter carefully. The women of the family, by the way, the only judges I have access to, do not see the force of your criticism.

I invited Fite to dinner the other day and was pleasantly impressed by him. He seems a bit battered physically as a result perhaps of what I surmise to have been a long and difficult struggle to get on academically. I had supposed that he was much younger. He has just been suffering from a fit of sleeplessness, brought on I believe by a prolonged and unsuccessful effort to discover an idea in Eucken.[23] The present age is in a sad way with Bergson and Eucken as its chief philosophers. – Do you think by the way that you would care for an article from me entitled "Bergson and Rousseau" to appear next September or October?[24] It would have a double appropriateness in view of the bicentenary of Rousseau and of Bergson's visit to this country. It might be possible to concoct something under the title that I suggest that would flutter the philosophical dovecotes, and also help prepare the way for your "Aphorisms." Apropos of my attitude toward Bergson I note that a prominent German review—the *Pädagogisches Archiv* of Leipzig—devotes its leading article for February (entitled *Gegen den Naturalismus*) to an examination from a philosophical point of view

---

21. See Babbitt 1940, esp. 23-24.
22. Babbitt 1912b.
23. Rudolph Christoph Eucken (1846–1926), a German philosopher and recipient of a Nobel Prize for Literature.
24. This article appeared in the November 14, 1912, issue of the *Nation*. See Babbitt 1912c.

of two books, one of which is "The New Laokoön." The author of the article, a Professor Albert Schneider, is a close and keen thinker but a hard writer, even I should suppose for Germans.[25] He is with me in almost all particulars as against James and Bergson whose points of view he declares to be pseudo-idealistic—a late product of romanticism. "Diese modernen Seelenbegriffe neigen allesamt zum Animalischen hin...."[26] Wenn die Neigung zur Verschwommenheit ein romantischer Zug ist, so hat Babbitt mit seiner Diagnose Bergsons recht."[27] etc.

I have given a card for you to President Foster[28] of Reed College, Portland, Oregon. Foster is a Harvard man, a friend and contemporary of Stuart Sherman's. He is very much down on Kittredge and claims to have been much influenced by your writing and mine. He has the income of an endowment and several millions to spend (almost without any restrictions) and is now getting together his faculty. He has a look of strong concentration about the eyes but I did not see enough of him to make sure of the soundness of his ideas.

I am just refusing an invitation from the Harvard Club of Cincinnati. I am mentioning to the President of the Club in my letter that I am likely to receive an invitation from the Un. of Cin. next year which I may accept and that I should be glad to meet the members of the Club in connection with this trip. I hope that there is no harm in my having put the matter in this way. You might in any case, if it is not too much trouble, mention the circumstances to your brother[29] when you next write him.

I should appreciate seeing a second proof of the second half of my article.[30]

Sincerely yours,
Irving Babbitt.

Is that foreign trip decided? What are likely to be the dates of your departure and return?[31]

---

25. Schneider 1912 (who misspells Babbitt's last name as "Babbit").
26. In the original letter, Babbitt marks the ellipsis here with "x x."
27. Schneider 1912: 72 (although Babbitt silently corrected Schneider's misspelling of his last name when quoting him).
28. William Trufant Foster (1879–1950), an economist and the first president of Reed College, which was founded in 1908.
29. More's younger brother Louis T. More was a physicist and dean at the University of Cincinnati.
30. Babbitt 1912b.
31. On More's summer trip to England, see above.

Cambridge
17 April, 1912

Dear More,

I have decided to do that paper on Bergson and Rousseau;[32] if any unexpected obstacle should supervene, I will let you know not later than August, which would still give you time, I suppose, to make arrangements elsewhere. The situation as regards the writing of serious essays in this country is as I see it distinctly exasperating. The *Atlantic* is losing intellectual caste under the present management, the Yale Review reaches too special a public and the *Nation* which reaches the right public imposes very severe restrictions in the matter of space. I agree with you as to the drawbacks of stretching an essay over two numbers and am as a matter of fact likely to keep within the bounds in anything I compose with the *Nation* directly in view. If I remember rightly 4,500 words is the extreme limit for a single issue. If I had tried to compress my essay on "English Criticism"[33] very much I am sure that it would have suffered seriously. As it is, men in the non-literary departments here (Taussig,[34] etc.) seem to have enjoyed it, and it is even more to the interests of the *Nation* that it should reach this wider circle of readers than it is to mine. – If I write the kind of essay on Bergson that I have in mind, my hat will be in the ring so far as the philosophical situation is concerned. I may want to come to New York and talk the paper over with you in detail before it actually goes into print.

Is the *Nation* not tending by the way, to overdo a certain kind of attack on Roosevelt? That seems to be the opinion of a certain number of people about here, and I should suppose that you might do your circulation some harm without any corresponding benefit. What I have in mind, of course, is not the attack on him in itself (that is very necessary), but the suggestion at times of violence and personal rancor.[35]

On what vessel have you engaged your passage? When I crossed on the *Adriatic* a few years ago, I remember that a comparison I made of the number of life-boats with the number of persons on board suggested to me the possibility of just such a disaster as has overtaken the *Titanic*. I returned on a cattle boat and a similar comparison showed room for everybody with a comfortable margin to spare. I am inclined to favor steamers that have

---

32. Babbitt 1912c.
33. Babbitt 1912a and b.
34. The Harvard economics professor Frank William Taussig (1859–1940).
35. Babbitt himself would criticize Theodore Roosevelt's imperialistic tendencies in *Democracy and Leadership*; see Babbitt 1924: 249, 269-70, 294.

only one class of passengers and not too many of them. Some of the Atlantic Transport steamers about satisfy (If I am not mistaken) this requirement. The only way that occurs to me for almost eliminating danger would be for boats to sail in pairs. With modern devices such as submarine signalling [sic], wireless, etc., they could keep at a uniform interval of about five miles from one another, say, in any kind of weather. I have never seen this idea set forth and it might be worth putting into print. Naval twins of this kind would appeal to all the timid old ladies and might be paying propositions.

You were misinformed about Wright.[36] He has received only an associate professorship. Not many men here are going to receive their full promotion if the President adheres to his present policy. His notion is that his faculty so far as the full professors are concerned should be a collection of jewels. The problem will be to find the jewels and especially to make sure they are not paste imitations.

Sincerely yours,
Irving Babbitt.

---

159 West Ninety-Second Street
New York
August 18, 191[2][37]

My dear Babbitt,

I have about got the MS. of my next volume ready for the printers, but before committing it to type I want very much to have your criticism of the Preface.[38] It was a difficult thing to write, and I am not at all sure that I have properly combined the personal note with an exposition of the purpose of the book. The definition of modern romanticism may seem to need development,[39] but that is precisely the main theme of the essays themselves. It seemed worth while in some such introductory way as this to give my particular point of view. Please let me have your impression of the Preface as a whole, and also any special criticism that may occur to you.

I have about made up my mind to give this volume to Houghton Mifflin Co., but there are certain difficulties in the way. It would be a very complicated matter to transfer to them the volumes already in print, and indeed my

---

36. Presumably, Babbitt and More were discussing C. H. Conrad Wright (1869–1957), one of Babbitt's colleagues in French at Harvard.
37. More's original letter is misdated, August 18, 1913.
38. More 1967a: vii-xiv.
39. See More 1967a: esp. ix-xi.

contracts with Putnams are such that they might hold me up for a number of years. The question then arises as to the name to be given to a new series begun with a new publisher. I feel sure that, in view of the end I contemplate, it is better to have some such general title. At the same time I intend hereafter to confine each volume to a particular period or movement, so that they may have the advantage of definite subtitles. For the general title I may continue the old name. Thus the present volume might stand as:

> Shelburne Essays
> Series VIII
> Types of Romanticism[40]

But I am not sure whether H. M. would like this plan, which, indeed has certain drawbacks. On the other hand I can think of no new title which is at once characteristic, sufficiently elastic, and not repellent. "Critical Essays" rather sins against the last requirement; "Epochs of Literature" against the second, and merely "Essays" against the first. I rather incline to the second of these, which would make the new volume stand as:

> Epochs of Literature
> I
> Types of Romanticism

Can you offer any suggestion? The seventh series of Shelburne Essays, you will remember, closed with a general index to the set,[41] so that the departure under a new name will not be awkward.

I gather from Dora's last letter to Net that your new volume on Modern French Criticism[42] is about ready for the press. That I suppose means that it will come out shortly after Christmas, when I expect my own venture to appear, so that what I have to say on certain tendencies of the nineteenth century will be reinforced and confirmed by your approach from another country. I take comfort from that, though I might dread the occasion of comparison if I thought any reviewer would be sufficiently alert to see the grounds of similarity and contrast. I hope you will let me read your book in proof, since from my editorial experience I shall probably be able to offer a number of profitable suggestions in small points.

---

40. More later settled on the title *The Drift of Romanticism: Shelburne Essays, Eighth Series.*
41. More 1910a: 271-73.
42. Babbitt 1912e.

I expected when I sat down to tell you something of my English experiences and impressions, but so much of my letter has gone to matters of business that my epistolary impulse, as Johnson might say, is already exhausted. I was in England altogether for about seven weeks, some three of which were spent in London. For the rest I gave most of my time to the cathedral and university towns. Oxford, particularly, gave me matter for reflection, and some of my conclusions I may work into a lecture on the Classics to be given at the University of Michigan in the Spring.[43] In brief I felt very strongly the paradoxical character of Oxford, the rather unstable union, that is to say, of classical and mediaeval Christian influences.[44] Say what you will, there is something false in the composition of a place created for the production of Christian ministers, which makes Greek and Latin the basis of its curriculum. To ground education on Pagan ideals and at the same time to insist on the ultimate inadequacy and even falseness of these ideals in comparison with the New Testament, is a contradiction in terms. One or the other must give way—unless both succumb, as appears to be the actual tendency. Perhaps Oxford in this respect is only typical of the modern world. And I am not sure that the very lack of traditions in America may not make the proper restoration of the Classics easier than in the old world—though there are few signs of such a restoration.

Give my kind regards to Dora. I trust we shall be able to see you both in New York this winter.

Sincerely,
Paul E. More.

The Nation, 20 Vesey Street
New York, August 29, 1912

My dear Babbitt, – Thank you heartily for your criticism of my Preface.[45] I am making all the changes you suggest. As for your Bergson,[46] I can promise to print it in one of the first three issues of November, but should prefer to have it a little earlier. In November I am always much crowded with current publications. At any rate you must have the MS in time to give me the option

---

43. According to Dakin (1960: 140), on April 4, 1913, More delivered a lecture at the University of Michigan devoted to "the conflict between the classical and the medieval Christian traditions."
44. On this topic, see More's essay "The Paradox of Oxford" from the ninth series of *Shelburne Essays* (More 1915a: 71-100).
45. More 1967a: vii-xiv.
46. Babbitt 1912c.

of two or three weeks. I see Longmans are advertising a book on Bergson by Hugh S. R. Elliot,[47] which perhaps you might take some notice of in your article.[48] At any rate I shall send the book to you when it appears. I hope you will be able to confine the discussion to a single article in the *Nation*, as I am more and more opposed to continued articles. The *Nation* cannot print and ought not to try to print the kind of thing suitable in a regular monthly or quarterly magazine. I know I have been the chief sinner myself in this respect, but I mean to reform. – It is pleasant to hear that your new volume has gone to the printer. Do you include La Harpe in this survey?[49] While in London I picked up the seventeen volumes of the Lycée, in good condition, for eight shillings. One night I dined at the Passmore-Edwardes Settlement and told of this purchase to a couple of young Frenchmen who were living there and lecturing on French literature. They both exclaimed that nobody ever thought of opening La Harpe and that I had paid high for him. I observe too that Lanson[50] does not give him any recognition in his *Histoire*.[51] Well, I have been reading in him, and I reckon him very high among critics— certainly above Brunetière, though of course he has not Brunetière's special kind of erudition. La Harpe is dry in places; he has unmistakably his limitations, e.g. the naïve and primitive make no appeal to him; but at his best he shows an extraordinary insight into human character and the expression of it in literature. For instance, I read on the same day his criticisms of La Rochefoucauld and Diderot. The former he censures for confounding *amour de soi* with *amour-propre*, the latter for confounding *amour-propre* with *amour de soi*.[52] Now he does not bring these two men into comparison, and he does not enter very deeply into the metaphysical meaning of his distinction; but taken together these two chapters are something more than suggestive, they are illuminating; they give a bird's eye view, so to speak, of a whole ethical revolution. Indeed the whole of the fifteenth and sixteenth volumes is a masterly, though somewhat repetitious, analysis of the motives and ideas of the *philosophes*. His critique of the *Code de la Nature*[53] made

---

47. Elliot 1912.
48. Babbitt chose not to mention it in his piece.
49. Although Babbitt mentions Jean-François de La Harpe (1739-1803) in *The Masters of Modern French Criticism* (see Babbitt 1912e: 3, 11, 51, 85, 152), he did not devote a chapter to him.
50. Gustave Lanson (1857–1934), a French literary critic, historian, and professor.
51. Lanson 1906.
52. On Rousseau's concepts of *amour de soi* and *amour-propre*, see, e.g., Chazan 1993.
53. An influential French utopian tract published anonymously in 1755 and often attributed to Étienne-Gabriel Morelly (1717–1778).

my blood tingle with joy. Take again his portrait of Retz;[54] here he is brief and very wise. I daresay you are wondering why I am carting all these coals to Newcastle. In the first place I am writing of La Harpe because my head is full of him, and in the second place I hope that you will give him proper recognition in your book—in the present volume or its chronological predecessor. – Have you seen the last number of the *Forum*? Your friend and pupil, Nickerson,[55] presents himself in it as one having a storm of chaff in his brain; he also makes you look ridiculous and me talk like a fool. He needs discipline. – With kind regards to Dora,

Sincerely
Paul E. More.

Dublin, N. H.
31 August, 1912

Dear More,

I shall be glad to see the book on Bergson by Elliot. I was under the impression that it had already been disposed of by a note in the *Nation*. I was planning to write only a single article on Bergson though I shall probably want the outside amount of space you are willing to grant. I am hoping to let you have the copy about Oct. 20 if this is agreeable to you.

I have not read La Harpe in a systematic way for years (and even then I did not read some of the parts of the Lycée you mention). I remember that my judgment on him at the time coincided with that of Sainte-Beuve in his entertaining double article in the *Lundis*.[56] (S. B. by the way strung his papers over two weeks in publications more or less similar to the *Nation*.) S. B. says of him "J'en ai profité mille fois" (I am quoting from memory).[57] He is

---

54. Jean François Paul de Gondi, the cardinal of Retz (1613–1679), was a memoirist and churchman.

55. Hoffman Nickerson (1888–1965) was a Harvard graduate, real estate developer, and writer who had studied with Babbitt. Although an admirer of Babbitt (he contributed a chapter to Manchester and Shepard's *Irving Babbitt: Man and Teacher* [1941: 91-94]), Nickerson drifted away from the New Humanism towards monarchism and Distributism. He was a contributor to Seward Collins's *Bookman* and *American Review*. The article to which More must be referring to here is Nickerson 1912, provided it appeared in print slightly earlier than its publication month of September, 1912. This piece, which invokes a conversation Nickerson had with More (333) and suggests Babbitt's and More's agreement with the author's views (335), is an apologia for musical comedy, a genre Babbitt and More disesteemed. On Nickerson, see, e.g., Stone 1960: 7; Tucker 2006: 104-5, 113-17.

56. Sainte-Beuve 1865: 103-44.

57. The exact quote is "j'en ai mille fois profité" (Sainte-Beuve 1865: 112).

excellent to give "une teinture première et générale," a first initiation into the humanistic tradition. But neither S. B. nor any other important Frenchmen, so far as I am aware, ever took La Harpe very seriously as a *thinker*.

La Harpe does not appear to an important extent in my present volume which covers only the 19th century. I translate a "thought" of Joubert about him for a special purpose. This "thought" is so disparaging that I may correct it by a cross-reference to Sainte-Beuve.[58]

I have not seen that article in the Forum to which you refer. Shortly after that trip to New York when he saw you, Nickerson came down with grip[pe] which settled in his head so that he had to be confined for several months in a sanatorium. He is distinctly unbalanced. I fear he may be planning to take one of my courses this year.

Sincerely
Irving Babbitt.

The Nation, 20 Vesey Street
New York, September 28, 1912

My dear Babbitt, – I have been obliged to run over the proof[59] rather hastily, but I have marked a number of small points, as you will see. It seemed necessary to make my marks on the proof, though this is stamped as the proof to be returned to the printer. As my marks are in pencil, you can easily erase any of them you choose. Reading as I did for minor matters of style and punctuation I got a poor grasp of the thing; as a whole there was much in it. I hope some of my suggestions will prove serviceable. Send on the other galleys as they come. – I have signed my contract with H. M. but the book[60] will not appear until after Christmas.

Yrs. etc.
Paul E. More.

P.S. I return proof under another cover.

---

58. Cf. Babbitt 1912e: 50-51.

59. A footnote in the typescript of the letter reads: "Of *The Masters of Modern French Criticism.*" See Babbitt 1912e.

60. A footnote in the typescript of the letter reads: "*The Drift of Romanticism*: Shelburne Essays, Eighth Series." See More 1967a.

6 Kirkland Road
Cambridge
5 December, 1912

Dear More,

One point has occurred to me in reflecting on your "Newman."[61] You speak of Newman's sister-in-law *Miss* Mozley (? I quote from memory). How can an unmarried man have a sister-in-law who is a *miss*?[62]

I should like to talk over with you certain analogies you discover between the scientific rationalist and the dogmatic religionist. One or two points in your argument are not clear to me. Perhaps you have clarified this passage in the revision you mention. One or two comments I have made in the margin do not imply that I think you should make changes but merely suggest the different angle from which I should view the same problem. I am struck by the truly Platonic quality of your thinking in this essay but also feel how hard it is to distinguish in words this Platonism from the romantic parody of it, (I refer especially to the gap you establish between the ideal and the real). I do not know whether it is a part of your plan to show that romanticism is subversive not merely of religious insight but of the humbler human virtues that can be compassed by good works and rest less immediately on a mystical illumination. Either the Platonic or the Aristotelian line of attack on romanticism is justifiable. If I prefer personally the latter it is because it does not lend itself to such subtle and baffling perversions.

Sincerely,
Irving Babbitt.

THE NATION, 20 Vesey Street (P.O. Box 794)
New York
December 7, 1912

My dear Babbitt,

Many thanks for your speed in returning proofs, and for the care you have taken in reading them. I think you will find the Beckford[63] and the

---

61. More's essay "Cardinal Newman," from the eighth series of *Shelburne Essays*. See More 1967a: 39-79.
62. See More 1967a: 60: "this has been supplemented by the two volumes of his letters edited by Miss Mozley."
63. More 1967a: 3-36.

Newman[64] clearer and sounder after my final revision, though the difficulties of the argument and the many subtle distinctions to be kept in mind have brought me almost to a state of despair. – As for your proposed review of the book, I should be glad to see that appear either in the *Yale Review* or the *Times Supplement*.[65] I suspect that an unsigned review in the latter would sell the greater number of copies, but a signed review in the former would in a way mean more κῦδος—judge thou for me. – One thing in your own book—a very trivial thing—I regret. On the strength of Scherer's[66] praise[67] of Doudan[68] I sent for the Letters and am now reading them—four large volumes, which I should be glad enough to have lengthened into ten. Doudan is indeed a delightful letter-writer and worthy of Scherer's encomium. He is not a great man; there was probably some lack of power or continuity in him which would have prevented him from accomplishing anything important in affairs or literature. Or, possibly, his *sagesse* without *illusion* kept him from that over-valuing of the world which, according to Halifax, makes what is called an "Able Man." I am not sure about that, but I am sure that he had the wit and disillusion and aloofness and fundamental melancholy that make a fascinating correspondent. The last letter I read this morning contained the following about Renan: "Celui-là est une grande coquette dans l'ordre des théologiens et des savants. Sa coquetterie est mêlée d'impertinence, mais il donne aux hommes de sa génération ce qu'ils désirent en toutes choses, des bonbons qui sentient l'infini."[69] That isn't bad for a casual remark, and his papers are full of them; sometimes a letter is almost a little essay, though never formal or formidable or *voulu*. It's not the *genre* that particularly appeals to you, but to me it is a substitute for good society. I do not get such wise gossip very often from the men I meet—and the women today have forgotten their rôle as sympathetic audience. Scherer was right.

Sincerely,
Paul E. More.

---

64. More 1967a: 39-79.

65. Babbitt ultimately reviewed the eighth series of More's *Shelburne Essays* for the *Yale Review*. See Babbitt 1913f.

66. The French literary critic and theologian Edmond Adolphe Schérer (1815–1889). For Babbitt's views on Schérer, see, e.g., Babbitt 1912e: 189-217.

67. The typescript of this letter contains a footnote that reads: "I. B. calls this praise 'almost exaggerated,' *Masters of Modern French Criticism*, pp. 205-206." See Babbitt 1912e, with the quote on 205.

68. The French journalist Ximénès Doudan (1800–1872).

69. See Doudan 1897: 143.

Cambridge
30 December, 1912

Dear More,

A second reading of your Definitions[70] has confirmed my first impression as to their rare philosophical distinction. I continue to regret however (for reasons that I will explain to you more fully when we meet) that you did not reserve them for a revised edition of your sixth volume.[71] You might have filled in the gap in this volume by an essay on Rossetti or something of the kind. – One other point occurs to me though it may be too late to do anything. An occasional phrase in the Definitions suggests romantic aloofness rather than the geniality and cheerfulness of true wisdom; for example, you speak of the *bitter* comfort to be found in the philosophers.[72] I fear that an epithet of this kind may alienate readers unnecessarily. – In one of your last Definitions you intimate that the strongest type of person can dispense with God, and then you put your final emphasis on the *amor Dei intellectualis*.[73] Will the ordinary reader see any contradiction here?

The *Revue Bleue* inserted my Bergson[74] on Dec. 7 in spite of my definite request that they should not do so without letting me see a proof. A number of serious blunders have naturally crept in—e.g. my humanism is rendered humanitarisme!

We are looking forward very much to seeing you and Mrs. More—the sooner the better. I for my part am hoping to take a trip to New York during the mid-year period or at least during the spring recess. With hearty good wishes for the New Year,

Sincerely yours,
Irving Babbitt.

---

70. More's piece "Definitions of Dualism," from the eighth series of *Shelburne Essays* (More 1967a: 247-302).

71. Since the sixth series of More's *Shelburne Essays* bore the subtitle *Studies of Religious Dualism*, Babbitt thought that it would have been best for More to include "Definitions of Dualism" in that volume.

72. See, e.g., More 1967a: 291-92.

73. More 1967a: 301-2.

74. A French translation by Jeanne Scialtiel of Babbitt 1912c. See Babbitt 1912d.

THE NATION, 20 Vesey Street (P.O. Box 794.)
New York
January 9, 1913

My dear Babbitt,

First of all let me thank you for careful reading of my proof. Your suggestions were particularly valuable in regard to the Definitions and I think you will find a notable improvement in some of these—particularly in the way of greater simplicity and clearness. I fairly shiver when I think what my bill for extra corrections will be. A second revise of the pages containing the Definitions has come this morning. This ends the business for me. I suppose the book will be out some time about the middle of February. – It seems to be the general opinion, in which I concur, that your "Masters"[75] is your best work so far. Mather, whom I met at the Authors Club[76] New Year's Eve was quite warm in his praise, even saying that the book had charm, which for him is the final word. I have sent it to Giese to review.[77] As he is in Switzerland the notice will be somewhat delayed, but he will probably send me something worth printing. – I am still uncertain about my projected visit to Cambridge, but, if Net comes with me, as she rather hopes to do, it will have to be sometime in February, when Mrs. Beck[78] will be in New York and on hand to look after the children.[79] I have a lecture engagement at Ann Arbor, the date of which has not yet been determined, and this prevents me from making any definite plans.[80] I expect daily to hear from the Michigan people. February our spare room will be in the possession of Mrs. Beck, but for the rest of the winter, so far as I know, it is very much at your service. Can't you come down the latter part of this month? With kind regards to Dora,

Sincerely,
Paul E. More.

P.S. I read the first book of Plato's *Republic* last night. What a miracle it is!

---

75. Babbitt 1912e.
76. On More's membership in the Authors' Club, see Dakin 1960: 163.
77. The unsigned review appeared in the February 13, 1913, issue of the *Nation*. See Giese 1913.
78. More's mother-in-law.
79. More ultimately spent two days in Cambridge visiting with Babbitt in late April of 1913 (see Dakin 1960: 140 and below).
80. More would lecture at the University of Michigan on April 4, 1913 (Dakin 1960: 140).

Cambridge
2 March, 1913

Dear More,

I have just finished reading a doctor's thesis, the last of an almost interminable series of small jobs I have had on hand, and am now ready to write those much-delayed book-notes[81] for you. I will mail them about the middle of this week. With two Radcliffe courses in addition to my work at Harvard, the reading of examination books has proved a rather formidable task this year.

I shall be glad to know that you are safely back from that Western adventure. Dualistic philosophers have been rather rare in Kansas but let us hope that your activities there may bear fruit.[82] I presume you have seen Cory's article on my book in *The Dial*.[83] You are really the hero of this paper. This just tribute should help forward your reputation in the great and exuberant West and prepare the way auspiciously for your eighth series.[84] I cannot say that I am greatly taken by the style of the article. If I were given to playing on words, I should say that it is a bit corybantic.

I hope the plans for that visit to Cambridge are holding good. With kind regards to Mrs. More,

Sincerely yours,
Irving Babbitt.

THE NATION, 20 Vesey Street (P.O. Box 794)
New York
April 16, 1913

My dear Babbitt,

You have already heard from Net that I have planned to visit you Friday of next week, arriving in Boston just before 6 P.M.[85] This will make my stay short, but I have been away from my desk so much this winter and am engaged to

---

81. According to the bibliography found in Babbitt 1940, More published four of Babbitt's anonymous reviews in the *Nation* that year, Babbitt 1913b, c, d, and e.
82. On More's lecture series at the University of Kansas from February 17 to 21, 1913, see Dakin 1960: 139.
83. Cory 1913.
84. Cory's review (1913) of Babbitt 1912e finds More's writing praiseworthy.
85. On More's two-day stay in Cambridge, see above.

be away so many days this spring, that I cannot do better. – Thank you for the list of German and French periodicals. I sent it to Houghton Mifflin and they have forwarded it to Constable, with what results remains to be seen. – I met Mrs. Kenyon Cox[86] the other day, and heard from her that her husband had been much impressed by your conversation and was now reading your books with pleasure and approval. – What you say about Schofield's book is no doubt true, in a way. It would be innocent enough, were it not for the eminence of the author's position. Bruce, however, did not write the review, but S. L. Wolff[87] (this, of course, sub sigillo).[88] Schofield complained to me in a letter that the notice was "malicious," evidently thinking it was by Fuller.[89] From Gunn[90] I heard recently that the younger men in Harvard were rather pleased to see Schofield brought up in this way. Certainly nothing could be more ludicrously banal than the extracts which Wolff gave at the end of his review. – You will not hesitate to let me know if my proposed visit falls at an inopportune time. I must leave Sunday night at the latest. – With kind regards to Dora, I am

Sincerely yours,
Paul E. More.

THE NATION, 20 Vesey Street (P.O. Box 794)
New York
May 3, 1913

My dear Babbitt,

First of all let me thank you and Dora for your pleasant way of being hospitable. I have made Net quite envious by the story of my two days in Cambridge.[91] She is thinking of making her excursion to Biddeford Pool the

---

86. The American painter Louise Howland King (1865–1945) was married to Kenyon Cox (1856–1919), himself an American painter. Hoeveler (1977: 13-14) considers Cox a minor figure in the Humanist movement.
87. Samuel Lee Wolff (1874–1941), was a professor of English at Columbia University and the author of *The Greek Romances in Elizabethan Prose Fiction* (1912).
88. For the review in question, a largely negative appraisal of William Henry Schofield's *Chivalry in English Literature*, see Wolff 1913. On Schofield, see above, chapter 2.
89. More means Harold de Wulf Fuller, an assistant editor at the *Nation*. See Dakin 1960: 111.
90. On Sidney Gunn, see above, this chapter.
91. On More's brief trip to visit the Babbitts in late April, see above.

last of this month, but whether she will stop off on the way I do not know.[92] – I am glad to report to you boastfully that in one instance at least my indulgence in the obnoxious spirit of laissez-faire in regard to my books has been more profitable than your militant policy of control. Mrs. Willcox[93] apparently is no longer the presiding daemon of the literary pages of the *North American*. At any rate I have just had the best review in the May issue that I have ever received.[94] It was written they tell me by a Clarence H. Gaines, who for some years past has been connected with *Harpers*.[95] – Did you ever have in your classes a Warren S. Archibald,[96] now of Pittsfield? I seem to associate his name with Harvard. He has sent me a paper on Newman which I felt obliged to return to him although it displayed unusual intelligence and an antipathy to humanitarianism which he certainly learned from you or from me. I have asked him whether he would care to review for the *Nation*, and should be glad to know anything definite in regard to his studies and preparation. – Spurred on by a remark of yours I have been rereading Leslie Stephen, with a confirmation of my old views.[97] His human criticisms, so to speak, as exhibited in his essays on Johnson and Pope, are extremely good; but when he comes to philosophy he is distinctly clever but almost always superficial, as befits a Utilitarian. Take his Jonathan Edwards. Here, so long as he deals with the man and with the influence of doctrine on character, he leaves nothing to be desired, but the moment he touches on the metaphysical problem he shows an acute logical faculty with complete inability to grasp the central issue. As I understand Edwards, that portent of New England had one of the clearest and profoundest conceptions of the dualism of good and evil the world has ever known. So far, good. But he was led by the spirit of the age to hypostasize these infinite principles of good and evil as two persons, God and the devil. In doing that there was nothing singular; all theologians have pretended to do the same thing. But Edwards was horribly logical and monstrously brave. The consequence is one of the most disastrous night-

---

92. On the Mores' summer travels in 1913, see Dakin 1960: 140-41, 143.
93. Louise Price Collier Willcox (1865–1929) was an American writer and suffrage activist. She was then on the staff of the *North American Review*.
94. See Gaines 1913.
95. Clarence H. Gaines was a professor of English at St. Lawrence University who was an editor of the *North American Review*; he wrote numerous pieces for *Harpers* and other periodicals.
96. Rev. Warren S. Archibald was a 1903 graduate of Harvard College.
97. Leslie Stephen (1832–1904) was an English critic and author.

mares in history. Most men either do not conceive good and evil, whatever their professions may be, as absolutes. However they may talk of infinity, they never really transcend in their imagination the relative quantities of the flux. Or else, if they are true dualists in their conception of good and evil, they do not really connect their absolute ideas with their religious personifications. They are illogical, but remain human. Not so Edwards. And, once grant that it is legitimate to accept a rigid personification of an absolute dualism, what is there left but the tremendous picture of a God dangling the poor souls of men gleefully over the mouth of an ever-lasting hell? Edwards is thus one of the most instructive illustrations in history of the consequences of mingling an unflinching mythology with a rigid philosophy, that is of confusing the personal and the super-personal. I do not find a word of explanation in Leslie Stephen of the real problem. And as he has treated Edwards[98] so he has dealt with others. – But the weather here is almost as hot as the Calvinistic pit, and a letter of this length is an heroic feat. – With kind regards to Dora,

Sincerely yours,
Paul E. More.

THE NATION, 20 Vesey Street (P.O. Box 794)
New York
June 5, 1913

My dear Babbitt,

There is to be something of a tumult over the celebration of Diderot's centenary, October 5. Wouldn't you like to give us a paper for the occasion? Let me have your decision soon, so that I may turn elsewhere if you are disinclined.[99] – Your work in the classroom is certainly redounding to my credit. Foerster[100] has reviewed the new volume favorably in the *Dial*,[101] and Maag[102]

---

98. For an essay by More on Edwards, see More 1967c: 33-65.

99. Babbitt produced this article: the October 9, 1913, issue of the *Nation* featured his "Bicentenary of Diderot" (Babbitt 1913a), which later appeared as a chapter in *Spanish Character and Other Essays* (Babbitt 1940: 105-20).

100. On Norman Foerster, a former student of Babbitt and an important and prolific second-generation Humanist, see his entry in the Biographical Register. For Foerster's reflections on Babbitt, see Manchester and Shepard 1941: 95-97.

101. Foerster 1913.

102. William F. Maag Jr. (1883–1968) was one of Babbitt's former students at Harvard. In 1924, he took over the editorship of the *Youngstown Vindicator* from his father. For his reflections on Babbitt, see Manchester and Shepard 1941: 57-88.

has contributed a fairly blazing notice to the *Independent*.[103] Blake[104] by the way leaves the latter journal this month and an arrangement has been made by which Trent[105] is to conduct the literary department, by long-distance connection so to speak. I have grave doubts of the feasibility of this plan. Trent, apparently, does not want the matter talked of yet. – I presume half of my family is now with you. The visit, I know will be a great pleasure to Net and Darrah.

Sincerely,
Paul E. More.

Cambridge
21 June, 1913

Dear More,

I have just finished up my college work for the year and am now in a position to give some attention to other tasks. I will let you have a short notice[106] of Guérard's "French Prophets of Yesterday" in a few days; also a few lines on the last volume of the "Annales J.-J. Rousseau."[107] About that article on Diderot you suggest I am hesitating. The subject tempts me, but I doubt whether it is wise to let anything divert me from the writing of my book. And then again the restrictions as to length that you place on your middle articles are rather galling from my point of view. Can you not let me have a few days more in which to consider the question?

The family went off to Dublin[108] last Wednesday. I am likely to stay on here for some time—possibly until the middle of July—rearranging and classifying my books and taking notes for my next volume. I am also arranging to have a large number of books bound. I had allowed my library to fall into a somewhat chaotic condition—partly as a result of my uncertain prospects at Harvard.

---

103. Maag 1913 (cf. Dakin 1950: 188, who misidentifies the author of this anonymous review as "Macy").

104. The journalist Warren Barton Blake (1883–1918) left the staff of the *Independent* in 1913 to become an editorial writer for *Collier's Weekly*.

105. Presumably, More here refers to his friend William Peterfield Trent. Since Trent was a professor at the University of the South, he would have to edit the *Independent*'s literary section remotely. On Trent, see above.

106. Babbitt 1913b.

107. Babbitt 1913d.

108. He means Dublin, New Hampshire, where the Babbitts occasionally summered.

I hope that you were not too much fatigued by that trip to St. Louis and now that you are the recipient of an honorary degree I look up to you with even more awe than before.[109] – I had a long call from Norman Foerster the other day and complimented him on his review of your book in *The Dial*.[110] I am also writing a note to Maag. I have just been damned, by the way, in both the *Yale Review*[111] and *Modern Language Notes*[112] for my attempt to foist philosophy upon the literary reader. Of my three books this one[113] is certainly faring the worst with the reviewers. I hope to hear better reports of the sales of your book than I have heard of mine thus far.

We were very glad to have that visit with Mrs. More. I presume she has already gone to Essex.[114] When are you planning to get away?

Sincerely yours,
Irving Babbitt.

THE NATION, 20 Vesey Street (P.O. Box 794)
New York
June 25, 1913

My dear Babbitt,

There is no pressing need to have your decision in regard to Diderot, but I ought to know at least by the first of August. – I rather envy you the quiet seclusion of your library, and the pleasure of bringing order out of confusion. But can't you get away long enough to visit us at Essex sometime in July while I am there? I go up next Tuesday. Darrah and Net would be delighted if you could bring Esther with you, and so should I. Dr. Houghton[115] says it is an easy trip from Dublin to Essex, and he too wants very much to see you. – I have in mind a scheme upon which I should like your judgment, and possibly your coöperation. This is nothing less than a series of open letters in

---

109. More received an honorary degree of Doctor of Laws from his alma mater Washington University in St. Louis on June 12, 1913, when he delivered the commencement address there. See Dakin 1960: 142.

110. Foerster 1913.

111. See Clarke 1913. This review, although partially faultfinding, is not as negative as Babbitt's comment here suggests.

112. See Blondheim 1913, a review far more complimentary overall than Babbitt insinuates.

113. *The Masters of Modern French Criticism* (Babbitt 1912e).

114. According to Dakin (1960: 143), the Mores and various visitors vacationed at Essex, New York, in July of this year.

115. Silas Arnold Houghton (1864–1916) was a physician in the Boston area friendly with both More and Babbitt.

the *Nation* addressed to President Lowell.[116] They would be a kind of middle articles, signed probably with a fictitious name, and dealing with education in general and Harvard in particular. I can see how such a series of letters might make a hit if I could get just the right man to coöperate. Secrecy of authorship would be essential. – I am sorry your book is not going off as well as it should. I saw the very shallow notice in the *Yale Review*, but not the one in the *Mod. Lang. Notes*.[117] As for England, it will take them ten years to become acquainted with you, then, having discovered you really are somebody, they will stick to you loyally for the rest of your life. Your own pupils, I suspect, think there is no need of coming out for you. I am not sure, too, but the very quality of your last book—what Mather calls its "charm"—militates against it in some quarters. Caught by that, such a fellow as your critic in the *Yale Review* only half sees the solid ground of austere thought below the surface, and is a little offended by what he does see. We both suffer a good deal from being at once literary and philosophical, and shall have to make our own audience. I think this is beginning to form—modestly enough as yet. But such little things as this are significant: the other day I received from a girl in Rochester a paper on English Metric which she wished me to read at least, if not to publish. She remarked in her letter that you and I were the only scholars in the country whose opinion she cared for. She may have been one of your Radcliffe students; but I suspect from the fact that she regarded you as particularly interested in metrics that her knowledge of you was from your books and of a more general character. However, time will answer all these things.

Sincerely,
Paul E. More.

THE NATION
Publication Office
20 Vesey Street
New York City
August 7, 1913

Dear Babbitt,

September 11th we have our autumn educational number. I have not so far planned for any signed article for that issue and I should like very well

---

116. On the legal scholar and political scientist A. Lawrence Lowell, then the president of Harvard University, see his entry in the Biographical Register.

117. On these reviews of Babbitt's *The Masters of Modern French Criticism*, see above.

to have something from you. Such a paper might be on any theme you have in mind and be quite short, two or three thousand words.¹¹⁸ Indeed it would have to be short, as I am planning to have a very long leading review on the Kittredge centenary volume.¹¹⁹ Perhaps you might be able to knock something together on the present French situation suggested by the book you spoke to me about. At any rate, please let me have an immediate reply, yes or no. I would much rather have this article than the Diderot, although I could very well carry both. As for the date, and subject of the Diderot, if you take it up, I am quite willing to leave this to your judgment; but whether you decide to take in the celebration or not, in either case we ought to have the article well in hand for the necessary date.¹²⁰

Very truly yours,
Paul E. More.

THE NATION, 20 Vesey Street (P.O. Box 794)
New York
August 11, 1913

My dear Babbitt,

The motto from Lowell is: "Before we have an American literature, we must have an American criticism."¹²¹ – I am glad to hear the Diderot is under way. Certainly one of two things ought to be done. We ought either to deal with the celebration in Paris (if there is to be one of any importance) or with the man without reference to the celebration. In the former case it would be necessary to wait until the French papers reach this country and to base the article on them, printing as speedily as possible. This, I fancy, you would not care to do. In the other case we must print our article immediately before or after the date of his birth, October 2 or 9.¹²² – My reviews from England have

---

118. Babbitt's brief unsigned review of William F. Giese's *Graded French Method* (Babbitt 1913e) appeared in the September 11, 1913, issue of the *Nation*.
119. See Sherman 1913. Although unsigned, the piece's later appearance in the posthumous collection *Shaping Men and Women* (Sherman 1928: 65-86) attests that it was the work of Sherman. Although not without criticisms, Sherman's article offers a rosier impression of George Lyman Kittredge than Babbitt would have supplied, since Babbitt deemed Kittredge the chief figure in Harvard's so-called Philological Syndicate.
120. On the bicentenary of Diderot, see above.
121. This quotation from James Russell Lowell serves as the epigraph on the title page of the first series of *Shelburne Essays* (More 1904: no pagination).
122. Babbitt's article on the bicentenary (Babbitt 1913a) appeared in the October 9, 1913,

been rather mixed and not very numerous. The *Athenaeum*[123] dealt with the book at length and very flatteringly although the writer fundamentally disagreed with my notion of romanticism. The *Times*[124] (the first time they have noticed me at all) was brief and rather colorless. The *News*[125] praised strongly and unreservedly. On the whole one feels as if one were straining one's lungs to be heard by a small audience sitting at the back of a great half-lighted hall. It is not very encouraging. There has been some recognition in this country; and the coupling of our names as engaged in the same campaign is a good sign—but the audience is very small and the hall very large!

Sincerely,
Paul E. More.

THE NATION, 20 Vesey Street (P.O. Box 794)
New York
August 29, 1913

My dear Babbitt,

My usual French reviewers are not within reach, and I wish very much to have some notice of Giese's book in our educational issue of September 11. I am accordingly sending the volume to you by post. Take an hour or two and let me have a note of some three or four hundred words, for friendship's sake—Giese's and mine. Copy must be in hand by September 5th if you care to see proof.[126] – You will be grieved, but scarcely surprised, to hear that I have at last resigned from the *Nation*.[127] My reasons are numerous. First of all it begins to grow only too clear that I can't carry the double work of editor and scholar, and, to me at least, the latter work is much the more important. Then there are changes coming in the office (*this second cause entre nous*) which will soon make it impossible for me to stand up against the current. I regret this, and I look forward to the career of the *Nation* with

---

issue of the *Nation*.

123. Anon. 1913a.

124. More may in fact refer to a short review in the *New York Times* (anon. 1913c), although this is obviously not an English newspaper. Dakin's list of reviews of More's *The Drift of Romanticism* (Dakin 1950: 188) does not include any from the *Times* of London or other English sources.

125. Anon. 1913b.

126. See Babbitt 1913e.

127. Dakin (1960: 144) notes that More informed his sister Alice about his resignation from the *Nation* on August 17, 1913.

considerable anxiety, but I feel perfectly sure that I have followed the right course. Fortunately I have been able to make the break without any ill feeling,[128] and am going to stay on until the staff is rearranged, probably through the winter.[129] I am not trying to keep my resignation secret. Fuller has an offer from Bryn Mawr, but not a good one, and is uncertain what to do. Villard[130] has told him flatly that he will not make him editor of the *Nation* when I leave.[131] Of Fuller's position you had better say nothing until his plans are settled. – With kind regards to Dora.

Sincerely,
Paul E. More.

THE NATION, 20 Vesey Street (P.O. Box 794)
New York
September 10, 1913.

My dear Babbitt,

Thank you for continuing your good work in regard to "The Drift."[132] I shall see that a copy of the book gets into the hand of Cestre, and may he deal mercifully with it. As for the Diderot, if it is to be printed October 9th (and that, or October 2nd, is the necessary date), I ought to have copy by the 1st or 2nd, so as to enable you to read the proof. – I am interested to know how the article on Kittredge[133] strikes you. We are keeping the authorship secret, but I suspect it will be guessed without difficulty. The portrait is a masterly

---

128. More's discussion of his resignation is interesting, in part because he does not mention the sizeable inheritance his wife received in early 1911 from her aunt (Dakin 1960: 113-14), which made the move financially feasible. (One presumes, however, that Babbitt and More would have discussed this topic when they saw one another in person, and thus More did not have to mention it in this letter.) More also does not directly discuss the political acrimony that encouraged his departure (see Dakin 1960: 145-46; cf. Mather 1938: 370, who calls the departure "stormy"), although Babbitt may have been aware of this already as well.

129. More had agreed to stay on as long as it was necessary to reorganize the staff, ultimately departing from the job on March 15, 1914 (see Dakin 1950: 7 and 1960: 144-46; and below). He would remain on the masthead of the *Nation* as an "advisory editor" from 1914 to 1917 (Dakin 1950: 7).

130. The journalist and editor Oswald Garrison Villard (1872–1949), as president of the New York Evening Post Company, was More's boss at the *Nation* and then an outspoken liberal who clashed with More politically (see Dakin 1960: 145-46).

131. Dakin (1960: 146) notes that as of January 23, 1914, Villard would make Harold de Wulf Fuller, More's colleague and friend, the acting editor of the *Nation* upon More's departure.

132. More 1967a.

133. Sherman 1913.

piece of writing, and if it doesn't stir things up at Harvard, then that place is defunct. The article does not, to be sure, hit the actually present conditions with entire accuracy, but it is close enough to be efficient. I think I have fulfilled my vow to get a knife into Kittredge's ribs before quitting. – As for quitting, nothing new has occurred. I shall probably go on with the work through the winter, and there is of course the barest possibility that some change may be made so that I may act as editor and do half work. But this is only a possibility. Fuller has not yet written his intentions in regard to Bryn Mawr, but Villard tells me he has written to him to let us have his decision. If Fuller leaves, have you in sight any-one you could recommend strongly for his place? As for myself, I have no definite plans for my life if I quit, or rather, when I quit. Only one thing is sure, I am not going to retire into any ivory tower. If a suitable college position is offered me which is not exacting, I shall probably take it. On the whole I should be happier, I think, and work as well, if not better, with some regular occupation which took part of my time. But I have made so many enemies here and there through the *Nation* that my prospects for such an offer are not very bright. – With kind regards to Dora.

Sincerely,
Paul E. More.

Dublin, N. H.
19 September, 1913

Dear More,

Taken purely from the literary point of view Sherman's paper on Kittredge[134] strikes me as capital. It should flutter the philological dovecotes. In its statement of facts and its line of argument, it seems to me that it might have been strengthened in places. I was quite prepared for the reply you printed this week.[135] I do not doubt that scores of Kittredge's pupils would testify that they have derived from him a love of literature. In fact about all the philologists I have ever known are certain they have a "love of literature" (this is also the pet phrase of the dilettante) and almost uniformly speak with awe of the literary sense of their philological colleagues. The true point at issue is not whether a man has a love of literature but whether he believes that

---

134. Sherman 1913.
135. See Stork 1913, a letter to the editor critical of Sherman 1913 for suggesting that Kittredge's pupils do not learn to love good literature in his courses.

there are any standards or discipline in life apart from the discipline of the scientific fact. If the basis of a sound humanistic *discipline* is once established the "love" will take care of itself. Furthermore Kittredge is a clever opportunist and saw the present danger coming years ago. Neilson was put in to handle the modern end and under his guidance the majority of the doctor's theses for years past have been in the modern field. I shall be surprised if you do not hear from some one of the Kittredge crowd on this subject.

I am planning to return to Cambridge tomorrow. The family follows early next week. I will see that you get the Diderot on or before Oct. 2. I hope you will let me go to the limit on space. I have a hard problem of condensation to bring so large and intricate a subject within these bounds at all. – I am greatly interested in seeing how the *Nation* situation works out and hope devoutly that you may be able to remain on part work. I do not think of any one for the moment whom I should be willing to recommend as Fuller's[136] successor. With kind regards to Mrs. More,

Sincerely yours,
Irving Babbitt.

THE NATION, 20 Vesey Street (P.O. Box 794)
New York
September 22, 1913.

My dear Babbitt,

What you say in regard to the situation at Harvard is true, no doubt, but I rather suspect that our article took the most direct and effective method of getting a knife into Kittredge and the English department. The writer's argument will be understood by everybody, and meet with wide assent, although a few of course will object—have already objected in letters. He did not follow out my request in one point. I suggested that it would be well to dwell on the result of mediaeval pedantry in fostering romanticism and dilettantism. If there had been time I should have sent the MS. back for revision in this matter, and in this way the present situation at Harvard would have been hit more squarely. I suspect however that the person who will be most cut by the article will be Neilson.[137] – It is good to hear that your Diderot is coming. Give me time to get proof to you, for I do not like to print such articles without the author's revision. As for length I must ask

---

136. Babbitt means Harold de Wulf Fuller. On this subject, see above.
137. On the Harvard professor of English William Allan Neilson, see above, chapter 2.

you to keep within the 4500 words. This is annoying but necessary. I had under this rule to cut out a large mass of stuff from the Kittredge paper all of which was as good as that which I printed. And in the case of a subject like Diderot, foreign and somewhat remote, I am positive that we ought not to print two successive articles. There is only one thing to do—select the principal theme and save the other subsidiary themes for the essay when you reprint in book form. This can be done, though it is painful. – I fear, if we are to meet this winter, you will have to come to New York; for I begin to feel that Cambridge is planted with enemies and that I may be insulted at any turn. But my enemies are not confined to Cambridge. You have made some for me in Princeton, and other dear friends have taken care of my reputation in other parts of the world—not to mention my own ability to say disagreeable things. The *Nation* is a siege perillous [sic]. Fuller by the way has thrown over his offer from Bryn Mawr and will stay here—hoping still, I suspect to occupy that same perillous [sic] seat. – With kind regards to Dora,

Sincerely,
Paul E. More.

THE NATION, 20 Vesey Street (P.O. Box 794)
New York
December 3, 1913.

My dear Babbitt,

I am in something of a maelstrom having the holiday issues of the *Nation* on my hands, but I must take time to ask you whether you are not coming to New York for part of the Christmas holidays. We shall be much disappointed if we do not see you. Let me know as soon as possible if you can come, so that we may reserve the guest room for you. No one else has proposed to visit us as yet, but some one may at any time.

My *Norton*[138] goes into the *Nation* this week. It was a hard thing to write and required constant balancing of judgment. If it seems to you in any way askew, let me know, so that I may make alterations for possible republication in a future volume.

Cordially yours,
Paul E. More.

---

138. More's article "Charles Eliot Norton" (More 1913), based on Norton's then recently published letters, later appeared in the eleventh series of *Shelburne Essays* (More 1967c: 97-113).

8 December, 1913

Dear More,

I am very much tempted by your invitation for the holidays though I should prefer to hold back my final decision for a few days longer. If I came I should probably reach New York on Thursday afternoon, Jan. 1, and leave the following Sunday morning. Would this suit you? I hope that we may see you in Cambridge later in the year. I see that you are on the Committee for visiting the graduate school and you should come up and visit some of Kittredge's graduate courses![139] That article of Sherman's[140] caused a good deal of stir here on the inside. Emerton and others have told me that I was suspected of having written it or at least of having had a hand in it. I have heard the suggestion that Kittredge might not be seriously offended. We are living in an age that cares very little for principles and a great deal for personal power and from this latter point of view the article is distinctly flattering.

You seem to me to have said the essential things in your paper on Norton[141] and though I have heard very little about it as yet, it will I imagine, meet with general approval. I am not quite sure about the structure of the article. The biographical details coming in where they do may give to some the impression of making a second start when you are already nearing the end. I remember that in the old days I rated Norton distinctly higher than you and that we used to argue on this point. I should suggest rather now that when you reprint you should hint a little more as to the limitations of his mind on the philosophical side—limitations somewhat similar to those of Leslie Stephen. I also think it would be well to quote more of his admirable commentary on Ruskin.

Cross[142] found my review of your "Drift"[143] too long and has cut out the middle third of it—all my comment on the Newman, the Fiona Macleod and most of the Nietzsche. He is planning I believe to print what is left in his December issue.

Give my kind regards to Mrs. More.

Sincerely yours,
Irving Babbitt.

---

139. Dakin (1960: 148 n. 1) notes that around March 20, 1914, More was in Cambridge to attend an advisory committee for the Harvard Graduate School. See below.
140. Sherman 1913.
141. More 1913.
142. A footnote in the typescript of this letter reads: "Wilbur L. Cross, editor of *The Yale Review*."
143. Babbitt 1913f.

Cambridge, Mass.
11 January, 1914

Dear More,

I had a prosperous homeward journey except that I had to chase my hat most of the way from your door to the entrance of the subway.[144] – It was not only a pleasure to see you and Mrs. More but I was glad to get certain information about your plans as well as a total feeling for the present situation that can only come through conversation. What you said about your work in Greek[145] interested me greatly as bearing upon the possibility of your taking a position here. I proceeded at once to take up the matter with Smyth.[146] I found, as I had supposed, that he is a genuine friend and admirer of yours. He expressed the opinion that you are the first essayist in the country, and warmly favored making an opening for you here if it is in any way possible. I also found E. K. Rand[147] favorable. I then took the matter to C. H. Moore,[148] the present head of the classics department, and learned from him the following facts which you are of course to regard as strictly confidential: they have a small sum of money available for the immediate future which they were planning to employ in calling here some person from the outside. The first offer is to go to Maurice Croiset[149] of the Sorbonne and if he refuses, as he probably will, the offer will be made next to Paul Shorey (now in Berlin). If both these men refuse, Moore, like Smyth and Rand, though less warmly I suspect, is in favor of you. What I suggested to Moore was that they offer you a lectureship in Greek, to run for three years, to involve not more than three or four hours a week, and to carry a salary of not less than $1,500.00. Moore thought that the Department would know where it stands by the middle of February. If the way is then open for you, the best plan, Moore

---

144. Obviously, Babbitt did visit More in New York City during the winter holiday season.

145. According to Duggan (1966: 89), More began to work on his book *Platonism* (More 1917b) soon after resigning from the *Nation*.

146. Herbert Weir Smyth (1857–1937) was a prominent scholar of ancient Greek literature then on the faculty at Harvard. Since he had overlapped with More in the classics department at Bryn Mawr, Smyth must have known More well. See Ward W. Briggs Jr.'s, entry on Smyth in the *Database of Classical Scholars*: dbcs.rutgers.edu.

147. Edward Kennard Rand (1871–1945) was a member of the Harvard classics department. He briefly discussed the New Humanism in an article on Cicero's *humanitas*, in which he referred to both Babbitt and More as his "friends" (Rand 1932: 207). On Rand, see Joseph Berrigan's entry on him in the *Database of Classical Scholars*: dbcs.rutgers.edu.

148. Clifford Herschel Moore (1866–1931) was a Greek and Latin philologist with particular interest in Roman religion. He would later provide a positive review of More's *Platonism* (see Moore 1919). For more biographical information, see Ward W. Briggs Jr.'s, entry on Moore in the *Database of Classical Scholars*: dbcs.rutgers.edu.

149. Maurice Croiset (1846–1935) was a French scholar of Greek literature.

and I both agreed, would be for you to make me a visit (I hope that you will do this in any case) and talk over things with Smyth and if you came to an understanding, we could then take the matter to the President. I hope that you will not buy a house at Princeton until you know how things are going to turn out here. The classical people have made fools of themselves once in your case and may do so again. Still, though I am not extremely sanguine, I see signs of a change of heart. The chief opposition is likely to come from Albert Howard.[150] I do not know what he and his intimate, Kittredge, will be able to accomplish. The only other serious obstacle may be lack of funds.

Give my kind regards to Mrs. More. I have the very pleasantest memories of her hospitality. I hope that Alice[151] is entirely back to her usual form.

Sincerely yours,
Irving Babbitt.

Cambridge
18 January, 1914

Dear More,

You will find a short notice of *The Drift of Romanticism* in the Dec. issue of the *Zeitschrift für Philosophie*[152] by James Lindsay, a professor of philosophy, I believe, at the Un. of St. Andrew.[153] The review is the most important of its kind in Germany, and perhaps in the world. Lindsay bestows warm praise on several of the essays especially the *Pater* and *Huxley* (which he deems the best treatment that has yet appeared), but he balks at the Definitions. They seem bloodless to him and an anti-climax after the vital criticism of the previous chapters! He has a notice of my "Masters"

---

150. Albert Howard (1858–1925) was a Latin philologist at Harvard. His scholarly interests (he wrote a dissertation on a minute linguistic topic and is most famous for his co-written *index verborum* for Suetonius) likely helped suggest to Babbitt his comparative hostility to the appointment of More. See William M. Calder III's entry on Howard in the *Database of Classical Scholars*: dbcs.rutgers.edu.

151. Presumably, Babbitt means More's older sister Alice (and not his daughter of the same name), who was often in ill health.

152. Lindsay 1913a. Dakin (1950: 188) does not include this review among his list of those devoted to *The Drift of Romanticism*.

153. Rev. James Lindsay (1852–1923) was a Scottish theologian and philosopher. On his life, see Lindsay 1924.

in the same issue—eulogistic but as it seems to me, very uninforming.[154] He fails to tell what either your book or mine is about and has no inkling apparently of their unity of spirit.

It has occurred to me that if you make a study of Platonism and wished to lecture here at Harvard, your material might be as suitable for the philosophical department as for the department of the classics. The classical people lack funds and Lowell I am told is very disinclined to increase the classical staff with the present diminution in students. The situation in the Dept. of Philosophy is very different. I may talk over the situation with Royce[155] one of these days. I should of course make perfectly clear as I have already done with the classical people that the initiative comes entirely from me and that you are not soliciting anything. You will therefore lose no "face" whatever happens.

Sincerely,
I. Babbitt.

P.S. – I am going to give Baldensperger[156] (exchange professor from the Sorbonne) a card for you. He will be in New York (probably with his wife) about Thursday of this week. Both he and his wife talk English and are worth meeting. He has been reading your "Drift" at my suggestion and being as he is a prolific reviewer will, I hope, help to make your work known in France.

I. B.

THE NATION, 20 Vesey Street (P.O. Box 794)
New York
January 22, 1914.

My dear Babbitt,

I much fear my admission to the Harvard philosophical department will depend neither on your efficient good-will nor on my readiness to accept. I have a feeling that Royce would not take the proposal seriously, as I have

---

154. Lindsay 1913b.
155. On Josiah Royce, a member of Harvard's philosophy department, see his entry in the Biographical Register.
156. Fernand Baldensperger (1871–1958), a scholar of comparative literature.

never identified myself in any way with the philosophical grinders. It seems to me that I am better fitted for a classical department,—but Barkis is willing!

At any rate I appreciate your zeal most thoroughly.

Net and the children are still at Lakewood, recuperating after the dissipations of Christmas, and I am like a monk in the house—although the other night I did have a wild debauchery with cards and whisky with some roaring boys.[157]

I shall look up the review in the *Zeitschrift* the first time I am at one of the large libraries.

Sincerely,
Paul E. More.

THE NATION, 20 Vesey Street (P.O. Box 794)
New York
January 23, 1914.

My dear Babbitt,

You will be interested to hear that the *Nation* affair is settled at last. On March 15 I am to turn over the authoritative blue pencil to Fuller, who is to have a chance to show what he can do. This is a bit sudden, but the design is to give Fuller an opportunity to display his hand before the dead Summer months. I am to have my name continued as "Advisory Editor." There is nothing to conceal in all this, except of course that Fuller is only on trial. He will appear to the world as full editor. He told me today that he had from Ayres[158] that they were working to get me into Columbia; but no one has approached me in the matter and I do not expect anything to happen. I suspect it would be hard to get through the (presumable) opposition of Matthews[159] and Brewster.[160] Do not, of course, say anything about this Columbia matter.

Sincerely,
Paul E. More.

---

157. On More's nights of cards and whisky, see, e.g., Dakin 1960: 125.

158. Presumably, More is referring to Harry Morgan Ayres (1881–1948), a professor of English at Columbia University.

159. More likely means Brander Matthews (1852–1929), a professor of literature at Columbia University with a focus on theater.

160. Presumably, More refers to William T. Brewster (1869–1961), a professor of English literature at Columbia University.

THE NATION, 20 Vesey Street (P.O. Box 794)
New York
February 24, 1914.

My dear Babbitt,

I have no wish to hurry or embarrass you, but if any thing definite, one way or the other, has taken place in Cambridge, please let me know. I ought of course to be proceeding with the negotiation for the Princeton house,[161] unless you feel there is sufficient reason for me to hold off. At any rate just drop me a line to advise me how things stand. I have felt that your effort to get me into Harvard was a desperate undertaking but I have great confidence in your diplomatic talents as developed by experience, and naturally the thought of working with you is alluring.

Sincerely,
Paul E. More.

P.S. Your letters henceforth had better be addressed to 159 W 92nd Street.[162]

THE NATION, 20 Vesey Street (P.O. Box 794)
New York
March 4, 1914.

Dear Babbitt,

Thank you for your note with the news and invitation it contains. I am on the Committee on the Graduate School which is to meet at 4:30, Friday, March 20. Dr. Shattuck,[163] chairman of the Committee, has asked me to take dinner with him at the Harvard Union after the meeting. Now the question is, would it be convenient to you and Dora if I came up to Cambridge Friday morning and stopped with you for two or three days, and would it be a good or ill thing for me to visit Cambridge while affairs are in their present state?

---

161. On the Mores' purchase of a house at 245 Nassau Street in Princeton, which was renovated prior to their move there, see Dakin 1960: 149.
162. More and his family had moved to this address on September 9, 1911 (see Dakin 1960: 115).
163. George Cheever Shattuck (1879–1972), a professor at the Harvard Medical School. On Shattuck, see Richardson 1972.

Please advise me frankly. And if you will reply immediately you will do me a service, for I must send my acceptance or regrets to Dr. Shattuck without delay.

Sincerely,
Paul E. More.

THE NATION, 20 Vesey Street (P.O. Box 794)
New York
March 6, 1914.

Dear Babbitt,

Thank you for your prompt and cordial response. Unless something happens to change my plans I shall leave here Friday morning, March 20, at 10 and reach Back Bay Station at 3:06. The meeting of the Committee is at 4:30, and I am to dine with the Committee that evening. I must I think return Sunday afternoon as I have a good deal of work on hand.

Sincerely,
Paul E. More.

P.S. I shall not write again unless my plans change.

---

159 West 92nd Street
New York, April 30, 1914

My dear Babbitt,

You will be interested to hear that we have signed the contract for the old house in Nassau Street, Princeton, and expect to have the title deeds in our hands the twelfth day of May. The Mathers[164] agree with us in thinking it an excellent purchase, and Net is filled with excitement over the alterations and improvements to be made. The grounds are lovely, about an acre and a half in extent, and you may some day see me playing tennis (!) in my own back garden. On the whole the move seems to me wise, although it cuts me off from what chance there may have been of putting my shoulder to yours in the μεγάλη μάχη[165] at Harvard. You have done shrewd work to get me there, but the gods evidently mean me to retire into my tower of ivory—but I

---

164. Frank Jewett Mather Jr., a good friend of Babbitt and More, was by now living in Princeton and teaching at the university there. See Dakin 1960: 114.
165. A footnote in the typescript of this letter reads: "Great battle."

expect to carry a gun or two with me into my retreat.[166] I am writing urgently now to get several tasks off my hands so as to be entirely free for the first volume of my Plato this summer. I have, in fact, already gone through several of the dialogues while smoking my after-breakfast pipe, and begin to see the outlines of the book—but only vaguely as yet. The revision of this work, with other engagements, will keep me well occupied next winter. – We shall begin alterations on the house as soon as possible, and shall probably come down from Essex to move in August, and then go back to Essex for the rest of the summer.[167] If we don't see you and Mrs. Babbitt in our Gasthaus sometime this vacation, we shall want to know the reason why.

Sincerely your friend,
Paul E. More.

P.S. If you have any criticisms to make on my articles in the January and April numbers of the *Unpopular*[168] I wish you would do so while the matter is fresh with you, so that I may be ready for revising for book form.

---

6 Kirkland Road
Cambridge
8 May, 1914

Dear More,

I do wish you could have given me a few days warning before taking the decisive step in regard to the Princeton house. The situation here is far from being hopeless, though Smyth who has had the matter in charge is naturally one of the slowest and ineffective of men. When I told him what you had done, he called a meeting to decide whether the matter should still be taken before the President. Present: Smyth, R. B. Perry,[169] Royce, Schofield, and myself. The sense of the meeting was that I should inquire of you whether

---

166. More would not begin to teach classes at Princeton for a few years.
167. On this subject, see Dakin 1960: 149.
168. More's essay "The New Morality" appeared in the January 1914 number of the *Unpopular Review* (see More 1914c) and later in the ninth series of *Shelburne Essays* (More 1915a: 193-217); his essay "Natural Aristocracy" was originally featured in the April 1914 issue of the journal (see More 1914a) and was also ultimately a part of the ninth series (More 1915a: 3-38). Dakin (1960: 151) notes: "For a few years after leaving *The Nation* More gave much attention to *The Unpopular Review* (by 1920 called *The Unpartizan Review*), which Henry Holt in his seventies financed and edited as an antidote to old age. Though, aside from being a regular contributor to it, he had at this time no official connection with the quarterly, he was virtually Holt's assistant editor."
169. Ralph Barton Perry (1876–1957), a professor of philosophy at Harvard.

your present action binds you irrevocably to Princeton. As a matter of fact I feel fairly sure of landing an offer for you here if I am given time. I probably could have done so this year if it were not for the present shortage of funds. The Dept. of Philosophy raised money on the outside in order to bring Hocking[170] here (a rather weak lecturer I fear). In the next year or so the financial situation will very likely change and, having got opinion prepared here in certain quarters, I can profit by some good opening. Let me know at once how you feel and if you hold out any encouragement Smyth will probably get his committee together and go to the President. Perhaps next year or the year after the offer might come to you in the form of a full professorship (with half work and half pay if you so desired). What I want is the authorization to work quietly for your interests as the opportunity offers itself. If you feel that the die is cast once and for all, you must say so. Unless you have made a bad bargain it should not be impossible to sell or rent the Princeton house.

I have not yet seen the last number of the *Unpopular*. I will read and report on your article.[171] I do not remember any suggestion on your article[172] in the first number of the *Unpopular* but will go over it again. I am going to be very much rushed between now and the middle of June when I leave for California.[173] I am already beginning to regret that I ever accepted that offer. With kind regards to Mrs. More.

Sincerely yours,
Irving Babbitt.

---

159 West 92nd Street,
New York, May 9, 1914.

Dear Babbitt,

I was convinced from the long pause that there was no longer any chance of an opening at Harvard this year, and, as there was some apprehension of losing the Princeton house, we acted. I have just heard however that the Insurance Company that is investigating the title deeds has found some difficulty, and we shall not get possession until May 19. Meanwhile we have

---

170. The American philosopher William Ernest Hocking (1873–1966), who left Yale for a job at Harvard in 1914.
171. More 1914a.
172. More 1914c.
173. According to an article in the *Sacramento Union* (anon. 1914a), Babbitt was to lecture on literature at the University of California at Berkeley as part of a summer school program there, which would run from June 22 to August 1, 1914.

paid an earnest of $1000 which will of course come back to us if the title is defective, but which we should forfeit if we threw up the purchase for any other reason. It looks as if, for the present at least, we were fixed in Princeton; for it is not likely that the difficulties now holding us up are insurmountable. The future is never fixed in this mutable world; but if we once get settled, it will naturally take a good deal to move us. When I talked with Royce in your library, he gave me to understand that the most feasible thing would be for me to give a series of lectures some semester as a visitor. Now I am pushing my work hard these weeks so as to get all my engagements off my hands by summer. This I believe I told you. I ought by next January to have the MS. of my volume on Plato[174] in pretty good shape, and it would be an excellent thing for me to give the matter as lectures at Harvard. This is a suggestion which may possibly be fruitful under the present circumstances, but I do not wish to embarrass you in any way. You have been so generous in your efforts to get me to Cambridge, that I feel almost like a deserter. But we really had to come to some decision about our home next year, and Princeton, as a place of residence, has many attractions. Mather seems to think that in time I shall drift into some lectureship there; but I am not calculating on that.

With kind regards to Dora,

Sincerely your friend,
Paul E. More.[175]

Cambridge, Mass.
8 June, 1914

Dear More,

I let Smyth have your letter regarding the Princeton house, having first struck out at the end the sentence in which you speak of your authorship of the editorial in the *Nation*.[176] The notes I enclose from Smyth and Royce may be of interest to you. Smyth has been curiously inefficient in this whole matter, though I have no reason to doubt the genuineness of his desire to see you here. Smyth is to spend next year abroad and will leave Cambridge in about a week. I am going to put your case in the hands of C. H. Moore. I am

---

174. More 1917b.
175. More's original letter included two handwritten lines of text, which Babbitt crossed out and rendered illegible. On Babbitt's decision to do so, see the next letter, below.
176. On Babbitt's crossing out of this sentence, see More's letter above. It is not clear to which editorial Babbitt here refers, though below he mentions More's anonymous attack in the *Nation* on the pedantry of medieval philologists (More 1914d). For bibliographical references to some of More's writings from around the relevant time, see Dakin 1950: 153-55.

not sure that he is so friendly to you, but at bottom he is a far more effective person. There are numerous complications here mainly due to the fact that you have been an editor, but if I have time I think I can overcome them. I should judge from what Mrs. More said to Dora that the Princeton title is far from clear and if this transaction falls through in consequence, you will of course inform me immediately.

When are you leaving New York for the summer? I am planning to start for California about June 16, and I might possibly arrange to stop with you in New York Tuesday afternoon and night and leave for Chicago about eleven on Wednesday morning. Please inform me on this point at once, as I must make my final arrangements by Wednesday or Thursday of this week at the latest. I am not sure yet that I shall be able to go by way of New York even if you are able to receive me.

Your editorial[177] in the *Nation* struck me as a good blow for the cause. The mediaevalists, I imagine, are beginning to feel that they are the victims of a persecution. I also read with much satisfaction your paper on a *Naughty Decade*.[178] The comment I have heard here has all been favorable. I have not been able as yet to get hold of a copy of the last *Unpopular*.[179] You are truly a most scribatious individual! Look up a very amusing skit at the end of the June *Atlantic* entitled *The Graduate's Choice*.[180] The author is a student of mine named Paul, a rich Baltimore youth who is planning to enter the diplomatic service. His verses render very well the bewildering effect on the student mind of the rival classic and romantic preaching to be heard here. With kind regards to Mrs. More.

Sincerely yours,
Irving Babbitt.

New York
June 9, 1914

My dear Babbitt,

First of all let me assure you that we shall both be glad to have you stop over with us the sixteenth. We shall certainly not get away by that date, and

---

177. More 1914d (which, although anonymous, Dakin 1950: 155 notes as More's work).
178. More 1914b. A later version of this piece appeared under the title "Decadent Wit" in the tenth series of *Shelburne Essays* (More 1967b: 279-304).
179. To which More contributed an article: see More 1914a.
180. Anon. 1914b.

may well enough be kept in New York considerably later. Our movements depend on the Princeton business, and that does not move at all. Mather was in town the other day and told me by telephone that as the matter came to his ears the only difficulty was in getting a quit-claim to the property from some one at a distance, and that this difficulty meant only time. I hope he was right. We telephoned this morning to our lawyer asking him to write again to the lawyer in Trenton and inquire how the affair was progressing. We may hear something in three or four days, and you shall be informed as soon as anything definite is known.

Thank you for the letters of Smyth and Royce. It would at least be a pleasant and profitable experience if I could give a course at Harvard the second half of next year, although of course my own plans and necessities might make this impossible. – Net tells me she is writing or has invited Dora to visit us at Essex this summer, and I hope you will be able to come at the same time or another time. – With sincere expectations that I may see you here next Tuesday, I am

Faithfully yours,
Paul E. More.

Crater Club
Essex, N. Y.
August 31, 1914

Dear Babbitt,

It is a misfortune to me that you cannot get here this summer, and I must add to the evil by saying that I shall not be able to visit you. On Wednesday Net goes down to New York on a flying trip and I meanwhile must be here to have an eye on the children. Visitors are coming after that, and then on the 16th we both go down to move, and shall not return. My time, in other words, is going to be so much broken up for the rest of the season that I cannot make any further engagement. Unfortunately too, as is the way with human plans, I have accomplished only a small part of what I had proposed to myself in Plato–διανεῦσαι τοιοῦτόν τε καὶ τοσοῦτον πέλαγος λόγων.[181] I am stuck now in the middle of the *Laws*, stuck and bewildered. How did so great a master of language come to write so barbarous and confused a

---

181. A footnote in the typescript of this letter reads: "To swim through such a fearful ocean of words. Plato, *Parm.* 137A."

style? I suspect that the text, which, owing to its comparative lack of interest, has received little attention, is in a state of sad corruption and that probably also it is the author's rough draft, never having been revised. Most of the discussion is tediously unrewarding; yet, on the other hand, parts of the first books that deal with education by means of ἡδονή and λύπη[182] are among the mellowest and ripest things Plato ever wrote. I have plotted my book[183] all out, and think what I have to say is worth-while; but the end is a long way off. – Your trip to the West must have been a pleasant success, notwithstanding the cruel cut it made in your time. What a strange comment is this war[184] on all our talk of peace! And no man can tell what the political and ethical upshot is to be; but I have little hope of wisdom accruing. The Humanitarians will return to their Vomit, crying out, as you say, "Conspiracy!" It looks almost as if Plato were right, and ὁ θεὸς εἰς τὴν ἑαυτοῦ περιωπὴν ἀπέστη[185]—a good phrase for you, by the way, to vary your "tower of ivory." I sit in my little study among the trees in a profound peace, thinking of things very ancient and withdrawn, and cannot realize in my imagination what is actually taking place in the present. Yet I presume that hidden under the quiet-seeming growth of these trees and grasses the same spirit of strife and envy is at work. I used to wonder why the prohibition of covetousness should have been placed among the Ten Commandments, but I have come to understand that in that passion lies the root of all evil. It is only the Greek πλεονεξία.[186] – But I am monotonously full of Greek, as you see, and my writing is not εἰς συναγυρμὸν φρονήσεως.[187] – With best regards to Dora, and hopes that we may see you both in Princeton this winter,

Sincerely,
Paul E. More.

---

182. A footnote in the typescript of this letter reads: "Pleasure and pain. Cf. *Laws* I, 644C."
183. More 1917b.
184. World War I, which commenced on July 28, 1914.
185. A footnote in the typescript of this letter reads: "God withdrew to his place of outlook. Plato, *Politikos*, 272E."
186. A footnote in the typescript of this letter reads: "Greediness (covetousness)."
187. A footnote in the typescript of this letter reads: "For collecting wisdom. Plato, *Politikos*, 272C."

CHAPTER FIVE
1915–1916

245 Nassau Street
Princeton, January 6, 1915.

My dear Babbitt,

It is very hard to write to a man who persists in maintaining himself as a bodiless idea and refuses to be materialized, and really this Platonic sort of pleasure is about all you allow me to get out of you—and you a stark anti-Platonist. Are you aware of the fact that I have not had a word from you since midsummer? Dora wrote that you had an engagement at Vassar the 22nd of this month, which might permit you to visit us, and then later she wrote that you thought you couldn't come—and there we are. I most earnestly hope we shall see you some time this winter, and the sooner the better. I know your Parthian trick (it is nothing but cursed Yankeeism) will be to ask me when I am coming to Cambridge. Well, though I may seem to be a man of infinite leisure, as a matter of fact I have never been more beaten about and harassed than these last three months. Moving and settling turned out to be something worse than the labors of Hercules; he never underwent any such ordeal as living in a house for weeks, with all sorts of workmen making messes about him faster than he could clear them away. Then my sister Alice was taken down very ill, so that I had to make frequent trips to Bridgeton[1] and to the Philadelphia hospital where I carried her. She is out of danger now, and gaining strength daily. With all this I had several pieces of writing on hand. You can see how much leisure I have had; and I have work ahead that will keep me busy until spring. My last piece was a chapter on Jonathan Edwards for the *Cambridge Hist. of Am. Lit.*[2] One thing I did was a long review of Burnet's Greek Philosophy, which appeared in the *Nation* of last week.[3] Withal I have gone over a considerable part of Plato again since my

---

1. More's sister had been residing at a house in Bridgeton, New Jersey, where she had lived with their mother, until More's mother passed away on April 10, 1914. See Dakin 1960: 148-49.
2. This piece would not appear in print until 1917. See More 1917a. It was later featured as "Jonathan Edwards" in the eleventh series of *Shelburne Essays* (More 1967c: 35-65).
3. More 1914e.

summer reading. Some time this winter I am going to lock out six or seven weeks for working on my Plato,[4] and nothing else.

What are you doing, besides existing pertinaciously in my mind as an Idea? Come and tell me. I think you will find Princeton agreeable and mildly profitable for a few days.

We of the house are well, except that Net seems rather jaded. She is going down to Bridgeton for a few days' rest. My own health has been very noticeably more robust than for many years.

With greetings of peace to Dora I am

Faithfully yours,
Paul E. More.

Cambridge
18 January, 1915

Dear More,

Your letter was very welcome and in view of my own long silence better than I deserved. I have had nothing very cheerful to write during the past two or three months. Early in November I came down with an attack of facial paralysis and had to knock off lectures for about a month. I am now about back to normal but the experience has been a depressing one. Mr. Hurd, I understand from the Houghtons, came down with a similar seizure. The doctors say that the trouble in my case came from the teeth and had nothing to do with my general health. My own theory is that it was the result of talking too much. I have been going a rather hot pace from this point of view at Harvard for the past year or two with the Un. of California thrown in for good measure.

I find that lectures go on here until a week from this coming Wednesday and so I shall be forced to be back here from my trip to Vassar next Monday. That will leave me very little time to see you at Princeton and I have been wondering whether it is wise to attempt the trip at all at this time. I can however reach Princeton at 1:06 on Saturday Jan. 23 and remain there until about Sunday morning. (I should need to connect, by automobile, I presume, with the 11:30 train at Princeton junction.) What do you think of this scheme? Unless I hear from you to the contrary I am inclined to put it through. We

---

4. More 1917b.

have just had a welcome but only too brief glimpse of Mather. My wife joins me in kind regards to you and Mrs. More. She is very eager to visit you but I have told her that it would have to be *pour la prochaine fois*.

Sincerely,
Irving Babbitt.

---

245 Nassau Street
January 28, 1915.

My dear Babbitt,

We were disappointed in not seeing you last Saturday, but if this really means that we shall have a more leisurely visit from you at the time of the Easter recess, all is for the better. I am sorry to hear about your facial trouble, not that I hesitate to believe what the doctors say about its comparatively innocent cause, but these things are all hints and warnings of the terrible brittleness of health and life. I seem for months to have heard of nothing but calamities and threatenings. Withal my own health is much better than it has been for years, and from this point of view at least my retiring from the *Nation* has been proved wise. Fuller and Went[5] by the way are keeping a firm grip on that periodical, though they have made it somewhat less literary than it was in my hands. They are working very hard and are ambitious.

I have boasted of my health, but as a matter of fact I am at the present moment in anything but fit condition. Four dinners last week, besides one night at the Century until two in the morning, and two dinners this week, have thrown my physical and moral machinery out of kilter, and played havoc with an essay on Henry Holt's[6] book which I am finishing for the *Harvard Theological Review*.[7] I have promised to close it up by Sunday, and meanwhile I have to discover and define the difference between the Cosmic Soul and God!—rather between the *Poltergeist* and Apollo. These dinners are an illustration of the hospitality and good cheer of Princeton. I came down here expecting that the college men would drop in for [?] an afternoon and chat with me over a pipe. Instead of that the society into which I seem to have

---

5. On Stanley Went, an Oxford graduate who, along with Fuller, had served as one of More's assistant editors at the *Nation*, see Dakin 1960: 125-26, 150-51, 224, 260.

6. On Henry Holt, see his entry in the Biographical Register.

7. More 1915e. This essay, a review of Holt's *On the Cosmic Relations* (1914), later appeared in the eleventh series of the *Shelburne Essays* (More 1967c: 143-66).

gravitated is headed by Armours, Morgans, McClellans,[8] and that sort—quite charming people and very intelligent, but a little more immersed in the good things of this world than suits either my purse or my soul. However, I dine with a philosopher on Saturday; and Mather is always at my side to glorify my kind of comp [?].

I wish you could find the time to let me hear from you oftener and at more detail. Bank your fires now and then, my dear boy; learn to think more as a mortal, which is to say: learn to think sometimes not at all. These are the precepts of Aesculapius.

Faithfully,
Paul E. More.

Cambridge
12 February, 1915

Dear More,

In view of the programme you had on hand at Princeton at about that time, I did well not to attempt that short visit. My stay at Vassar was pleasant enough though a dinner, a lecture, and a reception, one on top of the other are not very restful. My health has certainly been below normal this year. But the difficulty is not as you seem to suppose that I have been living in an almost superhuman contention of spirit. Honest thinking never killed anyone: and if one's thinking is not honest the sooner it kills him the better. The difficulty is much more prosaic! I have, for economic reasons, taken on too much lecturing: six hours a week at Radcliffe in addition to nine hours at Harvard. Taussig told me the other day that what broke him down was Radcliffe. Perhaps it would be well for me to move to a flat in Somerville if I could thereby get rid of this incubus.[9] I am planning to take a semi-sabbatical the first part of this coming year. I have made no plans as yet for the coming summer. I wish Essex was not so far from Cambridge. When are you planning to go up there? I will write you later as to that visit to you during the spring recess. I think it might do you good in the meanwhile to exchange for a few days the flesh pots of Princeton for the Spartan atmosphere of Kirkland

---

8. Presumably, More is referring to George B. McClellan Jr. (1865–1940), a former mayor of New York City who was then a professor of economic history at Princeton. Some small parts excised from this letter in the typescript of the correspondence were reintroduced from Dora Babbitt's handwritten copy of the original in the IBP, because More's original letter has been lost.

9. Babbitt suggests that the rent for a place in Somerville, MA, farther from the Harvard campus, would be cheaper than it was for his current home on Kirkland Road, Cambridge.

Road. You might acquire from contact with me something of that fierce militant quality which is the only thing the articles you have been publishing during the past few months seem to me to lack. I hope that you will not become too genial as a result of your retirement into your Princeton Arcadia. I recognized of course the authorship of the review of Burnet in the *Nation*.[10] Men who follow Plato have to spend an alarming amount of their time in explaining why they themselves are true disciples and others are not. When I think of you and Shelley and Bertrand Russell all setting up as Platonists I am troubled. To put the matter mildly Plato did not make it as clear as he should have done that the proper basis for philosophy is not geometry or any other form of mathematics but common sense. – I had a hasty glance the other day at your article on "The Philosophy of War" in the *Unpopular Review*.[11] The beginning struck me as impressive but I do not feel so sure about the effectiveness of your conclusion. I do not feel sure that I can say of the article: *Vires adquiret eundo*.[12] I am going to read it over again more carefully. Before seeing your article I had given the paper[13] I enclose as an address at Harvard. I develop a thesis somewhat similar to yours. The time seemed to me propitious for a demonstration against the humanitarians. I note that the *Atlantic* has been publishing some anti-humanitarian articles of late along with many of the other kind and I am going to send it to them first of all. I shall be grateful to you if you find time to glance it over and note any details that in your opinion need to be bettered. I shall need to get the paper back promptly in any case. With the general argument you will I fancy be in entire accord except that you are inclined to put greater stress on the religious side of the problem.

Cestre by the way has published a very favorable notice of the "Drift of Romanticism" in *La Revue Germanique*[14] (about the last number that appeared before the war). He takes some exception to your anti-humanitarian tendency.

With kind regards to Mrs. More.

Sincerely,
Irving Babbitt.

10. More 1914e.
11. More 1915g. This article later served as a chapter in the ninth series of More's *Shelburne Essays* (More 1915a: 221-43).
12. This Latin phrase can be translated as "It gathers strength as it goes."
13. A footnote in the typescript of this letter reads: "This paper appears as 'The Breakdown of Internationalism,' *The Nation*, June 17, 1915." A second part of this essay appeared in the June 24, 1915, issue of the *Nation*. See Babbitt 1915.
14. Cestre 1914. This review of More 1967a is listed neither by Young (see 1941: 35) nor Dakin (see 1950: 188).

245 Nassau Street
Princeton, N. J.
Feb. 15, 1915.

My dear Babbitt,

    I was in New York Saturday and Sunday—seeking the flesh pots of club life—or I should have got this manuscript[15] back to you a day earlier. I have read it carefully, most of it twice, but my judgment of it is still somewhat uncertain. I do, however, feel pretty sure that you will not get it printed in its present form. You have sown from the full sack, and thought more of what was in your own mind than of what your reader could take *and put together*. And so, if I gave any advice, it would be this: Strip the first five pages to a few sentences; condense 11–17 and cut out complications of humanitarianism with science and rationalism; note that about page 31 a certain amount of repetition is felt; and, I fear, all the later part of the essay, after the introduction of the idea of humanism, is scattered and ineffective. You have three subjects: nationalism, humanitarianism, expansion. Now, as it seems to me the task before you is to make the connection between these subjects more *continuous* and to strip off everything that is not immediately applicable to them. You will gather from these criticisms that I judge the essay as a whole very harshly. Well, in one way I do, in another I do not. The ideas are excellent, the construction is loose. Possibly Sedgwick[16] will not agree with me, but I suspect he will. I feel pretty sure that he would demand an abridgement by a fourth or third. The season is ripe for such a paper as you can make out of this, and I hope you can work it over. The idea of Nationalism, to my mind, is the special thing much considered today and gives you an admirable handle for your propaganda.

    I am myself putting the finishing touches on an essay entitled *Justice*[17] which I hope to ram down Holt's none too willing throat. It is a continuation and development of my paper on the War.[18] You are quite right, by the way, in thinking that that article weakened as it progressed. I thought the whole thing rather languid.

    I would continue this letter, were it not that it is about time for the postman to call, and I wish to get it off by the next collection.

---

    15. Of what would be published as Babbitt 1915.
    16. Ellery Sedgwick, then the owner and editor of the *Atlantic Monthly*.
    17. More 1915f. This essay later appeared in the ninth series of *Shelburne Essays* (More 1915a: 103-23).
    18. More 1915g.

My kindest regards to Dora. As for your health, I rather fancy you are not quite laid on the shelf yet. I expect to see you make some blood flow yet. But I can't forbear the human joy of the *tu quoque*. You tell me to exercise; I tell you to rest. Exercise and rest are both beastly bores; but the ability to rest properly is one of the first laws of humanism—it is the only law of humanism I could ever practice.

Faithfully yours,
Paul E. More.

---

245 Nassau Street
Princeton, N. J.
March 10, 1915.

My dear Babbitt,

Will it be any tax on you to read this proof[19] before I alter and revise? I dare say the argument needs expansion or precision here and there. The Essay ought logically to precede the one on *Property*[20] which is coming out in the April *Unpopular*, but Holt wanted to use the *Property* first for reasons of general make-up. Neither of the two essays suits me, and I am honestly surprised that Holt has accepted them.

Have you done anything with your paper on the War?[21] I hope my criticism did not tend to discourage you from revising it. It is so easy to pick out flaws, and so hard to indicate the strength of an argument.

And what are the prospects for your visit here? Give me good notice of the date, as Princeton is a place much given to dining, and I may not be able to bring together quickly the persons I should like you to meet.

I write hastily, having the proof of a whole book of Marshall's[22] on my hands and a deluge of proof for Holt.[23]

With kindest regards to Dora,

Sincerely,
Paul E. More.

---

19. More appears to be discussing the proof pages for his essay "Justice"; see More 1915f.
20. More 1915h. This essay later appeared in the ninth series of *Shelburne Essays* (More 1915a: 127-48).
21. Babbitt 1915.
22. A footnote in the typescript of this letter reads: "Henry Rutgers Marshall [1852-1927], architect and writer. *War and the Ideal of Peace* was published in 1915."
23. On More's role at Holt's *Unpopular Review*, see Dakin 1960: 151.

245 Nassau Street
March 14, 1915.

My dear Babbitt,

Will you be good enough to send me back the proof of my *Justice*[24] immediately. They have asked me to read something at the ΦBK here, Monday, the 22nd, and I think I shall make some alterations in this essay and use it on them.[25]

If you feel disposed to criticise the essay, but are pressed for time now, I can easily return the proof to you next week.

Excuse this hasty note.

Sincerely,
Paul E. More.

Cambridge
14 March, 1915

Dear More,

Your article on Justice[26] strikes me as a weighty and dignified piece of thinking with the substance of which I am in hearty agreement. It is so close knit in its argument as to give the impression perhaps of a certain density of texture and will even seem to some, I fear, a bit grayish and abstract, and lacking in any case in high lights, in the vivid illustrations and applications that give a fillip to the ordinary reader. If you make any changes they should be in the direction of expansion and more concrete examples. Still I shall be glad to see the article get into print as it is. It will be especially appreciated by those who are familiar with the general background of your thinking. Are you planning ultimately to use it as a chapter in a book? It reads a bit that way. I am not sure that the parallel you work out between reason and the feelings in their relation to justice in nature, in the heart of the individual and in society, is not at times in danger of seeming a little forced. For example, Nietzscheism, instead of being "based on the exclusive claim of the reason" is based rather on a free expansion of the *libido dominandi* unchecked by reason (supported by insight).[27]

---

24. More 1915f.
25. For his Phi Beta Kappa address, More ultimately decided to lecture on "Property and Law" (More 1915h) instead; see Dakin 1950: 159 and 1960: 158.
26. More 1915f.
27. Cf. More 1915a: 118-19, which appears to take into account Babbitt's criticism.

Your criticism of my own paper[28] was so drastic that it has quite put me out of conceit with it. I have made no attempt at revision as yet and am not sure that I shall attempt to do anything with it. At no time in the past has your judgment about my work differed so much from my own. As my articles go, this struck me as one of the most readable I had written. The structure I took to be sound though extremely condensed and overlaid with a certain redundancy of illustration. I can shorten the article by cutting out some of this illustrative material, but the fault of my plea for humanism at the end—which struck you as disjointed and ineffective—is less easy to correct. I assert that the great problem at present is to put conduct on a positive and critical basis and this is a thought that needs to be developed in a book rather than in an article; it would require a pretty thorough review of the present situation in philosophy. I am by the way accumulating a treasure of wrath against the professional philosophers and my next book will be aimed almost as directly at them as my first was at the philologists. I am beginning to attack them openly—especially the neo-realists in my lectures and in an address that I have been asked to give before the Philosophical Club two weeks from now I am planning to carry the warfare into the enemy's country.

I hope you will pardon my delay in returning the proof. My moments of leisure are rare this year and I was waiting until I could give it careful consideration. Convey also my apology to Mrs. More for not answering her note directly. I had half made plans to visit you in the week Apr. 19–26 but it is plain from her letter to Dora that this time would not suit you. The idea of a visit early in June is tempting. If it turns out to be possible I shall give you ample notice of the exact date of my (of our) coming. I return stamps for those used by you on my MS.

Sincerely,
Irving Babbitt.

---

245 Nassau Street
March 17, 1915.

My dear Babbitt,

Certainly there is good stuff in your war article,[29] and I may be mistaken in my reservations as to some parts of it. I wish you would submit it to other judgment besides mine. Why not let Sedgwick see it in its present form and

---

28. Babbitt 1915. For this criticism, see above.
29. Babbitt 1915.

see what he says. – It is good news to hear you are going to pitch into the New Realists and other professional philosophers. They are open to attack. Fite (though his name is not signed) is giving them some hard knocks in the person of Bertrand Russell.

And now what do you mean by sending me stamps to cover the return of your manuscript. I ought to express my opinion of such an act by sending you stamps for the return of *Justice*.[30] But I won't. As William James once said to me: Don't do it again! You have laid your finger on the weak point of my article. I shall try to strengthen the argument there. It is as you felt, really a chapter in a book, being written with a new volume of essays in view which will embrace my recent lucubrations on Natural Aristocracy[31] and other kindred topics. I hope to publish in the autumn.[32] And any criticism meanwhile of any *Unpopular* essays will be welcome.

When we wrote about your Easter visit we supposed your holiday would be the first of April, as they are here. Unfortunately the two Heard girls[33] will be here from the middle of the month to the end, as they are breaking up their present establishment then and temporarily will have no home. I hope you may come in June. One thing to tempt you here will be a tennis court on the grounds.

With kind regards to Dora,

Sincerely,
Paul E. More.

---

245 Nassau Street
Princeton, N. J., April 7, 1915.

My dear Babbitt,

Dora's letter announcing that you may spend your Sabbatical months in Princeton has caused a great flutter of excitement in this household. Such an event seems almost too happy to be hoped for in this Valley of tears. Net and I will do all we can by way of consulting agents and examining houses to find something suitable. If you come down in June, I hope we may

---

30. More 1915f.

31. More 1914a. This essay was later featured in the ninth series of *Shelburne Essays* (More 1915a: 3-38), to which More is alluding here.

32. According to Dakin (1960: 160), this volume (More 1915a) was first published in October of 1915.

33. Presumably, More refers to his nieces Katherine Heard and Anne Heard.

have something to show you. The difficulty is that Princeton rents are by no means low, but there is always a chance of striking a bargain. About how high would you be willing to go? The public school here is, I think, good. There is, of course, a very mixed crowd of children going to it, but a number of the professors send their children, and I think there would be no objection on this score. I am sure you would find three or four months here very pleasant and most convenient for work. The Princeton library is poor, but you could have books sent from Cambridge, and the New York libraries are within easy reach. Meanwhile don't let the thought of being here in the autumn deter you from visiting us for a week in June. Mather and I are quite hilarious at the notion of facing you on the tennis court, two fat duffers against a man. And Net has quite set her heart on seeing Dora.

I am finishing up a paper on Disraeli for the *Atlantic*,[34] writing with my left hand so to speak, while my right hand is engaged on Plato. The straddle is a bit disconcerting.

Sincerely,
Paul E. More.

P.S. On Friday of next week we go out to St. Louis and shall not be back for seven or eight days. I have a horrid address to give at the opening of the Library Mrs. Richardson left to the Museum there.[35]

Cambridge
27 April, 1915

Dear More,

It is not at all certain yet that I can come to Princeton in June. If I am thoroughly tired out as I frequently am after the final rush here, I should prefer to postpone the visit—to come to Essex, say, in August. My visit to Princeton should not interfere in any case with that trip of yours to Indiana.[36] I should most likely come about the middle of the month. If

---

34. "Disraeli and Conservatism," which first appeared in the September 1915 issue of the *Atlantic* (More 1915d) and was later featured in the ninth series of the *Shelburne Essays* (1915a: 151-89).

35. According to Dakin (1960: 158-59), More delivered this address at the St. Louis Art Museum on April 18, 1915.

36. Dakin (1960: 159) notes that More delivered a paper to the Phi Beta Kappa chapter of Indiana University on June 7, 1915.

you are not inconvenienced I should like to put off my final decision until about the third week in May.

Sedgwick returned my article[37] with a very complimentary letter saying that he was so crowded with war articles that he could not find room for anything so long. I fancy that his real difficulty was the fear that a paper of this kind would not go down the crop of humanitarian New England. The *Yale Review* has accepted the paper on condition that I cut it down about a thousand words. I am not sure that I am willing to do this. Do you think that it would have a chance—with suitable modifications—as a middle article in the *Nation* to run through two numbers? – If you think I can be of any service in looking over any of your proof or MS. send it to me by all means.

Sincerely,
I. B.

Princeton, N. J.
April 29, 1915.

My dear Babbitt,

It will not put us out at all if your decision about your visit lies in abeyance till the end of May, or later. And a visit to Essex in August or September will be a fair compensation for failing to see you in Princeton.[38]

As for the war article, my advice would be to cut out the thousand words and let the *Yale Review* have it. I cannot speak certainly for the *Nation*, but I know that, contrary to Fuller's expectations and plans, the *Nation* has been reduced in size, and that, as a consequence, he is crowded with middle articles waiting for publication. Under such circumstances he would probably hesitate to take a long article like yours at the present time. This, of course, is only my conjecture.[39] I would suggest the *Unpopular*, were it not that, in a very general way only to be sure, my own article[40] went over some of the

---

37. Babbitt 1915.

38. On More's vacation in Essex, New York, during the summer of 1915, see Dakin 1960: 160.

39. This conjecture turned out not to be sound, since the *Nation* ultimately published Babbitt's article (see Babbitt 1915) in two installments.

40. More 1915g.

same ground. This might influence Holt to reject yours. I wish you had had it ready for printing some months earlier.

It is quite likely that I shall call on you to read the proof of my book[41] while it is still in the compositor's hands.

Sincerely,
Paul E. More.

P.S. As for cutting, I have just cut down an article[42] for Sedgwick from some 10,000 words to 6,500. ἀνάγκη.[43]

Century Club
May 16, 1915

My dear Babbitt,

It is raining, and I have been sitting here all day, going over the magazines. One article I found which will interest you, if you have not already seen it—Bertrand's "Goethe et le Germanisme" in the *Deux Mondes* of April 15.[44] It is written quite frankly from the present inimical point of view, and leaves out of the account the whole better half, including most of what you care for, of Goethe. But it was to me extremely interesting, as showing how closely related Nietzscheism is to Romanticism, and how this element plays a predominating part in what might be called the native temperament and poetical inspiration of Goethe, while his classicism to the very end was something laid on from the outside and never thoroughly assimilated. Speaking of Goethe, I have been reading Plato's *Phaedrus again*. As a τεχνή[45] it is supremely good; pretty much the whole art of rhetoric is in it. As a treatise on Love it is disquieting, and contains most of the things you object to in him. In some places he is the first great Romantic, and the one comment to make is Goethe's: Classicism is health, romanticism is disease.

I am keeping my eye open for a furnished house or apartment, but nothing has turned up yet. You will be interested to know that Warner Fite is

---

41. More 1915a.
42. Presumably, More is referring to More 1915d.
43. A footnote in the typescript of this letter reads: "Necessity."
44. Bertrand 1915.
45. A footnote in the typescript of this letter reads: "An art (system of rules)."

coming to Princeton next year as a full professor. I have the vain satisfaction of feeling that I and the *Nation* have been the chief instrument in reëstablishing him in academic life. I suspect that Harvard should have taken him.

Sincerely,
Paul E. More.

Cambridge
23 June, 1915

Dear More,

I have had several very interesting letters from you this spring for which I have the somewhat guilty sense of having given nothing in return. The claims upon my time have multiplied as usual as the college year has drawn to its end. I have decided not to attempt a visit to Princeton at this time but hope that it will be possible for me to visit you at Essex sometime in August. I have many things that I should like to talk over with you but am too indolent to discuss in a letter. Remember that I shall be very glad to go over the MS. or proof of your next volume. When is it likely to appear? I wonder how the sales here and in England are likely to be affected by the war if it still continues. I was gratified to see that the *Spectator* in one of its recent issues made a flattering allusion to your work (in a review of Brander Matthews' selection of *American Essays*).[46] I attach importance to allusions of this kind. Your reputation in this country if it is to attain really respectable proportions may have to come on the ricochet from abroad. Left to its own instincts the American public is hopelessly provincial in such matters and can always be counted on to bark up the wrong tree. Such articles as Sherman's recent paper on Wells[47] and Wister's article in the June *Atlantic* on the *Quack Novel*[48] are good signs as far as they go. They tend to clear the atmosphere and prepare the way for the recognition of serious work.

I decided finally to withdraw my war paper[49] from the *Yale Review* and give it to the *Nation*. Your criticism of it was so severe that for a time I had

---

46. Anon. 1915. The reviewer criticizes Matthews for his failure to include "a single example of the work of Mr. Paul Elmer More, whose *Shelburne Essays* perhaps reach the high-water mark of contemporary American literary criticism, and whose delightful paper on 'The Paradox of Oxford' would have been peculiarly appropriate for insertion in this collection" (686).

47. Sherman 1915a.

48. Wister 1915. Owen Wister (1860–1938) was an American novelist and historian.

49. Babbitt 1915.

about determined to suppress it entirely and I am somewhat nervous about seeing it in print, as it is. Fuller seemed to be very nervous about accepting it, not apparently because of doubts as to the intrinsic quality of the article itself, but of fear as to how it might be taken by Villard.

The chances of our getting furnished quarters at Princeton next autumn seem rather faint just now though we have not given up that scheme entirely. My sister,[50] the children and maid went to Dublin[51] yesterday. Dora and I are planning to follow in about a week. With kind regards to Mrs. More.

Sincerely,
Irving Babbitt.

---

245 Nassau Street
Princeton, N. J.
June 27, 1915

My dear Babbitt,

I am sorry to hear that you have given up the visit to Princeton this spring, but console myself with the thought of your promised visit to Essex in August. Fuller told me you had sent your article on the war to him, and I was pleased to see he had enough faith in it to print it in extenso.[52] I feared he would be hindered from this by Villard's known humanitarian sympathies. You evidently have got the notion that my objections to the article were more radical than the fact warrants. I did not, and do not, think it in your best vein. The first part is strong and convincing, but somehow the second part does not seem to clinch matters. Yet, withal, the ideas are sound and of a kind which ought to be hammered into the public ear, and I am thoroughly glad to see them displayed in the *Nation*. My sister Alice, whose judgment means much to me in such matters, thinks the article fine and effective—notably so. As for my own essays, most of the manuscript[53] is now in the hands of Houghton Mifflin, and the rest will be there as soon as Holt returns the dedicatory introduction[54] to him which I sent to Burlington for his imprimatur. The bulk of the essays came out in the *Unpopular*.[55] In despair of a better

---

50. Katharine Babbitt.
51. Dublin, New Hampshire, where the Babbitts often vacationed.
52. Babbitt 1915.
53. Of More 1915a.
54. More 1915a: vii-x.
55. See More 1915a: 5.

title I am calling the volume *Aristocracy and Justice*. If H. M. give me time I shall certainly send you proofs. – My Plato[56] gets clearer and clearer in my head, and some twelve to thirteen thousand words are already written out, besides a large volume of notes. I rather hoped to finish the work next winter, but I have engaged myself to give the Turnbull lectures at Johns Hopkins next year,[57] and these will cut pretty heavily into my time. As the subject of the lectures is American Poetry, with special insistence on Sidney Lanier,[58] I am not altogether happy over this interruption. However, we take what we can from the high Academic authorities. Four college text books this year are including selections from my essays, which means more to me than the recognition from Johns Hopkins. The world do move, but monstrous slowly.

With best regards to Dora,

Sincerely,
Paul E. More.

P.S. Houses in Princeton will be scarce, owing to the fact that the war will keep men from going abroad, but I shall keep a vigilant look out for you.

Crater Club
Essex, N. Y.
August 5, 1915

My dear Babbitt,

I fully expected to find a letter from you here telling when you would make your visit. The Houghtons,[59] the Lou Mores,[60] the Paul Mores, even my mother-in-law, are all looking forward to that great and welcome event. When? The Wents will be here from the 18th to about the 22nd this month; but beyond that our time seems to be all free. You must plan, if possible, to stop with us a week. Bring your tennis racket, and bathing suit. You will of course need no evening clothes.

Faithfully yours,
Paul E. More.

---

56. More 1917b.

57. Dakin (1960: 161) notes that More delivered the Percy Turnbull Memorial Lectures at the Johns Hopkins University between March 29 and April 12, 1916.

58. The American poet, musician, and writer Sidney Lanier (1842–1881).

59. The family of Silas Arnold Houghton (1864–1916), a Harvard-trained physician who summered in Essex, New York. On Houghton, see anon. 1916c.

60. On More's brother Louis T. More, see his entry in the Biographical Register.

Monadnock, N. H.
9 August, 1915

Dear More,

About the only time that I seem to have free in August for a visit to Essex is from about Aug. 23 to Aug. 28. Things are a bit complicated by Kathleen's wedding[61] which takes place in Cambridge on Aug. 30. How would a visit from about Aug. 31 to Sep. 6 suit you? This later date might be more convenient for me. Will your brother and Dr. Houghton be at Essex at that time?

The first essay[62] in your new volume strikes me as a strong piece of writing—very much improved, I should say, by certain additions you have made since it appeared in the *Unpopular*.[63] (Holt by the way is I believe in Dublin at present though I have not yet seen him.) I am glad to see you doing writing of this kind. It is very much needed in itself and will give you a following more rapidly than your more strictly literary essays. As to your last paper in the *Nation*[64] I will make some comments when I see you. You are weaving a great many very subtle strands together in the essays you are publishing on this period and it may be that they will need to support one another in volume form if your whole point of view is to be brought out clearly. With kind regards to Mrs. More.

Sincerely,
I. Babbitt.

Crater Club
Essex, N. Y.
August 13, 1915

Dear Babbitt,

Thank you for the careful reading of the first batch of my proof. Unfortunately, however, I had to return these sheets before receiving your corrections and suggestions. Apparently the printers forgot my instructions

---

61. Dora Babbitt's younger sister Kathleen Drew (1886–1963) married the psychology professor Edward Chase Tolman (1886–1959) on August 30, 1915. See Carroll 2017: 47-48.
62. "Natural Aristocracy," the first chapter (3-38) in More 1915a.
63. More 1914a.
64. Perhaps Babbitt means More's essay on Swift (More 1915c), which was then recently published, and which later appeared in the tenth series of More's *Shelburne Essays* (More 1967b: 101-21).

and did not send you the sheets until, after long delay, I wrote and admonished them. Your criticism will be of no inconsiderable help to me.

Dr. Houghton and Lou both expect to be here from August 31 to September 6, and this time would suit Net and me very well. I have a favor to ask. Bring Esther[65] with you. There is plenty of room for her, and Net and I should both like to have Darrah[66] renew her acquaintance. The little necessary oversight of her Net will gladly take, and leave you quite free. You will disappoint us all very much if you refuse. If Esther has any studying she is obliged to do, this could easily be managed, as Darrah works at her books every morning.

With kindest regards to Dora, I am

Faithfully yours,
Paul E. More.

P.S. You will find Henry Holt well worth cultivating if you get a chance to meet him. You have already met him, have you not, at the Century?

Crater Club
Essex, N. Y.
August 27, 1915

Dear Babbitt,

Thank you for the last batch of proof which helped me at a number of places. Your plan to come September 1st suits us very well. There is a boat that leaves Burlington at 5:30 P.M. and reaches Essex at 6:20—but you can *almost* count on its leaving a little late. Let me know when and how you are coming, so that we can meet you.

Sincerely,
Paul E. More.

Monadnock, N. H.
9 September, 1915

Dear More,

I was tumbled out of the train at Keene yesterday morning at about 4:30 A.M. and set out on a very warm walk of about fourteen miles, mostly uphill,

---

65. Babbitt's daughter Esther Babbitt.
66. More's older daughter, Mary Darrah More.

to Dublin, arriving in time to find the family at breakfast. The weather has I gather been cooler here than at Essex though I did not find the weather at Essex really oppressive. The only out, as I told you, to the extremely good time I had on my visit is that I do not deserve it. I have got very little done with my book this summer and shall lose my self-respect if I do not accomplish something very soon. – I have just received a letter from one of my old French friends, A. Foucher,[67] telling me that he has been appointed exchange professor at Columbia for this coming year and that he will arrive in New York in a few days. I gather that he did not care for the appointment but looked on it as his duty to accept. He has high standing as you may know as an "indianiste," especially in Buddhist archaeology. He is a very quiet man but of sterling qualities. I shall be very grateful for anything you can do to make his stay in America more tolerable—especially perhaps in connection with the Century Club. He speaks English.

You will be amused to learn that I have just received a letter from Ray Stannard Baker,[68] the muckraker, in which he says that he finds a "great deal to sympathize with" in my article in the *Nation*.[69] I am beginning to think that you are right in saying that I do not make sufficiently clear to people what I am driving at. I do not expect to hear that Lincoln Steffens,[70] let us say, has applied to you for spiritual consolation.

When I spoke to you about spending a few months in California I had in mind the suggestion that one of your friends and admirers on the Faculty at Berkeley had made to me; that you might be willing to come out and give a course during the regular session of the University.[71] Very likely the plan of spending the winter there with your family in that way would not appeal to you, but it is surely not in itself absurd.

I should have been glad to carry further my talks with your brother about science.[72] The time is ripe in my opinion to insist not on what is most purely scientific in science but on what is most *real*, two very different things as it would seem. Only in this way will it be possible to work out an understanding between naturalists and humanists and this is in my opinion one of the

---

67. The French orientalist Alfred Foucher (1865–1952) and Babbitt were both Sylvain Lévi's students at the Sorbonne. See Lévi in Manchester and Shepard 1941: 34.
68. Ray Stannard Baker (1870–1946) was an American journalist, historian, and writer.
69. Babbitt 1915.
70. Lincoln Steffens (1866–1936) was an investigative journalist with left-wing political views.
71. More did teach for a semester at UC Berkeley, but not until 1930. See Dakin 1960: 279.
72. Louis T. More, a physicist.

great desiderata of the age. – Give my regards to him and also to your wife and to Mrs. Lou More. I had been intending to go over and bid her farewell before my departure.

Sincerely,
Irving Babbitt.

Dublin, N. H.
29 November, 1915

Dear More,

We have just been having a very pleasant but only too brief visit from my old friend Foucher who, as I believe I wrote you, is exchange professor at Columbia this year. He has been lecturing at San Francisco and Boston and in Canada in addition to Columbia, and returns home about Christmas. I wonder if there is any chance of your seeing him. He is a finished man of the world and a good talker in either French or English. Your awful experience with Giese may have made you suspicious of my friends. Foucher has spent several years in India and in Cochin China (as director of antiquities). He is deep in Sanskrit and is the chief authority I believe in certain departments of Buddhist art. You would in my opinion find him a very agreeable addition to your Saturday evening circle at the Century;[73] and it would be still better if he could manage to spend a few hours at Princeton and get a glimpse of you and Mather there. I have my designs in thus trying to get you to meet men who are in contact with influential circles at Paris. Cestre by the way should get a copy of your last volume.[74] His notice of the "Drift of Romanticism" in the *Revue Germanique* is of the kind that counts. I confess that if I got such a notice I should see that an excerpt from it was used for advertising. I see by the paper that you are now an academician![75] I hope that the recognition that is coming to you from various quarters will finally translate itself into sales. I noticed by the way in fingering a new history of American Literature at the Coöperative[76] the other day that

---

73. On this circle, see Dakin 1960: 126.
74. More 1915a.
75. A footnote in the typescript of this letter reads: "American Academy of Arts and Letters." Dakin (1960: 162 n. 46) notes that More was elected to the American Academy of Arts and Letters on November 18, 1915. Cf. Aaron 1963: 1.
76. The so-called Harvard Coop.

the author (Pattie?),[77] an instructor at the Un. of Pennsylvania, gives you a great send off at the end. His account of your work struck me from a hasty perusal as distinctly intelligent.

Our present plan is to come to Princeton about Jan. 1st. We are getting a very comfortable and even luxurious house here for a nominal rental and it hardly seems worth while to make the change until then. If we could have found a suitable furnished house at Princeton it would have been different. The autumn here has been beautiful—much better than the summer. With kind regards to Mrs. More.

Sincerely yours,
Irving Babbitt.

---

245 Nassau Street
Princeton, New Jersey
December 21, 1915

My dear Babbitt,

I have to thank you for a pleasant evening. Foucher dined with me at the Century and spent the evening, talking freely with a circle of men. He appears to have a pretty heavy burden of work at Columbia, and so enjoyed his escape—as I certainly did. He is entertaining and keen, a bit lacking in imagination I should suppose. One thing amused me: his desire to see Hindu and Chinese subjects introduced into the college curriculum! I protested that we couldn't even make our boys study Latin and Greek; but he seemed to regard this as an instinctive desire on their part for Sanskrit and Manchu.

Have you decided yet just when you are coming to Princeton? We should like to know long enough in advance to get a good crowd at a dinner, including the Hibbens,[78] who are of course much engaged.

With greetings of the season to Dora and yourself, I am

Faithfully yours,
Paul E. More.

---

77. A footnote in the typescript of this letter reads: "Fred L. Pattee." Fred Lewis Pattee (1863–1950) was a faculty member in the English department at the Pennsylvania State University. For the (highly complimentary) discussion of More's work to which Babbitt is referring, see Pattee 1915: 433-36.

78. John Grier Hibben (1861–1933) was the president of Princeton University from 1912 to 1932.

6 Kirkland Road
Cambridge
13 February, 1916

Dear More,

I scarcely need to tell you that we have been very much shocked and saddened by the death of Dr. Houghton.[79] He was one of the men about here—and they are not so extremely numerous—for whom I had a genuine liking. He will be missed by a wide circle. The last time I saw him—in Burlington last September—he was the picture of exuberant health. Perhaps his habit of taking very violent exercise at Essex for a few weeks in the summer and then going almost without exercise for months in winter may have put some strain on his heart. However if his failure to weather the crisis of the pneumonia was due to weakness of his heart this weakness was probably due first of all to the strain that had been put upon him for years by his special type of medical practice. – I recollect that he called my attention one day to the rather sinister fact that very few of the successful doctors and surgeons about Boston were living much beyond middle age.

Dora and I both have very agreeable memories of our stay in Princeton.[80] The place and its surroundings both pleased me and I was struck by the unaffected cordiality of most of the people I met. There are certainly advantages in a comparatively small and homogenous community. After the spring days of the end of January at Princeton we are now back in the depth of winter with a blizzard as a matter of fact raging at the present moment.

There is a real principle involved in the logomachy in which we were engaged at the Century Club over the word "modern." The modern spirit is synonymous with the positive and critical spirit (as opposed to the spirit which accepts things on traditional authority): it is not identical surely with the spirit of innovation and mere intoxication with the future. Matthew Arnold's essay on the "Modern Element" at the beginning of the so-called third series of Essays in Criticism[81] seems to me thoroughly sound in its definition of the word modern though not thoroughly satisfactory, as Arnold

---

79. Silas Arnold Houghton passed away from pneumonia on February 6, 1916. On Houghton, see above, this chapter.

80. Dakin (1960: 160-61) notes that Babbitt spent the month of January 1916 in Princeton, at the end of his "semi-sabbatical," having previously been in Dublin, New Hampshire.

81. For the essay to which Babbitt alludes, entitled "On the Modern Element in Literature," see Arnold 1910: 35-83.

himself came to feel, in all its specific judgments. Indeed a similar distinction is implied in your comparison of Burke and Plato ("Natural Aristocracy")[82] and I am surprised that you brought up the point at all. To admit at present that one is a Tory or even a reactionary is in my opinion to commit a tactical mistake of the first order. One is at once put on the defensive; and in the war of intellect as in other forms of warfare the advantage belongs with the offensive—especially when it takes the form of an unexpected flanking movement. *A positiviste positiviste et demi.* For example, cover with ridicule Sir Oliver Lodge for the more than medieval credulity he displays in the exploits he attributes to the "ether."[83] Insist that the scientist put the "law for thing" on a purely positive and critical basis[84] (for example do not allow him atoms except as a more or less useful "fiction"): and then emulate him in regard to the "law for man."[85] One should plant himself first of all here on the naked *fact* of a power of control in human nature and then bring in if he wishes all the experience of the past as collateral testimony.

Sherman has raised up a dangerous adversary against himself in George Dutton.[86] I saw a great deal of Dutton when he was working under me for the doctorate and look upon him as an unusually cautious and judicial person. I have not read Bennett but I fancy Dutton's estimate of him in the last *Nation* is pretty near the truth.[87] I see by the way that Boynton of whose critical

---

82. See More 1915a: 3-38.

83. Sir Oliver J. Lodge (1851-1940) was a British physicist. For his views on the now discarded ether theory, see Lodge 1889.

84. For a useful discussion of Babbitt's confusing references to himself as a "positivist," see Ryn 1995.

85. On the importance of Emerson's distinction between "law for man" and "law for thing" to Babbitt's Humanism, see above, chapter 2.

86. George Burwell Dutton (1881-1930), who was the class valedictorian at Williams College in 1907, received his M.A. (1908) and Ph.D. (1910) at Harvard University. He was an English professor at Williams College.

87. Sherman had stirred up a controversy with an essay on the novelist Arnold Bennett in the December 23, 1915, issue of the *Nation*, in which he demonstrated a preference for Bennett over H. G. Wells (see Sherman 1915b; cf. Sherman 1915a). More wrote to Sherman to criticize Sherman's unduly positive impression of Bennett, and Sherman partly defended his views in a response. See Zeitlin and Woodbridge 1929: 265-67. Babbitt's reference to Dutton's writing is unclear: the February 10, 1916, issue of the *Nation*—then the most recent one—does not contain any discussion of Bennett's work, by Dutton or by anyone else. Cf. Zeitlin and Woodbridge 1929: 820-21, which offers a bibliography on the controversy Sherman's piece launched and does not include any pieces by Dutton or by anonymous contributors.

acumen you think so highly ranks H. G. Wells with the prophets.[88] This is the kind of thing I find very exasperating.

I do hope that you will be able to visit us in May when Mrs. More is at the "Pool."[89] – Your wishes in regard to seeing people or not seeing them would be strictly respected. – Give my kindest regards to your wife. Dora and I both appreciate very deeply all she did to make our stay in Princeton agreeable.

Sincerely yours,
Irving Babbitt.

Princeton, N. J.
March 6, 1916

Dear Babbitt,

Dr. Houghton's death was indeed a shock, for the man seemed the very embodiment of exuberant health. His loss will be much felt at Essex, where he was a sort of universal solvent for all the diverse sets. – Your letter raises so many questions, that I could only answer it in an essay. To begin with, positivism is indeed a mark of the modern spirit, but it is certainly true also that the rejection of authority as authority has introduced a flimsiness of mind and a tendency to discredit anything settled in the mere wantonness of change. This has gone so far that I for one am not afraid of being called a reactionary, if only the word is properly taken.[90] I am reactionary in wishing to bring people back to a proper, not a superstitious, respect for sheer authority. Without that we must fall into the disintegration of an absolute individualism. As for Sherman's position on Wells and Bennett, I have just been writing to him on that head.[91] I am convinced that his view is essentially sound, that for fiction Bennett is ethically right whereas Wells is ethically wrong. But, as I have said, to Sherman himself, he has somewhat weakened his case by omitting the necessary reservations. Bennett has the common-sense of humanity on his side, but his common-sense runs to the Philistine; he lacks the note of inspiration that is needed for great art. Boynton as a

---

88. The literary critic Henry Walcott Boynton (1869–1947), who began writing regularly for the *Nation* and the New York *Evening Post* in 1912 (and thus worked with More), published a letter to the editor critical of Sherman's views in the February 3, 1916, issue of the *Nation* (see Boynton 1916).

89. Biddeford Pool, Maine, where the Mores occasionally summered. Dakin (1960: 162) notes that More visited Babbitt at Squam Lake, New Hampshire, in the middle of September, 1916.

90. For a similar sentiment, see More 1910a: 267-68.

91. For a discussion of More's and Sherman's correspondence on this topic, see above.

matter of fact feels towards Wells and Bennett as Sherman does; I know this from his reviews. But Boynton writes more from an instinctive sense of what is sound and interesting, than from any philosophical intuition. Hence he is up in arms against Sherman's intrusion of an ethical standard into the field. I am not afraid for Sherman.

This is a feeble reply to your letter, but I am in the throes of writing such a lecture about Sidney Lanier as will not outrage my conscience or provoke the disgust of the good Baltimorians.[92] It is a delicate task.

Your stay in Princeton has left most agreeable memories not only with us of the More clan, but with others who have referred to it. – With kind regards to Dora,

Faithfully yours,
Paul E. More.

"Woodlawn," Holderness
(P.O. address: Ashland
N. H., R. F. D. #1)
10 July, 1916

Dear More,

We gathered from Mrs. More that you are planning to visit your sister in Portland.[93] Would it not be possible for you to look in on us either on your way thither or on your return? We are only an hour's run from Concord, N. H., and would be directly on your way if you were going across from Portland to Essex (via Wells River Junction, Montpelier, etc.). We would meet you at Meredith. I wish that we might see more of one another during the summer. I was very much tempted by the suggestion that we take the Heard house at Essex[94] for August and September but felt that I ought not with the writing I have on hand to get so far away from Cambridge and the library. "Rousseau and Romanticism"[95] is not getting ahead so fast as I should like. The general structure of the book is giving me a great deal of difficulty. Still I hope to make better progress this summer.

---

92. On More's lectures at the Johns Hopkins University in Baltimore on American poetry, see above.

93. Dakin (1960: 162) informs his readers that More accompanied his sister Alice to the Maine General Hospital in Portland, where she underwent an exploratory operation. He remained with her for a few weeks in July, 1916. See also More's letter of August 22, 1916, below.

94. Dakin (1960: 106) notes that Henrietta More's sister, Katherine Beck Heard, first discovered the cottage in Essex, New York, where the Mores often summered.

95. Babbitt 1991.

The "Parmenides"[96] strikes me as one of your good papers—an unusually close and vigorous piece of thinking. It should make some of the professionals in the philosophical field sit up and take notice. Plato, though, does need a terrible amount of explaining! One moves along a narrow path with quaking bogs of misinterpretation on every hand. When is your volume on Plato[97] likely to be in shape?

I am going to do what I can to get them to invite you to give it in the form of lectures at Harvard though I am not very sanguine of accomplishing much.[98] – Why did you weaken so in the conclusion of that last paper[99] of yours in the *Nation*—otherwise excellent? Surely one had a right to expect something more ringing and stalwart from you at a time when the very foundations of civilizations are being menaced by ruinous fads in education.

I was glad to see that review in the *Spectator*.[100] It was not only favorable but it gave the reader an excellent notion of your point of view—and this is something that an author appreciates—if I may judge from my own experience—even more than praise. The notice in the *London Nation*[101] was unfavorable—as one might have expected—but not like the one in the *New Republic*[102] positively dishonest.

I should have said that we are occupying a large and comfortable house on Squam Lake and are unusually well situated to receive you. – I had a pleasant glimpse of Bruce[103] at Cambridge the other day. With kind regards to Mrs. More.

Sincerely,
Irving Babbitt.

96. More's essay "The Parmenides of Plato" appeared in the March, 1916, issue of the *Philosophical Review*. See More 1916b.

97. More 1917b.

98. More would instead base his Vanuxem Lectures at Princeton in October and November of 1917 on his material for *Platonism*; see Shafer 1935c: 206-7; Dakin 1960: 170.

99. Babbitt is referring to "The Old Education and the New" (More 1916a) from the June 22, 1916, number of the *Nation*.

100. Anon. 1916a, a review of More's *Aristocracy and Justice* (1915a).

101. Anon. 1916b. Babbitt presumably expected a negative review of More's *Aristocracy and Justice* (1915a) in the London *Nation* because it was a left-leaning publication.

102. Bourne 1916. In the review, Bourne polemically opined (246) that "Mr. More's ideal is a slave-society, as the Greek state to which he always reverts was a slave-state."

103. A footnote in the typescript of this letter reads: "Professor James Douglas Bruce of the University of Tennessee." Bruce (1862–1923) was a prominent literary scholar and longtime chair of the English department at Tennessee.

Biddeford Pool
July 13, 1916

Dear Babbitt,

Your letter has been forwarded to me here at the Pool, where I am waiting to take Alice[104] to the Portland Hospital. We go on Sunday, and after that my plans are of course indefinite. I should like mightily to visit you on my way back to New York, but as I have already been here a week and must remain still a number of days, I feel that I ought to return to my work the speediest way possible. Perhaps I can get the visit in some time in August or September, coming over from Essex, if it is agreeable to you. – I am now driving at my Plato,[105] having resolved to get it out next spring. Your proposal to have me give the lectures at Harvard is pleasant, but I rather wonder whether it would not be wiser, considering all the vain efforts in the past, to let me sink quite out of the Harvard mind and conscience. I don't want to be rammed down their throats, so to speak; and you won't want to outdo the importunate widow. This is only suggestion; I am quite willing to leave the decision in your hands. – The question of publishing rather bores me. Schofield has asked me several times and urgently to let him have the volume for his series. The Princeton Press wants it, and of course I can take it to H. M.[106] There would be a real advantage in adding it to the Shelburne series, as I shall almost certainly have occasion to refer to it in one or two volumes of English essays. On the other hand I may want to publish a supplementary volume on Plato that will not take the form of essays at all. What do you think? – I am sorry Rousseau proves so rebellious.[107] Make him suffer for it; no doubt you will. I think if we could talk the matter over, you would clear your mind. But that can't be for some time. – With kindest regards to Dora,

Faithfully yours,
Paul E. More.

---

104. A footnote in the typescript of this letter reads: "Miss Alice More, P. E. M's sister."
105. More 1917b.
106. Houghton Mifflin.
107. This is a reference to Babbitt's difficulties in writing *Rousseau and Romanticism* (Babbitt 1991).

248   Chapter Five

Ashland, N. H.
20 July, 1916

Dear More,

I am very sorry indeed to hear that your sister Alice has had to go to the hospital. Will you give her my kind regards and also my best wishes for a prompt and fortunate recovery. – We shall be most pleased to have you here at any time during the summer. If you come during August or September, I think it would be best, for your sake, to arrange if possible a date when we have no other guests, but we shall have plenty of room in any case. It is rather warm here at present and I should not be surprised to hear that at Princeton it has been positively oppressive.

I do not think that I lacked discretion in my way of bringing you to the attention of certain persons at Harvard at the time of your leaving the *Nation*. I have of course let the matter drop entirely since then. The question is whether I should not have done more pushing. I have to see Lowell on other matters next October and it strikes me that it might be expedient for me to mention your Plato to him. Lowell is supposed to have a great deal to do with the appointments to the Lowell lectures[108] which as you doubtless know are very well paid. I am not sanguine of accomplishing anything, but I do not see what harm can be done. If you feel differently let me know.

J. E. Creighton[109] of the *Phil. Review* has asked me to write an article or a short notice as I prefer on the new Cambridge edition of Rousseau's political writings in 2 vols. (which will I presume sell in this country for at least $15), and wishes me, if I cannot do the work myself, to suggest the right man. I have already arranged to write a review of this work for the *Nation*[110] and am suggesting you as one of the possibilities to Creighton. Do you think Fite would be competent for this job?[111] Another important work on R. has just come out—"The Religion of R." in 3 vols. By P. M. Masson. It is a mine of information on the development of the deistic movement and like tendencies in 18th century France. I have arranged to review the work for *Modern*

---

108. More would eventually deliver a series of Lowell Lectures at the Lowell Institute in Boston, but this would not take place until 1934 (Dakin 1960: 341).

109. James Edwin Creighton (1861–1924) was a distinguished professor of philosophy at Cornell University. On Creighton, see Carr 1924.

110. Babbitt 1917c.

111. The professor of French literature Albert Schinz (1870–1943) ultimately reviewed the book for the *Philosophical Review*; see Schinz 1917.

Philology.¹¹² If it comes in to Creighton, he might send it to the same person that undertakes the political writings.

I should suppose that it might be just as well to give the Plato to H. M. I do not feel that I have all the data requisite to give an opinion as to its inclusion in the Shelburne series. If we can get together this summer we can talk over this and many other matters that I am too indolent to discuss on paper.

Sincerely yours,
Irving Babbitt.

---

245 Nassau Street
Princeton, New Jersey
August 4, 1916

Dear Babbitt,

I left my sister in Portland still miserable from her operation, but out of danger, and I hear that everything now is doing well with her. Infantile paralysis[113] has played the mischief with our travelling plans. Darrah has been away visiting Westerly, R. I. and cannot come home through New York. The disease has struck Princeton, and it is desirable to get Alice[114] away as soon as possible. Net takes her by the Federal Express tonight, thus avoiding New York. They will pick Darrah up *en route* and go to Essex by way of Boston and Burlington—a long, tedious trip. I am staying here for another ten days, so as to finish up the essay on Plato on which I am now engaged. I am bound to have the volume ready for the press by January 1ˢᵗ. This urgency may prevent my visit to you, but I sincerely hope it will not. I shall of course write to you about the time of my coming—if I come. – I have never for a moment supposed that you were indiscreet in bringing me to the attention of the Harvard men when I left the *Nation*; my only question is whether it is worth while to propose anything now. I do not see how there could be any harm in approaching Lowell in the manner you suggest. Have you heard that Mather is to give the lectures this year or next?[115] – As for the Rousseau, I should not feel myself competent to write a review of his political writings. I might have enough to say about his ideas, but I am not up in the literature

---

112. For this review, see Babbitt 1917d.
113. More refers to the polio epidemic in New York City during the summer of 1916.
114. More's younger daughter Alice.
115. Mather's book *Modern Painting* (1927) was based on his 1916 Lowell Lectures. See Mather 1927.

of the subject. The Masson I might handle better, owing to my reading of the English deists. I shall certainly get the book one way or another. Is Masson's book in English? If not, what is the exact title? – I don't wonder you are having troubles with your book.[116] The subject is huge. I and some others are waiting for the results, hoping to see certain hard questions really answered. With kindest regards to Dora,

Sincerely yours,
Paul E. More.

Crater Club
Essex, N. Y.
August 22, 1916

Dear Babbitt,

Here I am in my summer quarters—a mighty hot hole these last few days—working along slowly in my Plato and asking myself how and when I may get to Squam. Would some time about the ninth or tenth of next month be convenient, or should the visit be later? Matters are a little complicated by my desire to drop Darrah off at St. Johnsbury, Vt., on my way to you, and to stop over with Holt in Burlington on my way back. Holt will not be at home until about the ninth. I am ill provided with time tables and cannot decipher the intricacies of the New England railway system. Have you the means at hand to tell me how I can most comfortably reach Squam from here, and if it is possible to come by way of St. Johnsbury? I have some fear that the intricacies of travel may drive me to forego my summer visit altogether, and to wait for an opportunity to see you in Cambridge after Christmas. However, I shall be genuinely disappointed if driven to this. – I left my sister Alice at the Portland hospital very weak but out of danger. The surgeon hopes that the removal of a decayed appendix will ultimately help her, but her recovery of strength is terribly slow, and makes me anxious. Net was frightened out of Princeton by the spread of infantile paralysis,[117] and had to bring the children here by a most devious route outside of New York and through Boston. I stayed behind for a week with Francesco,[118] feeding royally on Italian

---

116. Babbitt 1991.
117. On the 1916 polio epidemic centered in New York City, see above.
118. On Francesco, the Mores' Italian butler, see Dakin 1960: 163, 214.

cooking. Now I am in my summer harness. It galls a bit when the thermometer crawls up to 90°. – Let me hear from you as soon as you conveniently can. – Meanwhile with kindest regards to Dora, I am

Faithfully yours,
Paul E. More.

Crater Club
Essex, N. Y.
September 1, 1916

My dear Babbitt,

My last letter crossed yours, and since writing I have given half my days and nights to an intensive study of New England time tables. As a result I think I understand pretty well the various routes by which I can reach your rural prhontisterion.[119] But now comes the greater difficulty. It looks as if this threatened strike would put all travel out of the question and as if I should be compelled again to postpone my visit until the winter. If I find it possible to get to you this month, some time before the fifteenth I will warn you by telegram. I find that if I take Darrah with me to Greensborough I could most conveniently reach your part of the State by going to Plymouth. Is that town near enough to you to make meeting there as easy for you as at Meredith? Please let me know about this immediately. – And another thing. Some time ago I asked you for a good quotation from Rousseau showing his pretensions to Platonism. Your reply I have some where, but cannot lay my hands on it now. Can you without trouble send me this information again? And with it I should like to have a quotation to show the falseness of Rousseau's pretensions. The point is this. I am making the test of the true and spurious Platonism to lie in this: Plato makes the spirit an inhibition, just as Socrates always speaks of the δαιμόνιον[120] as a veto, never as a positive command. Hence when Goethe represents Mephistopheles as the *Geist der immer verneint* is he exactly reversing the Platonic doctrine? In like manner

---

119. A footnote in the typescript of this letter reads: "Place for meditation, thinking shop, = School of Socrates. (Aristophanes, *Clouds*, passim.)"

120. A footnote in the typescript of this letter reads: "Spiritual monitor. Almost impossible to translate. (Cf. Plato, *Thaet.*, 151 A; *Apol.*, 40 A.)" On More's link between the Socratic *daemon* and the "inner check," see, e.g., More 1917b: 145-46.

Rousseau's rejection of spiritual *restraint* is a false Platonism. This is the thesis I wish to fortify by a quotation similar to that from *Faust*. Can you help me out? – I am plunging through my last chapter, but I need at least two months for a complete rewriting. – Meanwhile I should like to talk with you on various points.

Sincerely,
Paul E. More.

Crater Club
Essex, N. Y.
September 18, 1916

Dear Babbitt,

It was a long way to Essex,[121] and for the most part a hot and dusty way, but it came to an end at last. And so I am here with the loveliness of Squam Lake in my memory and wondering whether I prefer it to the wider and more heroic outlook of Champlain. I dare say you found me rather a sluggish and intractable guest, but I enjoyed myself heartily and am grateful to you and the good ladies for their care of me. – Yesterday I finished the first draft of my Plato,[122] and now I look forward to two steady months of revision. It will be a happy day when the work is all behind me. – We have our eye here on a wonderful farm of some ninety acres with lake front and magnificent view. It may, we hope, be bought for something under $10,000, perhaps a good deal under that figure. We may ask you to go in with us, if we should take the place. I know that Essex is somewhat inconvenient for you, but there are good trains from Burlington to Boston, and this country has one supreme advantage in the absence of black flies and mosquitoes. However this is all very much in the air at present. – I have heard from my sister,[123] and she will stay in Portland until the first of October; so that I have two weeks for rest and idling. – Lou is much interested in my report of your comments on his book.[124]

Sincerely,
Paul E. More.

---

121. More is describing his journey back from the Babbitts' summer cottage at Squam Lake to the Mores' place in Essex, New York, which overlooked Lake Champlain. Dakin (1960: 162) notes that More visited with Babbitt at Squam Lake in the middle of September, 1916.

122. More 1917b.

123. Alice More.

124. A footnote in the typescript of this letter reads: "*The Limitations of Science* [1915], by Louis T. More."

Ashland, N. H.
24 September, 1916

Dear More,

I am glad to hear that the Plato is finished and am looking forward to reading the MS. From what I presume is a more or less selfish point of view, I wish that you were devoting to a careful study of Plotinus the time that you have been putting on Proclus. Plotinus is the source of much in modern thought that passes as mysticism and is also accounted genuinely Platonic.[125] The German romanticists in particular go back very largely to him and to Jacob Böhme.[126] Since you were here I have been looking over my notes and find that I already have a considerable body of evidence on this point. I can forward a number of precise references to you if the subject interests you. A point that seems to me to concern your subject is the way in which Böhme corrupted the idea of evil and at the same time the reality of dualism by making of evil only a manifestation of God; this point was seized upon with great avidity by the romanticists. Böhme at the same time encourages an expansive infinite of desire. Fire or desire (sulphur) is both a good and bad principle with him. One needs in dealing with him to distinguish carefully between the way in which one falls away from the original unity into what he calls *Zerbrechlichkeit* and the way in which one recovers this unity. Various authorities I have connect up this side of Böhme with Plotinus, and of course the name of Plato is constantly invoked. The youthful Novalis for example said that he was a Platonist and at the same time declared that there is no such thing as sin in the world. There is certainly here a line of tendency that bears on your subject and that antedates the corruption of conscience by Shaftesbury and the sentimentalists. As a result of romantic confusion the word Platonist has become well-nigh impossible. Any discriminations that are intended to make for a sound revival of Platonism ought I should suppose, to be at once clear-cut and concrete.

Your scheme for a summer colony sounds very tempting but the Champlain region is as you know very inconvenient for us. If you are planning to sell your present place why are you not willing to take a glance at the region about Monadnock? It is much nearer to New York than Essex with a good train service day or night (5½ hours) to Keene. Because of the altitude that district is cooler than either Champlain or Squam. Mosquitoes are getting pretty well cleaned up around Dublin. I wish that you might put in a summer at Dublin or thereabouts and get well acquainted with the Monadnock

---

125. This comment anticipates many of the criticisms of Plotinus More would articulate in his later volume *Hellenistic Philosophies* (see More 1923: 171-259).
126. Jakob Böhme (1575-1624) was a German philosopher and Christian mystic.

region before coming to a final decision of any kind. Dublin is less than 3 hours from Boston and this proximity to the Harvard Library means a good deal to me and might even at times mean something to you. – It was fine to have you at Squam, though I do not feel that you saw much of the country. If I got a place here it would probably be in a part of the lake entirely different from any you visited. – I am leaving tomorrow for Cambridge. The family stays on for another week. With kind regards to Nettie.

Sincerely yours,
Irving Babbitt.

Essex, N. Y.
September 28, 1916

Dear Babbitt,

I should of course be glad to have any notes bearing on the corruption of Platonism you may care to send me; but you must be cautious not to rob yourself of material. Proclus is merely a continuator of Plotinus and Iamblichus, and I already have notes showing the mischief of the emanation theory which they substituted for Plato's dualism. Plotinus I shall go through as soon as I return to Princeton. But the full discussion of this matter I shall leave for a later volume, merely indicating the sources of error in this present work. The bookseller whose address I am seeking is Weller, not Weil, but I suppose you do not know his place. – I go down to Princeton on Monday.

Sincerely,
Paul E. More.

CHAPTER SIX
1917–1918

245 Nassau Street
Princeton, New Jersey
January 24, 1917

Dear Babbitt,

At last the MS. of my Plato[1] goes to you by express. As I see the bulk of the thing I have qualms of conscience about asking you to read it now in your busy time; but it was your own generosity that prompted the act. And as I have been looking the papers over and making a few minor corrections here and there, I have become sadly aware of the need of general criticism and revision. Of course this is the moment of natural depression, when one's work is just finished, and one's enthusiasm has passed into something like the headache after a debauch; at least, I hope this is the case and that I shall be able to take more satisfaction in the thing when I come back to it after a rest.

The only person I have heard speak of your *Nation* paper[2] on Rousseau was Marshall,[3] and he praised it unstintedly. It certainly shows a masterly understanding of the subject.

Let me have a post card acknowledging the receipt of the MS., as I tremble for its security. And when you come to criticise, do not hesitate to speak your mind.

We are hoping to see you when you go South.[4]

Sincerely,
Paul E. More.

---

1. More 1917b.
2. Babbitt 1917c.
3. Presumably, More refers to his friend Henry Rutgers Marshall. On Marshall, see above.
4. On Babbitt's lecture at Randolph-Macon College in Virginia, see below.

Cambridge
27 January, 1917

Dear More,

Your MS. has just reached me safely. We are having the pleasure of entertaining the Mathers just at present and I shall scarcely have a chance to look at it until they go. I have put it for safe-keeping into my fire-proof room at Widener.[5] My general instinct will be to be rather chary of criticisms,—to confine myself to points of which I feel fairly certain. If you are not in a hurry to get the MS. back, might it not be a good idea for me to bring it with me when I go south? Would it be convenient for you to put me up on Feb. 7 (I am likely to reach Princeton on the 5:26). I would remain with you on Thursday and leave for Lynchburg on Friday morning (the 9th). If you prefer I can get your MS. back to you in about a week but am likely in any case to reserve most of my comment until we meet.

I am grateful to you for going over the Rousseau.[6] I gave it a careful revision after you saw it and then at the request of Fuller cut out the more technical parts of my review of Vaughan. The article in its abridged form is more accessible to the general reader, but it is not improved I should say, in other respects.

Mather's lectures[7] have been well received here. The last one was especially effective. I was hoping to get Lowell interested in your Plato for a similar course and was waiting to get the MS. before taking the matter up with him, but now that they are to be given at Princeton, I am not sure that they would be available for the Lowell foundation.[8] With best regards to Nettie.

Sincerely yours,
Irving Babbitt.

---

245 Nassau Street
Princeton, New Jersey
January 29, 1917

Dear Babbitt,

There is no obstacle at this end in the way of your proposed visit, and we shall both be delighted to see you. Suppose we regard it as settled that you

---

5. Widener is the main library at Harvard University.
6. Babbitt 1917c.
7. On Mather's Lowell Lectures in 1916, see above, chapter 5.
8. On More's Vanuxem Lectures at Princeton in late 1917, see above, chapter 5.

are to reach Princeton, the 7th, at 5:26, unless you write to the contrary. If you do change your plans, let me know at the earliest possible moment, as I may wish to have one or two people at the house to meet you. – As for the MS.[9] there is no haste about that at all, as I shall not take it up for revision for three or four weeks in any case. Bring it with you, if that is convenient; or, if your time is engaged, leave the reading until you return from Lynchburg. I know it is no light task to go through a MS. of that kind and bulk. – The Mathers, whom I saw this afternoon, report a thoroughly enjoyable visit in Cambridge.

Sincerely,
Paul E. More.

Cambridge
26 February, 1917

Dear More,

I should have written to you some time ago to tell of my safe escape from Lynchburg after my pleasant glimpse of you and Nettie. I faced an audience of between five and six hundred young women at the Randolph-Macon institution. They looked very attractive from the platform but I did not get any nearer view. If I had been young and good-looking there would not only have been a reception but it would have been the chief thing.

I could have wished more time to mull over that Plato of yours and regret also that I did not bring to it a fresher knowledge of Plato himself. I anticipate that the book will have a beneficent influence. It should coöperate in any case with my book on Rousseau. Like you I have a great deal to say about the distinction between pleasure and happiness. The first part of your volume did not leave as clear cut an impression on my mind as I could have desired. – Personally I hold with Aristotle that, if one does not wish to fall into metaphysical subtlety, the identification of virtue and knowledge is simply untenable. The Aristotelian position (video meliora proboque, etc.)[10] is here more obviously dualistic than that of Socrates.

I am feeling a good deal of worry about the English these days. The English people itself seems to be making a great effort but I have no confidence in the leaders. Northcliffe[11] seems to me the modern equivalent of Creon.

9. Of More 1917b.
10. Babbitt here quotes a portion of Ovid's *Metamorphoses*, 7.20: "I see and approve better things."
11. Alfred Harmsworth, the 1st Viscount of Northcliffe (1865–1922), was a publishing magnate who promoted a strong anti-German line as editor of the *Daily Mail*.

Can you not come up with Nettie when she makes her visit to us on her way to the Pool?[12] We do not see much of one another at best. I hope you made my excuses to Mrs. Mather for my failure to see her again before leaving Princeton.

Sincerely,
Irving Babbitt.

---

245 Nassau Street
Princeton, New Jersey
April 1, 1917

My dear Babbitt,

I too have returned from an incursion into the South—my first crossing of Mason and Dixon's line. They asked me to come down to Trinity College, Durham, N. C., and give a lecture; and as I had my essay on New England Poetry ready, I gave them that.[13] They seemed to accept it kindly enough.

Your criticism of the earlier chapters of my Plato[14] was certainly mild. On reading over the MS. I was not at all surprised that this part of the book did not make a clear impression on you. My revision has gone to the length of rewriting all the whole of the first four chapters. This makes the sixth actual rewriting of most of chapter I! It ought to be perfect; if it is clear I shall be satisfied. And when this work is finished, it is the last for me of the kind. There is something repellent to me in such an attempt to systematize truth, and I wonder how far such systematizing is really a betrayal of a mind like Plato's.

Late this month I am going out to Chicago to give one of the inaugural addresses for the newly established William Vaughn Moody lectures. My subject will be Canons of Taste.[15] The first word of the title at least ought to stimulate attention these days.

Sincerely yours,
Paul E. More.

---

12. Biddeford Pool, Maine, where the Mores occasionally vacationed.

13. Dakin (1960: 167) notes that More delivered an address called "The Spirit and Poetry of Early New England" at Trinity College (now Duke University) on March 23, 1917.

14. More 1917b.

15. Dakin (1960: 169) specifies that More delivered his William Vaughn Moody lecture, called "Standards of Taste," at the University of Chicago on April 26, 1917. He would later repurpose the material from this lecture; for details, see Dakin 1950: 167.

P.S. Can you send me the volume and page of Vaughan's Rousseau[16] where the words occur: "With modifications due to the influence of Montesquieu"—Rousseau remained "essentially a Platonist to the end?"

Princeton
May 9, 1917

Dear Babbitt,

Won't you be good enough to let me have immediately the volume and page for these two references: Vaughan's *Pol. Writings of J. J. R.*: "with modifications due to the influence of Montesquieu (Rousseau remained) essentially a Platonist to the end." Herford[17] in *Cam. Hist. Eng. Lit.*: "Shelley has given, in *Prometheus Unbound*, magnificent expression to the faith of Plato and of Christ."

My MS.[18] is all ready for the printer except for these references.

From something Dora said in her letter to Net, we have been indulging in the hope that you might possibly think of Essex as a place for part of the holidays. The country, and particularly the lake, is, I know, not perfectly suited to your needs and habits, but you would find some compensations. For one thing we have built a tennis court on our ground. Lou will probably play a good deal, and I may possibly make a try at it again.

My trip to Chicago was successful, so far as the lecturing went, and I met a few interesting people, including President and Mrs. Judson.[19] But these hurried journeys are tiresome and unsettling. The university buildings impressed me as they did you.

How does your Rousseau[20] progress? Will you not finish it this summer?

Sincerely,
Paul E. More.

---

16. More here refers to *The Political Writings of Rousseau*, edited by C. E. Vaughan, which Babbitt had reviewed for the *Nation* (Babbitt 1917c).

17. C. H. Herford (1853–1931), an English literary critic and professor of English literature, who contributed the chapter on Shelley (57–78) to Ward and Waller 1915. The quotation More was looking for can be found on 67.

18. Of More 1917b.

19. Harry Pratt Judson (1849–1927) was the president of the University of Chicago from 1907 to 1923.

20. Babbitt 1991.

P.S. Columbia is going to give me the *Doctor of Letters* this commencement. They wish the fact, of course, to be kept absolutely secret until after the event.[21]

Cambridge
11 May, 1917

Dear More,

You will find the references for which you ask on the enclosed slip. I should be glad to look over your Plato in proof if you think it would do any good. I am working on the last chapter of my Rousseau but it is proceeding rather slowly. I do not see much use in publishing a book of this kind until the war is over. There is not much room for quiet thinking in the present hurly burly. – I shall need to be in close touch with the Harvard Library this summer and so we shall probably take the Flint cottage at Dublin. It would mean a great deal for me to be near to you but Essex is at best very inaccessible. I am disappointed at not seeing you in Cambridge this spring. It seems doubtful now whether I am going to get a glimpse of Stuart Sherman. What do you think of his book on Arnold?[22] It strikes me as a model book for his special audience, but there are certain deeper questions about Arnold—such as you take up in your essay on criticism[23]—that he rather shirks. The reading of poetry, even of the best poetry, may turn out to be a very doubtful substitute for philosophy and religion in the case of the few and no substitute at all in the case of the many. This seems to me personally a time for keen dialectic and hard consecutive thinking. Arnold is not himself an aesthete but in his praise of poetry he tends at times to encourage aesthetic errors in others.

Sincerely yours,
Irving Babbitt.

---

21. Dakin (1960: 169) claims that More received "the honorary degree of Doctor of Letters from Columbia [University] and Dartmouth [College] in June 1918." But in both cases, Dakin appears to be incorrect about the year. On the honorary degree from Dartmouth, see below, this chapter.

22. Sherman 1917a. Babbitt would write a review of the book for the August 2, 1917, issue of the *Nation*. See Babbitt 1917b. This essay later appeared in the collection *Spanish Character and Other Essays* (Babbitt 1940: 48-65).

23. More 1910a: 213-44.

Cambridge
23 May, 1917

Dear More,

I wrote recently to Fuller asking him for Spingarn's[24] "Creative Criticism,"[25] and he informs me that the volume has been sent to you. If by any chance you are not anxious to do this bit of reviewing, I should be glad to take it over. I have traced this whole question of genius vs. taste with all the care of which I am capable from the early 18th century down to the present and I believe that in his general solution of it Spingarn is a dangerous anarchist. He is one of those who in my opinion need to bleed for the good of the cause. It may be that you yourself are eager for utterance on this subject and in that case of course I withdraw discreetly. If on the other hand you are not anxious to do the reviewing but would like a copy of the book let me know and I could supply myself independently.

Sincerely,
I. Babbitt.

---

245 Nassau Street
Princeton, May 25, 1917

Dear Babbitt,

You are more than welcome to Spingarn, and I am sending the *Nation* copy of his book to you by post. I have another copy, sent me with "compliments of the author." I should scarcely have returned compliments, had I reviewed him. As I have a number of other books on my hands, it is a relief to lighten myself of this one.

I am sorry that taste, convenience, and other matters divide us in the summer. This season it is your turn to visit, and I trust you will plan to give us a number of days at Essex any time in August or September. Net, of course, will be extending the invitation to Dora.

---

24. On Joel Elias Spingarn, see his entry in the Biographical Register.
25. Spingarn 1917. Babbitt would ultimately discuss this book in "Genius and Taste," an essay in the February 7, 1918, issue of the *Nation* (see Babbitt 1918).

My Plato[26] is in the printer's hands, and I suppose proof will be coming before long. I am going to accept your offer to read the proof. Let me know when you change your address.[27]

Sherman is preparing a volume of essays for Holt.[28] He sent me the Preface[29] today—a vigorous and unambiguous plea for discipline. His Arnold is as you describe it. The tone is admirably conciliatory, and not too high, for the audience he was looking to. But it is a pity that he should have written for such a series. Fuller wants me to review it. I do not want to do so. Can you?[30]

Faithfully,
Paul E. More.

---

245 Nassau Street
Princeton, New Jersey
June 15, 1917

Dear Babbitt,

I am ordering the Princeton Un. Press to send you the galley proofs of my *Platonism*. When you change your address, kindly notify the Press. I have told them you would keep them informed of your whereabouts. Slash away at the proof to your heart's content; I am ready to do any amount of rewriting that may be necessary. Next Wednesday I shall be getting another hood at Dartmouth;[31] what an iridical effect I might produce by wearing all my hoods at once!

How is this for a bit of wisdom from an old lame slave who kept a school at Nicopolis: τὸ παιδεύεσθαι τοῦτ' ἔστι, μανθάνειν τὰ ἴδια καὶ τὰ ἀλλότρια.[32] I am going through Epictetus to my great pleasure and profit. True wisdom is not quite so sad as he and Marcus Aurelius represent it to be. Their philosophy

---

26. More 1917b.
27. More refers to Babbitt's departure from Cambridge for the summer vacation.
28. Sherman 1917b. This book was published in November of 1917.
29. In the published book, these pages are called the Introduction: see Sherman 1917b: 3-17.
30. A footnote in the typescript of this letter reads: "Babbitt did review Sherman's book in *The Nation*, Aug. 2, 1917, and the review is reprinted in Babbitt's *Spanish Character and Other Essays*."
31. Dakin (1960: 169) claims that this occurred in June of 1918, but he appears to be wrong about the year.
32. A footnote in the typescript of this letter reads: "To be getting an education means this: to be learning what is your own and what is not your own. Arrian's *Discourses of Epictetus*, IV, 5–7. W.A. Oldfather in Loeb Class. Lib., *Epictetus* II, 1928, p. 333."

is nothing more than the Hindu doctrine of *works without attachment*, and if they miss the joy of the greater Hindus and of Plato there is nevertheless a certain steady consolation in their bravery. Do you know the stoics?

Faithfully,
Paul E. More.

Cambridge
16 June, 1917

Dear More,

You are receiving so many honorary degrees that apparently you have been forced to turn for consolation to stoicism. – If you are going back up to Dartmouth why not look in on us, preferably on your way back? I do not see that it will lengthen your journey greatly. We shall be much disappointed if we miss seeing you. I should like very much to visit you at Essex late in the summer, but I do not feel that I have earned the right to any such pleasure. I am not at all satisfied with the progress I have been making in my work and am planning a summer of hard toil. If things go very successfully—nous verrons. We are intending to remain here until about July 6, and then off to Dublin.[33]

Sincerely yours.
Irving Babbitt.

---

245 Nassau Street
Princeton, New Jersey
June 24, 1917

Dear Babbitt,

I do not pretend to have read the Renaissance literature of criticism, but I know enough of it to see that Shepard[34] has not been fair in his use of it. His review[35] is certainly learned and well written, but it doesn't leave an

---

33. Their summer cottage in Dublin, New Hampshire.
34. On Odell Shepard, see the entry on him in the Biographical Register.
35. The review in question (Shepard 1917) is of Clarissa Rinaker's book on Thomas Warton, in origin a dissertation written at the University of Illinois, under the direction of Stuart P. Sherman (see Rinaker 1913: no pagination). Odell Shepard was a student of Babbitt's who composed an extremely negative review of Rinaker's monograph for the *Journal of English and*

entirely pleasant impression on my mind; in fact I am not sure that it does not exhibit some of the worst faults of scholasticism in its over-emphasis on sources, and its delight in boggling over a gnat and swallowing the camel. Miss Rinaker's book is sufficiently open to criticism—how many doctoral theses are not?—and she does fall into the ordinary hero-worship, or rather subject-exaggeration, of the editor and biographer; but she does not do so to anything like the vicious extent that Shepard asserts. Shepard moreover fails to give her credit for some excellent writing; minimizes her scholarship, which is considerable, and in general slurs over her successful achievements in a way that is really dishonest—or, perhaps, merely youthful. He does not, in my judgement, show critical taste himself in his discriminations of eighteenth-century poets. Miss Rinaker writes as an avowed romanticist, and one or two of Shepard's attacks on this point are thoroughly deserved; here he seemed to be merely echoing what he had learned from you. - I wrote in my letter to Dora of my trip home, and of the great pleasure I had in my stop-over in Cambridge. - Tomorrow Darrah goes off on a visit, and Thursday Mrs. Beck[36] leaves, so that the house will be very quiet.

Faithfully yours,
Paul E. More.

---

245 Nassau Street
Princeton, New Jersey
July 13, 1917

My dear Babbitt,

You have certainly not erred by obscuring the work of Sherman; you are in fact very generous to him.[37] The paper is good and well constructed; but I think when you read it over again, you will see two or three places where the argument can be made clearer. I have indicated these places, as they appeared to me, by marginal notes. The proposed additions to the text are, of course, mere suggestions; I have thought nothing of my language. The least satisfactory part of the essay constructively is in pages 44–45. Consider the succession of points you take up: p. 44 newspapers are a sign of our folly; 45

Germanic Philology (Shepard 1917). Shepard used the term "hero-worship" (Shepard 1917: 155) in his review, which More repeats in this letter.

36. More's mother-in-law, Annie E. McMurray Beck (1845–1918).

37. More here discusses Babbitt's review of Sherman's book *Matthew Arnold: How to Know Him* (1917), which would appear in the August 2, 1917, issue of the *Nation*. See Babbitt 1917b.

melodrama; 46 the common; 48 the remnant; 49 optimism; 50 education; 53 quality, quantity, imperialism; 55 criticism. Now these points are all well made individually, and I dare say their sequence is logical. But as they stand their effect is scattered and dissipated. What is the source of them all? State this, and derive the others.

I am glad you have written the article. It will do Sherman good, and will help to clear up the ideas of some readers.

My Platonism is now in the composing room, and proof ought to be coming in immediately. Keep the Princeton University Press informed in advanced of your change of address.

Faithfully,
Paul E. More.

---

245 Nassau Street
Princeton, New Jersey
August 1, 1917

My dear Babbitt,

I leave for Essex tomorrow, and my address henceforth will be the Crater Club. I am disappointed that no proof has come yet, but I presume they will get at it now very soon.

As I was the traveller [sic] last summer, I am hoping that you will find it possible to visit us sometime in August or September. Of course Net will be glad to see Dora also. I gather from what Dora says that you are making steady but slow work with the revision of your MS.[38] You will probably find after a while that a relief from it for a few days will really be a help and not a retardation.

Yesterday was excessively hot and last night was one of the worst I have ever felt. It is scarcely any better today. If there is no change by tomorrow night it will be hard travelling. But these things lie in the lap of the gods.

Good luck to you, and may your brain work like a trusty machine. My own two months in the country will be almost free. I am taking Pindar and Vergil with me.

Sincerely,
Paul E. More.

---

38. Babbitt 1991.

Crater Club
Essex, N. Y.
August 29, 1917

My dear Babbitt,

This is an excellent piece of work,[39] in so far as it expresses some of your fundamental ideas—ideas, too, which it is important to have set before the public. But my editorial sense tells me that in its present form it will rather fail to carry conviction to the uninitiated. You have put too much into it. My advice is to prune somewhat rigorously, taking out many of the allusions and some of the secondary ideas. Could you not force more conclusively the derivation of the various themes from your first thesis "Man is ignorant *and* lazy?" And then, at the last, I should certainly develop the theme of the relation of expansiveness to war, and Buddhism-Aristotelianism to peace; and let the article conclude with this, rather than return to your first thesis. The matter of your article is too serious to be weakened by embroidering—though the embroidery itself, if you had sufficient space, is important enough. I think Holt would have looked kindly on an error of this sort.

I am vexed at the slowness of the Princeton University Press; but you must have the second installment of proof now in hand.

We are still hoping that your conscience will permit you to visit us. Darrah will have a friend here until about the middle of September, but our guest house will be free after that until we go home on the twenty-sixth.

Having finished up two or three odd jobs, I am now resting strenuously; but with some reading of Greek thrown in.

With kindest regards to Dora and Katharine, I am

Sincerely yours,
Paul E. More.

Monadnock, N. H.
30 August, 1917

Dear More,

The Plato proof came just after I had sent my letter to you. Your discussion of free will is about the most difficult and subtle thing in your book but I am not sure that it is possible for you or any one else to do better than you

---

39. A footnote in the typescript of this letter reads: "A review of 'Buddha and the Gospel of Buddhism' by Ananda Coomaraswamy in *The Nation*, Oct. 18, 1917." See Babbitt 1917a. The review was later featured in *Spanish Character and Other Essays* (Babbitt 1940: 150-69).

have done. The difficulties in the way of any discussion of this kind are so great that one is inclined at times to plant oneself with Dr. Johnson on free will as a primary perception anterior to argument. "We're free and we know we're free and that's the end of it." You may be able to clarify somewhat a few places I have marked but even here you should not attach undue weight to my comment.

I have so high a regard for your editorial sense and your literary sense in general that I am naturally disappointed by your judgment on my Buddha paper. You simply want a different paper from the one I have written. I might write two new articles in the time I would spend mulling over this one trying to bring it into line with your suggestions. I am inclined to send it on to Fuller very much as it is,[40] and then if he sends it back to lay it aside for the present. – I happen to be very sick of attempts at rewriting just now. I have had to recast the early chapters of my book[41] and do not feel sure even now that I have arrived at anything definitive. I am indeed very much discouraged at my rate of progress and do not feel that I have any right to that visit to Essex, as much as I am tempted. I understand by the way, that ordinary travel is likely to be much disturbed during September by movements of troops. With my kind regards to Nettie.

Sincerely yours,
Irving Babbitt.

Crater Club
Essex, N. Y.
September 14, 1917

Dear Babbitt,
What you say of my discussion of free will is sadly true. There, and in other places of the book, I have felt keenly that I was trying to accomplish the impossible; and yet, somehow, it seemed necessary to make some sort of metaphysical foundation for the moral fact on which true Platonism rests. And I can understand your dejection over the labor of recasting your work. I wrote the first chapter of my book over and over, a good deal of it six times! Yet after all that it is by no means in a satisfactory condition. The problem you are attacking is much more difficult than the three theses I was dealing with; there is nothing to do but to grit your teeth and have patience. I am sorry

---

40. As Babbitt appears to have done, since Fuller published the review in the *Nation* (Babbitt 1917a).
41. A footnote in the typescript of this letter reads: "*Rousseau and Romanticism.*"

my comments on your Buddha article were discouraging; but they were not meant to be so, and I am not sure that they ought to be so taken. I was criticizing from my own experience. It is easy to take too big a slice of thought for a short magazine paper, and one must recognize the limits of one's medium. More than once, many times in fact, I have written a long essay, and then cut out the heart of it, or perhaps one member of it, for periodical publication. This requires some force of intellectual renunciation, but, when that renunciation is once made, not so much intellectual labor. Probably, however, whatever discouragement my words conveyed, was owing rather to the fact that they were in the direction of the criticism of your writing I have been making at various times recently. Now, my general position, that your work does not carry as it might for the reason that you do not sufficiently lay bare the skeleton of your argument and that you tend to conceal the rigid cold syllogism under a mass of allusion and illustration,—my general position in this respect is undoubtedly true. Your work would be more effective if you first *wrote* out a skeleton of your argument, with an "it follows" at the head of each section and subsection, and if then, in putting flesh on the skeleton, you were diligent in keeping out of each section or paragraph every sentence that did not bear on the subject in the narrowed sense of the word.[42] Marshall has been here and we have been talking about your books and essays, and he agrees with me perfectly in this matter. I say all this by way of self-justification so to speak. But this is only one half of what I have to say; and the other half is far the more important. As you know, I owe my whole mental direction from what I have got from you in conversation, and some day, in the proper place, I shall state this in print. Now, in my criticism of your writing, I have that fact in mind. When I say that your writing is not so effective as it might be, I mean, not so effective as I have known you to be in another medium. And in my criticism of your method I am trying to lay my finger on the cause of this difference. But it does not follow that your writing, with no change in your method, may not be effective—ultimately, as readers get inside of your circle of ideas so to speak, very effective. I repeat that my comments were not intended to discourage, nor ought they to discourage. You are certainly winning your adherents, though slowly. Could you expect to get them rapidly in the present state of society? – We are all sorry that we shall not see you this summer, but bow to the decree of your New England conscience. At least we shall see you in Princeton this winter when you come down to enlighten the ladies,[43] and I may have a call that will bring me near

---

42. Cf. More's similar criticisms of Babbitt's writing style in his contribution to Manchester and Shepard 1941: 326.
43. Dakin (1960: 169) specifies that Babbitt lectured at Princeton on January 30, 1918.

Cambridge. I rather look for an easy winter, after I have got my Vanuxem lectures off my hands in October.[44] It is true that I need a rest. I have kept the bow string taut for too many years. And particularly I feel fatigue after the strain of my Platonism. Princeton is a good place for intellectual repose, and I shall indulge in it for a time. – With kindest regards to Dora and to your sister if she is with you.

Faithfully yours,
Paul E. More.

Princeton, N. J.
October 6, 1917

My dear Babbitt,

It has been good to hear that your threat of typhoid, in serious form, has not been realized. The βέλος[45] of Apollo is not ἐχέπευκες[46] this time. But don't write yourself down an ass, and go to work before you have got back your strength. I know how inconvenient absence from lectures must be at this time of the year, but it will be no economy to force matters—I can hold myself up as an example. After working for part of the summer, I came at last reluctantly to the conclusion that my *Platonism* had really strained my reserve of elasticity and that I needed a complete rest. And so for a month nearly I did what I have not done more than two or three times before in my life—I rested, writing nothing, reading no Greek and very little English. My proofs kept me rather anxious, and they are still hanging over me, but otherwise I am still taking things easily and shall probably do very little work this winter. The women's club of Lowell has asked me to read them my paper on *Taste and Tradition* the 31st of December, and, if it is convenient to you, I shall be glad to stop with you then in Cambridge for a day or two.[47] At the end of this month I have to read my Vanuxem lectures here.[48] I am aware that most of my book is ill suited for public delivery. But I shall pick out the easiest portions, and let the good people get out of this what they can. – You

---

44. More delivered the Vanuxem Lectures at Princeton in October and November of 1917 (Shafer 1935c: 206-7; Dakin 1960: 170).
45. A footnote in the typescript of this letter reads: "Arrow."
46. A footnote in the typescript of this letter reads: "Bitter or sharp. Homer, *Iliad*, I, 51."
47. On More's delivery of his "Standards of Taste" lecture at the Middlesex Women's Club in Lowell, Massachusetts, on December 31, 1917, and accompanying visit to the Babbitts in Cambridge, see Dakin 1960: 169.
48. On More's delivery of these lectures, which featured material from his book *Platonism*, see Shafer 1935c: 206-7; Dakin 1960: 170; and above.

have heard of the execution of poor Harry Dana.[49] I was told last spring that he had quite lost his balance on the subject of pacifism, and was making a nuisance of himself. The New England conscience is an ineradicable evil, it seems. On the other hand I have heard an amusing or pathetic story about Hibben.[50] It is said that two students had occasion to call on him at Prospect,[51] and that in the course of conversation one of them innocently spoke of certain young men as going into the army for a lark. Whereupon Hibben quite lost his head; shook the astounded boy by the shoulders, and asked him how he dared to make so vile an insinuation to him (Hibben) in his own house! Such is the stuff of the college president! I heard Hibben the other evening speak on the occasion of Pomeroy's[52] (the Episcopal clergyman) leaving for Princeton. Such soapy sentimentalism as he vented was enough to make one wonder whether the knowledge of human nature has fled the earth. – Thank Dora for her kindness in keeping us informed as to the stages of your disease. We are waiting to hear that you are entirely yourself again.

Sincerely,
Paul E. More.

Cambridge
21 November, 1917

Dear More,

I got the better of the typhoid very quickly so far as the actual fever was concerned but have had a rather tedious convalescence. I began my college lecturing on Oct. 27 but, to judge from certain symptoms, have not got the poison completely out of my system yet. I am about twenty pounds under my normal weight and though I seem to be gaining slowly still fall distinctly short of my usual strength and vitality.

I am distinctly concerned by what you tell me about your health. You have been going a rather rapid clip for years past and in a way it is not surprising that it should begin to tell on you. Since you do not seem inclined to imitate

---

49. Henry ("Harry") Wadsworth Longfellow Dana (1881–1950), the grandson of the poet Longfellow, was a professor of comparative literature at Columbia University from 1912 to 1917, when he lost his job due to his support for pacifism. By "execution," More here refers to Dana's loss of his job.
50. On John Grier Hibben, then the president of Princeton, see above, chapter 5.
51. Prospect House was then the president's residence at Princeton.
52. The Episcopal minister Ralph Brouwer Pomeroy (1876–1935) became an instructor at the Princeton Theological Seminary in 1917.

J. D. Rockefeller and take to golf, a brisk daily walk, gradually working up to five or six miles would probably do a great deal to restore your tone. Walking is not the most exciting thing in the world but it is probably the healthiest.

I shall be interested to learn that the lectures on Plato went off well but am still more interested of course in the reception the book gets. I assume that it will be out very shortly.[53] It is a pity that you are cut off from the English and continental public. I do not rate my fellow country men very high in these matters. Only the professional philosophers will be able to follow you in two or three of your chapters; and I fear that they will not agree with you. The chapter on the Parmenides is difficult but of a rewarding kind of difficulty, whereas the treatment of free will strikes me as just a bit jiggery. Your last chapter strikes me not only as excellent but of an excellence that should make a fairly wide appeal. You are at your best here as well as in various other parts of the volume.

Sherman's article in the *Nation*[54] is excellent as a satire on Roosevelt but as a piece of constructive thinking it is worse than negligible. Sherman's dubious side is his windy democratic "idealism." His declamations about the "plain people" and "never again" leave me very cold. I do not doubt he will awaken an ecstatic response in many quarters. Personally I should prefer never to get any recognition at all than to get it by flattering the enormous humanitarian illusions of the age. Most of what now passes as democracy, involving as it does the class war and the confiscation of property, is an even worse menace to civilization than the Kaiser.

I have noted very carefully what you said in a recent letter—and you have often said the same thing in conversation—about the structural defects in my writing that have stood in the way of its recognition. The failure to get recognition would seem indubitable. I should get more if only on the important principle laid down by Boileau:[55] *Un sot trouve toujours un plus sot qui l'admire*. The explanation of this failure, coming from so shrewd and sympathetic a critic as yourself, has of course great weight with me. In the meanwhile I have been running counter to all the main tendencies of the time and if I had syllogized my point of view quite so uncompromisingly as you suggest, I should have been thrown out of Harvard and very likely out of teaching altogether. I had a very close shave as it was. I am not planning a different method in my coming volume. I shall, however, have the advantage of the considerable background I have built up and shall also in view

---

53. According to Dakin (1950: 170), More's *Platonism* was published in December of 1917; this fits with More's statement in his December 9, 1917, letter below. Cf. Dakin 1960: 176.
54. Sherman 1917c.
55. The French poet and critic Nicolas Boileau-Despréaux (1636–1711).

of recent events be able to speak out more frankly. The result may be in the direction of what you desire.

We are much pleased at the prospect of seeing you in December and are hoping for as long a visit as possible. With kind regards to Nettie,

Sincerely,
I. Babbitt.

Princeton
December 9, 1917

My dear Babbitt,

I was glad to hear of your returning strength, and hope that by now you are quite yourself. What you say of your loss of weight touches me nearly. I was frightened several weeks ago to learn that in the past twelve months or so I had lost eighteen pounds. This, with other disagreeable symptoms, sent me to the doctor, who gave all my organs a thorough examination. Heart, kidneys, blood-pressure, etc. proved to be perfectly sound, but there were signs of colitis, a trouble which I have as a matter of fact always had. It is clear that I left the *Nation*, or at least gave up the attempt to carry on the double work of editor and scholar, just in time. I knew this when I made the change. I should have taken a year's rest, but instead of that plunged into my Plato, which turned out to be a vastly more wearing task than I had expected. Now that the book is published, the lectures given, and the matter off my mind, I am feeling like a new man. I shall take things easily this winter, and hope to get back my normal health, if not all my elasticity. The lectures went off fairly well—at least I had a fair audience of students, which is a good deal to say, considering the nature of the subject. But I do not like lecturing. I have no stage-fright, and I estimate the performance at its true value, but there is nevertheless a sort of factitious excitement about it which is quite distasteful to me. I came on a passage in Chrysostom the other day, which describes the state of mind admirably, though in exaggerated terms: πρὸ μὲν γὰρ τοῦ θεάτρου καὶ τῶν ἐν τῷ λέγειν ἀγώνων, ἐν ἀγωνίᾳ καὶ τρόμῳ κατέχεται· μετὰ δὲ τὸ θεάτρον, ἢ ἀποτέθνηκεν ἀπὸ τῆς ἀθυμίας, ἢ χαίρει πάλιν ἀμέτρως· ὅπερ λύπης ἐστὶ χαλεπώτερον.[56] I have no such excessive feelings of either

---

56. A footnote in the typescript of this letter provides the following translation: "Before the theatre and the oratorical performances one is in a state of agony and trembling; after the theatre either one is dead from despondency or one is full of joy beyond measure; which is worse

sort, but enough of them to make the return to the quiet oblivion of my study like the restoration of health. What you say of that part of my book that deals with the problem of free will, I heartily endorse. It is better to leave these subjects alone; no good comes of discussing them. I shall scarcely touch them again. – Your own book,[57] I presume, will be considerably delayed by your ill health; that is vexatious, but such a task as you have undertaken cannot be hurried. I am awaiting with keen interest your solution of the problem of the imagination. You are right in thinking that this is the key. – My lecture in Lowell the 31st will bring me to Cambridge, Saturday the 29th, if that will be agreeable to you and Dora. I shall be returning home almost immediately after the lecture. – Mrs. Beck[58] is not at all well, and Darrah has never entirely recovered from the exciting dissipations of the summer, but otherwise we are in good condition. – With kind regards to Dora,

Faithfully yours,
Paul E. More.

Princeton
January 2, 1918

My dear Babbitt,

I am home, but the process of getting here was no joke. Both trains were late, and when I arrived at the Junction at seven o'clock there was no train to meet us. Mrs. Mather and I and two others telephoned for a taxi, and so at last, tired and exasperated, I got home. I am deeply in your debt for your kindness in keeping me under such difficulties, and you must thank your sister especially for her obliging industry. I hope Dora is up now and enjoying the bad weather with the rest of you.

On the train coming down I read the Fifth Book of Chrysostom's *De Sacerdotio*, which I recommend to your prayerful consideration; it is a book ἀναγνωστέον μετὰ εὐχῆς.[59] Here are the subjects: (1) ὅτι πολλοῦ πόνος καὶ σπουδῆς αἱ ἐν τῷ κοινῷ ὁμιλίαι δέονται (2) ὅτι τὸν εἰς τοῦτο τεταγμένον καὶ ἐγκωμίων ὑπερορᾶν χρὴ, καὶ δύνασθαι λέγειν, (3) ὅτι ἂν μὴ ἀμφότερα ἔχῃ ἄχρηστος ἔσται τῷ πλήθει, (4) ὅτι μάλιστα βασκανίας τοῦτον δεῖ κατα

---

than pain." The quotation is from the homiletic works (*In Matthaeum*, homil. 40.443-444) of John Chrysostom (ca. AD 354–407).

57. Babbitt 1991.
58. More's mother-in-law.
59. A footnote in the typescript of this letter reads: "A book to be read with a prayer."

φρονεῖν, (5) ὅτι ὁ λόγους εἰδὼς πλείονος δεῖται σπουδῆς, ἢ ὁ ἀμαθής, (6) ὅτι τῆς ἀλόγου τῶν πολλῶν ψήφου οὔτε πάντη καταφρονεῖν οὔτε πάντη φροντίζειν δεῖ, (7) ὅτι πρὸς τὸ τῷ θεῷ ἀρέσκον μόνον δεῖ τοὺς λόγους ῥυθμίζειν (8) ὅτι ὁ μὴ κααφρονῶν ἐπαίνων, πολλὰ ὑποστήσεται δεινά.[60] – Really, change a few words—such as ὁμιλίαι[61] into "essays"—and this is one of the noblest, and at the same time most sensible, pieces of advice for the writer and teacher I have ever read. To find one of those old saints analysing the problems that confront us today is something more than entertaining; it is distinctly heartening. – But to return from Antioch to Princeton, I found that Darrah's operation is very slight. It is only to remove what was left over from her tonsils when these were not properly cut out. She is in New York today with Net, and will stay at a hospital tonight.

Sincerely yours,
Paul E. More.

P.S. Your lecture is the afternoon of Wednesday January 30th.[62] Of course you will stop with us.

Princeton
January 16, 1918

My dear Babbitt,

I got to New York nearly on time, but I passed a restless dreaming night, and I must sadly attribute most of my discomfort to too much champagne at the Harvard Club. The meeting[63] in University Hall was futile enough, as was

---

60. A footnote in the typescript of this letter provides the following translation: "(1) Public sermons require much effort and hard work. (2) The man who deals with this must despise praise and must be an orator. (3) He is useless to the people if he does not possess both qualities. (4) He must avoid envy above all. (5) The preacher who is well equipped with knowledge must work harder than the ignorant man. (6) One should neither entirely despise nor entirely take into consideration the unreasonable judgment of the masses. (7) One should compose sermons keeping in mind that they please God only. (8) The man who does not despise praises will face many terrible things." The Greek text appears as the summary of John Chrysostom's *De sacerdotio* 5.

61. Sermons, homilies.

62. Dakin (1960: 169) notes that Babbitt delivered a lecture at Princeton on this date.

63. Dakin (1960: 204) informs us that More attended a meeting of a Visiting Committee of the Graduate School of Harvard in early January of 1922. He previously attended a meeting of this committee in December of 1913 (see above, chapter 4). Presumably, More here refers to another meeting of this committee, unmentioned by Dakin. Franklin B. Dyer, discussed by More below, was a member of this committee in 1918. See anon. 1919b: 375-76.

to be expected. Moore,[64] Coolidge,[65] Bullock,[66] and Bagster spoke, and we asked a few questions, but of no special significance. One of the committee is a man named Dyer,[67] Superintendent of schools in Boston, a weasel-faced creature with a weasel brain, who tried to find fault with the economics department for not sending its students out as aides and runners for the mayors of Cambridge and Boston. I must say that Bullock answered him well by bringing up the ill-savory results of mixing education with politics and uplift in Wisconsin. But our pedagogue held on with his weasel tenacity, in a way that prolonged our session far beyond the necessary time. I could see that he might be effective in committees with popular legislators, but it is a disgrace to have such a man on the committee to criticise the Graduate School. I expressed my opinion of him to Lowell in frank terms. I sat near Lowell at the dinner, with Haskins[68] at my right and Kittredge at my left, and I was a good deal amused at the manners of the first and last of the three. Lowell evidently likes to play the rôle of omniscience. He held forth at length on all sorts of questions in physics and other subjects of which he might be supposed to know nothing. His information was sound so far as I could judge, but his enthusiasm in instructing was to say the least amusing. Kittredge was very cordial, but also had his rôle—the high pontifical manner of one who has never had his word disputed. I did however dispute his authority in a matter of good English, to his apparent surprise. What queer fellows these big men are. The dinner was elaborate, but poor; one course being chicken so tough I could scarcely masticate it. There was champagne which I detest, but which I always drink (when someone else pays for it) for the name of the thing. It always turns into miasmatic geysers in my stomach. I had some interesting talk with Haskins on the doctor's degree and other kindred matters. He was sensible for the most part, but I am always inclined to distrust the ultimate judgment of one so crammed with facts and figures as Haskins is. Of course he gets his power in that way; just as Eliot did. – And my budget of news is ended. Kindly thank the ladies of the household for their kindness to me, and believe me,

Faithfully yours,
Paul E. More.

---

64. Presumably, More here refers to the Harvard professor Clifford Herschel Moore. On his biography, see above.

65. More likely refers here to Archibald Cary Coolidge (1866–1928), a professor of history at Harvard.

66. More here refers to Charles J. Bullock (1869–1941), an economics professor at Harvard.

67. Franklin B. Dyer (1858–1938) was the superintendent of Boston schools from 1912 to 1918.

68. Charles Homer Haskins (1879–1937), a professor of history at Harvard.

P.S. You understand that your lecture is Wednesday, the 30th. Let us know when to expect you on Tuesday. There are trains to Princeton at 2:03 (slow), 4:04, and 5:02. Also 7 and 8.

Cambridge
2 February, 1918

Dear More,

I got home safely though about half an hour late on a noon train from New York (via Springfield), after my very pleasant but only too brief glimpse of you at Princeton.[69] I found Dora distinctly improved—temperature back to normal. She is likely though to have a rather slow convalescence. – One of the letters I found waiting for me was a very cordial one from Mussey[70] in which he assures me among other things that the Nation is very eager for further contributions from me. I gather that he and possibly also Villard are a bit anxious about the present situation and wish to avoid any appearance of a sharp break with the past of the paper. You will probably receive a like conciliatory epistle, if you have not already done so, and will I imagine deem it expedient to meet the new management halfway provided it does not do anything unduly compromising. – The irony of Sherman's last paper[71] is too intricate for my taste—in fact, it approaches in places the weird. I wish that his power of thought about fundamentals was equal to his literary gift.

Semi-annual report on my books just received shows sales almost down to zero point—possibly in sympathy with the weather. I hope that you are doing at least a little better. I take this kind of thing, I think, with a fair degree of philosophy, but cannot say that I find it a positive inspiration to further writing.

---

69. On Babbitt's January 30, 1918, lecture at Princeton, see Dakin 1960: 169 and above.

70. The typescript of this letter renders the name "Murrey" and underlines the name, presumably due to uncertainty. But Babbitt here means Henry Raymond Mussey (1875–1940), who was a managing editor at the *Nation* and would play a more prominent role there upon the departure of Fuller, More's former assistant. Dakin (1960: 179-80 n. 9) quotes a January 4, 1918, letter of More to Stuart Sherman, in which More laments Fuller's departure from the magazine. He also quotes an April 6, 1918, letter to Frank Jewett Mather Jr., which demonstrates More's dislike for Villard and Mussey.

71. Sherman wrote and reviewed so regularly for the *Nation* at this time that it is difficult to determine which piece Babbitt means here. For a bibliography of Sherman's work, see Zeitlin and Woodbridge 1929: 803-60.

Give my kind regards to Nettie and convey to her my appreciation of all she did to make my stay in Princeton pleasant.

Sincerely yours,
Irving Babbitt.

Crater Club
Essex, N. Y.
July 26, 1918

My dear Babbitt,

Now that we are here I am beginning to wonder how much truth there is in the rumors of your visit to Essex.[72] I do most sincerely hope you can come, and Net bids me add that she will "be perfectly furious" if Dora does not come too. Of your own work I am expecting to hear much. Perhaps the MS.[73] will be completed so that we can read it together. My own task, the continuation of *Platonism*, has taken pretty definite shape, and if I have no class this coming autumn term[74] I think I shall be able to turn off a good part of the next volume. – But more of these things when we meet. With kind regards to Dora, and Katharine if she is with you,

Faithfully yours,
Paul E. More.

Crater Club
Essex, N. Y.
August 19, 1918

My dear Babbitt,

I fear we must hold you to your consent to visit us, if we are to get together. As there is no one here with whom Net and I can leave the children, it is out of the question that we should go off together; and as far as you and I are concerned, it is your turn to make the perillous [sic] journey over the mountains. I do hope nothing will happen to obstruct your visit. We can take you in any

---

72. Dakin (1960: 182-83) notes that More would entertain Babbitt in Essex in mid-September of 1918. See below.
73. Of Babbitt 1991.
74. This is the first mention in the extant Babbitt–More correspondence of More's lectureship in the philosophy department at Princeton.

time in September, and for as long as you will stay. If you wish to work, the mornings can be entirely at your disposal. We return to Princeton about the twenty third or fourth. – I am glad to hear that your book is progressing so regularly. As for my reading it, arrange the matter as you think it will be most profitable. I am looking forward to having a number of ideas cleared up from its perusal. – I have been getting through a good deal of Greek this summer. Chrysostom is easy fun, but Origen's *Commentary on St. John*, without notes, and with no dictionary at hand, is about as tough a job as a man may desire. I find that a sentence rarely completely baffles me, but many of them I have to unravel as one would an intricate puzzle. I have begun translating the παλαιὸς λόγος[75] and its sequel in the *Laws*, which will form the opening chapter, or chapters, of my next volume. It is a difficult and unsatisfying kind of work, but necessary for my design. – With kindest regards to Dora,

Faithfully yours,
Paul E. More.

Essex, N. Y.
September 2, 1918

My dear Babbitt,

The first parcel of your MS. came several days ago, but I have not started to read it yet. I shall be careful not to mar it with pencil marks.

The boats begin to run on their autumn schedule Sept. 16, but the schedule is not yet published. I will send this to you as soon as it is out. The 9 a.m. train to Albany is running regularly.

We are all looking forward to your visit. I rather think Holt will be in Burlington when you pass through. Will you not stop over night with him?

Sincerely,
P. E. M.

Crater Club
Essex, N. Y.
September 11, 1918

My dear Babbitt,

The second parcel of MS. has come and I have read already through the fifth chapter. My criticisms will not be severe. But of one thing I

---

75. A footnote in the typescript of this letter reads: "Ancient doctrine."

wish you would think. Ought not the title to be changed? I feel strongly that Rousseau is not enough centralized to stand in the title. Some word denoting the modern spirit or the like ought to take the place of his name. Then, in the Introduction you could say something about the importance of Rousseau and excuse the frequent references to him. As a matter of fact English philosophy is more fundamentally in your argument than is Rousseauism; the former is the source, the latter is the shining example.

The schedule for the boat is not yet out. It is possible that there may be no boat running at all. Suppose then we leave it thus: unless I telegraph you to the contrary you may know there is a boat from Burlington on Tuesday the 17th, and I will meet you in Essex accordingly. But you had better inquire in Burlington whether it is running morning or afternoon. If it turns out that no boat is to be running, I will wire you to that effect as soon as I get the information—at the latest by Saturday.

Sincerely,
P. E. M.

Crater Club
Essex, N. Y.
September 13, 1918

My dear Babbitt,

I have just sent you a telegram stating that there is a boat from Burlington to Essex only on Wednesday and Thursday afternoons (leaving Burlington at 5:30). This would give you a very short visit with us, if you must leave on Saturday. Can you not get here Monday or Tuesday by way of Rutland and Whitehall?[76]

I have just finished your manuscript,[77] and am deeply impressed by the completeness of your treatment and by the union of force and moderation. The book ought really to tell. I am eager to read the concluding chapter. Some minor details I have to criticise, and possibly some matters of arrangement; but the work is essentially done.

Sincerely,
Paul E. More.

---

76. A railroad in Vermont.
77. Babbitt 1991.

245 Nassau Street
Princeton, New Jersey
October 2, 1918

My dear Babbitt,

It was good to hear from Dora and yourself that you got through your journey[78] without ill results. I trust that by this time you have mastered the hideous germs that were at war within the cave—the only warfare of this kind that the world seems willing to recognize.[79] So far our family has quite escaped the plague, though there is a good deal of it stalking about Princeton.

Your prostration, after so burdensome a trip and when we had so much to discuss, was certainly a calamity—but οὕτως ἐδόκει τοῖς θεοῖς.[80]

I am rather in despair over my lecture course. Owing to the absence of other available courses, it looks as if I were to have a considerable number of seminary men, who, to judge from their appearance, are only one degree removed above the ape—or oyster. However, I may have also a couple of moderately intelligent graduate students. Princeton is merely a war camp with nothing of the glamour of war.

Sincerely,
Paul E. More.

---

245 Nassau Street
Princeton, New Jersey
October 19, 1918

My dear Babbitt,

The passage you need from Xenophon is apparently in the Memorabilia IV, 3: ὁρᾷς γὰρ ὅτι ὁ ἐν Δελφοῖς θεός, ὅταν τις αὐτὸν ἐπερωτᾷ, πῶς ἂν τοῖς θεοῖς χαρίζοιτο, ἀποκρίνεται, "Νόμῳ πόλεως"· νόμος δὲ δήπου πανταχοῦ ἐστι κατὰ δύναμιν ἱεροῖς θεοὺς ἀρέσκεσθαι.[81] If this is not the passage in request let me know again just what the point is.

---

78. The journey from More's summer cottage in Essex, New York, which Babbitt had visited in mid-September. See Dakin 1960: 182-83.

79. More here is joking about Babbitt's insistence on recognizing "the civil war in the cave," a battle between one's impulsive desires and one's higher will—which, according to Babbitt, romanticists, with their monistic view of human existence, deny. See, e.g., Babbitt 1940: 155, 157 and 1991: 150, 187.

80. A footnote in the typescript of this letter reads: "Thus it was resolved by the gods."

81. A footnote in the typescript of this letter provides the following translation: "For you see that the god at Delphi whenever anyone asked him how he might please the gods would reply,

My class started out with rather formidable numbers, owing to the paucity of courses in philosophy offered this year by the Graduate School.[82] But I have weeded out a Korean and several pimply looking Seminarists,[83] so that now I have only four or five men left. One of these is a Rabbi from Trenton, who shows signs of wishing to play to the galleries, and will probably need to be mildly squelched. He is learned in Hebrew and mediaeval mysticism, but without any real critical sense. Then I have a Seminary graduate student, who is doing special research work in Apologetics; a college graduate man, kept out of service by a weak heart, a gentleman withal, but a bit flabby; and one or two (I am trying to eliminate one) other Seminarists. – How does your work go? Have you any advanced students?

Our Will has had the influenza, and Darrah and Alice have both had colds, but of the ordinary sort. Otherwise we are in good state.

You must remember that I am expecting to read the proofs of your book.

Faithfully yours,
Paul E. More.

'By the law of the city.' It is I presume the law everywhere to gratify the gods with sacrifices as far as possible." Babbitt referred to this passage (Xenophon, *Memorabilia* 4.16.3) in *Rousseau and Romanticism*. See Babbitt 1991: 175 n. 1.

82. On More's teaching in the philosophy department at Princeton, see the Introduction.
83. From the Princeton Theological Seminary.

CHAPTER SEVEN
1919–1921

Princeton
January 25, 1919

My dear Babbitt,

Dora's last letter brought the good news that you were engaged on your bibliography and would soon have your manuscript[1] ready for the press. It will be a lightsome day for you, I know, when the thing is off your hands. I wish you could go on with the sequel on politics, but I dare say you will need a time of rest; certainly you have been one of the πεφορτισμένοι.[2] I was talking with Mather the other day about your Rousseau and he expressed much eagerness to get the book in his hands. He has got his discharge from the navy and is back at his desk, but a sadly disillusioned man. It seems as if he could not get the fantoms of optimism out of his brain, and now the spectacle of our peace-makers indulging in rhodomontades of sentiment while practical matters are ignored is filling him with bitter dismay. What should he have expected? – I am just recovering from a week or ten days of wretched illness. The catalogue of my ailments would have made Voltaire mad with envy. My liver was all wrong I know, and I think I had the influenza and one or two other diseases. At least I am left weak and ignominiously in need of rest. But I hope soon to be at my books again. Just before the blow I had pretty well planned out my next volume. Now I am casting about for a title for the series. How does this strike you: The Message of Greece, From Plato to St. Chrysostom?[3] That exactly conveys the subject of the volumes, but the word "message" worries me as rather presumptuous and romantic. The separate volumes, so far as I now see, will be: (1) Platonism; (2) The Religion of Plato; (3) Pagan Philosophies; (4) Christian Theology; (5) Clement of Alexandria; (6) Philosophy and Religion. It is a large order you will say. It is, but I have to work on only one volume at a time. A certain amount of

---

1. Of Babbitt 1991.
2. A footnote in the typescript of this letter provides the translation "Heavily laden."
3. For the title of the series as a whole, More ultimately chose *The Greek Tradition: From the Death of Socrates to the Council of Chalcedon (399 B.C. to 451 A.D.)*.

repetition seems inevitable. – I hope you are all keeping well; I have been the only sick one here.

Faithfully yours,
Paul E. More.

Cambridge
7 February, 1919

Dear More,

I am heartily sorry to hear of your indisposition. It seems to be the common fate this year, though in your particular case I have my usual suspicion that you do not get enough of the open air. I wish that in this one respect you would emulate great men like Wilson and J. D. Rockefeller, and I have always been sorry that you gave up golf. – I am much interested in your account of your plans for the Plato but I do not feel moved to make any particular comments on your titles. As a matter of fact I had a somewhat different notion of the whole undertaking, but what you are planning to do, I scarcely need say, seems to me both interesting and important. I wish I could talk the whole thing over with you. I was hoping that I might see you this spring on my return from a lecturing trip I shall probably take in the Middle West, but at present that seems out of the question. I am invited to give one lecture at Cincinnati, as Lou[4] may have written you, and hope to have the pleasure of spending a day or so with him. I am also scheduled to give a few lectures at Indiana University in June and I may be able to take in Princeton then, either going or returning. All this lecturing means that I am trying to fortify my bank account against big printing bills. My book[5] is down for publication in April. You should have received about last Wed. the first batch of proof. I am not going to make any changes unless they seem imperative—in view of the present ruinous rates for type-setting—but I shall be very grateful for your help in the work of revision all the same. Give my kind regards to Nettie and to Mather.

Sincerely,
Irving Babbitt.

---

4. Louis T. More, Paul More's younger brother and a professor of physics at the University of Cincinnati.
5. Babbitt 1991.

245 Nassau Street
Princeton, New Jersey
April 17, 1919

My dear Babbitt,

   Can you spare time from your castigations of the Rousseauists to look over these sheets[6] and tell me what to do with them. Shall I print them or throw them away? It would cause me no particular pain to accept the latter alternative. They are written, as you will surmise, to introduce a volume of essays, a number of which deal with Pope and his contemporaries. But the book can appear just as well without this preface, or any preface, if you think it better. The writing is of a sort that it is impossible for me to judge.

Sincerely,
Paul E. More.

It is scarcely necessary to add that of the three bits of verse (pp. 5, 6, 7) only the first is from Pope, though a single line from him is embedded in each of the two latter. My intention was, without committing myself, to let the idle reader suppose all three are genuine quotations.

Cambridge
27 April, 1919

Dear More,

   I am very grateful to you for all the trouble you took with my proof. Your criticism is valuable even though it adds to my final reckoning with the printer. I wreaked my wrath on your Plato while it was still in MS. whereas your eagle eye seems to be aroused to its full activity only by the sight of the printed page. I have read with interest your proposed Introduction to your new volume of essays. It is amusing and I am glad to see you cultivate, at least for a change, this unwonted vein. The Popian imitations are effective. At the same time several reflections as to the expediency of this material in its present form occur to me. In the first place I am afraid that the reader may feel in one or two places at least a sub-suggestion of

---

   6. From Babbitt's April 27, 1919, letter below, it becomes clear that More is referring to a draft of the preface to his tenth series of *Shelburne Essays* (More 1967b: v-xii).

soreness, and this is of course a thing to be avoided. I have marked the passages. The second objection I have to make is rather more serious. You are a leader in what aspires to become an important movement, and should therefore consider with some care the question of tactics. Now it is in my judgment a tactical error to seem to identify the critical and satirical spirit with malice. Boileau has the very keenest satire and at the same time has very little malice in the sense that the word may properly have when one speaks of Pope. The satire of Horace is also genial rather than malicious. Dr. Johnson lacks the epigrammatic point of view of these writers but can do fairly well on occasion and is also free from malice in the Popian sense. That is one reason why the age of Johnson rather than the age of Pope is the true Augustan age of England—so far as it has had one.[7] It is both unsound in itself, therefore, and bad tactics to seem to identify a keen and crisp criticism with mere *Schadenfreude*. You can in my opinion make the necessary distinction by the insertion of a short paragraph, going on to say that even the satire of Pope would be welcome as a counterirritant to the present flabbiness.[8]

I had a pleasant though only too brief glimpse of your brother at Cincinnati. My trip was a distinctly strenuous one. Besides Cincinnati I visited the Uns. of Illinois, Minnesota, Wisconsin and Michigan—fourteen lectures and addresses and about nineteen formal dinners and receptions in two weeks! I stayed with Sherman at Urbana and had a good deal of interesting talk with him. In the latter part of June I am to give some lectures at Bloomington, Indiana. There is a chance that I may be able to look in on you at Princeton on my return about July 1. Would it be convenient for you to see me at that time? I hope very much to hear that you are getting back to your usual physical form. If not, I should suppose that you ought to hasten your departure for Essex. I hear that you spoke recently at Smith[9] and wish that you might have taken in Cambridge on your return. Talking of lectures I gave one about a week ago here to the Chinese students on Buddha and the meaning of Buddhism for contemporary China. A lively and entertaining discussion of about an hour followed. Among others a representative of young China arose and remarked that he "did not see any good in stirring up all this Nirvanic stuff"! – Remember that I shall be very

---

7. More took this criticism into account when revising the preface; cf. More 1967b: ix.

8. More included such a paragraph. See More 1967b: ix-x.

9. Smith College in Northampton, Massachusetts. Dakin (1960: 185) notes that More offered an opening address on the topic of humanism at the Latin Conference of Mount Holyoke, Smith, Vassar, and Wellesley on March 21, 1919.

glad to read the proof of your new book if you think I can be of any use. With kind regards to Nettie,

Sincerely yours,
Irving Babbitt.

---

245 Nassau Street
Princeton, New Jersey
April 29, 1919

Dear Babbitt,

Your advice in regard to my Preface is rather more favorable than I expected, and naturally pleases me. The passage which seems to you to reflect a feeling of "soreness" shall be eliminated; and I think I can add a paragraph which will meet your more serious objection. The imitations of Pope, I suspect, will puzzle the illiterate reviewers. How many of them will recognize the fact that they are not genuine quotations? I wrote them, indeed with the malicious design of worrying some of the ignorant.

Your book ought to be out soon. Mather and I are both looking for it eagerly. I am sorry to hear that my criticisms have brought extra expenses on you. Certainly the changes suggested were very few.

Mather, by the way, is in a state of black bleak pessimism over the world at large and this portion of the globe in particular. Like a true sentimentalist he swings from one extreme to the other. He is going to contribute regularly to the editorial pages of Franklin and Fuller's *Review*,[10] and this is giving him a little zest in life. I have some fear that Fuller, in his part of the paper, is going in for smartness; but this is to be seen. They tell me the response to their circular has been very encouraging; but they will need a large circulation to carry the heavy editorial charges they are assuming. Do you ever see Strauss's[11] *Villager*? It often has very good things. I am writing for it occasionally.[12]

---

10. The engineer, mathematician, and journalist Fabian Franklin (1853–1939) and Harold de Wulf Fuller had both departed from the editorial staff of the New York *Evening Post* and the *Nation* respectively, aiming to set up their own journal, first called the *Review*. See, e.g., Dakin 1960: 179-80. Both Babbitt and More would contribute to the publication.

11. The editor Samuel Strauss (1870–1953).

12. Dakin (1960: 180) writes: "Samuel Strauss, who ran *The Villager*, of Katonah, New York, so interested More in that little periodical that he not only wrote gratis for it but recommended to Strauss, as among other possible contributors, Sherman, Norman Foerster, Mather, Louis More, and Warner Fite." The *Villager* stopped publishing in 1925.

We shall be delighted to see you on your return from Bloomington if you take in Princeton on the way. You seem to be running the late H. W. Mabie and the living (generally intoxicated) Henry Van Dyke[13] close as a lecturer. – My health is rather better than it was last spring. We shall go to Essex probably about the middle of July. With kind regards to Dora,

Faithfully yours,
Paul E. More.

---

6 Kirkland Road
Cambridge
2 May, 1919

My dear More,

My Chinese friend, Mr. K. T. May,[14] is planning to look in on you at Princeton, and I hope that you will be able to spare him a few moments. He is hoping to translate some of your work into Chinese and this should be enough by itself to convince you of his intelligence. He is now President of the Chinese Club at Harvard and he has been offered the editorship of the new Chinese review that is to appear in Shanghai. His view of the political situation in China is not very hopeful; and certainly China should have turned to better account the respite she has had while the wild beasts of the Occident have been clawing one another. The surface indications at least, in both the East and the West, are not very pleasant right now. Still Wilson may succeed in bringing back from Paris his halo as the savior of humanity and in that case the lines in the preface to your new volume[15] will seem very ungracious indeed. – It occurs to me that you have perhaps given too much prominence to C. A. Moore in this preface. Would it not be just as well to make your acknowledgment in a note to the article in question?[16]

---

13. Henry van Dyke Jr. (1852–1933) was an author and professor of English literature at Princeton.

14. May (1890–1945) contributed to the collection *Irving Babbitt: Man and Teacher* under the name K. T. Mei (see Manchester and Shepard 1941: 112-27). Also known as Guandi Mei and Kuang-ti Mei, he studied with Babbitt from 1916 to 1919. He served as an instructor in the Chinese department at Harvard and later as a professor in China.

15. More 1967b.

16. See More 1967b: viii.

H. M. Co. are planning to publish my book[17] on May 24, a very unfavorable date for a volume that has to depend largely on the college public. They promised it for April 12! I expect to be well mulcted financially. With kind regards to Nettie,

Sincerely,
Irving Babbitt.

---

245 Nassau Street
Princeton, New Jersey
May 28, 1919

My dear Babbitt,

Your book came this morning and in appearance makes a good companion for the *Criticism*.[18] I shall be reading it again, and hope I may have an opportunity to write something about it somewhere. I have just concluded a bargain with H. M. for my tenth volume, *With the Wits*.[19] You will probably have the pleasure of reading the proofs.

Monday I go out to Alleghany College to give a ΦBK address,[20] but I shall be back Thursday morning. Your visit to Princeton, I believe, will not be until the first of July.

I am quite excited over the news from Net that you are thinking of coming to Essex this summer. I most sincerely hope you can find quarters there, but anything you may get will seem poverty-stricken in comparison with your ordinary summer houses. However, you know what the place is.

Faithfully yours,
Paul E. More.

P.S. Let me know when you change your address against the possibility of my sending proofs.

---

17. Babbitt 1991.
18. More means Babbitt's previous monograph, *The Masters of Modern French Criticism*.
19. More 1967b.
20. On More's June 3, 1919, address at Allegheny College, see Dakin 1960: 185.

Bloomington, Ind.,
24 June 1919.

Dear More:

Just a line to say that I am planning to look in on you next Saturday at Princeton and remain until Monday morning. I gathered from Nettie that a visit at this date would be convenient for you. If my train from the West is on time, I can catch the train from Philadelphia that reaches Princeton at 7:40 P.M.; if I miss this train, I may catch the one that makes Princeton at 8:27. If I miss this train I may spend the night in Philadelphia. I shall take my dinner on the train in any case.

I am earning my stipend here in the sweat of my brow in a very little [sic] sense of the word. The mingled heat and humidity this afternoon was something to remember.

Sincerely,
Irving Babbitt.

Cambridge
10 July, 1919

Dear More,

The Fite boy[21] proved to be well-behaved and the return to Cambridge was without incident. It was a very pleasant glimpse that I had of you all, but I cannot help wishing that it had been longer. There were so many things that I wished to talk over with you and I had barely got started. I wished to hear more in particular about the books you are planning on the Platonic influence. The general scheme is not as yet altogether clear to me. I fancy that your *Platonism* in spite of the ungracious reception it has received from various professionals is having a quiet and salutary influence. The reference to it in the letter I enclose from Patrick[22] may interest you. He is head of the Dep't of Philosophy at Iowa and has been president of the Western Section of the American Philosophical Association. I have no reason to think, however, that he is a very important person. I have just received a long letter from

---

21. Presumably, Babbitt refers to the son of his friend Warner Fite. Fite was a distinguished professor of ethics at Princeton.

22. Babbitt refers to George Thomas White Patrick (1857–1949), a philosophy professor at the University of Iowa.

Bruce. He approves apparently of *R. and R.* He believes, however, that the devil has at present a strangle grip upon this country, especially in the form of Deweyism, and so does not look, I gather, for much practical effect from my admonitions.

We have taken for the summer at a merely nominal rental, a house at Chesham, N. H., a little town between Dublin and Keene. The family is going up in a few days but I am likely to be in Cambridge for some time yet collecting material for *Democracy and Imperialism*.[23] I am working for the moment on Thomas Jefferson. The thermometer has on several occasions recently gone above 100—almost enough to make one regret Bloomington. – I wish that you might visit us this summer and get a notion of the Monadnock region with a view to spending a summer there later. I could take you on some walks—but the very thought of any such possibility will I fear prove a deterrent. Seriously in this matter of exercise I should advise you to go to a first class physician, have him look you over carefully and then follow his prescription whether it accords with your notions or mine. I am struck by the way in which persons of only moderate physique like Woodrow Wilson bear up under great pressure by following this method, and the method always involves, I notice, a great deal of exercise in the open air. With kind regards to Nettie,

Sincerely,
Irving Babbitt.

---

245 Nassau Street
Princeton, New Jersey
July 15, 1919

My dear Babbitt,
Your brief visit was a very great pleasure, and I wish these meetings could be more frequent. I may be able to get to Chesham this summer, but my plans now are all in the air. We leave this Thursday and shall return about the middle of September. I hardly think it will be worth while to bother you with the proofs of my new volume of essays,[24] as there is scarcely anything

---

23. A footnote in the typescript of this letter reads: "*Democracy and Leadership.*" Indeed, *Democracy and Imperialism* was Babbitt's first choice of title for the project (Babbitt 1924). For more on the title, see below.
24. More 1967b.

of a philosophical or controversial nature in the book. As usual H. M. are lagging; not a galley of proof yet!

Patrick's letter is interesting. These signs of recognition are always encouraging, but to me at least they come like angel visits very rarely. I had a good walk (!) with Gauss a couple of days after you left, and he talked with some glimmerings of intelligence on this question of the ethics of *Faust*. He seems to agree with much that one says, but deep down in his heart the leaven of the old Romanticism is working all the time. – Kemp Smith[25] has got the Edinburgh place; his absence will be a serious loss to me, for though his mind was often turbid he was honestly looking for the light.

My summer reading this year is Plutarch's *Moralia*. He is full of wisdom despite the smothering blanket of quaint pedantry over all. I feel him a kindred spirit.

Sincerely yours,
Paul E. More.

P.S. Strauss is writing to Foerster to do the *Rousseau*. Have you had the book sent to the *Villager*?[26]

Chesham, N. H.
7 August, 1919

Dear More,

I hope very much that you may be able to make that visit to Chesham which you suggest as a possibility. One train leaves Burlington at 8 A.M. and reaches Keene (where I should meet you) at 2:14 P.M.; another leaves Burlington at 11:38 A.M., reaching Keene at 4:27 P.M. This latter is, I believe, the better train and would be especially convenient if you happened to be visiting Holt. – There is of course some chance of a general tie-up at present. The insolence of organized labor is getting beyond all bounds. Unless it receives a pretty prompt set-back, the outlook is not bright for our form of government. I am hoping that the latent good sense of the people will rally at the last extremity. There is of course not much hope in the politicians at

---

25. Norman Kemp Smith (1872–1958) was a Scottish professor of philosophy. In 1919 he left Princeton for a position at the University of Edinburgh. Smith was in a discussion group with More, and thus More was dismayed by Smith's departure. See, e.g., Dakin 1960: 165. On More's friendship with Smith, see also Spaeth 1943: 539-40.

26. See Foerster 1919, an anonymous review in the *Villager* of Babbitt's *Rousseau and Romanticism*.

Washington unless they feel the pressure of a powerful public opinion. At the present rate the last hope for the rights of property may be the Supreme Court, though it may not prove easy to protect its less radical members from dynamite bombs. My mind is rather turned to problems of this order at present, as the result of reading I am doing for *Democracy and Imperialism*. I have been reflecting a good deal of late on the psychology of Thomas Jefferson. It seems to me to have a good deal in common with that of Woodrow Wilson.

Give my kind regards to Nettie.

Sincerely,
Irving Babbitt.

Essex, N. Y.
August 20, 1919

Dear Babbitt,

It looks very much as if I should not be able to visit you at Chesham this summer. It is a case of too much Babbitt. That book[27] of yours is causing me anguish. I find the writing of my article for the *Unpartizan*[28] excessively difficult and slow. Not only is the subject itself hard to treat adequately in brief compass, but to write so as not to misrepresent yourself or myself yet so as to make the thing acceptable to the editor is taxing all my ingenuity. And I find any sort of literary work troublesome in these summer conditions. All of which is to say that by the time my task is ended, we shall be having visitors here, and by the time that is over I shall have only a brief interval of complete rest before returning to Princeton. If things turn out so that I can get to you some time in September, I will let you know.

Meanwhile you will be pleased to hear that I am playing tennis and otherwise taking violent and foolish exercise. I am resolved to go home this autumn totally exhausted physically, so that no one will ever dare say exercise to me again.

Net joins me in sending best regards to Dora.

Faithfully yours,
Paul E. More.

---

27. Babbitt 1991.
28. Henry Holt had by then given his journal, the *Unpopular Review*, the new name of the *Unpartizan Review*; see Dakin 1960: 151. More did not review *Rousseau and Romanticism* for the *Unpartizan*. Rather, Frank Jewett Mather Jr. did. See Mather 1920. On this subject, see below.

Essex-On-Lake Champlain
New York
September 1, 1919

My dear Babbitt,

I have disappointing news. My article on your book for the *Unpartizan* has failed, and has been returned by Holt with a word of contemptuous rejection. I worked hard over the thing, but somehow, owing I suppose to the conditions under which I wrote, I could get no life into my words. I was chagrinned but scarcely surprised when Holt rejected it. My grievance is rather for you than for myself, as I had set my heart on giving the book adequate notice. Wright's review turned out to be a smart ironical piece of writing, disgracefully inadequate, even dishonest. Fortunately Fuller let me see the proof before printing, and I wrote a long letter to him pointing out the deficiencies and perversions of the article. What he will do I cannot say, as I have not heard from him since, except for a word of acknowledgement.[29] I am hoping that Foerster will do something worth while for the *Villager*;[30] but that is an obscure medium at best. Houghton Mifflin have not sent me a stick of proof yet of my new volume. The sun is shining very dimly in my literary heavens. One good thing the summer has brought me. I have found in several of Plutarch's *Moralia* a fine interpretation of certain dark passages of Plato's *Timaeus* which fortify me wonderfully in my own views. Plutarch grows upon me as a very great man. – With kind regards to Dora.

Faithfully yours,
Paul E. More.

Chesham, N. H.
4 September 1919

Dear More,

Your letter certainly contains a depressing budget of news. I am of course vexed both for your sake and mine that you should have worked in vain over the article. At bottom Holt has no real sympathy either with your outlook on life or mine and if, as you say, he rejected the paper with contempt I am

---

29. The ultimate reviewer of Babbitt's *Rousseau and Romanticism* for Fuller's journal (at this point called the *Review*) was Wilmon H. Sheldon; see Sheldon 1919. It is unclear who Wright is, or whether this man ended up publishing a review of the book.

30. See Foerster 1919 for his review in the *Villager*.

inclined to suspect an element of senile ὕβρις.³¹ Before giving up why do you not try the *Philosophical Review* or the *International Journal of Ethics* or the *Journal of Scientific Method* or perhaps the *Yale Review*. You see I am still a bit sceptical about the badness of the article. It might be a good idea in any case to let me glance over it. With the help of the women of the family I can probably arrive at a fairly accurate estimate. Parts may deserve to be salvaged even if the thing as a whole *laisse à désirer*.³²

In general I do not approve of your sticking so closely to the *Unpartizan*. The effect is one of a growing aloofness. Some of the papers you have given Holt should have gone to one or the other of the good English reviews that have a real public. Why do you not, by the way, write an article for the *Edinburgh* or the *Quarterly* with some such title as "The Attack on Romanticism" or "Romanticism and Imperialism." You might give as the usual references at the beginning: Lasserre's book, some of those of Seillière,³³ Maurras's³⁴ "Avenir de l'Intelligence,"³⁵ the German work of J. Bub, "Fortinbras or the struggle of the 19th century with the spirit of romanticism," Sherman's book on "Contemporary Literature"³⁶ and my last book. I could supply you if you wished with certain books from the Harvard Library. In presenting as part of an international movement the growing tendency to question romantic and naturalistic postulates you might do something really notable, something that would command attention in important quarters. There would be no harm in any case in sounding the English editors as to this project.

If Fuller allows an unfavorable and incompetent review of the Rousseau to appear, he will be guilty, to put the matter on no higher ground, of a rather serious tactical faux pas. The book of course coöperates in its general point of view with the campaign he himself is trying to conduct. I am grateful to you for the trouble you have taken in trying to enlighten him. His reviewer may have taken his cue from a would-be clever skit on the book that appeared in the *Sun* early last July.³⁷ Sherman published in the literary supplement of the *Evening Post* (July 26) an article³⁸ that seemed like a reply to the review in the *Sun*. It has unmistakable gusto and at the same time brings out with great skill my central thesis. It is on the whole the best review I have ever had.

---

31. A footnote in the typescript of this letter reads: "Pride."
32. More appears never to have reviewed *Rousseau and Romanticism* in print. See the bibliography of the relevant time-period in Dakin 1950: 174-76 and below.
33. On Ernest Seillière, see his entry in the Biographical Register.
34. On Charles Maurras, see his entry in the Biographical Register.
35. Maurras 1905.
36. Sherman 1917b.
37. Anon. 1919a.
38. Sherman 1919.

I leave here on Sep. 22. Have you given up all intention of making that visit? The weather has been very bad of late reminding me of a bit of what we had at Essex last year. With kind regards to Nettie,

Sincerely yours,
Irving Babbitt.

Essex, N. Y.
12 September, 1919

My dear Babbitt,

I think the best thing to do with my unfortunate article is to let it lie until I get home. In the quiet and familiarity of my Princeton study, I shall be able to examine the thing critically and see whether anything is to be made of it in whole or in part. As for the magazines I feel more and more inclined to follow your leadership and give them up entirely. I get little profit from reading them or writing for them. And the years remaining to a man begin to shorten.

We are going down on the twenty-fourth—I hope to better weather than we are having here.[39] It has been raining now for about three weeks, and the monotony of it is disheartening. I hope your summer has been more profitable than mine, though, as I think I told you, I have found Plutarch a treasure-house. I have just read G. F. Moore's[40] history of Judaism, Christianity, and Mohammedanism—the sort of book that any well-educated man might compose by condensing articles in the various religious encyclopaedias.[41] Yet I suppose Moore will reap κῦδος[42] from it. The mystery of the scholarly reputation grows every day more inexplicable to me.

Faithfully,
Paul E. More.

---

39. On More's time in Essex, New York, during the summer of 1919, see Dakin 1960: 186.

40. George Foot Moore (1851–1931) was a scholar of religion, Presbyterian minister, and professor at the Harvard Divinity School.

41. More composed an anonymous (faultfinding) review of this book, George Foot Moore's *The History of Religions*, for the January 24, 1920, issue of the *Villager*. See More 1920a. For More's negative estimation of Moore, see Dakin 1960: 243.

42. "Glory, renown."

245 Nassau Street
Princeton, New Jersey
25 December 1919

My dear Babbitt,

Did you see Foerster's review of your book in the last (December 13th) *Villager*?[43] It is I think quite an able piece of writing and ought to do some good, though of course the circulation of the magazine is small. I take a personal interest in having got the notice there, after my own dismal fiasco. I laid aside my article intended for the *Unpartizan* (née *Unpopular*) until I was home in the autumn. Then I read it dispassionately, and I can only say that it was a deplorable failure, and contained nothing that could be worked over. No doubt my extreme anxiety to do something super-excellent embarrassed me. I say that; but in fact the thing read as if my brain had softened. As the boys say, I'm sorry.

How are you progressing with your political treatise? I shall be glad to see it in print, but I begin to believe that the world is too much for us. A sapient critic has just damned my latest production on the ground that I am a gentleman and a scholar—his *ipsissima verba*![44]

Do you remember speaking to me once about Synesius?[45] I have just been reading him with the utmost delight. His letters especially fairly sparkle with good things. If I weren't too lazy I would quote you a few of them.

With kind regards to Dora, in which Net joins me, I am
Faithfully yours,
Paul E. More.

---

6 Kirkland Road
Cambridge
4 January, 1920

Dear More,

I have been through your last volume[46] very carefully, many parts of it more than once, and with the solid satisfaction that I usually get from your

43. Foerster 1919.
44. His "very words." According to Dakin (1950: 194), only one review of *With the Wits*, then More's latest book, had appeared in print by the time More composed this letter: see H. S. G. 1919. This review does not refer to More specifically as "a gentleman and a scholar," but it does deem More a learned critic whose work on contemporary authors suffers from squeamishness.
45. The Christian Neoplatonist Synesius of Cyrene (ca. AD 370–413).
46. More 1967b.

writing. It is not often that one finds nowadays this grave note of mature wisdom. I had forgotten how much good stuff there is in the Beaumont and Fletcher. In general the essays that are outside your central group are perhaps the ones that appeal to me the most—though I shall need some more rereading to make up my mind finally on this point. This central group leaves on my mind a tantalizing sense of incompleteness. You might without being unduly systematic have done a little more defining of the word wit itself, of the changes in its meaning (largely under French influence), of its relation to humor and humors, etc. The rôle of Addison was very important, surely more important than Shaftesbury (see p. 244), in making wit respectable, and I cannot help feeling that if you had included an essay on him, it would not only have been very interesting in itself but would have rounded out your whole treatment. – My own impression is that the high quality of your writing is increasingly recognized. The more intelligent college students nearly always take to it kindly. Two Chinese students, by the way, who were in my study at the Library recently complained that they had been trying to buy the complete sets of Shelburne Essays but had received a report from the publisher that two or three of the volumes were out of print! I hope that this is only a temporary condition.

I think that I detect a "defeatist" note in several of your recent letters. The odds are, I admit, overwhelming but instead of getting behind a stone fence, as recommended by your beloved master, it seems to me that it is just the time to be more aggressive than ever. I did not advise you in a recent letter to refrain from writing reviews but to choose, if possible, some review which has a real public and if necessary to go to England. Harold Cox,[47] editor of the *Edinburgh*, had a manly attack on socialism in his July number[48] and I wondered whether if you wrote him, he would not encourage you to send him an article on the anti-romantic and anti-naturalistic movement that is now beginning especially in France. This French movement is rapidly attaining important proportions and is one of the really encouraging signs at the present time. For Seillière and his general position see article in *La Revue Bleue*, Nov. 19 ('19).[49] You would not need to mention my work or mention it only in passing, since it seems to have a blighting effect on your genius. Foerster, by the way, writes me that the *Nation* refused to print a review of

---

47. Harold Cox (1859–1936) was a Liberal Member of Parliament who was a proponent of laissez-faire economics.
48. Cox 1919.
49. Lote 1919.

R. & R. that it had engaged from him, though it sent him a check for the full amount. Unfavorable notices of this book are snapped up with alacrity. Schinz notified me recently that he has an attack of goodly length (in which he will probably also glance at you) in the *Journal of Philosophy*.[50] Tufts[51] of Chicago has what seems to me a rambling and ineffective refutation of the book in the October issue of the *International Journal of Ethics*.[52]

In reading Synesius, I wish you would mark for me any passages in which he seems to recognize the supreme rôle of the imagination or asserts that men need to be deceived for their own good.

I am going West to deliver some lectures at Kenyon College in March[53] but shall scarcely find it possible to take in Princeton either going or returning. Is there no chance of seeing you in Cambridge this winter? An occasional foregathering of this kind is good for me and I am not sure that it is bad for you. Give my kind regards to Nettie.

Sincerely yours,
Irving Babbitt.

---

245 Nassau Street
Princeton, New Jersey
17 January, 1920

My dear Babbitt,

Your name has passed the written ballot for election to the Institute,[54] is proposed by the Committee, and will come up for final consideration at the dinner tonight. As this last vote is scarcely more than a matter of form, you are about the same as elected. However, I will keep my letter open and add a line after the dinner if all goes well. For diplomatic reasons I got Brownell to act as first sponsor. He welcomed the proposition, and said he was ready to propose you for Chancellor of the Academy; but that dignity must be

---

50. Schinz 1920. Babbitt replied to this review; see Babbitt 1920.
51. James Hayden Tufts (1862–1942) was a professor of philosophy at the University of Chicago who collaborated with John Dewey on a book devoted to ethics.
52. Tufts 1919.
53. Contra Slayton (1986: 233), who puts Babbitt's role as Larwill lecturer at Kenyon College in January of 1920. In a prefatory note in *Democracy and Leadership*, Babbitt mentions that these four Kenyon lectures were called "Democracy and Imperialism" (Babbitt 1924: no pagination).
54. The National Institute of Arts and Letters. Dakin (1960: 105-6) notes that on February 10, 1908, More had been elected to this body.

deferred. Mather acted as second sponsor and I as third. You are now on a level with Edgar Lee Masters and Robert Frost!

The most important statements of Synesius in regard to the imagination (φαντασία) are in his *De Insomniis*, and to save the trouble of copying I am sending you my notes on that treatise, which I will ask you to return. The numerals refer to the sections in the Migne edition, vol. 66 of the Greek series. In his 254th letter (to Hypatia) he tells a remarkable story about writing the treatise at a single sitting in a sort of trance and boasts that it contains δόγματα τῶν οὔπω φιλοσηθέντων Ἕλλησι.⁵⁵ How far this boast is true I cannot say, but Synesius was a pretty well-read man, and would probably know what he was talking about. At any rate it is a curious and notable work.

And while I am referring to my friends, the Greeks, let me quote from another of them in justification of what you call a "defeatist" note in my letters. I am not giving up the fight, but I am beginning to take myself out of it a little personally. My text is Epictetus' Chapter περὶ τοῦ ἀγωνιᾶν, on being anxious; and it is to be noted in the first place that ἀγωνιᾶν also has the meaning of ἀγωνίζεσθαι, to contend. But I see on referring to the book that the same idea is expressed more tersely in another chapter (II, xvi), and I quote from there: ἐπεὶ διὰ τί ὁ ῥήτωρ, εἰδὼς ὅτι γέγραφε καλῶς, ὅτι ἀνείληφε τὰ γεγραμμένα, φωνὴν εἰσφέρων ἡδεῖαν ὅμως ἔτι ἀγωνιᾷ; ὅτι οὐκ ἀρκεῖται τῷ μελετῆσαι. τί οὖν θέλει; ἐπαινεθῆναι ὑπὸ τῶν παρόντων. πρὸς μὲν οὖν τὸ δύνασθαι μελετᾶν ἤσκηται, πρὸς ἔπαινον δὲ καὶ ψόγον οὐκ ἤσκηται.... ἀλλ' οὐδ' αὐτὸ τὸ ἀγωνιᾶν τί ἐστιν οἶδεν, πότερον ἡμέτερον ἔργον. ἐστὶν ἢ ἀλλότριον, ἔστιν αὐτὸ παῦσαι ἢ οὐκ ἔστιν.⁵⁶ It is the Hindu doctrine of detachment, you see, expressed with Greek moderation; and it means, so far as I dare apply it to myself, that I am concerning myself more wholeheartedly with my work and thinking less about its effect—or perhaps I should say, less about praise and blame. I do feel too that the world for

---

55. A footnote in the typescript of this letter reads: "An inquiry…into some other points which have not yet been treated by any Greek philosopher. Translated by A. Fitzgerald, Oxford, 1926, p. 254."

56. A footnote in the typescript of this letter provides the following translation: "For why is it that the orator, although he knows that he has composed a good speech, has memorized what he has written and is bringing a pleasing voice to his task, is still anxious despite all that? Because he is not satisfied with the mere practice of oratory. What then does he want? He wants to be praised by his audience. Now he has trained himself with a view to being able to practice oratory, but he has not trained himself with reference to praise and blame.... Nay, he does not even know what this anxiety itself is, whether it is something that we can control, or beyond our powers, whether he can stop it or not. Arrian's *Discourses of Epictetus*, II, xvi, 5–6, 10; Loeb Class. Lib. *Epictetus*, I, pp. 323-325."

the present has gone beyond any care that I can offer; but nevertheless it is vastly important to keep the tradition alive for those who come after us. That also is a way of keeping up the fight, but perhaps it may not satisfy your more belligerent nature. – You are right, I think, in what you say about the relative merit of my essays on the Queen Anne wits and of those on men outside of the group. The tantalizing incompleteness of the former must be attributed in part to the fact that they were written independently one of the other. Addison certainly is a fine theme; I may come to him some day. – You do not tell me what you are working on, but I suppose it is your political diatribe. It will round out your other volumes most satisfactorily. – Mather still nurses his vein of ironical pessimism. My dentist, who had me in his chair yesterday, assured me that from the shape of my teeth he knew me to be sanguine and optimistic. There you are.

Faithfully yours,
Paul E. More.

P.S. I am just back from dinner. Thorndike[57] tells me that your name received the largest vote in the first written ballot. At the dinner your name was the only one that went through unanimously. You will of course receive formal notice of your election from the secretary, now J. B. Fletcher.[58]

---

6 Kirkland Road
Cambridge
5 April, 1920

Dear More,

Thank you for your efforts in my behalf in connection with my election to the Institute. Convey also my thanks to Mather and, if the proper occasion presents itself, to Brownell. I approve on principle of an organization of this kind though to be very effective it would have to be better known. A French writer describes it as a "*vague* imitation" of the French Institute.[59] The vagueness is above all, I fear, in the minds of the public. The selection of names is

---

57. Presumably, More refers to Ashley Horace Thorndike (1871–1933), a professor of English literature at Columbia University.
58. Jefferson Butler Fletcher (1865–1946), a professor of comparative literature at Columbia University and a 1918 inductee to the American Academy of Arts and Letters.
59. Babbitt would be elected to the French Institute in 1926. See Dora Babbitt in Manchester and Shepard 1941: xii; Brennan and Yarbrough 1987: 72–73.

no doubt about as good as one has a right to expect, though when I note in the number lightweights about twenty years my junior of the general style of Walter Prichard Eaton[60] I find it hard to be elated beyond all measure by my own election.

I note with interest that you are to run a review department in the *Unpartizan*.[61] I wish it were in some publication of a less hole-and-corner character. Sidney Gunn's article, by the way, in the last issue[62] seems to me to miss the point entirely and to be a confusion of good counsel. I wonder why such flimsy stuff gets into print at all.

Sherman's article about you in the *Review* struck me as a bit "fresh."[63] I have heard several of the graduate students here express a similar view. The political argument of the paper is of course very sophistical and certainly out of place in Fuller's sheet. Sherman's rhetoric has from the start run well ahead of his thinking power and I cannot see that the gap between the two is closing up. As for your reputation, the article should do you good. The suggestion that you are only for very superior persons should in sound psychology lead a number of people to say to themselves that that means them.

I have very heavy work at Harvard this year and this has interfered with the writing of my political volume. I have got the subject thought out, however, or think I have; the only question is whether I can present it convincingly to others. I am just back from Kenyon College (Gambier, Ohio) where I gave the gist of the book in four lectures,[64] with what effect it is hard to say. Kenyon is an interesting little institution with a sound tradition.

You may be interested in taking a glance at a review[65] of my last book in the *Athenaeum* (Feb. 27) by J. Middleton Murry,[66] the editor. He has sent me his last volume, just out, entitled the *Evolution of an Intellectual*, accompanied by an interesting letter in which he tells me that he is only thirty; and

---

60. Walter Prichard Eaton (1878–1957) was an American drama critic and a professor at Yale.

61. Henry Holt, the editor of the *Unpartizan Review*, had recently asked More to edit the book section of his journal; see Dakin 1960: 188. More edited this section from 1920 to 1921; in 1921 Holt stopped publishing the magazine. See Dakin 1960: 188, 190.

62. Gunn 1920.

63. Sherman 1920. The piece was reprinted under a new title as a chapter in Sherman's book *Americans* (Sherman 1923: 316-36).

64. On Babbitt's lectures at Kenyon College in March of this year, see above.

65. Murry 1920. In the review, Murry asserted about *Rousseau and Romanticism*, "Its style is, we admit, at times rather harsh and crabbed, but the critical thought which animates it is of a kind so rare that we are almost impelled to declare that it is the only book of criticism worthy of the name which has appeared in English in the twentieth century."

66. John Middleton Murry (1889–1957) was a prolific English author and critic.

this is his fifth volume! It would appear from some of his essays towards the end of his book that his ideas are undergoing a very significant clarification. He has certain essential distinctions still to make. Should he succeed in making them, being as he plainly is a very lively youth, he may exercise a salutary influence on contemporary English criticism.

Thank you for the excerpts from Synesius. I have been meaning to look into him for a number of years because I inferred from certain references I have seen that he realized certain truths about the rôle of the imagination that are not brought out with sufficient explicitness by Greek philosophy.

Is there no chance of seeing you in Cambridge? I hope that you will have to inspect somebody or something here in connection with those visiting committees you are on. Dora joins me in kind regards to Nettie.

Sincerely,
Irving Babbitt.

---

245 Nasssau Street
Princeton, New Jersey
June 18, 1920

My dear Babbitt,

Net gave a cheering account of you and your doings, and I have been meaning to write to you ever since her return. She tells me you are busy on your political diatribe and expect to be engaged on it all summer. Perhaps, if you are suitably settled and my own circumstances permit, I may get a chance to read the MS. this summer. It looks now as if I ought to be able to get away for a visit. I have not made any definite plans as yet, but shall probably go with Alice[67] to Essex some time after the middle of July. We shall thus be there without Net and Darrah for two or three weeks. The time of my going depends on the work now in hand. The last chapter of my volume *The Religion of Plato*[68] is under way, and indeed well on towards completion. Of course the entire book needs revision and in large part rewriting, but this I shall not undertake until the autumn. Meanwhile there are several minor tasks to get out of the way before I leave my library for the summer. – Did Net tell you, or have I told you, that the university is giving me a[n] honorarium of $1000 for my course? This will seem a pitiful sum to a Harvard

---

67. More's younger daughter Alice, one presumes, not More's sister of the same name.
68. More 1921.

professor since the new wealth has poured in, but it is a very comfortable addition to my income and a welcome sign that the work is approved. Fite was the procurer. He, by the way, has been smitten down suddenly with some strange disease with swollen glands and high fever. It may be only a temporary ailment, but I suspect his nervous energy is somewhat undermined. He does not take kindly to the world's rather cross-grained treatment of the one great "individualist" and is growing frightfully embittered. In fact with him on one side of me and Mather on the other I feel like Goethe's Weltkind, your only smiling optimist and romanticist. Really it isn't worth while to take the world so seriously— ἔστι δὴ τοίνυν τὰ τῶν ἀνθρώπων πράγματα μεγάλης μὲν σπουδῆς οὐκ ἄξια, κτλ.,[69] as no doubt I have quoted several times before in my letters. I have in mind an essay thereanent on Socrates as the true ἀπαθής[70] contrasted with St. Paul as typical of the much commoner mixture of spiritual insight and egotism.[71] But of that some other time. – With kind regards to Dora,

Sincerely yours,
Paul E. More.

---

245 Nassau Street
Princeton, New Jersey
June 19, 1920

My dear Babbitt,

I forgot to tell you in my letter that there will be a review[72] of your *Rousseau* in the July number of the *Unpartizan*. Mather wrote it for me, and it is moderately good, but by no means all that it might be. Holt thinks, on the basis of the review, that Mather and you and I are all three of us cracked; but I forced him to print the thing.

Sincerely,
Paul E. More.

---

69. A footnote in the typescript of this letter provides the following translation: "Human affairs are not worth bothering about too much [etc.]." This quotation is spoken by the Athenian stranger in Plato's *Laws* (803b).

70. A footnote in the typescript of this letter reads: "Dispassionate man."

71. On More's dislike for St. Paul, see, e.g., Duggan 1966: 98–99.

72. Mather 1920.

Crater Club
Essex, N. Y.
August 9, 1920

Dear Babbitt,

How would it do if I came Thursday the 19th and stayed a week? Would this suit the convenience of all the good folk male and female of Chesham?

I can not add anything more now, as the mail is about to go.

Net and Darrah come this Thursday, but Darrah has studying to do and cannot make any visits.

Sincerely,
Paul E. More.

P.S. Please reply immediately, as I have to make arrangements to take Alice to the Gausses[73] at the same time—if I go then.[74]

---

245 Nassau Street
Princeton, New Jersey
Nov. 12, 1920

Dear Babbitt,

After talking with Holt I have come to the conclusion that we had better drop the Murry.[75] My editorship[76] will probably terminate at an early date, and meanwhile the only course is to make things as smooth as possible.

My lecture at Bowdoin is to be the evening of the seventh. I have not yet looked into the matter of trains, and do not know what I shall do. An unconscionable rush of work—the *Unpartizan*, the *Weekly*, and the *Villager*—has thrown me behind in my writing, or revision of the Plato, and I may find

---

73. On Christian Gauss, see his entry in the Biographical Register.

74. Dakin (1960: 191) notes that in August of 1920 More left his daughter Darrah in their cottage at Essex, New York, to visit Christian Gauss in Greensboro, Vermont, and the Babbitts in Chesham, New Hampshire, for a week.

75. A footnote in the typescript of this letter reads: "This probably refers to a review of J. Middleton Murry's *The Evolution of an Intellectual*, Richard Cobden-Sanderson, London, 1920, which I. B. proposed to write for the *Unpartizan*."

76. On More's work as the book editor for the *Unpartizan Review*, see above.

it impossible to take an extra day. But of this I shall be able to speak more certainly at a later date.

Sincerely,
Paul E. More.

Cambridge
17 December, 1920

Dear More,

Dora's temperature is back at normal and she seems to be definitely on the mend. She is still weak, however, and the process of recuperation promises to be slow. We have had much more worry from her setback (pleurisy or pneumonia?) than from the original operation.

I have a letter from the editor of *La Revue hebdomadaire* (Paris) saying that he would like to publish some of my work. I am suggesting to him that he translate passages from *R. & R.* In the meanwhile I am encouraging Mercier[77] of the French department here to write an article for the *Revue heb.* that will present to the French public not merely my work but yours. I am supplying him with information about you. Faÿ's conclusions in the *Correspondant*[78] are inadmissible in regard to both of us but he is especially inadequate on you. – Give my kind regards to Nettie.

Sincerely,
Irving Babbitt.

---

245 Nassau Street
Princeton, New Jersey
December 20, 1920

Dear Babbitt,

We have been waiting anxiously ever since I returned for a word from you and your letter this morning was a great relief. I had begun to imagine that

---

77. On Louis J. A. Mercier, see his entry in the Biographical Register.
78. Faÿ 1920. This article includes extended discussion of the work of Babbitt and More, though Faÿ misspells the latter's name.

things were going very badly indeed. Net is writing to Esther[79] to ask her to send a few flowers to Dora.[80] Let them be our Christmas greeting.

I am interested to hear what you say about the *Revue hebdomadaire*. What a bull dog worker you are. In self protection I feel obliged to keep my hand free from all these outside tasks, and it is good that some one has the strength and courage to keep up the fight. The devil seems to have no weaknesses.

With hopes that Dora will soon be at ease, and in trust that the New Year will bear less heavily on you than the old has done,

Faithfully yours,
Paul E. More.

---

245 Nassau Street
Princeton, New Jersey
June 23, 1921

My dear Babbitt,

The University Press here expects to start the composition of my "Religion of Plato" next week, and I want very much to have the benefit of your criticism as the galleys come out. Please let me have word by return post, to what address the proof should be sent. I suppose you are still in Cambridge, but am not sure. And let me have a card notifying me of any change of address. I should have preferred to have you go through the MS., but as it is now the Press promises to let me have all the proof in July while I am in Princeton, whereas if I had sent you the MS. this could scarcely have been done. Parts of the book will scarcely meet with your entire approval; something in their tone I fear will displease you; but as a whole I hope you will think the work is better constructed than the *Platonism*.

I do hope Dora is gaining in strength, and that your summer will be untroubled. Your proximity to the Mathers will add to your pleasure. Possibly Net and I may come to the Ark[81] for a few days, so as to be of the party.

Sincerely,
Paul E. More.

---

79. Babbitt's daughter Esther Babbitt.
80. On Dora Babbitt's illness, see both above and below.
81. A footnote in the typescript of this letter reads: "At Jaffrey, New Hampshire." The Ark was a large farmhouse turned hotel near Mount Monadnock.

Jaffrey, New Hampshire
27 June, 1921

Dear More,

I am much interested to learn that you are getting ahead so fast with your "Religion of Plato." I shall of course be very glad to go over the galley proof. It is probable that I could have been of more help to you if I had had a chance at the book in MS. The title of this book is one that may attract purchasers. – I have been reading with great pleasure your eleventh Shelburne series.[82] The essays in this volume go well together and there is a greater evenness in execution than in some of the preceding volumes. The *Edwards* and the *Emerson* seem perhaps a bit perfunctory in places but in general you have achieved a geniality and mellowness of tone that befits your years. I am amused at a notice in the *Freeman*[83] by Newton Arvin[84] in which you are accused of "hideous frivolity" because, instead or promoting the class-war, you advise people to fear the Lord and keep his commandments. This youth has just graduated from Harvard with highest honors in English. His inverted psychology is more than an individual aberration; it is the direct outcome of the kind of "idealism" that now flourishes in academic circles.

My own book goes forward very slowly. The more I reflect on the subject the more I am impressed by its importance and also by its difficulty. I hope to make rapid progress and recover some of the ground I have lost this winter because of the disturbed domestic situation as well as other circumstances. The southern doctors diagnosed Dora's ailment as pernicious anemia, but the diagnosis was not confirmed by the physicians of the Peter Bent Brigham Hospital. As a matter of fact she seems to be gaining ground slowly and we hope that by autumn she will be entirely restored to her normal health.

We are much pleased at the prospect of seeing you and Nettie in Jaffrey. The most convenient plan would be for you to come down from Squam via Concord and Peterboro. You can get a good through train at Fitzwilliam, a few miles south of there that connects with the afternoon boat from Burlington for Essex. There is no reason why you should put up at the Ark since we have plenty of room and so far as we can see at present it will be perfectly convenient for us to entertain you. If any difficulty should arise in the meanwhile, we shall let you know frankly.

---

82. More 1967c.
83. Arvin 1921, a vituperative criticism of More and his political outlook.
84. Newton Arvin (1900–1963) was an American literary critic and professor at Smith College. He began writing for the *Freeman* while still an undergraduate, thanks to the invitation of Van Wyck Brooks, his favorite teacher at Harvard.

Mi Wu,[85] one of my Chinese graduate students at Harvard, tells me that he is planning to visit you at Princeton. He is a green-looking little runt but is a man of real cultivation both in his own and occidental literature. He is a great admirer of your work and will spread a knowledge of it in China.

Sincerely,
Irving Babbitt.

Camp Cedars
Crater Club
Essex, N. Y.
8 August, 1921

My dear Babbitt,

Has no proof[86] reached you? It should have been sent from Princeton last Monday. I find the reading, especially checking up the translations with Apelt's[87] new version before me, trying and irksome, and am keen to be done with it. There comes a time when one wonders why he has ever written a book.

Our weather here this past week has been beautiful, a great relief from the intense heat in Princeton. I presume you have been enjoying the same vigorous air. I hear from Mather that Dora is very well, playing tennis and that sort of thing. That is certainly good news.

We are looking forward to our visit to Jaffrey the last of the month.

Sincerely,
P. E. M.

Jaffrey, N. H.
10 August, 1921

Dear More,

I have just received the second batch of proof (completing the book), but have decided to send on the first batch before reading it. Any comment I can make at this late hour is of course very superficial and does not indeed go much beyond the details of the expression. If I went very deeply into the thought I should soon run up against certain clashes between your

---

85. On Wu Mi, see his entry in the Biographical Register.
86. Of More 1921.
87. Otto Apelt (1845–1932) was a German classical philologist.

underlying postulates and mine. Our conclusions when translated into actual conduct are practically identical but our philosophies certainly diverge at times very widely. In the book I am now writing,[88] I am covering some of the same ground that you have covered in your volume and I may deem it expedient to point out very frankly our agreements and disagreements, especially as regards Plato.[89]

I have retained a youthful impression that the *Timaeus* is almost impossibly difficult and obscure and this impression has not been entirely dissipated by your translation and comment. This part of the book is I think likely to be the least attractive to me. In various other passages you seem to me to strike a high level; from a first hasty glance I should say that you come in strong at the finish—an important achievement in a book of philosophy.

I remember remarking after reading one of James's[90] books and noting his hostility to capitals that he seemed determined to live in a lower-case universe. After scanning your pages and seeing how they are peppered with H's,[91] I am a bit inclined to bring against you the opposite charge. I am inclined especially to query this extreme holiness in your references to the deity of Plato.

I am reserving many other comments for your visit here at the end of August. We are all looking forward with great pleasure to your coming.

Sincerely yours,
Irving Babbitt.

---

88. Babbitt 1924.

89. Babbitt ultimately chose not to do this. There is only one mention of More in *Democracy and Leadership* (Babbitt 1924: 328) and it is supportive.

90. He means the philosopher William James.

91. Babbitt is referring to More's use of capital letters when referring to God as Him, Himself, etc. This seems a cheeky way for Babbitt to note More's drift in the direction of Christianity.

CHAPTER EIGHT
1922-1925

6 Kirkland Road
Cambridge
22 January, 1922

Dear More,

The publication that I mentioned to you when you were in Cambridge is the *Church Quarterly Review* (London). Your publisher will probably send it a copy of the *Religion of Plato* but it is just as well to make sure. I shall be heartily pleased at any recognition this last volume of yours receives. It will indicate that the sense of things religious is not so completely atrophied as I am at times inclined to believe.

I hope you are none the worse for your brief but rather strenuous sojourn in these parts.[1] I allowed the talk after luncheon at the Colonial Club to stretch to rather undue length in the hope of getting Mercier more interested in your writing and personality. The result may appear in the book he is contemplating (*Vers les Synthèses nécessaires*).

I have another letter from Sherman. He has heard that I have been expressing disapproval of his recent trend but he does not seem to take it very much amiss. I am planning to write him a rather frank letter. His introduction to Emerson is very nearly a pure panegyric;[2] as such it is excellent. His introduction to Flaubert ends on the note of love![3] Any one who wishes to clear up the present situation is going to have the ungracious task of submitting this word to a perfectly pitiless dialectic.

---

1. Dakin (1960: 204) notes that More traveled to Cambridge in early January of 1922 to attend a Visiting Committee of the Graduate School at Harvard. He further details that More, in a letter to his sister Alice from January 14, said that Babbitt looked "old and troubled" when he saw him in Cambridge.
2. This essay first appeared as the introduction to Sherman's collection of Emerson's essays and poems (Sherman 1921a: vii-xlv). It was later reprinted in Sherman 1923: 63-121.
3. This essay first appeared as the introduction to the George Sand–Gustave Flaubert correspondence (Sherman 1921b). It was later reprinted in Sherman 1924: 327-63.

With kind regards to Nettie,

> Sincerely yours,
> Irving Babbitt.

---

245 Nassau Street
Princeton, New Jersey
25 February 1922

My dear Babbitt,

I feel very much a sinner that I have never written to you or Dora to thank you for taking me in so kindly and treating me so well.[4] No doubt you will add that the time I have borne this feeling without a sound shows a very indurated conscience. I did enjoy my little visit most heartily. A wretched cold caught me on the way back and laid me prostrate in bed for two days. That started my delay in writing, and then the devil of laziness got in his work. – Thank you for the name of the magazine. I will see that a copy of the book is sent there. But my only hope for a sale is in my successive classes. I have just bullied twenty-three men into buying it. That is what I call direct action.

> Faithfully,
> Paul E. More.

Cambridge
8 April, 1922

Dear More,

It was pleasant to get a glimpse of Mather a few days ago. I presume he has told you something about the situation with us. Dora is back from the hospital but is under instructions to remain in bed for the next few weeks.[5] The cause of her anaemia (which seems definitely to be of the ordinary [?] type) is somewhat obscure. We hope to avoid any future operating.

I am leaving for California next Wednesday. In addition to the series at Leland Stanford I am to speak at the Un. of California, Northwestern and

---

4. On More's brief trip to Cambridge in early January of 1922, see above.
5. Zeitlin and Woodbridge (1929: 516-17) quote an April 11, 1922, letter from Stuart Sherman to Babbitt, in which Sherman worries about Dora Babbitt's grave illness.

the Un. of Chicago.⁶ I shall have to make a good part of my preparation on the train! – My special reason for writing you in the midst of the present rush is to tell you that Mercier inclines to write the article about you in *La Revue hebdomadaire*.⁷ He has an honest though rather plodding mind. I am not sure that he can do justice to your Platonic subtleties. He may, however, with my aid be able to turn out something respectable. I wonder whether it would not be a good plan for you to send him some of the Shelburne series—especially perhaps vols. I, VI, VIII, & IX; or perhaps it might be worth while to send him the series complete. Suit yourself in the matter. I could lend him the volume on Plato.

I am sending you a letter from Mi Wu in accordance with his own request (see last page). You may not care to read the whole document. I gather from another letter he has written me that Kuang-ti May⁸ is not turning out well. Wu has a great admiration for your work in general and a special affection I should say, for your *Indian Epigrams*. There is a certain pathos in the spectacle of this frail youth putting up a fight almost single-handed in behalf of traditional Chinese civilization against the on-rushing tide of Westernism.

Give my kind regards to Nettie. I [am] hoping that you are both having less anxiety about Darrah.

Sincerely yours,
Irving Babbitt.

---

245 Nassau Street
Princeton, New Jersey
April 10, 1922

My dear Babbitt,

I did hear about you from Mather, and should have written to express my disappointment at learning of the return of Dora's trouble. I do hope a few weeks of complete rest may bring back her strength. But resting must be a

---

6. Slayton (1986: 233) mentions that Babbitt lectured at Stanford in April of 1922. In a prefatory note in *Democracy and Leadership*, Babbitt informs us that this amounted to four lectures that he collectively called "The Ethical Basis of Democracy," supported by the West Foundation (Babbitt 1924: no pagination).
7. Mercier does not appear to have published an article on More for *La Revue hebdomadaire*, although a piece he wrote on Babbitt had appeared in the periodical's July 1921 issue (see Mercier 1928: iv). The material that would have appeared in the article on More can presumably be found in Mercier's 1928 book (see esp. 126-87).
8. On K. T. May, a former student of Babbitt, see above, chapter 7.

matter of sad monotony for her now after so much of it. Please give her our sympathy. – Will it be possible for you to stop over in Princeton on your way back after your lecture tour? I suppose you will be pressed for time, but we should love to see you, if only for a night. – Wu's letter is a brave and pathetic document. It must in a way encourage you to receive such homage; sure in this case the seed was sown in fertile soil. But for him, poor fellow, I do not see much comfort. China's tragedy apparently is her too great conservatism. She has held back so long that now it is difficult to see how there can be a readjustment without an almost complete bouleversement. Japan did of course weather a change of that sort—yet not the same. She had to adjust herself to a new mechanical civilization, but she did not have the devilish doctrines of men like Dewey to contend with or to assimilate. I see not much comfort in the East. As for my own world, I give the strong hours of the day to doing what I can to counteract the growing heresies without thinking much of what I may or may not accomplish; and thus for refreshment I am steeping myself[9]

Camp Cedars, Crater Club,
Essex, N. Y.,
August 21, 1922.

My dear Babbitt:

A letter from Dora a few days ago brought the welcome news that she is gaining notably in strength. No doubt the complete change has been good for her. She also said that you were to go over to the Sorbonne next spring, but gave no information as to what you are to do.[10] Are you going as exchange professor, or is this some special course of lectures you have been asked to deliver? And, in either case, will you give the substance of the book you are now working on, and will it be in French or English? I congratulate you most heartily on the opportunity; but I fear you will find Paris *quantum mutata*,[11] and I suspect it will not be quite easy to express your real views

---

9. A footnote in the typescript of this letter reads: "The last part of this letter is missing."
10. Between March and May of 1923, Babbitt was the James Hazen Hyde Lecturer and exchange professor at the Sorbonne (see Chesley Martin Hutchings in Manchester and Shepard 1941: 227; Marcus Selden Goldman in Manchester and Shepard 1941: 233; Slayton 1986: 233; Ryn 1991: xviii; Ryn 1995b: xxiv; Panichas 1999: 202; see also Dora Babbitt in Manchester and Shepard 1941: xii).
11. "Greatly changed."

without irritating the French nerves. From hearing Cestre lecture last spring and for other reasons I have the impression that the French are in a state of almost morbid exacerbation and ready to quarrel with any body [sic]. Meanwhile how is your book progressing? From the fact that I have received no answer to my note in the spring I suppose that you are too busy with your work to think of visiting this summer.

I am myself sitting tight—no strange occupation for me. Tomorrow Net and Alice and I go over to the Gausses in Vermont for a couple of days, but otherwise I shall not stir from Essex until we go back to Princeton in late September. I stayed behind for a couple of weeks in July after the family had left, and contrived to finish, or virtually finish, the first draft of my book.[12] But there is plenty of work by way of revision to keep my nose to the typewriter during my four months of complete freedom—i.e. until my lectures begin in February. This summer I am writing nothing, save notes. The back bone of my reading is Aristotle and Holtzmann's[13] great *Neutestamentliche Theologie*.[14] I have gone through the *Rhetoric* and am now well into the *Metaphysics*,—and strange reading as it is, sometimes profound, sometimes, as it seems to me, a mere debauchery of the analytic reason. Holtzmann's two huge volumes are a masterpiece. He gathers up all the literature on his subject for the past fifty years and presents the results in a manner which can scarcely be overpraised, except the language, which is absurdly difficult.

Let me have a word in one of your spare moments. With kindest regards to your sister, I am

Faithfully yours,
Paul E. More

Dublin, N. H.
13 September, 1922

Dear More,

I have been assuming all summer that there was not much chance of getting a visit from you, though we are unusually well situated to receive you. We have a rather large plastered house, with the kind of study that I find a

---

12. More 1923.
13. The name appearing in the typescript of this letter here and below is written as "Hollymann." But More was referring to the German theologian Heinrich Julius Holtzmann (1832–1910), the author of the two-volume *Lehrbuch der Neutestamentlichen Theologie*.
14. Holtzmann 1911.

distinct encouragement to writing. My experience with unplastered houses has not, from the point of view of real work, been a satisfactory one. Is there not just a chance that you will be able to look in on us on your return trip from Essex to Princeton? We are planning to be here until about 25 Sep. – Dora hopes to be back from California early in October. The reports about her are encouraging, though there is still much room for improvement.

And so you have another book well advanced towards completion. Comme vous y allez! I hope you feel that the series to which this book belongs is reaching an audience "fit though few." It is extraordinarily difficult to win attention for anything that is out of the current sociological trend. – I have just been looking through "Painted Windows" (by Harold Begbie?),[15] not much more than a bit of clever journalism with a disagreeably "intimate" tone in places. It gives, however, a notion of the confusion and ineffectiveness of contemporary religious thought in England.

My own book[16] goes forward slowly. I hope to have the first half on paper by the end of the summer and the rest completed before my departure for France. The extreme difficulty I have found in this task is perhaps due to my preoccupation with the question of method. It is in a way easy enough to see what is the matter with the present situation but not easy to state the difficulty in a way that will force attention and put the mere modernists on the defensive. I am planning to send you my MS. for criticism. It will be a pleasure for me, as you know, to go through your new volume either in MS. or in proof.

It will, as you say, be a very ticklish thing for me to expound my ideas at the Sorbonne. At the same time it is well to remember that Lowell nominated me for the exchange professorship at the request of the Sorbonne itself, which acted no doubt on the suggestion of a group of professors several of whom know me personally and all of whom are more or less familiar with my point of view. Cestre is a good chap personally but he has a Jacobinical streak in his psychology combined with a rather preternatural lack of sense of humor. Perhaps I may decide to give my public course on English literary criticism and a *cours fermé* on the political writings of Rousseau, an arrangement that should prove rather harmless.

I had a rather strenuous two weeks and a half in the West this spring. I gave four lectures at Leland Stanford, one at the University of California and, on the return trip, a Phi Beta Kappa address at Northwestern University and a "Moody" lecture at the University of Chicago—with the usual number of

---

15. *Painted Windows: A Study in Religious Personality* was originally published anonymously by "a Gentleman with a Duster." Its author was the English journalist Edward Harold Begbie (1871–1929), who used this nom de plume for other books as well. See Begbie 1922.

16. Babbitt 1924.

teas, dinners and receptions thrown in for good measure. I did my speaking from notes. I have found that it is not possible to establish contact with an audience when one keeps one's nose in a manuscript.

I lunched with "Uncle" Henry Holt the other day. One of his sons has just married a daughter of the Handasyd Cabots.[17] Uncle Henry noticed my absence at the ceremony, but I hope that he will forgive me. My sister joins me in kind regards to you and Nettie.

Sincerely yours,
Irving Babbitt.

---

245 Nassau Street
Princeton, New Jersey
January 2, 192[3][18]

My dear Babbitt,

I have been driving hard at the MS. of my volume on the Hellenistic Philosophies[19] for two reasons. In the first place I wish to place it with the publisher in time to have the proofs finished before we go abroad in the summer—if we go;[20] and, secondly, I wanted you to read it before your own exodus.[21] The work is nearing completion now and I hope to have it done by the first of next month. This ought to satisfy my first reason of urgency, but it will be too late to send it to you. I am sorry, for I should particularly like your judgment of the thing. It has been particularly hard, as you can imagine, to decide on what should be included and what omitted. Unless I am deceived in my judgment I have been able to treat the central theses of Epicureanism, Stoicism, Neoplatonism, and Scepticism in a fairly original manner, while keeping the general thesis of the series constantly in view; but to do this I have had to exclude a good deal of otherwise pertinent matter rather rigorously. The Sceptics bothered me the most; but as it stands I take my discussion of that subject to be the most important in the book. There is at present no history or discussion of Pyrrhonism and the Middle Academy in English even tolerably adequate. That is curious, since the work of these two schools is final and of the first significance.

---

17. Holt's son Henry Holt Jr. (1889–1941) married Elizabeth Dwight Cabot (1902–1975) on September 4, 1922.

18. This letter is dated "January 2, 1922," but the contents of the letter make clear that it was written on January 2, 1923—a misdating especially common at the start of a new calendar year.

19. More 1923.

20. More vacationed in upstate New York for much of September of 1923.

21. This is a reference to Babbitt's upcoming lectureship at the Sorbonne.

I presume your own writing has been pretty well shelved by the need of preparing for the Sorbonne; or will you just use your old material for those lectures? Our plan—so far as we have one—is to sail some time in July or later and pass our first few months in England. We shall probably make Oxford or Cambridge our headquarters. Later we shall travel through France and Italy, and certainly go to Greece. But as I said, nothing yet has been settled. For one thing, the whole venture depends on renting Net's Pool[22] houses, and perhaps on renting our Princeton place. It will be no great disappointment to me if we do not go, but Net and the girls have quite set their hearts on the trip. Darrah graduates in June.[23] She is not any too well, and her experience has brought me to the conclusion that a female college is a place where students go to acquire the vices of men and unlearn the virtues of women; but perhaps such instruction is proper preparation for life in the new world to be. In Darrah's case at least, I think that a year abroad will probably be a good cure for her frazzled nerves. I hope we shall have a glimpse of you in England, if we are there.

Have you seen Frye's new volume of essays, *Romance and Tragedy*, published by the Marshall Jones Co.?[24] It is a first rate piece of work, better than his earlier collection.[25] The essay in particular on the "Idea of Greek Tragedy" is superb, a really profound bit of thinking. Do not fail to get hold of the book; it will interest you. He is everything that Sherman is not. Sherman's recent work, by the way, *Americans*,[26] is no less than a compact signed with the Devil. Mather is so indignant that he has written Sherman a long letter of rebuke in his cleverly turned phrases. Mather, I ought to add, is fairly enthusiastic over the achievement of Frye, and will review it for the *Independent* or the *Evening Post*. I am debarred from reviewing by the fact that the book is dedicated to me, a beautiful dedication.

One more item of the shop. I have just received—the clipping came from Paris on Christmas day—a review of my *Platonism* by Robin[27] in the *Études Grecques* in 1921.[28] Robin is the most distinguished Platonist of France, and his notice is more than satisfactory.

---

22. Biddeford Pool, Maine.
23. According to Dakin (1960: 213-14), Darrah More graduated from Vassar College in the summer of 1923.
24. Frye 1922.
25. Presumably, More is referring to Frye 1908.
26. Sherman 1923. On Babbitt's and More's dislike for Sherman's move away from the New Humanism, see Zeitlin and Woodbridge 1929: 545-47. For Sherman's response to such criticisms, see Zeitlin and Woodbridge 1929: 548-50.
27. Léon Robin (1866-1947) was a French scholar of ancient Greek philosophy.
28. Robin 1921.

I hope the New Year finds Dora in better health. At any rate we send you our best wishes for the season.

Faithfully yours,
Paul E. More.

---

6 Kirkland Road
Cambridge
5 February, 1923

Dear More,

I am head over ears at present in preparation for my European trip but must find time for at least a word of reply to your very interesting letter of a month ago. I am at present planning to sail on the "France" (Comp. Gen. Transatlantique) from New York, Feb. 21. In spite of all things that are crowding upon me, I should like very much to have the pleasure of looking over the MS. of your new book. It might perhaps be possible for me to spend the evening and night of Feb. 20 with you in Princeton. Would this arrangement be convenient for you? It would give me an opportunity to talk over your MS. with you (in case you sent it to me in the next few days)—and also some other matters.

I was heartily glad to see Robin's notice of your "Platonism." It is the kind of thing that counts. Mercier, by the way, is preparing an article on you for *La Revue hebdomadaire*. He has a very un-Platonic mind and I am not sure that he will achieve anything very good but I hope to have a chance to read his paper before I leave Cambridge and make sure that it is correct as far as it goes. Frye's book I bought immediately on its appearance and also had copies of it put on my reserved shelf at Harvard and Radcliffe where it has been receiving the attention of fifty or sixty graduates, not to speak of a contingent of undergraduates. I look on him as a real ally in the classical campaign I am carrying on though I am not in agreement with all the details of his position. The proof-reading, like that of his last volume, is positively disreputable.

It is scarcely necessary for me to tell you what I think of the trend of Sherman's last volume. The type of idealism he defends is becoming increasingly impossible for me. From a purely literary point of view, however, the book deserves a high rating. I was especially struck by the effectiveness of the "Mencken."[29] The article on you[30] is of course a picturesque perversion.

---

29. Sherman 1923: 1-12. On H. L. Mencken and his feuds with the Humanists, see his entry in the Biographical Register.
30. Sherman 1923: 316-36.

I am inclined, however, to think that the harm it will do you is small compared with the benefit that you will derive from it as a piece of advertising. Sherman's ambition is to convince people that he has struck the golden mean between you and Mencken and in the current confusion of critical ideas he may win no small following.

Dora sails for Naples next Friday. She hopes to join me in Paris in April. I am much interested to learn of the trip abroad that you are yourself planning. I wonder whether it is going to be possible for us to meet you over there. With best regards to Nettie.

Sincerely yours,
Irving Babbitt.

---

245 Nassau Street
Princeton, New Jersey
2/9/23.

My dear Babbitt,

Unfortunately the MS. of my book is in the hands of the printer, and as they may possibly publish the book this spring, I can scarcely recall it, I say unfortunately for me; with all you must have on your mind these days, you really should not be burdened with reading 350 pages of manuscript. We shall of course be delighted to have you stop with us the night of the 20th. Let me know as soon as you have decided, as I may wish to ask one or two men to dinner that evening. I have a luncheon engagement for the noon of the 21st and shall be going in to New York in the afternoon; but I suppose you will be obliged to leave here in the forenoon. – I am interested in what you say about Mercier. These French certainly have a neat way of getting at the gist of a man's work. I thought Robin's review a masterpiece in that respect. Did I tell you that A. E. Taylor[31] had a laudatory notice of *The Religion of Plato* in *Mind*,[32] in which he virtually apologized for the tone of his previous review of the *Platonism*?[33] I thought it rather magnanimous of him. – Of Sherman's last book I got a different impression from yours. It seemed to me markedly inferior in literary quality from his earlier work. The "Mencken" I

---

31. The British philosopher and scholar of Plato A. E. Taylor (1869–1945).
32. Taylor 1922.
33. Taylor 1918. On More's and Taylor's critical letters to one another in response to this review, see Dakin 1960: 236 n. 8.

particularly disliked. I felt as if he had tried to attack the rascal with his own weapons, and showed himself unequal on that field. I can't believe that that is the way to go at the thing. The sketch of myself seemed to me quite the most brilliant piece of writing in the volume, though naturally I do not altogether enjoy that sort of caricature. I notice that in a California paper it was mentioned as "an established classic of American literature," which is more than was ever said of any of the poor victim's works.[34] – Our European plan is still very much in the air, depending chiefly on the state of the family purse. If we go we shall probably spend the late summer and autumn in England. It would be most pleasant to see you there. By the way, should you not come to Princeton before sailing, do not fail to let me have your Paris address. Dora I presume is sailing today.

Faithfully yours,
Paul E. More.

Hotel des Saints-Pères
65, Rue des Saints-Pères
Paris
26 March, 1923

Dear More,

The Easter recess has begun so that I am feeling less rushed than I did when I had to prepare three lectures a week for the Sorbonne in addition to numerous social engagements. I have not found Paris as much changed as I had anticipated—except for the jam of automobiles which in some parts of the city has got to the point where it reminds me of Harvard Square. In spite of deterioration of this kind Paris still remains one of the most fascinating of cities. The fascination is likely to grow on one the more one sees the place. I have never happened to have this experience in the case of London. In some ways the change in Paris is not as great as I should have liked. The cult of what Arnold calls the great goddess Lubricity still goes on unabated and *la femme nue* seems to have become a veritable obsession. – I have already met a number of the men prominent in the world of ideas and cannot say that I have become conscious of any important new direction in French thought. On the one hand are those who are for continuing 19th century

---

34. For a long list of reviews of Sherman's *Americans*, see Zeitlin and Woodbridge 1929: 831-33.

naturalism, on the other are those who favor what seems to me a mechanical return to the past. Still it is good to get occasionally out of the atmosphere of American philistinism.

How is your book getting on? I regretted on shipboard that I did not have your MS. with me, but I gathered from what you said that evening at Princeton that you would not have found it convenient to let me have a copy. As for the MS. I left with you,[35] it is as you remarked correctly, a book without a head or tail. The last chapter which is to be much longer than the others, is likely to determine the success or failure of the whole volume. I have got only about a third of this chapter on paper and that is only in a first rough draft. Any comment you can make on the total thought of the book at this stage must be of a very provisional character but I do not doubt that your criticism of details can be of great service to me. I should appreciate having you send the MS. to me (at the above address) as promptly as possible. The safest way to send it will I think be by registered first class mail. Will you not let me show my appreciation of all the trouble you are taking by sending you some French books that you desire to own? How about that trip abroad this summer? My own plans are somewhat unsettled but I am not likely to remain here much after the middle of July. – Dora is still at Taormina. I am hoping to see her at Paris towards the end of April. With kind regards to Nettie,

Sincerely yours,
Irving Babbitt.

---

245 Nassau Street
Princeton, New Jersey
April 16, 1923

My dear Babbitt,

Under another cover, by registered mail, I am sending you your MS. As you say, it is hard to judge a work which stands without head or tail, but I can see what you are driving at, and even as it is, I feel the force of your arguments. Only a few minor suggestions occurred to me as I read, and these I have noted in the margins. The weakest part of the book seems to

---

35. Of what would ultimately be Babbitt 1924.

me to be the first chapter on *Types of Political Thinking*.[36] I could not see that your critical thesis of ethos and government was worked out clearly, and the construction, or partition of subjects, did not strike me as very orderly or effective. I do not feel that this chapter, in its present form, adds much to your argument. On the whole I was most impressed by Chapter V on *Europe and Asia*.[37] Here you deal with fundamental ideas clearly and convincingly. My one criticism, and that tentative, might be the lack of a clear psychological definition of what you mean by "humility." You will retort that in a way the whole chapter is directed to the elucidation of this matter; and in a way that is true. But as when you dealt, in your former book, with imagination I wanted a clear, sharp definition of the faculty, so here I want the same thing for humility. Possibly I might desiderate the same thing for "awe" as contrasted with "wonder"; but these terms rather explain themselves.

The last chapter, on "True and False Liberals,"[38] is good and effective; but occasionally I felt that the motion was circular rather than straightforward. I have an overmastering desire to have one subject finished before another is taken up; but I admit that such construction is not always easy, and perhaps not always the most effective.

I shall await the completed book with interest, and hope that it may be influential. Of the last point I am doubtful, not from any feeling that the book is lacking, but because the generation of men today seems to me blind.

My own book[39] is announced for the autumn. Meanwhile I am more deeply interested in working up the material for the following volume[40] than I have ever before been. I even think, mirabile dictu, that I shall write something that will sell!

Our plans for travelling are still quite unsettled. The house here is still on the market. My sister Alice went to New York today and will sail Thursday for Naples.

Faithfully yours,
Paul E. More.

---

36. See Babbitt 1924: 27-69.
37. See Babbitt 1924: 158-85.
38. See Babbitt 1924: 186-238. In the printed book, this served as the sixth of seven chapters. As Babbitt notes in his letter directly above, he had not yet finished the manuscript, especially what would be the final chapter.
39. More 1923.
40. More 1924.

6 Kirkland Road
Cambridge, Mass.
17 Sep., '23

Dear More, – I have been back in America about two weeks and have been trying to put some hard licks on the uncompleted portions of my book before the rush of the college opening. My stay in Paris was so strenuous socially that I found it left no time for writing or for anything else except recuperating from numerous dinner parties and late hours. I had planned to have the book out of the way before going abroad. Under the circumstances I feel that I made a mistake in accepting the foreign job at all at this time. – I am deeply grateful to you for the trouble you took in going over the chapters I left with you just before sailing. I wish that I might have performed a similar office for your impending volume. It would have been a pleasure for me to do so and I might have made an occasional criticism that would have deserved your attention.

You will not be surprised to learn that I did not find the general tenor of your observations especially exhilarating. Your commendation (except of one chapter and that the shortest in the volume) is perfunctory, your strictures have about them an air of real conviction. You end with the encouraging remark that even if the book is all right in itself you do not anticipate that it will be influential. I understand your reserve in dealing with an incomplete MS. of this kind but even so was hoping that you would find it a somewhat less languid performance. I will send on my introduction and last chapter as soon as they are ready and shall be much interested in getting your judgment. My first chapter by the way does not deal primarily with the relation between ethos and government (I attempt to elucidate that point in my last chapter) but with the passage from the mediaeval emphasis on the divine will to the modern emphasis on the popular will. The whole book in fact is devoted to the problem of the will. In the part of it that you have not seen (about one third of the whole) I also discuss rather fully my use of the word imagination.

Literary influence is, as you know, a thing difficult to estimate especially in the case of work the appeal of which is not meant to be ephemeral. In my opinion your writing is gradually coming into the kind of influence to which it is entitled, though I am of course glad to learn that you anticipate for the book you are now starting a more immediate and obvious success. Mather, whom I met at Paris, gave me to understand that the laurels of

Papini[41] are disturbing your slumbers. You have too much taste to write anything resembling a life of Christ but I can imagine you writing something on the early Christian period that will have decided interest. – I saw the editor of the *Revue hebdomadaire* just before leaving Paris and he told me that he is planning to use Mercier's article on you. This is good news, for this publication has a wide circulation and an increasing influence. Reports that reach me of the growing recognition that is coming to Sherman would seem to indicate that he is measurably successful in his deliberate ambition—namely, to convince the public that he has struck the golden mean in criticism between you and H. L. Mencken. Truly we are a superficial folk!

Dora and my sister are still in Paris. They are planning to reach this country about the end of September. Have you been spending the whole summer in Princeton? With best regards to Nettie,

Sincerely yours,
Irving Babbitt.

---

245 Nassau Street
Princeton, New Jersey
November 1, 1923

My dear Babbitt,

I have been waiting to receive the unread chapters of your MS., but they do not come. I suppose you are delayed by the rush of college work. At least I hope that my last letter was not so inadequate as to discourage you from ever sending me anything else. Apparently I got a little mixed in my expression. There is no concealing the fact that I am despondent about the acceptance of any real thinking today. The change in our magazines during the past fifteen years shows how small the audience is growing for any serious literary work; and what I see of our college boys, at least those of Princeton, brings me no cheer for the coming generation—their ignorance is simply appalling. Think of this: a Junior who is studying for honors in English stops me in a lecture to ask how to spell Walter Pater! And that is typical. But I should not have

---

41. Giovanni Papini (1881–1956), an Italian writer whose biography of Jesus (Papini 1922) caused controversy because it suggested that Jesus may have had a homosexual relationship with John the Apostle. More (1924: 45 n. 2) called the book "a despicable piece of work."

permitted my discouragement to appear as if your MS. had anything to do with it. As for myself I won't say that I am aiming to rival Papini, whose book, by the way, is a perfectly despicable thing; but I am rather expecting that the subject will bring about a somewhat larger scale than I am accustomed to. If I should sell three thousand copies, I should be in the mood of Diogenes to ask what evil thing I had done to deserve such praise. I have finished the first draft and am now revising. Tomlinson[42] tells me that if I can have the MS. ready by the first of January, he will publish this spring. This is important for me, as we are again planning to go abroad and I should not like to let the thing hang over. If I sent you the MS. sometime about the first of December, could you read it immediately? I do not mean to urge you, for I know how deeply engaged is every moment of your time; but you see my situation. I am afraid there is a good deal in the book that will not altogether please you, and I shall not take it amiss if you decline the task of reading under the circumstances, much as I desire your criticism. The *Hellenistic Philosophies* will be out this month. – Frois-Wittman[43] tells me he came over with Dora and your sister and that they both looked well; I hope he is right. – Will you be passing this way any time during the winter? I need not say how glad we should be to see you. I should like to get your impressions of France. Frois-Wittman came back terribly distressed over the reactionary and militaristic state of the country; but he is a bit of a radical.

With kind regards to Dora,

Faithfully yours,
Paul E. More.

---

6 Kirkland Road
Cambridge, Mass.
5 November, 1923

Dear More,

It will be a great pleasure for me to read the MS. of your new book. I shall look for it about Dec. 1 and get it back to you as soon as possible. I am greatly impressed by the rapidity with which your books follow one

---

42. Paul G. Tomlinson (1888–1977), the director of the Princeton University Press from 1917 to 1938.

43. Jean Frois-Wittman (1892–1937) was a Paris-born psychoanalyst who received his Ph.D. from Princeton University in 1929. Prior to earning his doctorate, Frois-Wittman worked as an instructor of French at Princeton.

another—bowled over in fact. I should be incapable of any such performance even if I were not crowded with other engagements, as has been the case especially during the past few months. I have, however, finished my Introduction and am sending it to you under separate cover. I am just beginning to revise my concluding material and hope to be able to send it to you towards the end of this month. The present plan is to have the book appear early next April.[44] – Greenslet does not seem to warm up especially to the title "Democracy and Imperialism." Two other titles occur to me as possible: "Democracy and Civilization" and "Democracy and Leadership." I should very much appreciate your opinion on this matter.

I had a very pleasant glimpse of your brother[45] when he was in Boston in connection with the positions he is trying to fill in Cincinnati. His general plan strikes me as admirable, only he will not find it easy to discover men who deserve such good treatment—especially perhaps in philosophy.

My students are rather more numerous this year—about 135 at Harvard and Radcliffe. I find them somewhat less discouraging than the ones you describe at Princeton.

With kind regards to Nettie.

Sincerely yours,
Irving Babbitt.

---

245 Nassau Street
Princeton, New Jersey
November 11, 1923

My dear Babbitt,

I am glad to have read this introductory chapter, and think you have made your points sharply and clearly. Your position is summed up in a manner which ought to leave no room for misunderstanding. The subject has been considerably clarified by comparison with the views of Spengler and Seillière.[46] This part of the exposition seems to me very important. As you will see I have had no suggestions of detail to make. In two places however I think some improvement could be effected. Beginning on page 9, where you

---

44. It seems ultimately to have been published in May; see below.
45. Babbitt means Louis T. More, a faculty member in physics at the University of Cincinnati and by then the dean of its graduate school.
46. See Babbitt 1924: 20-22.

summarize your earlier books, the exposition seems to me somewhat confused. One does not always know just when you are speaking of a particular book, and when you are discussing your ideas in general. A more serious fault, as I see it, is in the paragraphs on the imagination. I still feel the need of a sharper definition of what you mean by this faculty. And your treatment of Plato and the Stoics seems to me inadequate, not to say erroneous. To speak of Plato's "disparagement of the fancy,"[47] as if this included the imagination as we understand it, is surely paradoxical at the least, when one considers Plato's use of *anamnesis*[48] in the *Phaedon* and of what we should call the imagination in the *Symposium*. Surely of all philosophers Plato is the one who has made the profoundest use of the imagination. Have you not been misled by the mere deficiency in his terminology? If the Ideal philosophy is not a philosophy of the imagination, then the world has been strangely deceived. As for the Stoics, φαντασία[49] is only the first step in the act of imagining; the word should not be translated fancy. Their nearest equivalent to the imagination is the χρῆσις τῶν φαντασιῶν,[50] which is the discriminating use of impressions and the basis of character. Read Epictetus. My book which will reach you, I hope, in a few days, has a good deal to say on this head. – These two sections I think need revision to bring them up to the high level of the rest of the chapter.

My present work is progressing, but is costing me infinite pains. I have read some hundredweight of German books for it, and have had to get up my Hebrew again. Pray heaven it may not be another case of *ridiculus mus*.[51]

Sincerely yours,
Paul E. More.

---

245 Nassau Street
Princeton, New Jersey
December 6, 1923

My dear Babbitt,

I sent my MS.[52] to you by express today, feeling that I was rather imposing on your kindness. I do hope it will not come to you at a particularly busy

---

47. Cf. Babbitt 1924: 11.
48. A footnote in the typescript of this letter reads: "Recollection."
49. A footnote in the typescript of this letter reads: "Imagination."
50. A footnote in the typescript of this letter reads: "Use of imagination."
51. "A laughable mouse." This is a reference to the Aesopian fable of the mountain in labor, mentioned in Horace's *Ars poetica* 136-9, which signifies overpromising and delivering little.
52. Of More 1924.

season. The point is that, owing to our projected trip abroad this summer,[53] I must have the MS. in the printer's hands early in January. And though this is now the third, in parts the fourth, draft, I fear the thing needs a good deal of drastic revision. Unless you are free to go through the book in a few days, I must ask you to return it unread. But I very much want your criticism; you will see why if you read the MS. Meanwhile let me have a post card assuring me that the parcel has reached you safely. A considerable part of the MS. I have not read over in its present form, so that you need not bother over obviously omitted words, and other details of that sort.

Net is doing well and beginning to get back some of her strength, though one of her wounds is still open and requires constant dressing. She has been much touched by the kindness of the Princeton women and their interest in her. I suppose the anxiety and the going back and forth tired me out, for I have been fighting a nasty cold that strikes one part of my anatomy and then another. Just now I am exasperated by a tickling throat. I shall rest strenuously for a few days.

With kind regards to Dora.

Faithfully yours,
Paul E. More.

---

245 Nassau Street
Princeton, New Jersey
December 26, 1923

My dear Babbitt,

I have held back your MS.[54] until after Christmas, until the post was less burdened and safer. This chapter has impressed me deeply. It seems to me about the strongest thing you have done, solid and at the same time epigrammatic. I do not see how it can fail to set a good many people to thinking. It is a fitting conclusion to the book and to those that preceded. At the same time—and I say this without withdrawing the judgment already passed—at about two thirds of the way through I began to feel you were repeating yourself and not going forward but moving about in a circle. I feel sure that the effect would be greater if you cut the length down by a third. And in

---

53. More would be in Europe from July of 1924 (Dakin 1960: 223) through early August of 1925 (Dakin 1960: 231).

54. A footnote in the typescript of this letter reads: "'Democracy & Leadership.'" The context of the letter demonstrates that Babbitt had sent More a version of the book's final chapter, "Democracy and Standards" (Babbitt 1924: 239-317).

some places the matter could be better sorted out, and more attention paid to speaking of one thing at a time. The three texts from the New Testament did not seem to me to be handled very efficiently. You may think this criticism severe, but it is not. As it stands the chapter has a note of telling finality, and needs only to be purged a bit.

Your criticisms of my book were helpful and I have followed your notes carefully. I am very much in your debt for your promptness, and shall have the MS. in the printers' hands by the second of January. He promises to give it the right of way and to have the book out this spring. But printers' oaths ought to be reckoned with those of lovers and dicers. Your remarks on the closing paragraph, where you draw a distinction between psychological and experimental truth, seem to me to head straight into modernism of the *als-ob* type upheld by Tyrrell[55] and Loisy.[56] Particularly in regard to the Incarnation I do not see how by taking it as a psychological truth a man can be saved from acting merely as if it were a fact, and there is no solid ground for morality or religion on that basis. I do not see how we can avoid the dilemma of accepting it as a true objective fact or dealing with it, in the manner of Santayana, as a pretty bit of poetry. Certainly the world will do one of these things. The middle ground is a quagmire. So at least it seems to me.

Our Christmas went off pleasantly, and with no more hilarity than a sexagenarian, or near sexagenarian, could tolerate comfortably. My sister[57] was here and is quite well for her. Net is beginning to go about. She drove to the church this noon, and walked back, nearly a mile. With kind regards and good wishes for the New Year.

Faithfully yours,
Paul E. More.

---

6 Kirkland Road
Cambridge
14 May, 1924

Dear More,

I should have written you weeks ago to thank you for the trouble you took with the last chapter of my book and also to acknowledge the receipt of your *Hellenistic Philosophies*. I did not see my way clear to cutting down my last

---

55. George Tyrrell (1861–1909) was an Irish modernist theologian.
56. Alfred Loisy (1857–1940) was a French modernist theologian and Roman Catholic priest.
57. Alice More.

chapter to the extent you suggested but I have removed to an appendix about fifteen hundred words in the portion of the chapter to which you objected especially. Your recollection of the earlier chapters must have been getting rather dim so that I do not feel quite so sure of your verdict on this last chapter as I should have felt if you had come to it with the rest of the book fresh in your mind.

My sentiments about your *Hellenistic Philosophies* are somewhat mixed. For both the form and substance of the greater part of the book I have only hearty approval. Your presentation of a subject like Stoicism has about it the note of definitive excellence. I agree with everything in fact except about fifty pages (pp. 205–259) of your treatment of Plotinus. My disagreement with some of the views you express in this portion of the book is rather serious. I wish that I had had the opportunity to see the book in MS. and to debate certain points with you. In order to set forth the nature of my difficulties I should have to write a counter-treatise. I may say in brief, however, that you seem to me too uncompromising in your attitude towards mysticism. The subject is one of appalling difficulty. It is hard to discredit the shams without seeming to discredit at the same time genuine religious meditation and the peace that passeth understanding. Furthermore I have the impression that you are building too vast a structure of generalization on your distinction between the self-moved mover and the unmoved mover. Can this latter conception be dismissed as a mere bit of heartless metaphysics? Quite apart from the intellect and its usurpation, one may have, in looking forth upon nature the intuition of

> central peace subsisting at the heart
> Of endless agitation.[58]

Plotinus and other men you mention seem to have been profoundly unaware of the Aristotelian derivation of their Absolute and mystical monism. I happen to know of very few authorities of any consequence (you mention Loofs)[59] who have asserted this derivation. Psychologically Plotinus and the gnostics seem to me utterly remote in *their total temper* (and that is surely the decisive test) from Aristotle in *his* total temper. The whole Aristotelian conception of life is dominated by the idea of work and energy and the closely related idea of end or purpose. Purposeful effort, which is the most Aristotelian thing in the world, is at the opposite pole from the type of

---

58. This is a quote from the last two lines of Wordsworth's *The Sea Shell*.
59. Friedrich Loofs (1858–1928) was a German theologian and historian of Christian dogma.

mysticism you attack. Master Eckhardt indeed, who derives directly from the pseudo-Denys and the Neo-platonists, and is himself the progenitor of a numerous line of mystics, says in so many words: "Din gotheit wirkt niht.... in ir ist kein werk," an idea that is commonly supposed to have influenced the great anti-Aristotelian Martin Luther. With Luther's discrediting of work in the spiritual sense the way is open for a one-sided naturalistic working and the utilitarian nightmare.

Apropos of usurpations of the intellect I suspect that one such usurpation (though other elements may enter in) is the tendency to project the idea of personality into the region of the infinite and the eternal. There is a whole class of questions, of which I take this to be one, that, when considered with sufficient psychological tact, turn out to be neither true nor false but meaningless or at any rate insoluble with our existing faculties. However that may be, the person who thus projects personality is likely to be led to abandon the Socratic *autarkeia* in favor of dogmatic and revealed religion. This is in itself an eminently respectable position; it does not, however, seem to me to follow from the main body of your previous writing of which I have been a careful student and admirer for many years; it seems in fact to involve a change of base line, and when a man at your age changes his base line, the effect is always a bit disquieting. The matter seems to me so important that if I had not been overwhelmed with work this spring, I should have come down to Princeton to talk it over with you in the hope that I might induce you to introduce certain qualifying clauses into your new book, especially the last chapter. As a result of your apparent refusal to recognize any valid intermediary position between the crude anthropomorphism of the Nicaean and Chalcedonian formulae and mere modernism, joined to your tendency to present Aristotle as the evil genius of occidental philosophy, effective coöperation between us is going to become more difficult; and this prospect does not, as you can well imagine, inspire in me very cheerful reflections.

I wish very much that I might get a glimpse of you before you start on your foreign trip. Is it not possible for you to run up to Cambridge? I shall be especially free after May 28 when lectures cease. There is a chance that I might be able to come down to Princeton in June but I should be afraid of taxing Nettie. I hope earnestly that she is gaining strength. – Is your new book to come out this spring according to the original plan? A copy of my own volume reached me today and you should receive it very shortly.

Sincerely yours,
Irving Babbitt.

245 Nassau Street
Princeton, New Jersey
May 24, 1924

My dear Babbitt,

I have delayed answering your letter for a few days, hoping I might have the pleasure of acknowledging the receipt of your book. But the book has not come, and I must not wait any longer. My own volume will probably be in your hands when this letter reaches you.[60] I hope it will not confirm the misgivings you felt on reading the MS. and which my chapter on Plotinus gave you in the preceding volume. I am afraid that in the end my only defence can be Luther's: Here I stand, so God help me; I cannot otherwise. My recent work does, I admit, show a change of base line; but the change has been very gradual, and has been forced on me by much reflection. I began with a disposition to waver between a materialistic agnosticism (very different from a true scepticism, as I now see it) and a complete mysticism. I now reject both those positions for what seems to me a sound mediation. In Aristotle I find two things; (1) a law of purposeful effort, which, as it seems to me, cannot be dissociated from personality, and (2) a metaphysic which abrogates such purpose and personality. He never seems to have seen the inconsistency of his position. Historically, I hold it certain that his metaphysic entered into the current that produced the Neoplatonic mysticism and Scholasticism. "The evil that men do lives after them." I see no incompatibility between "the peace that passeth understanding," "the central peace," and the true conception of personality. Both peace and personality seem to me to become meaningless in the extreme form of mysticism which I reject. If that is a crude anthropomorphism, then I must bear the reproach; I see no profit in peering into the ultimate void; I suspect that void is a pure creation of the *intellectus sibi permissus*.[61]

This is a shabby defence, and I would try to develop it more satisfactorily, were it not that I hope to have a chance to talk the matter over with you. Do come down to Princeton. You will not discommode Net in the least, and she adds her urgent invitation to mine. From June 13 to 17 Princeton is a little hell which the Graduates regard as heaven. But any other date will suit.

---

60. This suggests that More's *The Christ of the New Testament* (More 1924) was published in May of 1924. Cf. Mather 1938: 370; Duggan 1966: 89.
61. "The intellect having been left to itself."

Meanwhile I assure you that on my part I do not feel that my present position makes it impossible for me to coöperate in the work you are doing. I should regret that extremely.

Could not Dora come with you?

Sincerely yours,
Paul E. More.

P.S. We sail July 12.

---

6 Kirkland Road
Cambridge
9 July, 1924

Dear More,

It was, as usual, a pleasure to get a glimpse of you. My only regret is that our meetings cannot be more frequent. There is an accumulation of topics that I should like to talk over with you, most of them of a somewhat less abstruse character than those we actually discussed. Some of the passages in your last two books tempt one to a violation of the precept: "Presume not God to scan." The distinction between the self-moved mover and the unmoved mover in particular seems to me to come very near to overpassing the bounds of human faculty. The Aristotelian phrase, by the way, has always seemed to me to correspond to certain primary intuitions regarding the mysterious background of our conscious life. I was not even aware of the metaphysical argument that you cite on p. 208 ff. of your *Hellenistic Philosophies* and which, as you rightly affirm, has very little or no value. To project the idea of personality into the central element of calm that is, as I take it, a matter of primary intuition, is to depart from the Socratic reserve at the very point where it may be most needed. One is beginning at all events to abandon the positive and critical attitude toward life in favor of dogma and revealed religion. I am at least as anxious as you are to get rid of mere metaphysics but what I would substitute is not theology but psychology. To be sure there is much admirable religious psychology in your *Christ of the New Testament*, set forth in a style that is at once simple and dignified. The conclusion, however, is not from my point of view sufficiently psychological. There is still room for ample coöperation between us in view of our agreement on certain essentials of the inner life. A rather wide gap is likely to open, however, between our respective followers—assuming that either of us has any.

I fancy that rather frequently during your foreign trip you are going to wish yourself once more snugly ensconced in your Princeton study. Nevertheless, it is, if I may judge from my own experience, a good thing to escape occasionally from the somewhat stifling atmosphere of American Philistinism. Give my kind regards to Nettie and tell her how much I appreciate all she did to add to the pleasure of my stay in Princeton. With best wishes to you both for a prosperous voyage,

Sincerely yours,
I. Babbitt.

"The Isis," Iffley Road
Oxford, Sept. 5, 1924

My dear Babbitt,

Probably you have already seen this column of Inge's[62] in the *Morning Post*, but it is pleasant enough to read twice. Inge is so widely read and quoted over here that his notice ought to be a real service. There has been a meeting of the Church Congress here this past week, and on last Sunday we heard the Dean preach a good sermon but not brilliant. What most impressed me was the man's evident earnestness. And this brings to my mind a thought which may not surprise you from my lips, but may possibly vex you. Coming over in the boat we found the passengers of a very mixed sort—commonplace, loud and vulgar, a few refined. Sunday morning the captain read the service as usual, and I was struck by the fact that the occasion acted as a sort of shibboleth to distinguish the sheep from the goats. All the respectable and decent sort were there, the vulgar and offensive were conspicuous by their absence. That set me to thinking. Then at Stratford, at the tomb of Shakespeare I received something of a shock. Ordinarily I am not very sensitive to local associations, but here, rather to my amazement, I was overcome by a rush of emotion. It seemed to me that here in this old church where Shakespeare lies—that here, if anywhere, I stood at the heart of England. And since then I have felt again and again that the true life of the country is symbolized in the churches. And I have felt that if there is to be any genuine unity between England and America, as indeed between any peoples, it must come

---

62. William Ralph Inge (1860–1954), often called Dean Inge, was an English professor of divinity at the University of Cambridge, a prolific author, an Anglican priest, and the Dean of St. Paul's Cathedral. He had published an enthusiastic review of Babbitt's *Democracy and Leadership* in the London *Morning Post* (for a discussion of this review, see anon. 1924). For More's review of Inge's *The Philosophy of Plotinus* (1918), see More 1919.

through concord of worship. Visiting the rural churches, and the cathedrals too, though these affect one rather as mere museums of antiquity, I have had my old opinion confirmed that the greatest and most characteristic product of the English genius is its Prayer Book. And the conclusion? It is simply the query whether in these days of mental confusion and insolent materialism the first and most effective protest may not be simply to go to church. A lame and impotent conclusion, I fear you will say; but there is something in it, believe me. The greatest obstacle of course is the brainless character of most of the clergy, but then that would soon remedy itself if intelligent men took part in the service.

We have settled down as you see in this private hotel on the Iffley Road, which lies within convenient distance of Carfax. Until September we travelled about rather rapidly through the cathedral towns, the Lake country, Edinburgh too, staying at London for a couple of weeks. Then Net and Eleanor[63] took Alice and Catherine over to Lausanne, where the children are now at school. Finally we came to Oxford, stopping first at Micklem Hall, an old house near Christ Church which in the winter is used by students but in the summer is open to tourists. When driven out of that we came here. We have a private sitting room for the two families, and my bed room serves also for a separate study, having a gas heater which is more convenient than coal and throws out abundant heat. I do most of my Hebrew reading and other work there. This Thursday Net and Eleanor and Darrah go over to the Continent, leaving Louis and John and myself here. I do not know how long John will stay. Louis has to leave the first of January for his Vanuxem lectures in Princeton. I shall probably be here until the last of February, when I shall go to Italy and Greece. Term does not begin until the tenth, so that as yet very few of the University men are about. But Reggie Harris,[64] Fellow of All Souls[,] has called, and has invited us all to luncheon tomorrow in the College. Last Thursday Net and I had luncheon at Balliol with Duncan Macgregor,[65] tutor in Greek, his wife, and a Mr. & Mrs. Ridley,[66] also of Balliol. Tuesday I am going to give a dinner at the Mitre.

---

63. More, his wife Henrietta, and his daughters Darrah and Alice had traveled to Europe together with More's brother Louis T. More, his wife Eleanor, their son John, and their daughter Catherine. See Dakin 1960: 223.

64. C. R. S. Harris (1896–1979) was the author of *Duns Scotus* (1927) and *The Heart of the Vascular System in Ancient Greek Medicine, from Alcmaeon to Galen* (1973). On More's friendship with Harris, see Dakin 1960: 224, 262.

65. Duncan Campbell Macgregor (1888–1939) was a scholar of ancient Greek history. On More's meeting of Macgregor, see Dakin 1960: 225.

66. Presumably, More refers to Roy Ridley (1890–1969), a fellow and chaplain at Balliol College, Oxford.

I have not undertaken any special work, and probably shall not do any writing. In the main I shall give my time to Hebrew and the Old Testament—that will be enough to keep me out of mischief. I have also read the first two volumes of Bréhier's text and translation of Plotinus, published by the Association Budé, an excellent piece of work, which I recommend to you.[67]

You no doubt are in full swing of academic work. I trust that Dora has got back more of her strength and that the winter will pass pleasantly and profitably for you both. I should love to hear from you, but have no strong assurance in that direction.

Lou seems to think that Hack is doing admirably at Cincinnati.[68]

Faithfully yours,
Paul E. More.

THE ATHENAEUM
Pall Mall, S.W.I.
December 30, 1924

My dear Babbitt,

Louis is sailing on Thursday for New York to give the Vanuxem lectures, and I came down with him to London for a fortnight. Tomorrow I return to the *Isis* at Oxford, where I shall be quite alone. Our bachelor life has been very pleasant [in] every way, quite a renewal of old times when we lived together in the attic of our St. Louis house. But now I rather crave a spell of solitude, having a number of matters to ponder over, and settle for myself if they are ever to be settled in this life. I have not many books with me, and after a good pull at Greek and Hebrew I shall have many long hours before my fire for reflection. Probably I shall remain in Oxford until about the first of March. I have seen very few people in London—should have seen nobody but for my card to the *Athenaeum*—since everybody is full up with business and engagements at this season of the year. Possibly I may spend a week or two in London before sailing for Italy, in which case I shall expect to meet various men. It looks as if this next term at Oxford I should get to see something of the more intimate life of the colleges. My impression of the place is that we are quite on a par with the men here in exact scholarship, but that

---

67. Bréhier 1924.
68. Roy Kenneth Hack (1884–1944) was a classical scholar who left his position at Harvard University in 1923 to join the faculty of the Graduate School at the University of Cincinnati. More's younger brother Louis T. More was the dean of Cincinnati's Graduate School. On Hack, see Ward W. Briggs Jr.'s entry on him in the *Database of Classical Scholars*: dbcs.rutgers.edu.

we fall behind them in imagination. So few of our scholars have any large undertaking in hand, but most of them are squandering their energies in a succession of ephemeral papers. This is no doubt due in part to our system of forcing quick and constant publication; but in part also I should attribute it to lack of imagination and patience.

Clifford Moore has asked me to give Gulick's courses in Plato and Aristotle and some other subject for advanced students in the second term of next year.[69] I have replied that I should like very much to accept, but must first consult the Princeton men, and that at any rate I could not give more than two courses. As I must keep the first term free for my writing, acceptance of the offer would mean the suspension of my course at Princeton for two successive years. And then there is the question of family. They will scarcely wish to pull up stakes again so soon after returning, nor should I like to be separated for most of four months. I should be expected to reside in Cambridge. What draws me most is the chance I should have to be near you for so long a period.

With best wishes to you and Dora for the New Year,

Faithfully yours,
Paul E. More.

Florence
March 7, 1925

My dear Babbitt,

I have, as you probably already know, accepted the Harvard offer for next year—though with some misgivings. It will cost me heavy work to get up the machinery for the two courses. The Plato-Aristotle will be new for me and that on Hellenistic philosophy will be virtually new, as it will be given to graduate students of Greek. The experience will be pleasant and profitable, and should help me in my Princeton work when I return. Bowman[70] and

---

69. In the spring semester of 1926, More would replace Charles Burton Gulick (1868–1962), a Greek philologist in Harvard's classics department, lecturing on Plato and Greek philosophy and teaching a Greek course at Radcliffe. See Dakin 1960: 241; Duggan 1966: 16. On Gulick, see Arthur F. Stocker's entry on him in the *Database of Classical Scholars*: dcbs.rutgers.edu. More's residing in Cambridge, MA, for the term (see Dakin 1960: 240) allowed Babbitt and More to meet with regularity and attempt to hash out their philosophical and religious differences.

70. Archibald Allan Bowman (1883–1936) was a Scottish professor of philosophy then serving as the chair of Princeton's philosophy department.

Capps[71] both tell me I may teach whatever I choose, and probably I shall hereafter alternate year by year between the philosophical and the classical departments.[72] I have never felt that my lectures at Princeton were really successful. For one thing, they touched so near the quick of one's own inner life that I have always been conscious of holding myself very much in reserve. It is pleasant for that reason to find Bowman and Capps so well disposed. I hardly think I could accept a permanent place at Harvard, even if it were offered to me. I am rather old to pull up stakes and make a new start. Such an offer would of course be welcome nevertheless for various reasons. And even though I should cling to Princeton, I must acknowledge that society there is changing rapidly for the worse, under the intrusion of hordes of idle rich. It is a pity. And I feel that the college itself is not at all in a sound state. – Probably we shall try to rent our house for the second term, and take a house or apartment in Cambridge. If you hear of anything suitable, let me know about it. I have not heard whether Gulick's house will be on the market.[73] – I too welcome the opportunity of talking with you over various matters. Some of the questions you ask me to answer, will probably be taken up in my last volume (of miscellaneous essays), such, for instance, as the problem of Buddhism which offers a godless religion. Other questions I may prefer to leave in the penumbra of doubt. But it will be for me interesting and profitable just the same to discuss them with you. – Lou's lectures[74] on the *Dogma of Evolution* were a howling success, and drove the biologists to a frenzy of rage, some of which no doubt will fall upon my head when I return. The book I think ought to sell well.[75] It is a secret which no one knows—and even Lou seems to have forgotten—that a large part of the book was planned and suggested by me, even to the writing out of elaborate schemes for some of the chapters. I have not hinted this to any one except

---

71. Edward Capps (1866-1950) was a Greek philologist at Princeton, then serving as the chair of its classics department. On Capps, see William M. Calder III's entry on him at the *Database of Classical Scholars*: dcbs.rutgers.edu.

72. According to Dakin (1960: 236), on January 28, 1926, More accepted Capps's offer to teach two courses per year in Princeton's classics department. More thus transferred from Princeton's philosophy department, his previous affiliation, to the classics department. Given his lack of technical training in philosophy, More felt more at home in the classics department, despite his cordial relations with the philosophy faculty at Princeton. On this topic, see Dakin 1960: 236.

73. More ultimately chose to rent the house of the Harvard theologian James Hardy Ropes (1866-1933) at 13 Follen Street in Cambridge (Dakin 1960: 240). See below, chapter 9.

74. The Vanuxem Lectures at Princeton, which Louis T. More delivered in January of 1925. See above.

75. See Louis T. More 1925.

yourself, should not now hint it to the author. But so it is. I must say that the best things in the book, i.e. the criticisms of specific parts of Darwinism, are Lou's, not mine. – I am glad to hear that your own book[76] has been so widely reviewed, even though most of the notices are unsatisfactory—that was to be expected. I have seen only two or three insignificant reviews of my last volume.[77] I do not know whether this means that it treads so closely upon the heels of its predecessor as to need time to make its way. I have grown a bit callous in that part. – My last weeks at Oxford brought me many invitations to dinner and tea, and I feel that I got a pretty fair impression of life there. It is pleasant in many ways, but has its drawbacks. For one thing it is extremely difficult to get at current literature there, and in fact the scholars suffer a good deal in that way. And then I cannot but feel a very harsh discord between the spirit of the old buildings and the spirit of the students. Such a magazine as the *Isis*—so far as it represents the intellectual life of the undergraduates—is really shocking in its cheap cleverness and shallow modernism. In the end the ponderous stones of Oxford will probably win the victory in this contest between the old and the new. That is the great virtue of a noble and visibly embodied inheritance. I stayed only three days in Paris on my way to Lausanne, where I stopped to see Alice,[78] and then on to Florence. Here I am stopping at the Pension of Signorina Bertolini with Net (14 Piazza Independenza). Darrah[79] is elsewhere. I have not yet seen much of Florence. Curiously enough it looks just as I expected it would; it seems as if I had lived here before. Certainly the amount of beauty stored here is amazing. What a world! Of the few things I have seen, the dome of Michael Angelo in the new sacristy of San Lorenzo, a "Preparation for the Tomb" by Bartolommeo, and Giotto's incomparable tower have impressed me most. And yet, looking at all this loveliness and reading history, I understand Savonarola.

The first of April we go to Athens for a month, where our address will be the Hotel Majestic. The last week in July I have to be back in Oxford, to open a symposium of the Aristotelian society.[80] We shall sail for home soon after that.[81]

Net has not been very well for some time, and has suffered from anaemia. I think she is beginning to recover now. She was too energetic last summer.

---

76. Babbitt 1924.
77. More 1924.
78. More's younger daughter.
79. More's older daughter.
80. Dakin (1960: 231) specifies that More roomed at Balliol College from July 24 to 27, 1925, to attend "a joint session of the Aristotelian Society and the Mind Association."
81. Dakin (1960: 231) reports that More headed back to the United States on August 3, 1925.

I am in good condition, but sated with sight-seeing, weary of change, and homesick for my library. Travel I put down as the first mark of the insuperable stupidity of human nature.

I judge from what you say that Dora is still much below par. I do hope this winter will bring back her normal vigor.

Faithfully yours,
Paul E. More.

Crater Club
Essex, New York
September 15, 1925

My dear Babbitt,

I have just heard from Holt who tells me he is coming back to Burlington about the twentieth and wants me to visit him then. He says too that he is about to see you and ask you to come also. It would be jolly if we could meet there for a day or two. We came up here last Wednesday and shall stay until the last of next week. I have not written to Holt yet, but rather plan to visit him about that time, that is about the 25th. It would be pleasant of course if you could come here before that date and go over to Burlington with me; but I hesitate to press the invitation, owing to the fact that a young fellow, one of Alice's friends, may be in the guest home at that time, and you might not find it agreeable to sleep in the same room with him. Won't you let me have just a line by return post, advising me whether and when you could go to Burlington. I must answer Holt as soon as possible.

I shan't undertake to tell you anything about my later travels, but shall reserve that for our first meeting. The last five or six weeks I spent in England, most of the time alone, first in a small town among the Somerset hills and then at Malvern Wells, where I had from my window a wonderful view over the broad flat valley of the Severn. The meeting of the Aristotelian Society at Oxford was, as I expected it to be, an expense of spirit and a waste of words. It confirmed me in the opinion that modern philosophy is an intellectual nuisance. I never in my life felt so much out of place and so hopelessly stupid as when attending these sessions. Give my kindest regards to Dora and to your sister if she is with you. I am sending this at a venture, having heard only that you are in Dublin. Net and the girls wish to be kindly remembered.

Faithfully yours,
Paul E. More.

Crater Club
Essex, N. Y.
September 22, 1925

My dear Babbitt,

I am sorry you don't feel like coming over to Holt's, but can quite understand your reasons. For my part, I really must go straight home from Burlington. My work, as you may imagine, is terribly behind, and even these two weeks at Essex could ill be spared. When I left for Europe I had the plan and notes for my next volume well under way, and now I must take advantage of every possible day before I come up to Harvard for the second term. My two courses are going to exact lots of work as the machinery for them will all be new. It is an odd fact,—to me at least, perhaps not to you,—that this call to Harvard has brought me more *kúdos* than anything I have ever done. I hear about it from all sorts of strange places.

Our talk must wait, but will not grow stale.

Faithfully yours,
Paul E. More.

---

6 Kirkland Road
Cambridge
25 November, 1925

Dear More,

I have heart-breaking news to announce. About seven o'clock on Saturday evening, Nov. 14, my sister was struck by an automobile while trying to cross the highway that runs between the two parts of Miss Porter's school at Farmington.[82] She died in the hospital at Hartford on the following Tuesday morning. I scarcely need tell you how deeply I have been shaken by the cutting short in this way of a life that was so near to me. Katharine was not only the most devoted of sisters, but was in general the most unselfish person I have ever known. She was a real support to me in the struggle I have been attempting to carry on in a world of alien tendencies. She joined to her sisterly affection no small degree of critical discrimination. The resulting psychic bond was one of peculiar intimacy. Her death has made a void in my life that I feel can never be filled. The best

---

82. Babbitt's sister Katharine taught at Miss Porter's School. On Katharine Babbitt, see her entry in the Biographical Register.

remedy for a blow of this kind, so far as there is any[,] is, I presume, hard work, but for the time being at least, my work and everything else have ceased to have any meaning.

Sincerely yours,
Irving Babbitt.

---

245 Nassau Street
Princeton, New Jersey
November 27, 1925

Dear Babbitt,

    Your news is heart-breaking indeed, it leaves me dumb, like Tiberius not knowing what to say and what not to say. At least I can respond to your words about Katharine; I was well enough acquainted with her to know how loyal and helpful a sister she had been, and how utterly unselfish she was. To me she can be a beautiful memory, but I understand what her loss is to you. These years that are coming now take away one thing after another, and to that we have to grow reconciled; but there is something unspeakably painful in a death so sudden and so cruel and so needless. I have never been, and not now, able to take the common Christian view of these evils and say they must be providential and somehow for our good. Often they seem to me to bring irreparable loss. But on the other hand I cannot look at them as the Buddhist does and regard them as the essential of life. They strike me rather as hateful accidents, or as the working of some no less hideous fatality, breaking through and thwarting the real purpose of the world. Strange as it may sound, they have come to be for me in that way the last bulwark of faith and hope. Taken with the large beauty and many benevolences of the world they force me to believe that the universe is not governed by a dull, inhuman, passionless law, nor is yet a thing of chance and blank illusion, but is the result of purpose, understood quite anthropomorphically, working through mysterious obstacles of evil.

    But I am not in a mood to preach or to philosophize, least of all to you. I am sure you know how deeply I sympathize with you. There is no one in the world whose sorrow would mean so much to me. Nettie desires me to express her sympathy also.

    Faithfully yours,
    Paul E. More.

CHAPTER NINE
1926–1929

245 Nassau Street
Princeton, New Jersey
January 8, 1926

My dear Babbitt,

The enclosed clipping came to me some days ago from a London bureau as an advertisement, and I thought that perhaps you had not seen it. I don't know anything about the *British Weekly*, but have a vague notion that it is a Catholic organ.

My time here grows short. I have finished after a fashion the first, very rough draft of my next volume[1]—a strenuous bit of work, as I had to read over again a considerable amount of Greek to check up the vagaries of German critics. But it is done, and I have turned my mind to the Harvard courses. Already I have gone through several of Plutarch's essays, and shudder to think of setting the students at them, for they are tough reading. I sometimes think that Greek, as it is written, is the worst organ of speech ever devised by the brain of man. It can be so very easy; in fact it is commonly ambiguous and cumbrous to the last degree. Since I signed the contract Gulick has asked me to take the repetition of Greek 8 at Radcliffe. He has two schoolmarms (wretchedly prepared, he says) and a professor's wife who are keen to continue the course. I don't want to do it at all, but hate to be troublesome, and so have consented. The two courses alone are quite enough, and this third will drive me hard. I asked Gulick (whom I saw in N. Y. the other day) how many pages of Plato his class covered daily. He said six. From our man here I learn that three pages is all that can be got out of a Princeton class!

Alice is down with the mumps, and Darrah is suffering from a catarrhal trouble; but I hope we shall be able to come to Cambridge on February 1st. Ropes seems to be an easy and generous landlord.[2] Meanwhile luckily we

---

1. More 1927a.
2. While in Cambridge, More rented the home of the Harvard theologian James Hardy Ropes. See above, chapter 8.

have rented our house here. We all want to be quiet in Cambridge, and hope there will not be much entertaining, I on account of my work, the girls because they have been in a frightful whirl for months.

I think often of your great loss,[3] but can scarcely realize it as a fact. She seemed so full of life when I saw her last, and now the terrible silence.

Faithfully yours,
Paul E. More.

---

245 Nassau Street
Princeton, New Jersey
July 23, 1926

Dear Babbitt,

I have felt as if I ought to send a bread-and-butter letter to you and Dora after leaving Cambridge, to thank you for all you did to make our stay pleasant and profitable. I have no one here to drop in on an evening and stir me up to think of high matters, nor in fact shall I have when college opens. Fite comes in often, but our talk is mostly on smallish personal matters. We have signed the deed for the property out at Cedar Grove, but we have not sold this place yet, and may not do so for years.[4] But as Howe let us have the new lot with no restrictions, it is not a bad investment, whatever happens.

We have bought a Dodge touring car, resplendent in what they call pheasant green. Day before yesterday Darrah, Alice, and I all went to Trenton, passed the test and examination, and are now licensed drivers. Somehow I do not recognize myself in that rôle, and in fact my action has caused some scandal in the Town.

Just now I am revising my *Platonism* to be brought out as a "second edition." Tomlinson promises to have it ready next October if I get the copy to him promptly; but I told him I didn't believe him. As I read the book over it seems to me for the most part hard to understand and stiff in construction, with the exception of two or three chapters. I shall add a second (short) preface, admitting that in some respects the ideas of the book are not in accord with the later volumes of the series. – Certainly, whatever may be said

---

3. On the passing of Babbitt's sister Katharine, see above, chapter 8.
4. According to Dakin (1960: 251 n. 61), More's wife Henrietta would not buy the lot in Princeton known as 59 Battle Road until June 25, 1927. More would not sell the house on Nassau Street until July 7, 1929 (Dakin 1960: 274).

of these ideas, the volumes improve notably in ease and style as they come down. That is some comfort. The *Platonism*, to tell the truth, rather repels me by its scholasticism.

We leave here for Essex next Wednesday. I am addressing this letter to Cambridge, not knowing just where you are in Dublin.[5]

I enclose a letter from Rand, not because it means anything in particular, but because I thought you might care to see it. He is certainly what the boys call a "smooth proposition."

With kindest regards to Dora,

Sincerely yours,
Paul E. More.

Camp Cedars
Crater Club
Essex, New York
August 29, 1926

My dear Babbitt,

Thank you so much for reading and criticising the Preface to the second edition of the *Platonism*. One of your suggestions I have followed, but not the one about the *volte-face*. If there has been any such change in my attitude as you and others feel, it certainly has taken place between the writing of the *Platonism* and of *The Christ of the New Testament*. The former volume was composed from my reserve of study, and presents almost completely the same point of view as the sixth volume of *Shelburne Essays*. Whatever change occurred was caused by my reading and reflection after the composition of that volume. For this reason I have passed this part of the Preface without correction. In general my revision has touched only secondary matters, such as it has seemed scarcely worth while to bother you with. The proof is already beginning to come in abundantly, so that the book ought to be ready not too late in the autumn.

I am bound to be in Cambridge by the evening of September 13, Monday. How would it do if Darrah and Alice drove me over in the car on the 9th, or thereabouts?[6] Would it be perfectly convenient if they two stayed over the

---

5. Dublin, New Hampshire, where the Babbitts often summered.
6. On More's trip from Essex to Dublin, New Hampshire, in September of 1926 to talk with Babbitt and play cards with his wife Dora, see Dakin 1960: 247.

night with you? Dora intimated that you could take them in comfortably; but circumstances may have changed. I need them both, because I do not want one of them to drive back alone. Net cannot come, because such a journey overfatigues her. I should of course stay until Monday morning. I say the 9th, as that appears to be the first day we shall be free of company here; but our plans, or rather our guests', are still a bit uncertain.

Our weather has been cool with continual rains. Today for the first time it has turned really hot. I trust the heat won't last long. For my reading I am now deep in Bremond's[7] *Sentiment Religieux*,[8] the six volumes of which I have bought. The work is immensely interesting; but there undoubtedly is something at the very heart of Western Latin Christianity which leaves me uneasy and even rebellious. I feel quite otherwise when I take up some of the great Anglicans.

With regards to Dora, and to Esther whom we were delighted to see here, I am

Faithfully yours,
Paul E. More.

Camp Cedars
Crater Club
Essex, New York
19 September, 1926

My dear Babbitt,

I should have written earlier to thank you and Dora for the very good time you gave me in Dublin, but I really have been extraordinarily busy. What with proof-reading, lectures, and society my days were very full at Harvard, and when I got back here I found two great packages of proof, finishing the book—*Deo gratias ago*.[9] Except for the noise everything was salubrious in Cambridge.[10] Our suite was right on Boylston Street, and the uproar until two or three o'clock in the morning was incessant and terrific. I got precious

---

7. Henri Bremond (1865–1933) was a Catholic philosopher and literary scholar.
8. Bremond 1967.
9. "I give thanks to God."
10. Dakin (1960: 247-48) notes that More attended the Sixth International Congress of Philosophy in Cambridge, Massachusetts, in September of 1926. On this conference, which took place from September 13 to 17, see Brightman 1926 (with a full list of participants); Friess 1926.

little sleep. I managed to listen through about two lectures a day; but it took heroic resignation on my part. Really, this philosophical game is ended. Some of the papers, Sheldon's[11] and Starbuck's[12] for instance, were just rotten; and I heard nothing, absolutely nothing, that had the slightest value. I found that they had arranged to have two chairmen for each sectional meeting, so that I resigned my place to Brett[13] in my section and sat in the audience. He called on me to speak, but I said very little. Burnet[14] was not there, having had an epileptic stroke, and his paper was too fragmentary even to read. Shorey was not there either, but his paper, read by Levinson,[15] was pretty good, the best thing I heard. The pleasure of the Congress was in meeting the men. Robin, of whom I saw a good deal, was very flattering, and apologized for not having reviewed the later volumes of my series.[16] Several of my English friends were there, and I met others, one charming young Fellow of Trinity College, Oxford, who spent the evening with me. I dined with Woods[17] and several "Platonists" (including Spa[u]lding!)[18] in Boston, and had luncheon with Hocking in Cambridge. Mrs. H. is a walking nightmare, and H. is rather dull. But I had some good talk with Pratt[19] and Hoernle.[20] Lou and I left Friday morning. I found our house full of girls, but two of them went last night.

Fortunately my walks at Dublin had put me in good condition, so that the lack of sleep at Cambridge did not hurt.

Sincerely,
P. E. M.

---

11. More here refers to the philosopher Wilmon Henry Sheldon (1875–1980).
12. More refers to Edwin Diller Starbuck (1866–1947), a professor of philosophy at the University of Iowa.
13. The typescript of this letter reads "Britt," but More here refers to the Canadian psychologist and philosopher G. S. Brett (1879–1944). See Brightman 1926: lxiv.
14. The Scottish classicist John Burnet (1863–1926) was a scholar of ancient Greek philosophy. On Burnet's views on More's series *The Greek Tradition*, see Dakin 1960: 236. On his absence from the conference, see Friess 1926: 635.
15. More likely refers to Ronald B. Levinson (1896–1980), a scholar of ancient Greek philosophy.
16. On Robin's reviews of More's work, see above, chapter 8.
17. James Haughton Woods (1864–1935), a professor of Indic and Greek philosophy at Harvard.
18. The typescript of this letter offers the name as "Spalding," but More must mean Edward Gleason Spaulding (1873–1940), a philosophy professor at Princeton.
19. James B. Pratt (1875–1944), a professor of philosophy at Williams College.
20. The South African philosophy professor R. F. A. Hoernlé (1880–1943). On Hoernlé, see Sweet 2010.

6 Kirkland Road
Cambridge
19 December, 1926

Dear More,

Your MS.[21] reached me safely yesterday. I have not had time to look into it yet, beyond glancing at a few pages. I am not sure that any critique I can give you will be of much value because of my unfamiliarity with the field that the volume covers. I shall read the book with deep interest, in spite of my rather untheological turn of mind. I am hard pressed just now with a paper[22] I am preparing for the meeting of the Modern Language Assn, in Cambridge at the end of this month and this may delay somewhat my return of your MS. If you feel the matter is urgent you must let me know.

I was glad to receive the copy of the second edition of your *Platonism*. I have commended it to the students of my course in criticism in a way that has led to an immediate sale of at least thirty copies, with more sales, I hope, in the offing.

Mercier has turned over to me for my criticism the chapter of his forthcoming book[23] that concerns you. You will, I fancy, be gratified by the amount of space he gives to your *Christ of the New Testament*. As for me, I feel that such an elaborate theological argument may repel the general reader. I should even suggest cutting out about fifteen pages of summary at this point, retaining of course your important conclusions. You can decide for yourself when he sends on the MS. to you, as I presume he will.

Have you seen Giese's book on Victor Hugo?[24] One gets the effect of too much of a muchness, as one usually does in G's writing; yet the book abounds in smashing epigrams; and so far as Hugo's reputation is concerned, impresses one as being something definitive. Barry Cerf's book[25] on Anatole France is also worth reading. He shows no small subtlety in uncovering the spiritual anarchy that came to France from the romantic movement.

---

21. Of More 1927a.
22. A footnote in the typescript of this letter identifies the paper as "Dr. Johnson and the Imagination." Babbitt later turned this into an essay for the *Southwest Review* (Babbitt 1927), which, under the new title "The Problem of the Imagination: Dr. Johnson," was included in his collection *On Being Creative and Other Essays* (Babbitt 1968: 80-96).
23. Mercier 1928.
24. Giese 1926.
25. Cerf 1926.

As a preliminary to writing that article[26] on American literature you might find it worth your while to glance at Lovett's[27] article on *Am. Literature* (of the past fifteen years) in the new supplement to the *En. Britannica* (the so-called 13th edition). He there declares that Mencken is the chief critical force of the day. Mencken for his part avows that criticism as anything more than the irresponsible overflow of an individual temperament is impossible. See the volume *Literary Criticism in America*, p. 269. Here is surely a phenomenon that is worthy of comment.

With best regards to Nettie,

Sincerely,
Irving Babbitt.

---

245 Nassau Street
Princeton, New Jersey
January 19, 1927

Dear Babbitt,

The manuscript of my book came today, and I am much obliged to you for your careful reading of it in the midst of your many occupations. In making my final revision I shall have in mind your notes, especially those in regard to Aristotle and Western thought. The first four pages of the MS (pp 1 to 4) are missing. It is possible they have been mislaid in my study, but a careful search fails to discover them, and I am wondering whether possibly you still have them. It will not be a very serious matter if they are irretrievably lost, as I have them in the first draft.

I believe Net wrote to Dora, asking whether you and she could not visit us in the Easter holidays. I wish you could either then or earlier in the examination period—you could have a good rest, and perhaps your MS. of the *Dhammapada*[28] will be so far advanced that we can read all or part of it. I was talking with Mather about the book yesterday and he too is keen to see it.

---

26. More 1927b. This article, which was translated into French (see below for the specifics), later appeared in English in the January 1928 issue of the *Forum* (More 1928b) and as "Modern Currents in American Literature" in *The Demon of the Absolute* (More 1928a: 53-76).

27. Robert Morss Lovett (1870-1956) was an American professor of English literature.

28. Babbitt 1965.

I got Cons[29] here to translate my article on the *Courant moderne dans la Littérature américaine*,[30] and so far as I can judge he had made a satisfactory job. The article itself I have read here to the Ladies' Club and the Nassau,[31] and it has proved a good hit. I think it will do. At any rate the MS. went off to Paris yesterday.

Sincerely,
Paul E. More.

---

245 Nassau Street
Princeton, New Jersey
January 27, 1927

Dear Babbitt,

I dare say I mixed up those first four pages somehow when I was getting the parcel ready to express. At any rate this loss has caused no trouble. I have rewritten the whole of that chapter twice and parts of it three times since it was in your hands. It is in shape at last, I think.

Have you seen the January issue of the *London Quarterly*? The leading paper is a flaming review of your work.[32]

Thank you for the word to Aswell.[33] I have asked Thiebaut[34] for permission to print in an American magazine, but I do not know whether he will grant it.

Shafer[35] has been here two days, before sailing. He is very grateful to you for your kindness and hospitality.

Sincerely,
P. E. M.

---

29. Louis Cons (1879–1942) was then an associate professor of modern languages at Princeton. See Dakin 1960: 249 n. 54.

30. More 1927b.

31. Dakin (1960: 158) notes that More had been elected to the Nassau Club in Princeton in December of 1914. On More's delivery of this lecture in January of 1927, see Dakin 1950: 177-78.

32. Hough 1927.

33. More presumably refers to Edward Aswell (1900–1958), then a recent graduate of Harvard University who then served as an assistant editor for the *Atlantic Monthly*.

34. Marcel Thiébaut (1897–1961) was the editor of the *Revue de Paris*, which commissioned More to write an essay (More 1927b) on contemporary literature in the US.

35. On Robert Shafer, see his entry in the Biographical Register.

6 Kirkland Road
Cambridge
7 April, 1927

Dear More,

I have been holding off as long as possible in the hope that I might see my way clear to accepting your kind invitation for the Easter recess. Work has been piling up on me, however, at such a rate and I am so in arrears with work I already had on hand that I have been forced very regretfully to give up the trip for the present. I do not wish to come until I can bring the Introduction to the *Dhammapada* with me and though I am making progress, the completion of the work is still some way ahead. Would it be convenient for you to receive us if Dora and I came down during some weekend in May or perhaps in early June? I could promise to give you at least three weeks notice in any case.

I have been reading Mather's new book[36] with much pleasure and on the whole with approval. It is not often I encounter anything with which I can agree in what seems to me the present very black period of literature and art. Give my best regards to Nettie,

Sincerely,
Irving Babbitt.

---

245 Nassau Street
Princeton, New Jersey
April 11, 1927

Dear Babbitt,

We are naturally disappointed that your visit to Princeton is delayed, but the fact that a later date will enable you to bring with you the MS. of your *Dhammapada* is more than compensation. At present I can foresee no embarrassment from this end in May or June. Let me know a couple of weeks before you are free and I am sure we can arrange a date. – I too have been reading Mather's book with great interest. It is perhaps the most brilliant thing he has done, wonderfully penetrating and, so far as I can judge, sound in its individual criticisms. I do however feel a certain serious defect in the

---

36. Mather 1927.

work, which perhaps is unfairly emphasized in my mind from my knowledge of the writer. There is, for my taste, a little too much of mere balancing of meritorious traits against vicious traits, a failure to bring out the central cause at work behind the curiously intertangled lines of progress and decline. Why is it that in painting, as in the other arts, the development of technique—sound technique—beyond a certain point seems the inevitable prelude (is it the cause?) of retrogression in the substantial value of the art? These are questions which Mather does not touch. – The MS. of my own book[37] went to the printer today. Though the substance is the same, the writing has been so changed since you saw it that you would scarcely recognize it as the same work. It has cost me infinite labor, and I am still conscious of its inadequacy. But the point of saturation has been reached. Further rewriting threatened to take out whatever life I had got into it. – My two courses are going on very satisfactorily, and I am profiting from my experience at Harvard last year.

With kindest regards to Dora,

Faithfully yours,
Paul E. More.

P.S. The *Forum* is going to print my article on *Am. Lit.*,[38] though it runs to some 7000 words.

Dublin, N. H.
22 September, 1927

Dear More,

Esther's wedding went off with great éclat in spite of the unpropitious weather.[39] I should have preferred something simpler, more after the fashion of Darrah's wedding.[40] I fear, however, that the simplicity in her case was due at least in part to Nettie's health. I trust that she has not suffered unduly from the strain and excitement, as seems to be the case with Dora, and in general that she is better after her summer.

---

37. More 1927a.
38. More 1928b.
39. Babbitt's daughter Esther married the historian and teacher George Frederick Howe (1901–1988) on September 1, 1927.
40. More's daughter Darrah married the teacher and headmaster Harry Boehme Fine (1899–1959) at St. John's Episcopal Church in Essex, New York, on September 1, 1927—the same day as Babbitt's daughter's wedding (see Dakin 1960: 251).

The introduction to the *Dhammapada* is ready at last for your inspection. I am planning to print it also in my next volume of essays[41] and it will gain a good deal of any significance it may possess from its connection with other material that will appear there. Taken by itself the essay might suggest that I am trying to convert occidentals to Buddhism; when related to the other essays, it will be seen to be a part not of a religious but of a humanistic argument. I admit, however, that if the mediation of the humanist is to be effective it must have a background of religious meditation. I am therefore devoting a good deal of my effort to discriminating between genuine meditation and the pantheistic revery that has been promoted by the Rousseauistic movement.

Mercier's book[42] is, if my latest information is correct, to be published by Hachette. The contract that is being imposed on him is, however, rather iniquitous. The book seems to me so important for the diffusion of certain ideas that both you and I regard as important that I am planning to contribute $100 to the expense of the printing with the understanding that I am to have at my disposal a number of copies equal, at the retail price, to this amount.

Has your article[43] appeared in the *Revue de Paris*? I have just finished a paper on "The Critic and American Life" which I am sending to the *Forum*.[44] I rather regret the time I have given to writing it. It is my conviction, however, that if the critic is to exercise a useful function he cannot afford to get too much out of touch with the contemporary situation. – Please inform me whether you wish the MS. of my essay sent to you at Essex or Princeton. With best regards to Nettie,

Sincerely,
Irving Babbitt.

---

245 Nassau Street
Princeton, New Jersey
September 26, 1927

Dear Babbitt,

Your letter reached me only today, having been forwarded from Essex. I am glad to hear that Esther's wedding went off so well. Net has had in mind

---

41. See Babbitt 1968: 235-61, an earlier version of the essay affixed to Babbitt's translation of the *Dhammapada* (Babbitt 1965: 65-121).
42. Mercier 1928.
43. More 1927b.
44. This piece first appeared in the February, 1928, issue of the *Forum* (Babbitt 1928) and was later a chapter in *On Being Creative and Other Essays* (Babbitt 1968: 201-34).

to write to Dora in regard to some gift for the bride, but has been, and still is, deterred by the wretched state of her eyes. She thought of sending a nest of tables. Would that be acceptable, or would Esther prefer China or silver? How has the tide of presents been? Ask Dora to let us know as soon as she conveniently can. I am sorry to hear that the strain has fatigued Dora. In our house we had something more than fatigue. Everything was made as simple as possible, but shortly after the wedding (post hoc, perhaps not propter hoc) Net had a relapse which caused us very serious alarm. Fortunately there is an excellent doctor at Westport, and he pulled her through skillfully. She is much better, and I got her home on the twenty-first with no ill effects. But she can do scarcely anything.

I shall of course be glad to have the Introduction to the *Dhammapada* as soon as you can send it, and in reading it I shall remember what you say of its place in a volume of humanistic studies. Have you kept your plan of sending the translation to the Oxford Press?[45] My article[46] has not yet appeared in the *Revue de Paris*, but I see it announced in the current issue as to be printed "prochainement." I am preparing a volume of *Shelburne Essays* in which it is to be included.[47] Meanwhile I am sending you the new volume of my *Greek Tradition*.[48] You will find it at least smoother reading than it was in MS. I can vouch for the labor it cost me—"easy reading is curst hard writing!" If you are correct in your information about Mercier's book I shall be glad to contribute a hundred dollars towards the publication. I do not know how I could dispose of the equivalent number of copies, but I should be glad to have a score or so of them. Will you kindly tell Mercier this; or had I better write to him myself? I am sure Brownell would be glad to contribute something, and I should be glad to pass the word on to him if it be so desired—as coming from myself of course, and not from Mercier.

I hope you got rest and physical recuperation from your summer. My two months in Essex were about the laziest, intellectually, of my life. Owing to some fault in transmission, the books I ordered from Oxford did not come, and I had very little to read. I did however go through Cicero's *De Senectute*,

---

45. A footnote in the typescript of this letter reads: "The translation and the essay were published by the Oxford Press in 1936." See Babbitt 1965.
46. More 1927b.
47. More 1928a.
48. More 1927a. Dakin (1950: 178 and 1960: 253) specifies that More's *Christ the Word* was published in September of 1927.

which is fine rhetoric but quite misses the real sting of old age, and a good deal of Virgil. I was annoyed to find the *Georgics* difficult.

With kind regards to Dora,

Sincerely yours,
Paul E. More.

---

245 Nassau Street
Princeton, New Jersey
October 12, 1927

My dear Babbitt,

I have lost no time, having temporary leisure, in reading through your paper.[49] And I have commented so freely on the margins that there is little to add. In general my negative criticism would be put in the form of questions: What is the permanent or is there any permanent, that Buddha offers when the impermanent is escaped? Does Buddhism totally eliminate the sense of cosmic *purpose*? How is the doctrine of sympathy or love related to his doctrine of the will? What is the passage from inner to outer ἐνέργεια?[50] The first of these is of course the fundamental question, and is scarcely quieted by declaring Buddha's repudiation of metaphysical curiosity. He should have gone further and confined *karma* to this life only, or he should have gone further in the other direction and left room for a continuing ψυχή.[51] At least there is a difficulty here that must be faced more squarely than you have done. In one way or the other the later deviations in Buddhism seem to me to have arisen from this insistent and disquieting antinomy. But perhaps this is the sort of question which you bade me not to repeat.

Apart from these residual questions I very much admire the scope and conciliatory tone of the article. Its appeal to the modern man who is not hardened in his occidental optimism and conceit ought to be strong. My marginal criticisms represent only what I have found possibly in need of modification or completion, and thus do not convey my more general assent to your thesis and its development. I presume that when the article is

---

49. More refers to Babbitt's introductory essay that would accompany his translation of the *Dhammapada*.
50. A footnote in the typescript of this letter reads: "Actuality."
51. A footnote in the typescript of this letter reads: "Soul."

printed as an introduction to the *Dhammapada* you will add a more explicit statement of what the Dh. actually is.

Net[,] I am glad to report, is considerably better, so much so that we can hope for return to a moderately active life. But her eyes are still bad. She can scarcely use them at all for reading or writing, or even for cards. But there is perhaps a slight improvement here also.

Sincerely yours,
Paul E. More.

---

245 Nassau Street
Princeton, New Jersey
Friday morning
[January (20), 1928 – Ed.][52]

My dear Babbitt,

Saturday afternoon Nettie was struck by an acute attack of nephritis with dilation of the heart. She rallied, but had a second attack Sunday, and since then has been gradually failing. The first days were very distressing, but she has lapsed into total unconsciousness, and we are now only waiting for the end.[53] Fortunately Darrah was near and of course has been sleeping here in the house. I don't know what I should have done without her. What my future plans will be I do not know; I am only perplexed now. I wanted you and Dora to know what was happening.

I have read the proof of your *Forum* article[54] which the editor sent me, and naturally was very much interested in it. Also your article in the *Southwest*.[55]

Faithfully yours,
Paul E. More.

---

52. This parenthetic text appears in the typescript version of the letter. The specific date (i.e., the 20th) has been added to this text.

53. Dakin (1960: 253-54) notes that More's wife Henrietta suffered this attack on January 14, 1928, and passed away on January 20. See also Mather 1938: 371; Duggan 1966: 16. More held the funeral for her at his house on January 23 (Dakin 1960: 254).

54. Babbitt 1928.

55. Babbitt 1927.

245 Nassau Street
Princeton, New Jersey
April 23, 1928

Dear Babbitt,

I enclose my check for the contribution to Mercier's book. Thirty or forty copies of the volume will be enough I am sure to supply all my needs. It will help to prevent duplication if you will let me have a list of persons to whom you send copies; and please let me have this immediately. The thirty or forty copies had better be sent to me here by the publisher, so that I can distribute them myself. I have not written, and shall not write anything to Mercier on the subject.

My plan for coming abroad this summer is still in suspense. But I have gone so far as to engage passage on the *Cedric* sailing July 28.[56] It will be impossible to leave before that date, since, for one thing, I cannot close sale on the Pool property until some time in July.[57] The uncertainty of my plan otherwise depends on two things: the health of my sister and my bank account. As for the first, Alice is really somewhat better; her heart has gone back almost to normal, and the doctor assures me that she will gain a good deal more in strength. As for the second, so far as I am able to calculate in advance, I shall be able to meet the expenses; but of this there is some doubt. If I sail July 28th I ought to land at Southampton about the 6th of August. The Wents are going over on the same vessel, and, unless I can join up with you and Dora in England,[58] I shall probably go straight to Leicester and visit for about a week with Stanley Went's father. After that I hope to join Alice[59] somewhere. But these matters are uncertain. Will you be in England in August? Letters will

---

56. Dakin (1960: 260) specifies that More, along with Stanley Went, an old employee of his at the *Nation*, set sail on July 28, 1928, from New York City to England. More would start his return trip to the US on December 14 of that year (Dakin 1960: 267-68).

57. More's wife's family owned a vacation cottage in Biddeford Pool, Maine, at which some members of the family summered.

58. More did join up with the Babbitts on the trip; see Dakin 1960: 260. Babbitt took a trip for pleasure to Italy, Greece, France, and England (see Dora Babbitt in Manchester and Shepard 1941: xii). As the close of this letter indicates, Babbitt was at the time of its writing in France.

59. A footnote in the typescript of this letter reads: "His daughter, Mrs. Dymond." Alice More's husband, Edmund Gilbert Dymond (1900-1952), was a Scottish physicist. He and his wife, who had married on December 17, 1927 (Dakin 1960: 253), at this time resided at Cambridge.

reach me in England if addressed c/o E. Gilbert Dymond, 10 Hills Avenue, Cambridge—where, by the way, Alice will be glad to see you if you and she chance to be in Cambridge at the same time.

Quite recently I have heard that Frye has been in a hospital in Lincoln with a serious heart attack. He is already better, and has even been out to walk for a couple of blocks; but I am afraid his health will be permanently impaired. He may come East this summer, and I am urging him to go abroad for the first term, but I doubt if he will be able to afford this. I have been a good deal troubled by his illness; it seems as though, wherever I turn, death and sickness confront me. I need very much to get away for a period. A few days ago I gave a little talk to the Philosophical Club here on the subject "Philosophy and Literature." It was a frank disparagement of the kind of philosophy taught professionally today and a plea for humanism. The men appeared to be attentive and sympathetic, but I was told by one of them afterwards that their interest was only superficial and that any such appeal aroused their curiosity without really touching their conscience. I don't know. My book of essays on the *Demon of the Absolute*[60] is in the hands of the University Press and will be published in September. I have written a straightforward and rather personal preface for it.

I wonder whether after all you went to Greece. Your feelings at Delphi and Olympia and on the Acropolis would interest me. By the time this letter reaches Paris, I presume you will be there among your friends.

My regards to Dora,

Faithfully yours,
Paul E. More.

195, rue de l'Université
Paris, VIIe
3 July, 1928

Dear More,

I should have written you some time ago to acknowledge the receipt of your letter with enclosure of $100 for Mercier. I have forwarded this sum with a like amount of my own to him. In the meanwhile the publication of his book[61] is being delayed. It may not come out until next October.

---

60. More 1928a.
61. Mercier 1928.

Between now and then he hopes to get parts of it published in various French reviews. I am doubtful about the wisdom of all this postponement. – I am meeting many people here in Paris—men of letters, university people, business men, etc. My judgment on the total situation is not favorable, any more than it was when I was over here five years ago. The lines are very sharply drawn between the different groups but finally on political rather than on religious or humanistic grounds. I have not discovered any group to whom Mercier's volume is likely to make a special appeal. – The most thoughtful of the recent books I have seen is "La Trahison des clercs" by Julien Benda. I have promised to write an introduction for *Belphégor* by the same author which is to be published in an English translation next winter.[62]

Before coming to Paris, we spent two weeks about Naples—especially at Sorrento. From there we went to Athens where we also spent two weeks with an excursion to Delphi. I took this Grecian trip with some hesitation but found it distinctly rewarding. The Acropolis moved me deeply—in a way and to a degree of which, as you said, one can get no adequate notion from photographs. I was also greatly impressed by Delphi as well as delighted by glimpses I got of the Greek countryside on the way thither. Going abroad from Athens to Venice, we got a brief view from the deck of the steamer of the havoc wrought by the earthquake upon the modern town of Corinth.

I am much interested by what you tell me about your plans. I have deferred our sailing from England until Sep. 8 so that there should be a good chance of our getting together. There is only too much reason why you should be feeling depressed at present and some such change of scene would seem to be indicated for you. – We may not reach England until about Aug. 15, though our plans are still a bit uncertain. We have taken a very comfortable furnished "apartment" at Paris and I am likely to get more work done if I stay put for awhile.

I learn with real regret about Frye's illness both for his own sake and that of the humanistic cause. Give him my warm regards if you see him. I have just been reading Foerster's new book on *American Criticism*.[63] The last chapter is likely to do good though it glosses over certain issues that will have to be clarified if there is to be any genuine humanistic movement. G. R. Elliott[64] of Amherst has

---

62. This essay accompanied an English translation of Benda's *Belphégor* (Babbitt 1929b), appeared in the *Saturday Review of Literature* (Babbitt 1929a), and was reprinted as a chapter called "Julien Benda" in *On Being Creative and Other Essays* (Babbitt 1968: 187-200).
63. Foerster 1962.
64. On G. R. Elliott, see his entry in the Biographical Register.

just finished a book[65] in which he urges a return to Milton. It is likely to be free from the effect of "pussyfooting" that is one of Foerster's dangers.

Do you happen to have noticed T. S. Eliot's[66] article[67] in the *Forum* for July in which he takes issue with me, on the subject of humanism? As a statement and critique of my position it strikes me as confused and sophistical and in certain important respects positively inaccurate. It does, however, throw light on the spiritual difficulties of Eliot himself and of a portion at least of his numerous following of young intellectuals in England and America. – I took satisfaction on the other hand, in the exposition of my thought by Philip S. Richards[68] in *The Nineteenth [Century] & After* for April and May.[69] When Richards finally comes to the difficult subject of the relation of humanism to religion, the reader has some background. You will be pleased with his conclusion that I am not sufficiently Platonic, though it is not clear that your Platonism and his are of the same type.[70] I was pleased, by the way, at the warm appreciation Robin expressed to me the other evening of your writing. I gather that you are going to get another favorable notice in the *Revue des Études Grecques*[71]—which is very far from meaning that he is in agreement with you on all particulars. Address me until further notice c/o Bankers Trust Co., 5 Place Vendôme, Paris.

Sincerely,
Irving Babbitt.

---

245 Nassau Street
Princeton, New Jersey
July 11, 1928

My dear Babbitt,
   I am sending you a duplicate of the addresses to which I am asking Mercier to have copies of his book forwarded. I thought the simplest way to manage

---

65. Elliott 1965.
66. On T. S. Eliot's relationships with Babbitt and More, see the Introduction and Eliot's entry in the Biographical Register.
67. Eliot 1928.
68. Philip S. Richards was a classics teacher at Portsmouth Grammar School.
69. Richards 1928a and b.
70. Dakin (1960: 267) quotes a November 30, 1928, letter from More to his sister Alice, in which More notes that he is in touch with Richards, who, thanks to Babbitt's suggestion, is writing an article on More. For Richards' essay on More, see Richards 1929.
71. More's *Christ the Word* received a review in the journal soon after, though it was not notably favorable. See Puech 1929.

the business would be to have the order go to Hachette through him. Two weeks from this coming Saturday I sail. Up to the present I have been kept very busy with the lawyer and the bank and with my own work. The proof of my *Demon of the Absolute* has been read twice and the book will come out in September, unless it is held up for a month in order to permit the *Forum*, at their request, to print an essay from it in advance. Then I have completed the first draft of an essay for the next volume of the *Greek Tradition*.[72] Now I am sorting out my library as I mean to turn two or three thousand books over to the college. It is a dusty and unpleasant task. Among other things I have had frequent interviews with an architect here, with the result that I can begin to build at a moment's notice.[73] – My boat, the *Cedric*, is due at Liverpool, Monday, August the 6th. If you are in England I should love to see you. The best way to reach me is through Brown, Shipley & co., 123 Pall Mall. How long I shall stay over is very uncertain. My sister Alice's health is precarious, and I shall not want to be away if she begins to fail seriously. Otherwise I shall probably not return until about the first of January.

With kindest regards to Dora,

Faithfully yours,
Paul E. More.

---

10 Hills Avenue
Cambridge [England]
August 10 (1928)

Dear Babbitt,

I reached Liverpool last Monday and went on with the Wents straight to Leicester. From there I came to Cambridge day before yesterday. My plans depend somewhat on Gilbert's[74] motions. He starts for the Pyrenees next Thursday, and Alice and I shall stay on here until the following Monday (the 20th). We shall then for a week or so be travelling about in Norfolk and Suffolk. Are you and Dora going to be in this part of England at all? Certainly you will wish to see Cambridge and Ely. Alice's home is not large enough to take you in over night while I am here, but she would be delighted to have you make

---

72. More 1931.

73. Dakin (1960: 274) notes that More sold his house on Nassau Street in Princeton by July 7, 1929; More informed Prosser Hall Frye on that date that workmen were putting up a new house on his plot at 59 Battle Road. Around November 22, 1929, More and his sister Alice moved into this new abode.

74. A footnote in the typescript of this letter reads: "P. E. M.'s son-in-law, Mr. [Edmund Gilbert] Dymond."

this your headquarters any day except the 16th. Or if you are going into East Anglia we could no doubt arrange to meet you somewhere in those counties.

Let me know your plans as soon as they are formed.

Sincerely,
Paul E. More.

---

10 Hills Avenue
Cambridge [England]
August 13, 1928

Dear Babbitt,

I am delighted to hear that we have the chance of seeing you so soon. The two best hotels are the University Arms and the Bull; the former is rather the more expensive, but correspondingly the more desirable. We shall be in some confusion on Wednesday, as Gilbert will be preparing to leave for his travels the next morning. But if you come by the morning train, I can come in and see you in the afternoon. At any rate we hope that you and Dora will call Wednesday evening, so that Gilbert may see you before he leaves. Bus 6 which stops in front of the University Arms and from the Bull can be got opposite the Post Office, comes out by way of Hills Road. Get off at Hills Avenue, turn to the left and this house is a short distance from the corner. Bus 6 leaves the Post Office at 10, 30, and 50 minutes past the hour, and reaches University Arms in 3 or 4 minutes. The time from the Post Office to Hills Avenue is about 10 minutes. Let me know by telephone when you arrive and what your plans will be.

Sincerely,
Paul E. More.

---

10 Hills Avenue
Cambridge [England]
November 8, 1928

Dear Babbitt,

First of all my congratulations to you on attaining the dignity of being a grandfather.[75] Will you not pass on my good will to the mother and grand-

---

75. Irving Babbitt's daughter Esther gave birth to a daughter named Janet on September 9, 1928. Janet Howe Buttolph lived from 1928 to 1983.

mother. I too am expecting that honor in a few months.[76] Alas, our condition begins to resemble that of a traveller on a narrow path at the edge of a cliff, from which other and lustier passers-by will soon push him over. The motto of that great conqueror Time is, *Vae victis*.[77] – After some hesitation I have written to Richards, asking him whether he would care to receive any of my books, adding that of course their receipt would be laying him under no obligations.[78] Probably I shall not be in London again before I sail on the fourteenth of December, so that I shall not have an opportunity of meeting him or Roma. Of Eliot I saw a good deal while I was in Town, and feel that we know each other pretty well. I have already done a little writing for his *Criterion*, and may do more. What strikes me about him is the difficulty of reconciling his own damnable practice as a poet with his critical, particularly his later critical, views. There is something almost uncanny in this discrepancy. Personally I found him quite charming, but not so his wife. – After several weeks in London, most of the time alone, I went on to Oxford where again I stayed for about three weeks. Here I met a number of my old acquaintances—particularly the theologians—and also had some fun discussing the question of an infallible Church with the Jesuits, Puseyites and Dominicans in Giles Street. How those gentlemen—that is the first and third—did squirm under the inquisition! Here in Cambridge I am stopping, as you see, with Alice. I have dined at Corpus and a couple of times at St. John's, have an engagement with Cornford[79] at Trinity, and have met a few rather interesting men. But I can't say this English academic society is highly exciting. The younger men, particularly, are like most of ours, with very little background of any sort. – I am not sending a copy of Mercier's book—supposing there is such a book—to Richards, as I take it for granted you are doing this. I got a pleasant letter from Foerster about the *Demon*, but apart from that have heard very little as yet about it.[80] I suppose the bread is floating on the waters.

Faithfully yours,
Paul E. More.

---

76. Dakin (1960: 273 n. 20) notes that More's daughter Darrah gave birth to a daughter, Mary Darragh Fine (1929–2017) in early February of the next year. She was born on February 10.

77. "Woe to the conquered."

78. On More's contact with Philip S. Richards and Richards' ultimate choice to write an essay on him, see above, this chapter.

79. F. M. Cornford (1874–1943) was a classical scholar affiliated with Trinity College, Cambridge. His work focused chiefly on ancient Greek philosophy, religion, and historiography.

80. For a list of reviews of More's *The Demon of the Absolute* (More 1928a), see Dakin 1950: 201.

6 Kirkland Road
Cambridge
25 December, 1928

Dear More,

Just a line to welcome you back to "these states." I hope that you are in good shape physically. A rumor came to me from Oxford that you were a bit under the weather as the result of a bad cold.

Bernard Bandler,[81] a Jewish youth of twenty-three, of whom I think I spoke to you, is anxious to get a glimpse of you at Princeton during the Christmas recess. He has taken over "The Hound and Horn" and is planning to make of it a quarterly of national scope and humanistic leanings. The enterprise is already financed for five years ahead. His ideas are of course still immature but from what he has told me I should say that he is likely to do some good and that he may indeed accomplish a great deal in the way of influence on the younger intelligentsia. It might be well, by the way, to introduce him to Mather.

I have just received T. S. Eliot's new volume of essays.[82] Not only is there the weird contrast between his critical writing and his poetical practice that you mention but some of the essays likewise have an odd twist in them. He makes numerous acute observations which somehow do not result in a sound total estimate. If one had no other source of information than this volume one might infer that Machiavelli was a pure and dedicated spirit and Baudelaire not only a classicist but an example of true Christian humility.

I have been following with much interest the fortunes of your last volume.[83] I have the impression that it has been attracting more attention than anything you have written for years. Have you noticed Munson's[84] article in the December *Bookman*?[85] Mercier telephoned me today that he has just received two copies of his book from Paris. Enfin!

Is your brother Lou with you at present and is he coming to Boston? If so he must not fail to look me up. He wrote me some time ago that he might be East in December. Dora joins me in kind regards and in best wishes for the season.

Sincerely yours,
Irving Babbitt.

---

81. On Bernard Bandler II, then a co-editor of the *Hound & Horn*, a literary magazine co-founded at Harvard in 1927 by Varian Fry and Lincoln Kirstein, see his entry in the Biographical Register.
82. Eliot 1970.
83. More 1928a.
84. On Gorham B. Munson, see his entry in the Biographical Register.
85. Munson 1928.

245 Nassau Street
Princeton, New Jersey
December 27, 1928

Dear Babbitt,

Thank you for the welcome and for the pages from the *Hound and Horn*. I shall of course be glad to see Bandler if he will call on me here; I should like to talk with him and learn what brand of humanism he is going to purvey. – A copy of Mercier's book[86] has come to Mather, but none to me as yet or to anyone else, so far as I know, to whom I ordered it sent. From a glance over Mather's copy I should be inclined to think that the treatment of Brownell is the most adequate and interesting of the three.

My health is very good and the long rest has set me on my feet. I shall be scribbling again very soon. – What you say about the essays on Machiavelli and Baudelaire in Eliot's book is quite true. As a matter of fact I taxed him pretty directly about the wrong-headedness of the Baudelaire, and he admitted that it was journalistic and incomplete.

I am assuming that you are having a copy of Mercier's book sent to P. S. Richards; if you are not, I will do so. I had tea and dinner with him in London and we talked for five hours on end. We agreed in a vast number of things.

This is not a letter, but a scrap bag of notes. With the kindest New Year's greetings to Dora, I am

Sincerely,
P. E. M.

---

245 Nassau Street
Princeton, New Jersey
March 29, 1929

Dear Babbitt,

My lecture at Amherst is for April 17th, so that I shall be passing North just while you are in the West.[87] However, I could scarcely have stopped at Cambridge under any conditions, since I must make my excursion as brief as possible so as to miss no more of my class lectures here than necessary. I am sorry, as I should like very much to talk with you about Foerster's *Challenge*

---

86. Mercier 1928.
87. Dakin (1960: 273) notes that on April 17, 1929, More lectured at Amherst College on "Humanism and Religion." While at Amherst, More saw Dora Babbitt.

of Humanism.[88] It is with the utmost reluctance that I consented to contribute to that volume—and this for several reasons. Chiefly, because my theme, the relation of humanism to religion, must be handled with extreme delicacy and reserve so as not to run counter to much that the other contributors will probably have to say. I have already tried out my thesis at a little talk here at the Graduate School, and I am to speak on the same subject at Amherst. The reaction of my hearers in these two places will perhaps aid me in getting my thoughts into order.

I had heard from Richards that his article was accepted by the *Nineteenth Century*,[89] and I am naturally curious to read his criticism. From what he has said I judge that he has dealt almost exclusively with the *Greek Tradition* to the exclusion of my *Essays*, just as Mercier did. And from my conversation with him in London I judge also that in the main he is sympathetic with my point of view, but just how far and in what manner, remains to be seen.

Meanwhile I am deep in Aristotle.

Sincerely,
Paul E. More.

---

245 Nassau Street
Princeton, New Jersey
May 19, 1929

Dear Babbitt,

My brother tells me that you may possibly take a lot with us and build at Greensboro.[90] The news is almost too good to be true. I do not know a great deal about the place except that a number of my Princeton friends go there—the Gausses, Stuarts,[91] etc.—and that there are others from Harvard

---

88. More means the edited collection *Humanism and America* (Foerster 1930), not Mercier's later monograph *The Challenge of Humanism* (Mercier 1936). More had previously expressed reservations to others about contributing to Foerster's edited collection, the publication of which would help spark the attention-grabbing debate about the New Humanism among the American public.

89. Richards 1929.

90. Greensboro, Vermont, where More would summer in 1930 with his sisters Alice and May; see Dakin 1960: 292.

91. Duane R. Stuart (1873–1941) was a Roman historian and Latinist in Princeton's classics department. For more information on Stuart, see Ward W. Briggs Jr.'s entry on him at the *Database of Classical Scholars*: dbcs.rutgers.edu.

and Yale, quite an academic society. It is not at all fashionable. There are three or four lots for sale in what is said to be a good situation at $800 each, and they are to be held for me until July 1st. After that I might get an option on them, but I am not sure of this. If Lou can come down from Murray Bay to join me I may run up to Greensboro and look the property over late in June. Could you perhaps come too for a day or two? Of course I have my Essex place on my hands, but if the Greensboro lot seems very desirable I may buy and trust to selling the Essex place later.[92] I have actually sold the Biddeford Pool property, and I have very strong prospects of selling this house next month. It will be a relief to get this land off my hands. My plans are ready and I shall begin to build immediately if this house is taken.

It was a surprise and a delight to see Dora at Amherst. In fact my whole experience there was pleasant. But this lecturing business is hard on the nerves. I had of course some talk with Roy Elliott about the humanistic book.[93] As a matter of fact I should really prefer to keep out of the venture, and still may do so. I feel sure that I shouldn't contribute anything of much value, and that I could probably serve the cause better by writing *about* the book in some magazine than by writing *for* it.[94] However, Foerster is something of a slave driver and may compel me to come in. The last contributor he has corralled is T. S. Eliot.[95]

I suppose you will be going to Dublin this summer. Alice and Gilbert are coming over late in July. Gil will spend most of the vacation in the West, but Alice will stay with me, except for short visits, here and at Essex.

I may have to do some reading this summer for my new course and also for my present Plato course, which I am to conduct on an entirely different basis. Even so the first term—I am giving my two courses then instead of the second term—is going to be a very strenuous season for me. I feel like something of a sport, taking on such work at the age of sixty-five.

Sincerely,
Paul E. More.

---

92. Dakin (1960: 292) specifies that More leased his place in Essex, Vermont, for the 1930 summer season. But More would spend more time in Essex during the summer of 1931 (see Dakin 1960: 310).

93. More means Foerster 1930.

94. More ultimately both contributed to the volume (More 1930a) and reviewed it for the *Bookman* (More 1930b)—a review that later appeared in More's final volume of *New Shelburne Essays*, called *On Being Human* (More 1936d: 1-24).

95. See Eliot 1930.

370   Chapter Nine

6 Kirkland Road
Cambridge
23 June, 1929

Dear More,

I am much interested in what you tell me about your plans in connection with Greensboro. It would mean a great deal to me, as you know, if I could see more of you either in winter or summer. It is, however, out of the question for me to go to a region so remote from Cambridge. I have to do most of my writing in summer and need to keep within reasonable distance of the Harvard library. I wish that it were possible to get you and Lou interested in the Monadnock country which has many attractions and is far easier for both of you to reach than Greensboro. Greensboro is especially inaccessible from Dublin—even more so than Essex—and I should about have to give up hope of seeing you in summer if you were there. – I feel very strongly that we should get together from time to time not only for the pleasure, but also, in my case at least, for the profit of the meeting. There are certain matters that I should like greatly to talk over with you at the present moment—for example, Foerster's undertaking. He is a good impresario but I fear a failing on his part to grasp the full gravity of some of the issues involved. At the same time I am hoping that you will not only contribute something to his volume but that you will do your level best. I am planning to submit my own contribution[96] to you and am inclined to think that you would do well to reciprocate. You will probably agree with me that in this particular place it will be wise for us to emphasize our agreements rather than our differences. When I come to expand my essay for my next book I may enter into certain controversial matters.

The whole present situation strikes me as critical. Both of us are being assailed from various quarters. Have you seen Bernbaum's[97] savage attack[98] which was read originally before the Modern Language Association at Toronto? It then appeared in the *English Journal* and has since been mailed by his publisher to teachers of English all over the country. A few years ago Bernbaum wrote me that he was my disciple! I should have kept the letter as a curiosity. – The editor of *The Sewanee Review* has also raised a loud bray in the last issue of his periodical.[99]

---

96. Babbitt 1930.
97. Ernest Bernbaum (1879–1958) was a Harvard-trained scholar of English literature then on the faculty at the University of Illinois.
98. Bernbaum 1929.
99. Knickerbocker 1929: 260-64.

I was pleased with Elliott's article on you in the *Bookman*,[100] though I do not like his nagging of Matthew Arnold and am not enamored of some of his stylistic mannerisms. The last chapter in his new book[101] strikes me as notable. It really gets under the surface of the situation. I am writing a review of the volume for the *Forum*.[102] – J. D. M. Ford has a longish review of Mercier's book in the last number of the *Harvard Graduates' Magazine* which shows more knowledge of your work and mine than I gave him credit for.[103]

We are planning to go up to Dublin tomorrow. Can we not induce you to visit us there? We have a Ford at present so that, if you desire, you can inspect the country in all directions.

Sincerely yours,
Irving Babbitt.

Princeton
July 3, 1929

My dear Babbitt,

This place is actually sold and work has been begun on the new house in Battle Road. I believe the rascally Greek was right and πάντα ῥεῖ[104]—at least all my world seems afloat and I cannot guess where it will land me. Alice[105] lands the 22nd or 23rd of this month and stays over until September 21st. Of course my summer will be planned chiefly to meet her convenience. Darrah has had in mind to go with us to Essex for August, taking the baby. But a complication has arisen. Mr. Fine[106] is dying of a cancer. If his condition is very low this next month, as it may well be, Darrah thinks she will not want to leave Harry here alone for more than a week or two. Perhaps she will come back the middle of August and leave the baby with us under Mary's care for the rest of the month. But this is of course very uncertain. In short, I can make no plans at all as yet.

I thought Lou's report that you might build at Greensboro was too good to be true, and I can well understand your reasons for not doing so. On the other hand Dublin, apart from your presence there, would not give me what I want. Most part of my summers I shall probably spend in Princeton

100. Elliott 1929.
101. Elliott 1965.
102. Babbitt 1929c.
103. Ford 1928.
104. A footnote in the typescript of this letter reads: "All things are flowing. (Heraclitus)."
105. More's daughter.
106. Darrah's father-in-law.

working. The five or six weeks I am away, I want to read in the mornings, play golf in the afternoons, and with some frequency bridge in the evenings; and this I want to do among friends with whom I am at ease as with an old shoe. That is what draws me away from Essex to Greensboro, and what makes Dublin an unsuitable place for me.

I should be very glad indeed if you would send me the MS[.] of your essay for Foerster's book. For one thing it would help me to know how to go about writing my own contribution, or, on the other hand, it might help me to make up my mind not to contribute at all. There is a fair probability that you will forestall me in all that I might have to say unless I went into aspects of the question which perhaps had better not be touched on in this volume. It would scarcely be worth while to repeat your arguments or definitions. As a matter of fact I have from the first been very reluctant to come in, and Foerster knows that I am doubtful. – I have not seen Bernbaum's attack, but I did see the editorial in the *Sewanee*. The latter at least is mild and innocent compared with the sort of stuff that used to come out, and on the other hand the stream of eulogistic comment has very much increased. For one thing Mercier's book seems to have attracted a good deal of attention, and in one Swedish paper at least has brought out very complimentary notice of the humanistic movement. But in truth I don't take these matters very seriously; I have practiced too long, or tried to practice, the Hindu virtue of inattachment. – Ford's review was intelligent enough.

Lou is working for a Guggenheim fellowship to enable him to go over to England next February for the purpose of looking up material for his life of Newton.[107] I should love to go with him but fear it will not be possible. My courses here are to be the first term hereafter, but this winter in January—before our term has quite ended—I am going out to Berkeley to lecture at the University, and shall not be back until May.[108] As I shall have been in my new house for barely a month before leaving for California, I shall probably be disposed to settle down in quiet for a time. I know I shall be tired, as my work here will all be in a new field. I ought to be preparing for it now, but instead I am writing on mysticism—what a subject! The weather has been damp and depressing a good deal of the time, but I grind out my half-thousand words a

---

107. L. More 1962.
108. Dakin (1960: 279) specifies that More would head to Berkeley in January of 1930, to teach two courses—an undergraduate class on Plato and a graduate seminar on Aristotle—at the University. He would leave California in early May of that year (Dakin 1960: 288).

day with horrible regularity. *Onhe Hast onhe Rast*—that is about what is left for me in this life.

You did not give me your Dublin address, and I am therefore sending my letter to Cambridge with directions to forward.

Faithfully yours,
P. E. M.

Princeton
59 Battle Road
November 27, 1929

Dear Babbitt,

Thank you for the two letters, both of which I return herewith.

Collins[109] is an interesting chap, but I wonder how stable he is. I had already learned through Roy Elliott that he is the author of the review of Sherman, and that certainly is encouraging. I am quite disposed to help him so far as I can, but my energy for journalistic work is, as you know, reduced to a minimum.[110] I may offer to write for him a notice[111] of Foerster's menagerie.[112] In which case I shall, probably, try to explain more clearly and definitively my views of the relation of religion to humanism.

Robin's letter does not in fact contain anything new to me. The passages he quotes from [the] twelfth book of the *Laws* do indeed point back to the divination, so to speak, of τὸ ἀγαθόν[113] in the sixth book of the *Republic*; but Robin—I won't say errs, but—gives a wrong impression of Plato's position by failing to interpret the twelfth book of the *Laws* by the tenth book and by the *Timaeus*. At one moment in the *Republic* Plato was evidently drawing very near to a monistic metaphysic. His modification of this monistic idealism by the theism of the *Timaeus, Philebus,* and *Laws,* is one of the most significant and surprising events in the history of philosophy; and also it is, for very obvious reasons, surprisingly overlooked or viciously interpreted away by

---

109. Seward B. Collins, the socialite and journal editor whose later turn from the New Humanism towards a self-described American Fascism would cause a public-relations problem for Humanists. On Collins, see his entry in the Biographical Register and the Introduction.

110. Collins was then the editor of the *Bookman* and at this time sympathetic to the New Humanism.

111. More 1930b.

112. Foerster 1930.

113. A footnote in the typescript of this letter reads: "The good."

commentators of the nineteenth century who are almost all, despite their occasional protests, dominated by Hegel. It is a curious fact that Aristotle, *in his religious metaphysic*, derives from *Republic* vi and *Laws* xii, and brushes aside the intervening position of the *Timaeus* and *Laws* x.

I am as you see from the address now installed in the new house. Order is beginning to appear out of chaos, but I still feel like a man evicted into the street.

Sincerely,
Paul E. More.

CHAPTER TEN
1930–1934

59 Battle Road
Princeton, N. J.
November 10, 1930

My dear Babbitt,

I had not been informed of your election to the Academy[1] until your letter came this afternoon. I am glad to know that the "immortals" have seen the light at last, but frankly I do not think you will get much profit from the honour. If they had not elected you this year, I was in fact on the point of resigning. – I had not expected to attend any of the ceremonies this year, and had so written to the secretary. But I am writing tonight to inform her that I shall be present at the luncheon on Thursday. Unfortunately I have a dinner here in Princeton which makes it obligatory on me to come back by the 5.05 train. I shall be mightily glad to get at least a glimpse of you. As I said in my telegram, I wish you could come down Wednesday and pass the night here, or that you could come out Thursday evening. Unfortunately the last night train out leaves N. Y. at 10.25 and you could scarcely get that if you go to the dinner. There is a still later train for the junction 12.50, but it does not reach the junction until 2.26; it is a fortune. If you can come out Wednesday or Thursday, let me know, by wire.

It is a pleasant memory that Alice[2] so thoroughly enjoyed the summer. We rented a house at Greensboro, and filled it up with the family. I thought of coming over to Dublin to visit you if you could take me in, but felt rather bound to stay with Alice, as I knew it was almost certainly her last summer. I hardly expected her death so soon.[3] It was probably a blessing for she was

---

1. A footnote in the typescript of this letter reads: "American Academy of Arts and Letters." On Babbitt's election to the Academy, seemingly in November of 1930, see Dora Babbitt in Manchester and Shepard 1941: xii-xiii; Dakin 1960: 295; Slayton 1986: 235; Ryn 1991: xviii.

2. A footnote in the typescript of this letter reads: "P. E. M.'s sister."

3. Dakin (1960: 293) notes that More's sister Alice, aged 81, collapsed in September of 1930, soon before they were to leave Greensboro for Princeton. She passed away on October 5 of that year (Dakin 1960: 294).

getting very weak and I know she dreaded the winter. She was a brave soul. I am now quite alone in the house. It is rather ghastly.

With affectionate regards to Dora,

Faithfully yours,
Paul E. More.

---

59 Battle Road
Princeton, N. J.
March 30, 1931

My dear Babbitt,

I have been highly amused by the story of your lottery boys, which apparently has gone the rounds of the press over the country.[4] That is fame!

Saturday, the 4th, I am sailing for England to be gone until about the last of July.[5] My chief object is to be in Cambridge when Alice presents me with a British grandchild. If all goes as well with her as it has gone with Darrah and her boy, I can wish nothing better.[6] I tell Darrah she has brought a great philosopher into the world; for the boy, as they say down South, is the spitten [sic] image of Socrates. I may have other business in England, as a scheme is on foot to raise money to pay the salary for two years to some young English scholar to assist me in editing a "Library" of Seventeenth-century Anglo-ecclesiastical literature.[7] But the success of this project is highly doubtful. It will in fact be something of a relief for me if it falls through. But one bit of business is certain: I must be in Glasgow June 17th to receive an honorary L.L.D.[8] Meanwhile T. S. Eliot promises me long evenings in London over tobacco and whiskey, enlivened by counter charges of heresy[9]—an appetizing programme. I may ask Richards to take a brief tour in a car with me as my guest. I presume you know that my old friend C. R. S. Harris is now editor of the *XIXth Century*.

---

4. A footnote in the typescript of this letter reads: "*Time*, 16 March 1931." The story (anon. 1931) discusses the lottery amongst students in Babbitt's Comparative Literature II course, to see who can guess the (large) number of writers to whom Babbitt will refer in the course of a lecture.

5. According to Dakin (1960: 299, 302), More would be in Britain from April 4 to July 18, 1931. On the trip, see also Eliot 2015: 481 n. 1.

6. Soon after More arrived in England, More's daughters Alice and Darrah both gave birth to sons. See Dakin 1960: 299.

7. More and Cross 1935.

8. Cf. Dakin 1960: 300.

9. Cf. Eliot's August 10, 1930, letter to More (Eliot 2015: 292-93).

I have been working desperately hard to complete the MS. of a volume of essays for the *Greek Tradition*,[10] even sitting at the typewriter occasionally after midnight. Yesterday I gave the last revision to an essay on *Buddhism and Christianity* with which the volume opens, and today I turned the MS. over to the University Press. Now I don't want to print the essay on Buddhism without the benefit of your criticism, and the following would appear to be the only practical way of getting that. Tomlinson promises to have proof of the whole book ready for me when I return about August 1st—of course he won't, for no printer ever kept his word—but I may have it sometime in the summer or early autumn.[11] Would it be a burdensome task, if I had him at that time send you proof of the Buddhism, and could you read it promptly? By the way, are you familiar with De Lorenzo's[12] translations? The Italian seems to me to preserve the flavour of the Pâli in quite a wonderful way, better than English or German.

My address in England will be c/o Brown Shipley & Co., 123 Pall Mall. Won't you send me a line letting me know what your address will be about August 1st.

With kindest remembrance to Dora,

Sincerely,
P. E. M.

Brown's Hotel
London, W. I.
(Dover St & Albemarle St)
July 1, 1931

Dear Babbitt,

I am writing today to Tomlinson and asking him to send you proof of my essay on Buddhism. I sail from London on the Minnewaska July 18th, and ought to be in Princeton the 27th. If you could without inconvenience to yourself mail the proof with your criticisms so that I should receive it on the 27th or 28th, it would be a great help. I shall be in Princeton for only a few days before leaving for Essex,[13] and I should like to go through the proof of

---

10. More 1931.

11. Tomlinson at Princeton University Press got the proofs to More and Babbitt prior to August 1st; see Dakin 1960: 302 and below.

12. Giuseppe De Lorenzo (1871–1957) was an Italian professor who focused some of his scholarly attention on Buddhism.

13. On More's summer in Essex and Greensboro in 1931, see Dakin 1960: 310.

the book, or as much as possible of it, while in Princeton. Tomlinson has promised me the complete proof for that time.

I have travelled about so much and have seen so many places and people that I shouldn't know where to begin or to end, if I undertook a real letter. Most important of all is the fact that Alice gave birth to a sturdy little boy and is herself in excellent health. It seems highly venerable to be thrice a grandfather. As for places, I have pretty well made the circuit of England. After being in Cambridge four weeks, I went over to Oxford, from thence to Storrington, Sussex, then to Portsmouth with Richards (whose guest I had been at Storrington), across to Exeter (where I met up again with Louis), then to Tintagel and up through Devon and Somerset to Bath. So far I had been motoring. From there by train to Liverpool (where Louis met his family) and to Glasgow. Then across to Edinburgh and back to Oxford and Cambridge. Now I am in London for a few days, mainly for business in connection with the projected *Anthology*.[14] The conferring of degrees at Glasgow was a stately ceremony, but much like the same sort of thing anywhere. One rather novel bit of experience for me was sitting beside the Duke of Montrose[15] and chatting with him easily—except for his deafness. I was amused at the form given to my eulogy by the Dean. He made me out to be a monster of restless energy. I fear I must have looked to the audience a very mild sort of gentleman as I stood while he read his encomium. One of the pleasantest spots in my journey was a dinner at Kemp Smith's in Edinburgh with Grierson[16] and A. E. Taylor.[17] The latter's *Gifford Lectures*,[18] by the way, is a rather notable book, though exceedingly repetitious. I am seeing something of T. S. Eliot, who impresses me more and more as an enigma the better I know him. What his *Criterion* really stands for, only the Devil comprehends.

Give my kindest regards to Dora.

Faithfully yours,
Paul E. More.

---

14. More and Cross 1935. Around May 20, 1931, T. S. Eliot attempted to set up a meeting for More with an English publisher for this book (see Eliot 2015: 573).
15. James Graham (1878–1954), the 6th Duke of Montrose.
16. Sir Herbert J. C. Grierson (1866–1960) was a Scottish literary scholar and critic.
17. On this dinner, see also Dakin 1960: 300-1.
18. Taylor 1951.

59 Battle Road
Princeton, N. J.
August 2, 1931

My dear Babbitt,

Your labors were not wasted and I am very much obliged to you for the extreme care you have taken in going through my proof.[19] It has resulted in a considerable correction and rewriting of the essay, though I cannot flatter myself that you will find it to your taste in its present form. I do not quite concede that I leave Buddha the victim of a "ghastly illusion," unless in return it would be conceded by one who accepts the main thesis of the *Dharma* that Jesus was such a victim. Certainly if Buddha is right then Christ's doctrine of God is an illusion, if not a ghastly one. You must take your choice. As for the theory that the five *khandhas* pass from one life to another, I am familiar with Thomas's[20] exposition, but cannot believe it correct. How could they pass over? Certainly this body and this consciousness are dispersed at death. As for the rôle of *Karma* and *Tanha* in producing the new *Aggregates*, there I confess I do not see the matter clear. In deference to your judgment, however, I have cut out part of my statement of these riddles.

I should love to visit you at Dublin,[21] and may be able to do so. But at present my plans are all in abeyance. Mary (my cook) has developed tuberculosis, and I have got to establish her in a sanatorium.[22] And I do not know yet just what Darrah is going to do. I will write later if I find myself free of such obligations and of work.

After suffering for four months from cold and damp I find myself cast into a fiery furnace—from the ice-box into the frying pan, so to speak.

With best regards to Dora,

Faithfully yours,
Paul E. More.

---

19. Of a chapter of More 1931. On this topic, see above, this chapter.
20. The English scholar E. J. Thomas (1869–1958) wrote numerous books on Buddhism.
21. Dublin, New Hampshire, where the Babbitts often summered.
22. Mary had been More's cook for twenty-five years; see Dakin 1960: 310.

Dublin, N. H.
6 August, 1931

Dear More,

I meant to call your attention on the proof to a possible inaccuracy in your reference to Buddha's dialogue with Vaccha: the question asked, if I remember rightly, is not whether the saint is *reborn* but whether he continues to exist after death.

Though the ways of *Karma* are according to Buddha "unthinkable," he did not commit himself to the palpable absurdity of asserting that there is transmigration without any "self" to transmigrate. As bearing on the Buddhist attitude in this matter, I cite *Sutta* 143 of the *Majjhima-Nikāya* which contains the story of the illness and death of the rich merchant Anāthapundika who, after being reborn in the Tusita heaven, *returns to visit Buddha*. A number of the Saints (notably Mogullana) were supposed, by putting forth the appropriate psychic powers, to have visited the various heavens and hells and to have interviewed their denizens with a view to finding out what conduct on earth had brought them to a state of bliss or the opposite. The *Vimāna-vatthu* ("Heavenly Mansions") of the *Khuddaka-Nikāya* contains 85 interviews of this kind; the *Peta-vatthu* of the same *Nikāya*, dealing with the victims of bad *Karma* in the world to come, is constructed on a similar plan. I have seen the suggestion that Christian journeys to the other world, culminating in Dante's vision, reveal Buddhist influence, but the proof did not seem to me convincing.

At all events a Buddhist ghost is at least as substantial practically as a Christian ghost. The difference is that the Christian has traditionally conceived the "soul" to be immobilized at death for good or ill through eternity (with the partial exception of purgatory); whereas, according to the Buddhist, even future states are subject to the law of impermanence. Your own position is apparently that the opposition between the changeful and the unchanging is to go on indefinitely in the next world as in this. The Buddhist ambition to escape from the changeful once for all you condemn as leading to an "absolved dualism."

Your treatment of Buddhist *samādhi* in this connection strikes me as most unsatisfactory. It makes clear that we are coming to differ very gravely not only about Buddhism but about what is genuinely religious, psychologically speaking, in Christianity itself. From my point of view you are in danger of sacrificing essential aspects of the religious experience to a certain brand of theology. You lump together under the common denomination of "mysticism" things that are in reality as far apart as the poles. Do you really suppose that Buddha was a mystic in the same sense as Blake? Are you ready to maintain that because Dante tells towards the end of the *Divine Comedy* how he was rapt out of his ordinary consciousness by a mystic vision that he is therefore to be placed on the same level as some modern Rousseauist or Wordsworthian who calls himself a mystic simply because he has mixed himself up with the landscape? The truth is that there is an immense mass of alleged mysticism from the ancient Chinese Taoists down to the closing chapter of Eddington's "Nature of the Physical World"[23] which is not dualistic at all in your sense but unmistakably pantheistic. In distinguishing between true religious meditation and the various forms of pantheistic revery one needs to apply unflinchingly the maxim: "By their fruits ye shall know them." The substantial agreement of Christ and Buddha as to the *fruits* of the religious life is a fact not to be dismissed lightly on theological or other grounds. Buddhism should be used to give psychological support to Christianity—it needs all the support it can get these days; this becomes impossible if the culmination of the Buddhist "path" is dismissed as mere frustration and self-deception.

Both Dora and I are sorry to learn of Mary's illness.[24] In the meanwhile remember that we have a large house here with a room that you can use as a study if you have any work that can be done away from Princeton. Up here on the slopes of Monadnock you are practically sure to escape from the heat—except perhaps the kind that is engendered by theological discussion.

I did not gather from my conversations with Mather that he has gone Buddhist. He has in him, however, a touch of the fear [?] for [?] pink and always has had. He has a genuine perception of the humanistic position but, through an excessive open-mindedness, he is continually tempted to undertake a mediation between it and some other position with which it is incompatible. To anything that is specifically religious he seems to be blind. Some fundamental intuition is lacking. One encounters in purely eschatological form the [?] of the mystery of grace.

Sincerely,
I. B.

---

23. Eddington 2014.
24. More's longstanding cook. On her illness, see above, this chapter.

Camp Cedars
Essex, New York
August 12, 1931

My dear Babbitt,

    I am familiar with the *Maj.-Nik.* 143 and other similar texts that imply the continued existence of something corresponding to the Christian soul, and this I grant fully in my essay. The point is this, and I insist on it: What is it that is reborn? Something is reborn, and yet over and over again, in the *anathā* doctrine, Buddha so analyses the constituents of being that nothing would seem to be left for rebirth where there is only a stream of cause and effect. It is true also that he rejects the question of *what* is reborn as not for edification. But his psychological analysis, nevertheless, forces the question, and did force the question upon his disciples as many passages show. I cannot help thinking that the Western conception of the soul as something damnable at least, however unanalysable, is better logic and better psychology, unless one takes a purely agnostic position and denies any knowledge of moral responsibility carried into the future. Buddha's position is morally, to this point, irreproachable, it is philosophically impossible. And beyond this point the difficulties, both moral and philosophical, increase. His conception of *Nirvâna* does most certainly involve what I call an "absolved dualism" and does lead to the difficulties I enumerate. Up to a certain point the fruits of Buddhism and Christianity are extraordinarily alike, and for reasons, I think which I state. But I do not see how any one familiar with history, and unprejudiced, can fail to see that Christianity (despite its fanaticism, etc.—*corruptio optimi pessima*)[25] has produced a richer life than Buddhism. Nor does it seem to me possible to deny that this is because Christianity accepts the soul simply and refuses practically, despite the vagaries of certain metaphysical theologians, to advance to an absolved dualism. Whether Buddhism or Christianity is true in this respect is another question, though pragmatically the argument is on the side of the latter.

    I cannot quite understand your words about mysticism. I do ultimately reject mysticism of any brand; but I nowhere confuse a Rousseauistic with a Christian or Hindu mysticism; the two may be rejected on quite different grounds. The last essay in the book, by the way, is a long discussion of mysticism in which I endeavor to distinguish its various forms. In clinging to an "absolute" as against an "absolved" dualism I mean to say simply that the absolute, abstract element of our being that we express as unity and

---

25. "The corruption of the best (is) the worst."

immutability has no meaning for us apart from its conjunction with multiplicity and change. A. E. Taylor, by the way, has some profound observations in his recently published *Gifford Lectures*[26]—a great book by and large, though in places he indulges in rather dry metaphysics. In sum I cannot escape the feeling that, led by your desire to find the full value of religion without any "dogma" or "myth," you do not face quite squarely the actuality of Buddhism. I entirely agree with your statement that "Buddhism should be used to give psychological support to Christianity," and this I intimated in the last paragraph of the essay, to which you so strongly objected.

After a good deal of wire-pulling I got Mary placed in a sanatorium, where I hope she will receive adequate treatment. She must remain there for many months, and indeed I am not too sanguine of her recovery at all. Meanwhile William will carry on for me alone, with occasional help from the outside. My housekeeping will go on one foot, but I trust not too lamely.

I have not seen Mather since his excursion into Russia; but I know that he went there prejudiced in favour of Bolshevism, and from all accounts he has returned fully confirmed in his views.[27] He was wont to boast that he alone really believed in civilization. Then suddenly he was converted to Socialism by an article of Edmund Wilson's in the *New Republic*. I suspect that his antipathy to Christianity—enhanced I fear by controversies with me—has been a large factor in his acceptance of a theory which is militantly antireligious. What he will be tomorrow, heaven only knows. I tell him that his next enthusiasm will be paedo-baptism. I do not object to change—I have changed myself—but I draw the line at whirling about like a weather cock.

Faithfully yours,
Paul E. More.

---

59 Battle Road
Princeton, New Jersey
October 21, 1931

My dear Babbitt,

Your note about the Am. Acad. of Arts and Sciences[28] precipitates a letter which I have had in mind to write for some time. The principal thing that has

---

26. Taylor 1951.
27. Mather discussed this trip in an article for the *Atlantic Monthly* (Mather 1931). The piece provides a more supportive take on the Soviet Union than Babbitt or More would have offered.
28. Dakin (1960: 295 n. 17) notes that in November of 1931 More, with Babbitt's help, became a member of the American Academy of Arts and Sciences.

held me back, is the fact that I caught a damaging cold in Essex which quite took the life out of me, and from which even yet I have not fully recovered. I still have to be very sparing of my eyes.

I am sorry about the Academy. I must have read the documents carelessly, for I got the impression that dues were at least expected from non-resident members. My present obligations to other clubs and associations made me hesitate to assume any new obligation—especially as I frankly, like yourself I suspect, do not see much practical outcome from such organizations. But I should regret the appearance of offering even the mildest affront to the Academy in question, which I know to be a very honourable and distinguished body. If you can make it right with the Committee, I should be glad to accept the invitation to join.

As for the other Academy,[29] which meets in N. Y. I seem to have no record of the date of the session this year. I shall inquire about this, and, if my University obligations permit, will attend. I shall notify you of my decision as soon as possible. Could you not come out to Princeton? I can put you up for as long as you can stay, and, I need not add, should love to do so. I have put Mather up for membership, had doubt whether he passes. For seconders I called on men connected immediately with the practice and criticism of art.

My book[30] will be out, presumably, about the first of next month,[31] and of course a copy will be sent to you. Some changes I have made in the article on Buddhism as suggested by your comments; but I fear neither this essay nor the rest of the book will give you much satisfaction. As a matter of fact it does not satisfy me. I found on reading the proof that the ideas and arguments needed more over-hauling for clarification than was possible for matter already in type. As it is, the printer must have been aghast at the way I tore things up.

Mather has just escaped a horrid tragedy. By mistake he dashed ammonia into his eyes, with how painful results you can imagine. He was compelled to spend several days in bed with ice packs on his eyes, and still suffers.

With affectionate regards to Dora,

Sincerely,
Paul E. More.

---

29. Presumably, More means the American Academy of Arts and Letters, of which both Babbitt and More were members.
30. More 1931.
31. Dakin (1950: 179) specifies that More's book was published in November of 1931.

59 Battle Road
Princeton, New Jersey
February 14, 1932

My dear Babbitt,

Dean Eisenhart[32] has just telephoned me that he is asking you to give the ΦBK address some time before March 24th and that he would like me to join in urging you to accept. Naturally, I told him I would do what I could, and indeed I do wish you would come. You must have some lecture in your desk or in your head which you could use. I have a spare room, in fact two rooms if Dora would come too.

At present I am in a state of mental agony over an attempt to write an essay on Proust.[33] Why I ever undertook such a task I don't know, and whether I can make anything worth while out of it I know still less. But the subject calls for treatment. Seillière's book[34] has good stuff in it and is more orderly than most of his work, but it leaves much still to be said.

It was this burden on my mind that made me return Mercier's MS[35] after reading only the introductory chapter. I found so much to criticise in the English of these pages that I just balked at the work of reading through the whole work. I fear I hurt his feelings, which was the last thing I wanted to do. But if I sail for England in April, as I probably shall do,[36] my time for Proust and other tasks is very limited.

I was sorry you couldn't accept Mather's invitation. He has gone to Cornell, and will probably not be here if you come in March.

Sincerely,
Paul E. More.

---

32. The mathematician Luther Pfahler Eisenhart (1876–1965) was then the dean of faculty at Princeton.
33. This essay (More 1933) would be More's first contribution to Seward Collins's new journal, the *American Review*. It would later serve as a chapter of *On Being Human* (More 1936d: 43-68).
34. Seillière 1931.
35. More presumably refers to Mercier 1936.
36. More did not, in fact, travel to England at this time. He would instead go the following year; see Dakin 1960: 326; and below.

6 Kirkland Road
Cambridge
17 April, 1932

Dear More,

I have been under pressure for some time past in connection with putting a book through the press and at the same time writing parts of it. I therefore wrote to Dean Eisenhart that I could not accept his invitation for March but should be glad to come in April in case you had not sailed for Europe in the meanwhile. He replied that an April date would not be convenient because of a conflict with certain ceremonies in honor of Hibben.[37]

I owe you an apology for not having acknowledged sooner your volume *The Catholic Faith*. The truth is it is a rather alarming production for so indolent a correspondent as myself. To deal adequately with some of the questions it raises would require the writing of a countertreatise. From another point of view there is very little I can say. Like Iago I am nothing if not critical; and so far as the central issue is concerned you have put yourself beyond criticism. In certain portions of the book you have penetrated into regions that are simply alien to me and were almost equally alien to you only a few short years ago. Even in these portions I can admire the genuinely Platonic elevation of tone and the high distinction of style (except that I have no special affection for a few words like "costingness"). Perhaps I am most impressed by the essay on the mystics. There is material here that students of the subject will have to reckon with. I am not a mystic myself and, as regards the mystical experience, my mind is in a state of Socratic abeyance. If I did have to decide, it would be in favor of the mystics—at least of a few of them. Dante, for example, seems to me to be mystical in the fullest sense of the word in certain passages towards the end of the *Divine Comedy*. I am rather loath to admit that he is in these passages guilty of the self-deception of an "absolved dualism." In rejecting the absolute in its metaphysical form and at the same time reviving it in a theological form ("absolute dualism") you seem to me to have put yourself in a difficult position. Dualism, as you define it, is a present fact of experience—one of the immediate data of consciousness. But to project this dualism into the mysterious Beyond and

---

37. The Presbyterian minister and philosopher John Grier Hibben (1861–1933) served as the president of Princeton University from 1912 to 1932. The ceremonies referred to here must pertain to Hibben's impending retirement.

to insist that it is to endure *in saecula saeculorum*[38] is a very different matter. My own attitude towards such questions is summed up in the sentence of Dr. Johnson: "The good and evil of eternity are too ponderous for the wings of wit."

You have come out as a full-fledged theologian in this book and are at the same time receiving your chief publicity as a humanist—with no small risk of confusion. I have just for example received a clipping of an article by some Roman Catholic ecclesiastic who condemns your brand of theology not as theology but as humanism! I am the first to recognize that your total position, which you have summed up so admirably at the end of the present volume, not only implies a high type of religion, but also carries with it a high type of humanism. The question is whether humanism is necessarily dependent on a Platonic and Christian theism or something of the kind. Your defining of the issue in the early chapters of *The Demon of the Absolute* should in my opinion be acceptable to every genuine humanist. In your *Bookman* article,[39] however, you seem to strike a different note: humanism is well enough in its way, you seem to say, but is likely to prove ineffective except as *ancilla theologiae*.[40] This statement, coming from the most distinguished writer in the humanistic group, has been snapped up by a long series of persons from the Bolshevist Max Eastman[41] to the Jesuit Francis Burke[42] who are eager on very different grounds, to deny an independent status to humanism. If their interpretation of the *Bookman* article is correct, there will have to be some public explanation. If such an explanation takes place the area of disagreement between us should be reduced as much as possible. My explanation would probably appear in the appendix to a book I am preparing on *Humanism and Education* (a working up of the Clyde Fitch lectures I gave at Amherst).[43] Indeed I have already mentioned you several times both

---

38. "Into the ages of ages," i.e., eternity.
39. More 1930b.
40. "The servant of theology."
41. Max Eastman (1883–1969) was an American writer and radical political activist. Babbitt presumably refers to Eastman's discussions of More and Humanism found in Eastman 1969: esp. 32.
42. Rev. Francis Burke, S. J., was a philosophy professor at Georgetown University. For Burke's work on the potential compatibility of Humanism and Christianity/Catholicism to which Babbitt could be referring, see Burke 1931, 1932a and b. Burke also reviewed More's book *The Catholic Faith* (Burke 1932c).
43. Unfortunately, Babbitt never finished this book. Slayton (1986: 235) and Panichas (1999: 204) note that Babbitt was the Clyde Fitch lecturer at Amherst College in 1930.

by way of agreement and disagreement in the volume of essays[44] which is scheduled for publication early in May. I wish that we might get together and canvasss the whole present situation thoroughly. Could you not visit us (probably at Dublin) on your way to Essex this summer?

Dora joins me in hearty good wishes for your English trip. I am wondering whether this letter will reach Princeton before your actual departure.

Sincerely yours,
Irving Babbitt.

---

59 Battle Road
Princeton, New Jersey
May 17, 1932

My dear Babbitt,

I have been reading your book,[45] and for the most part with great satisfaction. The Introduction in particular impresses me by its gravity and its restrained moderation. On one small point I think love of the epigram[46] has somewhat misled you. The "central peace" I would be the last to deny; the difficulty, and of this there can be no doubt, with Aristotle is that he saw it absolutely abstracted from the "heart of endless agitation." To refuse to acknowledge that one side of Aristotle was the source of the mischievous tendency of scholasticism is just to shut one's eyes to the plain facts of history. That there is another side to Aristotle is also very true.

Of the rest of the book I do not know what part I should prefer. The little essay on Benda is perhaps easier to grasp than most of the others, and may claim precedence in clarity at least. On one or two matters I think you still have something to say to make your position clear. For myself I am even yet a little cloudy as to what you mean by imagination and the supernatural, and their relation one to the other; and I know that other readers have the same feeling of being baffled here. Certainly the imagination is not the perception of resemblances—that faculty, if it has any name, is the reason. You seem to agree with Joubert in his definition of it as that which "gives access to the supersensuous," and in this sense, I take it, you use the canon of "imitation" for

---

44. A footnote in the typescript of this letter reads: "*On Being Creative and Other Essays.*" See Babbitt 1968.

45. Babbitt 1968.

46. For Babbitt's epigraph for the book from Aristotle's *Metaphysics* (1027B), see Babbitt 1968: vii.

art. But what is this supersensuous or supernatural? It cannot be "a certain quality of will," as elsewhere you define the "superrational." One doesn't get access to a quality of the will; the will of right quality is that which is directed to, or by, the supernatural. Is this "supernatural," "supersensuous," "superrational," a reality in the sense of the Platonic Ideas, or is it God, or what? Or is there only "an illusion of a higher reality," given by the imagination, in the Joubertian phrase? And what then is meant by illusion? Does it mean that the supernatural is a reality, which becomes through the imagination an illusion in the sense that it appears to us clad in natural, or sensuous, forms? Or does the imagination simply give us the illusion of something as existent which really does not exist? I cannot escape the feeling that you are a little inclined to play fast and loose with your supernatural, dealing with it as a reality at one time, and then retracting it to a mere quality of the will. One can't, in this world, have his cake and eat it. And I may say that it is just impossible to get the psychological benefits of Christianity while rejecting the Christian (and Platonic) conception of the supernatural as a reality. Nor from Buddhism either, for that matter. Nirvâna is erected upon a vast foundation of the supernatural accepted in the most concrete form, though Nirvâna may be an ultimate escape from that supernatural reality. – Needless to say that these reflections, whether sound or not, have nothing to do with your inculcation of humanism on the purely human level of moderation, restraint, decency, etc, where I am heartily at one with you. And needless also to say that the length of my criticism (or interrogation) is out of proportion to the part of the book that bothers me.

I am myself, as usual, busy with several things at once—a bad habit which plagues me utterly and of which I do not seem to be able to break myself. Cross,[47] who is assisting me with the Anthology, has come and gone. I shall have to be with him at Oxford probably for several months next year; but I have decided that I need not go abroad this year. And this is a release, as Alice and her family are coming over for the summer. Meanwhile I am working hard on a series of Lowell Lectures to be given in the second term of 1933–34.[48] You will smile when you hear that the subject of my lectures—though not the title—is the theology of faith, or the faith of theology, whichever is the cart or the horse. I am not finding them easy to write.

---

47. A footnote in the typescript of this letter reads: "A young English theologian." Frank Leslie Cross (1900–1968) was an English scholar of patristics and an Anglican priest. For their co-edited book, see More and Cross 1935.
48. Dakin (1960: 341) specifies that More delivered his lectures at the Lowell Institute in Boston to small audiences on each Monday and Wednesday in February of 1934.

Mather, I am grieved to say, has turned into a raving fanatic. He has accomplished a great deal, but I never thought he would make himself notorious as a bore.

With affectionate regards to Dora,

Faithfully yours,
Paul E. More.

---

6 Kirkland Road
Cambridge
12 June, 1932

Dear More,

It was good to get that glimpse of you the other day.[49] I wish that such glimpses might be more frequent. I should benefit from the opportunity to talk over certain matters with you. I hope that I did not give you the impression in the *decousu* of conversation that I look upon you in any way as an ex-humanist. The religion of your Greek series, as I have already written you, seems to me not only to be of a high type in itself, but to carry with it a high type of humanism. I have no antipathy to Revelation *per se*. I should regard it as arrogant to make what I am myself capable of achieving in the way of belief the measure of what is desirable or attainable. There is a side of Christianity for which I do feel a real antipathy—namely the fanaticism and intolerance it has so often displayed as a historical religion, so much so that you yourself would have been persecuted for certain statements in your last volume during the genuine ages of faith.

On the basis of our conversations I may decide to write a short appendix to my next volume on "P. E. M. and Humanism." In that case I should probably submit it to you for revision. Certain statements that you made in your *Bookman* article[50] have added complications to a situation that was already complicated. This is of course a matter of regret to me. My regret would be still greater if my temper were primarily that of the crusader, something that in spite of all appearances to the contrary, it is not. I shall of course continue to do all I can to oppose the present naturalistic deliquescence and to coöperate with those who are making a similar effort, even though

---

49. Dakin (1960: 317-18) notes that Babbitt visited More May 1 and 2, 1932, after Babbitt delivered an address at Drew University in New Jersey.
50. More 1930b.

on postulates very different from my own. I am not sure that any of us can accomplish very much. The anti-naturalist who wishes to preserve his peace of mind these days would do well to recall the Hindu maxim and, while working to the utmost, to be not unduly attached to the fruit of his working.

The questions you raise regarding the higher will in its relation to the reason and imagination will receive further attention in my next volume. I do not doubt that my last book would have profited by receiving your criticism in MS., but I hesitated to inflict this task upon you. It is hard to define these ultimate operations of the spirit. One may, however, study them practically and concretely. I am myself a sort of pragmatist of the higher will—which does not mean much more than a thoroughgoing application of the maxim: "By their fruits ye shall know them." – I may say that I do not regard the higher will as subject to either the imagination or reason or as itself involved in the element of illusion. I accept it simply as a primordial *fact*, something of which one is immediately aware. I have always recognized this sense of the "numinous" in your work, though you interpret it apparently in less voluntaristic fashion than I do. On the other hand I am not able to discover much of it in the writings of T. S. Eliot.

I judge Giese's *Sainte-Beuve*[51] rather more favorably than you do. Perhaps I am unduly affected in my estimate by old friendship. My acquaintance with him antedates by several years even, my first meeting with you.

Sincerely,
Irving Babbitt.

---

59 Battle Road
Princeton, New Jersey
June 16, 1932

My dear Babbitt,

I have sent off the razor strop and hope it will reach you in good condition.

The other matters of your letter interested me very much, particularly what you said about religion and the supernatural. Those subjects are indeed difficult to deal with sharply, yet, after all, the Socratic method must be applied there as well as elsewhere. I think if you would define in writing your notion of the higher will as clearly as you defined it to me in conversation, you would satisfy some of your readers who cannot quite make out where

---

51. Giese 1974.

you stand and what you mean. It is another question whether the higher will, so defined, would be sufficient to supply the place in any but an extremely few men, of that sense of the supernatural which they need as a makeweight against the world and the flesh—not to say the devil. We are something more than bare will; we must reckon with the desires, with those of both orders. However you may be *entirely* right; and certainly you are half right.

The appendix on *P. E. M. and Humanism* would interest me at least immensely, and might interest others. But one thing you should bear in mind. I have, and admit that I have, changed in some of my views. Better men than I have done that—both Plato and Aristotle among them. This being so, it is not quite fair to quote two passages, one old the other new, as instances of *present* inconsistency.

I am plugging away at my Lowell Lectures. The fourth, in rough draft, will be finished in a few days; but I doubt if I shall be able to complete the fifth before leaving Princeton, as I had planned to do.

With kind regards to Dora,

Sincerely yours,
Paul E. More.

---

59 Battle Road
Princeton, New Jersey
September 19, 1932

My dear Babbitt,

Your letter came today, and I have forwarded it immediately to Mather. But I fear it will reach the Secretary too late. Will you, by the way, be coming down to the Academy meeting? There is room for you here, of course.

I am glad to hear of your projected book on *Humanism and Education*,[52] certainly a fruitful topic, and I can understand how the work proceeds slowly. As for myself, I did a little reading this summer: Bradley, Hocking (who is Bradley sentimentalized), Kant. I also went through Hooker making excerpts for the *Anthology*. But I wrote nothing. Most of my time was devoted to l'art d'être grand'père.

Sincerely,
P. E. M.

---

52. A footnote in the typescript of this letter reads: "This book was not written, but the material was given in lectures under the Clyde Fitch Foundation at Amherst." On these lectures, see above, this chapter.

59 Battle Road
Princeton, New Jersey
November 18, 1932

My dear Babbitt,

What you say about Mather is sadly true. I once, talking with a little group of men here, ventured the opinion that he was a man of enormous intelligence but totally devoid of principles. One of the group corrected me by saying he had always regarded Mather as incurably frivolous. I have meditated upon the two dicta, and incline to regard my own judgment as the sounder; but I am not too sure. Perhaps the two criticisms amount to the same thing. At bottom I suspect the trouble with Mather, however you formulate it, springs from a complete rejection of the supernatural, at least of the supernatural as a regulative principle.

It is very kind of you to think of me in connection with the Nobel prize; but I fear your energy is wasted. Two years ago my name was, I know, actively considered. A notice in an Italian newspaper stated in fact that at one time my name was the only one before the Committee on Literature. But the Committee decided for Sinclair Lewis. The decision brought out vehement protests in Sweden and England, but *dictum est*.[53] I have some reason to suppose that Bishop Soderblom[54] was behind the movement in my favour. But he is dead, and I should be very much surprised indeed if my name came up again. I have just received several long reviews from Sweden of the translation of *The Chr. Of the N. T.*[55] One of these Shellabarger[56] translated for me. It was highly eulogistic, but ended with the assertion that I had no Sense of religion!

I hope Mercier is not too scholastic to win attention. His earlier book[57] was extraordinarily clear.

---

53. "It has been spoken." In the summer of 1929 rumors circulated that More would win the Nobel Prize for Literature (see Dakin 1960: v, 275; Duggan 1966: 9; Tanner 1998: 186). But Sinclair Lewis received the award in 1930, and in his acceptance speech Lewis criticized the New Humanism (see Hindus 1994: 39). Rumors again circulated about the possibility of More winning the Nobel Prize for Literature in early 1933 (Dakin 1960: 324), but again he did not receive the award.

54. Nathan Söderblom (1866-1931) was a Swedish Lutheran theologian and archbishop who won the Nobel Prize for Peace in 1930.

55. For a list of reviews of the Swedish translation of *The Christ of the New Testament*, see Dakin 1950: 207-8.

56. Samuel Shellabarger (1888-1954) was an American scholar and novelist who taught at Princeton.

57. Mercier 1928.

I presume from your silence on the subject that you have not yet submitted to a thorough physical examination.[58] I wish that you would do this. In fact a man of our age ought to be examined regularly at not too long intervals. You never know where there may be a little breach which the enemy is secretly working to enlarge. And I would take it as a great favour if you would let me know, without delay, what your doctor says.

With kindest regards to Dora,

Faithfully yours,
Paul E. More.

P.S. Collins dined with me Thursday evening. He declares he has made money at some business venture, and is ready not only to continue the *Bookman* but to start a new quarterly. The first issue of the latter is scheduled for January. So he says.[59]

---

59 Battle Road
Princeton, N. J.
December 12, 1932

My dear Babbitt, –

I have heard from Mather that you must undergo some kind of exploratory operation.[60] It isn't pleasant news, but I am hoping that whatever the doctors find will not be serious. And your physical strength and health are all to the good. Nevertheless one can't but be a little anxious, and I shall feel very badly if you and Dora do not keep me promptly informed.

This is my birthday—the sixty-eighth—and not a very happy one. Trouble and anxiety seem to be everywhere about. Not the least of these is the precarious condition of Harry's school.[61] My own health I can say is

---

58. In January of 1932, Babbitt's health began to decline (see Dora Babbitt in Manchester and Shepard 1941: xiii; Slayton 1986: 235; Ryn 1995: xix; Panichas 1999: 204).

59. Seward Collins ultimately ceased publication of the *Bookman* in 1933 and established the *American Review* as its successor. The first issue of the latter would appear in April of 1933 (see Stone 1960: 4). On the *American Review* and its ultimately negative impact on the New Humanism, see the Introduction and Collins's entry in the Biographical Register.

60. A footnote in the typescript of this letter reads: "No exploratory operation was deemed necessary after all."

61. On More's son-in-law Harry Boehme Fine, a teacher and headmaster, see above, chapter 9.

excellent—perhaps I should say, would be excellent were it not that I am driven almost to a phrensy [sic] by my inability to get my Lowell Lectures into decent shape.

Faithfully yours,
Paul E. More.

---

59 Battle Road
Princeton, New Jersey
January 3, 1933

My dear Dora,

I hope your silence means that the Christmas season has kept you busy, and not that Irving is still in bed with no change. Do please let me know, a postal card will do, when any change for the better occurs.

My own Christmas, as you can imagine, wasn't exactly a joyous occasion. But Harry and Darrah brought the children here Sunday morning and a number of unopened presents, and there was a bit of the proper sort of racket for a while.

Let us hope the New Year will bring a bit of cheer to us all.

Sincerely yours,
Paul E. More.

---

59 Battle Road
Princeton, New Jersey
March 18, 1933

My dear Babbitt,

I am sailing for England on the *Westernland* the 7th of April, and shall not return until the middle of August or later.[62] Most of my time must be spent in Oxford finishing up the *Anthology* with Cross, and the date of my returning will depend on how far he has progressed in the work. It will be a joyous day for me when the task is ended. Meanwhile I am toiling over my Lowell Lectures for 1934. Some of the chapters have already been written over three or four times, and still need revision. It is rather humiliating that in all my long experience as a writer I have not gained at all in facility of

---

62. See Dakin 1960: 326.

expression. My days are thus heavily mortgaged. But I am going tomorrow to Williamstown to give a talk to Pratt's boys,[63] and Eliot's visit[64] will steal some of my time. Next autumn I shall be free for the final revision of the Lectures as my days of teaching are ended.[65] The axe has fallen.

But I am writing not so much to send news of myself as to hear about you. Do let me have a line before my sailing about your health. Have you quite got back your normal strength and are you giving your courses again as usual?

I am seeing these days a good deal of Asher Hinds,[66] a most loyal pupil of yours, and one of the very best of our younger men.

With kind regards to Dora,

Sincerely yours,
Paul E. More.

---

59 Battle Road
Princeton, New Jersey
March 24, 1933

My dear Dora,

Your letter, evidently written before the receipt of mine to Irving, came while I was away, giving a talk at Williamstown. I think I wrote about my plans. At any rate it won't do any harm to say again that I am sailing April 7th on the *Westernland*. Most of my time must be spent in Oxford, finishing up the *Anthology* with my collaborator, F. Leslie Cross. I shall of course be with Alice for a time, and have one or two visits to make in the South of England. If possible I shall be back in this country by the middle of August.[67] My address will be: Brown Shipley & co., 123 Pall Mall.

---

63. Dakin (1960: 325) notes that More's lecture at Williams College was "A Sceptical Approach to Religion." James Bissett Pratt (1875–1944) was a distinguished philosopher at Williams.

64. More introduced T. S. Eliot at Princeton, when the latter gave a talk about Biblical influences on English literature on March 23, 1933 (see Dakin 1960: 325). After the lecture, More entertained Eliot and some others at his home.

65. Dakin (1960: 321) notes that More officially retired from teaching at Princeton on April 13, 1933.

66. Asher E. Hinds (1894–1943) was a faculty member in the English department at Princeton. He was among More's group of friends there. Hinds had attended Colby College and then transferred to Harvard. On Hinds, see anon. 1943.

67. Dakin (1960: 332) specifies that More left Liverpool for Montreal on August 4, 1933. He would arrive in Essex, New York, on August 12 (ibid. 333).

T. S. Eliot is now here, though he leaves this afternoon. His lecture last night was rather disappointing as a whole, though lightened here and there by rich epigrammatic sentences. He looks worn to me. And if he has a habit of sitting up, talking, until two-thirty in the morning I can understand why.

I am sorry to hear that Irving is still troubled with that low fever. Is there no wise physician in Boston who can hunt down the ugly streptococcus to its lair?

From this end I can report general good health.

Sincerely yours,
Paul E. More.

"The Isis" Private Hotel
Iffley Road, Oxford
May 14, 1933

My dear Babbitt,

A letter from Dora just before I sailed on the 7th of last month said that you might write me while I was in England. Knowing your anti-epistolary habits I was sceptical of hearing from you; but knowing too the state of your health I cannot help but fear that your silence may be due to the fact of continued fever. I hate to think of you hampered by ill health. Do write me a line, or, if you don't feel like doing so, ask Dora to write. I shall be in England certainly at least until the first of August, and my constant address is: c/o Brown Shipley & Co., 123 Pall Mall. – The voyage over was uneventful and monotonous. From Southampton I got to Oxford the same day, and soon settled myself down here at the Isis, with bedroom and sitting-room at moderate price, very comfortable. My mornings I spend with Cross at the Bodleian or Pusey House going through masses of bulky volumes, some of which, as shown by uncut leaves, have never been read here before. It is pretty frightful; but in their own way some of these old boys were wonders. Their erudition is simply appalling. A book by Barrow[68] for instance on the Papacy makes the modern attacks, even Coulton's,[69] seem like the work of school children in comparison. Fortunately Cross and I get on admirably together, and occasionally I relieve the monotony of the job by telling him ribald tales of the clergy, which he apparently enjoys. For relaxation I get through five or

---

68. Isaac Barrow (1630–1677) was an English mathematician and theologian.
69. G. G. Coulton (1858–1947) was a scholar of medieval history and a critic of Catholicism.

six detective stories a week. What a place Oxford is for books—if you want to buy. A man could furnish a library here at an amazingly low cost. But otherwise books are very hard to come at, and I often wonder how the dons keep up with modern literature—as a matter of fact, they don't. Of course the Bodleian for a job like my present one is unsurpassable; but books are slow in coming, and the facilities for work are very inadequate. I find that the only thing one can get quickly there, is a cold; I have been running a nasty one for five days. – I expect to stay here through the month, pass June with Alice in Edinburgh (you may know she has a daughter), come back to Oxford for two or three weeks, and then to London and the South until I sail. I am hoping the Shafers will be with me here for a while. – No doubt you have seen the first issue of Collins's new venture.[70] I like the simplicity of the format and the lack of advertisements. And his programme is interesting, though it seems to me that Belloc and his henchman Chesterton in their scheme of "distributism" do not reckon with the necessary economic changes since the Renaissance and with the fact that machinery and mass production render any return to the old system practically impossible. As for me, I begin to despond. I see no release from our hideously industrial civilization until the oil wells are dry, and coal is scarce. Oxford from a quiet monkish retreat has become a roaring reality of Ezekiel's vision, wheels grinding incessantly. – I have not tried to go out much or see many people, but I have dined a number of times at Magdalen and have seen something of a rather nice group of Rhodes scholars at Oriel and Queen's.

With kindest regards to Dora,

Faithfully yours,
Paul E. More.

Kingsley Hotel
Hart Street
Bloomsbury Square
London, W.C.I.
July 10, 1933

My dear Babbitt,

I did not see Esther,[71] as she sailed the day after I reached London, but George Howe tells me today that he has received rather distressing news of

---

70. A footnote in the typescript of this letter reads: "*The American Review*." More contributed an essay on Proust to this first issue; see More 1933.

71. Babbitt's daughter, who was married to George Howe.

your condition.[72] The doctors and the hospital seem to have accomplished nothing for you. The news, I say, is most distressing to me. I still hope that you will pull through and take up your work, which, with all you have done, is still unfinished. Your book on humanism and education promised to add the capstone and to bind your theory to your first book on the American college; and now you are lying in bed, and the doctors look wise, no doubt, but bring no help. There are many besides myself who are hanging on the bulletin of your health, but none I am sure so anxiously as myself. My Lowell Lectures are scheduled for February; it will be a sad occasion for me if you have not made a turn for the better by then.

Day after tomorrow I go back to Oxford, where I shall give all my energy to the *Anthology* until I sail the 4th of August. The boat lands at Montreal, and I shall go directly from there to Essex and join Darrah and her family. It will be a happy arrival; Oxford no longer interests me very much. June I spent with Alice in Edinburgh, and went from there to Hereford to be present at the christening of the last grandchild in the cathedral.

Sincerely yours,
Paul E. More.

Kingsley Hotel
Hart Street
Bloomsbury Square
London, W.C.I.
July 10, 1933

My dear Dora,

I have just written to Irving, moved by the distressing news George Howe has given of his condition. I could not say all I felt, and so am adding a word to you. I just cannot reconcile myself to the thought of Irving lying weak and prostrate, and as it seems in real danger of his life. It seems impossible to realize that one so strong as he has been should be broken. I still hope, but meanwhile I want you to know that my heart is with you.

In all sympathy,
Paul E. More.

---

72. Dakin (1960: 328) specifies that on May 26, 1933, More had written to his brother Louis, explaining that Babbitt's daughter Esther had told Robert Shafer that Babbitt was bedridden and being taken care of by a nurse.

The Isis Private Hotel
Iffley Road, Oxford
July 17, 1933

My dear Dora,
Your letter of the 4th came just after I had written to Irving and to you. Then this morning came a note from George Howe announcing the end.[73] I cannot say that Irving's death was a shock to me in the sense that it took me by surprise. Ever since I saw him last November I have felt that something was radically wrong, that something had snapped. If I did not express my full anxiety in my letters you will understand the reason.

I do not know what to say now. It is easy to write or telegraph "sympathy," but the word sounds terribly inadequate. For me it is the breaking of the closest friendship of my life. And though in these latter years we did not often see each other or correspond frequently, he was always as it were the background of all my thinking. My own movement back to Christianity was never a real interruption.

I do hope that Roy Elliott or some other one of Irving's followers will be able to tell the world what it has lost. I say "lost," but I do not for a moment believe his work and ideas will be forgotten. I think he will be remembered as probably the greatest teacher this country has ever produced.

Sincerely and affectionately yours,
Paul E. More.

---

59 Battle Road
Princeton, New Jersey
November 4, 1933

My dear Dora,
I am much obliged to you for sending me a copy of the Bulletin, containing the notice of Irving. It was nicely written, but a very tardy recognition of his powers. You will be interested to know that somewhat reluctantly—for reasons you will understand—I have consented to write an article for the

---

73. Babbitt passed away on July 15, 1933, in his home on Kirkland Road in Cambridge, having completed all his work for the spring term at Harvard. See Dora Babbitt in Manchester and Shepard 1941: xiii; Hough 1952: 135; Slayton 1986: 235; Ryn 1991: xvii and 1995: xix; Panichas 1999: 205.

Toronto Quarterly.[74] It is primarily made up of my reminiscences of Irving as a talker. I sometimes think that he was greater as a teacher than a writer, and greater as a talker, particularly in his earlier years, than a teacher. But the subject is illusive, as you can imagine.

I was not at all well for a while after I came home from Essex, and the composition of my Introduction to the *Anthology*[75] took it out of me heavily. But the writing is done and my health is back to normal. In a few days after one or two minor jobs are finished, I shall be free to settle down to the revision of the Lowell Lectures. These, by the way, I am going to repeat in Cincinnati.[76] That means a little money, much needed,[77] and a long visit with Louis.

Darrah and the children are well. This afternoon I drove with Harry and her over to the George School some ten miles beyond Trenton. The day was just the finest that we produce in Autumn and that you know is very fine indeed. And we had a football victory.

Very sincerely yours,
Paul E. More.

---

59 Battle Road
Princeton, New Jersey
January 19, 1934

Dear Dora,

I am deeply pleased and relieved to hear that you liked my article on Irving.[78] My difficulty in writing was one you comprehended: I wanted to give an impression of his greatness and at the same time I had to make clear that on certain points our views were radically different. That I have succeeded in your estimation means a great deal to me. A copy of the magazine has not yet come to me, but no doubt will arrive before long, together with

---

74. More 1934. This piece later appeared in More's volume *On Being Human* (More 1936d: 25-42) and as the final chapter in *Irving Babbitt: Man and Teacher* (More in Manchester and Odell 1941: 322-37).
75. More and Cross 1935.
76. Dakin (1960: 342) notes that More's repetition of these lectures in Cincinnati in April of 1933 was more successful than their first delivery in February in Boston.
77. According to Dakin (1960: 321), by 1933 More was "living chiefly on property inherited from his wife, which he put in trust with a bank but the value of which the depression had so reduced that he had to relinquish some luxuries, including his car."
78. More 1934.

the fifty reprints which the editor promised me. If by chance you would care to have several of the reprints to send anywhere, I can easily provide them.

My Lowell Lectures have been on the anvil for a couple of years, but even yet are not in satisfactory shape. They will have to pass as they are. If you are interested in hearing any of them, you can get tickets by applying to the Institute—or I could send you a couple. My plan is to come up Monday morning and return each Wednesday night or Thursday morning. I am stopping with my brother at Higham [?], who insists that it will be convenient to drive me back and forth. I shall hope to see you sometime, of course, during the month.

I do not know that there would be any advantage in adding a motto to the book-plate. One however that occurs to me is the Pâli phrase at the end of the footnote on page 53 of *Literature and the American College*. Only I think there is a misprint and that the words should read: *appamādena* sampāde-tha.[79] If used, it would be well to have the diacritical marks verified by some one better versed in Pâli than I am.

Faithfully yours,
Paul E. More.

---

59 Battle Road
Princeton, N. J.
March 10, 1934

Dear Dora, --

Your letter in one sense does not call for an answer, but I should feel very remiss if I did not let you know how deeply I appreciate its intimate frankness. It seems to me that you have got to the heart of Irving's character. There was just that wall about his heart. It is a little thing in that connexion [?], but significant, that for all our long and close friendship we never addressed each other except by our last names. It was more significant that, though he fought with me pertinaciously over my defection, as he thought of it, yet he continued always to recommend my books to his classes. That was his magnanimity. I can imagine that as a husband he was sometimes irritating, but he was loyal to the core, and always, I know, proud of you.

But there is no need for me to go on in that vein. You understand these things better than I can do.

---

79. Cf. Babbitt 1986: 99 n. 9.

Our few talks together while I was in Boston mean a good deal to me. And if anything I said contributed to your memory of a great, one may say an heroic, man, I am more than glad. By the way, one of our best men here, a former pupil of Irving's, seems to have rather a low opinion of Manchester's ability to carry through the sort of book you have in mind.[80] Would Foerster be available?

This is a dull and crudely expressed letter. My excuse is that I have been in New York for several days, lecturing and talking.

Sincerely yours,
Paul E. More.

---

80. More here refers to what would ultimately be Manchester and Shepard 1941.

APPENDIX A

Undated letter, ca. early July 1909[1]

Dear More,

Print Gauss's letter either in whole or in part if you so desire, only in that case you should give me the privilege of reply. Unfortunately, Gauss carries on the discussion in a rather petty and quibbling way, and I should be forced more or less to meet him on his own ground. All this, I fear, would not be very exciting for the readers of the *Nation*, especially as Gauss's letter, from the point of view of literary form, seems to me almost impossible.

Gauss's proof of my "inaccuracy" rests upon an entire misunderstanding of certain statements in my opening paragraphs. There is a part of my second paragraph, especially, which is perhaps over-condensed, and in which I may have failed to make my meaning perfectly plain. I did not intend for a moment to assert that the *Journal of the Goncourts* discusses the incident of the "hundred francs and the smoking chimney," or the question of whether Sainte-Beuve in his small charities was "draping himself for posterity." This whole sentence, i.e. the one alluding to Renan, Taine etc. *is meant to refer only to the sentence that immediately goes before it*, and not to any of the preceding sentences, at least not in detail. What I am trying to say is that in estimating Sainte-Beuve's character, his degree of amiability and attitude toward contemporaries, we should turn to Scherer etc., rather than to the

---

1. This letter from Babbitt to More appears as "Appendix A" in the typescript version of the correspondence. A note in the typescript above it reads: "An undated letter from I. B. to P. E. M. after I. B.'s review of C. M. Harper's book on Sainte-Beuve had appeared in the *Nation*, June 24, 1909 [Babbitt 1909b]. Professor Gauss's criticisms of that review are answered." The letter criticizing Babbitt's review was presumably written by Christian Gauss, later More's friend on the Princeton faculty (see his entry in the Biographical Register). Ultimately, the staff of the *Nation* chose not to publish either Gauss's letter or Babbitt's response. Gauss likely wrote his criticisms soon after Babbitt's review was published; Babbitt's reply was likely composed in early July of 1909. Since the loss of Gauss's letter has rendered Babbitt's response less useful than it would be otherwise, it has been placed in the appendix, rather than in its chronological order in chapter 3.

Goncourts. With this preliminary explanation, I proceed to take up Gauss's points in detail, my numbers referring to the numbers I have jotted down on the margin of his MS.

(1) The book on Chateaubriand was not published until 1861, when Sainte-Beuve had no need to call attention to himself in this way. The incident has a connection with Chateaubriand, because it explains how Sainte-Beuve came to go to Liège and deliver the Chateaubriand lectures at all. Harper's fling at Sainte-Beuve would seem entirely gratuitous. The best proof of the genuineness of Sainte-Beuve's feelings about this absurd incident of the smoking chimney will be found in the letters he wrote at the time (i.e. 1848) and which are included in his collected correspondence.[2]

(2) Troubat's[3] testimony as to Sainte-Beuve may be backed up by that of another of his private secretaries—Jules Levallois.[4] The chapter in Levallois' book on Sainte-Beuve entitled *L'homme privé*[5] illustrates admirably both the genuine kindliness of Sainte-Beuve and his great irritability.

(3) It is Renan himself who says this, and not I. He refers to a certain priestly politeness he practiced in conversation, but did not of course adopt the same method in his writing. I have not time to collect all of Renan's passages about Sainte-Beuve. The first one I open up to, showing the esteem he had for Sainte-Beuve, is in *Souvenirs* p. 354 (French edition) "Je n'ai quelque temps fait cas de la littérature que pour complaire à M. Sainte-Beuve qui avait sur moi beaucoup d'influence. Depuis qu'il est mort, je n'y tiens plus" etc.[6]

(4) I have not accused Taine of lack of character but of excess of logic.[7] Regarding the Greene-Palgrave anecdote about Taine and Tennyson, I do indeed quote it in my text, but suggest in a note that it is not entirely fair to Taine in its implication.[8]

(5) Nothing, apparently, is to Professor Harper's purpose except small gossip. The whole of the article on Sainte-Beuve in Taine's *Derniers Essais*

---

2. On this incident in Babbitt's original review, see Babbitt 1909b: 622.
3. Jules Troubat (1836–1914) was Sainte-Beuve's final secretary, who published some of Sainte-Beuve's posthumous works.
4. Jules Levallois (1829–1903) served as Sainte-Beuve's secretary from 1855 to 1859.
5. Levallois 1872.
6. Renan 1902: 240.
7. Cf. Babbitt 1909b: 623-24.
8. There is no such note in the printed version of the review, so perhaps Babbitt here refers to an earlier draft.

*de critique et d'histoire*⁹ contains testimony of just the kind I had in mind—Gauss's quotation of a phrase from this essay is remarkably disingenuous. The phrase in its context, pp. 52–53, is as follows: "Il a aimé de tout son coeur la vérité vraie, et l'a cherchée de toutes ses forces...telle est l'intention suivie et constante que dissimulent parfois mais *que n'étouffent jamais* les petites malices, les irritations passagères, les complaisances *apparentes*" (*not* evident) "auxquelles il se laissait aller" etc.¹⁰ Taine concludes "On verra qu'à travers plusieurs engagements, il n'a servi qu'un maître, l'esprit humain."¹¹

(6) In the passage referred to (Etudes, Vol. VII, 285)¹² Scherer does not contradict but confirms the passage I take from Sainte-Beuve's "confession."¹³ "Ces hommes-là," (i.e. like Sainte-Beuve) says Scherer, "se posent parfois, mais comme l'oiseau qui a des ailes, et qui le sait; ils se livrent, *mais sans s'aliéner définitivement*; itls conservent ce que j'appellerais un esprit de retour" etc.¹⁴

However, the decisive passages of Scherer that I had in mind are in his *Etudes* Vol. IV,¹⁵ p. 101, where he says "*Sainte-Beuve avait au plus haut degré l'humanité.*"¹⁶ He was deeply touched by the sufferings of the lowly, Scherer goes on to say, and would have been led by his *âme compatissante* to be a good humanitarian if his intellectual keenness had not made it impossible for him to accept the humanitarian Utopias. On p. 109, Scherer says, "Sainte-Beuve a grandi jusqu'à la fin; il n'a pas eu une défaillance; ...Sainte-Beuve est le modèle de l'homme de lettres."¹⁷ p. 110: "On lui a reproché des injustices; je suis persuadé, au contraire, qu'il n'y a jamais eu de critique plus équitable,"¹⁸ (and Scherer goes on and applies this to Sainte-Beuve's criticisms of contemporaries.) p. 111: "Et maintenant il faut prendre congé de lui, congé

---

9. Taine 1929.
10. Taine 1929: 52-53 (the emphasis is Babbitt's).
11. Taine 1929: 61.
12. Scherer 1882.
13. Babbitt did not quote Scherer in his review, so the passage referred to must stem from Gauss's letter.
14. Scherer 1882: 285 (the emphasis is Babbitt's).
15. Scherer 1886.
16. Scherer 1886: 101. The exact quote is: "Il [Saint-Beuve] avait, au plus haut degré, l'*humanité*" (emphasis in the original).
17. Scherer 1886: 109.
18. Scherer 1886: 110. The typescript of this letter mistakenly reads "100," but the quotation is found on 110.

de cette lucide intelligence, de cet écrivain merveilleux, de ce causer charmant, de *cet indulgent ami*," etc.[19]

(7) Flaubert, like the Goncourts, was disgruntled at Sainte-Beuve for not doing justice, as he thought, to his own writings, especially to Salammbô. Sainte-Beuve as a humanist protested against the abuse of local color, the crudity and brutality of Flaubert's romanticism and naturalism. See articles on Salammbô in *Nouveaux Lundis* IV, and Flaubert's irritated reply, printed in the appendix. Besides, the insinuation of Flaubert quoted by Gauss, is something very different from asserting that a man is "draping himself for posterity," even in his small acts of charity.

(8) I should like to know what these "several" other instances of inaccuracy are.

(9) Why should the fact that a man is, like La Rochefoucauld, skeptical of the disinterestedness of human nature keep him from being a great literary portrait painter? What is meant by the Platonism of Sainte-Beuve? The whole argument here escapes me.

(10) I should think it ought to be plain that I have used the line from Herrick merely as a less dry and matter-of-fact way of saying that though Sainte-Beuve was unchaste in his private life, his writings are in general chaste.[20] He has kept this element "so completely" out of his writings—i.e. out of about forty-nine fiftieths of them. The remaining one-fiftieth in which he speaks of his love affairs is read only by Sainte-Beuve specialists and by people in search of scandal.

(11) This sentence should be interpreted in the light of the previous paragraph. Sainte-Beuve says he had passed through various parties but had not "bound himself to them irrevocably." Everybody who has studied Sainte-Beuve knows that for a time, to borrow his own phrase, he "alienated his will under the effect of a charm" (i.e. Madame Hugo). But he was not very long in breaking away from the romanticists, nor from any other groups with which he was at various times affiliated.

(12) This is just the petty personal way of interpreting Sainte-Beuve's opinions against which I protest. According to most French critics of any authority, the *Lily in the Valley* represents Balzac at his worst. Sainte-Beuve did substantial justice to Balzac in the article published shortly after Balzac's death. When the smoke of the romantic and naturalistic movements clears away, I believe that Sainte-Beuve will be seen to have come closer to the truth

---

19. Scherer 1886: 111 (the emphasis is Babbitt's).
20. See Babbitt 1909b: 622.

in his judgments on contemporaries than is generally supposed. In fact, I noticed when I was in Paris last year that opinion is already beginning to veer around on this point. Lasserre's book has been of help here.

You are free to send on any or all parts of this letter to Gauss. If I have answered his communication as fully as I have, it is because I am anxious not to embarrass you in any way in your editing of the "Nation."

Very sincerely yours,
Irving Babbitt.

APPENDIX B

Notes on More's "Definitions of Dualism" [ultimately published in More 1967a: 247-302], associated with Babbitt's letter to More of September 26, 1911.[1]

p. 4, line 2: I think I should substitute the word inner check or some other word for "it."[2]

p. 4-5, VII-VIII: I do not feel sure about your definition of emotion and pleasure and pain. So many different things are connoted by these words. The pains of child birth for example are said to be attended with a sense of elation.[3]

p. 6, XI (four lines from bottom): "Vanity....possession of joy and hope." Certain romanticists based their vanity on the fact that they were unique in suffering, unique, not in joy and hope but in sorrow and despair. Vanity has such manifold forms that some persons may think your definition a bit summary.[4]

p. 7, XII: "It may be...control of this check." Difficult. When I mark a passage in this way I do not always mean to imply that you can change it or that it ought to be changed but that even the reader of some philosophical training will, to judge from my own experience, find it obscure.[5]

p. 9, XVII: "The emotional...flux." Difficult.[6]

---

1. These notes pertain to a draft of More's "Definitions of Dualism," which was ultimately published in the eighth series of *Shelburne Essays*. Where possible, Babbitt's commentary has been juxtaposed with More's published version. For the letter of September 26, 1911, see above, chapter 3.
2. This comment likely corresponds to one of the sentences found in More 1967a: 248.
3. See More 1967a: 251-52.
4. Cf. More 1967a: 253-54. More obviously altered his discussion of vanity in response to Babbitt's criticisms.
5. In the published version of the definitions (More 1967a: 254) this sentence reads: "It may be surmised, but only surmised, that in some way the faculties themselves have been created by the action of a force within the flux obedient to the inner check, and that the regularity of their function depends on the fulness [sic] of the control of this check."
6. No sentence in section XVII in the published version of the definitions (More 1967a:

412   *Appendix B*

p. 10: (XIX)⁷ "impulses...units." Difficult.⁸

p. 12, XXII: "Beyond...motion." Difficult.⁹

p. 13-14, XXVI: This passage has imaginative quality. I wonder, however, whether in some of your illustrations ("stealthy instincts," etc.) you are not confusing *élan vital* and *frein vital*.¹⁰

p. 15, XXIX: "It differs...soul." Difficult.¹¹

p. 15, XXX: "Distinctions of the senses." Do you not need to add "or intellect"? Strictly speaking only the confusion of the arts (as opposed to the *genres* in the domain of each art) confuses the distinctions of the senses.¹²

p. 19, XXXVII: "But also" etc. I am not sure that also comes in very elegantly here. Possibly "But neither should it be" etc. might be better.¹³

p. 19, XXXVIII: "then proceeds...denied." This is clear enough on reflection. I wonder however whether you might not make it still clearer by adding a sentence or so.¹⁴

p. 20, XLI: In this very condensed form, your definition of stoics and epicureans is difficult, especially perhaps the word "reintegrated."¹⁵

p. 22, XLVII: (XLVI) "In all...power." Difficult.¹⁶

p. 22, XLVIII: (XLVII) Line 4. Do you not need some such word as spiritual with health?¹⁷

p. 24, LII: (LI) I do not like the transitive use of refraining.¹⁸

256-57) corresponds with this sentence. But cf. this part of the published section XVI (256): "The concrete emotion of passing time seems to spring from a divergence between the inner and the outer flux."

7. These parenthetical numbers, penciled in the typescript version of the notes, denote the proper section of the published version of "Definitions of Dualism."

8. Cf. More 1967a: 257: "The objective reason deals, not with the whole field of experience, but with the impulses that arise under the immediate impact of impressions from the outer world, by its perception of sameness and difference conceiving this material as more or less comprehensive units."

9. More evidently altered this sentence in light of Babbitt's criticism; cf. More 1967a: 258-59.

10. Cf. More 1967a: 261-62, with the quotation on 262.

11. Cf. More 1967a: 263: "It differs from the pathetic fallacy by implying a distinct and more or less revocable addition to nature rather than a fusion of nature and the soul."

12. Cf. More 1967a: 263-64.

13. Cf. More 1967a: 267: "But neither should it be forgotten that...."

14. More appears not to have added such a sentence. See More 1967a: 268.

15. Cf. More 1967a: 270. The word "reintegrated" was removed.

16. More appears to have altered this sentence. Cf. More 1967a: 272-73.

17. Cf. More 1967a: 273: "Philosophy and moral health may not wholly coincide in a man's life, but each is the natural reinforcement of the other, and in their perfection they cannot exist apart."

18. More apparently decided to keep the original phrase in the published version. Cf. More 1967a: 274: "Since the will is the result of eliminating or refraining detrimental impulses, it

p. 26, LVI: (LVII) "Unless the soul" etc. I think I should prefer "the soul, unless conceived as etc., is indistinguishable" etc.[19]

p. 28, LIX: "function of emotion" strikes me as heavy.[20]

p. 31, LXVI: (LXVII) "Chance and fate." I think I should add some such phrase as "in the deterministic sense" after fate or simply substitute "determinism." Fate in the Calvinistic and fate in the scientific or naturalistic sense are entirely different things and have entirely different moral effects on those who accept them.[21]

p. 33, LXIX: (LXX) "is to call...coming together." Difficult.[22]

p. 38, LXXIX: I am not sure I like the word "nature" here. Are you not giving to mythology a somewhat broader sense?[23]

p. 40: (LXXXIII) "The insoluble...attention." Difficult.[24]

p. 42, LXXXVII: I do not especially like "word of magic." Word to conjure by or some such expression would in my opinion be better. "Fundamental existence" does not seem to me very happy though I do not know that you can improve on it.[25]

p. 43, LXXXVIII: "heart...universe." Difficult.[26]

p. 43, LXXXIX: "unsupported...God." The word God by itself does not mean much. Personal God would of course convey something comparatively definite. I wonder whether this whole clause is not going to antagonize needlessly certain readers whose sympathies would be with you in nearly everything else you have said.[27]

---

may, by an easy transference of language, be called the will to refrain."

19. Cf. More 1967a: 279: "the soul, unless it is conceived as including the inner check...."

20. More appears to have struck this phrase. Cf. More 1967a: 280.

21. Cf. More 1967a: 285: "Chance and fate, in the deterministic sense, accident and natural law, are not contradictory ideas, but different aspects only of the flux."

22. Cf. More 1967a: 287: "Amid the ceaseless change and heterogeneous motion of the flux the effect of the inner check is to call a certain pause and so to create the opportunity of fusing a present and a past impulse."

23. More evidently took Babbitt's advice here. Cf. More 1967a: 294-95.

24. Cf. More 1967a: 297: "The insoluble paradox of grace and free-will is the mythological counterpart of the relation of the inner check and attention...."

25. Cf. More 1967a: 299. The phrase "word of magic" was removed and "fundamental existence" was changed to "fundamental reality."

26. Cf. More 1967a: 300-1.

27. Cf. More 1967a: 301.

APPENDIX C

A letter from Irving Babbitt to Louis T. More, Paul More's younger brother, which was included in the typescript version of the Babbitt-More correspondence.

6 Kirkland Road, Cambridge,
30 Dec. 1918

Prof. Louis T. More[1]
University of Cincinnati
Cincinnati, Ohio.

My dear More:
    I have taken the liberty of giving a card for you to Mademoiselle Marfaing,[2] Professor in the Lycée of Bordeaux, who is in this country on a travelling fellowship. Any little kindness you can show her will be greatly appreciated. She is on her way to the Pacific coast. I imagine that she would be glad to give a lecture if there is any opening for that sort of thing in Cincinnati. I believe she has lantern slides of Reims where she resided for some time. Her French is of the very best. The only out I discovered about her is that she is a little lacking in what Mrs. Drew[3] calls a "sense of departure"; and so you must have an "engagement" ready if she tends to encroach on your time.
    I am heartily glad to see your declaration of principles in the recent bulletin of the Assc'n of Un. Professors. It is the real stuff. I should think you would get a considerable following if only because of the clause relating to salaries.
    It seems practically certain now that I am going to go on a lecturing trip, probably next March, to various universities of the Middle West—especially Wisconsin, Minnesota, and Illinois. There is just a possibility that I might be

---

1. On Louis T. More, Paul More's younger brother, see his entry in the Biographical Register.
2. Marfaing appears to have been offering lectures on educational topics in the US around this time.
3. Presumably, Babbitt here refers to his mother-in-law, Anna Davis Drew (1851–1932).

able to include Cincinnati for one lecture on some such topic as "Rousseau and Contemporary Education" or a more specifically literary topic if preferred. My terms would be $75. I should know inside the next two or three weeks whether I can accept an offer from you and in the meanwhile shall understand perfectly if you do not feel in a position to make one.

Give my regards to Mrs. More. I hope that you are all keeping well these sickly times.[4]

Sincerely,
Irving Babbitt

---

4. Presumably, Babbitt here refers to the influenza epidemic of 1918.

Biographical Register

Dora (Drew) Babbitt (1877–1944): Irving Babbitt's wife Dora was born and raised in China, the daughter of the Commissioner of Imperial Customs at Tianjin. An undergraduate at Radcliffe College who had formerly taken one of Babbitt's classes, she began a romantic relationship with him as a senior in 1899. When Irving proposed to Dora, she returned to China to ponder her response; the two met in London during the summer of the following year and married. At that point Irving was 35 and Dora 23. The two then moved to a rented home at 6 Kirkland Road near the Harvard campus where they would raise a family. Their daughter Esther was born in 1901; their son Edward followed in 1903. Although her husband was not a churchgoer, Dora, raised as a Unitarian, attended non-denominational services at Harvard. The two had occasional disagreements about China: Irving stressed that he understood the country because he had studied Confucius, and Dora suggested that she knew China better because she had lived there. Dora was intimately involved in Irving's writing. After Irving had produced a draft of his books in shorthand, she would copy it out for him in longhand. Upon her husband's untimely death in 1933, Dora worked hard to aid his legacy. She, for example, had her husband's translation of *The Dhammapada* posthumously published in 1936. Dora donated the contents of the Irving Babbitt Papers to the Harvard University Archives, produced the typescript version of the Babbitt–More correspondence to be found among these papers, and contributed a helpful (albeit brief) biographical essay on her husband to Frederick Manchester and Odell Shepard's edited volume *Irving Babbitt: Man and Teacher* (1941). On Dora Babbitt, see, e.g., the references to her in Dakin 1960; Nevin 1984: 13, 17; and Brennan and Yarbrough 1987: 25-26, 65, 75.

Katharine Babbitt (1871–1925): Irving Babbitt's beloved younger sister Katharine was a French instructor at Miss Porter's School in Farmington, Connecticut. Like Irving a graduate of Woodward High School in Cincinnati, she took French courses at Radcliffe College. Irving had great respect for Katharine's intellect and asked for her feedback on his writings. Katharine was also on good terms with Paul More; in the Babbitt–More correspondence More refers to a tie she sent him, which he wore to great effect when lecturing at Bryn Mawr. In addition to her teaching duties, Katharine edited Ludovic Halévy's *L'Abbé Constantin* (1915) and translated René Nicolas's *Campaign Diary of a French Officer* (1917) and Henriette Cuvru-Magot's *Beyond the Marne* (1918). Unfortunately, on November 14, 1925, Katharine was struck by a car when crossing the highway between the two parts of Miss Porter's School. She passed away in a hospital in Hartford three days later. Always close with his sister, Irving Babbitt was greatly distraught over her death. On Katharine Babbitt, see the references to her in Dakin 1960 and Slayton 1986.

Bernard Bandler II (1904–1983): A native of New York, Bandler received an A.B. and an M.A. in philosophy from Harvard University, where he studied with and admired Irving Babbitt. In the summer of 1928 Bandler became one of the editors of the *Hound & Horn*, a literary quarterly founded in 1927 by the Harvard undergraduates Lincoln Kirstein and Varian Fry. Upon joining the *Hound & Horn*'s editorial staff, Bandler helped redirect the journal from a Harvard miscellany to a prominent cultural outlet focused on the New Humanism. Bandler wrote essays and reviews in the magazine on Babbitt and Paul More and even contributed to Norman Foerster's collective manifesto *Humanism and America* (1930). Although deeply impressed with Babbitt's learnedness and pedagogical skills, Bandler also had reservations about the movement, which he perceived to be lacking in a positive program. His mixed feelings about Humanism can be gleaned from his contribution to *A Critique of Humanism*, C. Hartley Grattan's book-length attack on the movement, which appeared later in 1930. Miffed that most of the Humanists—including Babbitt and More—would no longer contribute to the *Hound & Horn*, Bandler soon abandoned his revisionist Humanism in favor of Southern Agrarianism. He left the staff of the *Hound & Horn* in 1932 to enter medical school at Columbia University, ultimately to become a prominent psychiatrist and professor at the Boston University School of Medicine. On Bandler and the history of the *Hound & Horn*, see Greenbaum 1966; Hamovitch 1982; Eliot 2015 41 n. 3.

Van Wyck Brooks (1886–1963): A renowned literary critic, biographer, and historian, Brooks was born in Plainfield, New Jersey, the son of a stockbroker. After demonstrating great promise at local schools, he earned an A.B. at Harvard University in three years, graduating in 1907. There he wrote poetry, served as an editor of the university's literary magazine, and studied with, among others, Irving Babbitt. Brooks greatly respected Babbitt's intellect but disliked what he took to be his elitist and conservative sensibilities. In the first volume of his autobiography, he penned a vivid portrait of Babbitt's classes, likening his former teacher to a latter-day Dr. Johnson. For his part, Babbitt appears to have thought highly of Brooks: as the Babbitt–More correspondence documents, in 1909 Babbitt recommended Brooks as a possible editorial assistant for Paul More at the *Nation*. Having abandoned poetry for criticism soon after graduation, Brooks worked various jobs in the literary world, including a visiting instructorship at Stanford University, and wrote a series of books that established him as one of the most heralded critics of his generation. He won a Pulitzer Prize for history and a National Book Award for nonfiction. A promoter of Walt Whitman and kindred poets whose work underscored the democratic potential of the US, Brooks was naturally critical of the New Humanism. His book *Letters and Leadership* (1918), for example, provides a negative portrait of More. In part for similar reasons, Brooks despised the writings of his fellow Harvardian T. S. Eliot. On Brooks, see Brooks 1954; Spiller 1970; Hoopes 1977; O'Connor 1986.

W. C. Brownell (1851–1928): A morally engaged literary and art critic influenced by Sainte-Beuve and Matthew Arnold, William Crary Brownell shared much in common with Irving Babbitt and Paul More, whom he appears to have influenced. Born in New York City to a well-to-do family, he graduated from Amherst College and first worked in journalism, most notably at the *Nation*. From 1881 to 1884 Brownell and his wealthy wife lived in Europe. Returning to the US, Brownell joined the staff of the *Philadelphia Press*. Four years later he started at the Charles Scribner's Sons publishing firm, where he would serve as an editor and literary advisor for the remainder of his life. This firm published all his books; by the early years of the twentieth century Brownell enjoyed an enviable reputation as a literary critic and gentleman-scholar. His preference for creative restraint and his distaste for aestheticism unmoored from morals speak to his overlaps with what would become the New Humanism. The same may be said for Brownell's antipathy for the perceived decay of literary standards and concomitant avoidance of contemporary writers. Although such views allied him with Babbitt and More, Brownell had different political inclinations: throughout his life he was a moderate progressive. The Babbitt–More correspondence demonstrates that the two leaders of Humanism were on good terms with Brownell, although they occasionally questioned his literary judgments. For more on Brownell, see Mercier 1928: 1–48; Nevin 1988, which also supplies helpful bibliographical references.

Seward B. Collins (1899–1952): A native of upstate New York, Collins was a wealthy, well-connected journalist, editor, and writer. The heir of a tobacco fortune (his father Henry became a high-powered executive at the United Cigar Stores), he attended elite preparatory schools and then Princeton University. After a spell in the US propaganda office in Madrid, Collins inhabited a fancy residence on Park Avenue in New York City. His friends included F. Scott Fitzgerald, Theodore Dreiser, H. L. Mencken, and Edmund Wilson, the latter of whom secured employment for Collins at *Vanity Fair*. Although he thrived there, in either 1922 or 1923 Collins left for California, to recover from a case of tuberculosis. Upon his return, he moved to his family's opulent estate in Connecticut. In 1926 Collins had a stormy love affair with Dorothy Parker, whom he almost wed. He purchased the *Bookman*, then a middle-brow literary journal, in 1927. When he clashed with its editor, his erstwhile friend Burton Rascoe, Collins took over the position the following year. Up to this time, Collins was a liberal activist, strongly supporting Sacco and Vanzetti, for example. But by 1929 he had drifted rightwards. For a spell Collins embraced the New Humanism, turning the *Bookman* into a veritable house organ for the movement. A zealous and erratic convert, Collins was on friendly terms with Irving Babbitt and Paul More, but both men appear to have viewed him with suspicion. He closed the *Bookman* in 1933, replacing it with his new magazine, the *American Review*. Intended as a "Right-Wing miscellany," the *Review* was more openly political than its predecessor; it published articles by New Humanists, Southern Agrarians, Distributists, and monarchists, among others. By the appearance of its first issue, Collins had departed from the New Humanism in favor of Distributism and a self-styled American Fascism. The magazine published some disturbing content, which included anti-Semitism, anti-Catholicism, anti-Black racism, and praise for Mussolini. Even so, some of the New Humanists—including More—continued to contribute to the *Review*. The publication of a disastrous interview with Collins in a pro-Communist magazine in 1936 led to the failure of his magazine; the interview made Collins seem like a bigoted and malignant fool. An unreliable editor possibly suffering from clinical depression, Collins embarrassed his Southern Agrarian contributors, a number of whom stopped publishing in the *Review*. Starved of contributors, the magazine ended its run in 1937. After a failed attempt to operate a right-wing bookstore in New York City, Collins and his wife Dorothea Brande departed for New Hampshire. Although no longer actively contributing to journalism, Collins remained an FBI subject and aided various isolationist and right-wing political causes, prior to his death from a heart attack in 1952. Long reviled as the "Park Avenue Fascist," Collins harmed the New Humanist movement through his temporary association with it, even though Babbitt and More disagreed with him on many political issues. For more on Collins, see above all Tucker 2006. See also Stone 1960.

Charles W. Eliot (1834–1926): As the president of Harvard University from 1869 to 1909, Eliot was Irving Babbitt's longstanding curricular and pedagogical bête noir, although the two men appear to have been on cordial terms. Born into an influential Harvardian family from Boston, Eliot attended the Boston Latin School and then Harvard (class of 1853). A strong student, he became focused chiefly on chemistry and minerology. In part because Harvard gave short shrift to these subjects during his undergraduate days, Eliot grew critical of the institution's prescribed, classics-heavy curriculum. Appointed a tutor in mathematics at his alma mater after graduation, he earned a promotion to an assistant professorship in mathematics and chemistry in 1858 and a professorship in chemistry at Harvard's Lawrence Scientific School in 1861. Eliot soon showed a talent for administrative work, but he lacked the training requisite for scholarly research and hence was passed over for the coveted Rumford Professorship of Chemistry. Eliot thus resigned from Harvard in 1863, taking his family on a two-year trip to Europe, where he studied higher education on the continent. Upon his return, he took up a professorship in chemistry at the newly founded Massachusetts Institute of Technology. Two articles on polytechnic instruction and higher learning that appeared in the *Atlantic Monthly* in 1869 helped him land the position of Harvard's next president, at the tender age of thirty-five. As the institution's leader for forty years, Eliot modernized Harvard, replacing the remnants of its prescribed classical curriculum with almost complete curricular free-election. Eliot raised great sums of money for Harvard, ensuring the vast expansion of its faculty, which allowed it to offer numerous courses in a wide array of disciplines. He also established serious graduate study at Harvard and greatly improved the institution's professional schools. A pedagogical Darwinian whose curricular views were influenced by the British scientist and philosopher Herbert Spencer, Eliot was hostile to the classics and humanism. Hence Babbitt deemed him a "scientific naturalist" par excellence. Babbitt criticized Eliot's approach to education in many writings, especially *Literature and the American College* (1908) and "President Eliot and American Education" (1920). For more on Eliot, see, e.g., James 1930; Hawkins 1972; Adler 2020.

T. S. Eliot (1888–1965): The celebrated poet, critic, playwright, and editor Thomas Stearns Eliot, who won the Nobel Prize in Literature in 1948, was the most heralded writer associated with the New Humanism. A scion of blue-blooded New England stock (he counted Harvard president Charles W. Eliot among his relatives), Eliot was born and raised in St. Louis, Missouri, where he attended the Smith Academy (1898–1905). Paul More, who knew Eliot's family in St. Louis, had taught Eliot's brother Henry at the Smith Academy. After a year at Milton Academy in Massachusetts (1905–06), T. S. Eliot entered Harvard University, from which he would earn an A.B. (1909) and an A.M. (1911). During his senior year he enrolled in Irving Babbitt's course devoted to French literary criticism and was enthralled by him. One can spy Babbitt's influence especially in Eliot's early criticism, which often demonstrates both an anti-romanticism and deep regard for tradition linked to Babbitt's Humanism. After further graduate work at Harvard, the Sorbonne, and Oxford, Eliot ultimately settled in England, where he worked successively as a teacher, a banker, and an editor at the publishing house of Faber and Faber. All the while he became one of the most heralded poets and critics of the twentieth century. From 1922 to 1939, his small-circulation magazine the *Criterion* published highly esteemed writing, including his famous poem *The Waste Land* in its inaugural issue. Various contributors to Eliot's *Criterion*—including Eliot himself—weighed the pros and cons of the New Humanism in its pages. Although he was quick to note Babbitt's impact on him, by the later 1920s Eliot had become a more qualified proponent of Humanism. Eliot's baptism into the Anglican Communion in 1927 attracted him to Paul More, whose heterodox Anglo-Catholicism closely matched Eliot's own. Having previously met More at Babbitt's house when a student at Harvard, Eliot now grew close to More, who became a mentor and good friend. Eliot championed More's *The Greek Tradition* as his greatest work and tried diligently to secure a publisher for his books *Anglicanism* (1935) and *Pages from an Oxford Diary* (1937). Although a contributor to Norman Foerster's collective manifesto *Humanism and America* (1930), Eliot by that time had expressed doubts about Babbitt's decidedly ecumenical approach to revealed religion. He thereby increased the squabbles in the Humanist camp over religious matters. Eliot had also become a follower of the monarchist and proto-fascist Charles Maurras, whose reactionary politics Babbitt had sharply criticized. When Eliot returned to Harvard to deliver the prestigious Charles Eliot Norton lectures in 1932, he twice visited with Babbitt, until Babbitt's illness made further contact impossible. Eliot wrote tributes to both Babbitt (in Manchester and Shepard 1941: 101-4) and More (1937b), deeming them exceedingly wise men who had a lifelong impact on him. On Eliot's views on and relationship with Babbitt and More, see, e.g., T. S. Eliot 1928, 1930, 1937a and b, and in Manchester and Shepard 1941: 101-4; Tanner 1971; Jamieson 1986; Hindus 1994: 44-52.

G. R. Elliott (1883-1963): George Roy Elliott, a native of London, Ontario, who became a naturalized citizen of the United States, was an English professor and literary critic associated with the New Humanism. He earned a B.A. from the University of Toronto in 1904 and a Ph.D. from the University of Jena in 1908. After working as an instructor in English at the University of Wisconsin, Elliott joined the faculty of Bowdoin College in 1913. While there Elliott corresponded with Babbitt and ultimately met him after attending one of his class lectures at Harvard. This meeting helped turn Elliott into a prominent second-generation Humanist. A critic with particular interest in Shakespeare, he composed many books and essays, such as *The Cycle of Modern Poetry* (1929) and *Humanism and Imagination* (1938). From 1925 until his retirement in 1950, Elliott was a professor of English at Amherst College, where he befriended and was an important early booster of fellow faculty member Robert Frost. An Anglican, Elliott attempted to calm the waters in the religious disputes over the New Humanism. On Elliott, see his semi-autobiographical contribution to Manchester and Shepard 1941 (144-64); anon. 1963; and the references to him in Brennan and Yarbrough 1987.

Norman Foerster (1887-1972): The son of a composer, conductor, and music teacher in Pittsburgh, Pennsylvania, Foerster received an A.B. from Harvard University in 1910. There he edited the *Harvard Monthly*, wrote two prize-winning essays, and studied with Irving Babbitt. Foerster became one of Babbitt's most dedicated followers, especially in the realm of education. He attended graduate school at the University of Wisconsin, where he earned an M.A. in English in 1912. Chiefly interested in a career as a critic, essayist, and teacher in the Humanist vein, Foerster decided against further studies toward a Ph.D. In 1914 he landed an appointment as an associate professor of English at the University of North Carolina at Chapel Hill. By 1930 Foerster had earned a reputation as a prominent second-generation Humanist. His edited collection *Humanism and America* (1930), which included contributions from Babbitt and Paul More, jumpstarted the great public controversy over the New Humanism in the US. During the year this book was published, Foerster moved to the University of Iowa, where he would serve as the director of its newly founded School of Letters. As an administrator at

Iowa Foerster attempted—with varying degrees of success—to implement a curriculum more amenable to Humanism. He was instrumental in founding the famed Iowa Writers' Workshop. Clashes with administrators and faculty members hostile to his pedagogical ideals compelled him to resign his post at Iowa in 1944. He then returned to the University of North Carolina, where he taught until the early 1950s, when he retired and moved to California. In addition to his administrative work, Foerster contributed numerous books and essays on literary criticism and American higher education. In his writings on education, he demonstrated his steadfast devotion to Babbitt's ideas, although he grew more amenable to a populist approach to the humanities over time. On Foerster, see Mercier 1948: 165-88; Flanagan 1971; Barney 1974: 157-93; Hoeveler 1977: 19-22, 120-22; Graff 1987: 138.

Prosser Hall Frye (1866-1934): Born in New York City and raised in Andover, Massachusetts, Frye earned an A.B. from Harvard University in 1889. A recipient of an A.M. from Trinity College in Hartford, Connecticut, in 1892, he became a member of the rhetoric department at the University of Nebraska in Lincoln in 1896, a position he would hold for the remainder of his life. Although as a young man a materialist in the Darwinian-Spencerian mold, Frye turned to Humanism and Platonic dualism upon meeting Paul Elmer More's younger brother Louis, then a fellow faculty member at Nebraska. Having abandoned his earlier interest in writing poetry, Frye became a literary critic, contributing books in the New Humanist vein such as *Romance and Tragedy* (1922) and *Visions and Chimeras* (1929). In 1913 he founded the *Mid-West Quarterly*, a journal highly sympathetic to Humanism that lasted until 1918. Frye was a close and longstanding friend of Paul More, though in his approach to revealed religion he more closely matched Babbitt's outlook. On Frye, see the many references to him in Dakin 1960, as well as Stock 1975 and 1979.

Christian Gauss (1878-1951): The son of German immigrants, Gauss was a professor of French literature, an academic administrator, and a writer with broad interests. Born in Ann Arbor, Michigan, he earned an A.B. at the University of Michigan in 1898 and served as an instructor there, before taking a position in modern languages at Lehigh University in 1901. Four years later Woodrow Wilson made Gauss an assistant professor at Princeton; he became a full professor there in 1907. The chair of Princeton's modern languages department from 1912 to 1936, Gauss served as the Dean of the College from 1925 to 1945. Popular with students and highly dedicated to Princeton, he edited the *Princeton Alumni Weekly* and was a vice president of the Princeton University Press. He retired in 1946. A good friend of Paul More at Princeton, Gauss appears in Edmund Wilson's description of a visit to More's house in late 1929 (see Wilson 1948: 3-4). On Gauss, see anon. 1951a and b.

William F. Giese (1864–1943): A contemporary and friend of Irving Babbitt since their freshman years at Harvard, Giese was a professor of French and Spanish at the University of Wisconsin associated with the Humanist movement. His book *Victor Hugo: The Man and the Poet* (1926), a polemic in keeping with the Humanist viewpoint, contains an epigraph from Babbitt. When Babbitt's *Literature and the American College* (1908) proved a commercial failure, Giese lent Babbitt $500 to get his next monograph in print. He co-edited Babbitt's posthumous essay collection, *Spanish Character and Other Essays* (1940), along with his colleague Frederick A. Manchester and his daughter Rachel Giese. On William Giese, see Giese's useful contribution to Manchester and Shepard 1941 (1-25); Brennan and Yarbrough 1987: 10-12, 21, 23, 26.

Henry Holt (1840–1926): The Baltimore-born Holt, who earned an A.B. from Yale University in 1862, was widely considered the dean of American publishers. After becoming disenchanted with the legal profession while a student at the Columbia Law School, Holt turned to a career in publishing, first working at George P. Putnam's publishing house. He ultimately co-founded his own successful and influential firm, which was eventually called Henry Holt & Co. At age seventy-four, Holt in retirement decided to start a magazine, originally called the *Unpopular Review* but later rechristened the *Unpartizan Review*. He was on friendly terms with Paul Elmer More and, to a lesser extent, Irving Babbitt. More, in fact, served as both an unofficial and official editor of Holt's magazine, to which he contributed regularly, prior to Holt's decision to cease publication in 1921. Largely in tune with More's and Babbitt's political views, in the summer Holt occasionally hosted them at his estate in Burlington, Vermont, which he called "Fairholt." His books include *The Publishing Reminiscences of Mr. Henry Holt* (1910) and *The Cosmic Relations and Immortality* (1919). On Holt, see, e.g., anon. 1926.

George Lyman Kittredge (1860–1941): A renowned and decorated authority on Shakespeare, Chaucer, and *Beowulf*, Kittredge, known affectionately among his students as "Kitty," became something of a pedagogical legend at Harvard University, where he taught for almost fifty years. A Boston native of Mayflower stock, he graduated from Harvard with an A.B. in 1882. After six years teaching Latin at Phillips Exeter Academy in New Hampshire, Kittredge joined the English faculty at Harvard in 1888. By 1892 he had become the Gurney Professor of English there. Although he never earned a Ph.D., Kittredge, like his mentor Francis James Child, was a prominent proponent of the German-influenced philological school of scholarship. The author or co-author of thirteen books, he also edited numerous collections of poetry and the complete works of Shakespeare. Kittredge was famous at Harvard especially for his course English 2, an advanced and exacting examination of Shakespeare's plays. Irving Babbitt had enrolled in this course during his senior year, earning an uncharacteristically low grade from Kittredge. Babbitt condemned Kittredge as the chief figure in Harvard's Philological Syndicate, considering Kittredge's highly technical approach to literature trifling. Undoubtedly Kittredge's animus towards Babbitt's views impeded the latter's career at Harvard. In a hand-written note in his personal copy of the edited collection *Irving Babbitt: Man and Teacher*, Odell Shepard, who received his Ph.D. in English at Harvard in 1916, wrote, "Someone suggested that I. B. should be one of the readers of my Doctoral Thesis. G. L. Kittredge replied: 'I don't give a damn for Babbitt's opinions about anything!'" (Shepard's copy of Manchester and Shepard 1941: 295). When the *Nation* published Stuart P. Sherman's anonymous—and partly critical—estimation of Kittredge as a teacher (Sherman 1913), some Harvard faculty members believed that Babbitt had written it. For Babbitt Kittredge served as a prime example of the perniciousness of scientific naturalism's influence on literary study. On Kittredge see, e.g., anon. 1941; Hyder 1962.

Hammond Lamont (1864–1909): A journalist, critic, and academic, Lamont was born in Monticello, New York, and graduated from Harvard University with an A.B. and an M.A. in 1886. After a spell in journalism in Albany and Seattle, in 1892 he was appointed an instructor in Harvard's English department. Three years later Lamont joined Brown University as an assistant professor of English composition, soon thereafter earning a promotion to full professor. In 1901 he left academia for a position as the managing editor of the New York *Evening Post*. When Wendell Phillips Garrison retired from the editorship of the *Nation* in 1906, Lamont was chosen as his successor. He ran the *Nation* for less than three years, dying during an operation at Roosevelt Hospital in New York City on May 6, 1909. Upon his death, Paul More became the next editor-in-chief of the *Nation*. In their correspondence, More hinted to Babbitt that Lamont was skeptical of Babbitt's educational ideas. Lamont apparently cut much of Paul Shorey's review of Babbitt's *Literature* *and the American College* in the *Nation*, to make the review appear less positive. As a Harvardian who overlapped briefly with Babbitt as both a student and faculty member, Lamont may have grown skeptical of Babbitt, thanks to the latter's unfashionable views on scientific philology. But Babbitt provides no hints in his letters to More that he knew Lamont well. On Lamont see, e.g., anon. 1906, 1909a, b, and c; and the references to him in Dakin 1960.

Charles R. Lanman (1850–1941): Irving Babbitt's and Paul More's professor of oriental studies at Harvard University, Lanman was a native of Norwich, Connecticut, and a graduate of Yale (A.B. 1871, Ph.D. 1873), where he studied ancient Greek and Sanskrit. After further studies in Berlin, Tübingen, and Leipzig, Lanman earned one of the first appointments at the Johns Hopkins University when it opened in 1876. Four years later he became a professor of Sanskrit at Harvard, where he would stay until his retirement in 1926. A distinguished orientalist, Lanman served as the president of both the American Philological Association (1889–90) and the American Oriental Society (1907 and 1919). A productive scholar on many fronts, Lanman devoted much of his attention to editing the multi-volume Harvard Oriental Series. More, in fact, upon departing his cottage in Shelburne, New Hampshire, in 1899 aided Lanman with one volume in this series. As a scholar trained in both classical and oriental studies, Lanman appears to have earned both Babbitt's and More's great respect. He worked hard to secure More academic appointments at various stages of his early career. Lanman's home in Cambridge was near the house on Kirkland Road Babbitt and his family rented from 1900 onward. On Lanman, see Clark 1941; the references to him in Dakin 1960.

Sylvain Lévi (1863–1935): A distinguished French orientalist, Lévi, although only two years Irving Babbitt's senior, was Babbitt's professor for his graduate studies at the Sorbonne (1891–92). Born in Paris, Lévi became a lecturer at the École des Hautes Études in 1886. When Babbitt studied with him, Lévi was a special lecturer in Sanskrit in the Faculty of Letters of the University of Paris. Although principally a linguist, he did not confine his concerns to philology, a characteristic undoubtedly attractive to Babbitt. Lévi was also a careful student of Buddhism. Widely published and greatly respected, Lévi was arguably more akin to British than to German orientalists in his approach to scholarship. His brief but interesting reflection on Babbitt's days at the Sorbonne can be found in Manchester and Shepard 1941 (see 34-35). On Lévi, see, e.g., anon. 1935; Lévi et al. 1937.

A. Lawrence Lowell (1856–1943): The scion of wealthy Boston Brahmin stock, Abbott Lawrence Lowell was a legal scholar and political scientist who served as the president of Harvard University from 1909 to 1933. Lowell earned both his A.B. (in 1877) and a law degree (in 1880) from Harvard. A failure in private legal practice, he published sufficiently well to earn a part-time lectureship in government at his alma mater in 1897. Through his writing Lowell worked his way up the academic totem pole at Harvard, earning a full professorship and a strong scholarly reputation. A man with deep curricular interests and a critic of Charles W. Eliot's elective system, he actively campaigned for the Harvard presidency upon Eliot's resignation. In the early years of his presidency Lowell established both the concentration system (i.e., the major/minor system) and distribution requirements at Harvard. These innovations soon spread to many other American colleges and universities. Perhaps due to his erstwhile criticisms of Eliot, Lowell initially earned Irving Babbitt's support. But Babbitt would soon prove disappointed in Lowell's performance as president. In 1911 Lowell opposed Babbitt's promotion to a full professorship. Although this decision was reversed a year later, Babbitt had to acquire an external offer of employment from the University of Illinois to win his much-coveted promotion. Lowell's enthusiasm for the League of Nations also likely alienated Babbitt. Although earning a reputation as a progressive for attempting to compel Harvard undergraduates of disparate social and financial backgrounds to mix, Lowell also lobbied to limit the percentages of Jewish students at Harvard and to keep Black students from living in the freshman halls. On Lowell, see, e.g., Yeomans 1948; Dakin 1960: 116; the references to Lowell in Hawkins 1972; Brennan and Yarbrough 1987: 23-24, 111; and Geiger 2015.

Frank Jewett Mather Jr. (1868–1953): An art critic, journalist, and professor linked to the New Humanist movement, Mather was born in Deep River, Connecticut, the son of a corporate lawyer in New York City. He graduated from Williams College in 1889 and earned a Ph.D. in English philology and literature at the Johns Hopkins University in 1892, with a dissertation called *The Conditional Sentence in Anglo-Saxon*. Always a man of catholic tastes, Mather grew critical of the narrowness of professionalized academic scholarship. He was thus on firm footing for a lifelong friendship with Irving Babbitt, whom Mather met when both men began teaching at Williams in 1893. Increasingly disenchanted with academic life, Mather left his position as a literature professor in 1900 to join the world of journalism in New York. From 1901 to 1906 he was both an editorial writer for the New York *Evening*

Post and an assistant editor for the *Nation*. Paul More became his co-worker in 1903, and the two men developed a close friendship. A facile writer devoted to collecting art from a young age, Mather demonstrated increasing interest in art criticism during his tenure at the *Post* and the *Nation*. An attack of typhoid fever in 1905 prompted him to leave New York City with his wife for an extended stay in Italy. Although taking a break from his editorial duties, Mather continued to write journalistic pieces and reviews. In 1910 the wealthy fellow Hopkins Ph.D. Allan Marquand, the founder and chief benefactor of Princeton University's Department of Art and Archaeology, convinced Mather to teach art history at Princeton. Mather would do so from 1910 until his retirement from teaching in 1933. He also served as the director of the Princeton University Art Museum from 1922 to 1946. All the while Mather developed into a highly respected traditionalistic art critic and historian. He wrote many monographs that became standard college textbooks. Mather dedicated his book *Modern Painting* (1927), a much expanded and revised version of his Lowell Lectures from 1916, to Babbitt. Although he was on close terms with Babbitt and More during their lifetimes (upon his retirement from the *Nation* in 1914, More moved to Princeton in part because Mather was residing there), Mather's political inclinations differed from theirs. He had enthusiastically supported the American entry in World War I and found fault with Republican criticisms of Woodrow Wilson's League of Nations. Still, when the New Humanism became a lodestar of public controversy in 1930, Mather, who had contributed to Foerster's edited collection *Humanism and America*, took to the pages of the *Atlantic* and the *New Republic* to defend the movement. As a self-proclaimed "Humanist of the extreme left," Mather agreed that Babbitt, More, and their followers could prove too captious about science and too dogmatic in their views. But he still deemed the main ideas associated with Humanism sound. A celebrated critic, pellucid writer, and popular lecturer, Mather after his death has been overshadowed by Babbitt and More, the more vigorous proponents of Humanism. Edmund Wilson's essay "Mr. More and the Mithraic Bull" (Wilson 1948: 3-14) portrays Mather as a genial and witty companion of More. On Mather, see especially Morgan 1989: 105-49; Turner 2000.

Charles Maurras (1868-1952): A French anti-romantic literary critic, poet, and reactionary political polemicist, Maurras founded and edited *L'Action Française* (1908-44), the paper that served as the house organ for his far-right monarchist movement of the same name. A hyper-nationalistic and anti-Semitic opponent of democracy, Maurras was condemned by the Pope in 1926 and imprisoned by the French government in 1944 for his support of Pétain and Vichy. Despite the stark differences between Maurras's views and those of Irving Babbitt and Paul More, Maurras has been mentioned in tandem with the New Humanism because he, like Babbitt and More, served as an influence on T. S. Eliot. But it appears that Maurras's impact on Eliot compelled Eliot to step away from Babbitt's Humanism. According to More, who, like Babbitt, was skeptical of the *Action Française*, Maurras had been integral to Eliot's conversion to Christianity. Eliot's subsequent criticisms of Babbitt's ecumenism also speak to Maurras's influence. As it turns out, Babbitt had written critically of Maurras and kindred French anti-romantic reactionaries in writings as early as his second book. Although disapproving of romanticism and untampered democracy, Babbitt found the utopian, proto-fascist, royalist, and racist aspects of Maurrasian thought detestable. On Maurras, Eliot, and Babbitt, see the careful analysis and insights of Jamieson 1986. See also Brennan and Yarbrough 1987: 138.

H. L. Mencken (1880–1956): Born to a wealthy German-American family in Baltimore, Henry Louis Mencken became one of the most famous and controversial newspapermen and critics in US history. Largely an autodidact, he was well-read on a variety of subjects; this background enabled him to write meaningfully on politics, literature, and even English philology. But it was Mencken's caustic wit and literary inventiveness that earned him celebrity. He commenced his journalistic career in 1899 as a reporter for the *Baltimore Herald*. Three years later Mencken began his long-term association with the *Baltimore Sun*. A talented editor, he also helped grow the *Smart Set* and the *American Mercury* into prominent, albeit contentious, organs. An atheistic libertarian who championed Nietzsche and literary naturalists such as Theodore Dreiser and Sinclair Lewis, Mencken ridiculed the New Humanism, portraying the movement as an exercise in Puritanical gentility. Uncharacteristically, in his sparring with the Humanists Mencken received as many satirical jabs as he gave. Stuart Sherman criticized him in his book *Americans* (1923), Robert Shafer denigrated him as "an undiscriminating hard-boiled ranter" in *Paul Elmer More and American Criticism* (1935), and even Irving Babbitt, typically reluctant to join such battles, memorably dismissed Mencken's work as "intellectual vaudeville." Although disdainful of Humanism in numerous respects, Mencken had a grudging respect for More's scholarship and was friendly with Seward Collins. On Mencken, see, e.g., Miles 1982; Teachout 2002.

Louis J. A. Mercier (1880–1953): Born in Le Mans, France, as a youngster Mercier moved with his family to Chicago. There he earned his B.A. and M.A. at St. Ignatius College (now Loyola University). He completed further graduate work at the University of Chicago and Columbia University. Mercier taught French at the Francis W. Parker School in Chicago from 1906 to 1910 and then briefly joined the Romance languages faculty at the University of Wisconsin. In 1911 Mercier was appointed an instructor in Romance languages at Harvard University and thus became one of Irving Babbitt's colleagues. With the exception of a stint as an interpreter for the French Army from 1914 to 1917, he remained a faculty member at Harvard until his retirement in 1946. Mercier then moved to suburban Maryland, working as a professor of comparative literature and philosophy at Georgetown University. Highly sympathetic to the New Humanism, Mercier wrote numerous analyses of the movement, including *Le Mouvement humaniste aux États-Unis* (1928)—a book produced with Babbitt's and Paul More's encouragement and support—*The Challenge of Humanism* (1936), and *American Humanism and the New Age* (1948). The last of these books spied an essential connection between New Humanist approaches to higher education and the Great Books tradition associated with Mortimer J. Adler and Robert Maynard Hutchins. A Catholic, Mercier argued that Babbitt's Humanism agreed with and supported Christian doctrine. This view befuddled More, who believed that Babbitt was more hostile to the Christian church than his writings suggested. On Mercier, see anon. 1953a and b; Dakin 1960: 249–50, 338, 341.

Alice More (1849–1930) (sister of P. E. More): One of Paul More's elder siblings, Alice More was instrumental in Paul's upbringing and remained very close with him throughout her life. Fifteen years Paul's elder, she regularly read to both Paul and his younger brother Louis when they were children. Alice also saved Paul from potential disaster in college: during his first three years as an undergraduate at Washington University in St. Louis, he suffered from serious problems with his vision; Alice read his assignments in various languages out loud to Paul, so he could continue with his studies. An artist who had attended and taught at Washington University's St. Louis School of Fine Arts, Alice never wed. Paul corresponded with Alice regularly, informing her about his innermost thoughts and discussing his writing projects in detail. In a letter from 1895, Paul even suggested that one reason he had proposed to his childhood friend (and future wife) Henrietta Beck was that Alice had always gotten along with her. An invalid in later life, Alice intermittently lived with Paul's family or in nearby Bridgeton, New Jersey. Undoubtedly as a testament to his affection for his sister, Paul and Henrietta named their second daughter Alice. Edmund Wilson's discussion of a visit to More's house in 1929 (1948: 3-14) includes an unkind portrait of sister Alice, who was by then hard of hearing. On Alice More, see the many references to her in Dakin 1960.

Alice More (1906-1971) (daughter of P. E. More): The younger daughter of Paul and Henrietta More, Alice was unfortunately a difficult birth for her mother, whose health never fully recovered from the ordeal. On December 17, 1927, at her family's home in Princeton Alice married the Scottish physicist Edmund Gilbert Dymond (1901-1952), then a fellow of St. John's College, Cambridge. Paul More stayed for a time with his daughter and son-in-law in Cambridge during his 1928 and 1931 trips to Britain. Alice and her older sister Mary donated the Paul Elmer More Papers to the Princeton University Library. On Alice More, see the references to her in Dakin 1960.

Henrietta Beck More (1867-1928): A childhood friend of Paul More from St. Louis, Henrietta (typically called "Net" or "Nettie") became engaged to Paul in the autumn of 1895, after Paul had unsuccessfully proposed to a few other women. Since neither Henrietta nor Paul had much money, they did not officially wed until the summer of 1900, some months after Paul's extended retreat in remote Shelburne, New Hampshire. Once married, the couple moved to East Orange, New Jersey, and then to New York City, while Paul pursued a career in journalism. Henrietta gave birth to their two daughters: Mary Darrah More (b. 1902) and Alice More (b. 1906). The Mores appear to have had a very traditional domestic relationship, with the husband devoting long hours to his writing and editorial work and the wife taking care of the children and the household. Unfortunately, both births—but especially the second one—were trying for Henrietta. In addition to her familial duties, Henrietta had long cared for her paralytic aunt, Mary D. Richardson. When Richardson, the widow of a successful businessman, died in 1911, Henrietta received a surprisingly large inheritance. This financial windfall allowed her husband to leave his job as editor-in-chief of the *Nation* in 1914, so he could spend more time on his writing. When the Mores subsequently moved to Princeton, New Jersey, Henrietta paid for their home at 245 Nassau Street. Money from her inheritance also funded the construction of a new home at 59 Battle Road in Princeton. Although Henrietta appears to have been less involved in her husband's intellectual life than was Dora Babbitt in regard to that of her husband Irving, it seems likely that over the course of their marriage she helped push Paul closer to Christianity. Often in ill health after the birth of her second daughter, Henrietta passed away in January of 1928, after an attack of nephritis. On Henrietta More, see the many references to her in Dakin 1960.

Katharine Hay (Elmer) More (1825–1914): The mother of Paul Elmer More and seven other children, Katharine Hay Elmer was the third of four daughters of Lucius Quintius Cincinnatus Elmer (1793–1883), an attorney and justice of the New Jersey Supreme Court. In 1846 she married Enoch Anson More, Paul More's father. Ardent Calvinists, Katharine and Enoch moved from Dayton, Ohio, to St. Louis, Missouri, in 1859 to follow their minister, to whom they were strongly devoted. An avid reader of books, Katharine helped instill in Paul a love for the life of the mind. The inheritance she received upon her father's passing in 1883, furthermore, insured that Paul could attend college and kept the family afloat. Katharine was deeply distressed when young Paul announced his break from Christianity; although they remained on good terms, Paul's admission of his disbelief caused a lifelong rift between the two. Widowed in early 1899, Katharine along with her daughter Alice lived with Paul and his family at their home in East Orange, New Jersey, from 1901 to 1903. Katharine and Alice then moved to nearby Bridgeton, the hometown of Katharine's family. Paul More was at his mother's side when she died of pneumonia on April 10, 1914. On Katharine More, see the many references to her in Dakin 1960.

Louis T. More (1870–1944): The younger brother of Paul Elmer More, Louis Trenchard More was a physics professor, academic administrator, essayist, and biographer linked to the Humanist movement. He received a B.S. degree from Washington University in St. Louis in 1892 and a Ph.D. in physics from the Johns Hopkins University three years later. After a year as an instructor at Worcester Polytechnic Institute and four at the University of Nebraska, in 1900 Louis More was appointed a full professor and department head at the University of Cincinnati, where he would spend the remainder of his academic career. Although he first produced typical scholarly articles in his field of experimental physics, by 1909 he had grown disenchanted with what he took to be unsubstantiated and excessive theoretical trends in his field. Influenced by his older brother Paul, Louis transformed into a critic of scientism, writing numerous articles for popular organs to which Paul contributed. He also worked up such views into the books *The Limitations* *of Science* (1915) and *The Dogma of Evolution* (1925), the latter of which originated as the Vanuxum lectures at Princeton. Approached by Williams Jennings Bryan to testify in the infamous Scopes trial, Louis declined, noting that he agreed with evolution as a working hypothesis in biology and merely criticized its extension into the realm of philosophy. At Paul's urging, Louis wrote *Isaac Newton: A Biography* (1934), the research for which compelled Louis to accompany Paul on a trip to England in 1931. He later published a biography of Robert Boyle. As a public signal of his agreement with the New Humanism, Louis contributed the first chapter to Norman Foerster's edited collection *Humanism and America* (1930), called "The Pretensions of Science." A scientific positivist disenchanted with the speculative direction of his discipline, Louis decided to join the administrative ranks at the University of Cincinnati, serving as the Dean of the College of Arts and Sciences (1910-1913) and the Dean of the Graduate School (1912-1940). Through his efforts Cincinnati became something of a Humanist stronghold, appointing Robert Shafer to the faculty and offering speaking engagements to Irving Babbitt and Paul More. Louis retired in 1940. On Louis More, see L. T. More 1940 and 1942, L. T. More in Manchester and Shepard 1941: 36-39; Dakin 1960; Jensen no date.

Mary Darrah More (1902-1975): The elder child of Paul and Henrietta More, Darrah (as she was typically called) attended Vassar College. She worked at the Children's Island Sanatorium in Marblehead, Massachusetts, prior to her marriage in 1927 to Harry Boehme Fine (1899-59), then a mathematics and history teacher at the Princeton Preparatory School. A doting daughter, Darrah cared for her father at his home in Princeton when he was stricken with cancer. Around one month prior to her father's death, Darrah discovered the manuscript of his *Pages from an Oxford Diary*, which he had written during his European travels in 1924-25 and he now edited for publication as his final intellectual project. When her husband, then a teacher at the St. Mark's School in Southborough, Massachusetts, passed away, Darrah moved back to her hometown of Princeton, where she taught at a nursery school. She died at her home in Essex, New York. Darrah and her younger sister Alice donated the contents found in the Paul Elmer More Papers to the Princeton University Library. On Mary Darrah More, see the references to her in Dakin 1960.

Gorham B. Munson (1896-1969): Born in Amityville, New York, a graduate of Wesleyan University (B.A., 1917), Munson had one of the most interesting backgrounds of the second-generation Humanists. A prolific author and critic, in the early 1920s he lived in Europe and founded the avant-garde literary magazine *Secession*, which featured such writers as Hart Crane (Munson's good friend), Wallace Stevens, William Carlos Williams, and e. e. cummings. Originally a bohemian and Dadaist, by late in the decade he had made a break with his radical past and become a qualified advocate of the New Humanism. Although reluctant to be branded a Humanist, he was among the contributors to Norman Foerster's collective manifesto, *Humanism and America* (1930). Munson taught writing for decades at the New School for Social Research in New York City, prior to shorter stints at Wesleyan and Hartford University. His many books include a popular guide to writing called *The Written Word: How to Write Readable Prose* (1949), *Waldo Frank: A Study* (1923), *Robert Frost: A Study in Sensibility and Good Sense* (1927), and *The Dilemma of the Liberated: An Interpretation of Twentieth Century Humanism* (1930), the last of which provides Munson's views on the Humanist movement. He may have had the dubious distinction of introducing Seward Collins to Humanism; Munson dedicated *The Dilemma of the Liberated* to his "cherished" friend Collins (Munson 1967: vii-xi; quote on vii). When he penned this dedication, Munson was likely unaware of Collins's anti-Semitism; married to a Jewish wife, Munson was a consistent critic of anti-Jewish bigotry. Despite his link to Collins, Munson was a leftist advocate of the Social Credit movement who proved critical of Irving Babbitt's and Paul More's political and economic views. He further spied potential compatibility between the New Humanism and some brands of left-wing radicalism (see Munson 1967: 208-51). For some interesting autobiographical reflections by Munson, see Munson 1985. On Munson, see also anon. 1969; Hoeveler 1977: 22-23, 31-32.

Charles Eliot Norton (1827-1908): Scion of a prominent and wealthy Boston clan, Norton grew up at Shady Hill, his family's estate in Cambridge, Massachusetts. A Harvard graduate (class of 1846), Norton first worked in the trading firm of Bullard and Lee. A contributor of various essays and reviews, he gained much from a firm-sponsored trip to India and Europe from 1849 to 1851. In England, for example, he developed friendships with such eminent writers as Charles Dickens, William Makepeace Thackery, and Matthew Arnold. Upon returning to the United States, Norton joined Ralph Waldo Emerson, James Russell Lowell, and Oliver Wendell Holmes Sr. in founding the *Atlantic Monthly*. Although a staunch abolitionist and an agnostic with an early predilection for Transcendentalism, Norton had a conservative temperament; throughout his life he was skeptical of mass democracy and enamored of European high culture. Illness prompted another lengthy trip to Europe from 1855 to 1856, during which Norton befriended John Ruskin and, influenced by Ruskin's work, recognized his calling as a critic of medieval art and culture. Norton imbued medieval Italy with a moral mission; the study of it, he posited, could promote human betterment and unity. At this point in his life Norton also began translating and commenting on Dante, whose work he revered. The editor of the prestigious *North American Review* from 1863 to 1868 and a founder of the *Nation* in 1865, Norton became a major figure in American intellectual circles. Upon returning from another long stay in Europe in 1873, Norton accepted the offer of his cousin and Harvard president Charles W. Eliot to join the faculty of his alma mater. Starting as a lecturer in 1874, Norton soon became the nation's first professor of art history. He was also the chief architect of a rationale for modern humanistic study that ultimately earned the label "Western civilization." According to Norton, American students must learn about the history of their culture, which supposedly extended from Greek antiquity to the contemporary West. An exceedingly popular teacher, he provided a model for a moralistic approach to the humanities vastly preferable to the young Irving Babbitt and Paul More than those offered by the scientific philologists at Harvard. While in graduate school, Babbitt took Norton's course on Dante. Norton remained a moral and intellectual inspiration for Babbitt throughout his life. In fact, the walls of Babbitt's faculty study at Harvard's Widener Library featured the portraits of two men: Sainte-Beuve and Norton. Eventually Norton came to respect Babbitt as well; in the last year of his life, he wrote a letter of praise to Babbitt for his book *Literature and the American College*. Norton's anti-imperialism, criticism of Renaissance humanism, and distaste for an art-for-art's-sake approach to aesthetics also appear to have rubbed off on Babbitt. Babbitt's rationale for humanistic study, however, looked beyond Norton's focus on "Western civilization" toward a radical omni-culturalism. Though less close to Norton, More also respected him, as his essay on Norton's correspondence from the eleventh series of *Shelburne Essays* demonstrates. On Norton see, above all, Turner 1999. See also Vanderbilt 1959; Samson 2001.

Josiah Royce (1855–1916): An important philosopher, as well as a historian and novelist, Royce was among Irving Babbitt's neighbors in Cambridge and one of his very few close friends on the faculty at Harvard University. Born in the small mining town of Grass Valley, California, he received his B.A. from the University of California in 1875. After a year studying philosophy in Leipzig and Göttingen, Royce became one of the first graduate fellows at the newly founded Johns Hopkins University in 1876. He earned his Ph.D. from Hopkins two years later, with a dissertation called *The Possibility of Error*. Although principally a philosopher, Royce first earned an appointment in English at the University of California. Close contact with the Harvard pragmatist William James helped land Royce a temporary instructorship in philosophy at Harvard in 1882—a position that was soon made permanent. An absolute idealist philosopher especially attracted to Kant, Royce was far more enamored of the professionalized German-style research university, the romantic movement, and humanitarianism than was his friend Babbitt. But Royce's capacious approach to the life of the mind (he contributed much literary criticism and wrote valuable histories of California in addition to a novel) likely earned Babbitt's respect. Royce's status as a Californian without a blue-blood pedigree must have also attracted Babbitt, since Babbitt had a hard-scrabble background atypical of Harvard faculty members in his day. As one can tell from the Babbitt–More correspondence, Royce's stroke in 1912—likely spurred on by his hectic work schedule—underscored for Babbitt his preexisting ideas about the importance of leisure for the professoriate. When Paul More departed from his position at the *Nation* in 1914, Royce unsuccessfully attempted to help Babbitt win a spot on the Harvard faculty for More. On Royce, see, e.g., Buranelli 1964. On Royce and Babbitt, see Nevin 1984: 4, 13, 19, 24, 145-47; Brennan and Yarbrough 1987: 25, 73, 137-38.

Ernest Seillière (1866–1955): Born to a wealthy Lorraine family, the decorated literary critic and conservative political philosopher Baron Ernest Seillière was of a financial background that allowed him to devote his life to writing and scholarship. He attended the École Polytechnique and then studied philosophy and history for two years at Heidelberg. A prolific author (he penned more than sixty books and hundreds of articles, especially for the conservative paper *Le Journal des débats*), Seillière was an anti-romantic reactionary deeply hostile to the views of Jean-Jacques Rousseau. Seillière's anti-romanticism made him a natural ally of Irving Babbitt, whom Seillière claimed to have gotten elected to the French Institute in 1926. The two men were on good terms; Babbitt used to visit with Seillière when he traveled to Europe. But there were also important differences in their perspectives, as Babbitt himself noted, especially in his book *Democracy and Leadership* (1924). Whereas Seillière criticized "irrational" Rousseauistic imperialism and saw "rational" imperialism as its antidote, for example, Babbitt remained consistently anti-imperialistic in his political outlook. Seillière, moreover, flirted with collaboration under Vichy. Although Babbitt did not live to witness the horrors of Nazism, he proved critical of French proto-fascism of Seillière's ilk. For Seillière's interesting—albeit brief—reminiscences about Babbitt, see his contribution to Manchester and Shepard 1941 (244-45). For critical examinations of the similarities and differences between Seillière's work and the New Humanism, see Mercier 1931; and, above all, Leander 1937a.

Robert Shafer (1889-1956): The son of a successful businessman, Shafer was raised in Hagerstown, Maryland. After graduating from a local high school and a year at a preparatory academy, he attended Princeton University, earning his A.B. in 1912 and his Ph.D. in English literature in 1916, with a dissertation called *The English Ode to 1660: An Essay in Literary History*. He taught at various institutions, including the US Naval Academy, Goucher College, Wells College, and the University of Cincinnati. A student at Princeton prior to Paul More's association with the university, Shafer met More when he hosted him for a lecture at Wells College in October of 1922. Shafer became one of the most energetic of the second-generation Humanists, drawing particular attention (if not notoriety) for his polemical attacks on contemporary writers. His contribution to Norman Foerster's *Humanism and America* (1930), for example, was an excoriation of Theodore Dreiser. Shafer also crossed swords with the Southern Agrarian poet Allen Tate when Tate criticized Irving Babbitt's ecumenical approach to religion. A believing Protestant, Shafer had religious views that overlapped with More's, but he disliked More's open criticisms of Babbitt's latitudinarianism in the pages of the *Bookman*. Shafer's zeal for More's work was such that he produced the first monograph devoted to him; this uneven and meandering book, *Paul Elmer More and American Criticism* (1935), demonstrates that Shafer's chief contribution to Humanism was a fighting spirit. On Shafer, see, e.g., Bowler 1950; the relevant pages of Dakin 1960 and Eliot 2015.

Odell Shepard (1884-1967): The poet, critic, biographer, and English professor Odell Shepard was born outside of Chicago. He earned a Bachelor of Philosophy degree in 1907 and a Master of Philosophy degree a year later at the University of Chicago. Shepard received his Ph.D. in 1916 from Harvard University, where he studied with, among others, Irving Babbitt. From 1917 to 1946 he was a professor in the English department at Trinity College in Hartford, Connecticut. Among his published books are a collection of poems called *A Lonely Flute* (1917), *Bliss Carmen: A Study of His Poetry* (1923), and *The Joys of Forgetting* (1928). His most famous work, however, is *Pedlar's Progress: The Life of Bronson Alcott* (1937), for which he won a share of the 1937 Pulitzer Prize for Biography. A political supporter of the Democratic Party and the New Deal, Shepard served as the Lieutenant Governor of Connecticut from 1941 to 1943. Although Babbitt had influenced Shepard a good deal when the latter was in graduate school (sufficiently so that Shepard served as an editor and contributor to *Irving Babbitt: Man and Teacher* and Harris [1970: 49 n. 1] could deem him a Humanist), Shepard considered Babbitt insufficiently attuned to the aesthetic qualities of literature. For Shepard's reflections on Babbitt see Shepard in Manchester and Shepard 1941: 298-305. On Shepard's biography, see anon. 1967.

Stuart P. Sherman (1881–1926): Born in Anita, Iowa, Sherman, of English, Scotch, and Cornish descent, had a peripatetic early life, which featured stays in Los Angeles, Arizona, Vermont, and Williamstown, Massachusetts. A graduate of Williams College, where he was the salutatorian of his class, Sherman entered graduate school at Harvard University in 1903 to earn a Ph.D. in English literature. There he studied with, among others, the famous Shakespearean philologist George Lyman Kitteridge and Irving Babbitt. Sherman took Babbitt's courses in the history of criticism and Rousseau. In these classes Sherman became a convert to the New Humanism, albeit always with a more populist edge. At Harvard Babbitt introduced Sherman to Paul Elmer More, when More came to visit Cambridge. After completing his dissertation on the English playwright John Ford, Sherman taught at Northwestern University as an instructor in the English department, and then moved with his wife in the summer of 1907 to the University of Illinois, where he would spend most of his career. A compelling and seemingly effortless writer, Sherman was courted by the journalistic world: after a summer working as an editor for the *Nation* and the New York *Evening Post*, Sherman declined More's request for him to take up a permanent position on the staff. Once More replaced Hammond Lamont as the editor of the *Nation* in 1909, he continued cultivating Sherman's critical talents. More considered Sherman an exceedingly promising intellectual in the Humanist mold, and Sherman greatly appreciated More's wide learning and editorial acumen. As Babbitt had been the chief influence on Sherman at Harvard, More became such an influence in Sherman's early career. During what may be termed his Humanist phase, Sherman published the books *Matthew Arnold: How to Know Him* (1917) and *On Contemporary Literature* (1917), the former of which Babbitt reviewed in the *Nation* (see Babbitt 1940: 48-65) and the latter of which he dedicated to More. His polemical jousting with H. L. Mencken was one of the most attention-grabbing episodes in the history of the New Humanism prior to the great Humanist controversy of 1930. But Sherman ultimately drifted away from the New Humanist camp, and some considered him an intellectual turncoat. The aristocratic spirit he detected in the political, social, and educational criticism of Babbitt and More never won Sherman's favor. Sherman's faith in the democratic potential of the state universities mystified his former mentors. His enthusiastic support for Woodrow Wilson during World War I further marked his distance from Babbitt and More. Even prior to the publication of his books *Americans* (1923) and *The Genius of America: Studies in Behalf of the Younger Generation* (1923), both of which demonstrate Sherman's populist bona fides, Babbitt and More lamented that Sherman's perspective was no longer compatible with their own. Despite the criticism of his work found in the Babbitt–More correspondence, however, Sherman remained friendly with them both. In part as a result of More's efforts, for example, in early 1923 Sherman was elected to the American Academy of Arts and Letters. In 1924, after refusing a professorship at Yale University, Sherman departed from Illinois, to take a job as the editor of *Books*, the weekly literary supplement of the New York *Herald Tribune*. He only held this position for a short time. Sherman drowned on August 21, 1926, in a canoeing accident when vacationing in Michigan. Since he was among the most talented of the second-generation Humanists, Sherman's turn away from Babbitt and More, along with his untimely death, helped ensure that the New Humanism receded from the intellectual scene in the early 1930's. On Sherman's life and works, see, above all, the exhaustive two-volume biography of Zeitlin and Woodbridge (1929). On Sherman's relationship with More, see also Sherman and More 1929.

Paul Shorey (1857–1934): A native of Davenport, Iowa, Shorey was an influential and heralded scholar of ancient Greek philosophy, a vigorous defender of the classical languages in American higher education, and an outspoken political conservative. He earned an A.B. from Harvard University (1878) and a Ph.D. from the Ludwig Maximilian University of Munich (1884). After an appointment in Latin and philosophy at Bryn Mawr College (1885–92), Shorey spent most of his career at the University of Chicago as a professor of Greek. His books include *The Unity of Plato's Thought* (1903) and *What Plato Said* (1933). Partially sympathetic to the New Humanism, Shorey was commissioned by Paul More at the *Nation* to provide an anonymous review of Babbitt's *Literature and the American College* (see Shorey 1908b). As one can see from the Babbitt–More correspondence, Shorey's lukewarm review, much abridged by More's boss Hammond Lamont, irked Babbitt, who questioned More's selection of Shorey as the man for the task. Shorey also offered a respectful, but largely critical, review of More's *Platonism* in the *Nation* (see Shorey 1918). On Shorey, see, e.g., Kopff 1990; Kopff's entry on Shorey in the Database of Classical Scholars (dbcs.rutgers/edu).

Joel Elias Spingarn (1875–1939): A literary critic, professor, and social activist, Spingarn was born in New York City to Jewish immigrants from Europe. The son of a successful wholesale tobacco merchant, he earned an A.B. from Columbia in 1895. After graduate work in English and comparative literature at Harvard, Spingarn ultimately received his Ph.D. in 1899 from Columbia. He then taught in the comparative literature department at his alma mater, becoming a full professor in 1909. His clashes with Columbia's administration—especially for its firing of the classicist Harry Thurston Peck—led to his dismissal in 1911. From this point on Spingarn worked on various literary, critical, and political endeavors. Although a published poet and one of the founders of Harcourt, Brace and Company, Spingarn made his biggest cultural impact as a literary critic. In these writings Spingarn demonstrated the influence of Benedetto Croce's early approach to aesthetics, which hewed to an art-for-art's-sake point of view. Since Irving Babbitt had taken Croce to task for such a perspective, he similarly found fault with Spingarn. A firm proponent of racial justice, Spingarn became an early member of the National Association for the Advancement of Colored People, and in 1914 he succeeded his friend Oswald Garrison Villard—Paul More's former boss and antagonist at the *Nation*—as the chairman of its executive board. On Spingarn, see Martin 2000, which includes many helpful biographical references.

Frederick Cesar de Sumichrast (1845–1933): One of the senior members of the French department at Harvard when Irving Babbitt started to teach there, de Sumichrast was a staunch critic of Babbitt's views on literature. A native of Belgium, he lived in Scotland, England, and Canada prior to joining the Harvard faculty in 1889. His scholarship included multiple editions and translations of the work of the romantic writer and poet Théophile Gautier. De Sumichrast left Harvard in 1911 and headed to England, where he, a devoted Anglophile, wrote about and delivered lectures on British-American relations in retirement. On de Sumichrast, see Board of Governors 1872; anon. 1933; Brennan and Yarbrough 1987: 21.

William Roscoe Thayer (1859-1923): The son of a wealthy and influential merchant, the editor, biographer, and historian William Roscoe Thayer was born in Boston. He studied at the St. Paul's School in Concord, New Hampshire, with private tutors throughout Europe, and at Harvard College (class of 1881). Upon graduation from the latter, Thayer, formerly a writer for the *Harvard Advocate* and an editor of the *Harvard Crimson*, worked in journalism. He returned to Harvard for the 1885-86 academic year to earn an A.M. in literature and the fine arts. Like Irving Babbitt, Thayer admired his teacher Charles Eliot Norton immensely. Upon returning from a year in Europe, he took up residence in Cambridge, Massachusetts, where he, supported by income from a trust fund, studied and wrote. In 1888 Thayer was made an instructor in Harvard's English department, a position he held for only one academic year. From 1892 to 1915, in addition to writing various books and essays, he served as the first editor of the *Harvard Graduates' Magazine*. It was in this capacity that Thayer became a friend and supporter of both Babbitt and Paul More; both men published in Thayer's magazine. It was due to Thayer's recommendation that Houghton Mifflin published More's essay on Nietzsche as a short book in 1912. Although not strictly speaking a member of the New Humanist movement, Thayer was critical of President Eliot's elective system and sympathetic to Babbitt's and More's perspectives on literature and culture. On Thayer, see Hazen 1926; the references to Thayer in Dakin 1960.

Wu Mi (1894-1978): A native of Jingyang, Shaanxi, China, the critic, educator, and editor Wu Mi graduated from Tsinghua University in 1916. From 1918 to 1921 he was enrolled at Harvard University, from which he ultimately earned an A.M. At Harvard he studied with his academic advisor Irving Babbitt, whose Humanism deeply influenced him. Wu returned to China after graduation, where he became a professor and the chief member of the so-called Critical Review School—a group of traditionalistic Chinese intellectuals opposed to the anti-Confucian, scientistic New Culture Movement. Wu's group, as its name suggests, published a journal called the *Critical Review*, which broadcast its views in a print run lasting from 1922 to 1933. The journal, edited principally by Wu, aimed to apply Babbitt's ideas to a Chinese context. To this end, it published, inter alia, Chinese translations of many of Babbitt's essays. Other prominent members of the Critical Review school either studied with Babbitt or were highly influenced by his ideas. In Babbittian style, Wu and his group portrayed the New Culture Movement as inspired by a naïve naturalism that would ultimately lay waste to the best of Chinese traditions. As Babbitt had highlighted the grave ills that scientific and sentimental naturalism had introduced to the West, the Critical Review School argued that adopting this outlook would prove disastrous for China. Economic troubles caused the shutdown of the group's journal, and ultimately Mao Zedong's government persecuted some of its members. On Wu Mi, see, e.g., Ong 1999; Wu 2004; Zhu 2004; Hon 2015: 113-27; Zhang and Garrison 2020, esp. 262-66. See also Aldridge 1993.

Bibliography

Aaron, Daniel, ed. 1963. *Paul Elmer More's Shelburne Essays on American Literature*. New York: Harcourt, Brace and World.

Adams, George B. 1908. "Proper Work of a Graduate School [letter to the editor]." *The Nation* 86.2239 (May 28): 485.

Adler, Eric. 2016. *Classics, the Culture Wars, and Beyond*. Ann Arbor: University of Michigan Press.

Adler, Eric. 2020. *The Battle of the Classics: How a Nineteenth-Century Debate Can Save the Humanities Today*. New York: Oxford University Press.

Aldridge, A. Owen. 1993. "Irving Babbitt In and About China." *Modern Age* 35.4 (Summer): 332–39.

Anonymous. 1902. "M. Mabilleau's Lecture." *The Harvard Crimson* (Jan. 18): https://www.thecrimson.com/article/1902/1/18/m-mabilleaus-lecture-pm-leopold-mabilleau/.

Anonymous. 1906. "In Harness Forty-One Years." *The Independent* (Lincoln, NE) 19.943 (July 5): 1.

Anonymous. 1907. "An American Critic [review of More 1904]." *The Spectator* 99 (July 20): 91–92.

Anonymous. 1908a. "A Graduate School of Authorship." *The Nation* 86. 2237 (May 14): 439–40.

Anonymous. 1908b. "Notes." *The Nation* 87.2260 (Oct. 22): 385–88.

Anonymous. 1908c. "[Review of Frye 1908.]" *The Nation* 87.2259 (Oct. 15): 365–66.

Anonymous. 1909a. "Died." *New-York Tribune* May 8: 7.

Anonymous. 1909b. "Editor of 'The Nation' Dead." *Cameron County Press* May 13: 3.

Anonymous. 1909c. "Obituary: Hammond Lamont." *New-York Tribune* May 7: 7.

Anonymous. 1910. "Americans as Linguists." *The Nation* 90.2337 (Apr. 14): 869–70.

Anonymous. 1911. "Woman Holder of St. Louis Realty Dies in New York." *St. Louis Post-Dispatch* (Jan. 3): 4.

Anonymous. 1913a. "[Review of More 1967a.]" *The Athenaeum* 4468 (June 14): 644.

Anonymous. 1913b. "[Review of More 1967a.]" *The Daily News and Leader* (July 23): 4, col. 5.

Anonymous. 1913c. "Romanticism: Six Modern Leaders Who Illustrate a Popular Tendency [review of More 1967a.]" *The New York Times* (Apr. 27): 255.

Anonymous. 1914a. "Farmers to Have Summer School." *The Sacramento Union* (May 3): 9.

Anonymous. 1914b. "The Graduate's Choice." *The Atlantic Monthly* 113 (June): 851–53.

Anonymous. 1915. "American Essays [review of Brander Matthews, ed., *The Oxford Book of American Essays*]." *The Spectator* (London) 114 (May 15): 686–87.
Anonymous. 1916a. "Aristocracy and Justice [review of More 1915a]." *The Spectator* (London) 116 (May 20): 623–24.
Anonymous. 1916b. "[Review of More 1915a.]" *The Nation* (London) 19 (May 13): 193–94.
Anonymous. 1916c. "Silas Arnold Houghton, M.D." *Boston Medical and Surgical Journal* 174: 481–82.
Anonymous. 1919a. "Is Romanticism Re-Arming?" *The Sun* (New York) (July 20): 11.
Anonymous. 1919b. "Overseers' Records." *The Harvard Graduates' Magazine* 27 (Mar.): 375–78.
Anonymous. 1924. "Our 'Enthusiastic Degeneration': Irving Babbitt Indicts American Democracy." *Current Opinion* 77 (Nov.): 628–29.
Anonymous. 1926. "Henry Holt, Dean of Publishers, Dies." *The New York Times* (Feb. 14): 28.
Anonymous. 1928. "Rascoe Quits the Bookman." *The New York Times* (Apr. 17): 31.
Anonymous. 1930. "Humanists Start Wordy War." *The Boston Globe* (June 15): C7.
Anonymous. 1931. "Literary Lottery." *Time* 17.11 (Mar. 16): 28–30.
Anonymous. 1933. "Dr. de Sumichrast Is Dead in London." *The New York Times* (Feb. 11): 10.
Anonymous. 1935. "Prof. Sylvain Levi." *Nature* 136 (Nov. 30): 860.
Anonymous. 1941. "Prof. Kittredge of Harvard Dies." *The New York Times* (July 24): 17.
Anonymous. 1943. "Asher E. Hinds, '16." *The Colby Alumnus* (Feb.): 23.
Anonymous. 1951a. "Christian Gauss." *The New York Times* (Nov. 3): 16.
Anonymous. 1951b. "Dean Christian Gauss of Princeton Falls Dead in Pennsylvania Station." *The New York Times* (Nov. 2): 1, 24.
Anonymous. 1953a. "Dr. L. J. A. Mercier, Head of Philosophy Department of GU." *Evening Star* (Mar. 14): A6.
Anonymous. 1953b. "Prof. L. J. Mercier of Georgetown, 72." *The New York Times* (Mar. 14): 15.
Anonymous. 1963. "George Elliott, Educator, Dies." *The New York Times* (Oct. 19): 20.
Anonymous. 1967. "Odell Shepard, Writer, Is Dead; Won '37 Pulitzer for Biography." *The New York Times* (July 20): 37.
Anonymous. 1969. "Gorham Munson, Critic, Dies at 73." *The New York Times* (Aug. 17): 80.
Arnold, Matthew. 1910. *Essays in Criticism, Third Series*. Boston: The Ball Publishing Co.
Arvin, Newton. 1921. "The Everlasting No [review of More 1967c]." *The Freeman* 3 (June 1): 283–84.
Babbitt, Irving. 1897a. "Ferdinand Brunetière and His Critical Method." *The Atlantic Monthly* 79.476 (June): 757–66.

Babbitt, Irving. 1897b. "The Rational Study of the Classics." *The Atlantic Monthly* 79.473 (Mar.): 355–65.

Babbitt, Irving. 1898. "The Correspondence of George Sand." *The Atlantic Monthly* 82.492 (Oct.): 569–76.

[Babbitt, Irving.] 1899. "[Review of More 1899a.]" *The Atlantic Monthly* 84.504 (Oct.): 573–76.

Babbitt, Irving. 1902. "The Humanities." *The Atlantic Monthly* 89.536 (June): 770–79.

Babbitt, Irving. 1906a. "Academic Leisure." *The Harvard Graduates' Magazine* 15 (Dec.): 257–60.

Babbitt, Irving. 1906b. "Literature and the Doctor's Degree." *The Nation* 83.2151 (Sept. 20): 238–39.

[Babbitt, Irving.] 1906c. "[Review of Cestre 1905.]" *The Nation* 83.2149 (Sept. 6): 207–8.

Babbitt, Irving. 1907a. "Ferdinand Brunetière." *The Atlantic Monthly* 99.4 (Apr.): 530–36.

Babbitt, Irving. 1907b. "The Value of the Doctor's Degree [letter to the editor]." *The Nation* 84.2169 (Jan. 24): 78–79.

Babbitt, Irving. 1908. "On Being Original." *The Atlantic Monthly* 101.3 (Mar.): 388–96.

Babbitt, Irving. 1909a. "Racine and the Anti-Romantic Reaction." *The Nation* 89.2316 (Nov. 18): 480–82.

Babbitt, Irving. 1909b. "Sainte-Beuve [review of C. M. Harper's *Charles Augustine Sainte-Beuve*]." *The Nation* 88.2295 (June 24): 622–24.

Babbitt, Irving. 1910a. *The New Laokoon: An Essay on the Confusion of the Arts*. Boston: Houghton Mifflin Company.

Babbitt, Irving. 1910b. "Pascal." *The Nation* 91.2368 (Nov. 17): 466–69.

Babbitt, Irving, ed. 1910c. *Racine's* Phèdre. Boston: D. C. Heath and Co.

[Babbitt, Irving.] 1911. "[Review of J. Bézard's *De la Méthod Littéraire: Journal d'un Professeur dans une Classe de Première*.]" *The Nation* 93.2425 (Dec. 21): 609, cols. 2–3.

Babbitt, Irving. 1912a. "Are the English Critical?—I." *The Nation* 94.2438 (Mar. 21): 282–84.

Babbitt, Irving. 1912b. "Are the English Critical?—II." *The Nation* 94.2439 (Mar. 28): 309–11.

Babbitt, Irving. 1912c. "Bergson and Rousseau." *The Nation* 95.2472 (Nov. 14): 452–55.

Babbitt, Irving. 1912d. "Bergson et Rousseau," translated by Jeanne Scialtiel. *Revue Bleue* 90 (Dec. 7): 725–30.

Babbitt, Irving. 1912e. *The Masters of Modern French Criticism*. Boston and New York: Houghton Mifflin Company.

Babbitt, Irving. 1913a. "Bicentenary of Diderot." *The Nation* 97.2519 (Oct. 9): 329–32.

Babbitt, Irving. 1913b. "Leaders of Thought in France [review of A. L. Guérard's *French Prophets of Yesterday: A Study of Religious Thought under the Second Empire*.]" *The Nation* 97.2517 (Sept. 25): 288–89.

[Babbitt, Irving.] 1913c. "[Review of Gerhard Gran's *Jean Jacques Rousseau*.]" *The Nation* 96.2491 (Mar. 27): 313, col. 2.

[Babbitt, Irving. 1913d.] "[Review of *Annales de la Société Jean-Jacques Rousseau*, vol. 8.]" *The Nation* 97.2513 (Aug. 28): 191-92.

[Babbitt, Irving.] 1913e. "[Review of W. F. Giese's *Graded French Method*.]" *The Nation* 97.2515 (Sept. 11): 235, cols. 1-2.

Babbitt, Irving. 1913f. "[Review of More 1967a.]" *Yale Review* ser. 3.3: 386-89.

Babbitt, Irving. 1915. "The Breakdown of Internationalism." *The Nation* 100.2607 (June 17): 677-80 and 100.2608 (June 24): 704-6.

Babbitt, Irving. 1917a. "Interpreting India to the West [review of Ananda Coomaraswamy's *Buddha and the Gospel of Buddhism*]." *The Nation* 105.2729 (Oct. 18): 424-28.

Babbitt, Irving. 1917b. "Matthew Arnold [review of Sherman 1917]." *The Nation* 105.2718 (Aug. 2): 117-21.

Babbitt, Irving. 1917c. "The Political Influence of Rousseau [review of *The Political Writings of Jean-Jacques Rousseau*, edited by C. E. Vaughan]." *The Nation* 104.2690 (Jan. 18): 67-72.

Babbitt, Irving. 1917d. "[Review of Pierre Maurice Masson's *La Religion de J. J. Rousseau*, 3 vols.]" *Modern Philology* 15.7 (Nov.): 441-46.

Babbitt, Irving. 1918. "Genius and Taste." *The Nation* 106.2745 (Feb. 7): 138-41.

Babbitt, Irving. 1920. "Rousseau and Conscience." *The Journal of Philosophy* 17.7 (Mar. 25): 186-91.

Babbitt, Irving. 1921. "Humanistic Education in China and the West." *The Chinese Students' Monthly* 17.2 (Dec. 1): 85-91.

Babbitt, Irving. 1924. *Democracy and Leadership*. Boston and New York: Houghton Mifflin Company.

Babbitt, Irving. 1927. "Dr. Johnson and the Imagination." *Southwest Review* 13.1 (Oct.): 25-35.

Babbitt, Irving. 1928. "The Critic and American Life." *The Forum* 79 (Feb.): 161-76.

Babbitt, Irving. 1929a. "Benda and French Ideas." *The Saturday Review of Literature* 5 (Mar. 23): 808.

Babbitt, Irving. 1929b. "Introduction." In *Belphegor* by Julien Benda, translated by Sarah J. Lawson. New York: Payson and Clarke.

Babbitt, Irving. 1929c. "[Review of G. R. Elliott 1965.]" *The Forum* 82.4 (Oct.): xvii.

Babbitt, Irving. 1930. "Humanism: An Essay at Definition." In Foerster 1930: 25-51.

Babbitt, Irving. 1936a. "Buddha and the Occident." *The American Review* 6.5 (Mar.): 513-45.

Babbitt, Irving. 1936b. "Buddha and the Occident: Part II." *The American Review* 6.6 (Apr.): 66-97.

Babbitt, Irving. 1940. *Spanish Character and Other Essays*. Edited by Frederick Manchester, Rachel Giese, and William F. Giese. Boston and New York: Houghton Mifflin Company.

Babbitt, Irving. 1965. *The Dhammapada: Translated from the Pāli with an Essay on Buddha and the Occident*. New York: New Directions Publishing Corporation. Originally published in 1936.

Babbitt, Irving. 1968. *On Being Creative and Other Essays*. New York: Biblo and Tannen. Originally published in 1932.

Babbitt, Irving. 1986. *Literature and the American College: Essays in Defense of the Humanities*. Washington, DC: National Humanities Institute. Originally published in 1908.

Babbitt, Irving. 1991. *Rousseau and Romanticism*. New Brunswick, NJ, and London: Transaction Publishers. Originally published in 1919.

Babbitt, Katharine, ed. 1915. *L'Abbé Constantine* par Ludovic Halévy. Boston: Ginn and Company.

Badura, Catherine. 2000. "Reluctant Suffragist, Unwitting Feminist: The Ambivalent Political Voice of Corra Harris." *Southeastern Political Review* 28.3 (Sept.): 397–426.

Barnes, Eric Wollencott. 1959. "Charles Cestre." *Books Abroad* 33.2 (Spring): 151.

Barney, Joseph Aldo. 1974. "The Educational Ideas of Irving Babbitt: Critical Humanism and American Higher Education." PhD diss. Loyola University of Chicago.

Baur, Ferdinand Christian. 1973. *Das Manichäische Religionssytem nach den Quellen neu untersucht und entwikelt*. Hildesheim and New York: G. Olms. Originally published in 1831.

[Begbie, Edward Harold.] 1922. *Painted Windows: A Study in Religious Personality, by a Gentleman with a Duster*. London: Mills and Boon, Limited.

Bernbaum, Ernest. 1929. "The Romantic Movement." *The English Journal* 18.3 (Mar.): 221–30.

Bertrand, Louis. 1915. "Goethe et le Germanisme." *Revue des Deux Mondes* 26.4 (Apr. 15): 721–52.

Birzer, Bradley J. 2015. *Russell Kirk: American Conservative*. Lexington, KY: The University Press of Kentucky.

Blackmur, R. P. 1955. *The Lion and the Honeycomb: Essays in Solicitude and Critique*. New York: Harcourt, Brace and Company.

Blondheim, D. S. 1913. "[Review of Babbitt 1912d.]" *Modern Language Notes* 28.6 (June): 193–97.

Board of Governors. 1872. *Investigation of the Recent Charges Brought by Prof. Sumichrast against King's College, Windsor, with Letters, Reports, and Evidence*. Halifax, NS: James Bowes and Sons.

Bourne, Randolph. 1916. "Paul Elmer More [review of More 1915a]." *The New Republic* 6.74 (Apr. 1): 245–47.

Bowler, Richard N. 1950. "John Henry Newman and Robert Shafer Compared on a Liberal Education." MA thesis: University of Massachusetts.

Boyd, William. 1934. "President Eliot and Herbert Spencer." *Harvard Teachers Review* 4 (Feb.): 33–36.

Boynton, H. W. 1916. "Wells vs. Bennett Again [letter to the editor]." *The Nation* 102.2640 (Feb. 3): 133–34.

Bradby, G. F. 1907. *The Great Days of Versailles: Studies from Court Life in the Later Years of Louis XIV*. London: Smith, Elder and Co.

Bradford, Gamaliel, Jr. 1904. "The Mission of the Literary Critic." *The Atlantic Monthly* 94.564 (Oct.): 537–44.

Bréhier, Émile, ed. and trans. 1924. *Plotin: Ennéades*, vol. 1. Paris: Société d'Édition "Les Belles Lettres."
Bremond, Henri. 1967. *Histoire littéraire du sentiment religieux en France: Depuis la fin des guerres de religion jusqu'à nos jours*, 9 vols. Paris: Libraire Armand Colin. Originally published from 1916 to 1936.
Brennan, Stephen C. and Stephen R. Yarbrough. 1987. *Irving Babbitt*. Boston: Twayne Publishers.
Brightman, Edgar Sheffield. 1926. *Proceedings of the Sixth International Congress of Philosophy, Harvard University, Cambridge, Massachusetts, United States of America, September 13, 14, 15, 16, 17*. New York: Longmans, Green and Co.
Brody, Alter. 1930. "Humanism and Intolerance [letter to the editor]." *The New Republic* 61.791 (Jan. 29): 278.
Brooks, Van Wyck. 1918. *Letters and Leadership*. New York: B. W. Huebsch.
Brooks, Van Wyck. 1954. *Scenes and Portraits: Memories of Childhood and Youth*. New York: E. P. Dutton and Company.
Brooks, Van Wyck. 1973. *The Wine of the Puritans: A Study of Present-Day America*. Folcroft, PA: Folcroft Library Editions. Originally published in 1908.
Brown, Stuart Gerry. 1939. "Toward an American Tradition: Paul Elmer More as Critic." *The Sewanee Review* 47.4 (Oct.–Dec.): 476–97.
Brownell, W. C. 1909. *American Prose Masters: Cooper—Hawthorne—Emerson—Poe—Lowell—Henry James*. New York: Charles Scribner's Sons.
Buranelli, Vincent. 1964. *Josiah Royce*. New York: Twayne Publishers.
Burgess, R. L. 1934. "The Protestant Garrison in America." *The American Review* 2.4 (Feb.): 433–52.
Burke, Francis. 1931. "Humanism: Its Law of Thought." *Thought: A Quarterly of the Sciences and Letters* 5.4 (Mar.): 641–60.
Burke, Francis. 1932a. "The Faith of Dr. More." *Commonweal* 15 (Mar. 9): 516–18.
Burke, Francis. 1932b. "The Religious Trends of Humanism." *America* 46.15 (Jan. 16): 357–58.
Burke, Francis. 1932c. "[Review of More 1931.]" *America* 46.13 (Jan. 2): 317.
Bury, R. G. 1918. "[Review of More 1917b.]" *The Classical Review* 32.7/8 (Nov.–Dec.): 187–89.
Bush, Wendell T. 1922. "[Review of More 1917b and 1921.]" *The Journal of Philosophy* 19.20 (Sept. 28): 557–58.
Butts, R. Freeman. 1971. *The College Charts Its Course: Historical Conceptions and Current Proposals*. New York: Arno Press and *The New York Times*. Originally published in 1939.
Canby, Henry Seidel. 1930. "Post Mortem." *The Saturday Review of Literature* 6.47 (June 14): 1121–23.
Calverton, V. F. 1930. "Humanism: Literary Fascism." *The New Masses* 5.11 (Apr.): 9-10.
Carr, H. Wildon. 1924. "Obituary: Prof. J. E. Creighton." *Nature* 114.724 (Nov. 15): 724.
Carroll, David W. 2017. *Purpose and Cognition: Edward Tolman and the Transformation of American Psychology*. Cambridge: Cambridge University Press.

Cerf, Barry. 1926. *Anatole France: The Degeneration of a Great Artist*. New York: The Dial Press.
Cestre, Charles. 1905. *La Rèvolution Française et les poètes Anglais, 1789-1809*. Digon: Barbier-Marilier.
Cestre, C[harles]. 1914. "[Review of More 1967a.]" *Revue germanique* 10: 505-6.
Chalmers, Gordon Keith. 1941. "Rediscovery of a Radical [review of Babbitt 1940]." *The Kenyon Review* 3.3 (Summer): 388-92.
Chazan, Pauline. 1993. "Rousseau as Psycho-Social Moralist: The Distinction between Amour De Soi and Amour-Propre." *The History of Philosophy Quarterly* 10.4 (Oct.): 341-54.
Chesterton, G. K. 1929. "Is Humanism a Religion?" *The Bookman* 69 (May): 236-41.
Clark, Walter Eugene. 1941. "Charles Rockwell Lanman, 1850-1941." *Journal of the American Oriental Society* 61.3 (Sept.): 191-92.
Clarke, Charles C. 1913. "[Review of Babbitt 1912d.]" *The Yale Review* n.s. 2: 774-76.
Clemens, Cyril. 1939. "A Visit to Paul Elmer More, with Some Letters." *Mark Twain Quarterly* 3.3 (Summer-Fall): 18-20, 24.
Collins, Seward B. 1922a. "The Eagle Eye." *The Brooklyn Daily Eagle* (Feb. 11): 11.
Collins, Seward B. 1922b. "The Eagle Eye." *The Brooklyn Daily Eagle* (Mar. 18): 3.
[Collins, Seward.] 1930a. "Chronicle and Comment." *The Bookman* 70 (Jan.): 529-44.
[Collins, Seward.] 1930b. "Chronicle and Comment." *The Bookman* 71 (Mar.): 65-80.
[Collins, Seward.] 1933a. "Editorial Notes." *The American Review* 1.1 (Apr.): 122-27.
C[ollins], S[eward]. 1933b. "The Revival of Monarchy." *The American Review* 1.2 (May): 243-56.
C[ollins], S[eward]. 1934. "The American Review's First Year." *The American Review* 3.1 (Apr.): 118-28.
Colum, Mary M. 1930. "Debating Humanism." *Scribner's Magazine* 87 (May 24): 1063-64.
Copeland, Charles Townsend. 1898. "Unpublished Letters of Carlyle." *The Atlantic Monthly* 82.491 (Sept.): 289-307.
Cory, Herbert E. 1913. "Modern Humanism [review of Babbitt 1912e]." *The Dial* 54.640 (Feb. 16): 130-34.
Cowardin, Samuel Pendleton, Jr. and Paul Elmer More. 1936. *The Study of English Literature*. New York: H. Holt and Company.
Cowley, Malcolm. 1930. "Humanizing Society." In Grattan 1930a: 63-84.
[Cox, Harold.] 1919. "The Ethical Side of Socialism." *The Edinburgh Review* 230.469 (July): 190-206.
Cuvru-Margot, Henriette. 1918. *Beyond the Marne: Quincy, Huiry, Voisins before and during the Battle*, translated by Katharine Babbitt. Boston: Small, Maynard, and Co.
Dakin, Arthur Hazard, ed. 1950. *A Paul Elmer More Miscellany*. Portland, ME: The Anthoensen Press.
Dakin, Arthur Hazard. 1960. *Paul Elmer More*. Princeton: Princeton University Press.
Davidson, Thomas. 1898. *Rousseau and Education According to Nature*. New York: Charles Scribner's Sons.

Davies, Robert M. 1958. *The Humanism of Paul Elmer More*. New York: Bookman Associates.

Dewey, John. 1984. *The Later Works, 1925-1953, vol. 5: 1929-1930*. Edited by Jo Ann Boydston. Carbondale and Edwardsville: Southern Illinois University Press.

Domitrovic, Brian. 2003. "Paul Elmer More: America's Reactionary." *Modern Age* 45.4 (Fall): 343-49.

Doudan, Ximénès. 1879. *Lettres*, vol. 4. Paris: Calmann Lévy.

Duggan, Francis X. 1966. *Paul Elmer More*. New York: Twayne Publishers.

Dunham, Barrows. 1966. "Paul Elmer More." *The Massachusetts Review* 7.1 (Winter): 157-64.

Eastman, Max. 1969. *The Literary Mind: Its Place in an Age of Science*. New York: Octagon Books. Originally published in 1931.

Eddington, Arthur Stanley. 2014. *The Nature of the Physical World: Gifford Lectures of 1927*. Edited by H. G. Callaway. Newcastle upon Tyne: Cambridge Scholars Publishing. Originally published in 1928.

Eliot, Charles W. 1898. *Educational Reform: Essays and Addresses*. New York: The Century Co.

Eliot, Charles W. 1899. "Recent Changes in Secondary Education." *The Atlantic Monthly* 84.504 (Oct.): 433-44.

Eliot, Charles W. 1923. *Harvard Memories*. Cambridge: Harvard University Press.

Eliot, Charles W. 1926. *Charles W. Eliot: The Man and His Beliefs*, vol. 1. Edited by William Allan Nelson. New York and London: Harper and Brothers Publishers.

Eliot, T. S. 1928. "The Humanism of Irving Babbitt." *The Forum* 80.1 (July): 37-44.

Eliot, T. S. 1930. "Religion without Humanism." In Foerster 1930: 105-12.

Eliot, T. S. 1937a. "An Anglican Platonist: The Conversion of Elmer More [review of More 1937a]." *The Times Literary Supplement* (Oct. 30): 792.

Eliot, T. S. 1937b. "Paul Elmer More." *Princeton Alumni Weekly* 37.17 (Feb. 5): 373-74.

Eliot, T. S. 1964. *Selected Essays*. San Diego, New York, and London: Harcourt Brace Jovanovich.

Eliot, T. S. 1970. *For Lancelot Andrewes: Essays on Style and Order*. London: Faber and Faber. Originally published in 1928.

Eliot, T. S. 2015. *The Letters of T. S. Eliot, Vol. 5: 1930 - 1931*. Edited by Valerie Eliot and John Haffenden. New Haven and London: Yale University Press.

Elliott, G[eorge] R[oy]. 1929. "Mr. More and the Gentle Reader." *The Bookman* 69.2 (Apr.): 143-47.

Elliott, G[eorge] R[oy]. 1933a. "President Hyde and the American College: I. Collegiate Magnanimity." *The American Review* 2.1 (Nov.): 1-26.

Elliott, G[eorge] R[oy]. 1933b. "President Hyde and the American College: II. Collegiate Curriculum." *The American Review* 2.2 (Dec.): 143-69.

Elliott, G[eorge] R[oy]. 1936a. "Irving Babbitt as I Knew Him." *The American Review* 8.1 (Nov.): 36-60.

Elliott, G[eorge] R[oy]. 1936b. "T. S. Eliot and Irving Babbitt." *The American Review* 7.4 (Sept.): 442-54.

Elliott, G[eorge] R[oy]. 1937a. "More's Christology." *The American Review* 9.1 (Apr.): 35–46.

Elliott, G[eorge] R[oy]. 1937b. "*Othello* as a Love-Tragedy." *The American Review* 8.3 (Jan.): 257–88.

Elliott, G[eorge] R[oy]. 1937c. "The Religious Dissension of Babbitt and More." *The American Review* 9.2 (Summer): 252–65.

Elliott, G[eorge] R[oy]. 1938. *Humanism and Imagination*. Port Washington, NY: Kennikat Press.

Elliott, George Roy. 1965. *The Cycle of Modern Poetry: A Series of Essays toward Clearing Our Present Poetic Dilemma*. New York: Russell and Russell. Originally published in 1929.

Elliot, Hugh S. R. 1912. *Modern Science and the Illusions of Professor Bergson*. London: Longmans, Green, and Co.

Faÿ, Bernard. 1920. "De l'Esprit Classique et des Etats-Unis." *Le Correspondant* 281 (Oct. 10): 3–25.

Fite, Warner. 1911. "Pedagogy and the Teacher." *The Nation* 93.2410 (Sept. 7): 207–9.

Flanagan, Frances Mary. 1971. "The Educational Role of Norman Foerster." PhD diss. University of Iowa.

Foerster, Norman. 1913. "Romanticism in Light of Dualism [review of More 1967a]." *The Dial* 54.646 (May 16): 416–17.

[Foerster, Norman.] 1919. "The New Humanism [review of Babbitt 1991]." *The Villager* 3 (Dec. 13): 127–28.

Foerster, Norman. 1929. "Humanism and Religion." *The Forum* 82.3 (Sept.): 146–50.

Foerster, Norman, ed. 1930. *Humanism and America: Essays on the Outlook of Modern Civilisation*. New York: Farrar and Rinehart.

Foerster, Norman. 1933. "Education Leads the Way." *The American Review* 1.4 (Sept.): 385–408.

Foerster, Norman. 1937a. *The American State University: Its Relation to Democracy*. Chapel Hill: The University of North Carolina Press.

Foerster, Norman. 1937b. "The Religious Dissension of Babbitt and More." *The American Review* 9.2 (Summer): 252–65.

Foerster, Norman. 1946. *The Humanities and the Common Man*. Chapel Hill: The University of North Carolina Press.

Foerster, Norman. 1962. *American Criticism: A Study in Literary Theory from Poe to the Present*. New York: Russell and Russell. Originally published in 1928.

Foerster, Norman. 1969. *The Future of the Liberal College*. New York: Arno Press and the *New York Times*. Originally published in 1938.

Ford, J. D. M. 1928. "[Review of Mercier 1928.]" *Harvard Graduates' Magazine* 37 (June): 524–27.

Friess, Horace L. 1926. "The Sixth International Congress of Philosophy." *The Journal of Philosophy* 23.23 (Nov. 23): 617–38.

Frohock, W. M. 1940. "What about Humanism." *Southwest Review* 25.3 (Apr.): 322–34.

Frye, Prosser Hall. 1908. *Literary Reviews and Criticisms*. New York: G. P. Putnam's Sons.

Frye, Prosser Hall. 1922. *Romance and Tragedy*. Boston: Marshall Jones Company.

[Fuller, Harold de Wulf.] 1912. "Classical and Romantic [review of *Essentials of Poetry*, by William Allan Neilson]." *The Nation* 94.2434 (Feb. 22): 186–88.

[Gaines, Clarence H.] 1913. "[Review of More 1967a.]" *The North American Review* 197.690 (May): 716–18.

Garrison, Justin D. and Ryan R. Holston. 2020. *The Historical Mind: Humanistic Renewal in a Post-Constitutional Age*. Albany: State University of New York Press.

Geiger, Roger L. 2015. *The History of American Higher Education: Learning and Culture from the Founding to World War II*. Princeton and Oxford: Princeton University Press.

Ghent, W. J. 1902. "The Next Step: A Benevolent Feudalism." *The Independent* 54.2797 (Apr. 3): 781–88.

[Giese, William F.] 1913. "Criticism Applied to Life [review of Babbitt 1912e]." *The Nation* 96.2485 (Feb. 13): 151–53.

Giese, William F. 1926. *Victor Hugo: The Man and the Poet*. New York: Lincoln MacVeagh, the Dial Press.

Giese, William F. 1935. "Irving Babbitt, Undergraduate." *The American Review* 6.1 (Nov.): 65–94.

Giese, William F. 1974. *Sainte-Beuve: A Literary Portrait*. Westport, CT: Greenwood Press. Originally published in 1931.

Graff, Gerald. 1987. *Professing Literature: An Institutional History*. Chicago and London: The University of Chicago Press.

Grattan, C. Hartley, ed. 1930a. *The Critique of Humanism: A Symposium*. New York: Brewer and Warren Inc.

Grattan, C. Hartley. 1930b. "The New Humanism and the Scientific Attitude." In Grattan 1930a: 3–36.

Greenbaum, Leonard. 1966. *The Hound & Horn: The History of a Literary Quarterly*. The Hague: Mouton and Co.

Greenslet, Ferris. 1908. *The Life of Thomas Bailey Aldrich*. Boston and New York: Houghton Mifflin Company.

Gunn, Sidney. 1911. "Science and Literature." *Science* 34.878 (Oct. 27): 550–56.

Gunn, Sidney. 1920. "Rousseau and Bolshevism." *The Unpartizan Review* 13.26 (Jan.–Feb.): 323–28.

H. S. G. 1919. "Moral Moments of Mr. More [review of More 1967b]." *The Sun* (New York) (Dec. 14): 13.

Hamovitch, Mitzi Berger, ed. 1982. *The Hound & Horn Letters*. Athens: The University of Georgia Press.

Hancock, Albert Elmer. 1908. *John Keats: A Literary Biography*. Boston and New York: Houghton Mifflin Company.

Hanford, James Holly. 1961. "The Paul Elmer More Papers." *The Princeton University Library Chronicle* 22.4 (Summer): 163–68.

Harding, Joan N. 1954. "An American Thinker." *The Contemporary Review* 185 (Jan. 1): 34–39.

Harris, L. H. [=Corra Mae Harris]. 1899. "A Southern Woman's View [letter to the editor]." *The Independent* 51.2633(May 18): 1354–55.

Harris, Michael R. 1970. *Five Counterrevolutionists in Higher Education: Irving Babbitt, Albert Jay Nock, Abraham Flexner, Robert Maynard Hutchins, Alexander Meiklejohn*. Corvallis: Oregon State University Press.

Hawkins, Hugh. 1972. *Between Harvard and America: The Educational Leadership of Charles W. Eliot*. New York: Oxford University Press.

Hazen, Charles Downer, ed. 1926. *The Letters of William Roscoe Thayer*. Boston and New York: Houghton Mifflin.

Hazlitt, Henry. 1930. "Humanism and Value." In Grattan 1930a: 87–105.

Hindus, Milton. 1994. *Irving Babbitt, Literature, and the Democratic Culture*. New Brunswick, NJ, and London: Transaction Publishers.

Hoeveler, J. David, Jr. 1977. *The New Humanism: A Critique of Modern America, 1900-1940*. Charlottesville: University Press of Virginia.

Holston, Ryan R. 2020. "Irving Babbitt and Christianity: A Response to T. S. Eliot." In Garrison and Holston 2020: 145–67.

Holtzmann, Heinrich Julius. 1911. *Lehrbuch der Neutestamentlichen Theologie*, 2 vols. Tübingen: J. C. B. Mohr.

Hon, Tze-ki. 2015. *The Allure of the Nation: The Cultural and Historical Debates in Late Qing and Republican China*. Leiden and Boston: Brill.

Hoopes, James. 1977. *Van Wyck Brooks: In Search of American Culture*. Amherst: University of Massachusetts Press.

Hough, Lynn Harold. 1927. "Dr. Babbitt and Vital Control." *The London Quarterly Review* 147 (Jan.): 1–15.

Hough, Lynn Harold. 1924. "Paul Elmer More and Our American Civilization." *The Christian Century* 41 (Oct. 30): 1407–8.

Hough, Lynn Harold. 1952. *Great Humanists*. New York and Nashville: Abingdon-Cokesbury Press.

Hovey, Richard B. 1986. "*Literature and the American College*: Irving Babbitt Yesterday and Today." In Panichas and Ryn 1986: 201–25.

Hurley, Donna W. 1990. "Alfred Gudeman, Georgia, 1862–Theresienstadt, 1942." *Transactions of the American Philological Association* 120: 355–81.

Hyder, Clyde Kenneth. 1962. *George Lyman Kittredge: Teacher and Scholar*. Lawrence: University of Kansas Press.

James, Henry. 1930. *Charles W. Eliot: President of Harvard University, 1869-1909*, 2 vols. Boston and New York: Houghton Mifflin.

James, William. 1910. "A Great French Philosopher at Harvard." *The Nation* 90.2335 (Mar. 31): 312–14.

Jamieson, T. John. 1986. "Babbitt and Maurras as Competing Influences on T. S. Eliot." In Panichas and Ryn 1986: 155–77.

Jensen, William B. No date. "Critiquing Einstein and Darwin: The Humanism of Louis Trenchard More." Unpublished paper. Oct. 29, 2020.

Jewett, Andrew. 2012. *Science, Democracy, and the American University: From the Civil War to the Cold War*. Cambridge and New York: Cambridge University Press.

Johnson, Edward Gilpin, ed. 1891. *Sir Joshua Reynolds's Discourses on Art*. Chicago: A. C. McClurg and Company.

Jones, Howard Mumford. 1928. "Professor Babbitt Cross-Examined." *The New Republic* 54.694 (Mar. 21): 158–60.

Kazin, Alfred. 1982. *On Native Grounds: An Interpretation of Modern American Prose Literature*. San Diego, New York, and London: Harcourt Brace Jovanovich. Originally published in 1942.

Kimball, Bruce A. 1995. *Orators and Philosophers: A History of the Idea of Liberal Education*. New York: College Entrance Examination Board.

Kirk, Russell. 1960. *The Conservative Mind: From Burke to Eliot*, 3rd revised edition. Chicago: Henry Regnery Company. Originally published in 1953.

Knickerbocker, William S. 1929. "Asides and Soliloquies: Editorial Comment." *The Sewanee Review* 37.3 (July): 257–64.

Kopff, E. Christian. 1990. "Paul Shorey" In *Classical Scholarship: A Biographical Encyclopedia*, edited by Ward W. Briggs Jr. and William Calder III. 447–53. New York: Garland.

Krans, Horatio S. 1907. "Three Distinguished Critics: New Books by Brunetière, Paul Elmer More, and Bernard Shaw." *Putnam's Monthly and the Critic* (Mar.): 751–55.

Kuntz, Paul Grimely. 1980. "The Dualism of Paul Elmer More." *Religious Studies* 16.4 (Dec.): 389–411.

Lambert, Byron C. 1999. "The Regrettable Silence of Paul Elmer More." *Modern Age* 41.1 (Winter): 47–54.

Lanson, Gustave. 1906. *Histoire de la littérature française*, 9th edition. Paris: Librairie Hachette.

Le Roy, Édouard. 1912. "Une Philosophie nouvelle: M. Henri Bergson: I: La Méthode." *Revue des deux Mondes* 7.3 (Feb. 1): 551–80.

Leander, Folke. 1937a. *Humanism and Naturalism: A Comparative Study of Ernest Seillière, Irving Babbitt and Paul Elmer More*. Gothenburg: Göteborgs Högskola.

Leander, Folke. 1937b. "John Dewey and the Classical Tradition." *The American Review* 9.4 (Oct.): 504–27.

Leander, Folke. 1937c. "The Materialistic and the Humanistic Interpretations of History." *The American Review* 9.3 (Sept.): 380–406.

Leander, Folke. 1938. "More—'Puritan à Rebours.'" *The American Scholar* 7.4 (Autumn): 438–53.

Leander, Folke. 1970. "The Philosophy Underlying Paul Elmer More's Criticism of Life and Letters." Unpublished manuscript.

Leander, Folke. 1974. *The Inner Check: A Concept of Paul Elmer More with Reference to Benedetto Croce*. London: Edward Wright.

Levallois, Jules. 1872. *Sainte-Beuve: L'oeuvre du poete – La méthode du critique – l'homme public – l'homme privé*. Paris: Didier.

Lévi, Sylvain, et al. 1937. *Mémorial Sylvain Lévi*. Paris: P. Hartmann.

Levin, Harry. 1940. "Last Essays of Babbitt [review of Babbitt 1940]." *The New Republic* 103.1354 (Nov. 11): 670.

Levin, Harry. 1966. *Refractions: Essays in Comparative Literature*. New York: Oxford University Press.

Levin, Harry. 1991. "From Bohemia to Academia: Writers in Universities." *Bulletin of the Academy of Arts and Sciences* 44.4 (Jan.): 28–50.
Lewis, Sinclair. 1922. *Babbitt*. Toronto: George L. McLeod.
Lewis, Sinclair. 1927. *Elmer Gantry*. New York: Harcourt, Brace and Company.
Lindsay, James. 1913a. "[Review of More 1967a.]" *Zeitschrift für Philosophie und philosophische Kritik* 152: 252.
Lindsay, James. 1913b. "[Review of Babbitt 1912e.]" *Zeitschrift für Philosophie und philosophische Kritik* 152: 253–54.
Lindsay, James. 1924. *Autobiography of Rev. James Lindsay, D.D.* Edinburgh and London: William Blackwood and Sons.
Lodge, Oliver J. 1889. *Modern Views of Electricity*. New York and London: Macmillan and Co.
Lote, René. 1919. "La Psychologie de l'Impérialisme et l'Oeuvre de M. Ernest Seillière." *La Revue Bleue* 57 (Nov.): 659–64.
Lovejoy, Arthur O. 1920. "[Review of Babbitt 1991.]" *Modern Language Notes* 35.5 (May): 302–8.
Lumpkin, Grace. 1936. "I Want a King." *Fight Against War and Fascism* 3.4 (Feb.): 3, 14.
[Maag, William F., Jr.] 1913. "Romanticism and Its Reaction [review of More 1967a]." *The Independent* 74 (May 29): 1200–1.
Manchester, Frederick and Odell Shepard, eds. 1941. *Irving Babbitt: Man and Teacher*. New York: G. P. Putnam's Sons.
Martin, Robert F. 2000. "Spingarn, Joel Elias (17 May 1875–26 July 1939), Literary Critic and Social Activist." *American National Biography*. Oxford University Press: https://www.anb-org.
[Mather, Frank Jewett, Jr.] 1906a. "Aspects of Comparative Literature." *The Nation* 82.2126 (Mar. 29): 256–57.
[Mather, Frank Jewett, Jr.] 1906b. "Teaching Literature in Colleges." *The Nation* 82.2128 (Apr. 12): 296–97.
Mather, Frank Jewett. 1907. "An Art Museum for the People." *The Atlantic Monthly* 100.6 (Dec.): 729–40.
Mather, Frank Jewett, Jr. 1912. *Do the Arts Make for Peace?* New York: American Association for International Conciliation.
Mather, Frank Jewett, Jr. 1920. "The Cult of Eccentricity Examined [review of Babbitt 1991]." *The Unpartizan Review* 14.27 (July–Sept.): 178–83.
Mather, Frank Jewett, Jr. 1927. *Modern Painting*. Garden City, NY: Garden City Publishing Co.
Mather, Frank Jewett, Jr. 1930a. "The Babbittiad [review of Grattan 1930a]." *The New Republic* 63.812 (June 25): 156–59.
Mather, Frank Jewett, Jr. 1930b. "Humanism—Attitude or Credo?" *The Atlantic Monthly* 145.6 (June): 741–48.
Mather, Frank Jewett, Jr. 1931. "Glimpses of Russia." *The Atlantic Monthly* 148.2 (Oct.): 471–78.
Mather, Frank Jewett, Jr. 1938. "Paul Elmer More (1864–1937)." *Proceedings of the American Academy of Arts and Sciences* 72.10 (May): 368–72.

Maurras, Charles. 1905. *L'Avenir de l'Intelligence*, 2nd ed. Paris: Albert Fontemoing.

Maynard, Theodore. 1935. "The Rise and Decline of American Humanism." *Studies: An Irish Quarterly Review* 24.96 (Dec.): 573–88.

McGrath, Larry. 2013. "Bergson Comes to America." *Journal of the History of Ideas* 74.4 (Oct.): 599–620.

McMahon, Francis E. 1931. "The Humanism of Irving Babbitt." PhD diss. Catholic University of America.

Mencken, H. L. 1920. *Prejudices*, second series. New York: Alfred A. Knopf.

Mencken, H. L. 1922. *Prejudices*, third series. New York: Alfred A. Knopf.

Mercier, Louis J.-A. 1928. *Le Mouvement humaniste aux États-Unis: W. C. Brownell, Irving Babbitt, Paul Elmer More*. Paris: Librairie Hachette.

Mercier, Louis J.-A. 1931. "The Rational Imperialism of Ernest Seillière and the American Humanist Movement." *The Bookman* 74.2 (Oct.): 113–27.

Mercier, Louis J.-A. 1936. *The Challenge of Humanism: An Essay in Comparative Criticism*. New York: Oxford University Press. Originally published in 1933.

Mercier, Louis J.-A. 1948. *American Humanism and the New Age*. Milwaukee: The Bruce Publishing Company.

Miles, Elton. 1982. "H. L. Mencken (12 September 1880–29 January 1956)." In *American Humorists, 1800–1950*, edited by Stanley Trachtenberg. 323–31. *Dictionary of Literary Biography*, vol. 11. Detroit: Gale.

Moore, Clifford H. 1919. "[Review of More 1917b.]" *The Harvard Theological Review* 12.3 (July): 343–48.

More, Louis Trenchard. 1925. *The Dogma of Evolution*. Princeton: Princeton University Press.

More, Louis T[renchard]. 1940. "Shelburne Revisited: An Intimate Glimpse of Paul Elmer More." *The Sewanee Review* 48.4 (Oct.): 457–60.

More, Louis Trenchard. 1942. "The Priest and the Boy." *The Sewanee Review* 50.1 (Jan.–Mar.): 49–56.

More, Louis Trenchard. 1962. *Isaac Newton: A Biography*. New York: Dover Publications. Originally published in 1934.

More, Paul Elmer. 1890. *Helena and Occasional Poems*. New York and London: G. P. Putnam's Sons.

More, Paul Elmer. 1894. *The Great Refusal, Being Letters of a Dreamer in Gotham*. Boston and New York: Houghton, Mifflin and Company.

More, Paul Elmer. 1896. "The Influences of Hindu Thought on Manichaeism." *Proceedings of the American Oriental Society* 16: xx–xxv.

More, Paul Elmer, trans. 1898. *The Judgment of Socrates, Being a Translation of Plato's Apology, Crito, and the Closing Scene of Phaedo*. Boston and New York: Houghton Mifflin Company.

More, Paul Elmer. 1898a. "Two Famous Maxims of Greece." *The New World* 7.25 (Mar.): 18–35.

More, Paul Elmer. 1898b. "The Wholesome Revival of Byron." *The Atlantic Monthly* 82.494 (Dec.): 801–9.

More, Paul Elmer. 1899a. *A Century of Indian Epigrams: Chiefly from the Sanskrit of Bhartrihari*. Boston and New York: Houghton, Mifflin and Company. Originally published in 1898.

More, Paul Elmer. 1899b. "Nemesis, or the Divine Envy." *The New World* 8.32 (Dec.): 625–44.

More, Paul Elmer, trans. 1899c. *The Prometheus Bound of Aeschylus*. Boston and New York: Houghton, Mifflin and Company.

More, Paul Elmer. 1900. *Benjamin Franklin*. Boston and New York: Houghton Mifflin Company.

[More, Paul Elmer.] 1901. "The Gospel of Wealth." *The Independent* 53.2739 (May 30): 1263–64.

More, Paul Elmer. 1902. "Wealth and Culture." *The Independent* 54.2787 (May 1): 1058–1062.

[More, Paul Elmer.] 1903a. "Classical Teachers and the Public." *The Independent* 55.2830 (Feb. 26): 511–13.

[More, Paul Elmer.] 1903b. "Pedantry and Dilettantism in the Classics." *The Independent* 55.2827 (Feb. 5): 338–40.

[More, Paul Elmer.] 1903c. "What Are Our Classical Men Doing?" *The Independent* 55.2825 (Jan. 22); 216–18.

More, Paul Elmer. 1903d. "Zola's Truth." *The Independent* 55.2831 (Mar. 5): 562–64.

More, Paul Elmer. 1904. *Shelburne Essays, First Series*. New York and London: G. P. Putnam's Sons.

More, Paul Elmer, ed. 1905a. *The Complete Poetical Works of Lord Byron*. Boston and New York: Houghton Mifflin.

More, Paul Elmer. 1905b. *Shelburne Essays, Second Series*. New York and London: G. P. Putnam's Sons.

More, Paul Elmer. 1906. *Shelburne Essays, Fourth Series*. Boston and New York: Houghton Mifflin Company.

More, Paul Elmer. 1907. "The Forest Philosophy of India." *The Atlantic Monthly* 99.6 (June): 812–25.

More, Paul Elmer. 1908a. "The Dualism of Saint Augustine." *The Hibbert Journal* 6 (Apr.): 606–22.

More, Paul Elmer. 1908b. "A New Life of Lady Mary Wortley Montagu." *The Atlantic Monthly* 102.1 (July): 53–62.

More, Paul Elmer. 1908c. "Rousseau and Education." *The Nation* 86.2235 (Apr. 30): 393–96.

More, Paul Elmer. 1908d. *Shelburne Essays, Fifth Series*. Boston and New York: Houghton Mifflin Company.

More, Paul Elmer. 1908e. "The Teaching of the Classics." *The Independent* 65.3114 (Aug. 6): 327–29.

More, Paul Elmer. 1909a. *Shelburne Essays, Sixth Series: Studies of Religious Dualism*. Boston and New York: Houghton Mifflin Company.

M[ore], P[aul] E[lmer]. 1909b. "Tennyson." *The Nation* 88.2274 (Jan. 28): 82–85.

More, Paul Elmer. 1910a. *Shelburne Essays, Seventh Series*. Boston and New York: Houghton Mifflin Company.

M[ore], P[aul] E[lmer]. 1910b. "Victorian Literature (The Philosophy of Change)." *The Nation* 91.2362 (Oct. 6): 309–12.

More, Paul Elmer. 1912. *Nietzsche*. Boston and New York: Houghton Mifflin Company.

[More, Paul Elmer.] 1913. "Charles Eliot Norton." *The Nation* 97.2527 (Dec. 4): 529–32.

More, Paul Elmer. 1914a. "Natural Aristocracy." *The Unpopular Review* 1.2 (Apr.): 272–96.

M[ore], P[aul] E[lmer]. 1914b. "A Naughty Decade." *The Nation* 98.2550 (May 14): 566–68 and 98.2551 (May 21): 598–600.

[More, Paul Elmer.] 1914c. "The New Morality." *The Unpopular Review* 1.1 (Jan.): 47–62.

[More, Paul Elmer.] 1914d. "One of the Giants." *The Nation* 98.2549 (May 7): 535–36.

[More, Paul Elmer.] 1914e. "Socrates and Plato [review of John Burnet's *Greek Philosophy: Part I, Thales to Plato*]." *The Nation* 99.2583 (Dec. 31): 775–77.

More, Paul Elmer. 1915a. *Aristocracy and Justice: Shelburne Essays, Ninth Series*. Boston and New York: Houghton Mifflin Company.

M[ore], P[aul] E[lmer]. 1915b. "Children's Books." *The Nation* 101.2631 (Dec. 2): 651–52.

M[ore], P[aul] E[lmer]. 1915c. "Dean Swift: Reflections on an Enigma That Defies Solution." *The Nation* 101.2614 (Aug. 5): 171–73.

More, Paul Elmer. 1915d. "Disraeli and Conservatism." *The Atlantic Monthly* 116.3 (Sept.): 373–85.

More, Paul Elmer. 1915e. "Evolution and the Other World." *The Harvard Theological Review* 8.3 (July): 339–56.

[More, Paul Elmer.] 1915f. "Justice." *The Unpopular Review* 4.7 (July): 81–95.

[More, Paul Elmer.] 1915g. "The Philosophy of War." *The Unpopular Review* 3.5 (Jan.): 1–16.

[More, Paul Elmer.] 1915h. "Property and Law." *The Unpopular Review* 3.6 (Apr.): 253–68.

More, Paul E[lmer]. 1916a. "The Old Education and the New." *The Nation* 102.2661 (June 29): 694–96.

More, Paul E[lmer]. 1916b. "The Parmenides of Plato." *The Philosophical Review* 25.2 (Mar.): 121–42.

More, Paul Elmer. 1917a. "Edwards." In *The Cambridge History of American Literature*, vol. 1, edited by William Peterfield Trent, John Erskine, Stuart P. Sherman, and Carl Van Doren. 57–71. New York: Macmillan Co.

More, Paul Elmer. 1917b. *Platonism*. Princeton: Princeton University Press.

M[ore], P[aul] E[lmer]. 1919. "The Revival of Mysticism [review of W. R. Inge's *The Philosophy of Plotinus*]." *The Villager* 3.5 (May 24): 20.

[More, Paul Elmer.] 1920a. "Religions without Religion [review of George Foot Moore's *The History of Religions*]." *The Villager* 3.34 (Jan. 24): 152.

More, Paul Elmer. 1920b. "Theodore Dreiser, Philosopher." *The [Weekly] Review* 2.49 (Apr. 17): 380–81.

More, Paul Elmer. 1921. *The Religion of Plato*. Princeton: Princeton University Press.
More, Paul Elmer. 1923. *Hellenistic Philosophies*. Princeton: Princeton University Press.
More, Paul Elmer. 1924. *The Christ of the New Testament*. Princeton: Princeton University Press.
More, Paul Elmer. 1927a. *Christ the Word*. Princeton: Princeton University Press.
More, Paul Elmer. 1927b. "Le Courant moderne dans la littérature américaine," translated by Louis Cons. *Revue de Paris* 34.6 (Dec.): 858–79.
More, Paul Elmer. 1928a. *The Demon of the Absolute, New Shelburne Essays*, vol. 1. Princeton: Princeton University Press.
More, Paul Elmer. 1928b. "The Modern Current in American Literature." *The Forum* 79.1 (Jan.): 127–36.
More, Paul Elmer. 1930a. "The Humility of Common Sense." In Foerster 1930: 52–74.
More, Paul Elmer. 1930b. "A Revival of Humanism [review of Foerster 1930]." *The Bookman* 71.1 (Mar.): 1–11.
More, Paul Elmer. 1931. *The Catholic Faith*. Princeton: Princeton University Press.
More, Paul Elmer. 1933. "Proust: The Two Ways." *The American Review* 1 (Apr.): 50–75.
More, Paul Elmer. 1934. "Irving Babbitt." *University of Toronto Quarterly* 3.2 (Jan.): 129–45.
More, Paul Elmer. 1935a. "James Joyce." *The American Review* 5.2 (May): 129–57.
More, Paul Elmer. 1935b. "The Modernism of French Poetry." *The American Review* 5.3 (Summer): 329–48.
More, Paul Elmer. 1936a. "How to Read 'Lycidas.'" *The American Review* 7.2 (May): 140-58.
More, Paul Elmer. 1936b. "John Bailey." *The American Review* 7.1 (Apr.): 15–31.
More, Paul Elmer. 1936c. "Marginalia, Part I." *The American Review* 8.1 (Nov.): 1–30.
More, Paul Elmer. 1936d. *On Being Human: New Shelburne Essays*, vol. 3. Princeton: Princeton University Press.
More, Paul Elmer. 1937a. *Pages from an Oxford Diary*. Princeton: Princeton University Press.
More, Paul Elmer. 1937b. *The Sceptical Approach to Religion: New Shelburne Essays*, vol. 2. Princeton: Princeton University Press. Originally published in 1934.
More, Paul Elmer. 1967a. *The Drift of Romanticism: Shelburne Essays, Eighth Series*. New York: Phaeton Press. Originally published in 1913.
More, Paul Elmer. 1967b. *With the Wits: Shelburne Essays, Tenth Series*. New York Phaeton Press. Originally published in 1919.
More, Paul Elmer. 1967c. *A New England Group and Others: Shelburne Essays, Eleventh Series*. New York: Phaeton Press. Originally published in 1921.
More, Paul Elmer. 1972. *The Essential Paul Elmer More: A Selection of His Writings*, edited by Byron C. Lambert. New Rochelle, NY: Arlington House.
More, Paul Elmer and Frank Leslie Cross, eds. 1935. *Anglicanism: The Thought and Practice of the Church of England, Illustrated from the Religious Literature of the Seventeenth Century*. Milwaukee: Morehouse Publishing Co.

[More, Paul Elmer and C. M. Harris.] 1904. *The Jessica Letters: An Editor's Romance*. New York and London: G. P. Putnam's Sons.

Morgan, H. Wayne. 1989. *Keepers of Culture: The Art-Thought of Kenyon Cox, Royal Cortissoz, and Frank Jewett Mather, Jr.* Kent, OH and London: The Kent State University Press.

Morison, Samuel Eliot. 1942. *Three Centuries of Harvard, 1636–1936*. Cambridge: Harvard University Press.

Mumford, Lewis. 1930. "Towards an Organic Humanism." In Grattan 1930a: 337–59.

Munson, Gorham B. 1928. "The Embattled Humanists." *The Bookman* 68.4 (Dec.): 404–10.

Munson, Gorham [B]. 1967. *The Dilemma of the Liberated: An Interpretation of Twentieth Century Humanism*. Port Washington, NY: Kennikat Press. Originally published in 1930.

Munson, Gorham B. 1985. *The Awakening Twenties: A Memoir-History of a Literary Period*. Baton Rouge: Louisiana State University Press.

M[urry], J. M[iddleton]. 1920. "The Cry in the Wilderness [review of Babbitt 1991]." *The Athenaeum* 4687 (Feb. 27): 267–68.

Nevin, Thomas R. 1984. *Irving Babbitt: An Intellectual Study*. Chapel Hill and London: The University of North Carolina Press.

Nevin, Thomas R. 1988. "W. C. Brownell (30 August 1851–22 July 1928)." In *American Literary Critics and Scholars, 1880–1900*, edited by John Wilbert Rathbun and Monica M. Grecu. 44–49. *Dictionary of Literary Biography*, vol. 71. Detroit: Gale.

Nickerson, Hoffman. 1912. "In Defence of Musical Comedy." *The Forum* 48.3 (Sept.): 333–38.

Nickerson, Hoffman. 1933. "Napoleon and 20th-Century Disarmament." *The American Review* 1.3 (June): 290–307.

Nicolas, René. 1917. *Campaign Diary of a French Officer*, translated by Katharine Babbitt. Boston and New York: Houghton Mifflin Co.

Oates, Whitney J. 1946. "Paul Elmer More: A Quest of the Spirit." In *The Lives of Eighteen from Princeton*, edited by Willard Thorp. 302–17. Princeton: Princeton University Press.

O'Connor, Robert H. 1986. "Van Wyck Brooks (16 February 1886–2 May 1963)." In *American Poets, 1880–1945: First Series*, edited by Peter Quatermain. 59–66. *Dictionary of Literary Biography*, vol. 45. Detroit: Gale.

Oglesby, Catherine. 2008. *Corra Harris and the Divided Mind of the New South*. Gainesville: University Press of Florida.

Ong Chang Woei. 1999. "On Wu Mi's Conservatism." *Humanitas* 12.1: 42-55.

Otis, Brooks. 1965. "[Review of Dakin 1960.]" *Classical Philology* 60.1 (Jan.): 58–59.

Owsley, Frank L. 1933. "Scottsboro, the Third Crusade: The Sequel to Abolition and Reconstruction." *The American Review* 1.3 (June): 257–85.

Page, Curtis Hidden. 1909. "Poe in France." *The Nation* 88.2272 (Jan. 14): 32–34.

Panichas, George A. 1999. *The Critical Legacy of Irving Babbitt: An Appreciation*. Wilmington, DE: ISI Books.

Panichas, George A. and Claes G. Ryn, eds. 1986. *Irving Babbitt in Our Time*. Washington, D.C.: The Catholic University of America Press.
Papini, Giovanni. 1922. *Storia di Cristo*, 3rd ed. Florence: Vallecchi. Originally published in 1921.
Pattee, Fred Lewis. 1915. *A History of American Literature Since 1870*. New York: The Century Co.
Paulsen, Friedrich. 1906. *The German Universities and University Study*, translated by Frank Thilly and William W. Elwang. New York: Charles Scribner's Sons.
Place, Edwin B. 1960. "Jeremiah Denis Matthias Ford (1873–1958)." *Hispanic Review* 28.1 (Jan.): 94–96.
Proctor, Robert E. 1998. *Defining the Humanities: How Rediscovering a Tradition Can Improve Our Schools*, 2nd ed. Bloomington and Indianapolis: Indiana University Press.
Puech, A. 1929. "[Review of More 1927a.]" *Revue des Études Grecques* 42.197: 339.
Rand, E. K. 1932. "The Humanism of Cicero." *Proceedings of the American Philosophical Society* 71.4 (Apr.): 207–16.
Rascoe, Burton. 1930. "Pupils of Polonius." In Grattan 1930a: 109–27.
Renan, Ernest. 1902. *Souvenirs d'Enfance et de Jeunesse*, edited and introduced by Irving Babbitt. Boston: D. C. Heath and Co.
Richards, Philip S. 1928a. "Irving Babbitt: I. A New Humanism." *The Nineteenth Century and After* 103 (Apr.): 433–44.
Richards, Philip S. 1928b. "Irving Babbitt: II. Religion and Romanticism." *The Nineteenth Century and After* 103 (May): 644–55.
Richards, Philip S. 1929. "An American Platonist." *The Nineteenth Century and After* 105 (Apr.): 479–89.
Richardson, George S. 1972. "George Cheever Shattuck." *Proceedings of the Massachusetts Historical Society* 3rd ser. 84: 118–24.
Rinaker, Clarissa. 1913. "Thomas Warton: A Biographical and Critical Study." PhD diss. University of Illinois.
Rivet, P. 1928. "Philippe Belknap Marcou." *Journal de la Société des américanistes* 20: 379–81.
Robin, Léon. 1921. "[Review of More 1917b.]" *Revue des Études Grecques* 34.159: 466–70.
Ryn, Claes G. 1977. "The Humanism of Irving Babbitt Revisited." *Modern Age* 21.3 (Summer): 251–62.
Ryn, Claes G. 1978. *Democracy and the Ethical Life: A Philosophy of Politics and Community*. Baton Rouge and London: Louisiana State University Press.
Ryn, Claes G. 1991. "Introduction to the Transaction Edition." In Babbitt 1991: ix–lxvii.
Ryn, Claes G. 1995a. "How We Know What We Know: Babbitt, Positivism and Beyond." *Humanitas* 8.1: 6–25.
Ryn, Claes G. 1995b. "Introduction to the Transaction Edition." In *Character and Culture: Essays on East and West*, by Irving Babbitt. Ix–l. New Brunswick, NJ, and London: Transaction Publishers.

Ryn, Claes G. 1997. *Will, Imagination and Reason: Babbitt, Croce and the Problem of Reality*, 2nd ed. New Brunswick, NJ: Transaction Publishers.

Sainte-Beuve, C.-A. 1865. *Causeries du lundi*, vol. 5. 3rd edition. Paris: Garnier Frères.

Samson, M. David. 2001. "Charles Eliot Norton (16 November 1827-21 October 1908)." In *The American Renaissance in New England: Third Series*, edited by Wesley T. Mott. *Dictionary of Literary Biography*, vol. 235. 289-99. Detroit: Gale.

Santayana, George. 1900. *Interpretations of Poetry and Religion*. New York: Charles Scribner's Sons.

Scherer, Edmond. 1882. *Études sur la littérature contemporaine*, vol. 7. Paris: C. Lévy.

Scherer, Edmond. 1886. *Études sur la littérature contemporaine*, vol. 4. Paris: C. Lévy.

Schiller, F. C. S. 1906. "[Review of George Santayana's *The Life of Reason, or the Phases of Human Progress*, vols. 3-4 (1905-06).]" *The Hibbert Journal* 4.4: 936-40.

Schinz, Albert. 1917. "[Review of C. E. Vaughan's *The Political Writings of Jean Jacques Rousseau*.]" *The Philosophical Review* 26.2 (Mar.): 214-27.

Schinz, Albert. 1920. "[Review of Babbitt 1991.]" *The Journal of Philosophy* 17.1 (Jan. 1): 20-27.

Schneider. Albert. 1912. "Gegen den Naturalismus." *Pädagogisches Archiv* 54 (Feb.): 65-74.

Seillière, Ernest. 1931. *Marcel Proust*. Paris: Editions de la Novelle revue critique.

Shafer, Robert. 1935a. "Dean Inge and Modern Christianity." *The American Review* 5.1 (Apr.): 1-29.

Shafer, Robert. 1935b. "Dean Inge and Modern Christianity, Part II." *The American Review* 5.2 (May): 209-33.

Shafer, Robert. 1935c. *Paul Elmer More and American Criticism*. New Haven: Yale University Press.

Shafer, Robert. 1935d. "The Vitality of George Gissing." *The American Review* 5.4 (Sept.): 459-87.

Shafer, Robert. 1948. "Paul Elmer More: A Note on His Verse and Prose Written in Youth, with Two Unpublished Poems." *American Literature* 20.1 (Mar.): 43-51.

Sheldon, Wilmon H. 1919. "The Veto Power of Conscience [review of Babbitt 1991]." *The Review* 1.30 (Dec. 6): 644-45.

Shepard, Odell. 1917. "[Review of Clarissa Rinaker's *Thomas Warton: A Biographical and Critical Study*.]" *The Journal of English and Germanic Philology* 16.1 (Jan.): 153-63.

Sherman, Stuart P. 1908. "Graduate Schools and Literature [letter to the editor]." *The Nation* 86.2237 (May 14): 442.

[Sherman, Stuart P.] 1913. "Professor Kittredge and the Teaching of English." *The Nation* 97.2515 (Sept. 11): 227-30.

Sherman, Stuart P. 1915a. "H. G. Wells and the Victorians." *The Nation* 100.2603 (May 20): 558-61.

Sherman, Stuart P. 1915b. "The Realism of Arnold Bennett." *The Nation* 101.2634 (Dec. 23): 741-44.

Sherman, Stuart P. 1917a. *Matthew Arnold: How to Know Him*. Indianapolis: The Bobbs-Merrill Company.

Sherman, Stuart P. 1917b. *On Contemporary Literature*. New York: Henry Holt and Company.

Sherman, Stuart P. 1917c. "Why Mr. Roosevelt and the Rest of Us Are at War." *The Nation* 105.2733 (Nov. 15): 532–37.

Sherman, Stuart P. 1919. "The Romantic Movement and Its Consequences [review of Babbitt 1991]." *The Evening Post* (New York) (July 26): Book section, 1, 8.

Sherman, Stuart P. 1920. "Mr. P. E. More and the Wits." *The Review* 2.36 (Jan. 17): 54–56.

Sherman, Stuart P. 1921a. "Introduction." In *Essays and Poems of Emerson*. Vii–xlv. New York: Harcourt, Brace and Company.

Sherman, Stuart P. 1921b. "Introduction." In *The George Sand–Gustave Flaubert Letters*, translated by Aimee L. McKenzie. Ix–xxxvii. New York: Boni and Liveright.

Sherman, Stuart P. 1923. *Americans*. New York: Charles Scribner's Sons. Originally published in 1922.

Sherman, Stuart P. 1924. *Points of View*. New York and London: Charles Scribner's Sons.

Sherman, Stuart P. 1928. *Shaping Men and Women: Essays on Literature and Life*. Edited by Jacob Zeitlin. Garden City, NY: Doubleday, Doran, and Company.

Sherman, Stuart P. and Paul Elmer More. 1929. "Correspondence." Edited by Jacob Zeitlin. *The Bookman* 70.1 (Sept.): 43-53.

Shorey, Paul. 1903. *The Unity of Plato's Thought*. Chicago: The University of Chicago Press.

Shorey, Paul. 1908a. "Eduard Zeller." *The Nation* 86.2232 (Apr. 9): 326–27.

[Shorey, Paul.] 1908b. "[Review of Babbitt 1986.]" *The Nation* 86.2235 (Apr. 30): 403–4.

Shorey, Paul. 1911. "American Scholarship." *The Nation* 92.2393 (May 11): 466–69.

[Shorey, Paul.] 1918. "Interpretations of Plato [review of More 1917b]." *The Nation* 106.2747 (Feb. 21): 209–10.

Slayton, Mary E. 1986. "Irving Babbitt: A Chronology of His Life and Major Works, 1865–1933." In Panichas and Ryn 1986: 227–37.

Smilie, Kipton Dale. 2010. "Irving Babbitt's New Humanism: An Outsider's Perspective on Curricular Debates at the Turn of the 20th Century." PhD diss. University of Kansas.

Smilie, Kipton Dale. 2013. "Bookends of the Twentieth Century: Irving Babbitt, E. D. Hirsch, and the Humanistic Curriculum." *American Educational History Journal* 40.1-2: 153–70.

Smilie, Kipton Dale. 2016. "Unthinkable Allies?: John Dewey, Irving Babbitt, and the Menace of Specialized Narrowness." *Journal of Curriculum Studies* 48.1: 113-35.

Smith, William S. 2019. *Democracy and Imperialism: Irving Babbitt and Warlike Democracies*. Ann Arbor: University of Michigan Press.

Spaeth, J. Duncan. 1943. "Conversations with Paul Elmer More." *The Sewanee Review* 51.4 (Oct.–Dec.): 532–45.

Spanos, William V. 1985. "The Apollonian Investment of Modern Humanist Education: The Examples of Matthew Arnold, Irving Babbitt, and I. A. Richards." *Cultural Criticism* 1 (Autumn): 7-72.

Spiller, Robert E. 1963. "The Battle of the Books." In *Literary History of the United States: History*, 3rd ed., edited by Robert E. Spiller, Willard Thorp, Thomas H. Johnson, Henry Seidel Canby, and Richard M. Ludwig." 1135–56. New York: The Macmillan Company.

Spiller, Robert E., ed. 1970. *The Van Wyck Brooks–Lewis Mumford Letters: The Record of a Literary Friendship, 1921-1963*. New York: E. P. Dutton.

Spingarn, J. E., ed. 1908a. *Critical Essays of the Seventeenth Century*, vol. 1, 1605-1650. Oxford: Clarendon Press.

Spingarn, J. E., ed. 1908b. *Critical Essays of the Seventeenth Century*, vol. 2, 1650-1685. Oxford: Clarendon Press.

Spingarn, J. E. 1917. *Creative Criticism: Essays on the Unity of Genius and Taste*. New York: Henry Holt and Company.

Stephenson, Wendell H. 1946. "William Garrott Brown: Literary Historian and Essayist." *The Journal of Southern History* 12.3 (Aug.): 313–44.

Stock, R. D. 1975. "Prosser Hall Frye: Conservative Humanist." *Modern Age* 19.1: 61–70.

Stock, R. D. 1979. *The New Humanists in Nebraska: A Study of the Mid-West Quarterly (1913–1918)*. University of Nebraska Studies, new series 61. Lincoln: The University [of Nebraska] at Lincoln.

Stone, Albert E., Jr. 1960. "Seward Collins and the *American Review*: Experiment in Pro-Fascism, 1933–37." *American Quarterly* 12.1 (Spring): 3–19.

Stork, Charles Wharton. 1913. "Professor Kittredge as Teacher of Literature." *The Nation* 97.2516 (Sept. 18): 259–60.

Sweet, William. 2010. "R. F. A. Hoernlé and Idealist Liberalism in South Africa." *South African Journal of Philosophy* 29.2: 178 – 94.

Taine, H. 1929. *Derniers essais de Critique et d'Histoire*, 7th ed. Paris: Librairie Hachette. Originally published in 1894.

Taine, H. 1898. *Introduction à l'histoire de la littérature anglaise*. Edited by Irving Babbitt. Boston: D. C. Heath and Co.

Tanner, Stephen L. 1971. "T. S. Eliot and Paul Elmer More on Tradition." *English Language Notes* 8: 211–15.

Tanner, Stephen. L. 1987. *Paul Elmer More: Literary Criticism as the History of Ideas*. Provo: Brigham Young University.

Tanner, Stephen L. 1998. "Paul Elmer More and the Critical Temper." *Modern Age* 40.2 (Spring): 186–94.

Tate, Allen. 1930. "The Fallacy of Humanism." In Grattan 1930a: 131–66.

[Taylor, A. E.] 1918. "[Review of More 1917b.]" *The Times Literary Supplement* (Apr. 25): 192.

Taylor, A. E. 1922. "[Review of More 1921.]" *Mind* 31.124 (Oct.): 518–21.

Taylor, A. E. 1951. *The Faith of a Moralist: Gifford Lectures Delivered in the University of St. Andrews, 1926 – 1928*. London: Macmillan. Originally published in 1930.

Teachout, Terry. 2002. *The Skeptic: A Life of H. L. Mencken*. New York: HarperCollins.

Texte, Joseph. 1899. *Jean-Jacques Rousseau and the Cosmopolitan Spirit in Literature*, translated by J. W. Matthews. London: Duckworth and Co.

[Thayer, William Roscoe.] 1904. "[Review of More 1904.]" *The Harvard Graduates' Magazine* 13 (Dec.): 345–46.

[Thayer, William Roscoe.] 1905. "From a Graduate's Window." *The Harvard Graduates' Magazine* 14 (Dec.): 216–23.

[Thayer, William Roscoe.] 1910. "Babbitt's 'The New Laokoon' [review of Babbit 1910a]." *The Harvard Graduates' Magazine* 19 (Sept.): 32–35.

Tucker, Michael Jay. 2006. *And Then They Loved Him: Seward Collins and the Chimera of an American Fascism*. New York and Washington, DC: Peter Lang.

Tufts, J. H. 1919. "[Review of Babbitt 1991.]" *International Journal of Ethics* 30.1 (Oct.): 101–5.

Turner, James. 1999. *The Liberal Education of Charles Eliot Norton*. Baltimore and London: The Johns Hopkins University Press.

Turner, A. Richard. 2000. "Mather, Frank Jewett, Jr. (1868–1953), Writer, Art Collector, and Museum Director." *American National Biography*.

Twain, Mark. 1905. *Mark Twain's Seventieth Birthday: Record of a Dinner Given in His Honor: With Photographs of More than One Hundred Authors*. New York and London: Harper and Brothers.

Vanderbilt, Kermit. 1959. *Charles Eliot Norton: Apostle of Culture in a Democracy*. Cambridge, MA: Belknap Press.

Varel, David A. 2018. *The Lost Black Scholar: Resurrecting Allison Davis in American Social Thought*. Chicago and London: The University of Chicago Press.

Veysey, Laurence R. 1965. *The Emergence of the American University*. Chicago and London: The University of Chicago Press.

Voltaire. 1905. *Zadig and Other Stories*. Edited by Irving Babbitt. Boston, New York, and Chicago: D. C. Heath and Co.

Ward, A. W. and A. R. Waller, eds. 1915. *The Cambridge History of English Literature*, vol. 12, *The Nineteenth Century I*. Cambridge: Cambridge University Press.

Warren, Austin. 1936a. "George Herbert." *The American Review* 7.3 (Summer): 249–71.

Warren, Austin. 1936b. "Mr. Norton of Shady Hill." *The American Review* 8.1 (Nov.): 86–114.

Warren, Austin. 1937. "The Novels of E. M. Forster." *The American Review* 9.2 (Summer): 226–51.

Warren, Austin. 1956. *New England Saints*. Ann Arbor: The University of Michigan Press.

Warren, Austin. 1969. "Paul Elmer More: A Critic in Search of Wisdom." *The Southern Review* 5.4 (Autumn): 1091–111.

Wilson, Edmund. 1930. "Notes on Babbitt and More." In Grattan 1930a: 39–60.

Wilson, Edmund. 1948. *The Triple Thinkers: Twelve Essays on Literary Subjects*. New York: Oxford University Press.

Wilson, Edmund. 1977. *Letters on Literature and Politics, 1912–1972*, edited by Elena Wilson. New York: Farrar, Straus and Giroux.

Winters, Yvor. 1930. "Poetry, Morality, and Criticism." In Grattan 1930a: 301–33.

Wister, Owen. 1915. "Quack-Novels and Democracy." *The Atlantic Monthly* 115 (June): 721–34.

Withun, David. 2017. "W.E.B. Du Bois and Irving Babbitt: A Comparative Evaluation of Their Views on Education, Leadership, and Society." *Phylon* 54.1 (Summer): 25–42.

[Wolff, Samuel Lee.] 1913. "[A review of William Henry Schofield's *Chivalry in English Literature: Chaucer, Malory, Spenser, and Shakespeare.*]" *The Nation* 96.2489 (Mar. 13): 259–60.

Wu Xuezhao. 2004. "The Birth of a Chinese Cultural Movement: Letters between Babbitt and Wu Mi." *Humanitas* 17.1–2: 6–25.

Yeomans, Henry Aaron. 1948. *Abbott Lawrence Lowell, 1856–1943*. Cambridge: Harvard University Press.

Young, Malcolm. 1941. *Paul Elmer More: A Bibliography*. Princeton: Princeton University Press.

Yuang, Zhang and Justin D. Garrison. 2020. "Resistance and Renewal: Irving Babbitt and China." In Garrison and Holston 2020: 257–72.

Yunck, John A. 1963. "The Natural History of a Dead Quarrel: Hemingway and the Humanists." *The South Atlantic Quarterly* 62.1 (Winter): 29–42.

Zeitlin, Jacob and Homer Woodbridge. 1929. *Life and Letters of Stuart P. Sherman*, 2 vols. New York: Farrar and Rinehart.

Zhang Yuan and Justin D. Garrison. 2020. "Resistance and Renewal: Irving Babbitt and China." In Garrison and Holston 2020: 257–72.

Zhu Shoutong. 2004. "Chinese Reactions to Babbitt: Admiration, Encumbrance, Vilification." *Humanitas* 17.1–2: 26–45.

Index

About, Edmond François Valentin, 149
Adams, Charles Kendall, 93, 95
Adams, George B., 154
Addison, Joseph, 298, 301
Amiel, Henri-Frédéric, 88, 124
Anglicanism (More and Cross), 348, 376, 378
Apelt, Otto, 309
Archibald, Warren S., 197
Aristocracy and Justice (More), 33, 236
Aristotle, 12–14, 20, 37–38, 179
   Buddhism and the thought of, 266
   differences between Plato and, 257, 374
   Irving Babbitt's views on, 56–57, 191
   metaphysics of, 331, 334
   Paul Elmer More's views on, 315, 332–33, 368, 374, 388, 392
   unmoved mover in the thought of, 334
Arnold, Matthew, 32, 115, 153, 242, 321
   aesthetic thought of, 260
Arvin, Newton, 308
Ashley-Cooper, Anthony (1st Earl of Shaftesbury), 298
Aswell, Edward, 352
Atlantic Monthly, The, 25, 99–103, 108–9, 129–38, 218
   Irving Babbitt and, 141, 184, 218, 225, 234
   Paul Elmer More and, 143, 152, 231
Augustine, 135, 162
Aurelius, Marcus, 262
Ayres, Harry Morgan, 212

Babbitt, Augusta, 7
Babbitt, Dora (Drew), 10, 145, 186, 196, 218–19, 276
   biography of, 417
   health problems of, 273, 306–9, 312–16, 337, 341

Paul Elmer More's correspondence with, 395–96, 399–402
   previous efforts to publish the More-Babbitt correspondence by, 52–53
Babbitt, Edward Sturges, 122n46, 125
Babbitt, Edwin Dwight, 7–8
Babbitt, Irving, 3–20
   appraisal of Paul Elmer More's *Platonism* by, 253, 266
   death of, 400
   disagreements with Paul Elmer More, 35–37, 310
   dualism of, 13–15
   election to the American Academy of Arts and Letters, 375
   inner check in the thought of, 14–16, 19, 38, 41
   legacy of, 51
   lower will and higher will in the thought of, 19, 41, 324, 391–92
   on the emerging Christianity of Paul Elmer More, 332
   on the limited audience of Paul Elmer More's *Greek Tradition*, 284, 290, 316
   on the poetic sensibilities of Paul Elmer More, 108–9
   on the writing habits of Paul Elmer More, 327
   oriental studies and, 9, 380
   recovery from typhoid by, 270
   universalism of, 19–20, 47, 241
Babbitt, Katharine, 7, 102, 146, 163
   biography of, 417–18
   death of, 342–43
Bacon, Francis, 15, 136
Baker, Ray Stannard, 239
Baldensperger, Ferdinand, 211

Balzac, Honoré de, 149, 408
Bandler, Bernard, II, 366–67
   biography of, 418
Barce, Pedro Calderón de la, 112
Bartolommeo, 340
Barzun, Jacques, 4
Baudelaire, Charles, 366–67
Baum, Maurice, 57
Baur, F. C., 23
Beale, Joseph Henry, 130
Beaumont, Francis, 298
Beck, Annie E., 194
Beckford, William, 191
Beers, Henry Agustin, 121
Begbie, Edward Harold, 316
Belloc, Hilaire, 398
Benda, Julien, 361, 388
Bennett, Arnold, 243
Bergson, Henri, 13, 179, 181–84, 188
Bernbaum, Ernest, 370, 372
Bertolini, Signorina, 340
Bertrand, Louis, 233
Blackmur, R. P., 38
Blake, Warren Barton, 199
Blake, William, 381
Bôcher, Ferdinand, 10
Böhme, Jacob, 253
Boileau-Despréaux, Nicolas, 271, 286
Bolshevism, 383
Book of Common Prayer, The, 336
Bowman, Archibald Allan, 338–39
Boynton, Henry Walcott, 243, 244
Bradby, G. F., 128
Bradley, F. H., 392
Brank, Sarah Warfield, 87n4
Bréhier, Emile, 337
Bremond, Henri, 348
Brewster, William T., 212
Brody, Alter, 46
Brooks, Van Wyck, 4, 33, 165
   biography of, 418–19
Brown, William Garrott, 158
Browne, Sir Thomas, 161
Brownell, W. C., 148, 299, 367
   biography of, 419

Bruce, James Douglas, 196, 246, 291
Brunetière, Ferdinand, 99, 100, 128, 131, 188
Bryn Mawr College, 24, 88–92, 98–101, 204–7
Bub, J., 295
Buddha, 286, 357, 379–80
   Dhammapada, 353, 355–58
Buddhism, 20, 266, 286, 355, 377
   and Christianity, 377
   and cosmic purpose, 357
   and the concept of the soul, 382
   and the supernatural, 389
   view of immortality in, 343
Bullock, Charles J., 275
Burgess, R.L., 44
Burke, Edmund, 243
Burke, Rev. Francis, S.J., 387
Burnet, John, 221, 225, 349
Buttolph, Janet Howe, 364
Bynner, Witter, 120
Byron, George Gordon (Lord Byron), 105

Calverton, V. F., 46
Canby, Henry Seidel, 5
Capps, Edward, 339
Carlyle, Thomas, 115
Catholic Faith, The (More), 386
Century of Indian Epigrams, A (More) 25, 54, 98–99
Cerf, Barry, 350
Cestre, Charles, 118, 120, 125, 179, 204
   humanism and, 126
   Irving Babbitt on, 315–16
   Paul Elmer More and, 22, 240
Chateaubriand, François-René de, 90, 97, 116, 175, 406
Cheney, Mary Lyon, 135
Chesterton, G. K., 398
Christ of the New Testament, The (More), 56, 334, 347, 350
Christ the Word (More), 356
Christ, Jesus, 13, 259, 325, 379–82, 389
Chrysostom, John, 56, 272, 278
Cicero, Marcus Tullius, 12, 20, 356

Collins, Seward B., 42–46, 373, 394, 398
  biography of, 420–21
Columbia University, 166, 171, 179, 212, 239–42
  awarding of L.H.D. to Paul Elmer More by, 260
Confucius, 13, 19, 116
Cons, Louis, 352
Coolidge, Archibald Cary, 275
Copeland, Charles Townsend, 108
Cornford, F. M., 365
Cory, Herbert E., 195
Coulton, G. G., 397
Cox, Harold, 298
Cox, Kenyon, 196
Creighton, James Douglas, 248–49
Croce, Benedetto, 4
Cromwell, Oliver, 115
Cross, Frank Leslie, 376, 389, 395–97
Cross, Wilbur Lucius, 181, 208

Dabney, Charles William, 158
Dakin, Arthur Hazard, Jr., 50
Dana, Harry, 270
Dante, 115, 151, 380, 381, 386
Darwinism, 340
Davidson, Thomas, 155
Davis, Allison, 47
De Lorenzo, Giuseppe, 377
Democracy and Leadership (Babbitt), 12, 32–33, 46, 291–93, 316, 327
  composition of, 322–23, 328–30,
Demon of the Absolute, The (More), 360, 363, 387
Descartes, René, 131
Dewey, John, 38, 314
Dickens, Charles, 145
Dickinson, G. Lowes, 31
Diderot, Denis, 14, 188, 198, 200, 202, 204, 206, 207
Diehl, Charles, 178
Diogenes, 326
Disraeli, Benjamin, 231
  distributism, 398
Dos Passos, John, 29

Dostoyevsky, Fyodor, 40
Doudan, Ximénès, 192
Dreyfus Affair, The, 149
Drift of Romanticism, The (More), 186, 190, 204, 225
Du Maurier, George, 149
dualism, 13–16
  ethics in relation to, 30, 147, 197, 253
  religion in relation to, 152–53, 161–62, 175, 198, 380–86
Duggan, Francis, 40, 50
Dutton, George, 243
Dyer, Franklin B., 275
Dymond, Alice (More), 26, 221, 235, 247–49, 340
  biography of, 432
  birth of son Paul Philip Dymond, 376
  health of, 167, 171, 281, 345
Dymond, Gilbert, 360, 363, 364

Eastman, Max, 387
Eaton, Walter Prichard, 302
Eckhardt, Meister, 332
Eddington, Arthur Stanley, 381
Eddy, Mary Baker, 142–43
Edwards, Jonathan, 39, 197, 198, 221
Eisenhart, Luther Pfahler, 385–86
Eliot, Charles W., 89, 122–23, 156, 178, 275
  biography of, 421
  elective curriculum of, 8, 17
Eliot, T. S., 3–4, 49–50, 57
  biography of, 422–23
  Irving Babbitt and, 362, 391
  Paul Elmer More and, 365, 376, 378
Elliot, Hugh S. R., 188
Elliott, G. R., 10, 22, 361, 371
  biography of, 423
Elliott, Roy, 369, 373, 400
Emerson, Ralph Waldo, 14, 116, 118, 121, 311
Epictetus, 262, 300, 328
Epicureanism, 317
Eucken, Rudolph Christoph, 182

Fausböll, Viggo, 101

Faÿ, Bernard, 306
Few, William Preston, 92
Fielding, Henry, 107
Fine, Harry Boehme, 395
Fine, Mary Darragh (daugher of Mary Darrah Fine), 365
Fine, Mary Darrah (More), 26, 146, 167, 249–251, 356
  biography of, 434
  graduation from Vassar College by, 318
  recovery from tonsillectomy by, 274
  wedding of, 354
Fite, Warner, 176, 181–82, 233, 248, 346
  illness of, 304
  on Bertrand Russell, 230
FitzGerald, Edward, 31
Flaubert, Gustave, 311, 408
Fletcher, Jefferson Butler, 301
Fletcher, John, 298
Foerster, Norman, 4, 49, 198, 200, 292
  apprecation for *The Demon of the Absolute*, 365
  as contributor to *The Villager*, 294, 297
  biography of, 423
  Humanism and America, 367–370, 372
  publication of *American Criticism*, 361
  review of *Rousseau and Romanticism*, 298
Ford, Jeremiah D. M., 148n35, 371
Forman, Henry James, 146, 152
Foster, William Trufant, 183
Foucher, Alfred, 239, 240–41
Franklin, Benjamin, 25
Franklin, Fabian, 287
Frois-Wittman, Jean, 326
Frost, Robert, 300
Frye, Prosser Hall, 156, 158, 318, 319, 360–61
  biography of, 424
Fuller, Harold de Wulf, 196, 204–7, 267, 181
  as editor of *The Nation*, 212, 223, 235, 256, 261–62
  as editor of *The Review*, 287, 294–95

Gaines, Clarence H., 197
Galdós, Benito Pérez, 112
Garrison, Justin, 51

Gauss, Christian, 405–9
  biography of, 424–25
Ghent, W. J., 116
Giese, William F., 10, 149, 194, 203, 391
  biography of, 425
  Irving Babbitt and, 89–90, 94–95
  on Victor Hugo, 350
  Paul Elmer More's relations with, 240
Giotto, 340
Goethe, Johann Wolfgang von, 150, 161, 233, 251, 304
  Irving Babbitt on, 180
Goncourt, Jules, 406
Goncourt. Edmond, 406
Gondi, Jean François Paul de, 189
Goodell, Thomas Dwight, 145
Gorham, Maud, 133
Graham, James, 378
Grandgent, Charles Hall, 122, 148
Grattan, Hartley C., 37
Great Refusal, Being Letters of a Dreamer in Gotham, The (More), 24, 54, 87–88
Greek Tradition, The (More), 4, 28, 42, 50–51, 283–84, 377
Greenslet, Ferris, 171, 327
Gudeman, Alfred, 91
Guérard, Albert Leon, 199
Gulick, Charles Burton, 338, 339, 345
Gunn, Sidney Allen, 177, 196, 302
Guyau, Jean-Marie, 97

Hack, Roy Kenneth, 337
Hale, Rev. Edward Everett, 17
Hancock, Albert Elmer, 165
Hardy, R. Spence, 101
Harmsworth, Alfred, 257
Harper, George McLean, 160
Harris, C. R. S., 336, 376
Harris, Corra Mae, 25, 47
Harvard University, 7, 20–22, 25
  A. Lowell Lawrence and, 157, 178
  Charles W. Eliot and, 17, 156, 178
  Irving Babbitt's association with, 4, 8–11, 58, 89, 96
  Irving Babbitt's difficulty gaining promotion at, 90, 101, 169–72, 180, 199

Irving Babbitt's difficulty with colleagues at, 94, 99
Paul Elmer More's association with, 111, 205–6, 211–19
Paul Elmer More as a student at, 9, 23, 149
Paul Elmer More as a lecturer at, 246–49, 338–39, 342, 345, 348, 352
Haskins, Charles Homer, 275
Hauvette, Henri, 150
Hazlitt, William, 119
Heard, Augustine A., 178
Heard, Katherine Beck, 178
Hegel, George Wilhelm Friedrich, 374
Helena and Occasional Poems (More), 22
Hellenistic Philosophies (More), 56–57 317, 326, 330–31, 334
Heredia, José-Maria de, 106
Herford, C. H., 259
Herrick, Robert Welch, 408
Hibben, John Greer, 241n78, 270, 386
Hinds, Asher, 396
Hinduism, 263, 300, 372
Hocking, William Ernest, 216, 349, 392
Hoernlé, R. F. A, 349
Holston, Ryan, 51
Holt, Hamilton, 152
Holt, Henry, 223, 235, 250, 294
 as editor of *Unpopular Review*, 226–27, 233, 237
 biography of, 425
 Irving Babbitt's affection for, 317
 New Humanism and, 304–5
Holtzmann, Heinrich Julius, 315
Hooker, Richard, 392
Horace, 286
Houghton, Silas Arnold, 200, 237–38, 242, 244
Houston, Percy H., 36
Howard, Albert, 210
Howe, Esther (Babbitt), 124, 200, 238, 354
Howe, George, 346, 399
Hugo, Victor, 106, 114, 149, 350
 humanism, 12–20, 126, 136, 229, 360
 dualism and, 13–16, 23, 25, 161–62
 religion in relation to, 152–53, 175, 362, 368, 373, 387–390

humanitarianism, 48–49, 132, 220, 225–26, 271
 difference between humanism and, 136, 193
 in modern France, 150
 origins of, 15–16, 136
 perverted imagination and, 113–14

Iamblichus, 254
Independent, The, 25, 47–48, 117, 199, 318
 Paul Elmer More as literary editor of, 114, 152–56
Inge, Ralph William, 335

Jaeger, Werner, 4
James, William, 147, 168, 183, 230, 310
Jefferson, Thomas, 291, 293
Jessica Letters, The (More and Harris), 47, 54
Johnson, Samuel, 197, 267, 286, 387
Joubert, Joseph, 90, 97, 174–75, 190, 388
Joyce, James, 40
Judson, Harry Pratt, 259

Kant, Immanuel, 179, 392
Keats, John, 105
Kemp Smith, Norman, 292
King, Louise Howland, 196
Kipling, Rudyard, 31
Kirk, Russell, 50
Kittredge, George Lyman, 125, 183, 202, 205–10, 275
 biography of, 425–26
Krans, H. S., 128

La Fontaine, Jean de, 88
La Harpe, Jean François de, 188–90
La Rochefoucauld, François de, 188, 408
Lamb, Charles, 166
Lamont, Hammond, 127, 130, 133, 151–52, 154
 biography of, 426–27
 death of, 26, 162
Lanier, Sidney, 236, 245
Lanman, Charles R., 87, 95, 101, 103, 111
 biography of, 427

Lanman, Charles R. (*continued*)
  teacher to Paul Elmer More and Irving Babbitt, 9, 22–25
Lanson, Gustave, 188
Lasserre, Pierre, 132, 164, 295, 409
Leander, Folke, 14, 50
Leconte de Lisle, 106
Lemaître, Jules, 150
Lessing, Gotthold Ephraim, 164
Lévi, Sylvain, 9, 94
  biography of, 427
Levin, Harry, 47
Levinson, Ronald B., 349
Lewis, C. S., 51
Lewis, Sinclair, 5, 393
Lindsay, James, 210
Lippmann, Walter, 4
Literature and the American College (Babbitt), 12, 17–18, 34, 118, 131
  Paul Elmer More's suggestions on, 136
  publication of, 141
  reviews of, 145–46
Lodge, Sir Oliver, 243
Loisy, Alfred, 330
Loofs, Friedrich, 331
Lovejoy, Arthur O., 4, 42
Lovett, Robert Morss, 351
Lowell, James Russell, 148, 202
Lowell, A. Lawrence, 157
  as President of Harvard, 173, 178, 201–2, 211, 248–49, 256
  biography of, 428
  Irving Babbitt and, 316
Lumpkin, Grace, 45
Luther, Martin, 115, 135, 332–33

Maag, William F., Jr., 198, 200
Mabie, H. W., 288
Mabie, Hamilton Wright, 117
Mabilleau, Leopold, 113
Macgregor, Duncan, 336
Machiavelli, Niccolo, 366, 367
Macleod, Fiona, 208
Manchester, Frederick, 403
Marcou, Philippe Belknap, 104
Marks, Lionel Simeon, 92

Marshall, Henry Rutgers, 227, 255, 268
Masson, P. M., 248, 250
Masters, Edgar Lee, 300
Mather, Frank Jewett, Jr., 10, 27, 36, 87, 287
  approval for Paul Elmer More's *Christ of the New Testament*, 351
  biography of, 428–29
  Buddhism and, 381
  delivery of the 1916 Lowell Lectures, 249, 256
  disapproval of Stuart P. Sherman by, 318
  frienship with Irving Babbbitt, 114, 145, 172, 223–24, 240
  friendship with Paul Elmer More, 167–68, 181, 194, 224, 231
  literary criticism of, 141, 201
  opposition to the Harvard administration of, 122–25
  Paul Elmer More's evaluation of, 354, 393
  political views of, 57, 180, 283, 301, 383
  Princeton University and, 217–19
  publication of *Modern Painting*, 353
  recovery from typhoid fever, 117–21, 135, 144, 153–59, 162
  review of *Rousseau and Romanticism*, 304
  sponsorship of Irving Babbitt to the National Institute of Arts and Letters, 300–301
  Williams College and, 91
Mather, Rufus Graves, 144
Matthews, Brander, 212, 234
Maurras, Charles, 295
  biography of, 429–30
May, K. T., 288, 313
Mencken, H. L., 5, 320, 325, 351
  biography of, 430
Mercier, Louis J. A., 20, 36, 306, 356
  biography of, 431
  criticism of Paul Elmer More's work by, 311, 313, 319–20, 350, 368
  publication of *Le Mouvement humaniste aux États-Unis*, 356, 359–60
Milton, John, 180, 362
Mitchell, Donald G., 147
modernism, 332, 340
Mogullāna, 380

Molière (Jean-Baptiste Poquelin), 105
Moore, C. A., 288
Moore, Clifford Herschel, 209, 217, 275, 338
Moore, George Foot, 129, 135, 296
More, Alice, 135, 221, 235, 247
   biography of, 431–32
   death of, 375
   European travels of, 323, 336
   health of, 248–50, 359
More, Catherine, 336
More, Eleanor, 336
More, Enoch Anson, 21
More, Henrietta (Beck), 24, 27, 229, 245, 303
   biography of, 432–33
   death of, 358
   health of, 329–30, 332, 340, 348, 356–58
More, John, 336
More, Katharine Hay (Elmer), 21, 135
   biography of, 433
More, Louis Trenchard, 129, 183, 252, 259, 372
   biography of, 433–34
   Paul Elmer More's contributions to the work of, 339
More, Lucius Elmer, 113
More, Paul Elmer, 20–37
   and the label of reactionary, 244
   Christian Platonism of, 28–29, 50–51
   criticism of Buddhism, 382
   disagreements with Irving Babbitt, 35–37
   education of, 21–25
   ethical dualism of, 23, 41, 153, 161
   inner check in the thought of, 38
   journalistic career of, 27
   literary criticism of, 30–32, 40
   on being considered for the Nobel Prize in literature, 393
   on Irving Babbitt's *On Being Creative*, 388, 389
   on Stoicism, 262–63
   on the difficulties of translating Greek, 345
   on the education of women, 318
   on the hyper specialization of academic work in America, 338
   on Irving Babbitt's *Literature and the American College*, 136–39
   on the necessity of religion to humanism, 330
   on the Western influence of modernization in the East, 314
   resignation from *The Nation* by, 203
   thoughts on Spanish literature of, 112
   translation of *Prometheus Bound* by, 111
Morgan, J. Pierpont, 144–45
Morgan, Morris H., 104
Munson, Gorham B., 57, 366
   biography of, 434–35
Murry, John Middleton, 302
Mussey, Henry Raymond, 276
mysticism, 331, 332, 372
   Buddhism and, 381
   Neoplatonism and, 333
   Paul Elmer More's rejection of, 382

Nation, The, 26–27, 135, 142, 145, 147
   Harold de Wulf Fuller and, 181, 232–34
   Irving Babbitt and, 154–57, 169–70, 179, 187–89, 298
   Paul Elmer More and, 162–65, 168, 217–18, 221–23
   Paul Elmer More as editor of, 151, 177, 180, 198–201, 203–12
Neilson, William Allan, 131, 133, 135, 181, 206
Neoplatonism, 317, 332
New Humanism, 3–21, 37–49, 115
   criticisms of, 37–39
   diversity of political views within, 57
   impact of Seward Collins's association with, 46
   legacy of, 49–52
   on the compatibility of revealed religion with, 36
   public debates on, 37
New Laokoön, The (Babbitt), 12, 164, 171, 183
Newman, Cardinal John Henry, 191, 192, 197, 208
Newton, Sir Isaac, 372
New York Evening Post, 26–27, 130, 162, 170, 295
Nickerson, Hoffman, 190

Nietzsche (More), 178, 179, 181
Nietzsche, Friedrich, 39, 179, 208, 228
Norton, Charles Eliot, 9, 98–99, 156, 208
   biography of, 435–36
Norton, Richard, 96
Novalis, 253

Oglesby, Catherine, 38
On Being Human (More), 29
Origen, 278
Otis, Brooks, 4
Owsley, Frank L., 44
Oxford University, 187, 337, 349

Page, Curtis Hidden, 164, 165
Page, Walter Hines, 102, 108
Pages from an Oxford Diary (More), 29
Papini, Giovanni, 325, 326
Parker, Dorothy, 43
Pascal, Blaise, 129, 134–45, 161, 169–70, 172
Pater, Walter, 325
Patrick, George Thomas White, 290, 292
Pattee, Fred Lewis, 241
Paulsen, Friedrich, 125
Perry, Bliss, 114–15, 131, 134, 152,
   Irving Babbitt and, 119, 125, 141
Perry, Ralph Barton, 215
Petrarch, 13
Phelps, William Lyon, 121
Pindar, 265
Plato, 51, 328, 338, 345
   anamnesis and, 328
   divine element of the Good in, 373
   dualism in the thought of, 28, 41, 254
   Edmund Burke compared with, 243
   Irving Babbitt's analysis of, 191, 246, 257, 328, 362
   Laws, 219, 278, 373–74
   Paul Elmer More on the thought of, 219–20, 294
   Paul Elmer More on the concept of imagination in, 328
   Paul Elmer More's translation of, 111
   Paul Shorey and, 151
   Phaedo, 328
   Phaedrus, 233

   Philebus, 373
   Republic, 194, 373–74
   Symposium, 328
   Timaeus, 294, 310, 373–74
Platonism, 23, 191, 211, 408
   differences between Aristotelianism and, 56
   Irving Babbitt's and, 191, 221, 225, 246, 310
   metaphysical basis of, 267
   on the difference between true and false, 225, 251–54, 267
   Paul Elmer More's synthesis of Christinity and, 4, 28, 35–42, 259, 387–89
   problem of the One and the Many in, 18–19, 24
Platonism (More), 28, 56, 262, 269, 290, 307
   composition of, 252, 65, 267, 269, 277
   origins of, 215, 217, 236
   plans for follow up volume of, 277
   reviews of, 290, 318–20
   second edition of, 346–47, 350
Plotinus, 253, 254, 331, 333
   Emile Bréhier on, 337
   mystical Platonism of, 253
Plutarch, 31, 292, 294, 296, 345
Poe, Edgar Allan, 165
Pomeroy, Ralph Brouwer, 270
Pope, Alexander, 197, 286
positivism, 244
Pratt, James B., 349, 396
Princeton University, 10, 29, 168, 218–20
Proclus, 253–54
Proust, Marcel, 39, 385
Pseudo-Dionysius, 332
Pusey, Nathan, 4, 11
Pyrrhonism. *See* Skepticism

Quevedo, Francisco de, 112

Racine, Jean, 150, 164
Radcliffe College, 10, 94, 87, 94–96, 201
   Irving Babbitt and, 169, 195, 224, 327, 355
Rand, Edward Kennard, 209
Religion of Plato, The (More), 56, 303, 307, 311, 320

Renan, Ernest, 115–16, 192, 405–6
Reynolds, Sir Joshua, 121
Richards, Philip S., 362, 365–68 376, 378
Richardson, Mary D., 27, 144, 171, 231
Ridley, Roy, 336
Rinaker, Clarissa, 264
Robin, Léon, 318–20, 362, 373, 349
Rockefeller, John D., 271, 284
Ronsard, Pierre de, 88
Roosevelt, Theodore, 184, 271
Ropes, James Hardy, 345
Rossetti, Christina, 193
Rousseau and Romanticism (Babbitt), 12–16, 257, 283, 299, 306
  composition of, 164, 245–47, 259–60, 279
  reviews of, 291–306
  Rousseau, Jean-Jacques, 15, 32, 152, 182
  critical literature on, 124, 134
  Irving Babbitt on, 90, 131, 136, 182–84
  Paul Elmer More on, 147, 152
  Platonism in the thought of, 251, 259
  political writings of, 248–49, 259
Rousseauism, 15–17, 155, 279, 285, 355
Royce, Josiah, 178, 211, 215, 217, 219
  biography of, 436–37
Ruskin, John, 208
Russell, Bertrand, 225, 230
Ryn, Claes G., 51

Sainstbury, George, 180
Sainte-Beuve, Charles Augustin, 32, 97, 160, 189–90, 406–8
Sand, George, 107, 108
Santayana, George, 116, 127, 330
Savonarola, 340
Scherér, Edmond Adolphe, 192, 405, 407
Scherer, Wilhelm, 97
Schiller, Friedrich, 127
Schinz, Albert, 248n111, 299
Schneider, Albert, 183
Schofield, William Henry, 122–23, 144, 148, 215, 247
  Paul Elmer More and, 167, 196
Scholasticism, 264, 333
Scudder, Horace, 99, 100, 112
Sedgwick, Ellery, 152, 226, 229, 232

Seillière, Ernest, 295, 298, 327, 385
  biography of, 437–38
Shafer, Robert, 49, 352
  biography of, 438
Shaftesbury. *See* Anthony Ashley-Cooper
Shakespeare, William, 180, 335
Shattuck, George Cheever, 213, 214
Shelburne Essays, (More), 26, 30–32, 124, 174–75, 179
Sheldon, Edward Stevens, 95
Sheldon, William Henry, 349
Shellabarger, Samuel, 393
Shelley, Percy Bysshe, 105, 225, 259
Shepard, Odell, 58, 263–64
  biography of, 438–39
Sherman, Stuart P., 4, 49, 57, 183, 286
  biography of, 439–40
  early support for New Humanism, 154, 157, 205
  George Dutton and opposition to, 243
  Irving Babbitt and, 264, 276, 302, 234
  later departure from New Humanism, 311, 318–20, 325, 373
  on H.G. Wells and Arnold Bennett, 244–45
  on Matthew Arnold, 260, 262
  on Theodore Roosevelt, 271
  Paul Elmer More and, 265, 295–96, 302
  University of Illinois and, 162–63, 172–73
Shorey, Paul, 145, 148, 151, 154, 176, 349
  biography of, 440–41
Skepticism, 317, 333
Slaughter, Moses S., 95
Smith, William S., 51
Smyth, Herbert Weir, 209, 210, 215–17, 219
Socrates, 12, 20, 251, 304, 376
Söderblom, Nathan, 393
Spanos, William V., 39
Spaulding, Edward Gleason, 349
Spingarn, Joel Elias, 152, 261
  biography of, 441
Spinoza, Baruch, 174
Staël, Germaine de, 175
Starbuck, Edwin Diller, 349
Steffens, Lincoln, 239
Stephen, Leslie, 197, 198, 208

478 Index

Stoicism, 262, 263, 317, 328, 331
Strauss, Samuel, 287, 292
Studies of Religious Dualism (More), 158, 160, 347
Sumichrast, Frederick de Cesar, 101
  biography of, 441
Synesius, 297, 299, 300, 303

Taine, Hippolyte, 88, 405, 407
Tanner, Stephen, 50
Taoism, 381
Tate, Allen, 38, 438
Taussig, Frank William, 184, 224
Taylor, A. E., 320, 383
Tennyson, Alfred Lord, 162, 406
Terence, 137
Texte, Joseph, 124
Thackeray, William Makepeace, 149
Thayer, William Roscoe, 117, 119, 128, 170
  biography of, 442
Thiebaut, Marcel, 352
Thomas, Martha Carey, 24, 90, 99
Thoreau, Henry David, 147
Thorndike, Ashley Horace, 301
Tiberius, 343
Todd, Henry Alfred, 127
Tolman, Kathleen (Babbitt), 237
Tomlinson, Paul G., 326, 377–78
Toy, Crawford Howell, 109
Trarieux, Gabriel, 150
Trent, William Peterfield, 181, 199
Troubat, Jules, 406
Troyes, Chrétien de, 104
Tucker, Michael Jay, 45
Tufts, James Hayden, 299
Twain, Mark (Samuel Langhorne Clemens), 40, 119
Tyrrell, George, 330

University of Illinois, 11, 171, 286
University of Wisconsin, 89–95, 172

Van Doren, Carl, 5
Van Dyke, Henry, 288
Vaughan, C. E., 256, 259
Vesey, Laurence, 38
Villard, Oswald Garrison, 27, 204, 235, 276
Virgil, 151, 265, 357
Voltaire (François-Marie Arouet), 283

Warren, Austin, 4
Warren, Henry Clarke, 102
Wells, H. G., 244
Went, Stanley, 223, 359
Whitman, Walt, 31
Whittier, John Greenleaf, 107
Wilhelm II, 271
Willcox, Louise Price Collier, 197
Wilson, Edmund, 5, 42, 383
Wilson, Woodrow, 284, 288, 291, 293
With the Wits (More), 289
Wolff, Samuel Lee, 196
Woods, James Haughton, 349
Woodward, Robert Simpson, 128
Wordsworth, William, 30
Wortley, Lady Mary, 129
Wright, C. H. Conrad, 185, 294
Wu, Mi, 309, 313–14
  biography of, 442–43

Xenophon, 280

Yale University, 11, 119, 166

Zeller, Eduard, 154
Zola, Emile, 45, 151